Houghton Mifflin
Math

time

 HOUGHTON MIFFLIN   BOSTON

Program Authors & Consultants

Authors

Dr. Carole Greenes

Professor of Mathematics Education

Boston University
Boston, MA

Dr. Matt Larson

Curriculum Specialist for Mathematics

Lincoln Public Schools
Lincoln, NE

Dr. Miriam A. Leiva

Distinguished Professor of Mathematics Emerita

University of
North Carolina
Charlotte, NC

Dr. Jean M. Shaw

Professor Emerita of Curriculum and Instruction

University of Mississippi
Oxford, MS

Dr. Lee Stiff

Professor of Mathematics Education

North Carolina State University
Raleigh, NC

Dr. Bruce R. Vogeli

Clifford Brewster Upton Professor of Mathematics

Teachers College, Columbia University
New York, NY

Dr. Karol Yeatts

Associate Professor

Barry University
Miami, FL

Consultants

Strategic Consultant

Dr. Liping Ma

Senior Scholar

Carnegie Foundation for the Advancement of Teaching
Palo Alto, CA

Language and Vocabulary Consultant

Dr. David Chard

Professor of Reading

University of Oregon
Eugene, OR

Reviewers

Grade K

Hilda Kendrick
W E Wilson
Elementary School
Jefferson, IN

Debby Nagel
Assumption
Elementary School
Cincinnati, OH

Jen Payet
Lake Ave. Elementary School
Saratoga Springs, NY

Karen Sue Hinton
Washington Elementary
School
Ponca City, OK

Grade 1

Karen Wood
Clay Elementary School
Clay, AL

Paula Rowland
Bixby North Elementary
School
Bixby, OK

Stephanie McDaniel
B. Everett Jordan
Elementary School
Graham, NC

Juan Melgar
Lowrie Elementary School
Elgin, IL

Sharon O'Brien
Echo Mountain School
Phoenix, AZ

Grade 2

Sally Bales
Akron Elementary School
Akron, IN

Rose Marie Bruno
Mawbey Street Elementary
School
Woodbridge, NJ

Kiesha Doster
Berry Elementary School
Detroit, MI

Marci Galazkiewicz
North Elementary School
Waukegan, IL

Ana Gaspar
Lowrie Elementary School
Elgin, IL

Elana Heinoren
Beechfield Elementary
School
Baltimore, MD

Kim Terry
Woodland Elementary School
West
Gages Lake, IL

Megan Burton
Valley Elementary School
Pelham, AL

Kristy Ford
Eisenhower Elementary
School
Norman, OK

Grade 3

Jenny Chang
North Elementary School
Waukegan, IL

Patricia Heintz
Harry T. Stewart
Elementary School
Corona, NY

Shannon Hopper
White Lick Elementary School
Brownsburg, IN

Allison White
Kingsley Elementary School
Naperville, IL

Amy Simpson
Broadmoore Elementary
School
Moore, OK

Reviewers

Grade 4

Barbara O'Hanlon
Maurice & Everett Haines
Elementary School
Medford, NJ

Connie Rapp
Oakland Elementary School
Bloomington, IL

Pam Rettig
Solheim Elementary School
Bismarck, ND

Tracy Smith
Blanche Kelso Bruce
Academy
Detroit, MI

Brenda Hancock
Clay Elementary School
Clay, AL

Karen Scroggins
Rock Quarry Elementary
School
Tuscaloosa, AL

Lynn Fox
Kendall-Whittier Elementary
School
Tulsa, OK

Grade 5

Jim Archer
Maplewood Elementary
School
Indianapolis, IN

Maggie Dunning
Horizon Elementary School
Hanover Park, IL

Mike Intoccia
McNichols Plaza
Scranton, PA

Jennifer LaBelle
Washington Elementary
School
Waukegan, IL

Anne McDonald
St. Luke The Evangelist
School
Glenside, PA

Ellen O'Rourke
Bower Elementary School
Warrenville, IL

Gary Smith
Thomas H. Ford Elementary
School
Reading, PA

Linda Carlson
Van Buren Elementary
School
Oklahoma City, OK

Grade 6

Robin Akers
Sonoran Sky Elementary
School
Scottsdale, AZ

Ellen Greenman
Daniel Webster Middle
School
Waukegan, IL

Angela McCray
Abbott Middle School
West Bloomfield, MI

Mary Popovich
Horizon Elementary School
Hanover Park, IL

Debbie Taylor
Sonoran Sky Elementary
School
Scottsdale, AZ

Across Grades

Jacqueline Lampley
Hewitt Elementary School
Trussville, AL

Rose Smith
Five Points Elementary
School
Orrville, AL

Winnie Tepper
Morgan County Schools
Decatur, AL

Algebra Indicates lessons that include algebra instruction.

2 Compare, Order, and Round Whole Numbers and Money

Unit 1
Literature
Connection
Beyond Pluto
pages
644–645

Operations and Algebraic Reasoning

Algebra Indicates lessons that include algebra instruction.

Unit 2
Literature
Connection
Kid Camp
page 646

(WR) Indicates **WEEKLY (WR) READER** eduplace.com/map

Multiplication of Whole Numbers

SOLVE THIS PUZZLE.
WIN A PRIZE!
The product of 2 numbers is 24.
Their difference is 5.
What are the 2 numbers?

Algebra Indicates lessons that include algebra instruction.

7 Multiply by Two-Digit Numbers

Unit 3
Literature
Connection
Gone Prawning
page 647

Division of Whole Numbers

8 Understand Division

9 Divide by One-Digit Divisors

Algebra Indicates lessons that include algebra instruction.

Measurement and Graphing

Algebra Indicates lessons that include algebra instruction.

UNIT 5 Measurement and Graphing

Unit 5
Literature
Connection
*Lengths
of Time*
page 650

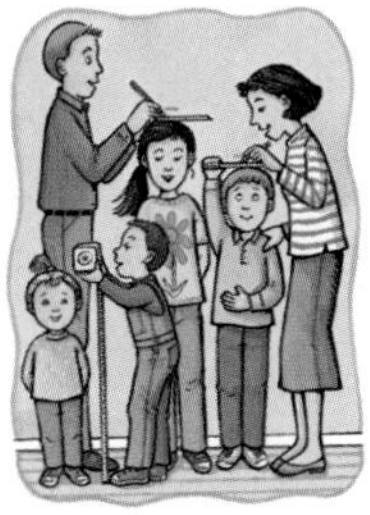

Geometry and Measurement

Algebra Indicates lessons that include algebra instruction.

18 Perimeter, Area, and Volume

FINISHING THE UNIT

Unit 6
Literature
Connection
*Dividing the
Cheese*
page 651

9 ft

6 ft

Fractions and Decimals

Algebra Indicates lessons that include algebra instruction.

UNIT 7 Fractions and Decimals

21 Understand Decimals

22 Add and Subtract Decimals

FINISHING THE UNIT

Unit 7 Literature Connection *Hold the Meat!* pages 652–653

WR Indicates WEEKLY WR READER eduplace.com/map

Probability/Algebra and Graphing

23 Probability

Algebra Indicates lessons that include algebra instruction.

UNIT **8** Probability/Algebra and Graphing

xx

Unit 8
Literature
Connection
*The Perfect
Present*
pages 654–655

Back to School

Welcome!

Scientists, athletes, artists, and health-care workers all use math every day—and you will too. This year in math you'll learn about numbers, patterns, shapes, and different ways to measure. You'll use the mathematics you know to solve problems and describe objects and patterns you see. You can get started by finding out about yourself as a mathematician and about the other students in your class.

Real Life Connection
Collecting Data

About Me

Write your math autobiography by answering these questions. You can draw a picture to go with your autobiography, if you want.

- Tell about a time you first remember doing math, even if you were very young.

- What are you good at in math?

- What would you like to improve or know more about?

- How do you (or someone in your family) use math outside of math class?

About My Class

Your classmates may be just like you in some ways and different in other ways. You can collect data to find out something about the whole class.

- Think of one topic you'd like to know about all your classmates.

- Write a survey question for your topic.

- Take a survey among your classmates. Use tally marks to collect the data.

- Make a bar graph or picture graph to show your results.

- Use your graph and data to write what you learned about your class.

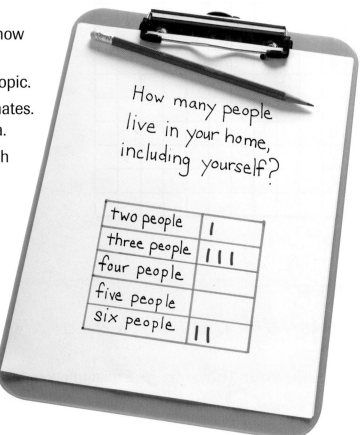

How many people live in your home, including yourself?

two people	I
three people	III
four people	
five people	
six people	II

Lesson

Problem Solving and Numbers

Objective Review basic number and problem-solving skills

Review and Remember

In this lesson, you will review the basic multiplication and division facts. You will also use basic facts to solve problems.

Guided Practice

1. Copy and complete a multiplication table like this one.

2. Highlight any facts that gave you trouble. These are facts to practice and learn.

×	0	1	2	3	4	5	6	7	8	9
0										
1										
2										
3										
4										
5										
6										
7										
8										
9										

Ask Yourself

• What strategies and patterns can I use to complete the table?

Divide.

3. $45 \div 5$ **4.** $42 \div 7$ **5.** $2 \div 2$ **6.** $56 \div 8$ **7.** $36 \div 6$

Explain Your Thinking ▶ Explain how to use your completed multiplication table to find answers to division facts.

Practice and Problem Solving

Multiply or divide.

8. 6×4 **9.** $54 \div 9$ **10.** 7×7 **11.** $35 \div 5$ **12.** 6×8

Solve each problem. Choose the strategy and computation method that works best for the problem.

13. How many students and teachers are in your classroom right now?

14. How many human elbows and knees are in your classroom right now? Explain how you found your answer.

15. An after-school group found that there were 28 elbows and knees. How many people were in that group?

16. **Multistep** Suppose that 15 students in your class are 10 years old and the rest are 9 years old. How many years have all the students in your class been living?

17. In one class, students built a pyramid. They put 9 cans on the bottom row, 8 cans on the next row up, and 7 cans on the third row. They continued building until they put 1 can on the top row. How many cans did they use in the entire pyramid?

You Choose

Strategy
- Find a Pattern
- Use Models
- Make a Table
- Write a Number Sentence

Computation Method
- Mental Math
- Estimation
- Paper and Pencil
- Calculator

Mixed Review and Test Prep

Open Response

Write each number in word form.
(Grade 3)

18. 7 hundreds, 6 tens, 5 ones

19. 120

20. $300 + 90 + 2$

Multiple Choice

21. Paula bought 8 beads for 7¢ each and 2 bracelets for $3 each. How much did she spend? (Grade 3)

   A. 56¢   **B.** 62¢

   C. $3.62   **D.** $6.56

Measurement

Objective Review basic measurement skills needed to start fourth grade.

Work Together

You can use math to describe objects in your classroom. First, review how to measure length with a ruler.

Work with a partner. Estimate the length of the pencil below to the nearest inch. Record your estimate; then measure.

Vocabulary

centimeter (cm)
foot (ft)
inch (in.)
meter (m)
yard (yd)

STEP 1 Line up the left end of the pencil with the zero mark of the inch ruler. If there is no zero mark, line up the pencil with the end of the ruler.

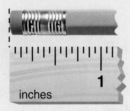
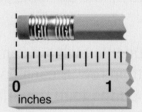

STEP 2 Find the inch mark closest to the right end of the pencil.

- What is the length of the pencil to the nearest inch?

- How close is your measurement to your estimate?

Repeat the steps above to estimate and measure the length of the pencil to the nearest centimeter.

On Your Own

**Find 3 classroom objects to measure. Copy each table.
Then follow the directions.**

- Estimate the length of each object to the nearest inch.
  Record your estimate.
- Measure the object. Record your measurement.

	Object	My Estimate	Length to the Nearest Inch
1.			
2.			
3.			

- Estimate the length of each object to the nearest centimeter.
  Record your estimate.
- Measure the object. Record your measurement.

	Object	My Estimate	Length to the Nearest Centimeter
4.			
5.			
6.			

**Use an inch ruler, a centimeter ruler, a yardstick,
or a meterstick to solve each problem.**

12 inches = 1 foot
3 feet = 1 yard
100 centimeters = 1 meter

7. Find three objects that you estimate
are each about 1 foot long. Measure
each object to check your estimate.

8. Find 3 objects that you estimate are
about 20 centimeters long. Measure
each object to check your estimate.

9. Find an object about 1 yard long or
wide. Measure to check your estimate.

10. Find an object about 1 meter long or
wide. Measure to check your estimate.

Talk About It • Write About It

11. Describe how to find the length of the pencil.

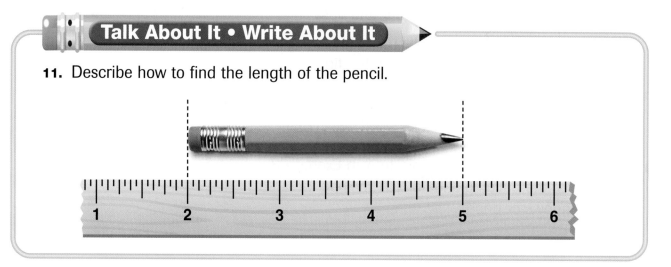

Hands On Lesson

Math Connections
Geometric Pieces

Materials
grid paper

The figure below was made by tracing around two rectangles on grid paper.

> Can you find each rectangle?

> Compare your answer with a classmate.

The distance around any figure is called the **perimeter** .

> Find the perimeter of this figure.

> Can you find the perimeter in more than one way?

> How do you label your answer?

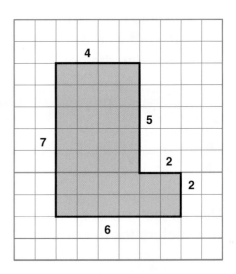

The **area** of a figure is the number of square units needed to cover the figure without overlapping.

> Find the area of the figure at the right.

> Can you find the area in more than one way?

> How do you label your answer?

Use grid paper. Follow the directions.

1. Draw a rectangle. Find its perimeter and area.

2. Draw a figure that combines two rectangles or squares. Find the perimeter and area of the entire figure.

3. Draw the front of a rectangular apartment building. Put in doors and windows. Use other geometric shapes to finish your picture.

4. Find the area of the building you drew in Exercise 3. The area of the building should NOT include the area of the windows or doors.

Reading Mathematics

Reviewing Vocabulary

Here are some math vocabulary words that you should know.

digit	any one of the ten number symbols 0, 1, 2, 3, 4, 5, 6, 7, 8, or 9
place value	the value of a digit determined by its place in a number
standard form	the usual, or common, way of writing a number, using digits
expanded form	a way of writing a number as the sum of the values of the digits
word form	a way of writing a number using words

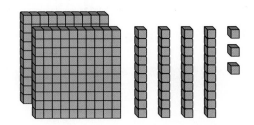

Reading Words and Symbols

Look at the base-ten blocks below. You can read and write the number they represent in these ways.

Read: There are 2 hundreds blocks

4 tens rods

3 ones cubes.

Write in standard form: 243

Write in expanded form: 200 + 40 + 3

Write in word form: two hundred forty-three

Use words or symbols to answer the questions.

1. What is the expanded form of 562?

2. What is the word form of 300 + 70 + 5?

Reading Test Questions

Choose the correct answer for each.

3. Select the answer that represents the blocks at the right.

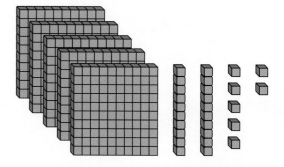

    a. 725   **c.** 527

    b. 572   **d.** 275

Select means "choose" or "pick."

---

4. What answer is equivalent to 318?

    a. 8 + 100 + 30

    b. 300 + 80 + 1

    c. 800 + 10 + 3

    d. 300 + 10 + 8

Equivalent means "equal."

5. Which of the following is not an alternate way to show the value of the number 89?

    a. 80 + 9   **c.** 8 tens 9 ones

    b. eighty-nine   **d.** 80 tens 9 ones

Alternate means "different."

Learning Vocabulary

Watch for these words in this unit. Write their definitions in your journal.

- ordinal number
- short word form
- period
- million
- hundred million

Education Place

At **eduplace.com/map**, see eGlossary and eGames—Math Lingo

Literature Connection

Read "Beyond Pluto" on Page 644. Then work with a partner to answer the questions about the story.

Place Value

INVESTIGATION

Using Data

The Statue of Liberty was a gift to the United States from France. Look at the facts about the statue. Which numbers are used to count? Which number is used to measure?

Use numbers to write 3 facts about another statue that you know.

The Statue of Liberty

- The statue was given to the United States on **July 4, 1884**.
- There are **25** windows in the crown.
- There are **354** steps from the base to the crown.
- The total weight of the statue is **450,000** pounds.

Use What You Know

**Use this page to review and remember
what you need to know for this chapter.**

VOCABULARY

Choose the best term to complete each sentence.

1. 1, 2, 3, 4, 5, 6, 7, 8, 9, and 0 are ____.

2. In the number 1,045, the 4 is in the ____ place.

3. 1st, 3rd, and 7th are examples of ____.

4. The number 400 + 30 + 5 is written in ____.

> **Vocabulary**
> tens
> digits
> standard form
> expanded form
> ordinal numbers

CONCEPTS AND SKILLS

**Copy the place-value chart and write each number in it.
Then write the value of the digit 7 for each number.**

5. 37
6. 785
7. 478
8. 1,075
9. 7,564

thousands	hundreds	tens	ones

Write each number in standard form.

10. 9 tens 3 ones

11. 6 hundreds 8 tens 5 ones

12. 800 + 20 + 4

13. 4,000 + 600 + 20

14. six hundred eighty-four

15. nine thousand, sixteen

Write the value of the underlined digit.

16. 6<u>3</u>4

17. <u>4</u>72

18. 7,<u>5</u>82

19. <u>4</u>,339

20. How many tens are there in 1,000? How many
    hundreds are there? Explain your answers.

Facts Practice, See page 664.

Audio Tutor 1/1 Listen and Understand

Uses of Numbers

Objective Use numbers in different ways.

Learn About It

Washington, D.C. became the capital of the United States in 1791. It has 3 famous monuments. It is the 21st largest city in the country.

Numbers are used in many different ways. How are the numbers **1791**, **3**, and **21st** being used?

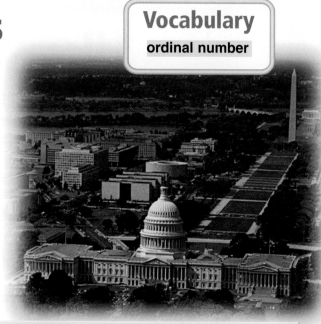

> **Ordinal numbers** are used to show position.
> - 2nd President
> - 1st President

John Adams was the 2nd President but the 1st President to live in the White House.

> **Numbers are used to count.**
> - 540 rooms
> - 658 windows

The U.S. Capitol building has 540 rooms and 658 windows!

> **Numbers are used to measure.**
> - 30 feet
> - 40 tons

The famous Bartholdi Fountain is about 30 feet high and weighs almost 40 tons.

> **Numbers are used to label.**
> - X-15
> - Apollo 11

At the Air and Space Museum, there is the X-15 airplane, and the Apollo 11 command module.

In the paragraph above, **1791** is used to measure, **3** is used to count, and **21st** is an ordinal number used to show position.

Tell how each number is being used.
Write *position, count, measure,* or *label*.

Ask Yourself

• Is the number an ordinal number?

• What does the number tell me?

1.

2.

3. 2,399 visitors

4. 25th person in line

Explain Your Thinking ▶ For each number on Page 4, tell if it is an estimate or an exact amount. Explain your reasoning.

Practice and Problem Solving

Tell how each number is being used. Write *position, count, measure,* or *label*.

5.
234

6.
Maximum Occupancy 250 persons

7.
George Washington 1st President

8. Carmel, IN 46033

9. 16th president of the U.S.

10. 750 pounds

11. 29 miles

12. 5 boxes of 12 pens each

13. Apartment 4B

14. 50 states

15. 3rd place

16. Row 65F

17. Reasoning Tanya went souvenir shopping. At the 3rd shop, she bought 4 souvenirs. The souvenirs weighed a total of 8 pounds. Which number in this problem is being used to count? Which number is used to measure? Explain how you decided.

Mixed Review and Test Prep

Open Response

Write each number in word form. (Grade 3)

18. 4,285

19. 2,049

20. 753

21. 14

22. 620

23. 359

24. 5,005

25. 290

26. During John's 5th trip to Washington, he traveled about 100 miles and bought 3 gifts. How is each number in the problem being used?

(Ch. 1, Lesson 1)

Audio Tutor 1/2 Listen and Understand

Place Value Through Hundred Thousands

Objective Read and write numbers through 999,999.

Vocabulary
period
standard form
expanded form
short word form
word form
base-ten

Learn About It

Anaya lives in Tallahassee, the capital of Florida. In the year 2000, the population of Tallahassee was 150,624.

What does the number 150,624 mean?

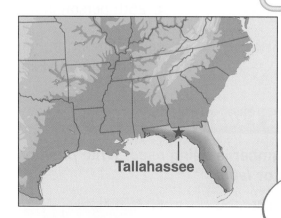

Tallahassee

Each group of 3 digits separated by a comma in a number is called a **period**.

▶ **A place-value chart can help explain what this number means.**

Thousands				Ones		
hundreds	tens	ones		hundreds	tens	ones
1	5	0	,	6	2	4

The value of the 1 is 100,000.

The value of the 5 is 50,000.

The value of the 6 is 600.

The value of the 2 is 20.

The value of the 4 is 4.

▶ **There are different ways to write 150,624.**

You can use **standard form**.	150,624
You can use **expanded form**.	100,000 + 50,000 + 600 + 20 + 4
You can use **short word form**.	150 thousand, 624
You can use **word form**.	one hundred fifty thousand, six hundred twenty-four

We use a **base-ten** place-value system. Each place is ten times greater than the place to the right of it.

Thousands			Ones		
hundreds	tens	ones	hundreds	tens	ones

× 10   × 10   × 10   × 10   × 10

Guided Practice

For Exercises 1–3, write each number in three other ways. You can use a place-value chart to help you.

1. 104,002   **2.** 104,020   **3.** 104 thousand, 200

4. What is the value of the 7 in 702,209?

Explain Your Thinking ▷ Do you think the population of a city is an estimated or exact amount? Why?

Ask Yourself

• What is the value of each digit?
• Do I need a comma?

Practice and Problem Solving

Write the value of the underlined digit.

5. 7<u>0</u>1   **6.** 5,<u>2</u>60   **7.** 63<u>9</u>,572   **8.** 5<u>6</u>,112

9. <u>1</u>2,048   **10.** 3<u>5</u>0,237   **11.** <u>7</u>63,299   **12.** 890,<u>0</u>973

Write each number in both short word form and word form.

13. 1,201   **14.** 300,200   **15.** 99,909   **16.** 332,332

17. 70,000 + 4,000 + 100 + 3   **18.** 500,000 + 20,000 + 1,000 + 600 + 3

Write each number in three other ways.

19. 80,000 + 4,000 + 200 + 2   **20.** 200,000 + 60,000 + 7,000 + 100 + 80 + 1

21. 405 thousand, 603   **22.** twenty thousand, eight hundred

23. 170 thousand, 815   **24.** six hundred four thousand, ninety-nine

Go On

Algebra • **Equations** Find each missing number.

25. $6{,}000 + 400 + 30 + \blacksquare = 6{,}439$

26. $2{,}000 + 900 + \blacksquare = 2{,}950$

27. $\blacksquare + 600 + 50 + 1 = 1{,}651$

28. $8{,}000 + \blacksquare + 4 = 8{,}204$

29. $\blacksquare + 5{,}000 + 60 = 905{,}060$

30. $70{,}000 + 8{,}000 + \blacksquare + 7 = 78{,}067$

Rewrite the number to show each change.

31. 2,146
  a. Increase by 10,000.
  b. Increase by 100,000.

32. 279,153
  a. Decrease by 1,000.
  b. Decrease by 10,000.

33. 509,986
  a. Decrease by 10,000.
  b. Decrease by 100,000.

34. 90,884
  a. Increase by 1,000.
  b. Increase by 10,000.

35. 192,906
  a. Increase by 10,000.
  b. Decrease by 1,000.

36. 99,090
  a. Decrease by 1,000.
  b. Increase by 1,000.

 Data Use the table for Problems 37–40.

37. What is the population of Austin, Texas? Write this number in three other ways.

38. Which cities have at least 200,000 people?

39. **Write About It** In which city's population does the digit 8 have the greatest value? Explain.

40. **Create and Solve** Use the table to write a problem. Give it to a friend to solve.

State Capital Populations in the Year 2000

Capital	Population
Indianapolis, IN	781,870
Austin, TX	656,562
Raleigh, NC	276,093
Frankfort, KY	27,741
Montpelier, VT	8,035

Extra Practice See page 21, Set B.

Visual Thinking
Benchmark Numbers

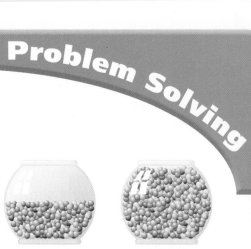

Benchmark numbers like 50, 100, and 200 can help you estimate an unknown amount.

If you know Jar A holds 250 marbles, you can use it as a benchmark to estimate how many marbles are in Jar B.

Jar A **Jar B**

Think There are about twice as many marbles in Jar B as Jar A.

So, there are about 500 marbles in Jar B.

Use each benchmark to choose the best estimate.

1.

Benchmark
25 marbles

a. 50 marbles
b. 100 marbles

2.    

Benchmark
500 gallons

a. 10,000 gallons
b. 1,000 gallons

Check your understanding of Lessons 1–2.

Tell how each number is being used. Write _position, count, measure,_ or _label._ (Lesson 1)

1. 2,305 books on a shelf   **2.** 350 inches long   **3.** Room 5C

Write each number in three other ways. (Lesson 2)

4. 45,207   **5.** 50 thousand, 203   **6.** 900,000 + 6,000 + 700 + 80 + 4

Write the place of the underlined digit. Then write its value. (Lesson 2)

7. 4<u>5</u>7,239   **8.** 12<u>7</u>,488   **9.** <u>5</u>64,220

Solve. (Lesson 1)

10. Sophia went to the mall to find a pair of X-20 sneakers. She bought the sneakers she wanted at the 3rd store she went into. How is each of the numbers in this problem being used?

Extra Practice at **eduplace.com/map**

 **Audio Tutor 1/3 Listen and Understand**

Problem-Solving Strategy
Use Logical Reasoning

Objective Use logical reasoning to solve problems.

Iris, Tennessee

Magnolia, Louisiana

Camellia, Alabama

Bluebonnet, Texas

Problem Al, Ron, Jo, and Di are each holding one of the state flowers shown. Di's flower is white. Al's flower is not red. Ron's flower is not purple. Jo's flower is not blue or red. Which color flower is each person holding?

 UNDERSTAND

This is what you know.

- Di's flower is white.
- Al's flower is not red.
- Ron's flower is not purple.
- Jo's flower is not blue or red.

PLAN

How can you use logical reasoning to solve?
You can make a chart to show what you know and then use logical reasoning to complete it.

SOLVE

Use logical reasoning to fill in the chart.
Write *yes* or *no* for the facts you know.

- Di's flower is white, so it is not red, purple, or blue.

- Jo's flower is purple because it is not white, blue, or red.

- Al's flower is blue, because it is not white, red, or purple.

- Ron's flower must be red.

When you write *yes* in the chart, you can write *no* in the rest of that row and column.

	White	Red	Blue	Purple
Di	yes	no	no	no
Jo	no	no	no	yes
Al	no	no	yes	no
Ron	no	yes	no	no

Solution: The flower Al is holding is blue. Ron's is red. Jo's is purple. Di's is white.

LOOK BACK

Look back at the problem.
Does the solution match the facts in the problem?

Extra Help at **eduplace.com/map**

Guided Practice

Use the Ask Yourself questions to help you solve each problem.

1. Rita, Gail, Rae, and Barb each have a state flag that is either red, blue, green, or black. Barb's flag is not red or green. Rita's is not red. Rae's is black. What color is each person's flag?

2. Dana, Nell, Bob, and Raj each take either Exit 1, 2, 3, or 4 off the state highway. Dana does not take Exit 1. Bob takes Exit 2. Raj does not take Exit 4. Nell does not take Exit 1 or Exit 4. Which exit does each take?

   (Hint) What are the heads of the columns and rows in my chart?

Ask Yourself

 UNDERSTAND **What facts do I know?**

 PLAN **Can I use logical reasoning?**

SOLVE
- **Did I fill in a chart with what I know?**
- **Did I use logical reasoning to complete the chart?**

LOOK BACK **Does my solution match the facts in the problem?**

Independent Practice

Use logical reasoning to solve each problem.

3. Mai, Lu, and Jo are playing a game about U.S. states. Their scores are 20, 25, and 30. Mai does not have the most points. Jo does not have the fewest points. Lu has 30 points. How many points does each girl have?

4. Vicki, Mary, and Tyra each own either a motorcycle, a car, or a van. Vicki does not own a vehicle with 4 wheels. Tyra owns a van. What vehicle does each person own?

5. Joe, Tom, Hal, and Bob are standing in line. Tom is first, Hal is not second or fourth. Joe is directly behind Hal. Bob is in front of Hal. In what order are the boys in line?

Go On

Mixed Problem Solving

Solve. Show your work. Tell what strategy you used.

6. **Multistep** Choi and Ana are playing a game. Choi scored 50, 40, and 80 points. If Ana has scored 60 and 70 points, how many more points does she need to tie Choi's score?

7. Tony and Aaron collect state patches. Tony has 4 more patches than Aaron. Together they have 14 patches. How many patches does each boy have?

8. Jeff bought a shirt for $12.00 and a pair of pants for $15.00. He paid with a $10 bill and a $20 bill. How much change did he receive?

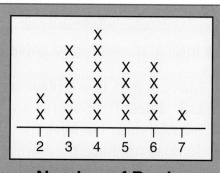

You Choose

Strategy
- Guess and Check
- Solve a Simpler Problem
- Work Backward
- Write an Equation

Computation Method
- Mental Math
- Estimation
- Paper and Pencil
- Calculator

 Data The line plot shows the number of books about the U.S. read by students in a class. Use the line plot for Problems 9–11.

9. How many students are in the class?

10. Students who read 4 or more books get certificates. How many students will get certificates?

11. Before the survey, Juan guessed that most people in his class had read more than 4 books. Was his guess correct? Explain.

12. **Reasoning** Erin, Hal, KC, and Juan each read either 3, 4, 5, or 6 books. Juan did not read 6 books. KC read 4 books. Hal did not read 5 or 6 books. How many books did each student read?

```
            X
      X     X
      X     X   X   X
      X     X   X   X
  X   X     X   X   X
  X   X     X   X   X   X
 ─┬───┬───┬───┬───┬───┬─
  2   3   4   5   6   7
```

**Number of Books
Read by Students**

Problem Solving on Tests

Multiple Choice

Choose the letter of the correct answer. If the correct answer is not here, select NH.

1. Leon has 7 pencils. His sister has 2 fewer pencils than he does. They want to share all the pencils equally among 3 people. How many pencils will each person get?

    A 4   C 12

    B 6   D 24

    (Grade 3)

2. The number below is being used to _____.

    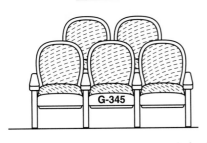

    F count   H label

    G show position   J NH

    (Chapter 1, Lesson 1)

Open Response

Solve each problem.

3. Rita's piano lesson starts at 11:35 A.M. and lasts for an hour. What time does it end?

    Explain how you know.

    (Grade 3)

4. The instruments below belong to Ned, Tom, and Belle. Ned's instrument does not have strings. Tom does not play the guitar.

    violin   clarinet   guitar

    Tell which instrument each person plays. Explain how you solved the problem.

    (Chapter 1, Lesson 3)

Extended Response

5. Alex went shopping for clothes to bring to camp. He bought 4 shirts: a yellow, a green, a red, and a white T-shirt. He also bought 2 pair of shorts: one brown and one black. Will he have enough clothes to wear a different outfit each day for 7 days? Make a list showing how he might plan to wear his clothes each day at camp.

    Information you need:

    • Alex decided he would not wear his yellow shirt with the black shorts.

    • He doesn't want to wear the same shorts or shirt two days in a row.

    • On Sunday, Alex would like to wear his brown shorts and the white shirt.

    • Camp starts on Monday.

    (Chapter 1, Lesson 3)

 Education Place

See **eduplace.com/map** for more Test-Taking Tips.

Hands On Lesson 4

How Big Is One Million?

Materials
Newspapers

Objective Relate one million to hundreds and thousands.

Work Together

Randy claims that he reads more than one million words each day. How many words is that?

A place-value chart can help explain what this number means.

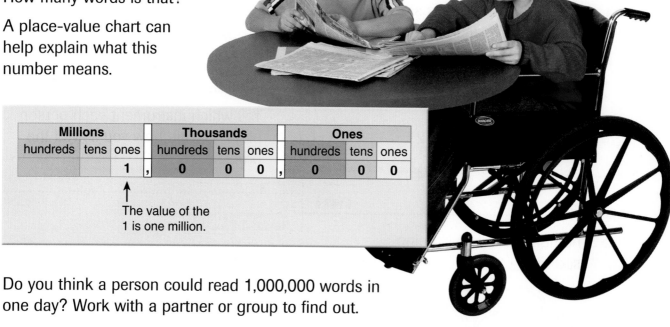

Millions			Thousands			Ones		
hundreds	tens	ones	hundreds	tens	ones	hundreds	tens	ones
		1 ,	0	0	0 ,	0	0	0

↑
The value of the
1 is one million.

Do you think a person could read 1,000,000 words in one day? Work with a partner or group to find out.

STEP 1 Take a page from a newspaper. Count and circle 100 words in an article. Write "100 words" on the circle.

STEP 2 Make a chart like the one shown. Estimate how many groups of 100 are on the first page. Write your estimate on the chart.

How many groups of 100 words are on the page?	
How many pages to read 1,000 words?	
How many pages to read 10,000 words?	
How many pages to read 100,000 words?	
How many pages to read 1,000,000 words?	

14

STEP 3 Estimate how many pages you will need to read 1,000 words. Write your estimate on the chart.

STEP 4 Use a calculator to complete the chart.

MILLIONS		THOUSANDS			ONES		
	millions	hundred thousands	ten thousands	thousands	hundreds	tens	ones
	1	0	0	0	0	0	0

On Your Own

Use your chart to answer each question.

1. How many thousands are there in 10,000?

2. How many thousands are there in 100,000?

3. How many thousands are there in 1,000,000?

4. How many hundreds are there in 1,000,000?

5. Describe the patterns you see in your charts.

6. Do you think Randy could read 1 million words in one day? How many newspaper pages would he have to read?

Talk About It • Write About It

You learned how 100 and 1,000 are related to one million.

7. How many thousands are in half of a million? Explain.

8. Would you use hundreds, thousands, or millions to count the following things? Explain your reasoning for each.

a. the people in your state

b. the students in your school

c. number of miles from New York to California

Place Value Through Hundred Millions

Objective Read and write numbers through 999,999,999.

Learn About It

Derek is collecting state quarters. The first state quarter the U.S. Mint made was the Delaware quarter in 1999.

The Denver mint made 401,424,000 Delaware quarters that year. A place-value chart can help you understand the value of the digits in the number 401,424,000.

▶ **A place-value chart can help explain what this number means.**

Millions				Thousands				Ones		
hundreds	tens	ones		hundreds	tens	ones		hundreds	tens	ones
4	0	1	,	4	2	4	,	0	0	0

The value of the 4 is 400,000,000.

The value of the 1 is 1,000,000.

Remember
Each group of 3 digits separated by a comma in a number is called a **period**.

▶ **There are different ways to write 401,424,000.**

You can use **standard form**.	401,424,000
You can use **expanded form**.	400,000,000 + 1,000,000 + 400,000 + 20,000 + 4,000
You can use **short word form**.	401 million, 424 thousand
You can use **word form**.	four hundred one million, four hundred twenty-four thousand

Guided Practice

For Exercises 1–5, write each number in three other ways.

1. 560,790,341   **2.** 56,298,743

3. 506,709,341   **4.** 500,000 + 200

5. 914 million, 887 thousand

6. Write 2<u>3</u>0,207,090 in expanded form. Then write the value of the underlined digit.

Explain Your Thinking ▶ What pattern do you see in the place-value chart on Page 16?

Practice and Problem Solving

Write each number in word form and short word form.

7. 6,007,002   **8.** 606,707,202   **9.** 45,213,450   **10.** 911,394,116

11. 4,000,000 + 200,000 + 30,000 + 6,000 + 400 + 20 + 5

12. 900,000,000 + 60,000,000 + 6,000,000 + 40,000 + 600 + 5

Write each number in standard form and expanded form.

13. 16 million, 201 thousand, 856   **14.** 439 million, 898 thousand, 312

15. sixty-three million, seven hundred ninety-six thousand, nine hundred three

16. five hundred twenty-seven million, nine hundred thousand, six hundred forty

Solve.

17. In one year, the U.S. Mint made a total of 939,932,000 Georgia quarters. Write this number in short word form.

18. Write About It Write a 9-digit number that has a 3 in the ten millions place, a 5 in the hundred thousands place, and a 2 in the ones place. Is this the only number you could have written? Explain.

The Georgia quarter was the 4th state quarter to be minted.

Go On

Write the place of the 7 in each number. Then write its value.

19. 708,993,040   **20.** 37,990,841   **21.** 16,007,845   **22.** 122,799

23. 20,895,227   **24.** 78,901   **25.** 107,912   **26.** 19,870,001

Match each standard-form number to its expanded or short word form.

27. 567,890,000   **a.** 243 million, 500 thousand

28. 56,789,000   **b.** 243 thousand, 500

29. 243,500,000   **c.** 567 million, 890 thousand

30. 243,500   **d.** 50,000,000 + 6,000,000 + 700,000 + 80,000 + 9,000

 Data The table shows the corn produced by four states. Use the table for Problems 31–34.

31. How many bushels of corn did Kansas produce? Write this number in two ways.

32. Which number has a 7 in the hundred thousands place?

33. Which states produced at least 100 million bushels of corn?

34. **Explain** How many bushels of corn did Oklahoma produce? In this number, does the digit 7 or the digit 8 have a greater value? Explain.

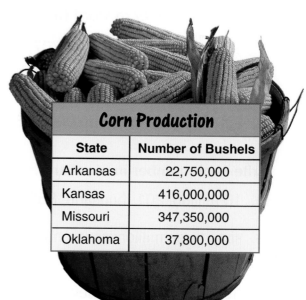

Corn Production	
State	Number of Bushels
Arkansas	22,750,000
Kansas	416,000,000
Missouri	347,350,000
Oklahoma	37,800,000

Mixed Review and Test Prep ✓

Open Response

For each pair of measurements, tell which is greater. (Grade 3)

35. 4 ounces or 4 pounds

36. 2 yards or 2 feet

37. 1 meter or 10 centimeters

Multiple Choice

38. What is NOT another way to write the value of the underlined digit in 7̲8,206? (Ch. 1, Lesson 2)

A 70 thousands   **C** 70,000

B 7 ten thousands   **D** 70 hundreds

Extra Practice See page 21, Set C.

Math Reasoning
Different Bases

Our place-value system is based on tens. Other systems use different bases.

Base Ten

Each place value in base ten is 10 times greater than the one to the right of it.

To read the number, add the values.

	×10	×10	×10
thousands	hundreds	tens	ones
1,000	100	10	1
2	**1**	**0**	**4**

Base 10 uses the digits 0 – 9.

$2 \times 1{,}000 + 1 \times 100 + 0 \times 10 + 4 \times 1$
$2{,}000 \quad + \quad 100 \quad + \quad 0 \quad + \quad 4 \quad = 2{,}104$

Base Two

Each place value in base two is 2 times greater than the one to the right of it.

To read 1101 in base ten, add the values.

	×2	×2	×2
8	4	2	1
1	**1**	**0**	**1**

Base 2 only uses the digits 0 and 1.

$1 \times 8 + 1 \times 4 + 0 \times 2 + 1 \times 1$
$8 \quad + \quad 4 \quad + \quad 0 \quad + \quad 1 \quad = 13$

Base Five

Each place value in base five is 5 times greater than the one to the right of it.

To read 1403 in base ten, add the values.

	×5	×5	×5
125	25	5	1
1	**4**	**0**	**3**

Base 5 uses the digits 0, 1, 2, 3, and 4.

$1 \times 125 + 4 \times 25 + 0 \times 5 + 3 \times 1$
$125 \quad + \quad 100 \quad + \quad 0 \quad + \quad 3 \quad = 228$

Write each base-two number in base ten.

1. 100   **2.** 101   **3.** 11   **4.** 110

Write each base-five number in base ten.

5. 201   **6.** 332   **7.** 41   **8.** 224

9. Challenge Look at the charts above. What are the next 2 place values in base two and base five? Explain your answers.

Chapter Review/Test

VOCABULARY

Choose the best term to complete each sentence.

1. A number that is used to show position is an ____.

2. Our place-value system is a ____ system.

3. 10,000,000 + 5,000 + 20 + 9 is the ____ for 10,005,029.

CONCEPTS AND SKILLS

Tell how each number is being used. Write *position, count, measure,* or *label.* (Lesson 1, pp. 4–5)

4. 4th in line

5. 16 ounces

6. 25 marbles

Write each number in three other ways. (Lesson 2, pp. 6–9, Lesson 4–5, pp. 14–19)

7. 395,123

8. 1 million, 619

9. 56 million, 432 thousand

10. 500,000,000 + 8,000 + 600 + 9

11. 20,000,000 + 300,000 + 4,000 + 1

12. seven hundred fifty-six million, six

13. three hundred nine thousand, fifty-one

Write the place of the underlined digit. Then write its value.

(Lesson 2, pp. 6–9, Lesson 5, pp. 16–19)

14. 1̲09,377

15. 2̲5̲6,300

16. 3̲,589,605

17. 48,5̲56,215

18. 2̲0̲6,000,015

19. 3̲46,157,021

PROBLEM SOLVING

Solve. (Lesson 3, pp. 10–13)

20. Four children stand in line to see a movie. Elise is second in line. Brian is not last. John is directly in front of Elise. Chris is not second or third in line. List the children in order from first to fourth.

Write About It

Show You Understand

Why do we call our system of numbers a base-ten system? Explain your thinking.

Extra Practice

Set A (Lesson 1, pp. 4–5)

Tell how each number is being used. Write *position*, *count*, *measure*, or *label*.

1. 52 miles
2. Charlotte, NC 08088
3. 50th anniversary
4. 76 people
5. Apartment 9C
6. 325 pounds

Set B (Lesson 2, pp. 6–9)

Write each number in three other ways.

1. 59 thousand, 505
2. 200,000 + 6,000 + 60
3. 300,991
4. 230,000
5. five hundred six thousand
6. 49,300
7. 800,000 + 50,000 + 400 + 70
8. 400,000 + 20,000 + 900 + 70 + 7
9. thirty thousand, nine hundred
10. five hundred fifty thousand, three

Write the place of the underlined digit. Then write its value.

11. 5<u>0</u>,862
12. <u>5</u>05,432
13. 99,9<u>9</u>0
14. 4<u>9</u>,887
15. 110,02<u>2</u>
16. 8,<u>8</u>92
17. <u>7</u>28,683
18. 1<u>4</u>6,170

Set C (Lesson 5, pp. 16–19)

Write each number in three other ways.

1. 4,005,000
2. 909,990,099
3. 15 million, 304 thousand, 794
4. 700,000,000 + 5,000,000 + 40,000 + 600 + 7
5. seventy-six million, two hundred fifty-seven thousand, four hundred forty-two

Write the place of the 9 in each number. Then write its value.

6. 780,090,001
7. 97,341,203
8. 109,866
9. 923,011,233
10. 65,901,235
11. 573,280,908
12. 59,605,511
13. 600,390,885

Compare, Order, and Round Whole Numbers and Money

INVESTIGATION

Using Data

A student claims that, according to the graph on the right, there are more species of fish than mammals in the Grand Canyon. Is she correct? Why, or why not?

What other comparisons could you make, using the information in the graph?

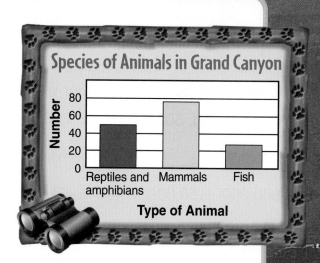

Species of Animals in Grand Canyon

(Bar graph showing Number (0, 20, 40, 60, 80) versus Type of Animal: Reptiles and amphibians, Mammals, Fish)

 **Use What You Know**

**Use this page to review and remember
what you need to know for this chapter.**

VOCABULARY

Choose the best term to complete each sentence.

Vocabulary
digit
estimate
less than
greater than

1. The symbol < means _____.

2. A symbol used to write numbers is called a _____.

3. A number that is close to an exact amount is an _____.

CONCEPTS AND SKILLS

Compare. Write >, <, or = for each ⬤.

4. 86 ⬤ 85   5. 75 ⬤ 57   6. 260 ⬤ 260   7. 400 ⬤ 500   8. 362 ⬤ 326

**Tell whether the digit 6 is in the hundreds,
thousands, or ten thousands place.**

9. 6,723   10. 1,645   11. 63,908   12. 86,709   13. 2,603

Write the numbers in order from least to greatest.

14. 65   73   45   15. 175   204   192   16. 1,973   1,745   1,945

**Write *true* or *false* for each.
If false, write a statement that is true.**

17. You can write forty-five cents as $0.45 or 45¢.

18. You can use two coins to give someone 31¢.

19. The value of two quarters and one nickel is less than the value of five dimes.

Write About It ▶

20. What two bills are equal to the value
of 4 five-dollar bills? Are there other
combinations of bills that would equal
that same amount? Explain your answer.

Facts Practice, See page 665.

Audio Tutor 1/4 Listen and Understand

Compare Numbers

Objective Compare numbers up to nine digits.

Vocabulary
compare

Learn About It

Our country has many beautiful national parks. **Compare** the number of acres each park occupies. Which park has the greater number of acres?

20,454 acres

20,766 acres

Different Ways to Compare Numbers

Way ❶ You can use a number line.

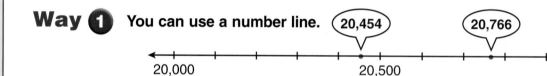

20,766 is to the right of 20,454 on the number line. So 20,766 > 20,454.

Way ❷ You can use place value.

STEP 1 Begin at the greatest place. Find where the digits are different.

```
20,766
20,454
  ↑ ↑
Same Different
```

STEP 2 Compare the digits that are different. Write > or <.

```
20,766
20,454
   ↑
```

7 hundreds > 4 hundreds

So, 20,766 > 20,454.

Solution: The park that occupies 20,766 acres has the greater number of acres.

Guided Practice

Compare. Write >, <, or = for each ⬤.

1. 1,001 ⬤ 979

2. 968,305 ⬤ 968,305

3. 19,009 ⬤ 19,090

4. 2,300,062 ⬤ 2,030,062

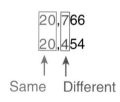

Ask Yourself

• Which digits do I compare first?

• What should I do when digits in the same place are the same?

Explain Your Thinking ▶ In Exercise 1, did you need to compare the digits in the hundreds, tens, or ones places? Explain.

Extra Help at **eduplace.com/map**

Compare. Write >, <, or = for each ⬤.

5. 808 ⬤ 880

6. 1,207 ⬤ 1,207

7. 2,347 ⬤ 2,487

8. 5,648 ⬤ 6,548

9. 1,035 ⬤ 1,340

10. 72,066 ⬤ 72,600

11. 11,001 ⬤ 92,876

12. 135,734 ⬤ 55,724

13. 869,621 ⬤ 879,566

14. 112,311 ⬤ 99,902

15. 190,098 ⬤ 19,098

16. 495,339 ⬤ 494,340

17. 98,760,032 ⬤ 98,790,032

18. 444,440,004 ⬤ 404,004,004

19. 40,000 ⬤ 400 thousands

20. 7 ten thousands ⬤ 7,000

21. 5,000 ⬤ 500 thousands

22. 9 thousands ⬤ 9,000

 Data Use the table for Problems 23–25.

The table shows the number of people who took part in activities at Colorado National Monument during one fall month.

23. Which activity was the most popular? Which was the least popular?

24. Did more people choose to go bicycle riding or mountain climbing?

25. **You Decide** Do you think the data would be similar or different for a month in summer? Explain.

Activities at Colorado National Monument	
Activity	**Number of People**
Auto Tour	11,908
Bicycle Riding	834
Horseback Riding	11,025
Mountain Climbing	943
Wildlife Tour	10,169

Mixed Review and Test Prep ✓

Open Response

Write the value of the underlined digit.
(Ch. 1, Lesson 5)

26. 2,090

27. 92,001

28. 120,900

29. 20,090,029

30. 379,536,221

31. 639,726,503

32. A museum has two thousand sixteen gems and one thousand ninety-eight minerals on display. Are there more gems or minerals on display? (Ch. 2, Lesson 1)

Audio Tutor 1/5 Listen and Understand

Order Numbers

Objective Order numbers up to nine digits.

Vocabulary
order

Learn About It

The Wright Brothers National Memorial in North Carolina is a fun place to visit! One summer, there were 72,566 visitors in June, 77,465 visitors in July, and 71,324 visitors in August. Which month had the most visitors? Which month had the least number of visitors?

This monument honors the first successful airplane flight achieved on December 17, 1903.

Different Ways to Order Numbers

Ordering numbers is like comparing numbers.

Way ① You can use a number line.

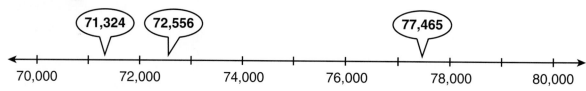

71,324 is farthest to the left. 72,566 is between 71,324 and 77,465.

77,465 is farthest to the right.

So, 71,324 < 72,566 and 72,566 < 77,465.

Way ② You can use place value.

STEP 1 Line up the digits by place value. Begin at the greatest place value. Find the place where the digits are different.

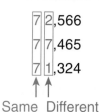

7**2**,566
7**7**,465
7**1**,324

↑ ↑
Same Different

STEP 2 Compare the digits that are different. Write < or >.

7**2**,566
7**7**,465
7**1**,324

7 > 2   So, 77,465 > 72,566.
2 > 1   So, 72,566 > 71,324.

Ordered from least to greatest, the numbers are: 71,324   72,566   77,465

Solution: July had the most visitors. August had the fewest visitors.

Other Examples

A. Order 4- and 5-digit Numbers

Order these numbers from greatest to least.
12,345   12,700   7,890

      7,890 ← This is the least
  12,700   number. It has the
  12,345   fewest digits.
  ↑ ↑

same   7 > 3

7 > 3. So 12,700 > 12,345.

So, the order from greatest to least is
12,700   12,345   7,890

B. Order Greater Numbers

Order these numbers from least
to greatest.
719,264,198   708,345,562   719,263,001

  719,264,198
  708,345,562
  719,263,001
    ↑   ↑
  0 < 1   3 < 4

0 < 1. So, 708,345,562 is the least number.

3 < 4. So, 719,263,001 < 719,264,198.

So, the order from least to greatest is
708,345,562   719,263,001   719,264,198

Guided Practice

Write the numbers in order from least to greatest.

1. 1,209   12,909   9,102

2. 69,541   689,541   68,541

3. 1,202,334   1,220,334   1,022,030

4. 993,457,601   994,574,601   993,574,601

Ask Yourself

- Am I ordering from least to greatest or from greatest to least?
- Which digits do I compare first?

Explain Your Thinking ▶ How does looking at the number of digits in some numbers help you order the numbers? Explain.

Practice and Problem Solving

Write the numbers in order from greatest to least.

5. 4,040   4,404   4,044   4,004

6. 102,000   12,000   100,200   10,200

7. 85,407,363   8,407,363   85,073,630

8. 225,522,145   25,522,145   252,522,145

The glider shown here was one of several used by the Wright brothers.

Write the numbers in order from least to greatest.

9. 3,199   2,233   8,872

10. 2,110   1,911   2,345   2,350

11. 19,588   10,002   9,855

12. 57,601   574,601   576,601   506,960

13. 365,844   365,448   356,882

14. 642,951,316   645,746,892   604,682,637

Find each missing digit.

15. 6,106 > 6,■19

16. 2,117 = ■,117

17. 4,382 < 4,3■2

18. 91,472 > 9■,472

19. 114,899 < 114,■99

20. 703,9■1 = 703,981

21. 11,234 > 1■,785

22. 67,813 > 67,8■3

23. 82,■88 = 82,588

24. 179,00■ < 179,001

25. 856,■34 < 856,134

26. 683,129 < 6■3,129

Solve.

27. Use the information in the picture. Thomasville's population is 30 more than Lincolnton's. Write the populations in order from greatest to least.

28. Mr. Marcel drove 1,038 miles, Ms. Lok drove 752 miles, and Mrs. Alba drove 1,093 miles. Order the distances they drove from least to greatest.

29. A seven-digit number has a 7 in the millions place and a 3 in the ten thousands place. All other places have ones. Write the number in words.

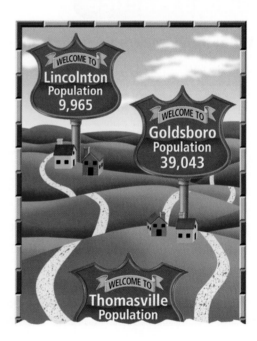

WELCOME TO
Lincolnton
Population
9,965

WELCOME TO
Goldsboro
Population
39,043

WELCOME TO
Thomasville
Population

Mixed Review and Test Prep

Open Response

Write the missing number. (Grade 3)

30. 5 + ■ = 11

31. 9 × ■ = 27

32. 14 − 7 = ■

33. 42 ÷ 6 = ■

34. 8 × 7 = ■

35. 13 − ■ = 6

36. ■ ÷ 4 = 9

37. 9 − 7 = ■

Multiple Choice

38. Look at the numbers below. Which number is greatest? (Ch. 2, Lesson 2)

A 62,102

C 62,109

B 61,902

D 61,002

Extra Practice See page 45, Set B.

Social Studies Connection
Thai Numerals

Students in Thailand use both Arabic and Thai numerals. The Thai number system is very similar to the base ten number system.

Here are the Thai symbols for 0–9.

• Think about how we put our symbols for 0–9 together to make the numbers from 10 to 20.

• Then look at the Thai symbols for 11, 17, and 19 in the chart. Now write the missing Thai symbols to complete the chart.

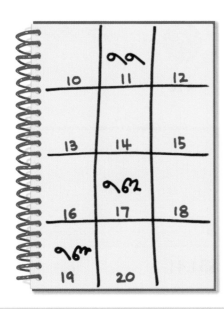

Math Reasoning
How Big is 100,000?

• 100,000 is big if you are carrying that many pounds of rocks.

• 100,000 is small if you are filling a bucket with that many grains of sand.

Choose the best number.

1. The number of people that would fit in an elevator

   a. 100 people   **b.** 10 people

2. The time it takes to brush your teeth

   a. 2,000 minutes   **b.** 2 minutes

3. When might 2,000 minutes seem like not enough time?

Brain Teaser

Use the clues to find the mystery number.

• It is a four-digit number.

• Its tens digit is 2.

• Its thousands digit is 4.

• Its hundreds digit is the sum of its ones digit and its tens digit.

• Its ones digit is two times its tens digit.

What is the number?

Education Place

Visit *Education Place* at **eduplace.com/map** to try more brain teasers.

Compare and Order Money

Objective Count and compare amounts of money.

Learn About It

Sean and Maria are visiting the Kennedy Space Center. They are buying a gift for $32.00. They have 1 twenty-dollar bill, 2 five-dollar bills, 1 one-dollar bill, 1 quarter, 1 dime, 1 nickel, and 1 penny. Do they have enough money?

Follow these steps to find out.

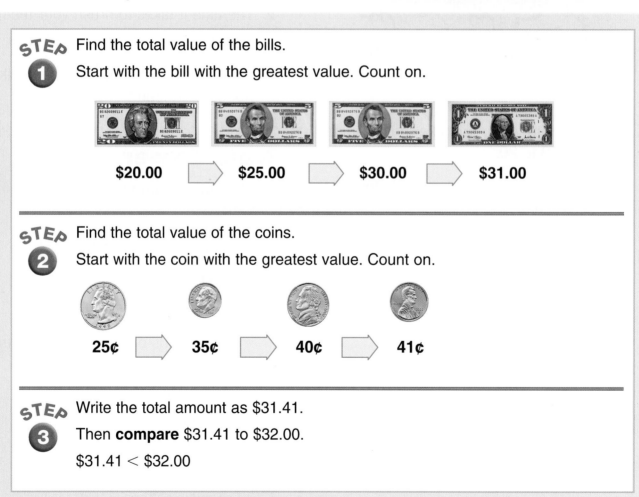

STEP 1 Find the total value of the bills.

Start with the bill with the greatest value. Count on.

$20.00 ▷ $25.00 ▷ $30.00 ▷ $31.00

STEP 2 Find the total value of the coins.

Start with the coin with the greatest value. Count on.

25¢ ▷ 35¢ ▷ 40¢ ▷ 41¢

STEP 3 Write the total amount as $31.41.

Then **compare** $31.41 to $32.00.

$31.41 < $32.00

Solution: No, they do not have enough money, since $31.41 is less than $32.00.

Follow these steps to order $25.30, $21.00, and $25.20 from least to greatest.

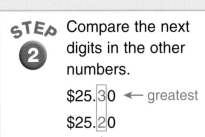

STEP 1 Find the greatest place value with different digits.

$2[1].00 ← least
$2[5].30
$2[5].20
↑
1 < 5

STEP 2 Compare the next digits in the other numbers.

$25.[3]0 ← greatest
$25.[2]0
↑
3 > 2

STEP 3 Write the amounts in order.

$21.00 < $25.30
and $25.30 > $25.20

So, from least to greatest,
$21.00 < $25.20 < $25.30

Solution: From least to greatest, the amounts are
$21.00 $25.20 $25.30

Guided Practice

Write each amount. Then write the greatest amount and the least amount.

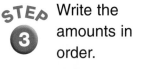

Ask Yourself

- In what order will I count the bills?
- In what order will I count the coins?

1.

2.

3.

4.

Explain Your Thinking ▶ Is it usually easier to count the bills or coins with the greatest value first? Why or why not?

Go On

Practice and Problem Solving

Write each amount. Then write the greater amount.

5.     **or**

6.    **or**

7. 6 dimes, 2 quarters, 4 nickels
or
7 nickels, 2 half-dollars

8. 4 one-dollar bills, 6 quarters,
or
1 five-dollar bill, 4 dimes

9. 3 five-dollar bills, 8 quarters
or
1 twenty-dollar bill, 5 dimes

10. 7 ten-dollar bills, 6 quarters
or
1 fifty-dollar bill, 3 five-dollar bills

11. 2 fifty-dollar bills, 5 quarters
or
5 twenty-dollar bills, 6 dimes

12. 13 one-dollar bills, 9 dimes
or
1 ten-dollar bill, 6 quarters, 8 dimes

Data Use the pictures for Problems 13–16.

13. Which souvenir is most expensive? Which is least expensive?

14. Adela has 1 twenty-dollar bill, 3 quarters, and 1 five-dollar bill. Does she have enough money for a Space Blanket and two NASA Travel Mugs?

15. **Estimate** About how much would it cost to buy one calendar and two T-shirts?

16. Using the least number of bills and coins, how would you pay the exact amount for a NASA Travel Mug?

17. **Write About It** Explain how you compare $53 and the sum of 4 ten-dollar bills, 3 five-dollar bills, and 2 one-dollar bills.

32

Extra Practice See page 45, Set C.

Real World Connection
Braille Numbers

Braille is a code made with raised dots. A blind person can read letters, words, numbers, and symbols by touching the raised dots. Here are the Braille symbols for the numbers 0–9:

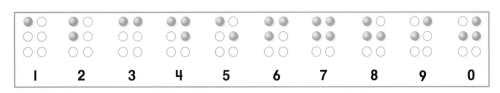

| 1 | 2 | 3 | 4 | 5 | 6 | 7 | 8 | 9 | 0 |

▶ This symbol appears before a number.   ▶ So this is the number 12.

Write each of these Braille numbers.

1. (Braille numbers)   2. (Braille numbers)

Check your understanding of Lessons 1–3.

Compare. Write >, <, or = for each ●. (Lesson 1)

1. 6,057 ● 12,032   2. 5,564 ● 5,654

3. 204,568 ● 204,567   4. 567,034,789 ● 593,694,129

Write the numbers in order from least to greatest. (Lesson 2)

5. 212   2,002   1,212   6. 4,004   4,440   4,044

7. 43,120   39,021   26,707   8. 512,678   34,762   710,094

Write each amount. (Lesson 3)

9. 6 ten-dollar bills, 4 quarters, 2 dimes, 4 pennies

10. 3 twenty-dollar bills, 2 five-dollar bills, 3 nickels, 2 pennies

---

Make Change

Objective Count on to make change.

Learn About It

The Bailey family is vacationing at Mammoth Cave in Kentucky. They are buying a poster of the stalactites and stalagmites in the Great Onyx Cave. The poster costs $23.89. They give the clerk $30.00. What amount will the Baileys get as change?

You can count on from the cost of the poster to make change.

Stalactites form downward from the roof of a cavern. Stalagmites form upward from the floor. Both are caused by the dripping of mineral-rich water.

Follow the steps below to find the change that the Bailey family will receive.

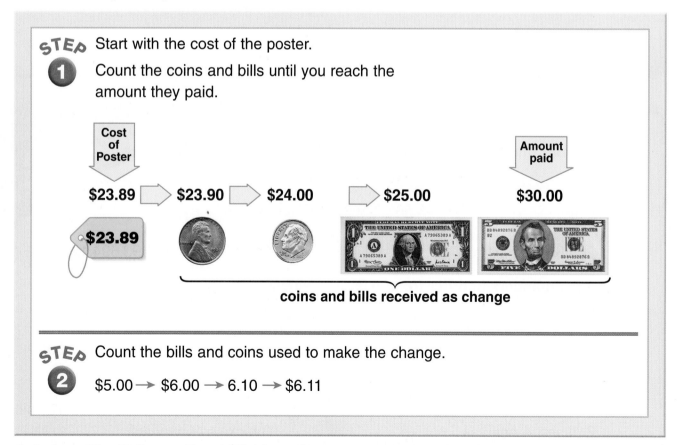

STEP 1 Start with the cost of the poster.

Count the coins and bills until you reach the amount they paid.

Cost of Poster

$23.89 ⟹ $23.90 ⟹ $24.00 ⟹ $25.00 $30.00   Amount paid

$23.89

coins and bills received as change

STEP 2 Count the bills and coins used to make the change.

$5.00 → $6.00 → 6.10 → $6.11

Solution: The Baileys will get $6.11 as change.

Guided Practice

A $10 bill was used to buy each item below. List the coins and bills you would use to make change.

Ask Yourself
- What amount do I start with?
- What coins and bills do I need to count up to the price?

1.  $3.28

2.  $8.77

3.  $5.99

Explain Your Thinking ▶ Look at Problems 1–3. Why do you start with coins when making change?

Practice and Problem Solving

A $20 bill was used to buy each item below. List the coins and bills you would use to make change.

4.  $12.75

5.  $8.29

6.  $6.55

7.  $4.35

8. $5.98

9.  $18.19

Write the amount of change you would receive for each.

10. You bought popcorn for 79¢. You paid with 4 quarters.

11. You bought a pen for $0.86. You paid with 1 five-dollar bill.

12. You bought a CD for $7.74. You paid with 2 five-dollar bills.

13. You bought a sandwich for $3.17. You paid with 1 ten-dollar bill.

Data The table on the right gives information about tours of Mammoth Cave. Use the table for Problems 14–18.

14. Mr. Orestes and his 12-year-old son are going on the Great Onyx tour. How much will they pay?

15. Mrs. Tyler goes with her two children on the Travertine tour. She pays with 1 twenty-dollar bill and 1 ten-dollar bill. How much change does she receive?

16. The Trog tour is planned only for 8- to 12-year-olds. If Pam and Tom's parents pay for their tickets with 1 twenty-dollar bill and 1 ten-dollar bill, how much change will they get?

17. You buy 1 adult ticket and 1 youth ticket to the Discovery tour. If you pay with 4 one-dollar bills and 1 five-dollar bill, how much change should you receive?

18. **Create and Solve** Use the data in the table to write a new problem. Exchange your problem with a friend and solve.

Mammoth Cave Tours

Tour	Adult	Youth
Discovery	$5.00	$3.50
Frozen Niagara	$11.00	$8.00
Grand Avenue	$21.00	$15.00
Great Onyx	$15.00	$11.00
Historic	$11.00	$8.00
Travertine	$10.00	$8.00
Trog	—	$14.00
Violet City	$15.00	$11.00

Mixed Review and Test Prep

Open Response

Tell what time it will be. (Grade 3)

19. in 20 minutes

20. in 2 hours

21. in 15 minutes

22. in 35 minutes

23. Jason bought the game below. What are the fewest coins and bills he could have used to pay for it if he received no change?

(Ch. 2, Lesson 4)

$14.87

Extra Practice See page 45, Set D.

Dollar Dunk

Activity

2–4 Players

What You'll Need • 40 index cards or Learning Tool 4

1¢ 10 cards

5¢ 10 cards

10¢ 8 cards

25¢ 8 cards

50¢ 4 cards

Practice using money by playing this game.

Dollar Dunk is like the game Go Fish. Try to be the first to use all your cards.

How to Play

1 Make 40 cards like the ones shown or use Learning Tool 4.

2 Shuffle and deal 5 cards to each player. Stack the rest facedown.

3 Players look at their cards. The object is to get rid of the cards by making $1.00 with some or all of the cards. Whenever players can make $1.00, they place those cards faceup in front of them.

4 If a player cannot make $1.00, he or she asks another player for a card. For example, the player might ask, "Do you have 25¢?" If that player has the card, it must be given to the first player. If not, the first player "dunks" into the deck by taking the top card.

5 Players take turns repeating Steps 3 and 4. The first player with no cards is the winner.

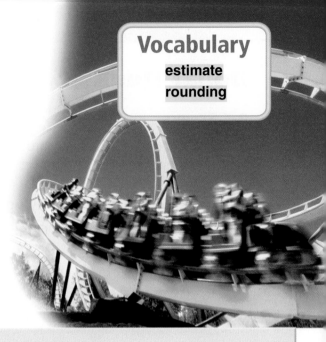

Audio Tutor 1/6 Listen and Understand

Round Numbers

Objective Round numbers and money amounts.

Vocabulary
estimate
rounding

Learn About It

Jeff visited an amusement park on his vacation. He rode a roller coaster that is 5,843 feet long. About how long is the roller coaster?

Since you do not need an exact number, you can **estimate** by **rounding** the number.

Different Ways to Round 5,843

Way ❶ You can use a number line.

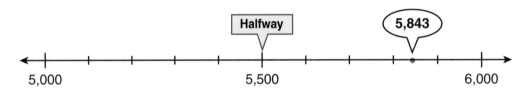

Halfway   5,843

5,000   5,500   6,000

5,843 is closer to 6,000 than to 5,000.
So, round 5,843 to 6,000.

Way ❷ You can use place value.

STEP 1
Find the place you want to round to. Underline the digit in that place.

<u>5</u>,843
↑
thousands place

STEP 2
Look at the digit to its right. Circle that digit.

5,⑧43
↑
digit to the right

STEP 3
• If the circled digit is 5 or greater, round up.

• If the circled digit is less than 5, round down.

• 8 is greater than 5, so

5,843 rounds to➤ 6,000

Solution: The roller coaster is about 6,000 feet long.

Guided Practice

Round each number to the place of the underlined digit.

1. <u>3</u>,812
2. 14,731,200
3. $44.92
4. 12<u>5</u>,601
5. $1<u>5</u>7.72
6. 792,3<u>6</u>9

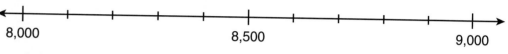

Explain Your Thinking ▶ Can a three-digit number round to 1,000? Use an example to explain why or why not.

Practice and Problem Solving

Use the number line to round each number to the nearest thousand.

```
←—+——+——+——+——+——+——+——+——+——+——→
8,000            8,500          9,000
```

7. 8,900
8. 8,210
9. 8,350
10. 8,732
11. 8,499

Round each number to the place of the underlined digit.

12. 2<u>6</u>,754
13. 19,8<u>8</u>7
14. 3<u>3</u>,501
15. 1<u>1</u>3,772
16. 42<u>8</u>,001,674
17. 209,<u>1</u>21,456
18. 7<u>8</u>,901,223
19. 7,<u>4</u>25,333

Round to the nearest ten cents. Then round to the nearest dollar.

20. $4.57
21. $9.45
22. $13.84
23. $578.34
24. $827.16
25. $391.72
26. $4,398.79
27. $3,287.95

Solve.

28. Rosemarie rode one of the longest roller coasters in the world. It is 8,133 feet long. How long is that to the nearest hundred feet?

29. There were 2,638 riders for the roller coaster. A park official rounded that number to 3,000. To which place was the number rounded?

Mixed Review and Test Prep

Open Response

Complete each number sentence. (Grade 3)

30. ■ + 9 = 16
31. 8 × ■ = 48
32. 18 − 5 = ■
33. 42 ÷ 7 = ■
34. 4 × ■ = 24
35. ■ + 3 = 12

36. Round 99,603 to the nearest ten thousand. Then round it to the nearest thousand. What do you notice about your answers? Explain. (Ch. 2, Lesson 5)

Problem-Solving Application
Use a Bar Graph

Objective Use a bar graph to compare data.

Vocabulary
bar graph

You can use a bar graph to compare data.

Problem A community center takes people on day trips. The bar graph shows how many people went on various trips last summer.

Which activity had twice as many people participate as the zoo?

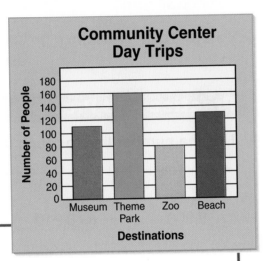

Community Center Day Trips

UNDERSTAND

This is what you need to find.

You can use the height of the bars on the graph to compare the number of people on each trip.

PLAN

Get information from the graph.

Find the bar that is about twice as tall as the bar for zoo.
Then find the number of people for the two trips.

SOLVE

Use the bar graph to compare data.

The bar for the zoo reaches to 80. The bar for the theme park is twice as tall as the bar for the zoo. It reaches the 160 line.

160 is twice as much as 80.

Solution: Twice as many people went on the theme park trip as went to the zoo.

LOOK BACK

Look back at the problem.

How could you check to see if your answer is reasonable?

Guided Practice

Use the bar graph on Page 40 to solve Problems 1–4.

1. How many people visited the theme park?

2. Did more people visit the museum or the zoo?

3. Did fewer people visit the beach or the theme park?

4. About how many more people visited the beach than the museum?

(**Hint**) Estimate each number, then subtract.

Ask Yourself

UNDERSTAND — What does the question ask me to find?

PLAN — Can I get the information from the graph?

SOLVE — Did I read the graph correctly?

LOOK BACK — Is my answer reasonable?

Independent Practice

 Data Use the bar graph for Problems 5–10.

The graph shows the coins that Gabriel has saved for summer trips.

5. Which coin does Gabriel have the most of?

6. Which coin does he have the least of?

7. **Mental Math** How much money does Gabriel have in pennies?

8. Does Gabriel have more quarters than nickels? How do you know?

9. **Multistep** If Gabriel gives all of the nickels and dimes to his younger brother, how much money will he give his brother?

10. **Create and Solve** Write a problem about the graph. Then exchange problems with a friend and solve.

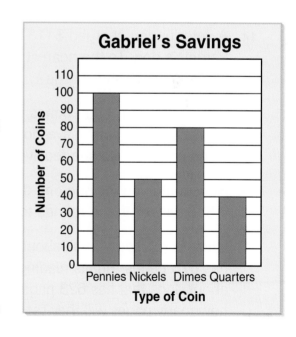

Gabriel's Savings

Go On

Mixed Problem Solving

Solve. Show your work. Tell what strategy you used.

11. **Reasoning** Ali, Jim, and Sue are members of either hockey, soccer, or swimming teams. Ali doesn't play soccer. Jim doesn't play soccer or swim. Each person plays one sport. What team is each person on?

12. Mark added 36 in. to his race car track. Then he removed 4 in. This made his track 94 in. long. How long was the track before he started changing it?

13. The prize for a competition doubles each day. The prize was $1 for the first day. What will the prize be on the seventh day?

Solve. Tell which method you chose.

14. A veterinarian charged $113 for treating Patricia's dog. To the nearest ten dollars, how much did she charge?

15. Patricia bought 3 dog bones for $0.60 each. She paid with 1 five-dollar bill. What coins and bills did she receive as change?

16. How could you change one digit in 7,856,041 so that it rounds to 7,800,000?

17. Laura is reading a book about horses that has 578 pages. Tina is reading a book about dogs that has 623 pages. About how many pages will they read altogether?

18. **Multistep** Maria earned 3 ten-dollar bills, 4 quarters, and 2 nickels. Alex earned 5 five-dollar bills, 3 one-dollar bills, and 3 quarters. Who has more money?

You Choose

Strategy
- Draw a Picture
- Find a Pattern
- Use Logical Reasoning
- Work Backward

Computation Method
- Mental Math
- Estimation
- Paper and Pencil
- Calculator

Logical Reasoning
Around They Go

Some friends ride the Marvel Wheel at an amusement park. The Marvel Wheel turns clockwise.

The wheel has stopped. Now Kathy has the best view. Tanya is between Hank and Luke. Luke's car is just starting up. Sara is between Clark and Emma. Kathy is just ahead of Hank and behind another boy.

Use logical thinking to find who is in which car.

- Kathy has the best view of all.

- Kathy is just ahead of Hank and behind another boy.

- Luke's car is just starting up.

Use the rest of the clues to solve the puzzle.

- Tanya is between Hank and Luke.
- Sara is between Clark and Emma.

Create your own logical thinking puzzle, using the Marvel Wheel as a guide.

Choose the names of 7 people you know, and assign each name to a car on the Marvel Wheel. You may want to draw your own Marvel Wheel as a guide. Then write clues that tell about the location of each person. Give the clues to your classmates to see if they can solve your puzzle.

Chapter Review/Test

VOCABULARY

Choose the best term to complete each sentence.

1. To tell about how much is to ____.

2. To compare numbers you can use ____.

3. One way to display data is to use a ____.

Vocabulary

order
estimate
bar graph
place value

CONCEPTS AND SKILLS

Compare. Write >, <, or = for each ⬤. (Lessons 1, 3, pp. 24–25, 30–32)

4. 8,032 ⬤ 8,132

5. 82,435 ⬤ 83,435

6. 1,111,111 ⬤ 1,111,011

7. $0.60 ⬤ 12 dimes

8. $2.35 ⬤ 9 quarters

9. 4 ten-dollar bills ⬤ $25

Write the numbers in order from least to greatest. (Lesson 2, pp. 26–28)

10. 1,653 1,335 1,356

11. 45,397 54,201 45,937

12. 202,765 201,777 202,762

13. 426,729 426,792 426,279

Round each number to the place of the underlined digit. (Lesson 5, pp. 38–39)

14. 56,<u>7</u>64

15. 2,3<u>4</u>3,890

16. 1,<u>1</u>43,251

17. $234.<u>5</u>6

18. $<u>6</u>51.22

PROBLEM SOLVING

Use the graph for Problems 19–20.

(Lesson 6, pp. 40–42)

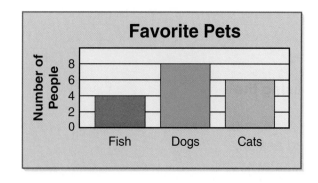

19. How many more people prefer cats than fish?

20. How many people were surveyed?

Write About It

Show You Understand

Carol bought three books. She gave the clerk 3 ten-dollar bills. Her change was 2 quarters, 1 nickel, and 2 one-dollar bills. What was the cost of the books ?

Explain how you got your answer.

Extra Practice

Set A (Lesson 1, pp. 24–25)

Compare. Write >, <, or = for each ●.

1. 125,427 ● 125,407   **2.** 501,100 ● 500,001

3. 60,000 ● 60 thousands   **4.** 3 ten thousands ● 3,000

Set B (Lesson 2, pp. 26–28)

Write the numbers in order from least to greatest.

1. 33,503 31,000 23,427   **2.** 126,522 126,351 130,000

3. 5,416,000 15,000,000 9,333,151   **4.** 122,341,984 122,347,000 122,347,050

Set C (Lesson 3, pp. 30–32)

Write each amount. Then write the greater amount.

1. 5 quarters, 3 dimes, 2 pennies **or** a one-dollar bill, 5 dimes, 6 pennies

2. 1 five-dollar bill, 4 quarters, 7 dimes **or** 4 one-dollar bills and 7 quarters

---

Set D (Lesson 4, pp. 34–36)

Write the names of the coins and bills you would use to make change for each of the following.

1. You bought a pen for $0.63. You paid with a five-dollar bill.   **2.** You bought a book for $7.52. You paid with a twenty-dollar bill.

3. You bought a game for $14.89. You paid with a twenty-dollar bill.   **4.** You bought a sandwich for $3.47. You paid with a ten-dollar bill.

Set E (Lesson 5, pp. 38–39)

Round each number to the place of the underlined digit.

1. 1,<u>5</u>67   **2.** 6,3<u>5</u>2   **3.** <u>9</u>,884   **4.** $1<u>7</u>.42

5. <u>1</u>6,276   **6.** <u>7</u>87,322   **7.** <u>4</u>,295,401   **8.** $<u>5</u>.98

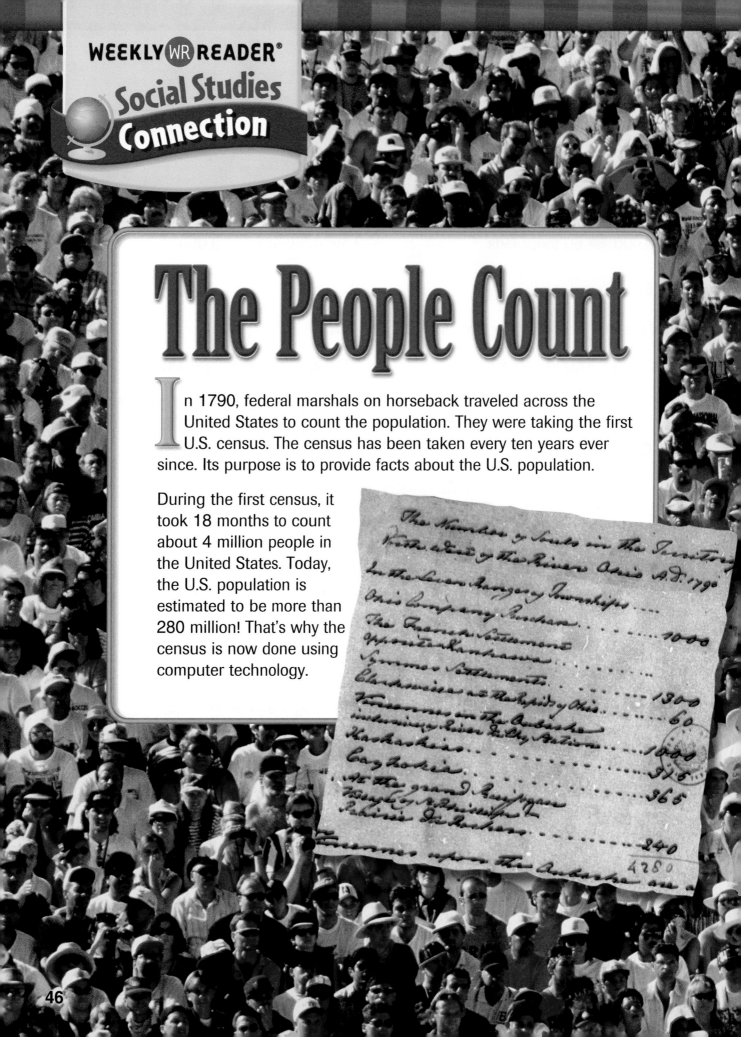

The People Count

In 1790, federal marshals on horseback traveled across the United States to count the population. They were taking the first U.S. census. The census has been taken every ten years ever since. Its purpose is to provide facts about the U.S. population.

During the first census, it took 18 months to count about 4 million people in the United States. Today, the U.S. population is estimated to be more than 280 million! That's why the census is now done using computer technology.

Problem Solving

This map shows the location of 5 major cities in the United States. The table below shows how the populations of the cities have grown.

Census Data of Major Cities in 1900 and 2000

City	Population in 1900	Population in 2000
Chicago, Illinois	1,698,575	2,896,016
Houston, Texas	44,633	1,953,631
Jacksonville, Florida	28,429	735,617
Los Angeles, California	102,479	3,694,820
New York, New York	3,437,202	8,008,278

1. What was the population of Jacksonville in 1900? Write the number two ways.

2. Did Houston or Chicago have the greater population in 2000?

3. Even in 1900, New York had a large population. Compare the population of New York in 1900 to each of the four other cities in 2000. Use > and < for each comparison.

4. Which city had the second greatest population in 1900? in 2000?

5. This city's population in the year 2000 has the same digit in the ones, thousands, and millions places. Which city is it?

Education Place

Visit Weekly Reader© Connections at **eduplace.com/map** for more on this topic.

Roman Numerals

When we write the numbers 0, 1, 2, 3, 4, 5, 6, 7, 8, and 9, we are using the Arabic number system. When you look at a clock or a building, sometimes you will see letters that represent numbers. These are called Roman numerals.

The picture at the right shows Roman numerals and their equivalent Arabic numerals.

- When Roman numerals are alike or the values decrease from left to right, add to find the value.

  III = 1 + 1 + 1 = 3

  VI = 5 + 1 = 6

- When a numeral of lesser value appears to the left of a numeral of greater value, subtract the value of the lesser numeral from the value of the greater numeral.

  IV = 5 − 1 = 4

  CM = 1,000 − 100 = 900

- A numeral never repeats more than 3 times.

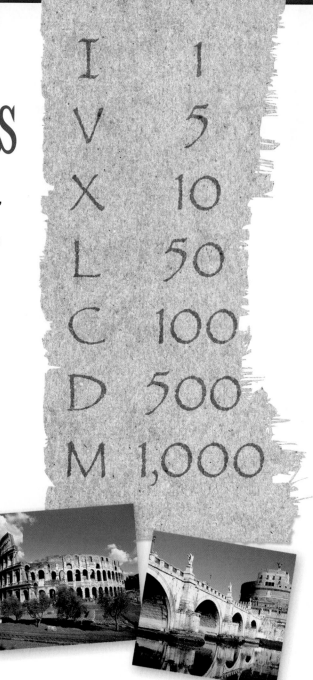

I	1
V	5
X	10
L	50
C	100
D	500
M	1,000

Try These!

Write these Arabic numerals as Roman numerals.

1. 7   **2.** 111   **3.** 56   **4.** 341   **5.** 2000

Write these Roman numerals as Arabic numerals.

6. XVII   **7.** CLXXIII   **8.** CXLV   **9.** XXIV   **10.** CIX

11. Analyze Write the year that you were born in Arabic numerals. Then write it in Roman numerals. Which system is easier to use? Why?

Change, Please

Joshua spent $5.53 on lunch. He gave the clerk a ten-dollar bill. What coins and bills should he get in change?

You can use the coin and bill models found on Education Place at eduplace.com/map/ to help you make change.

- At **Change Mat,** choose **Two Numbers Mat.**

- To show the amount Joshua spent:
  Put your pointer over the **Stamp** tool.
  Click the five-dollar bill.
  Then click the quarter 2 times.
  Next, click the penny 3 times.

- Click anywhere in the right workspace.

- Look at the cost of the meal. Add coins and bills to the right workspace until you reach the amount Joshua paid.

- Click **[123]** to show the amount of change Joshua should receive.

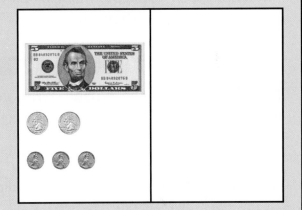

Solution: Joshua should receive $4.47 in change.

Use the coins and bills models to make change for each of the following. List the coins and bills you would use.

A $10 bill was used to buy each item below.

1.  $8.21

2.  $5.90

3.  $1.49

4.  $9.36

5.  $5.66

6. $6.25

Unit 1 Test

VOCABULARY Open Response

Choose the best term to complete each sentence.

Vocabulary
round
period
estimate
base-ten
ordinal number

1. Each place is tens times greater than the place to the right of it in a ____ system.

2. To show the order or position of something, you would use an ____.

3. Each group of 3 digits in a number is separated by a comma and is called a ____.

4. Words such as *about* or *almost* tell you that a number is being used to show an ____.

CONCEPTS AND SKILLS Open Response

Tell how each number is used. Write *position, count, measure, label,* or *location* for each. (Chapter 1)

5. 3rd fastest sprinter

6. 15 cats

7. Apartment 42A

8. 124 Hayward Street

9. 523 kilometers

10. 34 marbles

Write the place of the digit 4 in each number. Then write its value. (Chapter 1)

11. 645,312,978

12. 798,132,465

13. 321,654,987

Compare. Write >, < , or = for each ⬤. (Chapter 2)

14. 555,505 ⬤ 505,555

15. $1,987,654 ⬤ $1,978,654

Order the numbers from greatest to least. (Chapter 2)

16. 44,044 44,440 44,404

17. 716,844 617,488 761,844

A $20 bill was used to buy each item below. List the coins and bills you would use to make change. (Chapter 2)

18.

19.

Round to the place of the underlined digit. (Chapter 2)

20. 754,8̲42,182   **21.** 9̲89,434,123   **22.** 672,81̲8,432

PROBLEM SOLVING (Open Response)

Use the bar graph to solve Problems 23–24.

23. The zoo has the most of which reptile? the least?

24. About how many reptiles are at the zoo?

25. Reasoning Rae, Tai, and Gia either have a turtle, a lizard, or a snake. Rae's pet does not have legs. Gia loves the feel of her pet's shell. What reptile belongs to each girl?

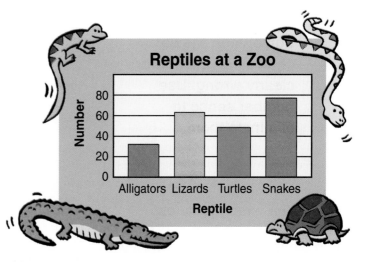

Performance Assessment

(Extended Response)

Task Georgia has $20.00 to buy her school supplies.

Use the information above and at the right. How should Georgia spend her $20.00 to get everything she needs and still have money left over? Explain your thinking.

Information You Need

- She needs twelve pencils.
- A notebook and two red pens are required for her science class.
- Georgia loves crayons, and she also needs them for art class.
- She needs a new backpack.
- She wants to buy either a box of markers or a calculator, but not both.

Cumulative Test Prep

Solve Problems 1–10.

Test-Taking Tip

Sometimes answer choices on a test are clearly wrong. Use number sense to eliminate them.

Look at the example below.

Ming went to the grocery store with $10.00. She purchased food items that totaled $7.51. What was her change?

A $4.39   C $2.49

B $3.49   D $1.49

THINK

You know that $10.00 − $7.00 is $3.00.
So $10.00 − $7.51 < $3.00.

So you can eliminate choices **A** and **B**.

Multiple Choice

1. Josias bought a hot dog for $1.75, a bottle of water for $0.75, and an apple for $0.68. He gave the clerk $5.00. What was his change?

   A $0.82   C $3.82

   B $1.82   D $5.82

   (Chapter 2, Lesson 4)

2. Which of the following shows 45,987 rounded to the nearest hundred?

   F 45,990   H 46,000

   G 45,900   J 50,000

   (Chapter 2, Lesson 5)

3. How many thousands are in 2,000,000?

   A 2   C 200

   B 20   D 2,000

   (Chapter 1, Lesson 4)

4. Amy has 2 one-dollar bills, 5 quarters, 1 nickel, and 6 pennies. Sao has 1 one-dollar bill, 9 quarters, and 1 dime. How much more money does Amy have than Sao?

   F $0.01   H $1.00

   G $0.10   J $10.00

   (Chapter 2, Lesson 3)

For Test-Taking Tips, See page 664.

5. Start at the left. Which number is in the sixth place?

5   10   15   20   25   30   35   40

(Chapter 1, Lesson 1)

6. Write the number eighty million, twenty-three thousand, one in standard form.

(Chapter 1, Lesson 5)

7. The bar graph shows the number of apples Bernadette's friends picked.

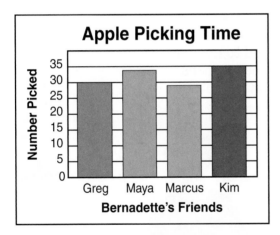

Bernadette picked 33 apples. Which of her four friends picked almost the same number as Bernadette?

(Chapter 2, Lesson 6)

8. Oscar and Yvette each have 5-digit numbers. Yvette's number has 4 sixes. Oscar's number has 3 sixes. Yvette is sure she has the greater number. Could she be wrong? Explain.

(Chapter 2, Lesson 1)

9. Use each number tile below once.

6   **4**   **1**   **5**

A Make the greatest number possible.

B Make the least number possible.

C What two numbers can you make if the six is in the tens place and the five is in the thousands place?

(Chapter 1, Lesson 2)

10. The chart below shows the prices of art supplies.

Art Supplies	
Item	Price
Crayons	$1.85
Scissors	$2.19
Markers	$3.39

A Caroline bought an item with 1 five-dollar bill. She received 6 quarters, 1 nickel, and 6 pennies in change. What item did she buy?

B List 3 ways the store clerk can make change for Carol if she buys crayons and scissors and pays with 1 five-dollar bill.

(Chapter 2, Lesson 4)

 Education Place

Look for Cumulative Test Prep at **eduplace.com/map** for more practice.

Vocabulary Wrap-Up for Unit 1

Look back at the big ideas and vocabulary in this unit.

Big Ideas

You can write a number in standard form, expanded form, short word form and word form.

You can compare numbers using a number line and using place value.

Key Vocabulary

standard form

expanded form

word form

compare

Math Conversations

Use your new vocabulary to discuss these big ideas.

1. Write nine hundred nine thousand, nine hundred ninety in three ways.

2. Explain how to round 8,934 to the nearest ten, hundred, and thousand.

3. Show how to order these numbers from greatest to least.

   2,765   2,739   2,768

4. Explain how you would make change from $20.00 for an item that costs $17.38.

5. **Write About It** Brainstorm a list of five places you want to visit. Research how far they are from where you live. Order them from farthest to nearest.

I need to compare the numbers in my data.

You might try using a number line.

UNIT 2

Operations and Algebraic Reasoning

Reading Mathematics

Reviewing Vocabulary

Here are some math vocabulary words that you should know.

dividend	the number that is divided in a division problem
factors	numbers that are multiplied together to give a product
quotient	the answer in a division problem
regroup	to use 1 ten for 10 ones, 10 tens for 1 hundred, 15 ones for 1 ten 5 ones, and so on

Reading Words and Symbols

You can use words and symbols to show addition, subtraction, multiplication, and division.

Write:	**Read:**
$12 + 8 = 20$	Twelve plus eight equals twenty.
$15 - 5 = 10$	Fifteen minus five equals ten.
$2 \times 9 = 18$	Two times nine equals eighteen.
$24 \div 3 = 8$	Twenty-four divided by three equals eight.

Use words and symbols to answer the questions.

1. Use the numbers 4, 6, and 10 to write an addition sentence and a subtraction sentence.

2. Use the numbers 2, 8, and 16 to write a multiplication sentence and a division sentence.

Reading Test Questions

Choose the correct answer for each.

3. Which number sentence describes the array at the right?

   a. $3 \times 4 = 12$ **c.** $3 \times 6 = 18$

   b. $3 \times 5 = 15$ **d.** $4 \times 5 = 20$

Describes means "represents."

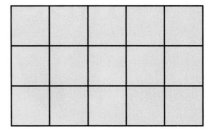

---

4. The sum of $430 + 135$ is between which two numbers?

   a. 450 and 500   **c.** 550 and 600

   b. 500 and 550   **d.** 600 and 650

Between two numbers means "after the first number and before the second number."

5. Which number is the best estimate of the difference?

$$324 - 155$$

   a. 100   **c.** 160

   b. 140   **d.** 200

Best estimate means "closest estimate."

Learning Vocabulary

Watch for these words in this unit. Write their definitions in your journal.

Zero Property of Addition

Commutative Property of Addition

variable

inverse operations

expression

equation

Literature Connection

Read "Kid Camp" on Page 646. Then work with a partner to answer the questions about the story.

Education Place

At **eduplace.com/map**, see eGlossary and eGames—Math Lingo

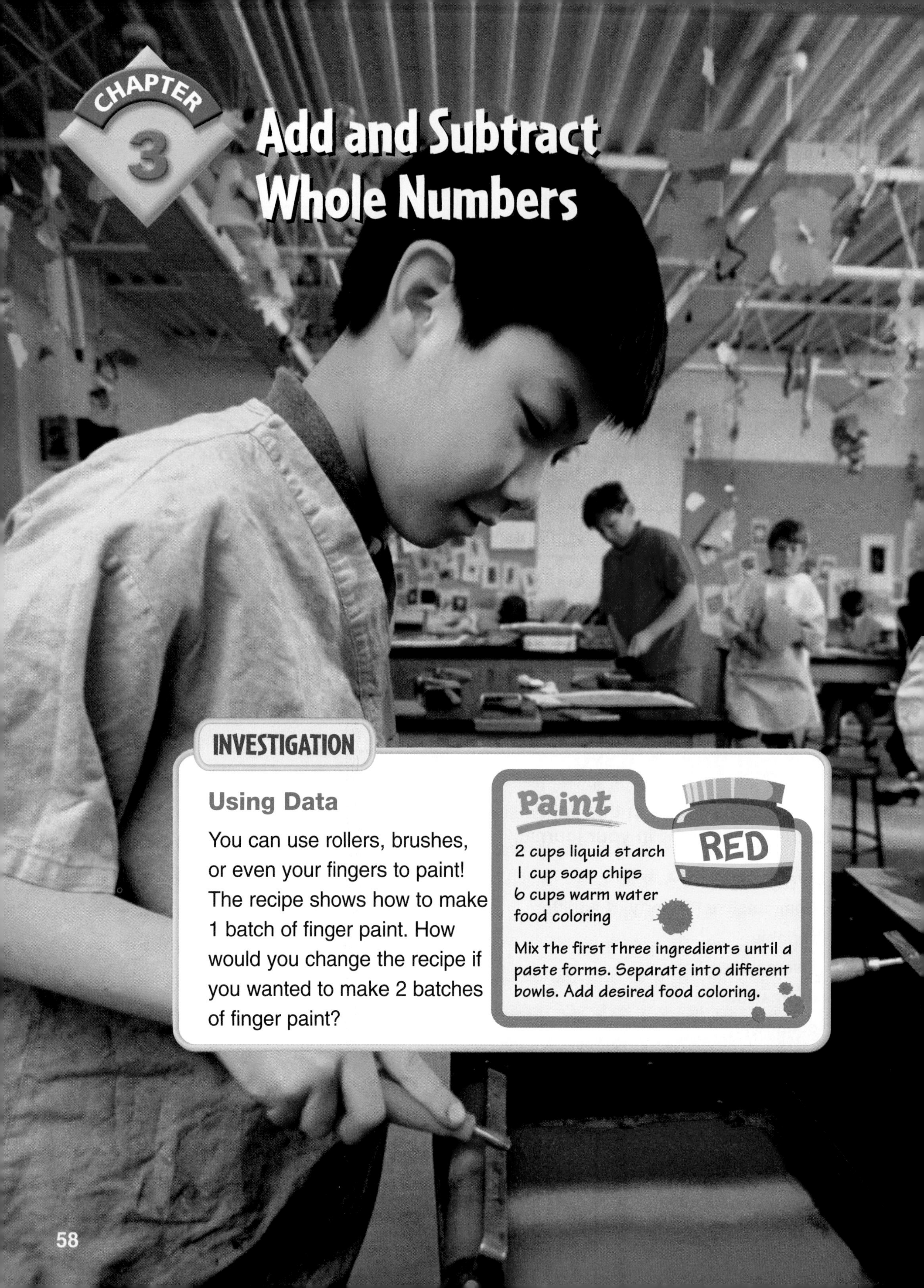

Add and Subtract Whole Numbers

INVESTIGATION

Using Data

You can use rollers, brushes, or even your fingers to paint! The recipe shows how to make 1 batch of finger paint. How would you change the recipe if you wanted to make 2 batches of finger paint?

Paint

RED

2 cups liquid starch
1 cup soap chips
6 cups warm water
food coloring

Mix the first three ingredients until a paste forms. Separate into different bowls. Add desired food coloring.

Use What You Know

**Use this page to review and remember
what you need to know for this chapter.**

VOCABULARY

Choose the best term to complete each sentence.

1. In 6 + 3 = 9, 6 is an ____.

2. In 7 + 5 = 12, 12 is the ____.

3. You can subtract two numbers to find their ____.

4. A ____ shows how numbers are related.

5. When you change 1 ten to 10 ones you are ____.

> ### Vocabulary
> sum
> addend
> difference
> estimating
> regrouping
> number sentence

CONCEPTS AND SKILLS

Add or subtract. Regroup if you need to.

| 6. | 62 + 37 | 7. | 40 + 28 | 8. | 87 + 54 | 9. | 56 − 19 | 10. | 71 − 32 |

Round each number to the place of the underlined digit.

11. 4$\underline{2}$5 12. 3$\underline{8}$5 13. $\underline{2}$,476 14. 14\underline{4}$.69 15. 92,$\underline{2}$39

Compare. Write >, <, or = for each ⬤.

16. 18 − 9 ⬤ 4 + 4   17. 8 − 3 ⬤ 9 − 4   18. 7 + 7 ⬤ 9 + 6

19. 9 + 6 ⬤ 10 + 5   20. 4 + 5 ⬤ 6 + 2   21. 15 − 7 ⬤ 14 − 6

22. 8 + 3 ⬤ 12 − 1   23. 12 − 4 ⬤ 11 − 5   24. 13 − 5 ⬤ 6 + 5

 **Write About It**

25. There are 175 more boys than girls at the
hobby show. There are 256 girls there. How
many boys are at the hobby show? Explain how
you know.

> Facts Practice, See page 666.

Algebra

Addition Properties and Subtraction Rules

Objective Use properties of addition and rules of subtraction.

Learn About It

Here are some properties and rules you can use when you add and subtract.

Properties of Addition

▶ **Zero Property of Addition**

• When you add zero to a number, the sum is that number.

$7 + 0 = 7$

▶ **Commutative Property of Addition**

• When you change the order of the addends, the sum stays the same.

$5 + 7 = 12$
$7 + 5 = 12$

Remember
Do what is in the parentheses first.

▶ **Associative Property of Addition**

• When you change the way addends are grouped, the sum stays the same.

$(3 + 5) + 6 = 3 + (5 + 6)$
$8 \quad + 6 = 3 + \quad 11$
$14 \quad = \quad 14$

Rules of Subtraction

▶ **Zeros in Subtraction**

• When you subtract zero from a number, the difference is that number.

$7 - 0 = 7$

• When you subtract a number from itself, the difference is zero.

$7 - 7 = 0$

Guided Practice

**Copy and complete each number sentence.
Tell which property or rule you used.**

Ask Yourself

• Is one of the numbers zero?

• If there are parentheses, what do I do first?

1. $11 + 0 =$ _____

2. $45 + 34 =$ _____ $+ 45$

3. $17 - 17 =$ _____

4. $(4 + 6) + 8 =$ _____ $+ (6 + 8)$

5. $25 - 0 =$ _____

6. $3 + (3 +$ _____$) = (3 + 3) + 1$

Explain Your Thinking ▶ How could you group $50 + 387 + 950$ to make it easier to add?

Practice and Problem Solving

**Copy and complete each number sentence.
Tell which property or rule you used.**

7. $34 + 99 =$ _____ $+ 34$

8. $342 + 0 =$ _____

9. $(7 + 3) + 67 = 7 + (3 +$ _____ $)$

10. $24 + (7 + 8) = (24 + 7) +$ _____

11. $(7 - 0) + 3 =$ _____ $+ 3$

12. $5 + (9 + 0) = 5 +$ _____

Use the Associative Property to help you find each sum mentally.

13. $75 + 25 + 46$

14. $92 + 421 + 8$

15. $179 + 345 + 21$

16. $490 + 84 + 10$

17. $328 + 291 + 9$

18. $820 + 78 + 80$

Solve.

19. Marta needs to find the sum of 24, 105, and 66. How can she group the addends to make it easier to add?

20. Cara had 92 stamps. Leah gave her 48 more. If Mel gives her 8 more stamps, how many will Cara have?

Mixed Review and Test Prep

Open Response

Round each number to the greatest place or to the nearest dollar.
(Ch. 2, Lesson 5)

21. 481

22. 3,597

23. $5.25

24. $316.37

25. 32,877

26. 481,921

27. Do you think there is a Commutative Property for subtraction? (Ch. 3, Lesson 1)

Why or why not?

Extra Practice See page 81, Set A.

Mental Math Strategies

Objective Use mental math to add and subtract
two- and three-digit numbers.

Vocabulary
breaking apart
compensation

Learn About It

Mental math strategies can help you add and subtract.

You can use breaking apart to add or subtract mentally.

▶ **Find 44 + 18.**

- Break apart $44 = 40 + 4$
  the numbers. $18 = 10 + 8$

- Add the tens. $40 + 10 = 50$

- Add the ones. $4 + 8 = 12$

- Add the tens and ones. $50 + 12 = 62$

So, $44 + 18 = 62$.

▶ **Find 58 − 25.**

- Break apart $58 = 50 + 8$
  the numbers. $25 = 20 + 5$

- Subtract the tens. $50 - 20 = 30$

- Subtract the ones. $8 - 5 = 3$

- Add the tens and ones. $30 + 3 = 33$

So, $58 - 25 = 33$.

You can use compensation to add or subtract mentally.

▶ **Find 38 + 56.**

$$38$$
$$+56$$

Add 2 to 38
to make 40.

$$40$$
$$+56$$
$$\overline{96}$$

Subtract 2 to
compensate for
adding 2.

$$-\ 2$$
$$\overline{94}$$

So, $38 + 56 = 94$.

▶ **Find 145 − 17.**

$$145$$
$$-\ 17$$

Add 3 to 17
to make 20.

$$145$$
$$-\ 20$$
$$\overline{125}$$

Add 3 to
compensate for
subtracting 3 extra.

$$+\ 3$$
$$\overline{128}$$

So, $145 - 17 = 128$.

Use mental math to add or subtract.
Tell which strategy you used.

1.   27
   + 31

2.   34
   + 29

3.   68
   − 24

4.   116
   − 97

Ask Yourself

• Which strategy makes the calculation easier?

• If I use compensation, what number should I adjust?

Explain Your Thinking ▶ Would you use mental math or paper and pencil to find 361 − 174? Explain.

Practice and Problem Solving

Use mental math to add or subtract.

5. 34 + 27

6. 33 + 49

7. 88 + 96

8. 314 + 498

9. 78 − 15

10. 59 − 22

11. 391 − 58

12. 212 + 107

 **Algebra • Symbols** Compare. Write <, >, or = for each ●.

13. 48 + 26 ● 46 + 28

14. 76 − 16 ● 92 − 20

15. 173 − 45 ● 120 + 45

16. 453 − 53 ● 224 + 176

17. Carolyn collected 136 colored beads. She traded 25 of them for 13 wooden beads. How many beads does she have now?

18. Jim removed 16 silver beads from a necklace. The necklace now has 65 beads. How many beads did the necklace have before?

Mixed Review and Test Prep

Open Response

Find the next two numbers in the pattern.
(Grade 3)

19. 14, 12, 10, 8, 6, _____, _____

20. 125, 120, 115, 110, _____, _____

21. 2, 4, 8, 16, 32, _____, _____

22. 3, 6, 5, 10, 9, 18, _____, _____

Multiple Choice

23. Lily used 294 beads for her craft project. Patty used 193 beads. How many beads were used?
(Ch. 3, Lesson 2)

A 397

C 487

B 401

D 497

Extra Practice See page 81, Set B.

○ **Audio Tutor 1/7** Listen and Understand

Estimate Sums and Differences

Objective Use rounded numbers to estimate sums and differences.

The Community Center in Riverville offers an after-school arts program. 478 grade school students and 188 middle school students sign up for the program. The Community Center has enough space for 675 students. Does the center have enough space for all of the students that signed up?

You do not need to know the exact number of students that signed up. You only need to know if the total is less than 675. So, you can estimate the sum.

> **Remember**
> To estimate is to find a number close to an exact amount.

Estimate the sum of 423 and 188.

Round each addend to the nearest hundred. Then add the rounded numbers.

478	rounds to	500
+188	rounds to	+200
		700

Since both addends were rounded up, the actual number will be less than 700. But will it be less than 675?

To get a closer estimate, round to the nearest ten. Then add.

478	rounds to	480
+188	rounds to	+190
		670

Both addends were rounded up and their sum is less than 675. So, you know the actual total is less than 675.

Solution: The Community Center has enough room for all the students.

Other Examples

A. Round to the Nearest Dollar

$4.89	rounds to	$5.00
+$1.59	rounds to	+$2.00
		$7.00

B. Round to the Nearest Thousand

6,742	rounds to	7,000
−2,575	rounds to	−3,000
		4,000

C. Round to the Nearest Ten Thousand

73,465	rounds to	70,000
−19,287	rounds to	−20,000
		50,000

Extra Help at **eduplace.com/map**

Ask Yourself
- Which place am I rounding to?
- Am I finding a sum or a difference?

Round each number to the nearest ten. Then estimate.

1. $45 + 32$ **2.** $586 - 98$ **3.** $4,567 + 1,111$

Round each number to the nearest hundred or dollar. Then estimate.

4.
$$\begin{array}{r} \$4.52 \\ + 3.26 \end{array}$$

5.
$$\begin{array}{r} 873 \\ - 256 \end{array}$$

6.
$$\begin{array}{r} 6,359 \\ + 1,703 \end{array}$$

7.
$$\begin{array}{r} 87,623 \\ - 24,401 \end{array}$$

Explain Your Thinking ▶ If both addends are rounded down, will the sum of the rounded numbers be greater than or less than the actual sum?

Practice and Problem Solving

Round each number to the nearest ten. Then estimate.

8. $526 + 313$ **9.** $672 - 259$ **10.** $427 + 777$ **11.** $821 - 482$

12.
$$\begin{array}{r} 5,426 \\ + 479 \end{array}$$

13.
$$\begin{array}{r} 3,550 \\ - 1,743 \end{array}$$

14.
$$\begin{array}{r} 724 \\ + 255 \end{array}$$

15.
$$\begin{array}{r} 10,207 \\ - 4,520 \end{array}$$

Round each number to the nearest hundred or the nearest dollar. Then estimate.

16. $266 + 142$ **17.** $397 - 151$ **18.** $701 + 884$ **19.** $925 - 478$

20.
$$\begin{array}{r} 2,436 \\ + 553 \end{array}$$

21.
$$\begin{array}{r} 4,444 \\ - 3,858 \end{array}$$

22.
$$\begin{array}{r} \$34.99 \\ + 96.78 \end{array}$$

23.
$$\begin{array}{r} \$49.99 \\ - 46.27 \end{array}$$

24.
$$\begin{array}{r} 25,492 \\ + 2,321 \end{array}$$

25.
$$\begin{array}{r} 46,591 \\ - 25,427 \end{array}$$

26.
$$\begin{array}{r} \$135.61 \\ - 93.48 \end{array}$$

27.
$$\begin{array}{r} 359,513 \\ + 233,642 \end{array}$$

Go On

Round each number to the greatest place. Then estimate.

28.	57,834	29.	23,509	30.	346,899	31.	3,277
	−53,619		− 837		+271,585		6,503
							+5,499

 Algebra • Functions Find a number at the right that makes each number sentence true. Use each number only once.

32. 453 + ■ < 800

33. 325 − ■ = 215

34. 755 < 169 + ■

35. ■ − 256 = 344

36. ■ + 662 > 1,000

37. ■ − 372 > 400

587   600
360   110
792   289

 Data Use the poster for Problems 38–41.

38. Doug bought 4 canvases. About how much money did he spend?

39. Karen bought a paint box and 3 tubes of paint. About how much money did she spend?

40. **Money** Ramon bought a canvas and a paint brush. About how much change should he get back if he paid with a $10 bill?

41. Emma estimated the cost of an easel and a paint brush by rounding each price to the nearest dollar. Was her estimate more or less than the actual amount? By how much?

Painting Supplies	
Canvas	$3.79
Paint brush	$2.29
Tube of paint	$1.95
Easel	$10.38
Frame	$7.49
Paint box	$14.67

Mixed Review and Test Prep

Open Response
Round each number to the greatest place. (Ch. 2, Lesson 5)

42. 3,496

43. 62,549

44. 876

45. 752,385

46. 5,689

47. 24,985

48. Rob sold 674 tickets to a play. About how many tickets did Rob sell? (Ch. 3, Lesson 3)
Explain how you got your answer.

Math Reasoning
Front-End Estimation and Clustering

You learned that one way to estimate is by rounding. Here are two other ways to estimate.

Activity

Vocabulary

front-end estimation

clustering

You can use front-end estimation to estimate.

▶ **Estimate 573 + 228.**

• Add the front-end digits.

573
+ 228
700

500 + 200 is 700.

• Adjust the estimate.

573
+ 228
800

73 + 28 is about 100 more. 700 + 100 = 800.

The estimate is about 800.

▶ **Estimate 311 − 196.**

• Subtract the front-end digits.

311
− 196
200

300 − 100 is 200.

• Adjust the estimate.

311
− 196
100

96 is about 100. So subtract another hundred.

The estimate is about 100.

You can use clustering to estimate sums. Clustering is used to estimate addends that have similar values.

▶ **Estimate 117 + 105 + 91.**

117 + 105 + 91 is about 300

The addends are all close in value. I can skip count by 100s. 100, 200, 300.

The estimate is about 300.

Use front-end estimation to estimate each sum or difference.

1. 663 + 141   2. 441 + 248   3. 866 − 450   4. 937 − 297

Use clustering to estimate each sum.

5. 48 + 49 + 52   6. 214 + 206 + 187   7. 375 + 407 + 389

Problem-Solving Decision
Estimate or Exact Answer

Objective Decide whether an estimated or an exact answer is needed to solve a problem.

Sandy's photography club at school sold photos to raise money for their club. The table shows what type of photos they took and how many of each were sold.

Look at these examples. They show when to use an estimate and when to use an exact answer.

Photography Fundraiser	
Type of photo	Number sold
Landscapes	123
People	105
Animals	216
Other	87

▶ **Sometimes you can estimate to solve a problem.**

About how many photos of people and animals were sold?

Since the question asks you to find *about how many* photos were sold, you can estimate the sum.

105	rounds to	100
+ 216	rounds to	+ 200
		300

About 300 photos of people and animals were sold.

▶ **Sometimes you need an exact answer to solve the problem.**

How many more photos of landscapes than photos of people were sold?

Since the question asks you to find *how many more,* you need to find the exact difference.

123 ← number of landscape photos
− 105 ← number of people photos
18

18 more photos of landscapes than people were sold.

Try These

Solve. Tell whether you need an exact answer or an estimate.

1. Were there more than 700 photos sold at the fundraiser?

2. How many photos of animals and of landscapes were sold altogether?

3. The club raised $193 selling photos of people and $212 selling photos of animals. About how much was raised by selling photos of people and animals?

4. The club raised a total of $685. About how much more do they need to reach their goal of $1,200?

Social Studies Connection
Magic Squares

A Chinese tale from B.C.E. 2200 tells about a turtle with a magic square on its back. Look at the rows, columns, and diagonals of numbers in the picture on the right. The numbers add to 15 each time!

**Copy the magic squares.
Then fill in the missing numbers.**

1.

2		6
9	5	1
	3	8

2.

6	1	
	5	3
2	9	4

3.

	3	4
1		9
6		2

Check your understanding of Lessons 1–4.

Copy and complete each number sentence. (Lesson 1)

1. 85 − _____ = 85

2. (24 + 21) + 9 = 24 + (21 + __)

Use mental math to add or subtract. (Lesson 2)

3. 128 + 139   4. 72 + 46   5. 215 − 98   6. 481 − 57

Round each number to the greatest place. Then estimate. (Lesson 3)

7. $81.31 − $23.66   8. 2,693 + 5,396   9. $426.18 − $162.27

Tell whether you need an exact answer or an estimate. (Lesson 4)

10. This year 1,285 people competed in a fishing contest. Last year 974 people competed in the contest. About how many people competed both years?

Lesson 5

Add Whole Numbers and Money

Vocabulary
regroup

Objective Add numbers using regrouping.

Learn About It

Mr. Shaw has a large collection of model trains. He has 129 pieces of track. He plans to buy 97 more pieces of track. How many pieces of track will he have altogether?

Add. $129 + 97 = \blacksquare$

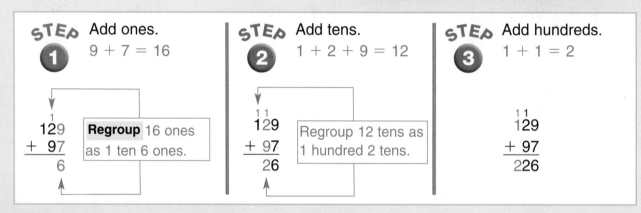

STEP 1 Add ones.
$9 + 7 = 16$

$$\begin{array}{r} \overset{1}{1}29 \\ +\ 97 \\ \hline 6 \end{array}$$

Regroup 16 ones as 1 ten 6 ones.

STEP 2 Add tens.
$1 + 2 + 9 = 12$

$$\begin{array}{r} \overset{1\ 1}{1}29 \\ +\ 97 \\ \hline 26 \end{array}$$

Regroup 12 tens as 1 hundred 2 tens.

STEP 3 Add hundreds.
$1 + 1 = 2$

$$\begin{array}{r} \overset{1\ 1}{1}29 \\ +\ 97 \\ \hline 226 \end{array}$$

Solution: Mr. Shaw will have 226 pieces of track.

Other Examples

A. Add Thousands

$$\begin{array}{r} \overset{1\ \ \ 1\ 1}{1}8{,}293 \\ +\ \ 2{,}048 \\ \hline 20{,}341 \end{array}$$

B. Add Money

$$\begin{array}{r} \overset{1\ 1}{\$}15.64 \\ +\ \ \ 3.87 \\ \hline \$19.51 \end{array}$$

Remember
Bring down the decimal point and the dollar sign.

Guided Practice

Find each sum.

1. $\begin{array}{r} 283 \\ +\ 55 \\ \hline \end{array}$

2. $\begin{array}{r} 6{,}582 \\ +\ 298 \\ \hline \end{array}$

3. $\begin{array}{r} \$27.93 \\ +\ \ 5.24 \\ \hline \end{array}$

4. $\begin{array}{r} 4{,}571 \\ +2{,}714 \\ \hline \end{array}$

Ask Yourself
- Are the digits lined up correctly?
- Do I need to regroup?

Explain Your Thinking ▶ How can adding numbers in a different order help you check that your answer is correct?

Add. Check by adding in a different order or by estimating.

5. 652
    + 145

6. 732
    + 88

7. 6,714
    +8,600

8. $51.95
    + 32.61

9. $37.80
    + 6.47

10. 894
     + 4,717

11. 5,182
     + 3,957

12. 9,832
     + 761

13. 3,431
     + 768

14. 3,984
     + 1,079

15. 8,623
     + 382

16. $143.21
     + 78.99

17. 54,186
     +11,983

18. $142.31
     + 56.28

19. $323.05
     + 184.95

 Data Use the price list for Problems 20–23.

20. What is the cost of 1 railroad station and 1 colonial house?

21. Is $30 enough to buy the railroad station and the hardware store?

22. Harold bought a barber shop and a hardware store. What coins and bills would he receive if he paid with a $20 bill?

23. **Create and Solve** Use the information in the price list to write an addition word problem. Then solve it.

Miniature Village

Building	Price
Barber Shop	$5.59
Railroad Station	$26.35
Colonial House	$15.67
Hardware Store	$13.25
Butcher Shop	$11.79

Mixed Review and Test Prep

Open Response

Write each amount. (Ch. 2, Lesson 3)

24.

25.

Multiple Choice

26. Janai collected 139 cans to recycle. Roy collected 242 cans. Ed collected 526 cans. How many cans were collected?

(Ch. 3, Lesson 5)

A 907   C 927

B 897   D 807

Audio Tutor 1/9 Listen and Understand

Subtract Whole Numbers

Objective Subtract whole numbers with up to five digits.

Learn About It

Can you imagine spending hours creating something only to knock it down? You might if you like building domino lines!

Suppose a domino line has 2,865 dominoes in it. If 868 dominoes are knocked down, how many dominoes are left standing?

Subtract.   2,865 − 868 =

 Subtract ones.

$$
\begin{array}{r}
\overset{5\ 15}{2,86\cancel{5}} \\
-\ \ \ 868 \\
\hline
7
\end{array}
$$

Regroup a ten as 10 ones.

 Subtract tens.

$$
\begin{array}{r}
\overset{\ \ \ 15}{\overset{7\ \cancel{6}\cancel{15}}{2,\cancel{86}\cancel{5}}} \\
-\ \ \ 868 \\
\hline
97
\end{array}
$$

Regroup a hundred as 10 tens.

STEP 3 **Subtract hundreds.**

$$
\begin{array}{r}
\overset{17\ 15}{\overset{1\ \cancel{7}\ \cancel{6}15}{\cancel{2},8\cancel{6}\cancel{5}}} \\
-\ \ \ 868 \\
\hline
997
\end{array}
$$

Regroup a thousand as 10 hundreds.

STEP 4 **Subtract thousands.**

$$
\begin{array}{r}
\overset{1715}{\overset{1\ \cancel{7}\ \cancel{6}15}{\cancel{2},8\cancel{6}\cancel{5}}} \\
-\ \ \ 868 \\
\hline
1,997
\end{array}
$$

Check Your Work.

You can check by adding because addition undoes subtraction. Addition and subtraction are **inverse operations**.

$$
\begin{array}{r}
2,865 \\
-\ \ 868 \\
\hline
1,997
\end{array}
\qquad
\begin{array}{r}
1,997 \\
+\ \ 868 \\
\hline
2,865
\end{array}
$$

The numbers are the same, so the difference is correct.

Solution: 1,997 dominoes are left standing.

Another Example
Subtract Money

$$
\begin{array}{r}
\overset{\ \ \ \ 12}{\overset{1\ \ \cancel{2}14}{\$8\cancel{2}.\cancel{8}\cancel{4}}} \\
-\ \ \ 21.59 \\
\hline
\$60.75
\end{array}
$$

Remember
Bring down the decimal point and the dollar sign.

Subtract. Use addition to check your answer.

1. 483
    − 262

2. 4,674
    − 1,833

3. $65.72
    − 49.81

4. 839 − 45

5. $53.59 − $3.48

Explain Your Thinking How could you use estimation to see if your answer is reasonable?

Practice and Problem Solving

Subtract. Use addition or estimation to check.

6. 967
    − 815

7. 8,397
    − 5,067

8. 7,927
    − 2,639

9. $97.48
    − 46.27

10. $28.13
    − 9.24

11. 757
    − 486

12. 324
    − 77

13. 5,188
    − 1,434

14. $73.59
    − 26.84

15. 9,634
    − 4,967

16. 9,526 − 8,410

17. $83.61 − $61.75

18. $75.26 − $29.58

 Algebra • **Find each missing number.**

19. 39 + ____ = 58

20. ____ − 178 = 113

21. ____ + 412 = 938

22. ____ − 247 = 429

23. 342 + ____ = 829

24. ____ − 276 = 634

25. A club has 1,985 dominoes. A group used 928 of these dominoes to make a domino line. How many dominoes were not used?

26. **Multistep** Josh and Meg each used 350 dominoes. If 2,658 dominoes were used altogether, how many were used by other club members?

Mixed Review and Test Prep

Open Response

What color is the next shape in each pattern? (Grade 3)

27.  ____

29. Mr. Tyson flew 1,224 miles in May and he flew 2,145 miles in June. How many more miles did he fly in June than in May?

(Ch. 3, Lesson 6)

28. ●●●●●●●●●● ____

Audio Tutor 1/10 Listen and Understand

Subtract Across Zeros

Objective Subtract when some digits are zero.

Learn About It

Painting eggs in colorful designs using wax and dye is an old tradition in the Ukraine.

Leah guesses there are 2,500 triangles on the Ukrainian egg shown at the right. There are actually 2,206 triangles on the egg. What is the difference between Leah's guess and the actual number of triangles?

Subtract. 2,500 − 2,206 =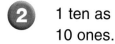

The world's largest Ukrainian egg is in Alberta, Canada. It is over 27 feet high.

STEP 1	STEP 2	STEP 3
Subtract ones. 6 > 0, so you need to regroup. There are no tens, so regroup 1 hundred as 10 tens.	Regroup 1 ten as 10 ones.	Then subtract.
$$\begin{array}{r} 4\,10 \\ 2,\cancel{5}\cancel{0}0 \\ -\ 2,206 \\ \hline \end{array}$$	$$\begin{array}{r} 9 \\ 4\,\cancel{1}0\,10 \\ 2,\cancel{5}\cancel{0}\cancel{0} \\ -\ 2,206 \\ \hline \end{array}$$	$$\begin{array}{r} 9 \\ 4\,\cancel{1}0\,10 \\ 2,\cancel{5}\cancel{0}\cancel{0} \\ -\ 2,206 \\ \hline 294 \end{array}$$

Solution: There are 294 fewer triangles than Leah thought.

Guided Practice

Subtract. Estimate or add to check.

1. $\begin{array}{r} 306 \\ -\ 94 \\ \hline \end{array}$
2. $\begin{array}{r} \$8.02 \\ -\ 4.88 \\ \hline \end{array}$
3. $\begin{array}{r} 4,055 \\ -1,572 \\ \hline \end{array}$
4. $\begin{array}{r} \$70.46 \\ -\ 23.15 \\ \hline \end{array}$

5. 500 − 156

6. 9,070 − 2,305

7. 4,000 − 2,843

8. 6,003 − 2,346

Ask Yourself
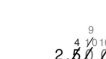
- Do I need to regroup?
- Do I need to regroup more than once before I can subtract at all?

Explain Your Thinking ▶ Where should you start regrouping if the number you are subtracting from has no ones, no tens, and no hundreds?

74

Subtract. Estimate or add to check.

9. 404
    − 159

10. 710
    − 572

11. $9.00
    − 7.48

12. 605
    − 94

13. 7,038
    − 3,251

14. 2,004
    − 1,413

15. 8,080
    − 637

16. $70.00
    − 53.94

17. $50.50
    − 32.56

18. $29.00
    − 17.07

19. 9,055 − 8,215

20. $60.00 − $41.20

21. 8,009 − 5,506

 Algebra • **Functions** Follow the rule to complete each table.

Rule: Add 2,376		
	Input	Output
22.	1,542	▪
23.	3,721	▪
24.	▪	6,922

Rule: Subtract 3,118		
	Input	Output
25.	5,307	▪
26.	7,200	▪
27.	▪	1,433

Rule: Subtract 4,628		
	Input	Output
28.	5,000	▪
29.	▪	1,053
30.	6,204	▪

Solve.

31. A Ukrainian egg artist plans to paint 400 stars on an egg. So far, he has painted 215 stars. How many stars still need to be painted?

32. A gift store ordered 6,500 Ukrainian eggs. They sold 6,221 eggs. How many Ukrainian eggs were not sold?

Mixed Review and Test Prep

Open Response

Write each amount. (Ch. 2, Lesson 3)

33. one $10 bill, 1 quarter, 1 dime

34. four $20 bills, 3 nickels, 7 pennies

35. two $50 bills, 6 quarters, 3 dimes

36. six $5 bills, 8 dimes, 5 nickels

Multiple Choice

37. There are 1,000 seats in a theater. So far, 762 seats have been filled. How many more seats are available? (Ch. 3, Lesson 7)

    A 362   C 248

    B 338   D 238

Add and Subtract Greater Numbers

Objective Add and subtract whole numbers with up to six digits.

Learn About It

Most murals are painted, but at the Corn Palace in Mitchell, South Dakota, they are made out of corn!

One mural at the Corn Palace uses 42,936 ears of corn. Another mural uses 75,658 ears of corn. How many ears of corn are used for the two murals?

Corn and grain are used to design murals on the walls of the Corn Palace.

Add. 42,936 + 75,658 = ▩

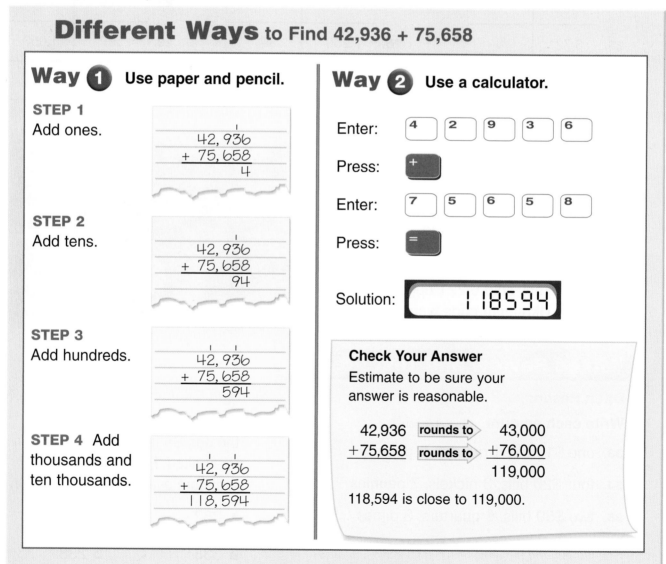

Different Ways to Find 42,936 + 75,658

Way ❶ Use paper and pencil.

STEP 1
Add ones.

```
    1
  42,936
+ 75,658
       4
```

STEP 2
Add tens.

```
    1
  42,936
+ 75,658
      94
```

STEP 3
Add hundreds.

```
  1 1
  42,936
+ 75,658
     594
```

STEP 4 Add thousands and ten thousands.

```
  1 1
  42,936
+ 75,658
 118,594
```

Way ❷ Use a calculator.

Enter: [4] [2] [9] [3] [6]

Press: [+]

Enter: [7] [5] [6] [5] [8]

Press: [=]

Solution: | 118594 |

Check Your Answer
Estimate to be sure your answer is reasonable.

42,936	**rounds to** ⇒	43,000
+75,658	**rounds to** ⇒	+76,000
		119,000

118,594 is close to 119,000.

Solution: 118,594 ears of corn are used for these two murals.

Subtract. 275,000 − 182,500 = ■

Different Ways to Find 275,000 − 182,500

Way ① Use paper and pencil.

STEP 1
There are no tens or ones, so write zeros.

```
  275,000
− 182,500
       00
```

STEP 2
Subtract hundreds.

```
      4  10
  275,000
− 182,500
      500
```

STEP 3
Subtract thousands.

```
      4  10
  275,000
− 182,500
    2 500
```

STEP 4
Subtract ten thousands and hundred thousands.

```
  1 17 4  10
  275,000
− 182,500
   92,500
```

Way ② Use a calculator.

Enter: 2 7 5 0 0 0

Press: —

Enter: 1 8 2 5 0 0

Press: =

Solution: 92500

Check Your Answer
Estimate to be sure your answer is reasonable.

275,000	rounds to	280,000
−182,500	rounds to	−180,000
		100,000

92,500 is close to 100,000.

Solution: 275,000 − 182,500 = 92,500

Guided Practice

Add or subtract. Estimate to check.

1. 43,396
   + 12,594

2. 78,396
   − 46,239

3. 456,912
   − 37,800

4. $312.75 + $357.39

5. 415,607 + 206,834

Ask Yourself
- Should I use paper and pencil or a calculator?
- How can I check that the answer is reasonable?

Explain Your Thinking ▶ Why should you always estimate when using a calculator?

Practice and Problem Solving

Add or subtract. Estimate to check.

6. 14,659
  − 11,584

7. $235.74
  + 20.97

8. 14,508
  − 13,639

9. 468,397
  + 457,107

10. 125,975
  − 109,300

11. 73,880 + 48,659

12. 64,340 − 8,621

13. 525,024 + 25,386

14. 413,816 + 253,109

15. 407,001 − 184,652

16. $387.91 + $413.28

Find each missing digit.

17.   53,268
   +25,▇35
     79,103

18.   145,397
   + 94,444
     23▇,841

19. $36▇.22
   −   99.97
     $267.25

20.   843,▇02
   − 564,763
     278,239

 Algebra • Symbols Compare. Write <, >, or = for each ⬤.

21. 342 + 471 ⬤ 620 + 233

22. 692 − 437 ⬤ 529 − 340

23. 1,273 − 836 ⬤ 236 + 201

24. 52,648 + 1,690 ⬤ 83,141 − 19,302

Choose a Computation Method

Mental Math • Estimation • Paper and Pencil • Calculator

Solve. Tell which method you chose.

25. Exactly 275,000 ears of corn will be used to make the murals this year. If 182,500 ears have been delivered so far, how many more are needed?

26. One mural requires 37,200 ears of corn. A different mural requires 30,100 ears. How many ears of corn are needed for both murals?

27. On Monday, 2,359 people visited the Corn Palace. On Tuesday, 4,697 people visited. About how many people visited altogether?

28. Each year over $100,000 is needed to make the murals. About how much money was spent in the last 10 years?

Every winter, the Corn Palace becomes one of the world's largest bird feeders!

78

Extra Practice See page 81, Set G.

Open Response

Add. (Ch. 3, Lesson 5)

29. 2,124 + 310

30. 5,073 + 759

31. 1,119 + 477

32. 141 + 3,994

33. 334 + 568 + 1,724 + 4,120

34. 1,902 + 758 + 98 + 2,742

35. When a baseball stadium was built, it had 42,521 seats. 1,295 seats were added. How many seats does the stadium have now? (Ch. 3, Lesson 8)

Visual Thinking
Venn Diagrams

Problem Solving

Venn diagrams show how two or more groups are related.

Each fourth-grader in Mr. Ames' class completed at least one writing project. Some students wrote a story, some wrote a poem, and some wrote both.

The Venn diagram on the right shows which writing projects students did.

1. How many students are in Mr. Ames' class?

2. Which students wrote both a story and a poem?

3. Which students only wrote a poem?

4. Make up a story about some friends who might play one or two sports, or who might play both sports. Use a Venn diagram to illustrate it.

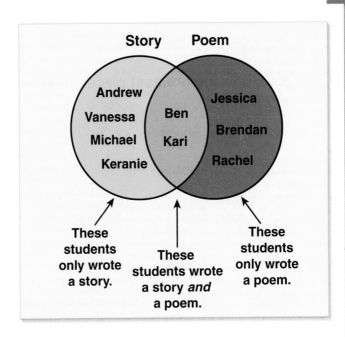

Chapter Review/Test

VOCABULARY

Choose the best term to complete each sentence.

1. The number sentence $3 + 5 = 5 + 3$ is an example of the ____.

2. The different ways in which addends can be grouped is an example of the ____.

3. Addition and subtraction are ____.

> **Vocabulary**
> inverse operations
> Associative Property
> Commutative Property
> compensation

CONCEPTS AND SKILLS

Copy and complete each number sentence.
Tell which property of addition you used. (Lesson 1, pp. 60–61)

4. $56 + 12 = 12 +$ ■   5. $5 + (5 + 9) = (5 +$ ■$) + 9$ 6. $582 +$ ■ $= 582$

Use mental math to add or subtract. Tell the strategy you used. (Lesson 2, pp. 62–63)

7. $12 + 27 + 38$ 8. $53 + 67$ 9. $38 + 47$ 10. $297 - 105$

Round to the greatest place. Then estimate each sum or difference. (Lesson 3, pp. 64–66)

11. $\$6.73 + \$5.29$ 12. $3,476 - 1,015$ 13. $883 - 316$ 14. $23,820 + 46,216$

Add or subtract. (Lessons 5–8, pp. 70–79)

15. $\begin{array}{r} 5,039 \\ + 698 \\ \hline \end{array}$ 16. $\begin{array}{r} \$63.25 \\ - \$26.42 \\ \hline \end{array}$ 17. $\begin{array}{r} 4,020 \\ - 1,546 \\ \hline \end{array}$ 18. $\begin{array}{r} 304,798 \\ + 96,312 \\ \hline \end{array}$

PROBLEM SOLVING

Solve. Tell whether you need an exact answer or an estimate. (Lesson 4, p. 68)

19. Aba has $20.00. She wants to buy a necklace for $12.59 and a bracelet for $9.99. Does she have enough money?

20. Sal's lunch costs $7.56. He pays with a twenty-dollar bill. How much change should the cashier give Sal?

Write About It

Show You Understand

Explain how you would use compensation to solve the following problem.

$27 + 18 =$ ■

Extra Practice

Set A (Lesson 1, pp. 60–61)

Copy and complete. Tell which property of addition you used.

1. $98 + \blacksquare = 76 + 98$ **2.** $\blacksquare + 0 = 15$ **3.** $50 + (25 + 38) = (50 + \blacksquare) + 38$

Set B (Lesson 2, pp. 62–63)

Use mental math to add or subtract.

1. $69 + 56$ **2.** $87 - 34$ **3.** $28 + 17$ **4.** $16 + 75$ **5.** $16 + (59 + 4)$

Set C (Lesson 3, pp. 64–66)

Round to the greatest place. Then estimate each sum or difference.

1. $\$6.35 - \$2.93$ **2.** $759 + 385$ **3.** $55{,}883 - 15{,}751$ **4.** $88{,}015 - 22{,}673$

Set D (Lesson 5, pp. 70–71)

Add.

1. $778 + 397$ **2.** $\$153.98 + \$72.35$ **3.** $25{,}846 + 16{,}985$ **4.** $62{,}141 + 37{,}436$

Set E (Lesson 6, pp. 72–73)

Subtract.

1. $\$73.14 - \$9.08$ **2.** $3{,}152 - 981$ **3.** $6{,}424 - 2{,}375$ **4.** $4{,}191 - 2{,}763$

Set F (Lesson 7, pp. 74–75)

Find each difference.

1. $\$9.05 - \$2.47$ **2.** $3{,}040 - 1{,}942$ **3.** $10{,}600 - 5{,}251$ **4.** $27{,}000 - 3{,}688$

Set G (Lesson 8, pp. 76–79)

Add or subtract.

1.
$$47{,}902 + 72{,}135$$

2.
$$563{,}399 + 26{,}302$$

3.
$$85{,}206 - 63{,}479$$

4.
$$942{,}385 - 461{,}803$$

Multiplication and Division Basic Facts

INVESTIGATION

Using Data

A group of people took Mexican folk dance lessons. The total cost of the lessons was $15. How many people might have been taking dance lessons? Is there more than one possible answer?

Mexican Folk Dance Lessons

Price List
$3 per student
$5 per family

 **Use What You Know**

Use this page to review and remember
what you need to know for this chapter.

VOCABULARY

Choose the best word to complete each sentence.

> **Vocabulary**
> equal
> addition
> division
> multiply
> product

1. You can ____ two factors to find the product.

2. Multiplication can be written as repeated ____.

3. In division, items are separated into ____ groups.

4. ____ can be written as repeated subtraction.

For each fact tell if 8 is a *factor, product, dividend, divisor,* or *quotient*.

5.
$$5\overline{)40} = 8$$

6.
$$\begin{array}{r} 4 \\ \times\ 2 \\ \hline 8 \end{array}$$

7.
$$2\overline{)8} = 4$$

8.
$$\begin{array}{r} 9 \\ \times\ 8 \\ \hline 72 \end{array}$$

9. $8 \times 4 = 32$

10. $32 \div 4 = 8$

11. $16 \div 8 = 2$

12. $2 \times 4 = 8$

CONCEPTS AND SKILLS

Write a multiplication sentence for each picture.

13.

14.

15.

Complete each number sentence.

16. $4 + \blacksquare + 4 = 12$

17. $3 + 3 + 3 + 3 = \blacksquare \times 3$

18. $8 + 8 + 8 + 8 = 4 \times \blacksquare$

19. $7 + 7 + 7 + 7 + 7 = \blacksquare \times 7$

 **Write About It** ▶

20. Look at Exercise 14. How does it show
$16 \div 4 = 4$? Use correct vocabulary to
explain your answer.

Facts Practice, See page 667.

Algebra

Multiplication Properties and Division Rules

Objective Use multiplication properties and division rules.

Learn About It

Multiplication and division have special properties and rules.

Multiplication Properties

 Commutative Property

$3 \times 2 = 6$ $2 \times 3 = 6$

- When you change the order of the factors, the product stays the same.

▶ **Property of One**

$1 \times 6 = 6$

- When you multiply any number by 1, the product is equal to that number.

▶ **Zero Property**

◯ ◯ ◯ ◯
$4 \times 0 = 0$

- When you multiply any number by 0, the product is 0.

▶ **Associative Property**

- When you group factors in different ways, the product stays the same. The parentheses tell you which numbers to multiply first.

$(3 \times 2) \times 4$
$6 \times 4 = 24$

$3 \times (2 \times 4)$
$3 \times 8 = 24$

▶ Division rules can help you divide with 1 or 0.

Division Rules

- When you divide a number by itself, the quotient is 1. This is true for all numbers except 0.

$5 \div 5 = 1$ or $5)\overline{5}$ with quotient 1

- When you divide a number by 1, the quotient is the same as the dividend.

$5 \div 1 = 5$ or $1)\overline{5}$ with quotient 5

- When you divide 0 by a number other than 0, the quotient is 0.

$0 \div 5 = 0$ or $5)\overline{0}$ with quotient 0

- You cannot divide a number by 0.

$5 \div 0$ $0)\overline{5}$

Guided Practice

Use properties and rules to solve. If there is no solution, explain why.

1. $1 \times 93 = \blacksquare$
2. $(2 \times \blacksquare) \times 4 = 16$
3. $9 \times (9 \times 0) = \blacksquare$

4. $0 \div 3 = \blacksquare$
5. $9 \div 9 = \blacksquare$
6. $4 \times \blacksquare = 0$

7. $8 \div 0 = \blacksquare$
8. $\blacksquare \times 1 = 18$
9. $11 \div \blacksquare = 1$

Ask Yourself

- Did I multiply what was in the parentheses first?
- Is 0 the dividend?

Explain Your Thinking ▶ Do you need to multiply 6×9 to find $(6 \times 9) \times 0$? Use multiplication properties to explain.

Solve. Name the multiplication property you used.

10. $1 \times 4 = \blacksquare$

11. $5 \times 8 = \blacksquare \times 5$

12. $0 \times 72 = \blacksquare$

13. $3 \times 7 \times 8 = 3 \times \blacksquare \times 7$

14. $\blacksquare \times 1 = 5$

15. $3 \times 2 = \blacksquare \times 3$

16. $(3 \times 2) \times 4 = 3 \times (\blacksquare \times 4)$

17. $8 \times \blacksquare = 0$

18. $(4 \times \blacksquare) \times \blacksquare = 4$

Solve. Explain the division rule you used. If there is no solution, tell why.

19. $0 \div 10 = \blacksquare$

20. $\blacksquare \div 17 = 0$

21. $12 \div \blacksquare = 1$

22. $\blacksquare \div 1 = 92$

23. $12 \div 0 = \blacksquare$

24. $10 \div 10 = \blacksquare$

 Algebra • Properties Compare. Write >, <, or = in each ●.

25. $6 \div 6 \ \bullet \ 6 \div 1$

26. $7 \div 1 \ \bullet \ 6 \div 1$

27. $0 \div 4 \ \bullet \ 4 \div 4$

28. $0 \div 19 \ \bullet \ 0 \div 7$

29. $8 \div 8 \ \bullet \ 0 \div 9$

30. $24 \div 24 \ \bullet \ 692 \div 692$

31. $15 \times 1 \ \bullet \ 15 \div 1$

32. $0 \div 63 \ \bullet \ 2 \times (7 \times 1)$

33. $81 \times (0 \times 1) \ \bullet \ 0 \div 81$

Solve.

34. When the product of two numbers is 0, what do you know about one of the numbers?

35. When the quotient of two numbers is 1, what do you know about the two numbers?

36. Analyze Miguel multiplied two non-zero numbers. The product was equal to one of the numbers. What was the other number? Use properties to explain your answer.

37. Reasoning Tiara is thinking of three whole numbers. The product of the three numbers is 8. Their sum is 7. What are the numbers? Explain how you got your answer.

Mixed Review and Test Prep

Open Response

Add or subtract. (Ch. 3, Lessons 5–7)

38. $109 + 93$

39. $\$243 - \$66$

40. $462 + 215$

41. $750 - 172$

42. $\$6.08 - \$1.99$

43. $586 + 709$

Multiple Choice

44. Which is an example of the Zero Property of Multiplication?
(Ch. 4, Lesson 1)

A $0 \times 6 = 0$

C $6 + 0 = 6$

B $6 \times 1 = 6$

D $6 \times 6 = 36$

Extra Practice See page 107, Set A.

Game
Mystery Number

Play this mystery number game with a partner.

Step 1: Player 1 picks a two-digit "mystery number."
Without showing Player 2, Player 1 enters that number
into a calculator, presses , enters a one-digit number

(any digit but zero), then presses [=] .
Step 2: Player 2 writes down the number shown on the
calculator, and uses the number to guess the mystery
number. If Player 2 guesses incorrectly, he or she must
give the calculator back to Player 1. Repeat steps 1 and 2,
using the same mystery number but a different one-digit
factor. Continue repeating all steps until Player 2 guesses
the mystery number. Record the number of guesses
made. Then switch roles. The player with the least
number of guesses is the winner.

> What are the factors of 42?

Algebraic Thinking
How Do They Relate?

Complete each sentence.

1. 3×4 is to 4×3 as
   6×7 is to _____.

2. $0 \div 13$ is to 0 as
   _____ $\times 13$ is to 0.

3. $(4 \times 5) \times 7$ is to $4 \times (5 \times 7)$ as
   $(6 \times 8) \times 2$ is to _____.

Brain Teaser

Choose digits from 0 to 9 to complete
each problem.

A.
```
    1 ■ 3
  + ■ 2 ■
  -------
    8 1 2
```

B.
```
   1, ■ 5 ■
  + 4 ■ 6
  --------
  2,0 0 3
```

C.
```
    4,5 ■ 3
  + 9, ■ 6 ■
  ---------
  1 ■, 6 3 1
```

D.
```
  8, 0 4 ■
  - 9 ■ 7
  --------
  ■, ■ 4 6
```

Education Place

Check out **eduplace.com/map**
for more brain teasers.

Algebra

Relate Multiplication and Division

Objective Use multiplication facts to help you divide.

Learn About It

A community theater stores hats on shelves. There are 15 hats arranged on 3 shelves with the same number of hats on each shelf.

A group of objects arranged in equal rows and columns like this is called an **array**.

You can write two multiplication number sentences about the array.

$$3 \times 5 = 15$$
↑   ↑   ↑
rows   hats in   hats
     each row   in all

$$5 \times 3 = 15$$
↑   ↑   ↑
columns   hats in   hats
     each column   in all

You can also write two division number sentences about the array.

$$15 \div 3 = 5$$
↑   ↑   ↑
hats   rows   hats in
in all   each row

$$15 \div 5 = 3$$
↑   ↑   ↑
hats   columns   hats in
in all   each column

Like addition and subtraction, multiplication and division are **inverse operations**. One operation undoes the other.

▶ The multiplication and division number sentences you can write using two factors and a product form a **fact family** . Fact families show how multiplication and division are related.

Fact Family for 4, 6, and 24	
4 × 6 = 24	24 ÷ 4 = 6
6 × 4 = 24	24 ÷ 6 = 4

Extra Help at **eduplace.com/map**

Guided Practice

Write the fact family for each array or set of numbers.

1. ● ● ● ●
   ● ● ● ●

2.

3. 4, 4, 16   4. 5, 6, 30   5. 3, 5, 15

Ask Yourself
• What are the factors?
• What is the product?

Explain Your Thinking ▶ Look back at Exercise 3. Why are there only 2 number sentences in the fact family?

Practice and Problem Solving

Write the fact family for each array or set of numbers.

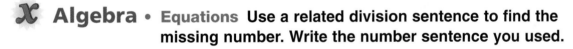

9. 3, 3, 9   10. 1, 10, 10   11. 4, 8, 32   12. 5, 8, 40

Complete each fact family.

13. $4 \times \blacksquare = \blacksquare$ $\blacksquare \div 4 = 6$

    $6 \times \blacksquare = 24$ $24 \div \blacksquare = 4$

14. $8 \times \blacksquare = 72$ $\blacksquare \div 8 = 9$

    $9 \times 8 = \blacksquare$ $\blacksquare \div 9 = \blacksquare$

✴ **Algebra • Equations** Use a related division sentence to find the missing number. Write the number sentence you used.

15. $8 \times \blacksquare = 64$ 16. $\blacksquare \times 6 = 54$ 17. $\blacksquare \times 9 = 81$ 18. $7 \times \blacksquare = 56$

19. $\blacksquare \times 9 = 45$ 20. $7 \times \blacksquare = 49$ 21. $7 \times \blacksquare = 63$ 22. $\blacksquare \times 20 = 20$

23. Can you form a fact family using 2, 7, and 27? Explain why or why not.

24. There are 2 different fact families that contain 3 and 6. Write the 4 number sentences for each fact family.

Mixed Review and Test Prep

Open Response

Write each number in expanded form.
(Ch. 3, Lessons 5–8)

25. 742

26. 4,909

27. 65,015

28. 608,926

29. A theater group has 48 students. Two students drop out. Can the remaining students be arranged in 6 equal rows? (Ch. 4, Lesson 2)

Extra Practice See page 107, Set B.

Algebra

Patterns in Multiplication and Division

Objective Use multiplication facts to help you divide.

Vocabulary
square number
multiple

Materials
multiplication table
(Learning Tool 5)

Work Together

You can use a multiplication table to multiply and discover patterns.

column ↓

×	0	1	2	3	4	5	6	7	8	9
0	0	0	0	0	0	0	0	0	0	0
1	0	1	2	3	4	5	6	7	8	9
2	0	2				10				
3	0	3				15				
4	0	4				20				
5	0	5				25				
6	0	6	12	18	24	⭐30				
7	0	7								
8	0	8								
9	0	9								

row → (points to row 6)

↑ product

STEP 1

Use a table like the one shown.

Look across the row for 6 and down the column for 5 to find 6 × 5.

• What is the product?

Use this method to fill in the rest of the products in the table.

STEP 2

A **square number** is the product of two factors that are the same.

> 4 × 4 = 16, so 16 is a square number.
> 7 × 7 = 49, so 49 is a square number.

• Find the other square numbers in the table.

• Describe how you found them.

STEP 3

A **multiple** of a number is the product of that number and any whole number. The row for 6 shows the multiples of 6.

• List 5 multiples of 6 shown in the table.

• Where else can you find multiples of 6 in the table? Where can you find multiples of 8?

You can also use a multiplication table to divide.

STEP 4

To find 40 ÷ 8, look down the column for 8 until you find 40. Follow that row to the left to find the quotient.

- What is the quotient of 40 ÷ 8?
- Use your table to find 21 ÷ 7. Describe how you found it.

×	0	1	2	3	4	5	6	7	8
0	0	0	0	0	0	0	0	0	0
1	0	1	2	3	4	5	6	7	8
2	0	2	4	6	8	10	12	14	16
3	0	3	6	9	12	15	18	21	24
4	0	4	8	12	16	20	24	28	32
5	0	5	10	15	20	25	30	35	40

STEP 5

Find the number 24 in four different places in the table. Write a division sentence for each 24 you find.

- How are your division sentences the same? How are they different?

On Your Own

Use your multiplication table to answer each question.

1. Write a division sentence using a square number as the dividend. Write the fact family for the set of 3 numbers in your division sentence. Is there another division sentence that uses the same dividend and factors? Why or why not?

2. Find the product of 4 and 8 in two places in the table. Write two multiplication sentences using 4 and 8 as factors. What property do the number sentences show?

Talk About It • Write About It

You learned how to use patterns in a multiplication table to multiply and divide.

3. **Analyze** Look at the multiples of 3 and 6 in the table. What do you notice? Why do you think this is true?

4. What division rule does the row for 0 show?

5. **Challenge** How could you extend the table to show multiples of 10?

Audio Tutor 1/13 Listen and Understand

Multiplication and Division Facts to Five

Objective Learn different ways to multiply and divide.

Learn About It

Kerry Connolly belongs to an Irish step dance company. In one dance, there are 4 lines with 3 dancers in each line. How many dancers are there?

Multiply. $4 \times 3 = $ ■ or $\begin{array}{r} 3 \\ \times 4 \\ \hline \end{array}$

Different Ways to Find 4×3

Way ① Use skip counting.

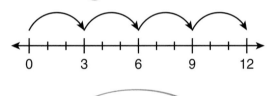

Think
3, 6, 9, 12
So $4 \times 3 = 12$.

Way ② Use doubles.

You know 4 is double 2 and $2 \times 3 = 6$.

Since $2 \times 3 = 6$

Then $4 \times 3 = 6 + 6$

$4 \times 3 = 12$

Solution: There are 12 dancers.

▶ You can also use different strategies to divide.

Different Ways to Find $20 \div 4$

Way ① Use repeated subtraction.

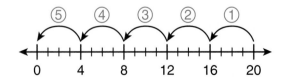

The number of 4s you subtract is the quotient.

So $20 \div 4 = 5$

Way ② Use a related multiplication fact.

$20 \div 4 = $ ■

Think
$4 \times $ ■ $= 20$
$4 \times 5 = 20$

So $20 \div 4 = 5$.

Guided Practice

Multiply or divide. Use one of the methods shown.

1. 6×2 **2.** 5×4 **3.** 5×6 **4.** 4×4

5. $2\overline{)10}$ **6.** $4\overline{)24}$ **7.** $18 \div 3$ **8.** $20 \div 5$

Ask Yourself

• Can I skip count or use doubles to multiply?

• Can I use repeated subtraction or related facts to divide?

Explain Your Thinking ▶ How can knowing that $4 \times 4 = 16$ help you find 5×4?

Practice and Problem Solving

Multiply or divide. Show your work with a drawing.

9. $\begin{array}{r} 3 \\ \times\, 3 \\ \hline \end{array}$ **10.** $\begin{array}{r} 4 \\ \times\, 2 \\ \hline \end{array}$ **11.** $\begin{array}{r} 4 \\ \times\, 7 \\ \hline \end{array}$ **12.** $\begin{array}{r} 3 \\ \times\, 8 \\ \hline \end{array}$ **13.** $\begin{array}{r} 4 \\ \times\, 6 \\ \hline \end{array}$

14. $5\overline{)5}$ **15.** 5×4 **16.** $36 \div 4$ **17.** $45 \div 5$ **18.** 3×7

✗ Algebra • **Equations** Complete each number sentence.

19. $4 \times \blacksquare = 0$ **20.** $\blacksquare \times 3 = 18$ **21.** $\blacksquare \times 2 = 18$ **22.** $5 \times \blacksquare = 35$

23. $30 \div \blacksquare = 6$ **24.** $25 \div \blacksquare = 5$ **25.** $27 \div 3 = \blacksquare$ **26.** $\blacksquare \div 5 = 8$

Solve using one of the methods shown.

27. Multistep Dancers' hair ribbons cost $5 a box. There are 8 ribbons in each box. How many ribbons can you buy for $15?

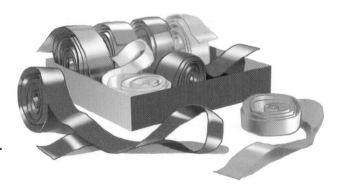

28. Explain Write and solve a multiplication number sentence for $5 + 5 + 5 + 5 = \blacksquare$. Explain how you got your answer.

Mixed Review and Test Prep ✓

Open Response

Order the numbers from least to greatest. (Ch. 2, Lesson 2)

29. 23, 33, 32, 20   522, 252, 325

30. 77, 71, 87, 18   203, 320, 302

Multiple Choice

31. Which number sentence can help you find $32 \div 4$? (Ch. 4, Lesson 4)

A $15 \div 3 = 5$ **C** $32 - 4 = 28$

B $8 \times 4 = 32$ **D** $32 \times 1 = 32$

Lesson 5

Multiplication and Division Facts to Ten

Objective Learn different methods to multiply and divide facts to ten.

Learn About It

An African theater company is putting on a puppet show using spider puppets. Each spider has 8 legs. How many legs do 6 spider puppets have altogether?

Multiply. $6 \times 8 = \blacksquare$ or $\begin{array}{r} 8 \\ \times\, 6 \\ \hline \end{array}$

Different Ways to Find 6×8

Way ❶ Use a known fact.

You know $5 \times 8 = 40$ and 6×8 is one more group of 8.

Since $5 \times 8 = 40$
Then $6 \times 8 = 40 + 8$
$6 \times 8 = 48$

Way ❷ Use doubles.

You know 6 is double 3 and $3 \times 8 = 24$.

Since $3 \times 8 = 24$
Then $6 \times 8 = 24 + 24$
$6 \times 8 = 48$

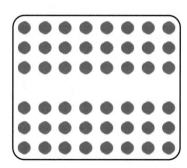

Solution: Six spider puppets have 48 legs.

▶ Omari is assembling spider puppets for the show. He has 24 spider legs. How many spider puppets can he make?

Divide. $24 \div 8 = $ ■ or $8\overline{)24}$

Different Ways to Find $24 \div 8$

Way ① Use a related multiplication fact.

$24 \div 8 = $ ■

Since $\quad 8 \times 3 = 24$

Then $\quad 24 \div 8 = 3$

Think
$8 \times $ ■ $= 24$
$8 \times 3 = 24$

Way ② Use doubles.

8 is double 4, so $24 \div 8$ will be half of $24 \div 4$.

Since $24 \div 4 = 6$

Then $\quad 24 \div 8 = 6 \div 2$

$24 \div 8 = 3$

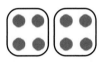 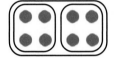

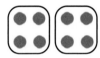 

$24 \div 4 = 6 \qquad\qquad 24 \div 8 = 3$

Way ③ Use a related division fact.

If you know $\qquad 24 \div 3 = 8$

then you know $\quad 24 \div 8 = 3$.

Solution: Omari can assemble 3 spider puppets.

Guided Practice

Multiply or divide.

1. $\begin{array}{r} 6 \\ \times 6 \\ \hline \end{array}$

2. $\begin{array}{r} 7 \\ \times 2 \\ \hline \end{array}$

3. $\begin{array}{r} 7 \\ \times 5 \\ \hline \end{array}$

4. $\begin{array}{r} 6 \\ \times 8 \\ \hline \end{array}$

5. $8\overline{)24}$

6. $6\overline{)54}$

7. $8\overline{)56}$

8. $10\overline{)70}$

Ask Yourself

- What strategy can I use to multiply?
- What strategy can I use to divide?

Explain Your Thinking ▶ How can knowing that $36 \div 6 = 6$ help you find $42 \div 6$?

Go On

Multiply or divide.

9. $\begin{array}{r} 8 \\ \times\ 0 \\ \hline \end{array}$ 10. $\begin{array}{r} 8 \\ \times\ 6 \\ \hline \end{array}$ 11. $\begin{array}{r} 6 \\ \times\ 7 \\ \hline \end{array}$ 12. $\begin{array}{r} 9 \\ \times\ 7 \\ \hline \end{array}$ 13. $\begin{array}{r} 7 \\ \times\ 8 \\ \hline \end{array}$ 14. $\begin{array}{r} 10 \\ \times\ 8 \\ \hline \end{array}$

15. $6\overline{)6}$ 16. 8×9 17. $40 \div 10$ 18. $27 \div 9$ 19. $40 \div 8$ 20. $8\overline{)16}$

21. 6×8 22. 9×3 23. $35 \div 7$ 24. 10×8 25. $63 \div 7$ 26. $42 \div 6$

Compare. Write >, <, or = in each ⬤.

27. $16 \div 2$ ⬤ $24 \div 3$ 28. 10×3 ⬤ 9×3 29. $80 \div 10$ ⬤ $81 \div 9$

30. 10×4 ⬤ 6×7 31. $32 \div 4$ ⬤ 8×1 32. $18 \div 2$ ⬤ $90 \div 10$

✳ Algebra • Functions Complete each table.

Rule: Multiply by 8	
Input	Output
33. 4	⬛
34. 6	⬛
35. ⬛	56
36. ⬛	80

Rule: Divide by 7	
Input	Output
37. ⬛	4
38. 14	⬛
39. 42	⬛
40. ⬛	9

41.

Rule: _____	
Input	Output
9	3
24	8
27	9
12	4

📊 Data Use the graph for Problems 42–46.

42. How many tickets did the children in Room C sell?

43. How many more tickets did Room B sell than Room A?

44. Write 2 number sentences to show the number of tickets sold by Room B.

45. **Money** Tickets cost $5. What is the cost of the tickets sold by Room A?

46. **Analyze** Suppose Room D sold 36 tickets. How would you show this on the graph? Explain your answer.

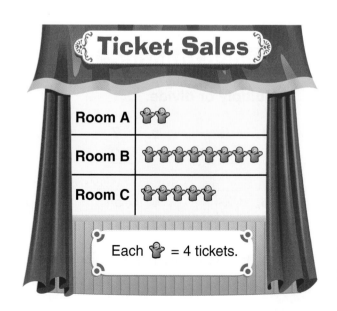

Extra Practice See page 107, Set C.

Math Reasoning
Common Multiples

You can use multiples to solve problems.

What is the least number of packages of hot dogs and rolls that you can buy to have the same number of hot dogs and rolls?

- Make two tables as shown.

Packages	1	2	3	4	5	6	7	8	9	10
Hot Dogs	10	20	30	**40**	50	60	70	**80**	90	100

Packages	1	2	3	4	5	6	7	8	9	10
Rolls	8	16	24	32	**40**	48	56	64	72	**80**

- Look for common numbers in the second row of both tables. Since you want the least number and 40 < 80, choose 40.

- To find the answer, look above the 40 in each table.

You will need to buy 4 packages of hot dogs and 5 packages of rolls.

Find how many bags you need to buy of each kind of balloon to get the same number of each.

1. Small balloons: 6 in each bag
   Medium balloons: 5 in each bag

2. Red balloons: 12 in each bag
   Blue balloons: 8 in each bag

Check your understanding of Lessons 1–5.

Use properties and rules to solve. If there is no solution, explain why. (Lesson 1)

1. $1 \times 27 = \blacksquare$
2. $\blacksquare \div 0 = 2$
3. $(4 \times 3) \times 3 = 4 \times (\blacksquare \times 3)$

Write the fact family for each set of numbers. (Lesson 2)

4. 7, 9, 63
5. 4, 4, 16
6. 10, 6, 60

Multiply or divide. (Lessons 3–5)

7. $4\overline{)36}$
8. 6×7
9. 10×7
10. $56 \div 8$

Multiply and Divide With 11 and 12

Materials
multiplication table
(Learning Tool 6)

Objective Use a multiplication table to multiply and divide with 11 and 12.

Work Together

You can use a multiplication table and patterns to multiply and divide with 11 and 12.

×	0	1	2	3	4	5	6	7	8	9	10	11	12
0	0	0	0	0	0	0	0	0	0	0			
1	0	1	2	3	4	5	6	7	8	9	10		
2	0	2	4	6	8	10	12	14	16	18	20		
3	0	3	6	9	12	15	18	21	24	27	30		
4	0	4	8	12	16	20	24	28	32	36	40		
5	0	5	10	15	20	25	30	35	40	45	50		
6	0	6	12	18	24	30	36	42	48	54	60		
7	0	7	14	21	28	35	42	49	56	63	70		
8	0	8	16	24	32	40	48	56	64	72	80		
9	0	9	18	27	36	45	54	63	72	81	90		
10	0	10	20	30	40	50	60	70	80	90	100		
11													
12													

STEP 1

Use a multiplication table like the one shown.

• What pattern do you see in the row and column for 10?

STEP 2

Now fill in the table for the 11 row and column.

• How can you use the 10 facts to find the 11 facts?

• How can you use patterns to find the 11 facts?

STEP 3

Fill in the table for the 12 row and column.

• How can you use the 11 facts to find the 12 facts?

• How can you use the 6 facts to find the 12 facts?

STEP 4

Use the table to find 4 × 12.

- What is the product?
  Describe how you found it.

- In what two ways can you find the product of 8 and 12 on the completed table?

×	0	1	2	3	4	5	6	7	8	9	10	11	12
0	0	0	0	0	0	0	0	0	0	0	0	0	0
1	0	1	2	3	4	5	6	7	8	9	10	11	12
2	0	2	4	6	8	10	12	14	16	18	20	22	24
3	0	3	6	9	12	15	18	21	24	27	30	33	36
4	0	4	8	12	16	20	24	28	32	36	40	44	48

STEP 5

Use the table to find 44 ÷ 11.

- What is the quotient?
  Describe how you found it.

- In what two ways can you find 33 ÷ 3 on the table?

×	0	1	2	3	4	5	6	7	8	9	10	11
0	0	0	0	0	0	0	0	0	0	0	0	0
1	0	1	2	3	4	5	6	7	8	9	10	11
2	0	2	4	6	8	10	12	14	16	18	20	22
3	0	3	6	9	12	15	18	21	24	27	30	33
4	0	4	8	12	16	20	24	28	32	36	40	44

On Your Own

Multiply or divide. Use your table to help you.

1. 11 × 6   2. 12 × 7   3. 9 × 11   4. 11 × 4   5. 12 × 12

6. 5)55   7. 12)120   8. 77 ÷ 11   9. 96 ÷ 12   10. 132 ÷ 11

Talk About It • Write About It

You learned how to use a multiplication table to multiply and divide with 11 and 12.

11. Write a fact family in which 96 is the product. Use the table to help you.

12. **Explain** Look at the multiples of 6 and the multiples of 12 on the table. What do you notice? Why is this true? Use an example to explain.

Algebra
Multiply Three Factors

Objective Use multiplication facts to help you divide.

Learn About It

Upright bass strings come in sets of 4. Suppose one box holds 2 sets of strings. If a musician orders 3 boxes, how many strings will there be?

Multiply. $4 \times 3 \times 2 = $ ▨

String instruments, such as the upright bass, guitar, and violin, are used to play many different types of music.

▶ You can use the Associative Property to group factors together. The parentheses show which factors to multiply first.

You can multiply 4×3 first.

$4 \times 3 \times 2 = $ ▨

$(4 \times 3) \times 2 = $ ▨

$12 \times 2 = 24$

You can multiply 3×2 first.

$4 \times 3 \times 2 = $ ▨

$4 \times (3 \times 2) = $ ▨

$4 \times 6 = 24$

No matter how you group the factors, the product is the same.

Solution: There will be 24 strings.

Guided Practice

Find each product.

1. $5 \times (3 \times 2) = $ ▨

2. $9 \times (2 \times 5) = $ ▨

3. $(2 \times 2) \times 11 = $ ▨

4. $(6 \times 1) \times 3 = $ ▨

Ask Yourself

• Which two numbers should I multiply first?

• What is the third factor?

Use parentheses to show two different ways to multiply. Then find the product.

5. $2 \times 3 \times 4$

6. $4 \times 3 \times 4$

7. $9 \times 12 \times 1$

8. $12 \times 0 \times 12$

9. $6 \times 2 \times 5$

10. $4 \times 2 \times 6$

Explain Your Thinking ▶ How can you use the Commutative and Associative Properties to make it easier to multiply $3 \times 9 \times 3$?

Practice and Problem Solving

Use parentheses to show two different ways to multiply. Then find the product.

11. $2 \times 2 \times 4$

12. $5 \times 2 \times 1$

13. $6 \times 2 \times 6$

14. $3 \times 4 \times 1$

15. $8 \times 1 \times 7$

16. $4 \times 3 \times 3$

17. $9 \times 8 \times 0$

18. $3 \times 3 \times 2$

 Algebra • **Properties** Find each missing number.

19. $\blacksquare \times 12 \times 3 = 0$

20. $7 \times 4 \times 1 = \blacksquare$

21. $3 \times 2 \times 6 = \blacksquare$

22. $(3 \times 3) \times \blacksquare = 9$

23. $4 \times (\blacksquare \times 2) = 24$

24. $(\blacksquare \times 3) \times 3 = 18$

25. $(2 \times 3) \times 6 = \blacksquare$

26. $\blacksquare \times (4 \times 2) = 32$

27. $(3 \times 3) \times \blacksquare = 108$

Data A Color Guard often marches with a marching band twirling colorful flags. Use the table for Problems 28–30.

28. Elaine bought a box of rainbow flags. What is the cost?

29. **Compare** Which costs more, 1 box of red flags or 1 box of blue flags? Explain how you got your answer.

30. Lee bought a box of each kind of flag. What was the total cost?

31. **What's Wrong?** Gina says that to find $8 \times 7 \times 0$, you have to multiply 8×7. What is wrong with her thinking? Use properties to explain.

Price List			
	Cost for 1 flag	Flags in a set	Sets in a box
Blue flags	$5	3 flags	2 sets
Red flags	$4	3 flags	2 sets
Gold flags	$3	4 flags	2 sets
Rainbow flags	$11	2 flags	1 set

Mixed Review and Test Prep

Open Response

Write the numbers in order from least to greatest. (Ch. 2, Lesson 2)

32. 413   431   143

33. 978   798   789

34. 511   600   499

35. 990   909   999

Multiple Choice

36. A box has 6 pairs of marching-band gloves. How many gloves are in 2 boxes? (Ch. 4, Lesson 7)

A 10

c 20

B 12

D 24

Lesson 8
Division With Remainders

Objective Learn how to divide when there are remainders.

Vocabulary
remainder

Learn About It

The Shanghai Acrobats use plates in their performances. Suppose there are 9 acrobats that each need the same number of plates. If there are 56 plates, how many plates does each acrobat get? How many plates are left?

When you divide, the **remainder** tells how many are left. The remainder is always less than the divisor.

The Shanghai Acrobats study for 7 years to learn how to perform incredible acrobatic feats!

Divide. $56 \div 9 \to \blacksquare$ or $9\overline{)56}$

STEP 1 Think of multiplication facts that have 9 as a factor and products close to 56.

$9 \times \blacksquare = 56$

$9 \times 6 = 54$

$9 \times 7 = 63$

7 is too many.
Try 6 as the quotient.

STEP 2 Divide. Multiply, then subtract.

$$\begin{array}{r} 6 \\ 9\overline{)56} \\ -54 \\ \hline 2 \end{array}$$

← Multiply. $9 \times 6 = 54$
← Subtract. $56 - 54 = 2$
There are no groups of 9 in 2, so 2 is the remainder.

STEP 3 Show the remainder next to the quotient.

$$\begin{array}{r} 6 \text{ R2} \\ 9\overline{)56} \\ -54 \\ \hline 2 \end{array}$$

← remainder
$2 < 9$

Solution: Each acrobat gets 6 plates. There are 2 plates left.

Guided Practice

Divide.

1. $2\overline{)11}$
2. $4\overline{)7}$
3. $3\overline{)14}$
4. $6\overline{)20}$

5. $32 \div 8$
6. $25 \div 3$
7. $25 \div 7$
8. $20 \div 9$

Ask Yourself
- What multiplication facts can help me?
- Is there a remainder? Is it less than the divisor?

Explain Your Thinking ▶ Why must the remainder always be less than the divisor?

Divide.

9. $4\overline{)6}$ **10.** $2\overline{)9}$ **11.** $5\overline{)12}$ **12.** $2\overline{)17}$ **13.** $4\overline{)23}$

14. $50 \div 7$ **15.** $15 \div 2$ **16.** $33 \div 9$ **17.** $49 \div 5$ **18.** $18 \div 6$

19. $6\overline{)16}$ **20.** $12\overline{)100}$ **21.** $8\overline{)32}$ **22.** $3\overline{)23}$ **23.** $2\overline{)25}$

24. $69 \div 7$ **25.** $44 \div 9$ **26.** $101 \div 9$ **27.** $39 \div 6$ **28.** $20 \div 4$

Find each missing number.

29. $3 \div \blacksquare \rightarrow 1\ R\ 1$ **30.** $9 \div 4 \rightarrow 2\ R\ \blacksquare$ **31.** $26 \div 9 \rightarrow 2\ R\ \blacksquare$

32. $15 \div 3 \rightarrow \blacksquare$ **33.** $\blacksquare \div 8 \rightarrow 2\ R\ 4$ **34.** $125 \div 11 \rightarrow \blacksquare\ R\ 4$

35. $34 \div \blacksquare \rightarrow 4\ R\ 2$ **36.** $\blacksquare \div 7 \rightarrow 4$ **37.** $150 \div \blacksquare \rightarrow 12\ R\ 6$

38. Suppose 9 acrobats each balance 5 sets of candles. Are 46 sets of candles enough for all the acrobats? Will there be any sets left over?

39. Mrs. Kim bought 2 adult tickets for $7 each and one senior ticket for $5 to an acrobat show. She paid with a $20 bill. What was her change?

40. **What's Wrong?** After the show, Chang packs 53 glasses into boxes. He says he can divide them evenly into 8 boxes. Use a division sentence to explain why he is wrong.

Mixed Review and Test Prep

Open Response

Add or subtract. (Ch. 3, Lessons 5–8)

41. $267 + 324$ **42.** $\$3.52 - \$1.09$

43. $\$678 + \$491$ **44.** $701 - 645$

45. $\begin{array}{r} \$72.79 \\ + \$13.21 \\ \hline \end{array}$ **46.** $\begin{array}{r} 6{,}005 \\ -\ 953 \\ \hline \end{array}$

47. Is this division example correct? If not, explain why not and then correct it. (Ch. 4, Lesson 8)

$$\begin{array}{r} 5\ R\ 6 \\ 6\overline{)36} \\ -\ 30 \\ \hline 6 \end{array}$$

Audio Tutor 1/15 Listen and Understand

Problem-Solving Decision
Choose the Operation

Objective Decide what operations to use to solve problems.

You need to use different operations depending upon what question is asked.

Ian the Great can juggle 6 rings in each hand at the same time! He has 4 assistants who can juggle several bowling pins at the same time. Ian has 20 juggling rings and 12 bowling pins.

Sometimes you add to find the total. How many pieces of juggling equipment does Ian have? 20 + 12 = 32 pieces	**You can multiply to find the total if you have equal groups.** How many rings can Ian juggle at the same time? 6 × 2 = 12 rings
You subtract to find the difference. How many more juggling rings than bowling pins does Ian the Great have? 20 − 12 = 8 more rings	**You divide to find equal groups.** Suppose each assistant juggles the same number of bowling pins. How many pins does each juggle? 12 ÷ 4 = 3 bowling pins

Try These

Solve. Explain why you chose each operation.

1. Ian's 4 assistants have 16 juggling balls. If they each juggle an equal number of balls, how many balls does each assistant juggle?

2. Manuela can juggle 5 rings. Carl can juggle 3 rings. Ian can juggle 12 rings. How many more rings can Ian juggle than Manuela and Carl together?

3. Ian needs to buy more juggling equipment. He buys 3 packages of juggling balls. Each package contains 5 balls. How many balls did he buy?

4. Ian's assistants can each juggle 3 rings or 5 balls at a time. Ian wants them to juggle a total of 15 balls. How many assistants does he need?

Math Challenge
Exponents

Becca decided to start a jogging routine last month. The first week, she ran 2 miles. Each week after that, she doubled the distance that she ran. How many miles could Becca run by the 4th week?

On the 4th week, Becca ran **2 × 2 × 2 × 2 miles**, or **16 miles**.

What is an easy way to write the product of **2 × 2 × 2 × 2**? You can write the product as an exponent. **2 × 2 × 2 × 2** written as an exponent is 2^4. This number is read as "two to the fourth power." So, Becca ran 2^4 miles last month.

▶ The **base** is the number that is being multiplied.

▶ The **exponent** shows the number of times that the base is used as a factor. In this case, the base 2 was multiplied by itself 4 times, so the exponent is 4.

$$2^4$$

exponent

base

Here are some more examples of exponents:
$3 × 3 × 3 = 3^3$ (Three to the third power)
$8 × 8 × 8 × 8 × 8 = 8^5$ (Eight to the fifth power)

Look at the table below. Use what you know about exponents to fill in the missing information.

Expression	Exponent	Spoken form
2 × 2	2^2	Two to the second power
	5^3	
6 × 6 × 6 × 6		
		Four to the fourth power
	3^8	
7 × 7 × 7 × 7 × 7		
		Eight to the third power

Choose an exponent from the table above. Write an example of how that exponent might be used in a real-world situation.

Chapter Review/Test

VOCABULARY

Choose the best term to complete each sentence.

1. You can find $7 \times 0 = \blacksquare$ using the ____.

2. $3 \times 4 = 4 \times 3$ is an example of the ____.

3. $6 \times 6 = 36$ and $36 \div 6 = 6$ are a ____.

4. The number left after you divide is called the ____.

> **Vocabulary**
> fact family
> remainder
> Commutative Property
> Zero Property
> Property of One

CONCEPTS AND SKILLS

Use properties and rules to solve. If there is no solution, tell why. (Lesson 1, pp. 84–86)

5. $9 \div \blacksquare = 9$ 6. $0 \times 84 = \blacksquare$ 7. $(5 \times 3) \times 2 = 5 \times (\blacksquare \times 2)$

Write the fact family for each set of numbers. (Lesson 2, pp. 88–89)

8. 3, 6, 18 9. 3, 4, 12 10. 2, 8, 16

Multiply or divide. (Lessons 3–8, pp. 90–103)

11. 5×3 12. $4\overline{)32}$ 13. $(9 \times 6) \times 2$ 14. $65 \div 6$

15. 12×7 16. $2 \times 4 \times 6$ 17. $7\overline{)80}$ 18. $25 \div 4$

PROBLEM SOLVING

Solve. (Lesson 9, pp. 104–105)

19. Jina has 12 stuffed bears. Her sister has half as many. How many bears does Jina's sister have?

20. Vanna reads for 10 minutes every night. Pete reads 3 times as long every night. How many more minutes does Pete read than Vanna each night?

Write About It

Show You Understand

Don has 12 coins in his coin collection. How many different rectangular arrays can he make with the coins?

Draw the arrays. Then explain how you found them.

Extra Practice

Set A (Lesson 1, pp. 84–87)

Use properties and rules to solve. If there is no solution, tell why.

1. $4 \times 9 = \blacksquare \times 4$

2. $4 \div 4 = \blacksquare$

3. $0 \div 6 = \blacksquare$

4. $5 \times (6 \times 4) = (5 \times 6) \times \blacksquare$

5. $5 \div 0 = \blacksquare$

6. $\blacksquare \times 16 = 0$

Set B (Lesson 2, pp. 88–89)

Write the fact family for each set of numbers.

1. 2, 3, 6

2. 3, 7, 21

3. 4, 9, 36

4. 5, 8, 40

5. 7, 4, 28

6. 3, 6 ,18

7. 4, 2, 8

8. 8, 8, 64

Set C (Lessons 4–5, pp. 92–93, 94–97)

Multiply or divide.

1. 3×3

2. $30 \div 5$

3. 7×4

4. $4\overline{)32}$

5. $24 \div 6$

6. 7×10

7. $9\overline{)63}$

8. 8×6

9. 7×9

10. $9\overline{)90}$

11. 5×6

12. $80 \div 8$

13. 9×4

14. $8\overline{)72}$

15. $32 \div 4$

Set D (Lesson 7, pp. 100–101)

Find each product.

1. $7 \times 6 \times 2$

2. $5 \times 6 \times 2$

3. $(4 \times 5) \times 2$

4. $(9 \times 3) \times 4$

5. $7 \times 3 \times 3$

6. $10 \times (2 \times 4)$

7. $5 \times (3 \times 2)$

8. $8 \times 7 \times 1$

Set E (Lesson 8, pp. 102–103)

Divide.

1. $3\overline{)19}$

2. $6\overline{)61}$

3. $4\overline{)15}$

4. $3\overline{)37}$

5. $9\overline{)103}$

6. $7\overline{)51}$

7. $6\overline{)41}$

8. $8\overline{)94}$

9. $9\overline{)85}$

10. $5\overline{)63}$

11. $11\overline{)121}$

12. $9\overline{)98}$

13. $8\overline{)60}$

14. $6\overline{)53}$

15. $12\overline{)100}$

CHAPTER 5

Algebraic Reasoning

INVESTIGATION

Using Data

Some animals spend most of their day sleeping! The table shows the average number of hours some animals sleep in a 24-hour period. Myra wrote the following number sentence using the data in the table:

$n = 19 \times 3$

What fact do you think Myra's number sentence might show?

Snoozing Animals	
Name of Animal	**Average Amount of Sleep Per Day**
Gerbil	13 hours
Koala	20 hours
Opossum	19 hours
Squirrel	15 hours
Tiger	16 hours

Use What You Know

**Use this page to review and remember
what you need to know for this chapter.**

VOCABULARY

Choose the best term to complete each sentence.

1. The number sentence $3 \times 5 = 5 \times 3$ is an example of the ____.

2. The ____ tells you the product of 0 and 218.

3. The number sentence $(2 \times 4) \times 5 = 2 \times (4 \times 5)$ is an example of the ____.

> **Vocabulary**
> Associative Property
> Commutative Property
> Zero Property
> Property of One

CONCEPTS AND SKILLS

Find the missing number.

4. $\blacksquare + 6 = 11$ 5. $15 + \blacksquare = 18$ 6. $\blacksquare + 22 = 45$ 7. $19 + \blacksquare = 63$

8. $6 \times \blacksquare = 30$ 9. $\blacksquare \times 8 = 0$ 10. $7 \times \blacksquare = 63$ 11. $\blacksquare \times 8 = 96$

12. $\blacksquare - 14 = 6$ 13. $17 - \blacksquare = 13$ 14. $45 \div \blacksquare = 9$ 15. $\blacksquare \div 3 = 12$

Copy and complete each table.

Rule: Add 6	
Input	Output
3	9
16. 5	$\blacksquare$
17. 8	$\blacksquare$
18. $\blacksquare$	15

Rule: Subtract 8	
Input	Output
19. $\blacksquare$	11
22	14
20. 35	$\blacksquare$
21. 47	$\blacksquare$

Rule: Divide by 7	
Input	Output
21	3
22. 42	$\blacksquare$
23. $\blacksquare$	5
24. 56	$\blacksquare$

 Write About It

25. Explain why you can multiply two factors in any order. Draw a picture to support your explanation.

Facts Practice, See page 668.

Algebra

Order of Operations

Objective Use the order of operations to simplify expressions.

Learn About It

The Sea Turtle Patrol in Florida helps protect green-turtle nests. One turtle made 3 nests on the beach. Three other turtles each made 4 nests. Then 1 nest was destroyed in a storm. How many nests were left?

You can write an expression to solve the problem. An **expression** is a number or group of numbers with operation symbols.

$3 + (3 \times 4) - 1$ is an expression that shows the number of nests that were left.

To simplify or find the value of $3 + (3 \times 4) - 1$, you need to follow the rules for the **order of operations**.

Order of Operations

• First, do operations inside the **parentheses** ( ).

• Then do multiplication and division in order from left to right.

• Finally, do addition and subtraction in order from left to right.

$3 + (3 \times 4) - 1$

$3 + 12 - 1$ ← There is no more multiplication or division.

$15 - 1$

14

Solution: There were 14 nests left.

Other Examples

A. Simplify $12 \times (4 - 2)$.

$12 \times (4 - 2)$ First, work inside parentheses.

12×2 Then multiply.

24

B. Simplify $14 + 10 \div 2 \times 3$.

$14 + 10 \div 2 \times 3$ Multiply and divide left to right.

$14 + 5 \times 3$

$14 + 15$ Then add.

29

Guided Practice

Simplify. Follow the order of operations.

1. $(14 - 7) + 3$
2. $(5 + 2) \times 3$
3. $6 + 12 \div 3$
4. $27 \div 9 - 1$

Ask Yourself

- Are there parentheses?
- Which operation should I do first?

Explain Your Thinking ▶ Does $48 - (16 - 6)$ equal $(48 - 16) - 6$? Why or why not?

Practice and Problem Solving

Simplify. Follow the order of operations.

5. $42 \div 7 \div 2$
6. $8 + 12 \div 4$
7. $8 \times (5 + 2)$
8. $3 \times 9 - 3 + 1$
9. $3 \times (9 - 3) + 1$
10. $15 \div 5 \times 8 - 4$

Copy the expression. Then insert parentheses to make the expression equal 24.

11. $13 - 1 \times 2$
12. $4 + 2 \times 4$
13. $6 + 6 \times 2$
14. $3 \times 11 - 3$
15. $8 \times 8 - 5$
16. $2 + 2 + 2 \times 4$

Solve.

17. Write this expression four times.

    $8 + 12 \div 4 \times 3 - 2$

    Add one set of parentheses to each expression to get different answers.

18. **Multistep** Two pails of turtle eggs hold 8 eggs each. There are 4 more pails of eggs with 10 eggs in each pail. Find the total number of eggs in the pails.

19. **Explain** There are 20 hatchlings, or baby green turtles, in a nest. If two groups of 5 hatchlings leave the nest, how many are left? How did you get your answer?

Mixed Review and Test Prep

Open Response

Round each number to the nearest hundred. Then estimate. (Ch. 3, Lesson 3)

20. $943 + 512$
21. $872 - 543$
22. $5,109 + 2,286$
23. $3,679 - 1,882$

24. Jamie simplified $15 - 3 + 9$ and got 3. What mistake did he make? What is the correct answer? Explain. (Ch. 5, Lesson 1)

Audio Tutor 1/17 Listen and Understand

Algebra

Words Into Expressions

Objective Use variables to write expressions.

Vocabulary
variable
evaluate

Learn About It

Many people have worked to help endangered grizzly bears in the wilderness areas of Yellowstone National Park. Suppose a park ranger saw 2 cubs in each of the dens she found. How many cubs did she see?

Since you don't know how many dens she found, you can use a **variable** to stand for that number and write an expression.

Remember
An expression is a number or group of numbers with operation symbols.

- Let *n* stand for the number of dens. ← You may choose any letter or symbol for the variable.

- Then express the number of cubs.
  2 × *n* or **2 • *n*** or **2*n***   ← You read all these expressions as "2 times *n*."

Solution: The ranger saw 2*n* cubs.

▶ Now suppose the ranger found 3 dens. How many bear cubs did she find?

Evaluate 2*n* when *n* = 3.

STEP 1 Write the expression.

2*n*

STEP 2 Replace *n* with 3.

2*n*
2 × 3

STEP 3 Simplify the expression.

2*n*
2 × 3
6

Solution: If the ranger found 3 dens, she found 6 cubs.

Extra Help at **eduplace.com/map**

▶ Which expression matches these words?

The ranger saw 2 more cubs this week than last week.

2y   **y − 2**   **y ÷ 2**   **y + 2**

> Let the variable *y* stand for the number of cubs the ranger saw last week.
>
> • 2*y* means twice the number seen last week.
>
> • *y* − 2 means 2 less than the number seen last week.
>
> • *y* ÷ 2 means half the number seen last week.
>
> • *y* + 2 means 2 more than the number seen last week.

Solution: The expression *y* + 2 matches the words.

Guided Practice

Choose the expression that matches the words.
Let *p* stand for the number of bears.

Ask Yourself

• What is the variable?

• Do I add, subtract, multiply, or divide to write the expression?

1. 5 more than the number of bears

   a. $5p$ **b.** $5 - p$ **c.** $5 + p$ **d.** $p \div 5$

2. half as many bears

   a. $p \div 2$ **b.** $2p$ **c.** $p - 2$ **d.** $p + 2$

3. three times the number of bears

   a. $p + 3$ **b.** $p - 3$ **c.** $3p$ **d.** $p \div 3$

Evaluate each expression when *n* = 6.

4. $5n$ 5. $n \div 3$ 6. $4n$ 7. $n + 7$ 8. $43 - n$

9. $n - 4$ 10. $15 - n$ 11. $12 \div n$ 12. $10n$ 13. $n + 35$

Explain Your Thinking ▶ When writing an expression, how do you know when to use a variable?

Go On

Practice and Problem Solving

Write the expression. Let *n* stand for the number of bear cubs seen yesterday.

14. 5 fewer cubs than seen yesterday

15. 3 more cubs than seen yesterday

16. half as many cubs as seen yesterday

17. four times the number seen yesterday

Evaluate each expression when $p = 7$.

18. $11p$

19. $p - 7$

20. $2 \times p + 5$

21. $0 + p$

22. $9 - p$

23. $28 + p$

24. $2p \div 7$

25. $3p + 1$

26. $7p - 4$

27. $6 + 2p$

28. $70 - 2p$

29. $4p \div 4$

Match each statement with the correct expression.

30. When *n* is 6, the value of this expression is 2.

    a. $n - 4$

31. When *n* is 2, the value of this expression is 8.

    b. $n \div 2$

32. When *n* is 10, the value of this expression is 5.

    c. $n + 2$

33. When *n* is 6, the value of this expression is 8.

    d. $4n$

Write an expression for each problem. Choose your own variables.

34. There are 3 more bear dens this year than last year. How many bear dens are there this year?

35. Bob and Joe collect animal figures. Bob has half as many figures as Joe. How many figures does Bob have?

36. On Saturday, 572 more people visited the zoo than on Friday. How many people visited the zoo on Saturday?

37. Multistep Kendi has 5 times as many wildlife books as mysteries. She gives 3 wildlife books away. How many wildlife books does she have now?

Open Response

Find each product. (Ch. 4, Lesson 7)

38. $5 \times 9 \times 1$

39. $6 \times 7 \times 0$

40. $3 \times 2 \times 8$

41. $3 \times 3 \times 7$

42. $4 \times 3 \times 2$

43. $2 \times 5 \times 6$

Multiple Choice

44. Which expression means "three less than a number n"? (Ch. 5, Lesson 2)

A $3 - n$ **C** $3 + n$

B $n - 3$ **D** $n \div 3$

Game

Expression Match-up

2 Players

What You'll Need • 16 Index Cards (Learning Tool 9)

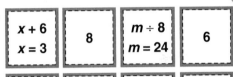

How to Play

1 Make 16 cards like the ones shown.

2 Shuffle the cards. Place them face-down in any order in a 4 × 4 array.

3 A player turns over any two cards. If the cards show an expression and its value, the player keeps both cards. If not, the player turns the cards face-down in the same positions.

4 Players take turns repeating Step 3 until all 8 matches have been made. The player with the greater number of cards is the winner.

$x + 6$ $x = 3$	8	$m \div 8$ $m = 24$	6
$4 + y$ $y = 2$	5	$2p$ $p = 4$	4
$z - 8$ $z = 10$	3	$5q$ $q = 2$	2
$9 - m$ $m = 4$	9	$d \div 6$ $d = 24$	10

Create your own Expression Match-up game. Make 16 cards—8 with expressions, and 8 with the value of each expression. Challenge a pair of classmates.

Algebra
Compare Expressions

Objective Use variables to compare expressions.

Learn About It

One morning, two giant pandas ate the same amount of bamboo. In the afternoon, the male panda ate 15 pounds of bamboo. The female panda ate a total of 44 pounds of bamboo during the morning and afternoon. Which panda ate less?

Let b = the amount the male panda ate in the morning.

male panda → $b + 15$ ⬤ 44 ← female panda

You can compare these expressions if you know the value of b. Let's suppose the value of b is 22.   Let $b = 22$.

STEP 1 Evaluate the expression, $b + 15$. Substitute 22 for b.	$b + 15$ ⬤ 44 $22 + 15$ ⬤ 44 37 ⬤ 44
STEP 2 Compare the expressions.	37 ⬤ 44 $37 < 44$, so $b + 15 < 44$

Solution: If b equals 22, the male panda ate less.

▶ Expressions are **equal** if they have the same value. When equal expressions are connected by an equal sign (=), they form an **equation**.

▶ When expressions are not equal, they form an **inequality**. The symbols $>$, $<$, and $\neq$ show an inequality.

Remember	
$=$	is equal to
$\neq$	is not equal to
$>$	is greater than
$<$	is less than

Another Example Evaluate and Compare

Let's suppose the value of b is 29.

Evaluate the expression $b + 15$.	$b + 15$ ⬤ 44
Substitute 29 for b.	$29 + 15$ ⬤ 44
Compare the expressions.	44 ⬤ 44
	$44 = 44$, so $b + 15 = 44$ when $b = 29$

Copy and compare. Let $n = 5$. Write = or ≠ for each ⬤.

Ask Yourself
- What is the value of the variable?
- What symbol makes the sentence true?

1. $25 \div n$ ⬤ 5

2. $2n$ ⬤ $10 - n$

3. $20 + n$ ⬤ 5×5

4. $n + 6$ ⬤ $3n - 7$

Explain Your Thinking ▶ Compare $2h + 3$ and $16 - 3$ when $h = 5$. Explain your answer.

Practice and Problem Solving

Copy and compare. Let $y = 3$. Write = or ≠ for each ⬤.

5. $6 + (14 - 8)$ ⬤ $(14 - 8) + y$

6. $(14 - 7) \times y$ ⬤ $(9 \times y) - 1$

7. $(15 - 9) \div y$ ⬤ $(18 \div 6) + y$

8. $(y + 9) \times 1$ ⬤ $44 - (4 \times 8)$

Copy and compare. Write >, <, or = for each ⬤.

9. $8 + (16 \div 4)$ ⬤ 2×9

10. $38 + (24 + 9)$ ⬤ $38 - (24 + 9)$

11. $(23 - 10) + 7$ ⬤ $23 - (10 + 7)$

12. $6 \times (8 - 3)$ ⬤ $(4 - 1) \times 10$

Compare the expressions. Write *equal* or *not equal* for each.

13. 24 and $(3 \times 9) - 4$

14. $15 + 1$ and $7 + (3 \times 3)$

15. $56 \div 8$ and $19 - (2 \times 6)$

16. $64 \div (2 \times 4)$ and $27 \div 3$

Solve.

17. The expression $2p + 2$ represents the weight of one panda cub. The weight of a second panda cub is $p + 10$. If p is 3 pounds, which panda cub weighs more?

18. Multistep One panda is 3 years older than a second panda. The second panda is 2 years older than a third one. Write expressions to show the ages of the first two pandas if the third one is 5 years old.

Mixed Review and Test Prep

Open Response

Find each product. (Ch. 4, Lesson 7)

19. $2 \times 5 \times 9$

20. $2 \times 4 \times 3$

21. $7 \times 1 \times 8$

22. $3 \times 2 \times 3$

23. Write *true* or *false* for the expressions compared below. Explain your answer. (Ch. 5, Lesson 3)

$12 + (3 \times 2) = 6 \times 3$

Algebra

Variables and Equations

Objective Write and solve equations.

Learn About It

Volunteers knit tiny wool sweaters to help penguins affected by oil spills. Lynn knit 4 more sweaters than Eva. Lynn knit 7 sweaters altogether. How many sweaters did Eva knit?

You can write an equation to solve this problem. Every equation has an equals sign to show that both expressions are equal.

Let the variable s stand for the number of sweaters Eva knit. Then write and solve this equation: $s + 4 = 7$.

This expression shows that Lynn knit 4 more sweaters than Eva. → $s + 4 = 7$ ← This expression shows the total number of sweaters Lynn knit.

Solve $s + 4 = 7$.

Different Ways to Solve $s + 4 = 7$

Way ① Use an addition fact.

$s + 4 = 7$
$s = 3$

Think
$3 + 4 = 7$
So s must be 3.

Way ② Use inverse operations.

$s + 4 = 7$
$s + 4 - 4 = 7 - 4$ ← Subtract 4 from each side.
$s = 3$

Check the solution.

$s + 4 = 7$
$3 + 4 = 7$ ← Substitute 3 for s.
$7 = 7$

Both sides of the equals sign are the same, so the solution is correct.

Solution: Eva knit 3 sweaters.

Other volunteers clean oil from the penguins.
Max cleaned 4 times the number of penguins
that Sara did. Max cleaned 40 penguins.
How many penguins did Sara clean?

Let the variable p stand for the number of penguins Sara
cleaned. Then write and solve this equation: $4p = 40$.

This expression shows that Max
cleaned 4 times the number of $\;\rightarrow\;$ $4p = 40$ $\;\leftarrow\;$ This expression shows the total
penguins Sara cleaned. $\qquad\qquad\qquad\qquad$ number of penguins Max cleaned.

Solve $4p = 40$.

Different Ways to Solve $4p = 40$

Way ① Use a related multiplication fact.

$4p = 40$
$p = 10$

Think
$4 \times 10 = 40$
So p must be 10.

Way ② Use inverse operations.

$4p = 40$

$p \times 4 \div 4 = 40 \div 4$ $\;\leftarrow\;$ Divide each side by 4.

$p = 10$

Solution: Sara cleaned 10 penguins.

Remember to Use Inverse Operations	
If the problem has addition, use subtraction to solve.	$s + 4 = 7$ $s + 4 - 4 = 7 - 4$ $s = 3$
If the problem has subtraction, use addition to solve.	$t - 5 = 11$ $t - 5 + 5 = 11 + 5$ $t = 16$
If the problem has multiplication, use division to solve.	$4p = 40$ $p \times 4 \div 4 = 40 \div 4$ $p = 10$
If the problem has division, use multiplication to solve.	$v \div 6 = 3$ $v \div 6 \times 6 = 3 \times 6$ $v = 18$

Go On

Guided Practice

Match each equation with its solution.

1. $n + 6 = 10$

2. $9 = n - 3$

3. $5n = 30$

a. $n = 12$

b. $n = 4$

c. $n = 6$

Ask Yourself

- What related fact can I use?
- Did I substitute the solution for the variable in the equation to check?

Explain Your Thinking ▶ If you multiply or divide equal expressions by the same number, will the expressions remain equal? Give examples.

Practice and Problem Solving

Solve each equation. Check the solution.

4. $m + 10 = 35$

5. $7n = 42$

6. $r - 7 = 43$

7. $5 = s \div 3$

8. $6m = 18$

9. $r \div 7 = 7$

10. $m + 12 = 20$

11. $13 = k - 1$

12. $6 + y = 12$

13. $27 = 9n$

14. $63 \div a = 9$

15. $12 + 5 = d$

Match each equation with the words that describe it. Then solve.

16. $20 = 10 + m$

17. $10 - m = 6$

18. $3m = 15$

19. $m \div 2 = 8$

a. Three times a number is 15.

b. Twenty is 10 more than the number.

c. A number divided by 2 is 8.

d. A number subtracted from 10 is 6.

Solve.

20. **Analyze** Oliver made 7 sweaters. This is half as many as Sam made. How many sweaters did Sam make? Write and solve an equation.

21. **Multistep** Tony has packed 27 sweaters and has 45 more to pack. A box holds 8 sweaters. Write an equation to find how many boxes Tony needs to pack all the sweaters. Then solve the equation.

120

Extra Practice See page 131, Set D.

Visual Thinking
Balance Equations

Use the picture below to find the weight of one cat.

- First, remove a bird from each side. The sides still balance because equal weights were removed from each side.

- Let *c* stand for 1 cat. Let *d* stand for 1 dog. Write an equation: $d = 2c$.

If the dog weighs 16 pounds, what does 1 cat weigh?

Write an equation for each picture. Let *b* = the weight of a ball and *c* = the weight of a can. Solve for *c* if *b* = 10 lb.

1.

2.

Check your understanding for Lessons 1–4.

Simplify. Follow the order of operations. (Lesson 1)

1. $6 + 7 \times 2$ **2.** $(12 - 7) \times 7$ **3.** $18 \div (12 - 9)$

Evaluate each expression when *h* = 3. (Lesson 2)

4. $3h + 5$ **5.** $13 - h$ **6.** $21 \div h + 4$

Copy and compare. Write >, <, or = for each ●. (Lesson 3)

7. $3 \times (4 + 5)$ ● $35 - 8$ **8.** $16 \div 4 + 3$ ● $5 \times (8 - 6)$

Solve each equation. Check the solution. (Lesson 4)

9. $4x = 20$ **10.** $18 - x = 12$

Extra Practice at **eduplace.com/map**

Problem-Solving Strategy
Write an Equation

Objective Write equations to represent and solve problems.

Problem On Adopt-a-Pet Day, Teva adopted two cats. She paid a total of $22 for the adoption fees and rabies shots. If the rabies shots were $6 per cat, how much was each adoption fee?

 **UNDERSTAND**

This is what you know.

- Two cats were adopted.

- The total fees were $22.

- Rabies shots were $6 per cat.

PLAN

Write an equation.
You can write an equation to help you solve the problem.

SOLVE

Choose variables and solve.

- Let *a* stand for the adoption fee for one cat.

$$22 = (2 \times a) + (2 \times 6)$$

↑   ↑   ↑
total   adoption   rabies
fees   fees for   shots for
2 cats   2 cats

- Solve the equation.

$$22 = 2a + 12$$
$$22 - 12 = 2a + 12 - 12$$
$$10 = 2a$$
$$10 \div 2 = 2a \div 2$$
$$5 = a$$

Solution: Each adoption fee was $5.

LOOK BACK

Check if the equation is true.
Substitute $5 for *a* in the equation. Are both expressions equal?

Guided Practice

Use the Ask Yourself questions to help you solve each problem.

1. Puppies are exercised 15 minutes longer than adult dogs. Puppies are exercised 45 minutes daily. Write and solve an equation to find the number of minutes that an adult dog is exercised daily.

2. Amy bought 1 cat toy and 5 large cans of cat food. She paid $14 in all. The cat toy cost $4. Write and solve an equation to find the cost of 1 can of cat food.

   (Hint) How can you show the cost of the food without the toy?

Ask Yourself

UNDERSTAND **What facts do I know?**

PLAN **Can I write an equation?**

SOLVE **What does the variable represent?**

LOOK BACK **If I substitute my solution for the variable, are both expressions equal?**

Independent Practice

Write an equation to solve each problem.

3. A student volunteer group has 38 members. Twenty-five of the members are boys. How many members are girls?

4. David has 10 pets. All his pets are either fish or hamsters. He has two more fish than hamsters. How many hamsters does David have?

5. There are twice as many cats as dogs in a kennel. The kennel has 21 animals. If there are only cats and dogs, how many cats are there?

6. A shelter has 7 poodles, 5 beagles, and 12 retrievers. The other dogs are mixed breed. There are 40 dogs. How many are mixed breed?

Go On

Mixed Problem Solving

Solve. Show your work. Tell what strategy you used.

7. A large flowerpot costs $5 more than a medium pot. A medium pot costs $4 more than a small pot. A small pot costs $2. If you buy one of each size pot, what will the total cost be?

8. **Multistep** Use the digits 5, 2, 8, and 3 to make the greatest 4-digit number. Then use the same digits to make the least 4-digit number. What is the difference?

9. A scarf has 13 stripes. The first stripe is red. The second stripe is blue. The third stripe is white. Then the pattern is repeated. What color is the last stripe?

Data **Use the target to solve Problems 10–14.**

10. Two of Megan's 5 darts landed in the inner circle. Her last 3 darts landed in the outer ring. What was her score?

11. Yuri scored 165 using 4 darts. Two darts landed in the outer ring. One dart landed in the inner circle. Where did his last dart land?

12. Using 4 darts, what is the greatest score possible? If all darts land on the target, what is the least score possible?

13. Where can 4 darts land to give a score of 180?

14. **Create and Solve** Write a word problem about the target. Then give it to a classmate to solve.

You Choose

Strategy
- Draw a Picture
- Find a Pattern
- Guess and Check
- Use Logical Reasoning
- Write an Equation

Computation Method
- Mental Math
- Estimation
- Paper and Pencil
- Calculator

Problem Solving on Tests

(Multiple Choice)

Choose the letter of the correct answer.

1. Which numbers are not in order from greatest to least?

   A 5,784   5,449   5,198   5,099

   B 7,039   6,999   6,689   6,679

   C 8,057   8,051   8,055   8,050

   D 9,483   9,238   948   923

   (Chapter 2, Lesson 2)

2. Mrs. Shu buys one of each state key ring. What is the total cost?

   $4.60   **$4.00**   **$2.40**

   F $6.40   **H** $10.00

   G $8.60   **J** $11.00

   (Chapter 3, Lesson 2)

(Open Response)

Solve each problem.

3. Mr. James will bake muffins for the 22 students in his class. Each muffin pan bakes 6 muffins. How many pans of muffins will he bake?

   Explain Will Mr. James have any muffins left over? How did you decide?

   (Chapter 8, Lesson 3)

4. Lee's height is represented by the expression $3h + 8$. Lee's friend Sam is 2 inches taller than Lee.

   Represent Write an expression to represent Sam's height. Then use >, <, or = to compare Lee's height and Sam's height.

   (Chapter 5, Lesson 2)

(Constructed Response)

5. Neighbors are planning a block party for 48 people. All the families on the street are bringing supplies.

Package Sizes	
Items Needed	**Number in Package**
Hamburgers	4
Hamburger buns	8
Paper plates	96
Plastic cups	20

   a. Each person will have one hamburger and one bun. Three families each will buy the same amount of hamburgers and buns, and they will buy enough for everyone. How many packages will each family buy?

   b. One family will buy cups and paper plates. They expect each person to use 1 plate and 2 cups. How many packages of cups are needed? How many extra cups and plates will there be?

   (Chapter 1, Lesson 3)

 Education Place

See **eduplace.com/map** for more Test-Taking Tips.

Algebra

Function Tables

Objective Relate equations to function tables.

Learn About It

Mr. Webb works part-time for a wildlife conservation group. He earns $8 an hour. Suppose Mr. Webb works 4 hours. How much will he earn?

Use a function table to solve the problem.

In the function table at the right, the input shows the number of hours, h, and the output shows how much Mr. Webb earns, e.

A **function table** is a table of ordered pairs that follow a rule. The rule lets you find the value of one variable if you know the value of the other.

The rule for this function table is multiply by 8, or $8h = e$. This means you multiply the number of hours (h) Mr. Webb works by 8 to find how much he earns (e).

Rule: $8h = e$		
Input (h)	Output (e)	
1	8	← 1 × 8
2	16	← 2 × 8
3	24	← 3 × 8
4	32	← 4 × 8

$8 \times h = e$

Substitute 4 for h. → $8 \times 4 = 32$

Solution: Mr. Webb will earn $32.

Another Example

Use Earnings to Find Hours

Suppose Mr. Webb earns $72. How many hours did he work?

$8 \times h = e$

$8 \times h = 72$ ← Substitute 72 for e.

$h = 72 \div 8$ ← Divide to find a missing factor.

$h = 9$

Mr. Webb worked 9 hours.

Wild turkeys were once almost extinct, but thanks to conservationists, there are now about 5,400,000 of them.

Write the rule for each function table.

1. Rule: _____

Input (a)	Output (b)
4	1
5	2
7	4

2. Rule: _____

Input (m)	Output (n)
9	11
15	17
18	20

Explain Your Thinking ▶ If another row was added to the function table in Exercise 2, what could the input and output be? Explain how you know.

Practice and Problem Solving

Copy and complete each function table or rule.

Rule: $b = a + 4$

	Input (a)	Output (b)
3.	6	▣
4.	3	▣
5.	2	▣

Rule: $q = p \times 6$

	Input (p)	Output (q)
6.	4	▣
7.	8	▣
8.	▣	54

9. Rule: _____

Input (x)	Output (y)
21	3
63	9
77	11

Solve.

10. Dan worked 7 hours a day helping to save wild turkeys. Make a function table to show how many hours he worked in 1 day, 5 days, 8 days, and 10 days. Write an equation to show the rule.

11. Create and Solve Ms. Rose earns $9 an hour. Write a problem that can be answered by using this information and a function table. Ask a classmate to solve the problem.

Mixed Review and Test Prep

Multiple Choice

Write >, <, or = for each . (Ch. 2, Lesson 1)

12. $7 + 8 \bullet 9 + 6$

13. $9 - 7 \bullet 5 - 2$

14. $5 + 9 \bullet 18 - 3$

15. If $y = 9 - x$ and $x = 4$, what is the value of y?

(Ch. 5, Lesson 6)

A 94   **C** 13

B 36   **D** 5

Problem-Solving Decision
Explain Your Solution

Objective Explain your solution.

Problem One Asian elephant weighs 4,875 pounds. An African elephant weighs 5,672 pounds more. About how much does the African elephant weigh? Explain your solution.

When you are asked to explain a solution, you should explain every step of your thinking.

African Elephant

Asian Elephant

▶ **Denise explained her solution with a picture.**

I needed an estimate, so I rounded the numbers before adding. The long rectangle shows the total weight of the African elephant. You can see you need to add the amounts. The solution is about 5,000 + 6,000 or 11,000 pounds.

African elephant

Asian elephant | + 6,000 lbs more

5,000 lbs

▶ **Paul explained his solution by labeling his work.**

The African elephant weighs more, so I knew I needed to add. The word "about" told me to find an estimate. First, I rounded each addend to the nearest thousand. Then I added the numbers. My answer is about 11,000 pounds.

4,875 rounds to> 5,000 lbs
5,672 rounds to> + 6,000 lbs
_____
11,000 lbs

Are both explanations good? Tell why or why not.

Try These

Solve. Explain your solution.

1. Elephants have 4 molars. One molar can weigh 5 pounds. In a lifetime, many elephants have 6 sets of molars. How many molars is that?

2. A sanctuary for endangered Asian elephants was founded in 1995 in Hohenwald, Tennessee. How many years ago was that?

Algebraic Thinking
Always, Sometimes, or Never

Write *always, sometimes,* or *never* to answer each question.

You can use the properties of multiplication to solve problems, even when you don't have all the information.

1. When does the value of $m + 1$ equal m?

2. When does the value of $3p$ equal the value of 0 times p?

3. When does the value of $n + 0$ equal the value of $0 + n$?

4. When does the value of $x + 1$ equal the value of $x - 1$?

5. When does the value of $r + 5$ equal the value of $5 + r$?

6. When does the value of z equal the value of $2z$?

7. When does the value of $2 \times (b + 4)$ equal the value of $2 \times b + 4$?

8. When does the value of $2a$ equal the value of $3a$?

9. When does the value of $m + 1$ equal m?

10. Write three questions about the value of variables. The answer to your questions should be *always*, *sometimes*, and *never*.

Chapter Review/Test

VOCABULARY

Choose the correct term to complete each sentence.

1. A letter that stands for a number is a ____.

2. A mathematical sentence with an equals sign is an ____.

3. The rule that says to do the operations in parentheses first is the ____.

CONCEPTS AND SKILLS

Simplify. Follow the order of operations. (Lesson 1, pp. 110–111)

4. $13 - (3 \times 3)$ **5.** $2 + (5 \times 3)$ **6.** $2 \times 6 \div 3 + 9$

Evaluate each expression when $n = 8$. (Lesson 2, pp. 112–115)

7. $9n$ **8.** $n \div 2$ **9.** $n + 24$ **10.** $63 - n$

Write >, <, or = for each ●. (Lesson 3, pp. 116–117)

11. $(64 \div 8) \times 3$ ● $100 - 67$ **12.** $3 \times (6 + 5)$ ● $(3 \times 6) + (3 \times 5)$

13. $25 + (36 - 9)$ ● $(25 + 36) - 9$ **14.** $5 \times (72 \div 8)$ ● $(6 \times 3) + 36$

Solve each equation. Check the solution. (Lesson 4, pp. 118–120)

15. $p + 12 = 75$ **16.** $9n = 63$ **17.** $x - 16 = 98$ **18.** $6 = y \div 8$

PROBLEM SOLVING

Solve. (Lessons 5, 7, pp.122–124, 128)

19. One ticket cost $10. The total cost was $60. Write an equation to show how to find the number of tickets bought.

20. On Friday, 1,976 people visited a zoo. On Monday, 786 people visited. About how many more people visited on Friday? Explain your solution.

 Write About It

Show You Understand

Explain how to decide if the rule is correct. Then copy and complete the function table.

Rule: $2x + 4 = y$	
Input (x)	Output (y)
4	12
9	■
■	26

Extra Practice

Set A (Lesson 1, pp. 110–111)

Simplify. Follow the order of operations.

1. $(3 \times 9) + 8$ **2.** $16 \div (2 \times 4)$ **3.** $20 - 5 \times 2$ **4.** $3 \times 4 \div 2$

5. $3 + 4 \div 2$ **6.** $8 + 12 \div 4$ **7.** $(21 \div 3) \times 2$ **8.** $9 \times (8 \div 4)$

Set B (Lesson 2, pp. 112–115)

Evaluate each expression when $x = 5$.

1. $x - 0$ **2.** $4x$ **3.** $2x + 39$ **4.** $52 - x$ **5.** $45 \div x$

6. $20 \div x$ **7.** $6 \times (4 + x)$ **8.** $x + 43$ **9.** $x + 9 \div 3$ **10.** $x + 4x$

Set C (Lesson 3, pp. 116–117)

Copy and compare. Let $y = 4$. Write = or $\neq$ for each ●.

1. $6y$ ● 28 **2.** $63 - y$ ● 51 **3.** $3y + 7$ ● 19 **4.** $28 \div y$ ● 7

Set D (Lesson 4, pp. 118–120)

Solve each equation. Check the solution.

1. $3x = 15$ **2.** $y + 5 = 19$ **3.** $m - 3 = 16$ **4.** $n \div 7 = 6$ **5.** $y + y = 10$

Set E (Lesson 6, pp. 126–127)

Copy and complete each function table or rule.

1.

Rule: $y = x + 5$	
Input (x)	Output (y)
3	8
■	11
2	■
8	■

2.

Rule: $y = 3x$	
Input (x)	Output (y)
5	15
6	■
7	■
■	24

3.

Rule: _____	
Input (x)	Output (y)
10	2
15	3
20	4
25	5

Extra Practice at **eduplace.com/map**

The Wright Stuff

Since people have walked on Earth, they have longed to fly. Some early attempts to fly used birdlike machines with flapping wings. These devices were doomed to failure.

In the winter of 1903, the Wright brothers did what those before them had not. Wilbur and Orville Wright built and flew the first engine-powered, heavier-than-air flying machine—the airplane.

The Wrights' airplane was hard to control, but Wilbur and Orville were able to make it fly for almost a minute. Their invention helped make modern planes possible.

Use the table showing the Wright brothers' first flights for Problems 1–3.

First Flights of the Wright Brothers			
Flight	Pilot	Distance (in feet)	Time (in seconds)
1	Orville	120	12
2	Wilbur	175	12
3	Orville	200	15
4	Wilbur	852	59

1. Estimate the total distance of Orville's two flights. Estimate the total distance of Wilbur's two flights. Who flew farther?

2. Who had a longer total time in the air, Wilbur or Orville? How much longer?

3. Suppose Orville flew an equal distance for each second of his first flight. How far would he have flown in 1 second?

4. Imagine that a pilot is flying an antique plane. Complete the table on the right to show how far she travels in 1 minute. Write an equation to show the rule.

Antique Plane Flight	
Time t (in seconds)	Distance d (in feet)
12	120
24	240
36	
48	
60	

Education Place

Visit Weekly Reader® Connections at **eduplace.com/map** for more on this topic.

Enrichment: Logical Thinking

All, Some, and None Statements

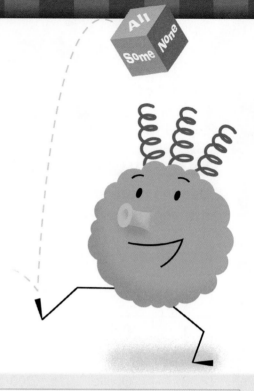

The words *all*, *some*, and *none* are used in logical thinking. They refer to a group of things.

- *All* means "every one" in the group.
- *Some* means "at least one" in the group.
- *None* means "not any" in the group.

Look at these creatures called frommets.
Then read the statements below about the frommets.

These statements are true.

- All frommets have one nose.
- Some frommets have yellow hair.
- None of the frommets have red feet.

These statements are false.

- All frommets have straight hair.
- Some frommets have stripes.
- None of the frommets have smiles.

Try These!

**Look at the go-carts.
Then write *true* or *false*
for each statement.**

1 All go-carts have green frames.

2 Some go-carts have stripes.

3 None of the go-carts have red wheels.

4 All go-carts have a steering wheel.

I Need Some Order!

You know how to follow the order of operations but your calculator may not. To see if your calculator follows the order of operations, press:

Does your display look like this?	Does your display look like this?
5	1
That means your calculator divided and then subtracted. So, it followed the order of operations.	That means your calculator subtracted and then divided. So, it did **not** follow the order of operations.

If your calculator does not follow the order of operations, you must enter the numbers in the correct order yourself.

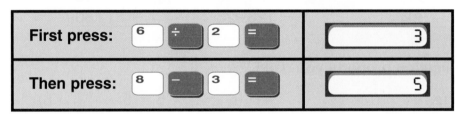

| First press: | 6 ÷ 2 = | 3 |
| Then press: | 8 − 3 = | 5 |

Use your calculator to simplify each expression.

1. $6 + (15 - 3) \times 4$

2. $8 - 20 \div (4 + 1)$

3. $(7 + 9) - 12 \div 2$

Write operation signs in the ▇ and place parentheses to make these number sentences true. Use your calculator to help you.

4. 35 ▇ 2 ▇ 3 = 7

   35 ▇ 2 ▇ 3 = 11

5. 24 ▇ 8 ▇ 4 = 6

   24 ▇ 8 ▇ 4 = 2

6. 32 ▇ 8 ▇ 6 = 4

   32 ▇ 8 ▇ 6 = 16

7. 27 ▇ 6 ▇ 3 = 9

   27 ▇ 6 ▇ 3 = 11

8. 7 ▇ 3 ▇ 9 = 90

   7 ▇ 3 ▇ 9 = 36

9. 6 ▇ 3 ▇ 7 = 63

   6 ▇ 3 ▇ 7 = 21

Unit 2 Test

VOCABULARY Open Response

Choose the correct term to complete each sentence.

1. A letter or symbol that stands for an unknown value in an expression is a _____.

2. The property that states that the order of factors does not change the product is the _____.

3. The property that states that when you multiply any number by 0, the product is 0, is called the _____.

CONCEPTS AND SKILLS Open Response

Complete each number sentence. Tell which addition property you used. (Chapter 3)

4. $54 + 78 = \blacksquare + 54$ 5. $154 + 0 = \blacksquare$ 6. $(89 + 11) + 32 = 89 + (\blacksquare + 32)$

Find each sum or difference. (Chapter 3)

7. $\begin{array}{r} 3,400 \\ + 201 \\ \hline \end{array}$ 8. $\begin{array}{r} 7,906 \\ - 804 \\ \hline \end{array}$ 9. $\begin{array}{r} 180,009 \\ - 123,923 \\ \hline \end{array}$ 10. $\begin{array}{r} 450,189 \\ + 312,809 \\ \hline \end{array}$

Solve. Tell which multiplication property you used. (Chapter 4)

11. $3 \times 9 = 9 \times \blacksquare$ 12. $54 \times 0 = \blacksquare$ 13. $(5 \times 2) \times 6 = 5 \times (\blacksquare \times 6)$

Solve. (Chapter 4)

14. $11 \times \blacksquare = 99$ 15. $12 \times 7 = \blacksquare$ 16. $\blacksquare \div 31 = 0$ 17. $21 \div \blacksquare = 1$

Simplify. Use the correct order of operations. (Chapter 5)

18. $(3 + 9) \times 3$ 19. $32 - 5 \times 2 + 8$ 20. $10 - (3 \times 2)$

21. $1 + (5 \times 7) - 9$ 22. $4 + 15 \div 5 + 2$ 23. $2 \times 8 + 9 \div 3$

Evaluate each expression when $t = 8$. (Chapter 5)

24. $12t$ 25. $t - 5$ 26. $7 \times (t - 3)$

Solve each equation. Check the solution. (Chapter 5)

27. $8k = 12 \times 4$ **28.** $45 = 4g + 5$ **29.** $5 + 25 = 6b$

PROBLEM SOLVING Open Response

Write an equation to solve each problem.

30. Shea Stadium seats 57,775 fans. Wrigley Field seats 38,902 fans. About how many more fans fit in Shea Stadium?

31. The soccer team won 3 times as many games as they lost. They played 28 games in all. How many games did they lose?

32. Frank draws a picture using 30 shapes. He draws 8 stars, 4 circles, and 11 triangles for the picture. The remaining shapes are squares. How many shapes are squares?

33. There are 11 children in Uli's drawing class. If each child draws 5 pictures on Monday and 3 pictures on Tuesday, how many total pictures are drawn? Explain your solution.

Performance Assessment

Extended Response

Task An environmental group is hosting a fundraiser breakfast. They have to decide what ingredients they need.

Use the recipes above and the information at the right to decide how many batches of each recipe to make. Then find the total amount of each ingredient that is needed to prepare the entire breakfast. Explain your thinking.

Information You Need

- The group will make at least one batch of each recipe.

- 50 people have purchased tickets for the breakfast.

- Each person will be served either 2 pancakes or 1 biscuit with an egg.

- The group wants to have no more than 8 pancakes or 8 biscuits left.

Cumulative Test Prep

Solve Problems 1–10.

Test-Taking Tip

Sometimes when you take a test, you can draw a model to help you.

Look at the example below.

Mary wants to put a 1-inch border on a picture. The picture is 8 inches wide. How wide is the picture with the border?

A 2 inches   **C** 9 inches

B 8 inches   **D** 10 inches

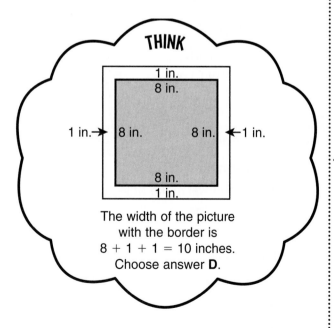

THINK

1 in.
8 in.

1 in. → 8 in.   8 in. ← 1 in.

8 in.
1 in.

The width of the picture
with the border is
8 + 1 + 1 = 10 inches.
Choose answer **D**.

Multiple Choice

1. Kia lives at number 18 Maple Street. Houses that are north of Kia's all have greater house numbers. Which house numbers are north of Kia's?

A 21, 49, and 85   **C** 11, 50, and 87

B 10, 17, and 59   **D** 8, 48, and 52

(Chapter 2, Lesson 1)

2. A number on a number line is between 15 and 25. The number is a multiple of 6 and 8. What is the number?

F 16   **H** 21

G 18   **J** 24

(Chapter 2, Lesson 2)

3. Which number can go in the box to make the number sentence true?

$$8 \times \blacksquare = 72$$

A 9   **C** 7

B 8   **D** 6

(Chapter 4, Lesson 5)

4. A band is practicing for a concert. The flute plays for x minutes. The tuba plays 3 times longer than the flute. Which expression shows how much time the tuba plays?

F $x - 3$ **H** $3 + x$

G $3x$ **J** $3 - x$

(Chapter 5, Lesson 4)

For Test-Taking Tips, See page 658.

5. Look at the graph. Which team won about half as many games as the Lions?

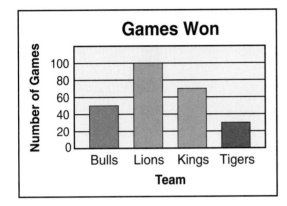

(Chapter 2, Lesson 6)

6. Simplify the expression $3 \times (4 + 1)$. Move the parentheses to write an expression with a different value.

(Chapter 5, Lesson 1)

7. Latrell wants to jump rope 200 times. He has already jumped 98 times. Write an equation to find how many more times Latrell must jump.

(Chapter 5, Lesson 5)

8. Beads cost $2.00 a bag. There are 30 beads in a bag. How many beads can you buy for $12.00?

(Chapter 4, Lesson 9)

9. There are 40 students in the library. There are between 6 and 9 tables. The same number of students sits at each table. How many tables are there?

(Chapter 4, Lesson 5)

10. The Ramirez family went on vacation. It took three days to drive from White Plains, New York, to Houston, Texas. The table shows how many miles they drove each day.

Ramirez Family Vacation	
Day	Miles Driven
Monday	559
Tuesday	573
Wednesday	476

A How many miles did the Ramirez family drive?

B How many miles is a round trip between White Plains and Houston?

C If the Ramirez family drove only 500 miles on Monday, how many miles would they have to drive altogether on Tuesday and Wednesday to reach Houston in 3 days? Explain how you found your answer.

(Chapter 3, Lesson 8)

Education Place

Look for Cumulative Test Prep at **eduplace.com/map** for more practice.

Vocabulary Wrap-Up for Unit 2

Look back at the big ideas and vocabulary in this unit.

Big Ideas

Addition and subtraction are inverse operations.

Multiplication and division are inverse operations.

You can follow the correct order of operations to simplify an expression.

Key Vocabulary

inverse operations

order of operations

expression

Math Conversations

Use your new vocabulary to discuss these big ideas.

1. Explain how to use mental math to find $56 + 35$.

2. Explain how you can use rounding to estimate $1,238 - 476$.

3. Explain the steps needed to find $21 \div 6$.

4. Explain how to use the correct order of operations to find $3 \times (5 - 2) - 4$.

5. **Write About It** Think of a problem in your everyday life that requires addition and multiplication to solve. Write the problem using words and symbols. Give the problem to a classmate to solve.

I need to simplify a long expression. Where do I start?

Use the order of operations. That will help!

Multiplication of Whole Numbers

Reading Mathematics

Reviewing Vocabulary

Here are some math vocabulary words that you should know.

estimate	to find a number close to an exact amount
factor	a number that is multiplied in a multiplication problem
product	the answer to a multiplication problem
square number	the product of a number and itself; a number that can be shown by a square array

Reading Words and Symbols

When you multiply, you find the total number of objects that are in equal groups. Look at the arrays below. You can use words and symbols to describe the ladybugs.

- Four groups of three ladybugs equals 12 ladybugs.

  factors → 4 × 3 = 12 ← product

- Three groups of four ladybugs equals 12 ladybugs.

  factors → 3 × 4 = 12 ← product

Use words and symbols to describe each picture.

1.

2.

Reading Test Questions

Choose the correct answer for each.

3. Which of the following is not an example of an array?

a.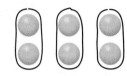

c.

b.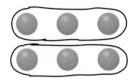

d.

Example means "a sample" or "something that shows a general rule."

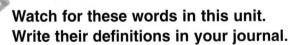

4. Which number sentence is accurate?

   a. $4 \times 4 = 8$

   b. $5 \times 2 = 10$

   c. $3 \times 6 = 3$

   d. $6 \times 2 = 8$

Accurate means "true" or "correct."

5. Which number sentence is inaccurate?

   a. $4 + 2 = 6$

   b. $2 \times 4 = 8$

   c. $8 = 4 \times 2$

   d. $8 = 2 + 4$

Inaccurate means "false," or "not correct."

Learning Vocabulary

Watch for these words in this unit. Write their definitions in your journal.

Associative Property
Distributive Property

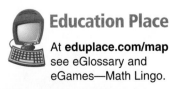

Education Place

At **eduplace.com/map**
see eGlossary and
eGames—Math Lingo.

Literature Connection

Read "Gone Prawning" on Page 647. Then work with a partner to answer the questions about the story.

CHAPTER 6

Multiply by One-Digit Numbers

INVESTIGATION

Using Data

The Mall of America in Bloomington, Minnesota is the largest mall in the United States. The table shows facts about the mall. How can you find the number of minutes you would need if you spent 8 minutes in each Arts and Crafts store at the mall? What if you spent 7 minutes in each of the types of stores listed in the table? How much time would you need? What is the best way to solve?

The Mall of America

Type of Store	Number
Arts and Crafts	7
Furniture	9
Jewelry	17
Toys and Games	11

Use What You Know

Use this page to review and remember
what you need to know for this chapter.

VOCABULARY

Choose the best term to complete each sentence.

1. In $3 \times 8 = 24$, 3 is a ____.

2. The number 12 is a ____ of 3.

3. The answer to a multiplication problem is the ____.

4. You can use an ____ to represent a multiplication fact.

> **Vocabulary**
>
> array
> factor
> quotient
> product
> multiple

CONCEPTS AND SKILLS

Complete the number sentence for each array.

5.
★ ★ ★ ★ ★ ★
★ ★ ★ ★ ★ ★

$2 \times 6 = \blacksquare$

6.
♥ ♥ ♥ ♥ ♥ ♥ ♥
♥ ♥ ♥ ♥ ♥ ♥ ♥
♥ ♥ ♥ ♥ ♥ ♥ ♥

$3 \times \blacksquare = \blacksquare$

7.
▲ ▲ ▲ ▲ ▲
▲ ▲ ▲ ▲ ▲

$\blacksquare \times \blacksquare = \blacksquare$

Draw an array to show each multiplication fact.

8. 3×6 9. 7×4 10. 5×6 11. 4×4

Find each product.

12. $\begin{array}{r} 7 \\ \times\, 6 \\ \hline \end{array}$ 13. $\begin{array}{r} 8 \\ \times\, 8 \\ \hline \end{array}$ 14. $\begin{array}{r} 9 \\ \times\, 3 \\ \hline \end{array}$ 15. $\begin{array}{r} 6 \\ \times\, 6 \\ \hline \end{array}$

16. $\begin{array}{r} 8 \\ \times\, 7 \\ \hline \end{array}$ 17. $\begin{array}{r} 10 \\ \times\, 3 \\ \hline \end{array}$ 18. $\begin{array}{r} 11 \\ \times\, 5 \\ \hline \end{array}$ 19. $\begin{array}{r} 12 \\ \times\, 6 \\ \hline \end{array}$

Write About It

20. How can you use arrays to tell that 4×6
is greater than 4×5 without multiplying?
Use a picture to help explain your answer.

Facts Practice, See page 667.

Multiply Multiples of 10, 100, and 1,000

Objective Use basic facts and patterns to multiply using mental math.

Learn About It

Stuart and his father are shopping at Music World. They are picking out some CDs to buy.

Music World displays their CDs in display racks. Each rack holds 300 CDs. How many CDs can 4 displays hold?

Multiply. $4 \times 300 = n$

300 is a multiple of 100. When multiplying a multiple of 10, 100, or 1,000, you can use basic facts and patterns of zeros to help you multiply.

$$4 \times 3 = 12 \qquad (4 \times 3 \text{ ones})$$
$$4 \times 30 = 120 \qquad (4 \times 3 \text{ tens})$$
$$4 \times 300 = 1,200 \qquad (4 \times 3 \text{ hundreds})$$

Think
What do you notice about the number of zeros in the factors and in the product?

Solution: Four displays can hold 1,200 CDs.

Guided Practice

Use basic facts and patterns to find each product.

1. 5×7
5×70
5×700
$5 \times 7,000$

2. 9×6
9×60
9×600
$9 \times 6,000$

3. 5×8
5×80
5×800
$5 \times 8,000$

4. 9×4

5. 9×40

6. 9×400

7. $9 \times 4,000$

Ask Yourself
• What basic fact can I use?
• How many zeros should be in the product?

Explain Your Thinking ▶ Look at Exercise 3. Why are there more zeros in the product than in the factors?

Use basic facts and patterns to find each product.

8. 4×4
4×40
4×400
$4 \times 4,000$

9. 7×3
7×30
7×300
$7 \times 3,000$

10. 6×7
6×70
6×700
$6 \times 7,000$

11. 9×8
9×80
9×800
$9 \times 8,000$

12. 6×5

13. 6×50

14. 6×500

15. $6 \times 5,000$

16. 2×80

17. 9×300

18. 6×70

19. 5×900

20. 3×200

21. 7×700

22. $8 \times 5,000$

23. $3 \times 6,000$

 Algebra • **Expressions** **Find the value of each expression when $n = 8$.**

24. $700 \times n$

25. $900 \times n$

26. $n \times 8,000$

27. $n \times (40 \times 10)$

28. $6 \times (n \times 0)$

29. $2,000 \times n$

30. $300 \times (n \times 5)$

31. $(n \times 1,000) \times 3$

Solve.

32. Music World displays CDs on racks. If each rack holds 200 CDs, how many CDs do 3 racks hold?

33. At the video store, one display shelf holds 200 videos. One display case holds 300 videos. Which holds more videos, 5 shelves or 3 cases? Explain your thinking.

34. **Multistep** At a computer super store, there are 40 display tables. Each table has 6 computer programs and 10 games. How many programs and games are there?

Open Response

Write the standard form of each number.
(Ch. 1, Lesson 2)

35. four thousand, five hundred two

36. five hundred thousand, two hundred sixty

Multiple Choice

37. What is 400×5?   (Ch. 6, Lesson 1)

A 20

C 2,000

B 200

D 20,000

Extra Practice See page 169, Set A.

Estimate Products

Objective Estimate products by rounding factors.

Learn About It

During Kindness Week, each fourth-grader in Hunter School bought 2 small toys to donate to a children's charity. If there are 419 fourth-graders, about how many toys were donated?

You can estimate **products** by rounding **factors** to their greatest place.

Estimate 2 × 419.

- First, round 419 to the nearest hundred.   419 **rounds to** 400
- Then multiply.   2 × 400 = 800
  2 × 419 is close to 2 × 400, or 800.

Solution: About 800 toys were donated.

Other Examples

A. Nearest Thousand

Estimate 3 × 7,911.

7,911 **rounds to** 8,000

3 × 8,000 = 24,000
So 3 × 7,911 is close to 24,000.

B. Money

Estimate 8 × $21.85.

$21.85 **rounds to** $20

8 × $20 = $160
So 8 × $21.85 is close to $160.

Guided Practice

Estimate each product by rounding the first factor to its greatest place value.

Ask Yourself
- What does the greater number round to?
- Do I need to write a dollar sign in the answer?

| 1. | 82
× 5 | 2. | $4.23
× 9 | 3. | 781
× 6 | 4. | $8.47
× 8 |

5. $28 × 2   6. 180 × 4   7. $19.95 × 7

Explain Your Thinking ▶ How can estimating a product help you check if the answer to a multiplication problem is reasonable?

Estimate.

8. 55
    × 4

9. 639
    × 2

10. $4,598
    ×   3

11. $8.74
    ×   6

12. 637
    × 4

13. 73
    × 7

14. 298
    × 5

15. 1,904
    ×   2

16. $7.35
    ×   3

17. 993
    × 6

18. 8 × 46

19. 9 × 663

20. 5 × 5,294

21. 7 × $96.32

22. This year 583 schools participated in Kindness Week. Next year this number is expected to triple. About how many schools are expected to participate next year?

23. A toy store donated 102 games, 3 times as many dolls as games, and 2 times as many craft kits as dolls to a children's charity. To the nearest hundred, how many of each item was donated?

24. Explain The first 5 customers to arrive at a toy store during Kindness Week will get a free toy. After that, every 5th person will get a toy. Sally is the 30th person to arrive. Will she get a toy?

25. Reasoning Mike's school collected about 900 children's books to donate. To the nearest hundred, what is the least number of books that could have been collected? What is the greatest number? Explain.

Mixed Review and Test Prep

Open Response

Solve each equation. (Ch. 5, Lesson 4)

26. $16 - n = 9$

27. $x \div 7 = 8$

28. $y + 15 = 19$

29. $t \times 3 = 12$

30. $z - 16 = 20$

31. $108 \div m = 9$

32. Jeanne has a bookcase with 3 shelves. She puts 78 books on each shelf. About how many books is this? Explain your thinking. (Ch. 6, Lesson 2)

Audio Tutor 1/20 Listen and Understand

Materials
base-ten blocks

Model Multiplication by One-Digit Numbers

Objective Use base-ten blocks to model multiplication.

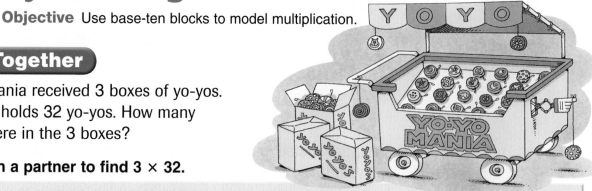

Work Together

Yo-Yo-Mania received 3 boxes of yo-yos. Each box holds 32 yo-yos. How many yo-yos were in the 3 boxes?

Work with a partner to find 3 × 32.

 STEP 1   Use base-ten blocks to show 3 groups of 32.

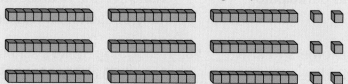

- How many tens blocks did you use?
- How many ones blocks did you use?

STEP 2   Record your work in a chart like this one.

Tens	Ones
9	6

- What is 3 × 32?
- How many yo-yos did the store receive?

What if the store received 2 boxes of 26 yo-yos?

Now find 2 × 26.

 STEP 1   Use base-ten blocks to show 2 groups of 26.

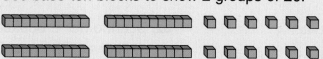

- How many tens blocks did you use?
- How many ones blocks did you use?

When the number of ones blocks is 10 or greater, you need to regroup 10 ones as 1 ten.

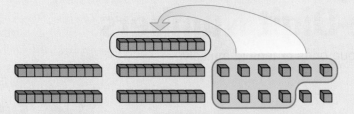

• How many tens blocks and ones blocks do you have now? Record your work in your chart.

• What is 2 × 26?

On Your Own

Tell what multiplication sentence is shown by the blocks.

1.

2.

Use base-ten blocks to find each product.

3. 3 × 31   **4.** 2 × 18   **5.** 4 × 21   **6.** 3 × 22

7. 5 × 15   **8.** 2 × 27   **9.** 7 × 13   **10.** 4 × 16

11. Analyze In which of Exercises 3–10 did you have to regroup? How can you tell if you need to regroup just by looking at the numbers in the problem?

Talk About It • Write About It

You have learned how to model multiplication using base-ten blocks.

12. Which is less, 2 × 35 or 2 × 36? Explain how you can tell without multiplying.

13. Represent How can you use 3 × 15 and 6 × 15 to find 9 × 15? Use a drawing to help you explain.

Lesson 4

Audio Tutor 1/21 Listen and Understand

Multiply Two-Digit Numbers by One-Digit Numbers

Objective Regroup ones or tens to multiply.

Learn About It

Joseph's favorite section of the Discover Science store displays dinosaurs on 3 shelves. Each shelf has 26 dinosaurs. How many dinosaurs are on the shelves?

Multiply. $3 \times 26 = n$

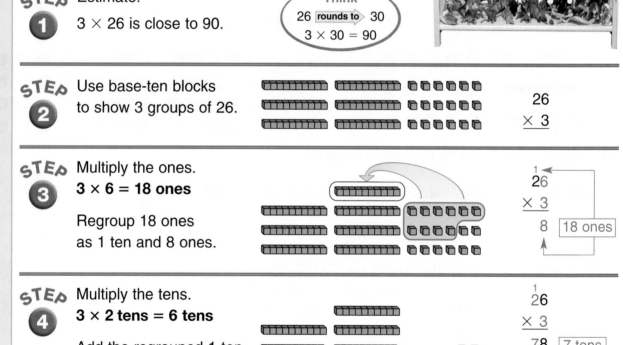

STEP 1 Estimate.

3×26 is close to 90.

Think
26 rounds to 30
$3 \times 30 = 90$

STEP 2 Use base-ten blocks to show 3 groups of 26.

$$\begin{array}{r} 26 \\ \times\ 3 \\ \hline \end{array}$$

STEP 3 Multiply the ones.

$3 \times 6 = 18$ **ones**

Regroup 18 ones as 1 ten and 8 ones.

$$\begin{array}{r} \overset{1}{2}6 \\ \times\ 3 \\ \hline 8 \end{array}$$ 18 ones

STEP 4 Multiply the tens.

3×2 **tens** $= 6$ **tens**

Add the regrouped 1 ten.

6 tens + 1 ten = 7 tens

$$\begin{array}{r} \overset{1}{2}6 \\ \times\ 3 \\ \hline 78 \end{array}$$ 7 tens

Solution: There are 78 dinosaurs on the shelves.

Since 78 is close to 90, the answer is reasonable.

Other Examples

A. No Regrouping

$$\begin{array}{r} 43 \\ \times\ 2 \\ \hline 86 \end{array}$$

B. Regrouping Tens as Hundreds

$$\begin{array}{r} 71 \\ \times\ 4 \\ \hline 284 \end{array}$$ 4×7 tens $= 28$ tens or 2 hundreds, 8 tens

152

Guided Practice

Find each product.

1. 2 × 14

2. 5 × 21

Ask Yourself

- What do I multiply first?
- Do I need to regroup ones as tens?
- Do I need to add any tens?

Estimate. Then multiply.

3.   14
   × 7

4.   11
   × 8

5.   19
   × 5

6.   31
   × 4

Explain Your Thinking ▶ What is the greatest number of ones you can have before you need to regroup? Why?

Practice and Problem Solving

Find each product.

7. 3 × 15

8. 4 × 23

9. 3 × 20

Estimate. Then multiply.

10.   73
    × 2

11.   11
    × 6

12.   90
    × 3

13.   13
    × 5

14.   46
    × 2

15.   31
    × 9

16. 2 × 29

17. 50 × 7

18. 29 × 3

19. 20 × 3

20. 2 × 42

21. 4 × 16

22. There are 50 pieces in one dinosaur skeleton model. How many pieces are in 7 models?

23. **Money** A toy Tyrannosaurus Rex costs $8. A toy Stegosaurus costs $6. Mrs. Suarez buys 12 Tyrannosaurus Rex toys and 14 Stegosaurus toys for her class. How much does she spend?

Go On

**Megan and Mark multiplied 29 × 4 in different ways.
Use their work for Questions 24 and 25.**

Megan
I think of 29 as 20 + 9.
29 × 4 = (20 + 9) × 4
= (20 × 4) + (9 × 4)
= 80 + 36
= 116

Mark
I think of 29 as 30 − 1.
29 × 4 = (30 − 1) × 4
= (30 × 4) − (1 × 4)
= 120 − 4
= 116

24. a. How does thinking of 29 as 20 + 9 help Megan multiply?

b. Use Megan's way to complete this multiplication problem.

$$17 \times 9 = (10 + \blacksquare) \times 9$$
$$= (10 \times 9) + (\blacksquare \times 9)$$
$$= (90) + \blacksquare$$
$$= \blacksquare$$

25. a. How does thinking of 29 as 30 − 1 help Mark multiply?

b. Use Mark's way to complete this multiplication problem.

$$38 \times 7 = (40 - \blacksquare) \times 7$$
$$= (40 \times \blacksquare) - (2 \times 7)$$
$$= 280 - \blacksquare$$
$$= \blacksquare$$

𝒳 Algebra • Properties Use properties to compare expressions.
Write >, <, or = for each ⬤.

26. 81 × 3 ⬤ 3 × 81

27. 72 × 5 ⬤ 9 × 8 × 4

28. 8 × 92 ⬤ (8 × 90) + (8 × 2)

29. 61 × 3 ⬤ 4 × 61

30. 7 × 2 × 2 ⬤ 2 × 7 × 3

31. 53 × (2 + 4) ⬤ 53 × (2 + 3)

32. 79 × 9 ⬤ (10 − 2) × 79

33. 65 × 5 ⬤ (60 × 5) + (6 × 5)

Solve.

34. The Discover Science store displays toy bugs on shelves. The first shelf has 10 bugs. The second shelf has 20. The third shelf has 40 and the fourth has 80. How many bugs do you think are on the fifth shelf? Why?

35. Write About It What do you think happens to a product when you double one of its factors? Give two examples to support your answer.

Extra Practice See page 169, Set C.

Social Studies Connection

Mayan Numbers

In C.E. 600 the Mayan civilization lived in Mexico and Central America. The Maya developed a number system using just three symbols.

The chart shows the numbers from 0 to 19.

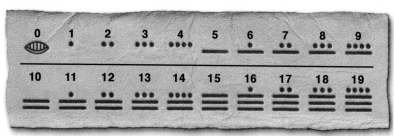

For greater numbers, the Maya drew the symbols in a column. Then they multiplied the top number by 20 and added the bottom to the product.

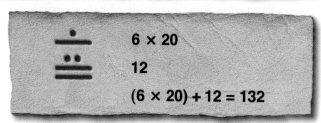

6 × 20

12

(6 × 20) + 12 = 132

Write the number sentence that these Mayan numbers show.

1.

2.

3.

4.

5. **Challenge** Write your own Mayan number problem and give it to a classmate to solve.

WEEKLY (WR) READER eduplace.com/map

Check your understanding for Lessons 1–4.

Use basic facts and patterns to find each product. (Lesson 1)

1. 6×700
2. $5 \times 4,000$
3. $8 \times 9,000$

Estimate each product. (Lesson 2)

4. 639×7
5. $\$23.18 \times 5$
6. $9,812 \times 9$

Estimate. Then multiply. (Lessons 3–4)

7. $\begin{array}{r} 23 \\ \times\ 2 \\ \hline \end{array}$

8. $\begin{array}{r} 24 \\ \times\ 3 \\ \hline \end{array}$

9. $\begin{array}{r} 18 \\ \times\ 4 \\ \hline \end{array}$

10. $\begin{array}{r} 81 \\ \times\ 6 \\ \hline \end{array}$

Problem-Solving Strategy
Guess and Check

Objective Guess and check to solve a problem.

Problem Math Marvel is shopping at the Nifty Numbers Store. He wants to solve the puzzle and win the prize. Which numbers should he pick?

SOLVE THIS PUZZLE.
WIN A PRIZE!
The product of 2 numbers is 24.
Their difference is 5.
What are the 2 numbers?

UNDERSTAND

This is what you know.

• The product of two numbers is 24.

• The difference between the two numbers is 5.

PLAN

You can use Guess and Check to solve the problem.

Guess two numbers. Check to see if they are correct.
If not, continue guessing numbers until you find the ones that work.

SOLVE

Make a reasonable guess.

Think of two numbers that have a product of 24.

1st Guess Try 4 and 6.	2nd Guess Try 2 and 12.	3rd Guess Try 3 and 8.
Multiply. $4 \times 6 = 24$ ✔	Multiply. $2 \times 12 = 24$ ✔	Multiply. $3 \times 8 = 24$ ✔
Subtract. $6 - 4 = 2$ ✘	Subtract. $12 - 2 = 10$ ✘	Subtract. $8 - 3 = 5$ ✔
4 and 6 do not work. The difference is not 5.	2 and 12 do not work. The difference is not 5.	3 and 8 work. The difference is 5.

Solution: Math Marvel should pick numbers 3 and 8.

LOOK BACK

Look back at the problem. How can you check to be sure the answer is correct?

Guided Practice

Use the Ask Yourself questions to help you solve each problem.

1. Math Marvel wants to buy two numbers with a product of 30 and a sum of 13. Which numbers should he buy?

2. Math Marvel wants to buy 2 numbers. The sum of the numbers is 26. One number is 4 more than the other. What numbers should he buy?

3. The sum of 3 numbers is 11. The product of the numbers is 36. What are the numbers?

   (Hint) What are the factors of 36?

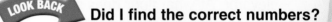

Ask Yourself

UNDERSTAND — What facts do I know?

PLAN — Can I use Guess and Check?

SOLVE
- What numbers have the correct product?
- Do these numbers have the correct sum or difference?

LOOK BACK — Did I find the correct numbers?

Independent Practice

Use Guess and Check to solve each problem.

4. Together Otto and Zoe have 28 Math Superhero trading cards. Otto has 4 more cards than Zoe. How many cards does each have?

5. Sue has 3 times as many trading cards as Tanya. If they have 12 cards altogether, how many cards does Sue have?

6. Tara is thinking of two numbers. One number is 6 more than the other. The sum of the numbers is 30. What are the numbers?

7. Two numbers have a product of 36 and a difference of 5. What are the numbers?

Go On

Mixed Problem Solving

Solve. Show your work. Tell what strategy you used.

8. **Measurement** A water park has one slide that is 538 feet long and another that is 615 feet long. How much longer is the second slide than the first?

9. Anna gets on an elevator at the fifth floor. She rides 6 floors up, then 3 floors down, then 8 floors up. Then Anna gets off the elevator. At what floor does she get off?

10. Two numbers have a product of 18 and a sum of 9. What are the numbers?

11. What is the rule for this pattern?

| 3 | 6 | 10 | 15 | 21 | 28 |

Use the rule to find the next number.

You Choose

Strategy
- Draw a Picture
- Find a Pattern
- Guess and Check
- Work Backward
- Write an Equation

Computation Method
- Mental Math
- Estimation
- Paper and Pencil
- Calculator

Data Allen School collects soup can labels for computer equipment. The table shows the labels collected in 1 month. Use the table for Problems 12–15.

12. How many more labels did the fourth grade collect than the third grade?

13. The fourth-grade students collected about twice the number of labels than what other class? Explain how you got your answer.

14. **Multistep** If Allen School needs 3,000 labels to get computer software, how many more labels are needed?

15. **Create and Solve** Write a problem using data from the table. Exchange problems with a classmate and solve.

Soup Label Collection

Class	Number of Labels
Third Grade	105
Fourth Grade	316
Fifth Grade	160
Sixth Grade	275

Problem Solving on Tests

Multiple Choice

Choose the letter of the correct answer. If the correct answer is not here, choose NH.

1. A movie ticket costs $5. A bucket of popcorn costs $3. How much do 9 movie tickets and 10 buckets of popcorn cost?

   A $90   C $45

   B $75   D NH

   (Chapter 4, Lesson 5)

2. Suppose twice as many students like soccer as softball. If 499 students like softball, about how many students like soccer?

   F about 400   H about 800

   G about 500   J about 1,000

   (Chapter 6, Lesson 2)

Open Response

Solve each problem.

3. Patrick has 5 quarters, 4 dimes, 13 nickels, and 16 pennies in his pocket. He wants to buy the book titled *Mystery at the Falls.* How much more money does he need? Explain.

   (Chapter 2, Lesson 4)

4. Fran buys 2 shirts and 1 pair of shorts. The total cost is $23. Each of the shirts costs the same amount.

   Write and solve an equation to find the cost of 1 shirt.

   (Chapter 5, Lesson 5)

Extended Response

5. The Lillyville Library is planning a book-making project for fourth-grade students. The librarian posted this sign on the bulletin board.

COME CREATE WITH US
Fourth-graders are invited to *Make Your Book* at the Lillyville Library.
Your book will have a beautiful blue cover and 16 white pages for stories of your own.
All supplies will be provided by the library. Sign up here.

   A Write and solve an equation to show the number of white pages needed for 19 students to make books.

   B Blue covers cost $1.00 each. One white page costs $0.25. How much does it cost to make one book? Show how you know.

   (Chapter 5, Lesson 5)

Education Place

See **eduplace.com/map** for more Test-Taking Tips.

Multiply Three-Digit Numbers by One-Digit Numbers

Objective Multiply three-digit numbers by one-digit numbers.

Learn About It

The Party Store ordered American flags to sell for the 4th of July. They ordered 2 boxes of flags. Each box had 235 flags. How many flags did they order?

Multiply. $2 \times 235 = n$

STEP 1 Estimate.

> **Think**
> 235 rounds to 200
> $2 \times 200 = 400$

2×235 is close to 400.

STEP 2 Multiply the ones.
$2 \times 5 = 10$ ones

$$\begin{array}{r} \overset{1}{2}35 \\ \times\ \ 2 \\ \hline 0 \end{array}$$

Regroup 10 ones as 1 ten 0 ones.

STEP 3 Multiply the tens.
2×3 tens $= 6$ tens

Add the 1 ten.
6 tens + 1 ten = 7 tens

$$\begin{array}{r} \overset{1}{2}35 \\ \times\ \ 2 \\ \hline 70 \end{array}$$ 7 tens

---

STEP 4 Multiply the hundreds.
2×2 hundreds $= 4$ hundreds

$$\begin{array}{r} \overset{1}{2}35 \\ \times\ \ 2 \\ \hline 470 \end{array}$$ 4 hundreds

---

Solution: They ordered 470 flags. Since 470 is close to 400, the answer is reasonable.

Other Examples

A. Zeros

$$\begin{array}{r} \overset{4}{2}07 \\ \times\ \ 7 \\ \hline 1{,}449 \end{array}$$

> **Think**
> 7 times 0 is 0.
> 0 plus 4 equals 4.

B. Money

$$\begin{array}{r} \$1.32 \\ \times\ \ \ \ 3 \\ \hline \$3.96 \end{array}$$

> Place a dollar sign and a decimal point in the answer.

Estimate. Then multiply.

Ask Yourself
- Do I need to regroup the ones, tens, or hundreds?
- Do I need to add any regrouped tens or hundreds?

1. 215
    × 4

2. $1.84
    × 2

3. 621
    × 3

4. $5.98
    × 7

5. 805 × 5

6. $4.20 × 6

7. 909 × 9

Explain Your Thinking ▶ When multiplying, what must you do with the numbers that you regroup?

Practice and Problem Solving

Estimate. Then multiply.

8. 321
    × 2

9. $3.08
    × 5

10. 197
     × 4

11. $725
     × 3

12. 790
     × 3

13. 398
     × 2

14. 109
     × 8

15. 514
     × 6

16. 136
     × 7

17. $9.21
     × 9

18. 199 × 7

19. 508 × 9

20. 982 × 6

21. $4.53 × 8

Solve.

22. Tahni buys 2 rolls of blue streamers and 4 rolls of red streamers at the Party Store. Each roll is 972 inches long. How many inches of streamers does she buy?

23. **Estimate** There are 175 balloons in 1 package. How many of these packages would you have to buy to have at least 1,000 balloons?

24. **Money** If 3 packages of confetti cost $5.25, how much would 9 packages cost? Explain how you got your answer.

Go On

Algebra • **Functions** Copy and complete each function table.

Rule: $y = 10x$	
Input (x)	Output (y)
25. 5	■
26. ■	80
27. 32	■
28. ■	170

Rule: $y = x \div 4$	
Input (x)	Output (y)
29. 20	■
30. ■	7
31. 32	■
32. ■	25

Solve.

33. The Party Store sells banners for $9.85 each. What is the cost of 7 banners?

34. Linh spent $51 on balloons. If red balloons cost $15 a box and blue balloons cost $7 a box, how many boxes of each type of balloon did Linh buy?

35. Ana buys 3 boxes of notes and 6 boxes of party invitations. Each box contains 20 cards. How many more invitations than notes does Ana buy?

36. **Multistep** Josh buys 8 sheets of stickers that are 5 stickers wide and 4 stickers long. He buys 2 sheets that are 10 stickers wide and 5 stickers long. How many stickers does Josh buy?

37. **Represent** Draw base-ten blocks to show 3×143. Explain how you regroup.

Mixed Review and Test Prep

(Ch. 3, Lesson 3)

Open Response

Estimate each to the nearest dollar.
(Ch. 3, Lesson 3)

38. $5.38 + $2.11   **39.** $8.49 − $3.61

40. $9.43 + $8.16   **41.** $7.32 − $1.76

42. If you double each factor in a multiplication problem, what happens to the product? Use examples to explain your answer.
(Ch. 6, Lesson 6)

Extra Practice See page 169, Set D.

Algebraic Thinking
Calculator Patterns

Use a calculator to find patterns when multiplying by 9.

1. To multiply any number by 9, press 9 . Then enter the number and press [=].

2. Multiply 9 by 1 through 15. Record the answers in a chart. Look for patterns.

   • What is the pattern in the hundreds place? the tens place? the ones place?

3. Find the sum of the ones and hundreds digits for each number on your list. What do you notice? Add other sets of digits. What patterns do you find?

4. **Challenge** Predict the next 4 numbers in the pattern. Use your calculator to check your prediction.

Algebraic Thinking
Fill Them In

Copy and complete these factors and products. Use each of the digits 0–9 once.

1. ■ × 40 = 28■

2. ■ × 1■ = 90

3. 3 × ■1 = 12■

4. ■ × 84 = 16■

5. ■ × 16 = ■44

Brain Teaser

Think about multiplication. Which number doesn't belong? Explain why.

Education Place
Check out **eduplace.com/map** for more brain teasers.

Multiply Greater Numbers

Objective Multiply with four-digit and five-digit numbers.

Learn About It

The All Sports Store has a display of 1,950 cans of tennis balls. If each can holds 3 balls, how many tennis balls are in the display?

Multiply. $3 \times 1{,}950 = n$

First, estimate. **Think** $3 \times 1{,}950 \longrightarrow 3 \times 2{,}000 = 6{,}000$

Remember
To estimate is to find a number close to an exact amount

STEP 1	Multiply the ones. **3 × 0 ones = 0 ones**	$\begin{array}{r} 1{,}950 \\ \times\quad 3 \\ \hline 0 \end{array}$
STEP 2	Multiply the tens. **3 × 5 tens = 15 tens**	$\begin{array}{r} \overset{1}{1}{,}950 \\ \times\quad 3 \\ \hline 50 \end{array}$ Regroup 15 tens as 1 hundred 5 tens.
STEP 3	Multiply the hundreds. **3 × 9 hundreds = 27 hundreds** Add the regrouped 1 hundred. **27 + 1 = 28 hundreds**	$\begin{array}{r} \overset{2\ 1}{1}{,}950 \\ \times\quad 3 \\ \hline 850 \end{array}$ Regroup 28 hundreds as 2 thousands 8 hundreds.
STEP 4	Multiply the thousands. **3 × 1 thousand = 3 thousands** Add the regrouped 2 thousands. **3 + 2 = 5 thousands**	$\begin{array}{r} \overset{2\ 1}{1}{,}950 \\ \times\quad 3 \\ \hline 5{,}850 \end{array}$

Solution: There are 5,850 tennis balls on the shelves. Since 5,850 is close to 6,000, the answer is reasonable.

Extra Help at **eduplace.com/map**

► **You can use a calculator to check the answer.**

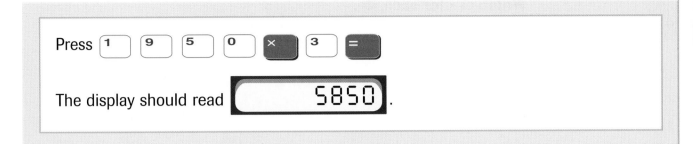

Press ① ⑨ ⑤ ⓪ ✕ ③ ＝

The display should read ⌜ 5850 ⌟.

Other Examples

A. Five-Digit Number

$$\begin{array}{r} {\scriptstyle 4\ \ 5} \\ 40{,}809 \\ \times\qquad 6 \\ \hline 244{,}854 \end{array}$$

B. Money

$$\begin{array}{r} \$62.21 \\ \times\qquad 4 \\ \hline \$248.84 \end{array}$$

Guided Practice

Multiply. Use a calculator to check.

1. $\begin{array}{r} 1{,}112 \\ \times\quad 2 \\ \hline \end{array}$

2. $\begin{array}{r} \$41.26 \\ \times\quad 2 \\ \hline \end{array}$

3. $\begin{array}{r} 3{,}089 \\ \times\quad 5 \\ \hline \end{array}$

4. $38.05 × 7   5. 6,253 × 8   6. 4,002 × 6

> **Ask Yourself**
> • Do I need to regroup the ones, tens, or hundreds?
> • Do I need to add any regrouped tens, hundreds, or thousands?

Explain Your Thinking ▶ Is $4,000 or $400 a reasonable estimate for 8 × $52.71? Explain your reasoning.

Practice and Problem Solving

Multiply. Use a calculator to check.

7. $\begin{array}{r} 321 \\ \times\ 2 \\ \hline \end{array}$

8. $\begin{array}{r} \$37.08 \\ \times\quad 5 \\ \hline \end{array}$

9. $\begin{array}{r} 7{,}342 \\ \times\quad 9 \\ \hline \end{array}$

10. $\begin{array}{r} 7{,}095 \\ \times\quad 3 \\ \hline \end{array}$

11. $\begin{array}{r} 7{,}490 \\ \times\quad 3 \\ \hline \end{array}$

12. $\begin{array}{r} \$90.25 \\ \times\quad 6 \\ \hline \end{array}$

13. $\begin{array}{r} 3{,}562 \\ \times\quad 7 \\ \hline \end{array}$

14. $\begin{array}{r} 14{,}208 \\ \times\quad 5 \\ \hline \end{array}$

15. $\begin{array}{r} \$64{,}836 \\ \times\quad 4 \\ \hline \end{array}$

16. $\begin{array}{r} 20{,}054 \\ \times\quad 8 \\ \hline \end{array}$

17. 2,731 × $4   18. 20,120 × 6   19. $34.83 × 2   20. 4,089 × 7

Go On

Algebra • Symbols Estimate to compare.
Write > or < for each ⬤.

21. 697×5 ⬤ $1{,}244 \times 2$

22. $2{,}987 + 3{,}980$ ⬤ 387×7

23. $2{,}700$ ⬤ 3×945

24. 2×999 ⬤ $10{,}000$

25. $5{,}978 - 879$ ⬤ 2×912

26. 79×9 ⬤ $1{,}111 \times 2$

27. 660×5 ⬤ 6×660

28. 798×5 ⬤ $3{,}500$

Choose a Computation Method

Mental Math • Estimation • Paper and Pencil • Calculator

Suppose the map shows the train routes Anne uses to visit her grandchildren. Use the map for Problems 29–33. Tell which method you chose. Hint: Remember that a round trip begins and ends in the same place.

29. In one year, Anne makes 5 round trips between Jacksonville and Florida City. About how many miles does she travel?

30. Anne travels from Birmingham to Jacksonville. Her son, Bill, travels from Birmingham to Charleston. Who travels farther? How much farther?

31. Anne lives in Jacksonville. She travels to Florida City and back, then to Pensacola and back, and finally, to Birmingham and back. About how many miles does she travel in all?

32. **Analyze** One of Anne's grandsons lives in Atlanta. On one round trip, he travels 1,445 miles and visits 3 of the cities shown on the map. What cities does he visit?

33. **Create and Solve** Use the map to write a multiplication problem. Then give it to a classmate to solve.

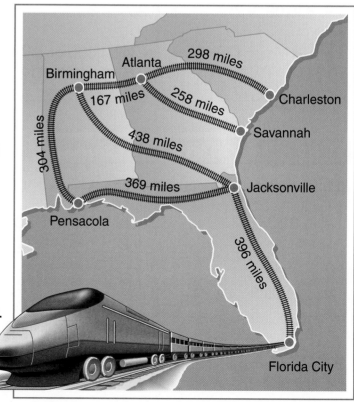

166

Extra Practice See page 169, Set E.

Mixed Review and Test Prep

Open Response

Use properties and rules to solve.

(Chapter 4, Lesson 1)

34. $1 \times 57 = $ ■

35. $21 \times 0 = $ ■

36. $14 \div 14 = $ ■

37. $0 \div 32 = $ ■

Solve. (Chapter 6, Lesson 7)

38. Amelia buys pendants for each of her 5 nieces. After tax, the pendants each cost $35.07. How much does Amelia spend altogether?

Math Reasoning
Venn Diagrams

Kyle used colored pasta to make the Venn diagram shown at the right.

A Venn diagram shows how sets or groups of things are related to each other.

Write *true* or *false* for each statement. If false, rewrite the statement to make it true.

1. Some wheels are red.

2. All shells are green.

3. None of the blue pasta are bow ties.

4. **What's Wrong?** Kyle says all red pasta are bow ties because all the bow ties are red. Why is he wrong?

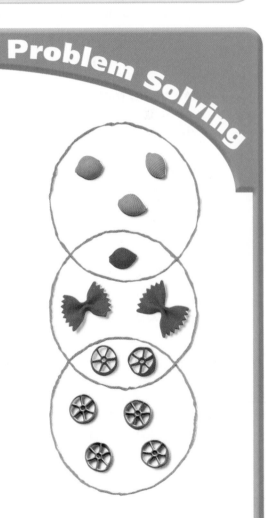

Problem Solving

Chapter Review/Test

VOCABULARY

Choose the best term to complete each sentence.

1. The number 18 is a _____ of 6.

2. You can _____ products by rounding factors to their greatest place.

3. If a product has more than 10 tens, you have to _____ tens as hundreds.

Vocabulary

factor
multiple
regroup
estimate

CONCEPTS AND SKILLS

Use basic facts and patterns to find each product. (Lesson 1, pp. 146–147)

4. 5×70　　　　**5.** 4×800　　　　**6.** 8×500　　　　**7.** $6 \times 9{,}000$

Estimate each product. (Lesson 2, pp. 148–149)

8. 3×38　　　　**9.** 4×509　　　　**10.** $5 \times 4{,}850$　　　　**11.** $7 \times \$82.70$

Multiply. (Lessons 4, 6–7, pp. 152–155, 160–167)

12. 2×41　　　　**13.** $3 \times \$16$　　　　**14.** 4×51　　　　**15.** 5×91

16. $\$6.09 \times 8$　　　　**17.** 712×5　　　　**18.** $\$725 \times 3$　　　　**19.** 923×4

20. $1{,}629 \times 6$　　　　**21.** $5{,}082 \times 8$　　　　**22.** $\$79.15 \times 6$　　　　**23.** $50{,}401 \times 4$

PROBLEM SOLVING

Solve. (Lesson 5, pp. 156–159)

24. The product of two numbers is 48. Their difference is 8. What are the two numbers?

25. Mike has twice the number of video games as John. Together they have 36 video games. How many games does each boy have?

 **Write About It**

Show You Understand

Explain how you can use this model to find the product of 3×15.

Extra Practice

Set A (Lesson 1, pp. 146–147)

Use basic facts and patterns to find each product.

1. 3×40 **2.** $4 \times 6,000$ **3.** 5×800 **4.** $7 \times 9,000$

5. 4×50 **6.** 8×60 **7.** 4×700 **8.** $7 \times 6,000$

Set B (Lesson 2, pp. 148–149)

Estimate each product.

1. 4×22 **2.** 3×68 **3.** 5×583 **4.** $8 \times \$7.15$

5. $9 \times \$0.95$ **6.** 7×366 **7.** $3 \times 8,549$ **8.** $2 \times \$21.07$

Set C (Lesson 4, pp. 152–155)

Estimate. Then multiply.

1. $\begin{array}{r} 11 \\ \times\ 5 \\ \hline \end{array}$ **2.** $\begin{array}{r} 22 \\ \times\ 3 \\ \hline \end{array}$ **3.** $\begin{array}{r} 20 \\ \times\ 6 \\ \hline \end{array}$ **4.** $\begin{array}{r} 18 \\ \times\ 5 \\ \hline \end{array}$ **5.** $\begin{array}{r} 27 \\ \times\ 3 \\ \hline \end{array}$

6. 5×16 **7.** 54×2 **8.** 19×4 **9.** 9×30 **10.** 48×2

Set D (Lesson 6, pp. 160–163)

Estimate. Then multiply.

1. $\begin{array}{r} 212 \\ \times\ 3 \\ \hline \end{array}$ **2.** $\begin{array}{r} 325 \\ \times\ 2 \\ \hline \end{array}$ **3.** $\begin{array}{r} \$2.46 \\ \times\ 4 \\ \hline \end{array}$ **4.** $\begin{array}{r} 376 \\ \times\ 3 \\ \hline \end{array}$ **5.** $\begin{array}{r} 202 \\ \times\ 4 \\ \hline \end{array}$

6. 510×3 **7.** $\$7.04 \times 8$ **8.** 526×5 **9.** $\$612 \times 8$ **10.** 914×8

Set E (Lesson 7, pp. 164–167)

Multiply. Use a calculator to check.

1. $\begin{array}{r} 4,007 \\ \times\ 8 \\ \hline \end{array}$ **2.** $\begin{array}{r} \$5,891 \\ \times\ 6 \\ \hline \end{array}$ **3.** $\begin{array}{r} 9,021 \\ \times\ 5 \\ \hline \end{array}$ **4.** $\begin{array}{r} \$45.09 \\ \times\ 4 \\ \hline \end{array}$ **5.** $\begin{array}{r} \$1,932 \\ \times\ 5 \\ \hline \end{array}$

6. $\$27.44 \times 8$ **7.** $\$603.40 \times 7$ **8.** $16,517 \times 2$ **9.** $\$80,175 \times 3$

Multiply by Two-Digit Numbers

INVESTIGATION

Using Data

Dedham Elementary School invited four people to talk about their careers as part of Career Day. The graph at the right shows the number of students that attended each presentation. If the speakers gave 2 pamphlets to each student at their presentations, what method could you use to find the total number of pamphlets handed out?

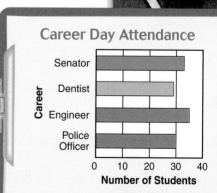

Career Day Attendance

Career (y-axis): Senator, Dentist, Engineer, Police Officer

Number of Students (x-axis): 0, 10, 20, 30, 40

Use What You Know

Use this page to review and remember what you need to know for this chapter.

VOCABULARY

Choose the best term to complete each sentence.

1. 9 is a _____ of 3.

2. When you multiply 126 by 5, the _____ is 630.

3. A number that is multiplied is a _____.

4. When you write $15.65 as $20, you _____ to the greatest place.

CONCEPTS AND SKILLS

Use basic facts and patterns to find each product.

5. 8×20

6. 4×600

7. $5 \times 3,000$

8. $2 \times 5,000$

Write each number in expanded form.

9. 27

10. 312

11. 4,520

12. 35,064

13. 105,869

Find each product. Estimate to check.

14.
$$\begin{array}{r} 76 \\ \times\ 4 \\ \hline \end{array}$$

15.
$$\begin{array}{r} 425 \\ \times\ 9 \\ \hline \end{array}$$

16.
$$\begin{array}{r} 1,451 \\ \times\ 3 \\ \hline \end{array}$$

17.
$$\begin{array}{r} \$21.59 \\ \times\ 7 \\ \hline \end{array}$$

18.
$$\begin{array}{r} \$12.89 \\ \times\ 4 \\ \hline \end{array}$$

19.
$$\begin{array}{r} 201 \\ \times\ 9 \\ \hline \end{array}$$

20.
$$\begin{array}{r} 357 \\ \times\ 7 \\ \hline \end{array}$$

21.
$$\begin{array}{r} 2,005 \\ \times\ 4 \\ \hline \end{array}$$

22.
$$\begin{array}{r} 12,506 \\ \times\ 3 \\ \hline \end{array}$$

23.
$$\begin{array}{r} \$35,154 \\ \times\ 5 \\ \hline \end{array}$$

Write About It

24. How does estimating a product help you know if your answer is reasonable?

25. What does it mean to say that multiplication and division are inverse operations?

Facts Practice, See page 668.

Patterns With Multiples of 10, 100, and 1,000

Objective Use patterns and basic facts to multiply mentally.

Learn About It

A construction worker is helping to build a 60-floor building. Each floor needs 300 tons of steel. How much steel will be used for the entire building?

Multiply. $60 \times 300 = n$

> **You can use basic facts and patterns of zeros to multiply.**
>
> $6 \times 3 = 18$ Use the basic fact $6 \times 3 = 18$.
> $6 \times 30 = 180$ Count the number of zeros in the factors.
> $60 \times 30 = 1,800$ Write that number of zeros to the right of 18.
> $60 \times 300 = 18,000$

Solution: The building will use 18,000 tons of steel.

Other Examples

A. Find 50×60.

$5 \times 6 = 30$
$5 \times 60 = 300$
$\boxed{50 \times 60 = 3,000}$

B. Find $40 \times 2,000$.

$4 \times 2 = 8$
$4 \times 20 = 80$
$40 \times 20 = 800$
$40 \times 200 = 8,000$
$\boxed{40 \times 2,000 = 80,000}$

Guided Practice

Use basic facts and patterns to find each product.

1. 70×8
   70×80
   70×800
   $70 \times 8,000$

2. 40×5
   40×50
   40×500
   $40 \times 5,000$

3. 30×9
   30×90
   30×900
   30×9000

Ask Yourself
- What basic fact can I use?
- How many zeros should be in the product?

Explain Your Thinking ▶ How many zeros are in the product of 50 and 800? Explain how you know.

Use basic facts and patterns to find each product.

4. 3 × 40
30 × 40
30 × 400
30 × 4,000

5. 7 × 30
70 × 30
70 × 300
70 × 3,000

6. 6 × 90
60 × 90
60 × 900
60 × 9,000

7. 9 × 80
90 × 80
90 × 800
90 × 8,000

8. 30
× 2

9. 30
× 20

10. 300
× 20

11. 3,000
× 20

12. 200
× 30

13. 60
× 60

14. 70
× 90

15. 600
× 60

16. 3,000
× 80

17. 900
× 20

18. 80
× 40

19. 60
× 50

20. 200
× 50

21. 6,000
× 10

22. 400
× 90

 Algebra • **Expressions** Write >, <, or = for each ●.

23. 40 × 20 ● 80

24. 50 × 200 ● 10,000

25. 600 ● 300 × 20

26. 5 × 40 ● 6 × 20

27. 30 × 50 ● 20 × 200

28. 20 × 30 ● 200 × 3

29. Sarah's mom earns $20 an hour as a construction worker. How much will Sarah's mom earn on a job that takes 40 hours?

30. Multistep There are 60 doors on each floor of an 80-story skyscraper. Each door has 3 hinges. How many hinges are there?

31. A construction worker used 20-inch wood panels to cover a large wall. She put 20 panels side-by-side. How wide is the wall? How many zeros are in the answer? Explain.

32. Money Kimberly bought two tickets to visit a building's observation deck. Each ticket cost $7.98. She got four $1 bills and four pennies for change. What bill did she use to pay?

Mixed Review and Test Prep

Open Response

Add or subtract. (Ch. 3, Lesson 8)

33.   24,571
+ 18,125

34.   193,374
− 102,487

35. 359 + 406

36. 1,290 − 1,146

Multiple Choice

37. What is the product of 40 and 600? (Ch. 7, Lesson 1)

A 240

C 24,000

B 2,400

D 240,000

Audio Tutor 1/23 Listen and Understand

Estimate Products

Objective Use rounding to estimate products.

Learn About It

Mark's dentist orders toothbrushes in boxes of 32. About how many toothbrushes does the dentist receive if she orders 18 boxes?

You can estimate products by rounding factors to their greatest place.

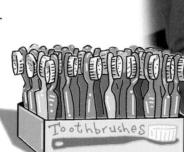

Estimate. 18 × 32 = n

STEP 1	Round 18 and 32 to the nearest 10.	18 rounds to> 20 32 rounds to> 30
STEP 2	Then multiply the rounded numbers.	20 × 30 = 600

Solution: The estimate shows that the dentist receives about 600 toothbrushes.

Guided Practice

Estimate each product by rounding each factor to its greatest place.

1. 23
   × 41

2. 233
   × 27

3. 4,125
   × 16

4. $12.35
   × 32

5. 53 × 127

6. 66 × 1,504

7. 85 × 79

Ask Yourself
- What does each number round to?
- Do I need to write a dollar sign in the product?

Explain Your Thinking ▶ How would you estimate the product of 59 × 63? What basic fact and pattern of zeros could help you find the product?

Estimate each product.

8. 42
    × 28

9. 15
    × 12

10. $1.46
    ×   37

11. 4,128
    ×   89

12. 575
    × 62

13. 45 × 91

14. 82 × 325

15. 11 × $28.48

16. 63 × 57

17. 18 × 5,629

18. 76 × 407

19. 24 × 926

20. 52 × 5,802

Use mental math or estimation. Write +, −, or × for each ■.

21. 69 ■ 700 > 40,000

22. 25 ■ 1,000 < 19 × 1,100

23. 49 ■ 576 = 25 ■ 25

24. 56 ■ 395 > 20,694 ■ 5,123

Solve.

25. Five dental assistants together perform about 185 cleanings a week. At that rate, about how many cleanings do they perform in a year?

26. A retired dentist visits schools to give information about dental health. Last year she made 11 visits a month. This year she plans to make 18 visits a month. About how many more visits will she make this year than last year?

27. **Analyze** Dr. Smith and Dr. Brown are dentists. In one month, Dr. Smith had 52 more patients than Dr. Brown. Together they had 548 patients. How many patients did Dr. Brown have?

Mixed Review and Test Prep

Open Response

Use the rule to find _y_ for each value of _x_.

(Ch. 5, Lesson 6)

Rule: $y = 5x$

28. $x = 48$

29. $x = 123$

30. $x = 2,547$

31. $x = 16,125$

32. Coach Davis wants to purchase 18 basketballs for $17.95 each. He has $425. Is that enough money to pay for the basketballs?

(Ch. 7, Lesson 2)

Explain how you got your answer.

Extra Practice See page 191, Set B.

Audio Tutor 1/19 Listen and Understand

Algebra
Model Multiplication

Objective Use models and the Distributive Property to multiply 2 two-digit numbers.

Work Together

The **Distributive Property of Multiplication over Addition** can help you multiply.

Materials
grid paper
colored pencils

Look at this example of the Distributive Property:

$4 \times 12 = \blacksquare$
$4 \times 12 = 48$

12
4

$4 \times 12 = \blacksquare$
$4 \times (10 + 2) = \blacksquare$
$(4 \times 10) + (4 \times 2) = \blacksquare$
$40 + 8 = 48$

10   2
4

Work with a partner. Use models and the Distributive Property to find 15×26.

STEP 1 Draw a rectangle on grid paper to show 15×26.

• How many rows are there?

• How many squares are in a row?

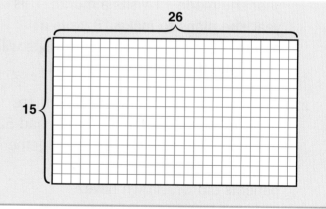

26
15

STEP 2 Draw a line to separate the factor 15 into the tens place and the ones place. Show 15 as $10 + 5$.

• Into how many rectangles have you divided the larger rectangle?

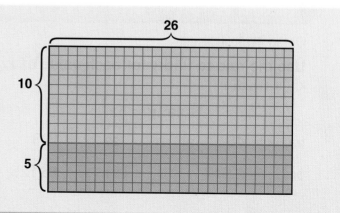

26
10
5

STEP 3 Draw another line to separate the factor 26 into the tens place and the ones place. Show 26 as 20 + 6. Label the grid.

• What multiplication does the grid show?

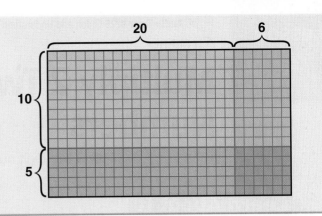

STEP 4 Multiply to find all the products. Then add the products.

• What is the sum of the products?

• How many squares are there in all?

10 rows of 20	→	10 × 20	=	200
10 rows of 6	→	10 × 6	=	60
5 rows of 20	→	5 × 20	=	100
5 rows of 6	→	5 × 6	=	+ 30
				390

STEP 5 Use the Distributive Property to record your work.

• What is 15 × 26?

$(10 \times 20) + (10 \times 6) + (5 \times 20) + (5 \times 6) = \blacksquare$

$200 + 60 + 100 + 30 = 390$

On Your Own

Use models and the Distributive Property to find each product. Record your work.

1. 23 × 11
2. 13 × 15
3. 20 × 32
4. 12 × 12
5. 18 × 28

6. 21 × 25
7. 14 × 19
8. 31 × 17
9. 16 × 22
10. 26 × 24

Talk About It • Write About It

You learned to use models and the Distributive Property to multiply two-digit numbers.

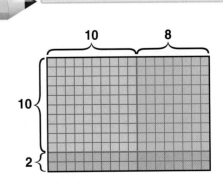

11. Write a multiplication problem that the model on the right represents.

12. Which number would you express as a sum to multiply 20 × 26? Explain.

Lesson 4

Algebra

Multiply 2 Two-Digit Numbers

Objective Multiply 2 two-digit numbers.

Vocabulary

Distributive Property

Associative Property

Learn About It

Dr. Sanchez is a geoscientist. He is putting minerals in a display case for a science exhibit. There are 14 rows in the case. Each row of the display case will hold 13 minerals. How many minerals can Dr. Sanchez place in the case?

Multiply. $14 \times 13 = n$

STEP 1 Multiply 14 by 3 ones.

$$\begin{array}{r} \overset{1}{14} \\ \times\ 13 \\ \hline 42 \end{array}$$

STEP 2 Multiply 14 by 1 ten.

$$\begin{array}{r} \overset{1}{14} \\ \times\ 13 \\ \hline 42 \\ 140 \end{array}$$

STEP 3 Add the products.

$$\begin{array}{r} \overset{1}{14} \\ \times\ 13 \\ \hline 42 \\ +\ 140 \\ \hline 182 \end{array}$$

$42 \leftarrow 3 \times 14$

$+ 140 \leftarrow 10 \times 14$

$182 \leftarrow (3 \times 14) + (10 \times 14)$

The **Distributive Property** shows why this works.

$13 \times 14 = (10 + 3) \times 14$

$13 \times 14 = (10 \times 14) + (3 \times 14)$

Solution: Dr. Sanchez can place 182 minerals in the case.

▶ When you multiply by multiples of 10, you can use the Associative Property.

Find 25×30.

You can think of 30 as 3×10.

$$\begin{aligned} 25 \times 30 &= 25 \times (3 \times 10) \\ &= (25 \times 3) \times 10 \\ &= 75 \times 10 \\ &= 750 \end{aligned}$$

The **Associative Property** says that changing the grouping of the factors does not change the product.

$25 \times (3 \times 10) = (25 \times 3) \times 10$

Ask Yourself

• What numbers are multiplied first?
• What numbers are multiplied next?
• What do I add to find the product?

Multiply.

| 1. | 31
 $\times 23$ | 2. | 49
 $\times 17$ | 3. | 52
 $\times 36$ | 4. | $22
 $\times 45$ |

Use the Associative Property to multiply.

5. $33 \times 20 = 33 \times (\blacksquare \times 10)$

   $= (\blacksquare \times 2) \times \blacksquare$

   $= \blacksquare \times \blacksquare$

   $= \blacksquare$

6. $74 \times 20 = \blacksquare \times (\blacksquare \times 10)$

   $= (\blacksquare \times \blacksquare) \times \blacksquare$

   $= \blacksquare \times \blacksquare$

   $= \blacksquare$

7. $51 \times 50 = 51 \times (\blacksquare \times \blacksquare)$

   $= (\blacksquare \times \blacksquare) \times 10$

   $= \blacksquare \times 10$

   $= \blacksquare$

8. $62 \times 30 = \blacksquare \times (\blacksquare \times 10)$

   $= (\blacksquare \times \blacksquare) \times \blacksquare$

   $= \blacksquare \times \blacksquare$

   $= \blacksquare$

Explain Your Thinking ▶ How does the Distributive Property show how each step works when you multiply?

Practice and Problem Solving

Multiply.

| 9. | 26
 $\times 16$ | 10. | 21
 $\times 31$ | 11. | $34
 $\times 24$ | 12. | 84
 $\times 42$ | 13. | 71
 $\times 63$ |

| 14. | 52
 $\times 25$ | 15. | 63
 $\times 53$ | 16. | 89
 $\times 92$ | 17. | $65
 $\times 29$ | 18. | 25
 $\times 78$ |

Multiply. Use the Associative Property.

19. 18×30 20. 41×50 21. 93×70 22. 55×60 23. 98×90

24. 68×20 25. 15×40 26. 27×70 27. 54×90 28. 16×30

Go On

Algebra • **Equations** Find each value of *n*.

29. $12 \times 5 = (10 \times n) + (2 \times 5)$

30. $(n + 4) \times 15 = 14 \times 15$

31. $21 \times 18 = (20 \times n) + (1 \times 18)$

32. $(n + 7) \times 12 = 17 \times 12$

33. $(10 \times n) + 9 = 349$

34. $34 \times 21 = n + 34$

35. $39 \times 20 = n - 20$

36. $25 \times (n \times 3) = 750$

 Use each of the digits 2, 3, 4, 5 once to write a multiplication sentence.

37. What is the greatest possible product you can make?

38. What is the least possible product you can make?

 Data Use the graph for Problems 39–41.

39. The ammonites each weigh 19 grams. How much do all the ammonites weigh?

40. **Multistep** The shark teeth weigh about 64 grams each. The bugs in amber weigh about 14 grams each. Which weigh more, all the shark teeth or all the bugs in amber? How much more?

 41. **Write About It** The number of fossils found by another team is 15 times the number of fossils found by Dr. Sanchez's team. Describe how you could find the number of fossils found by the other team.

42. At a science store, a leaf fossil costs $5.95, a geode costs $8.50, and a space pen costs $6.75. How much less would it cost Tim to buy 6 leaf fossils than 6 pens as gifts?

43. Teva collected some rocks on Monday. On Tuesday, she collected 3 more than on Monday. On Wednesday, she collected 6 more than on Tuesday. She collected 12 on Wednesday. How many rocks did she collect on Monday?

Fossils Found by Dr. Sanchez's Team

Open Response

Multiply. (Ch. 6, Lesson 7)

44. 4 × 53

45. 8 × 262

46. 9 × 3,005

47. 7 × 43,715

48. 5 × 24,608

49. 6 × 5,319

50. 3 × 7,539

51. 2 × 86,425

Multiple Choice

52. Each of 76 art students will decorate 15 ceramic tiles for a mural. How many tiles will be in the finished mural? (Ch. 7, Lesson 4)

A 456

C 1,110

B 760

D 1,140

Game Activity

Multiplying Does It!

2–4 Players

What You'll Need • 2 sets of number cards labeled 0 to 9 (Learning Tool 10)

How to Play

1 Use Learning Tool 10 or make two sets of cards like the ones shown.

2 Shuffle the cards. Place them facedown in a stack.

3 Each player draws four cards from the stack to make a multiplication problem. Each player decides to make either 2 two-digit factors or 1 one-digit factor and 1 three-digit factor and then multiplies.

4 Players compare their products. The player who has the greatest product gets one point. Play until one player gets 5 points.

How fast can you multiply? As an extra challenge, award 1 extra point to the player who correctly multiplies his or her factors the fastest.

Extra Practice See page 191, Set C.

Problem-Solving Decision
Reasonable Answers

Objective Decide whether the answer to a problem is reasonable.

After you have solved a problem, remember to look back and decide whether your answer is reasonable.

Look at these examples.

▶ **Sometimes incorrect information is used.**

Ms. Kerr is a cartoonist who draws 30 cartoon strips each month. She multiplied to find the number of strips she draws in a year.

$$30 \times 52 = 1,560 \text{ strips}$$

Ms. Kerr's answer is not reasonable. She multiplied by the number of weeks in a year instead of by the number of months in a year.

The correct solution should be:

$$30 \times 12 = 360 \text{ strips}$$

▶ **Sometimes the calculations are incorrect.**

A cartoonist drew 12 Sunday strips. For each strip, he drew 16 panels. He multiplied to find the number of panels he drew.

```
    12
 ×  16
    72
 +  12
 84 panels
```

The answer is not reasonable. An estimate of 12×16 is $10 \times 20 = 200$. The number 84 is not close to 200.

The correct solution should be:

```
    12
 ×  16
    72
 + 120
 192 panels
```

Try These

Solve. Explain why your answer is reasonable.

1. Each student in art class needs 16 pastel pencils. How many pencils will 24 students need?

2. Kelly used three times as many pens as pencils in one year. She used 150 pens. How many pencils did she use?

3. Roberto buys 5 boxes of markers for $2.79 each. He pays with a $20 bill. What is his change?

4. Sonia uses about 30 sheets of paper a month to draw cartoons. About how many sheets does she use in a year?

Math Challenge
Odd or Even?

You may remember that **even numbers** are numbers that are multiples of 2, and **odd numbers** are numbers that are not multiples of 2.
Explore multiplying by odd and even numbers.

> **Remember:**
> Even numbers always end in an even digit.
> Any whole number that does not end in 0, 2, 4, 6, or 8 is odd.

1. Multiply 2 odd numbers. Is the product even or odd? Multiply 5 more pairs of odd numbers.

2. Now multiply 2 even numbers. Is the product even or odd? Multiply 5 more pairs of even numbers.

3. Multiply an even number by an odd number. Is the product even or odd? Multiply 5 more even/odd pairs.

4. What are the multiplication rules for even and odd numbers? Write a statement to explain how you can tell whether a product will be even or odd without multiplying.

WEEKLY (WR) READER eduplace.com/map

Check your understanding of Lessons 1–5.

Use basic facts and patterns to find each product. (Lesson 1)

1. 60×90 2. 40×700 3. 30×500

Estimate each product by rounding each factor to its greatest place. (Lesson 2)

4. $\begin{array}{r} 23 \\ \times\, 36 \\ \hline \end{array}$

5. $\begin{array}{r} 547 \\ \times\, 89 \\ \hline \end{array}$

6. $\begin{array}{r} \$38.25 \\ \times\quad 41 \\ \hline \end{array}$

Find each product. (Lessons 3–4)

7. 41×23 8. 74×42 9. 24×52

Solve. (Lesson 5)

10. Charlotte bikes 48 miles every month. How many miles does she bike in a year? Tell why your answer is reasonable.

Extra Practice at eduplace.com/map

Audio Tutor 1/26 Listen and Understand

Multiply Three-Digit Numbers by Two-Digit Numbers

Objective Multiply three-digit numbers by two-digit numbers.

Learn About It

Some people get their exercise while they work! The table shows the number of miles that some people in a town walk every month on their jobs. How many miles does each person walk in a year?

Let's find out how many miles the mail carrier walks in a year.

Miles Walked in a Month	
Police officer	136
TV reporter	84
Salesperson	67
Mail carrier	116
Teacher	60

Multiply. $116 \times 12 = n$

STEP 1 Multiply 116 by 2 ones.	STEP 2 Multiply 116 by 1 ten.	STEP 3 Add the products.
$\begin{array}{r} \overset{1}{1}16 \\ \times\ 12 \\ \hline 232 \end{array}$	$\begin{array}{r} \overset{1}{1}16 \\ \times\ 12 \\ \hline 232 \\ 1160 \end{array}$	$\begin{array}{r} \overset{1}{1}16 \\ \times\ 12 \\ \hline 232 \\ +\ 1160 \\ \hline 1,392 \end{array}$ ← 116×2 ← 116×10 ← $(116 \times 2) + (116 \times 10)$

Solution: The mail carrier walks 1,392 miles in a year!

Other Examples

A. Zero in the Tens Place

$\begin{array}{r} \overset{2}{\underset{}{\cancel{4}}} \\ 205 \\ \times\ 59 \\ \hline 1845 \\ +\ 10250 \\ \hline 12,095 \end{array}$

B. Zero in the Ones Place

$\begin{array}{r} \overset{5}{\cancel{2}} \\ 490 \\ \times\ 63 \\ \hline 1470 \\ +\ 29400 \\ \hline 30,870 \end{array}$

C. Multiple of 10

$\begin{array}{r} \$1.35 \\ \times\ 10 \\ \hline 000 \\ +\ 1350 \\ \hline \$13.50 \end{array}$

Guided Practice

Multiply.

1. 241
    × 14

2. 305
    × 32

3. $1.32
    × 60

4. 574
    × 82

5. 86 × 427

6. 64 × 285

7. 42 × 975

Ask Yourself

- What numbers are multiplied first?
- What numbers are multiplied next?
- What do I add to find the product?

Explain Your Thinking ▶ What are the least and the greatest number of digits possible in the product when you multiply a three-digit number by a two-digit number?

Practice and Problem Solving

Multiply. Estimate to make sure your answer is reasonable.

8. $1.32
    × 20

9. 121
    × 43

10. 208
     × 52

11. 496
     × 71

12. 500
     × 85

13. $4.30
     × 50

14. 734
     × 24

15. 260
     × 65

16. 109
     × 72

17. 482
     × 39

18. 30 × $1.49

19. 46 × 544

20. 94 × 263

21. 81 × 719

 Algebra • Inequalities Compare. Write >, <, or = for each ⬤.

22. 56 × 24 ⬤ 25 × 56

23. (16 + 14) × 30 ⬤ 900

24. 2 × 425 ⬤ 2 × 400

Data **Use the table on Page 184 for Problems 25–26.**

25. In 12 months, Ms. Crawford walks 1,008 miles on her job. What is Ms. Crawford's job?

26. **Multistep** How many miles more does a police officer walk in a year than a mail carrier?

Mixed Review and Test Prep

Open Response

Multiply. (Ch. 6, Lesson 7)

27. 9 × 78

28. 6 × 325

29. 7 × 2,040

30. 5 × 13,125

31. Hala works 20 hours and earns $9.50 an hour. Bill works 30 hours and earns $7.50 an hour. Who earns more? (Ch. 7, Lesson 6)

Extra Practice See page 191, Set D.

Multiply Greater Numbers

Objective Multiply four- and five-digit numbers by two-digit numbers.

Learn About It

Ms. Julian is designing a Web site for her company. The company expects about 2,250 hits a day when the site is online. How many hits does the company expect in 31 days?

Multiply. $31 \times 2,250 = n$

Different Ways to Multiply $31 \times 2,250$

Way 1 Use pencil and paper.

STEP 1 Multiply 2,250 by 1 one.

```
  2,250
×    31
  2250
```

STEP 2 Multiply 2,250 by 3 tens.

```
    1
  2,250
×    31
  2250
 67500
```

STEP 3 Add the products.

```
     1
  2,250
×    31
  2250   ← 2,250 × 1
+ 67500  ← 2,250 × 30
 69,750  ← (2,250 × 1) +
           (2,250 × 30)
```

Way 2 Use a calculator.

Enter: 2 2 5 0

Press: ×

Enter: 3 1

Press: =

Solution:  69750

Check Your Answer
Estimate to be sure your answer is reasonable.

31 rounds to 30
2,250 rounds to 2,000
30 × 2,000 = 60,000

69,750 is close to 60,000.

Solution: The company expects 69,750 hits in 31 days.

Other Examples

A. Five-Digit Number

```
   1 1 1
   2 3 2
  21685
×    24
  86740
+ 433700
 520,440
```

B. Money

```
     1 2
  $12.45
×     41
   1245
+ 49800
 $510.45
```

C. Multiply with Zeros

```
   1   1
  3,506
×    20
   0000
+ 70120
  70,120
```

Guided Practice

Multiply. Estimate to check your work.

1. $31.45 × 10   2. 64 × 3,950

3. 40 × $241.28   4. 26 × 19,275

Ask Yourself
- Did I record all the zeros?
- How can I estimate to check my work?

Explain Your Thinking ▶ How do you know where to place the decimal point in the answer to Exercise 3? Explain.

Practice and Problem Solving

 Multiply. Estimate to check your work.

5. 1,342 × 23	6. 5,121 × 43	7. 5,004 × 85	8. $26.96 × 70	9. 21,814 × 52

10. 4,832 × 50	11. 7,534 × 24	12. 4,862 × 93	13. 1,019 × 32	14. $312.65 × 60

15. 60 × 1,249   16. 46 × 6,225   17. 90 × $58.25   18. 17 × 9,644

Use mental math, paper and pencil, or a calculator to solve.

19. 190 × 51   20. 18 × 326   21. 38 × 41,624   22. 90 × 2,000

Go On

Use the Distributive Property to find each missing number.

23. $40 \times \blacksquare = (40 \times 5{,}000) + (40 \times 20) + (40 \times 5)$

24. $50 \times 62{,}159 = (50 \times \blacksquare) + (50 \times \blacksquare) + (50 \times 100) + (50 \times 50) + (50 \times 9)$

25. $\blacksquare \times 45{,}783 = (30 \times \blacksquare) + (\blacksquare \times \blacksquare) + (\blacksquare \times \blacksquare) + (\blacksquare \times \blacksquare) + (\blacksquare \times \blacksquare)$

Choose a Computation Method

Mental Math • Estimation • Paper and Pencil • Calculator

Solve. Tell which method you chose.

26. Kara's dad charges $85.50 an hour to design a Web site. He designed a Web site for 60 hours. How much did he earn?

27. An electronics superstore sells about 175 computers a day. About how many computers does it sell in 2 weeks?

28. **Money** Shelly purchased 3 gifts from an online auction store. Each gift cost $19.99. What was the total amount that she paid?

29. An online store filled 807 orders in January, 723 in February, and 1,026 in March. How many orders did it fill in these three months?

Data The pictograph shows the number of hits to a music Web site. Use the pictograph for Problems 30–33.

30. How many hits did the Web site have in November?

31. How many more hits did the site have in November than in December?

32. What was the total number of hits in October and November?

33. **Multistep** If the average sale of CDs on the site was $15 per hit, about what were the sales during September?

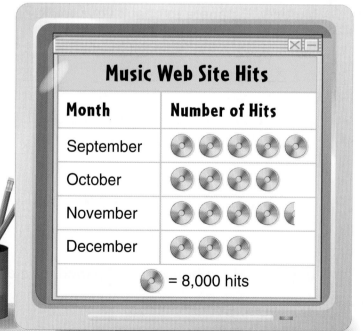

Music Web Site Hits

Month	Number of Hits
September	💿 💿 💿 💿 💿
October	💿 💿 💿 💿
November	💿 💿 💿 💿 💿
December	💿 💿 💿

💿 = 8,000 hits

Extra Practice See page 191, Set E.

Open Response

Use basic facts and patterns to find each product. (Chapter 7, Lesson 1)

34. 3 × 40

35. 30 × 40

36. 300 × 40

37. 3,000 × 40

Use a calculator to solve.
(Chapter 7, Lesson 7)

38. Tom's Web site gets about 4,650 hits every month. About how many hits will it get in 22 months?

Math Reasoning
Missing Products

Problem Solving

Farmer Brown is not happy because Hungry Harry, his goat, took a few bites out of his farm bill. The partly eaten bill below shows how many of each item Farmer Brown ordered. It also shows how much 1 item cost.

What's missing? Write a new bill for Farmer Brown that is complete.

Farmer Brown's Bill			
Quantity	**Item**	**Each**	**Total**
5	Alfalfa Bunches	$4.50	$22.50
30	Corn Kernel Packets	$1.55	$
	Bags of Fertilizer	$11.00	$110.00
18	Patches of Grass	$3.35	$
		Total	$239.30

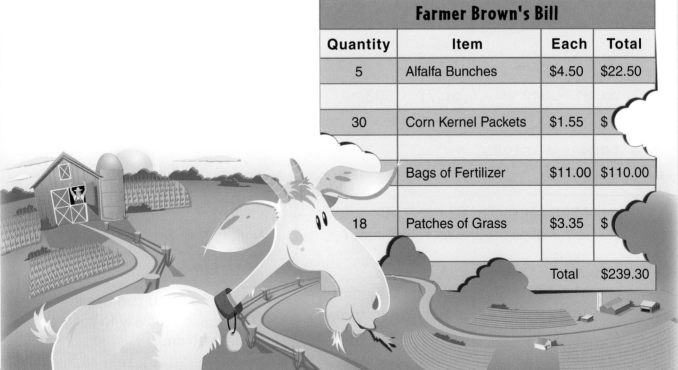

Chapter Review/Test

VOCABULARY

Choose the best term to complete each sentence.

Vocabulary
round
estimate
Distributive
Property
Associative
Property

1. A reasonable ____ of 29 × 52 is 1,500.

2. An example of the ____ is
4 × (5 + 6) = (4 × 5) + (4 × 6).

3. An example of the ____ is
2 × (3 × 8) = (2 × 3) × 8.

CONCEPTS AND SKILLS

Use basic facts and patterns to find each product. (Lesson 1, pp. 172–173)

4. 50 × 30 **5.** 60 × 400 **6.** 80 × 5,000 **7.** 20 × 7,000

Estimate each product. (Lesson 2, pp. 174–175)

8. 23 × 79 **9.** 87 × 498 **10.** 15 × 2,137 **11.** 91 × $18.75

Multiply. (Lessons 3, 4, 6, 7, pp. 176–181, 184–188)

12.	3,741	**13.**	3,847	**14.**	$18.95	**15.**	36,124
	× 14		× 60		× 20		× 26

16. 12 × 15 **17.** 13 × 22 **18.** 24 × 39 **19.** 67 × 59

20. 21 × 642 **21.** 77 × 803 **22.** 40 × $6.50 **23.** 38 × 720

PROBLEM SOLVING

Solve. (Lesson 5, p. 182)

24. Martin multiplies 62 by 99. His answer is 1,116. Is his answer reasonable? Explain.

25. Mrs. Lee bakes muffins for a muffin swap. She needs a dozen muffins for each of 25 people at the swap. Will 300 muffins be enough? Explain.

 Write About It

Show You Understand

• Explain how you can use the Associative Property to multiply 25 by 20.

• Explain how you can use the Distributive Property to solve the same problem.

Extra Practice

Set A (Lesson 1, pp. 172–173)

Use basic facts and patterns to find each product.

1. 30 × 90   **2.** 60 × 400   **3.** 80 × 7,000   **4.** 50 × 600

5. 70 × 70   **6.** 30 × 80   **7.** 20 × 900   **8.** 50 × 8,000

Set B (Lesson 2, pp. 174–175)

Estimate each product.

1. 12 × 18   **2.** 16 × 22   **3.** 39 × 416   **4.** 55 × 621

5. 44 × $52.35   **6.** 19 × 5,688   **7.** 61 × 3,195   **8.** 73 × 6,796

Set C (Lesson 4, pp. 178–181)

Multiply.

1. 43	**2.** 27	**3.** 39	**4.** 58	**5.** 82
× 22	× 18	× 46	× 75	× 61

Set D (Lesson 6, pp. 184–185)

Multiply.

1. 190	**2.** 206	**3.** 399	**4.** $5.07	**5.** 729
× 14	× 28	× 37	× 60	× 15

Set E (Lesson 7, pp. 186–188)

Multiply.

1. 1,960	**2.** 5,040	**3.** 16,142	**4.** $263.99	**5.** 41,038
× 20	× 86	× 29	× 50	× 18

Trips Around the Sun

Each planet in our solar system takes a different amount of time to orbit, or travel in its path around, the Sun. The amount of time it takes to complete one orbit is called a year. The farther away from the Sun a planet is, the larger its orbit is. That means its year is longer, too.

A year on Earth is about 365 days. Just think, for each birthday you have, Earth completes one orbit of the Sun. That's a trip of many millions of miles!

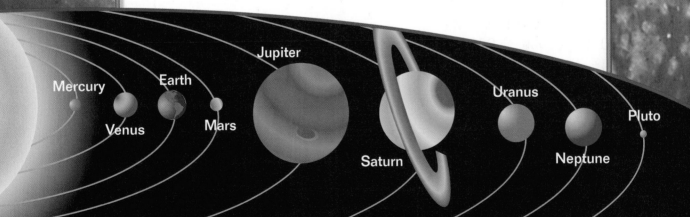

Mercury

Venus

Earth

Mars

Jupiter

Saturn

Uranus

Neptune

Pluto

Not to scale.

Problem Solving

The table shows the length of one year on some planets in our solar system. Use the table to solve Problems 1–5.

Planet Years	
Planet	**Time for One Orbit Around Sun (in Earth Years)**
Earth	1
Jupiter	12
Mars	2
Neptune	164
Pluto	248
Saturn	29
Uranus	84

1 Saturn has a larger orbit than Earth has. If Saturn makes 10 orbits around the Sun, how many years will have passed on Earth?

2 Suppose Jupiter makes 7 orbits around the Sun. How many orbits can Uranus make in the same amount of time?

3 Are six Neptune years greater than or less than a millennium on Earth? (Hint: a millennium is 1,000 years.)

4 In the last 1,500 Earth years, about how many times has Pluto orbited the Sun?

5 **Analyze** How do you think the distance from Mars to the Sun compares to the distance from Earth to the Sun? Explain your reasoning.

Education Place

Visit Weekly Reader Connections at **eduplace.com/map** for more on this topic.

Enrichment: Gelosia Multiplication

Before people had calculators and computers, they had other ways to multiply large numbers. One way became popular in Europe in the 1400s. It is known as Gelosia Multiplication.

You can use this method to find the product of 423 and 57.

 STEP 1 Make a grid like the one on the right.

 **STEP 2** Begin at the top right. Multiply 3 × 5. Write the product as shown, with the tens digit above the diagonal.

STEP 3 Continue to fill in the grid by multiplying the numbers for each box.

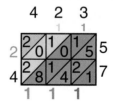 **STEP 4** Begin at the lower right. Add numbers in the diagonals. Regroup tens to the next diagonal on the left. Read the answer from top to bottom and left to right.

423 × 57 = 24,111

Try These!

Use Gelosia Multiplication to solve.

1. 48 × 35   2. 26 × 13   3. 487 × 83   4. 528 × 76   5. 2,017 × 21

6. **Analyze** How is Gelosia Multiplication like the multiplication method you know?

Did You Know?

Use a calculator to help you solve the problems below.

Suppose an opossum sleeps 18 hours a day and a giraffe only sleeps 2 hours a day.

1. About how many hours does an opossum sleep in a week? a year?

2. About how many hours does a giraffe sleep in a week? a year?

3. About how many hours do you sleep each day? About how many hours do you sleep in a week? a year?

Did you know that an elephant's heart beats about 28 times a minute? A shrew's heart beats about 1,100 times a minute!

4. About how many times does an elephant's heart beat in a day?

5. About how many times does a shrew's heart beat in a day?

6. In one week, about how many more times does a shrew's heart beat than an elephant's?

7. How many times does your heart beat in a minute? About how many times does it beat in a year? Explain how you got your answer.

Unit 3 Test

VOCABULARY ⬤ Open Response

Choose the correct term to complete each sentence.

Vocabulary

factors
product
Associative Property
Distributive Property
Commutative Property

1. The number sentences 5 × 4 = 20 and 4 × 5 = 20 are examples of the ____.

2. Two or more numbers that are multiplied together are called ____.

3. You can change how the factors of a multiplication problem are grouped by using the ____.

4. If you find 24 × 13 by thinking (24 × 10) + (24 × 3), you are using the ____.

CONCEPTS AND SKILLS ⬤ Open Response

Use mental math to find each product. (Chapters 6, 7)

5. 70 × 4

6. 900 × 3

7. 500 × 4

8. 8,000 × 2

9. 60 × 20

10. 500 × 60

11. 300 × 40

12. 70 × 4,000

Estimate each product. (Chapters 6, 7)

13. 88
    × 7

14. 511
    × 3

15. 701
    × 8

16. $48.02
    × 6

17. 73
    × 18

18. 303
    × 97

19. 213
    × 12

20. 2,345
    × 31

Find each product. (Chapters 6, 7)

21. 62
    × 9

22. 590
    × 5

23. $54.12
    × 7

24. 31,242
    × 3

25. 71
    × 23

26. 237
    × 56

27. 365
    × 34

28. 4,812
    × 33

29. 88 × 3

30. 372 × 9

31. 4,820 × 5

32. 34 × 15

33. $7.14 × 40

34. 36,009 × 42

196

Use the Distributive Property to find each product. (Chapter 7)

35. 43×12 **36.** 24×11 **37.** 37×21 **38.** 62×17

PROBLEM SOLVING   Open Response

Solve. Explain why your answer is reasonable. (Chapters 6, 7)

39. The product of Joan's age and her younger brother's age is 36. The sum of their ages is 15. How old are Joan and her brother?

40. Angelo's book has 388 pages. Angelo reads 20 pages a night for one week. At the end of the week, how many pages does he have left to read?

Performance Assessment

Extended Response

Fundraiser Prices		
Item	**Cost to Buy**	**Selling Price**
CD	$2.50	$7.00
T-shirt	$3.00	$8.00
Hat	$2.00	$5.00
Magnet	$0.00	$1.00

Task Mrs. Rhodes runs fund-raisers at school chorus concerts. She has $200 to buy items to sell at the next concert. She wants to have sales of at least $500.

Use the information above and on the right to decide what items Mrs. Rhodes should buy. Be sure to decide how many of each item she should buy. Explain the reasons for your choices.

Information You Need

- Mrs. Rhodes wants to sell at least 3 different types of items.
- All items must be ordered in sets of 10.
- Mrs. Rhodes has never sold more than 30 T-shirts at one event.
- The Parent Organization donated 50 magnets for Mrs. Rhodes to sell.

Cumulative Test Prep

Solve Problems 1–10.

Test-Taking Tip

Sometimes it is helpful to look for the key words in a problem. Sometimes they are capitalized, in italics, or in bold print.

Look at the example below.

For which of the following would you *not* use the number sentence 80 × 30 to estimate the product?

  A 83 × 34

  B 84 × 31

  C 86 × 32

  D 82 × 33

THINK

The key word is *not*. You need to find a factor that does not round to 80 or 30. In answer choice **C**, 86 rounds to 90, so the correct answer is **C**.

Multiple Choice

1. Olga picked 28 apples. She gave some to her brother. Now she has 13 apples. Which equation shows what happened?

  A $28 - x = 13$ **C** $28 - 13 = b$

  B $z - 28 = 13$ **D** $13 - c = 28$

(Chapter 5, Lesson 4)

2. How is three hundred one thousand, thirteen written in standard form?

  F 31,013   **H** 301,013

  G 31,113   **J** 301,130

(Chapter 1, Lesson 2)

3. Marisa had $20.50 to buy a present. She wanted to have at least $8.00 left over. What is the *greatest* amount she can spend and still have $8.00?

  A $8.00   **C** $12.50

  B $10.00   **D** $13.00

(Chapter 3, Lesson 7)

4. One small glass of orange juice costs $1.50 and 1 large glass costs $2.25. Which amount is a possible cost for 4 glasses of orange juice?

  F $3.75   **H** $5.50

  G $4.25   **J** $7.50

(Chapter 7, Lesson 5)

For Test-Taking Tips, See page 658.

5. What is the difference when you subtract 763 from 3,872? Explain how you can check your answer.

(Chapter 3, Lesson 6)

6. Devon has 87 sunflower seeds. He gives each of his 9 friends an equal number of seeds. If he gives each friend as many seeds as possible, how many will Devon have left for himself?

(Chapter 4, Lesson 8)

7. Describe the pattern. Then tell how many squares will be in the next figure.

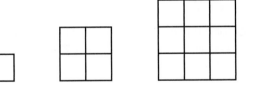

(Chapter 4, Lesson 3)

8. Explain how you can use mental math to determine which product is greater, 600 × 20 or 600 × 200.

(Chapter 7, Lesson 1)

9. The product of two numbers is 130. Their sum is 23. What are the two numbers? What strategy did you use to get your answer?

(Chapter 6, Lesson 5)

10. Study the table below.

X	Y	Z
1	8	8
3	11	33
■	16	■
7	23	■
■	■	288
11	■	473

A Describe the pattern in column X. Then find the missing numbers.

B Describe the pattern in column Y. Then find the missing numbers.

C How can you use columns X and Y to find the missing numbers in column Z? Find the missing numbers in column Z.

D Suppose there was one more row across the bottom of the chart. What numbers would be in columns X, Y, and Z?

(Chapter 7, Lesson 7)

Education Place

Look for Cumulative Test Prep at **eduplace.com/map** for more practice.

Vocabulary Wrap-Up for **Unit 3**

Look back at the big ideas and vocabulary in this unit.

Big Ideas

You can estimate the product by rounding the factors.

You can use the Commutative, Distributive, and Associative Properties to rewrite multiplication problems.

Key Vocabulary

product
factor
Commutative Property
Distributive Property
Associative Property

Math Conversations

Use your new vocabulary to discuss these big ideas.

1. Explain how you would use the Distributive Property and mental math to multiply 25 and 14.

2. Explain how multiplying 627×8 and 627×38 are similar. Explain how they are different.

3. Explain how you can use mental math to multiply $5,000 \times 4,000$.

4. Explain how to regroup to multiply 4×167.

5. **Write About It** What is the cost of one issue of your favorite magazine? What is the cost of a one-year subscription? Does it cost more or less to subscribe than to buy each issue separately? Why do you think the publisher does this?

According to my calculator, $14 \times 7 = 98$.

If that's true, then $7 \times 14 = 98$, as well.

UNIT

4

Division
of
Whole
Numbers

Reading Mathematics

Reviewing Vocabulary

Here are some math vocabulary words that you should know.

array   an arrangement of objects, pictures, or numbers in columns and rows

dividend   the number that is being divided

divisor   the number by which the dividend is divided

quotient   the answer in a division problem.

Reading Words and Symbols

When you divide, you separate a number into equal groups. All of the statements below, and the image below, can be used to represent the same division problem.

- Fifteen divided by three equals what number?
- 15 divided by 3 = ?
- $15 \div 3 = n$
- $3\overline{)15}$

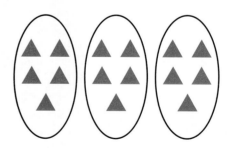

Use words and symbols to describe each array.

1.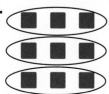

2.

3.

Reading Test Questions

Choose the correct answer for each.

4. Which number statement below is not correct?

    a. $15 \div 3 = 5$

    b. $14 \div 2 = 7$

    c. $11 \div 3 = 4$

    d. $9 \div 3 = 3$

A **number statement** uses symbols to show how numbers are related.

5. Which of the following tells how to divide 30 oranges into 3 equal groups?

    a. 2 groups of 15

    b. 3 groups of 5

    c. 3 groups of 10

    d. 10 groups of 3

Equal groups means "groups with the same number of objects."

6. Tell what the variable stands for in this problem.

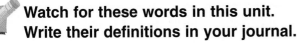

$$4 \overline{)n} \quad 6$$

    a. dividend   **b.** divisor

    c. quotient   **d.** remainder

A **variable** is a letter or a symbol that stands for a number. The variable in the problem above is *n*.

Learning Vocabulary

Watch for these words in this unit. Write their definitions in your journal.

    factor

    multiple

    prime number

    composite number

Education Place

At **eduplace.com/map**
see eGlossary and
eGames–Math Lingo.

Literature Connection

Read "But I'm Not Tired" on Pages 648–649. Then work with a partner to answer the questions about the story.

Understand Division

INVESTIGATION

Using Data

Ricardo and Mike bought a box of baseball cards for their collections. Look at the table. How can you find out how many cards Ricardo will get if the two boys share the cards equally?

Baseball Cards in Box

Position	Number of Cards
Baseman	25
Catcher	6
Outfielder	36
Pitcher	10
Shortstop	3

Use What You Know

**Use this page to review and remember
what you need to know for this chapter.**

VOCABULARY

Choose the best word to complete each sentence.

1. In the division sentence 8 ÷ 2 = 4, the _____ is 2.

2. In the division sentence 15 ÷ 3 = 5, the _____ is 15.

3. When you divide 12 by 3, the _____ is 4.

CONCEPTS AND SKILLS

Write a division fact for each picture.

4.    5.

6.   7.

Write two related multiplication facts for each division fact.

8. 6 ÷ 3 = 2	9. 18 ÷ 9 = 2	10. 24 ÷ 4 = 6	11. 35 ÷ 5 = 7
12. 56 ÷ 8 = 7	13. 42 ÷ 6 = 7	14. 54 ÷ 9 = 6	15. 72 ÷ 8 = 9

Divide.

16. $6\overline{)6}$ 17. $6\overline{)60}$ 18. $9\overline{)81}$ 19. $7\overline{)35}$

 **Write About It**

20. Explain how you could use multiplication
to find the missing numbers.

32 ÷ ■ = 8   ■ ÷ 7 = 2

Facts Practice, See Page 668.

Audio Tutor 1/27 Listen and Understand

Model Division

Objective Use models to understand division.

Materials
base-ten blocks

Work Together

You can use base-ten blocks to model division.

Work with a partner to divide 84 by 4.

STEP 1

Use base-ten blocks to show 84.

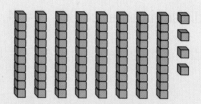

STEP 2

Start by dividing the 8 tens into 4 equal groups.

- How many tens are in each group?

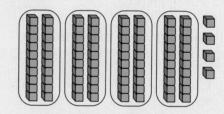

STEP 3

Next, divide the 4 ones into the same 4 equal groups.

- How many ones are in each group?

- How many tens and ones are in each group?

Write a number sentence to show the division.

▶ **Remember:** A number that is left when you divide is called the **remainder**.

Work with a partner to find 65 ÷ 2.

STEP 1   Use base-ten blocks to show 65.

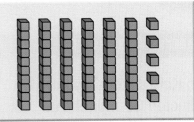

STEP 2   Divide the 6 tens into 2 equal groups.
 - How many tens are in each group?

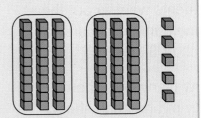

STEP 3   Try to divide the 5 ones into 2 equal groups.
 - How many ones are in each group?
 - How many ones are left?

Write a number sentence to show the division.

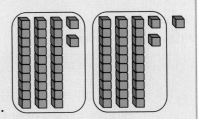

On Your Own

Use base-ten blocks to complete the table.

	Number	Number of Equal Groups	Number in Each Group	Number Left	Number Sentence
1.	85	4	■	1	85 ÷ 4 → 21 R1
2.	63	3	■	■	■
3.	28	■	14	■	■

Talk About It • Write About It

You learned to use models to show division.

4. Explain how dividing tens is like dividing ones.

5. **What's Wrong?** Ali divided 14 tennis balls into 4 groups as shown on the right. Explain what is wrong.

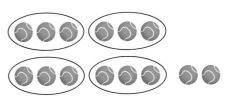

$14 \div 4 = 3$

Lesson 2

◉ **Audio Tutor 1/28** Listen and Understand

Divide With Remainders

Objective Find two-digit quotients with and without remainders.

Learn About It

Mr. King's students have collected 38 model cars to put on display. The students want to put the same number of cars on each of 3 shelves.

How many cars should they put on each shelf?

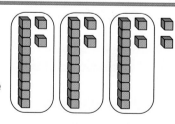

Remember

The remainder is the amount that is left over when a number cannot be divided equally.

Divide. $38 \div 3$ **or** $3\overline{)38}$

STEP 1	You can use base-ten blocks to represent the 38 cars.	number of groups → cars in each group $3\overline{)38}$ ← cars in all

STEP 2	Divide the 3 tens into 3 equal groups. Put 1 ten in each group.	$\begin{array}{r} 1 \\ 3\overline{)38} \\ -3 \\ \hline 0 \end{array}$ Multiply. 1 ten × 3 ← Subtract. 3 − 3 Compare. 0 < 3

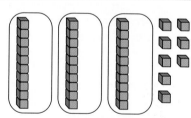

STEP 3	Try to divide the 8 ones into 3 equal groups. Put 2 ones in each group. There are 2 ones left.	$\begin{array}{r} 12 \text{ R2} \\ 3\overline{)38} \\ -3\downarrow \\ \hline 08 \\ -6 \\ \hline 2 \end{array}$ Bring down 8 ones. ← Multiply. 2 ones × 3 Subtract. 8 − 6 Compare. 2 < 3

The amount left is called the remainder. → 2
It should always be less than the divisor.

Solution: The students should put 12 cars on each shelf.
There will be 2 cars left over.

208

Extra Help at **eduplace.com/map**

Guided Practice

Divide. Tell if there is a remainder.

1. $3\overline{)39}$ **2.** $2\overline{)85}$ **3.** $2\overline{)47}$ **4.** $5\overline{)57}$

5. $66 \div 3$ **6.** $85 \div 4$ **7.** $34 \div 3$ **8.** $94 \div 3$

Ask Yourself
- Can I divide the tens?
- Can I divide the ones?
- Are there any ones left?

Explain Your Thinking ▶ How can you tell if the remainder is too large?

Practice and Problem Solving

Divide. Tell if there is a remainder.

9. $4\overline{)87}$ **10.** $5\overline{)55}$ **11.** $2\overline{)63}$ **12.** $3\overline{)68}$ **13.** $2\overline{)69}$

14. $78 \div 7$ **15.** $69 \div 6$ **16.** $26 \div 2$ **17.** $65 \div 3$ **18.** $29 \div 2$

X Algebra • **Symbols** Write > or < for each ⬤.

19. $24 \div 4$ ⬤ $48 \div 2$ **20.** $36 \div 3$ ⬤ $60 \div 3$ **21.** $48 \div 3$ ⬤ $48 \div 4$

22. $66 \div 3$ ⬤ $60 \div 2$ **23.** $99 \div 3$ ⬤ $99 \div 9$ **24.** $39 \div 3$ ⬤ $48 \div 4$

Solve.

25. José has 67 model cars in his collection. He wants to share them equally among 3 friends. How many cars will each friend get?

26. Money Jennifer has $29. She buys 2 model-car kits. Each kit costs the same amount. She has $1 left. How much does each kit cost?

27. How many different ways can 16 model cars be arranged in equal rows so there are at least 3 cars in each row and 1 car in a row by itself?

28. Multistep A shop sells 25 model cars for $9 each. It also sells 35 model trucks for $10 each. How much more does the shop receive for the model trucks than for the model cars?

Mixed Review and Test Prep

Open Response

Round each number to the nearest thousand. (Ch. 2, Lesson 5)

29. 3,762   **30.** 112,155   **31.** 876

32. 16,023   **33.** 7,864   **34.** 35,561

35. Can 58 model cars be divided into 5 equal groups? Why or why not? (Ch. 8, Lesson 2)

Extra Practice See page 225, Set A.

Audio Tutor 1/29 Listen and Understand

Problem-Solving Application
Interpret Remainders

Objective Interpret a remainder to find
a reasonable answer.

When you solve a problem that has a remainder,
you need to decide how to interpret the remainder.

▶ **Sometimes you increase the quotient.**

Mrs. Ross puts 4 old post cards on
each page of her scrapbook.
How many pages does she need
for 49 post cards?

Mrs. Ross needs 13 pages.

$$
\begin{array}{r}
12\ \text{R1} \\
4\overline{)49} \\
-4 \\
\hline
09 \\
-8 \\
\hline
1
\end{array}
$$

Twelve pages will hold 48 cards.
Another page is needed for the 1 extra
card. So increase the quotient.

▶ **Sometimes you drop the remainder.**

An exhibit of old post cards is on
display at a museum for 79 days.
How many full weeks is that?

Seventy-nine days are 11 full weeks.

$$
\begin{array}{r}
11\ \text{R2} \\
7\overline{)79} \\
-7 \\
\hline
09 \\
-7 \\
\hline
2
\end{array}
$$

There are 7 days in a week.
So 79 days are 11 full weeks and 2 days.
Drop the remainder.

▶ **Sometimes the remainder is the answer.**

Mrs. Ross has 86 post cards.
She divides them equally among
4 children and keeps the extras.
How many post cards does she
keep?

Mrs. Ross keeps 2 post cards.

$$
\begin{array}{r}
21\ \text{R2} \\
4\overline{)86} \\
-8 \\
\hline
06 \\
-4 \\
\hline
2
\end{array}
$$

Each child will get 21 post
cards. There are 2 extra post cards.
The remainder is the answer.

Look Back How does thinking about the question help you decide
what to do with the remainder?

Guided Practice

Use the Ask Yourself questions to help you solve each problem.

1. Mrs. Webster wants to buy a post card for each of 68 fourth-graders. The post cards come in packages of 3. How many packages does Mrs. Webster need to buy?

2. Every day, Mr. Lun displays 3 post cards for his class. Mr. Lun has 38 post cards. He will not display fewer than 3 cards on any day. How many days will Mr. Lun display post cards?

Ask Yourself

- Do I need to increase the quotient?
- Do I need to drop the remainder?
- Is the remainder the answer?

Independent Practice

Solve. Explain why your answer makes sense.

3. Suzanne is placing post cards in her scrapbook, beginning with page 1. She puts 3 post cards on each page. She is placing the ninety-fifth post card. Which page is it on?

4. **Money** Mr. Greene buys as many $6 post-card books as he can with $68. How much money does Mr. Greene have left after he buys the post-card books?

5. Fifty-nine fourth-graders are touring a printing plant. Only 5 students can see a printing demonstration at one time. How many times does the demonstration have to be given so that all 59 students can see it?

6. **Create and Solve** Write two word problems, one that you solve by dropping the remainder and one in which the remainder is the answer.

Go On

Chapter 8 Lesson 3 **211**

Mixed Problem Solving

Solve. Show your work. Tell what strategy you used.

7. Vicky has twice as many shells as fossils in her collection. If she has 45 fossils and shells, how many fossils does she have?

8. Ruth and Paul sold 34 tickets to a play. Ruth sold 6 more tickets than Paul. How many tickets did each person sell?

9. Look at the sequence of numbers.

   | 5 | 10 | 15 | 20 | 25 |

   If the pattern continues, what will be the tenth number in the sequence?

10. Use these clues to find a mystery number.
    - It is less than 40.
    - When you divide it by 5 or 6, the remainder is 1.

You Choose

Strategy
- Find a Pattern
- Guess and Check
- Make an Organized List
- Make a Table
- Write an Equation

Computation Method
- Mental Math
- Estimation
- Paper and Pencil
- Calculator

Solve. Tell which method you chose.

11. **Multistep** A band has 2 rows of 3 saxophones, 3 rows of 4 clarinets, 4 rows of 2 flutes, 2 rows of 5 trumpets, and 1 row of 3 drums. How many musicians are in the band?

12. Seats in an auditorium are arranged in 12 rows of 20 seats. Each seat is filled, and 9 people are standing. How many people are in the auditorium?

13. One collector spent $98.75 on stamps. A second collector spent $67.68 on stamps. How much more did the first collector spend than the second?

14. **Money** Is $10 enough to buy a grilled-cheese sandwich for $3.60, a salad for $2.75, and a small juice for $1.25?

212

Math Challenge
Side-by-Side Division

Materials: Paper Squares (Learning Tool 12)

Make square cards like the ones shown or use Learning Tool 12.

- When you find a number on one card that is the exact divisor of a number on another card, place the numbers side by side.

- Find other matches. Every time you match sides, give yourself one point. The most points you can get are 12.

The number 3 is an exact divisor of 36.

$$36 \div 3 = 12$$

Score 1 point.

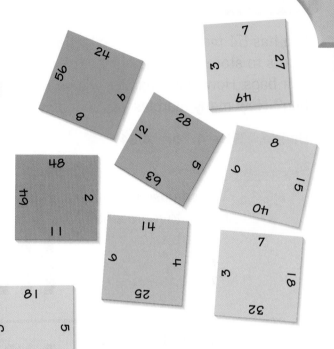

Check your understanding of Lessons 1–3.

Divide. (Lessons 1–2)

1. $2\overline{)42}$
2. $3\overline{)36}$
3. $4\overline{)48}$
4. $3\overline{)96}$

5. $5\overline{)56}$
6. $2\overline{)85}$
7. $3\overline{)65}$
8. $6\overline{)68}$

Solve. (Lesson 3)

9. Sarah has 49 coins in her collection. If she wants to place 4 coins on each page of her coin album, how many pages will she use?

10. Mr. Torres has 23 chairs in his class. He wants to divide the chairs into 2 equal rows. How many chairs will not be in the 2 rows?

Regroup in Division

Objective Regroup to divide two-digit numbers.

Vocabulary

divisor

quotient

dividend

regroup

Learn About It

Ella has 54 marbles in her collection. She wants to store the same number of marbles in four bags. How many marbles will be in each bag? How many marbles will be left?

Divide. $54 \div 4$ **or** $4\overline{)54}$

STEP 1 You can use base-ten blocks to represent the 54 marbles.

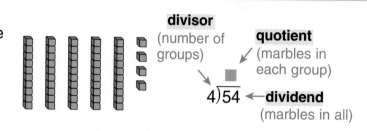

divisor (number of groups)

quotient (marbles in each group)

$4\overline{)54}$ ← **dividend** (marbles in all)

STEP 2 Try to divide 5 tens into 4 equal groups. Put 1 ten in each group. There is 1 ten left.

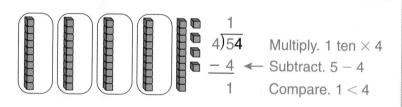

$\begin{array}{r} 1 \\ 4\overline{)54} \\ -4 \\ \hline 1 \end{array}$

Multiply. 1 ten × 4
← Subtract. 5 − 4
Compare. 1 < 4

STEP 3 **Regroup** the 1 ten left as 10 ones.

10 ones + 4 ones = 14 ones

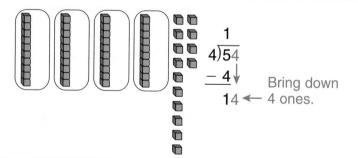

$\begin{array}{r} 1 \\ 4\overline{)54} \\ -4\downarrow \\ \hline 14 \end{array}$

Bring down
← 4 ones.

STEP 4 Divide the 14 ones. Put 3 ones in each group. There are 2 ones left. 2 is less than the divisor, so it is the remainder.

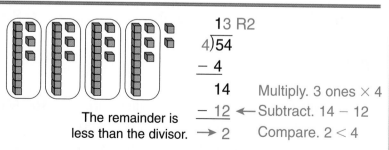

The remainder is less than the divisor.

$\begin{array}{r} 13 \text{ R2} \\ 4\overline{)54} \\ -4 \\ \hline 14 \\ -12 \\ \hline 2 \end{array}$

Multiply. 3 ones × 4
←Subtract. 14 − 12
Compare. 2 < 4

Solution: Thirteen marbles will be in each bag. There will be 2 marbles left.

Here is a way to check that an answer is correct.

Check 54 ÷ 4 → 13 R2.

- Multiply the quotient by the divisor. $13 \times 4 = 52$
- Add the remainder. $52 + 2 = 54$

The sum equals the dividend, so the answer is correct.

Other Examples

A. Remainder of Zero

$$
\begin{array}{r}
15 \\
5\overline{)75} \\
-5 \\
\hline
25 \\
-25 \\
\hline
0
\end{array}
$$

Check:
$$
\begin{array}{r}
15 \\
\times 5 \\
\hline
75 \\
+0 \\
\hline
75
\end{array}
$$

B. Zero in the Dividend

$$
\begin{array}{r}
12\text{ R6} \\
7\overline{)90} \\
-7 \\
\hline
20 \\
-14 \\
\hline
6
\end{array}
$$

Check:
$$
\begin{array}{r}
12 \\
\times 7 \\
\hline
84 \\
+6 \\
\hline
90
\end{array}
$$

Use place value columns to help.

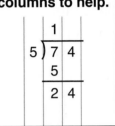

Guided Practice

Divide. Check your answers.

1. $5\overline{)74}$
2. $4\overline{)50}$
3. $6\overline{)79}$
4. $3\overline{)72}$

5. $40 \div 3$
6. $84 \div 5$
7. $78 \div 6$
8. $63 \div 4$

Ask Yourself
- When I divide the tens, are there any left?
- What should I do with any tens that are left?

Explain Your Thinking ▶ Look back at Example A. What would be a simpler answer check?

Practice and Problem Solving

Divide. Check your answers.

9. $2\overline{)62}$
10. $8\overline{)92}$
11. $6\overline{)74}$
12. $7\overline{)94}$
13. $8\overline{)96}$

14. $3\overline{)63}$
15. $2\overline{)76}$
16. $5\overline{)81}$
17. $4\overline{)49}$
18. $3\overline{)82}$

19. $80 \div 6$
20. $99 \div 7$
21. $65 \div 3$
22. $81 \div 7$
23. $64 \div 4$

Go On

Algebra • **Functions** Copy and complete each table.

	Rule: $y = x \div 3$	
	x	**y**
24.	54	■
25.	■	15
26.	66	■
27.	■	13

	Rule: $y = x \div 6$	
	x	**y**
28.	72	■
29.	66	■
30.	■	15
31.	■	14

32.

Rule: ___	
x	**y**
7	1
14	2
49	7
91	13

Data The graph shows the number of marbles in Ella's collection. Use the graph for Problems 38–40.

33. Ella wants to divide her aggies equally into two bags and give the leftover marbles to her sister. How many marbles will Ella give to her sister?

34. **Multistep** Ella and two friends are playing with all of Ella's marbles except the fiestas. If the marbles are divided equally, how many does each of the three girls have? How many marbles are left?

35. **Analyze** Ella wants to trade all her cat's eyes for twisters. She can get one twister for 3 cat's eyes. How many twisters will she have after the trade?

36. **Reasoning** Four marbles have prices of $1, $2, $3, and $5. An aggie costs less than a twister but more than a cat's eye. A fiesta is the most expensive. What is the cost of each marble?

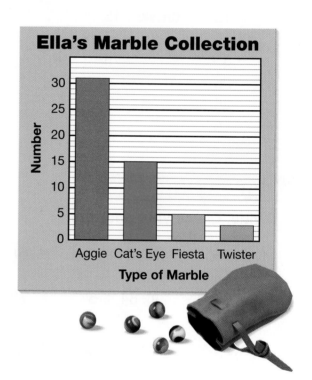

Ella's Marble Collection

Mixed Review and Test Prep

Open Response

Solve for _n_. (Ch. 5, Lesson 4)

37. $n = (2 \times 7) + 3$

38. $n + 15 = 3 \times 7$

39. $26 = (4 \times n) + 2$

40. $n = 4 + (5 \times 5)$

Multiple Choice

41. Abdul has 67 stamps. He places an equal number of stamps on each of 4 pages. How many stamps are left? (Ch. 8, Lesson 4)

A 1 stamp   **C** 3 stamps

B 2 stamps   **D** 5 stamps

216

Extra Practice See page 225, Set B.

Race for the Remainder

Activity

2 Players

What You'll Need • A number cube labeled 1 to 6
• A number cube labeled 4 to 9

How to Play

1 The first player rolls both number cubes to make a two-digit dividend.

2 The first player rolls a number cube labeled 4 to 9. The number rolled is the divisor.

3 The first player divides the dividend by the divisor. The second player checks that the quotient is correct.

4 The remainder is the number of points the first player receives.

Repeat steps 1 to 4.
Have players take turns.
The player to reach a
total of 30 or more
points first wins.

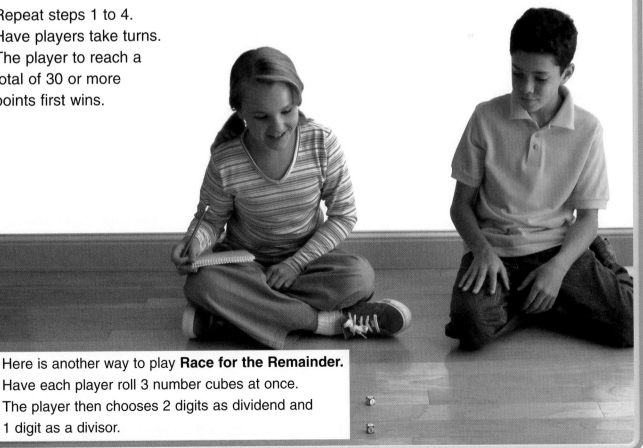

Here is another way to play **Race for the Remainder.**
Have each player roll 3 number cubes at once.
The player then chooses 2 digits as dividend and
1 digit as a divisor.

Divide Multiples of 10, 100, and 1,000

Objective Use basic facts and patterns to divide mentally.

Learn About It

The Delmar family collected pennies. When the jar was full, Mrs. Delmar gave the pennies to her three sons. They counted 1,500 pennies and shared them equally. How many pennies did each boy get?

Divide. $1,500 \div 3 =$ ■ or $3\overline{)1,500}$

Use the basic fact $15 \div 3 = 5$.

$$15 \div 3 = 5$$
$$150 \div 3 = 50$$
$$1,500 \div 3 = 500$$

2 zeros ⬑   ⬏ 2 zeros

What do you notice about the pattern of zeros?

Solution: Each boy got 500 pennies.

Guided Practice

Divide.

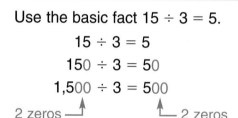

1. $48 \div 8 = 6$
    $480 \div 8 = 60$
    $4,800 \div 8 =$ ■

2. $21 \div 7 = 3$
    $210 \div 7 =$ ■
    $2,100 \div 7 =$ ■

3. $4,500 \div 9$

4. $900 \div 3$

5. $5,400 \div 9$

6. $4,000 \div 5$

Ask Yourself
- What basic fact can I use?
- How many zeros should be in the quotient?

Explain Your Thinking ▶ As the number of zeros in the dividend increases, what happens to the number of zeros in the quotient?

Divide.

7. $8 \div 4 = \blacksquare$
$80 \div 4 = \blacksquare$
$800 \div 4 = \blacksquare$

8. $9 \div 3 = \blacksquare$
$90 \div 3 = \blacksquare$
$900 \div 3 = \blacksquare$

9. $6 \div 2 = \blacksquare$
$60 \div 2 = \blacksquare$
$600 \div 2 = \blacksquare$

10. $270 \div 3 = \blacksquare$

11. $120 \div 2 = \blacksquare$

12. $160 \div 4 = \blacksquare$

13. $240 \div 8 = \blacksquare$

14. $120 \div 3 = \blacksquare$

15. $350 \div 7 = \blacksquare$

𝒳 Algebra • Equations Solve each equation.

16. $3{,}200 \div 4 = n$

17. $5{,}600 \div 8 = s$

18. $2{,}500 \div 5 = p$

19. $320 \div 8 = x$

20. $420 \div 6 = d$

21. $m \div 5 = 90$

22. $7{,}200 \div 8 = p$

23. $1{,}400 \div k = 700$

24. $b \div 9 = 700$

Solve.

25. Sela has 6 times as many coins now as she had 4 months ago. If Sela has 240 coins now, how many coins did she have 4 months ago?

 26. Write About It Robert sees a rare 1937 penny. The cost is $210. If he saves $3 every week, will Robert have enough money to buy the coin after one year? Explain your thinking.

27. Multistep Chip collected 289 dimes. Sue collected 191 dimes. They divided all their dimes into 8 stacks. If each stack had an equal number of dimes, how many dimes were in each stack?

Mixed Review and Test Prep

Free Response

Multiply. (Ch. 7, Lesson 7)

28. $\begin{array}{r} 352 \\ \times\ 11 \\ \hline \end{array}$

29. $\begin{array}{r} 1{,}468 \\ \times\ \ \ 32 \\ \hline \end{array}$

30. $\begin{array}{r} 12{,}914 \\ \times\ \ \ \ \ 26 \\ \hline \end{array}$

31. $\begin{array}{r} 621 \\ \times\ 43 \\ \hline \end{array}$

32. $\begin{array}{r} 3{,}823 \\ \times\ \ \ \ 27 \\ \hline \end{array}$

33. $\begin{array}{r} 20{,}584 \\ \times\ \ \ \ \ \ 30 \\ \hline \end{array}$

Multiple Choice

34. Which number sentence is **not** correct? (Ch. 8, Lesson 5)

A $150 \div 5 = 30$

C $4{,}500 \div 9 = 500$

B $400 \div 8 = 5{,}000$

D $5{,}600 \div 7 = 800$

Audio Tutor 1/30 Listen and Understand

Estimate Quotients

Objective Estimate quotients.

Learn About It

Maya Littlefeather collects and sells Native American crafts. One morning she sold 8 necklaces for $166. If each necklace sold for the same amount, about how much did each necklace sell for?

When you don't need an exact answer, you can estimate. An **estimate** tells about how much.

One way to estimate $166 ÷ 8 is to use basic facts and multiples of 10. Think of a new dividend close to $166 that is divisible by 8.

Estimate. 8)$166

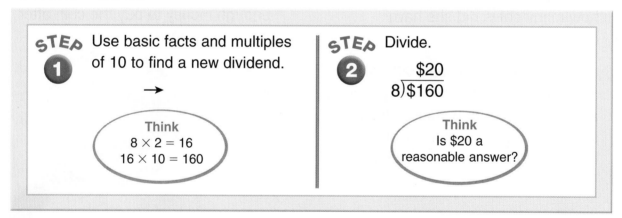

STEP 1 Use basic facts and multiples of 10 to find a new dividend.

→

Think
8 × 2 = 16
16 × 10 = 160

STEP 2 Divide.

$20
8)$160

Think
Is $20 a reasonable answer?

Solution: Each necklace sold for about $20.

Guided Practice

Estimate. Write the basic fact you used.

1. 5)28

2. 3)268

3. 8)310

4. 19 ÷ 4

5. 177 ÷ 6

6. 627 ÷ 9

Ask Yourself
• Which basic fact can help me choose a new dividend?
• Does the answer seem reasonable?

Explain Your Thinking ▶ How does the divisor help you choose a basic fact?

Practice and Problem Solving

Estimate. Write the basic fact you used.

7. $2\overline{)15}$ **8.** $3\overline{)25}$ **9.** $6\overline{)31}$ **10.** $4\overline{)35}$

11. $5\overline{)103}$ **12.** $7\overline{)409}$ **13.** $3\overline{)188}$ **14.** $2\overline{)157}$

15. $51 \div 6$ **16.** $22 \div 3$ **17.** $37 \div 6$ **18.** $338 \div 4$

19. $189 \div 5$ **20.** $123 \div 2$ **21.** $172 \div 8$ **22.** $263 \div 5$

Decide whether the actual quotient is greater than or less than the estimate given. Write < or > for each ⬤.

23. $13 \div 3$ ⬤ 4 **24.** $15 \div 4$ ⬤ 4 **25.** $41 \div 5$ ⬤ 8

26. $48 \div 5$ ⬤ 10 **27.** $19 \div 2$ ⬤ 9 **28.** $52 \div 5$ ⬤ 9

Solve.

29. Ms. Littlefeather has a collection of 128 Zuni carvings. She wants to place them in a display case. If she puts about the same number in each of 3 rows, about how many carvings will she put in each row?

30. At a craft fair, small beaded belts cost $8 and large beaded belts cost $25. Write an equation in which n is the cost of 3 small belts and 2 large belts. Solve for n.

Bird

31. **Write About It** Anna estimates that $205 \div 3$ is about 60. Raymond estimates that the quotient is about 70. Which estimate is closer to the actual quotient? Explain your reasoning.

Bear

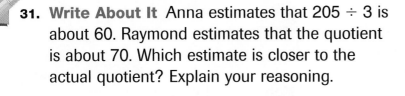

Rabbit

Wolf

Toy

Drum Rattle

Belt

Necklace

32. Multistep Joseph bought a necklace and one other item. He paid with four $10 bills. He received $6 as change. What other item did Joseph buy?

33. You Decide You have a $30 gift certificate. What two items could you buy? How much money would you receive as change?

34. Algebra Emily wrote this equation to find the cost of 5 items.

$$n = (2 \times 29) + (3 \times 5)$$

What were the 5 items? How much did they cost altogether?

35. Create and Solve Use at least three of the items pictured above to write a word problem that uses two operations. Give your problem to a classmate to solve.

Choose a Computation Method

Mental Math • Estimation • Paper and Pencil • Calculator

Solve. Tell which method you used.

36. The table on the right shows the number of miles a family drove each day on a trip from Miami to Phoenix. How far did they drive?

37. Multistep Red beads cost $3 per bag. Gold beads cost $7 per bag. If 38 bags of red beads and 12 bags of gold beads were sold, what was the total sales amount?

38. Analyze Joyce and 3 friends spent $44 on jewelry. If each person spent the same amount, how much did each person spend?

Mon.	Tue.	Wed.	Thu.	Fri.	Sat.
403	379	457	385	488	456

Extra Practice See page 225, Set D.

Open Response

Divide. Check your answers. (Ch. 8, Lesson 4)

39. 70 ÷ 6

40. 84 ÷ 3

41. 62 ÷ 5

42. 73 ÷ 3

Solve.

43. There are 8 children at a birthday party. Mrs. Mehta has 65 pieces of candy. She wants to give the same number of candies to each child. About how many pieces of candy will each child receive?

(Ch. 8, Lesson 6)

Social Studies Connection
Egyptian Multiplication

Activity

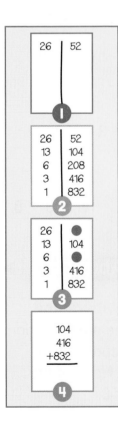

Ancient Egyptians multiplied two numbers by halving and doubling them. Find 26 × 52 with this method.

❶ Write 26 in the left column. Write 52 in the right column.

❷ Divide 26 by 2. Write the result below 26. Then multiply 52 by 2. Write the result below 52. Continue dividing each number in the left column by 2 and multiplying each number in the right column by 2. Ignore the remainders. Stop when the number in the left column is 1.

❸ Find all the even numbers in the left column. Cover the numbers across from them in the right column.

❹ Add the remaining numbers in the right column. Check your answer by multiplying 26 and 52.

WEEKLY WR READER eduplace.com/map

Chapter Review/Test

VOCABULARY

Choose the best word to complete each sentence.

Vocabulary
divisor
quotient
dividend
remainder

1. In a division problem, the number to be divided is the _____.

2. In the division sentence 24 ÷ 2 = 12, the number 12 is the _____.

3. A number that divides another number is the _____.

CONCEPTS AND SKILLS

Divide. (Lessons 1, 2, 4, pp. 206–209, 214–216)

4. $2\overline{)44}$ 5. $3\overline{)95}$ 6. $4\overline{)86}$ 7. $5\overline{)59}$

8. $2\overline{)51}$ 9. $4\overline{)68}$ 10. $6\overline{)72}$ 11. $7\overline{)80}$

Solve each equation. (Lesson 5, pp. 218–219)

12. $250 \div 5 = n$ 13. $3{,}600 \div a = 600$ 14. $b \div 3 = 80$

Estimate. Write the basic fact you used. (Lesson 6, pp. 220–222)

15. $3\overline{)23}$ 16. $7\overline{)346}$ 17. $276 \div 9$ 18. $573 \div 8$

PROBLEM SOLVING

Solve. (Lesson 3, pp. 210–212)

19. Lia keeps 19 dolls on 4 shelves. If there are 5 dolls on each shelf except the top one, how many dolls are on the top shelf?

20. Daniel keeps his marble collection in boxes. Each box holds 4 marbles. If Daniel has 27 marbles, how many boxes does he use?

 **Write About It**

Show You Understand

Each symbol in the multiplication sentence below represents a different number. None of the symbols stand for 0.

 ● × ■ = ▲

Extra Practice

Set A (Lesson 2, pp. 208–209)

Divide. Tell if there is a remainder.

1. $2\overline{)24}$ 2. $3\overline{)35}$ 3. $4\overline{)47}$ 4. $3\overline{)69}$ 5. $7\overline{)77}$

6. $2\overline{)67}$ 7. $5\overline{)59}$ 8. $4\overline{)85}$ 9. $8\overline{)89}$ 10. $6\overline{)68}$

11. $99 \div 9$ 12. $84 \div 2$ 13. $68 \div 6$ 14. $56 \div 5$ 15. $96 \div 3$

Set B (Lesson 4, pp. 214–216)

Divide. Check your answers.

1. $5\overline{)60}$ 2. $3\overline{)41}$ 3. $2\overline{)93}$ 4. $4\overline{)55}$ 5. $3\overline{)70}$

6. $4\overline{)62}$ 7. $7\overline{)87}$ 8. $3\overline{)84}$ 9. $5\overline{)66}$ 10. $7\overline{)98}$

11. $50 \div 2$ 12. $85 \div 5$ 13. $47 \div 3$ 14. $75 \div 6$ 15. $53 \div 4$

Set C (Lesson 5, pp. 218–219)

Divide.

1. $4 \div 2 = \blacksquare$ 2. $54 \div 9 = \blacksquare$ 3. $63 \div 7 = \blacksquare$
   $40 \div 2 = \blacksquare$ $540 \div 9 = \blacksquare$ $630 \div 7 = \blacksquare$
   $400 \div 2 = \blacksquare$ $5,400 \div 9 = \blacksquare$ $6,300 \div 7 = \blacksquare$

Solve each equation.

4. $1,000 \div 5 = n$ 5. $490 \div 7 = p$ 6. $640 \div 8 = d$ 7. $3,600 \div 4 = q$

8. $270 \div k = 30$ 9. $b \div 5 = 40$ 10. $420 \div a = 70$ 11. $s \div 9 = 50$

Set D (Lesson 6, pp. 220–222)

Estimate. Write the basic fact you used.

1. $3\overline{)28}$ 2. $5\overline{)29}$ 3. $4\overline{)33}$ 4. $6\overline{)47}$ 5. $9\overline{)56}$

6. $5\overline{)395}$ 7. $4\overline{)330}$ 8. $3\overline{)251}$ 9. $6\overline{)477}$ 10. $9\overline{)550}$

11. $131 \div 4$ 12. $243 \div 5$ 13. $179 \div 3$ 14. $250 \div 6$ 15. $642 \div 9$

CHAPTER 9

Divide by One-Digit Divisors

INVESTIGATION

Using Data

A wildlife preserve provides 5,000 pounds of food for elephants each day. How many elephants could be living at the preserve? Can you find an answer in more than one way?

The African Elephant	
Weight	8,800–15,500 pounds
Height	10–13 feet
Life Span	50–60 years
Food	About 528 pounds per day

Use What You Know

Use this page to review and remember what you need to know for this chapter.

VOCABULARY

Choose the best word to complete each sentence.

1. In $42 \div n = 6$, n is the ____.

2. The answer in division is called the ____.

3. If equal groups cannot be made when you divide, you will have a ____.

4. When you divide, the ____ is divided into equal groups.

CONCEPTS AND SKILLS

Match the division example with the better estimate.

5. $7)\overline{645}$ a. $7)\overline{630}$ (90)   b. $7)\overline{700}$ (100)

6. $6)\overline{200}$ a. $6)\overline{180}$ (30)   b. $6)\overline{240}$ (40)

7. $5)\overline{468}$ a. $5)\overline{500}$ (100)   b. $5)\overline{450}$ (90)

Find each quotient.

8. $4)\overline{12}$ 9. $7)\overline{56}$ 10. $9)\overline{63}$ 11. $3)\overline{15}$

12. $9)\overline{39}$ 13. $7)\overline{20}$ 14. $5)\overline{12}$ 15. $3)\overline{19}$

16. $4)\overline{48}$ 17. $5)\overline{65}$ 18. $3)\overline{77}$ 19. $6)\overline{78}$

 Write About It

20. A number is divided by 6. What numbers could the remainder be? Explain how you know.

Extra Practice at **eduplace.com/map**

Audio Tutor 1/31 Listen and Understand

Three-Digit Quotients

Objective Divide a three-digit number by a one-digit number.

Learn About It

Students in the third, fourth, and fifth grades made 525 origami animals to display in the library. If each grade made the same number of animals, how many animals did each grade make?

Divide. $525 \div 3 = \blacksquare$ or $3\overline{)525}$

Origami is the Japanese art of folding paper into different shapes.

STEP 1 Divide the hundreds.

$$\text{Think: } \frac{? \text{ hundreds}}{3\overline{)5 \text{ hundreds}}}$$

$$\begin{array}{r} 1 \\ 3\overline{)525} \\ -\ 3 \\ \hline 2 \end{array}$$

Multiply. 1×3
← Subtract. $5 - 3$
Compare. $2 < 3$

Remember
After you divide the hundreds, tens or ones place, the remainder should **always** be less than the divisor.

STEP 2 Bring down the tens. Divide the tens.

$$\text{Think: } \frac{? \text{ tens}}{3\overline{)22 \text{ tens}}}$$

$$\begin{array}{r} 17 \\ 3\overline{)525} \\ -\ 3\downarrow \\ \hline 22 \\ -\ 21 \\ \hline 1 \end{array}$$

Bring down the tens.
Multiply. 7×3
← Subtract. $22 - 21$
Compare. $1 < 3$

STEP 3 Bring down the ones. Divide the ones.

$$\text{Think: } \frac{? \text{ ones}}{3\overline{)15 \text{ ones}}}$$

$$\begin{array}{r} 175 \\ 3\overline{)525} \\ -\ 3 \\ \hline 22 \\ -\ 21\downarrow \\ \hline 15 \\ -\ 15 \\ \hline 0 \end{array}$$

Bring down the ones.
Multiply. 5×3
← Subtract. $15 - 15$
Compare. $0 < 3$

Check.
Multiply.

$3 \times 175 = 525$

The product equals the dividend.

Solution: Each grade made 175 origami animals.

Other Examples

A. With a Remainder

$$\begin{array}{r} 168 \text{ R4} \\ 5\overline{)844} \\ -\ 5\downarrow \\ \hline 34 \\ -\ 30\downarrow \\ \hline 44 \\ -\ 40 \\ \hline 4 \end{array}$$

Check:
$$\begin{array}{r} 168 \\ \times\ 5 \\ \hline 840 \\ +\ 4 \\ \hline 844 \end{array}$$

Multiply, then add the remainder.

$4 \leftarrow$ 4 is less than 5, so it is the remainder.

B. Zero in the Dividend

$$\begin{array}{r} 117 \\ 6\overline{)702} \\ -\ 6\downarrow \\ \hline 10 \\ -\ 6\downarrow \\ \hline 42 \\ -\ 42 \\ \hline 0 \end{array}$$

Check:
$$\begin{array}{r} 117 \\ \times\ 6 \\ \hline 702 \end{array}$$

Divide. Check your answers.

1. $2\overline{)394}$ 2. $2\overline{)962}$ 3. $4\overline{)450}$ 4. $7\overline{)802}$

5. $685 \div 6$ 6. $945 \div 2$ 7. $775 \div 2$ 8. $697 \div 6$

Ask Yourself
- Can I divide the hundreds?
- Can I divide the tens?
- Can I divide the ones?

Explain Your Thinking ▶ Think about $482 \div 4$. Without dividing, how do you know the quotient will have 3 digits?

Practice and Problem Solving

Divide. Check your answers.

9. $2\overline{)836}$ 10. $4\overline{)709}$ 11. $3\overline{)519}$ 12. $3\overline{)404}$

13. $5\overline{)762}$ 14. $6\overline{)913}$ 15. $8\overline{)923}$ 16. $8\overline{)889}$

17. $4\overline{)633}$ 18. $6\overline{)822}$ 19. $4\overline{)746}$ 20. $7\overline{)934}$

21. $578 \div 3$ 22. $710 \div 5$ 23. $535 \div 2$ 24. $864 \div 5$

Solve.

25. Each origami crane is made with either red, blue, or silver paper. The number of cranes in each color is the same. If there are 342 cranes in all, how many of them are blue?

26. An artist made 455 origami animals in 5 days. If she made the same number of animals each day, how many origami animals did she make each day?

Mixed Review and Test Prep

Multiple Choice

Choose the best unit of measure. (Grade 3)

27. distance from Boston to Chicago

   a. miles   b. yards

28. length of a room

   a. inches   b. feet

29. Fran read a 306-page book in 2 days. She read the same number of pages each day. How many pages did she read each day?

(Ch. 9, Lesson 1)

A 108   c 135

B 153   D 612

Extra Practice See page 249, Set A.

Place the First Digit of the Quotient

Objective Decide where to write the first digit in the quotient.

Learn About It

Reggie has 237 photographs of insects. If he puts them into 5 groups of the same size, how many photos will be in each group?

Divide. 237 ÷ 5 or 5)237

STEP 1 Estimate to place the first digit.

237 is between 200 and 250, so use these numbers to estimate.

$$\dfrac{40}{5\overline{)200}} \qquad \dfrac{50}{5\overline{)250}}$$

The quotient will be between 40 and 50. The first digit will be in the tens place.

STEP 2 Divide the tens.

$$\text{Think:}\ \dfrac{?\ \text{tens}}{5\overline{)23\ \text{tens}}}$$

$$\begin{array}{r} 4 \\ 5\overline{)237} \\ -\ 20 \\ \hline 3 \end{array}$$

Multiply. 4 × 5
← Subtract. 23 − 20
Compare. 3 < 5

STEP 3 Bring down the ones. Divide the ones.

$$\text{Think:}\ \dfrac{?\ \text{ones}}{5\overline{)37\ \text{ones}}}$$

$$\begin{array}{r} 47\ \text{R2} \\ 5\overline{)237} \\ -\ 20\downarrow \\ \hline 37 \\ -\ 35 \\ \hline 2 \end{array}$$

← Bring down the ones.

Multiply. 7 × 5
← Subtract. 37 − 35
Compare. 2 < 5

Check.
Multiply. Then add.

(5 × 47) + 2 = 237

The sum equals the dividend, so the answer is correct.

Solution: There will be 47 photographs in each group. Two photographs will be left over.

Other Examples

A. Multiple of 10

$$\begin{array}{r} 83\ \text{R6} \\ 8\overline{)670} \\ -\ 64\downarrow \\ \hline 30 \\ -\ 24 \\ \hline 6 \end{array}$$

Check:
$$\begin{array}{r} 83 \\ \times\ 8 \\ \hline 664 \\ +\ 6 \\ \hline 670 \end{array}$$

B. Multiple of 100

$$\begin{array}{r} 85\ \text{R5} \\ 7\overline{)600} \\ -\ 56\downarrow \\ \hline 40 \\ -\ 35 \\ \hline 5 \end{array}$$

Check:
$$\begin{array}{r} 85 \\ \times\ 7 \\ \hline 595 \\ +\ 5 \\ \hline 600 \end{array}$$

 Extra Help at **eduplace.com/map**

Guided Practice

Ask Yourself
- Can I divide the hundreds?
- Can I divide the tens?
- Can I divide the ones?

Divide. Check your answers.

1. 6)384　　2. 8)672　　3. 7)542　　4. 4)348

5. 437 ÷ 6　　6. 235 ÷ 5　　7. 341 ÷ 9　　8. 473 ÷ 6

Explain Your Thinking ▶ When you divide a three-digit dividend by a one-digit divisor, what is the least number of digits that can be in the quotient?

Practice and Problem Solving

Divide. Check your answers.

9. 4)396　　10. 8)272　　11. 5)394　　12. 3)485

13. 2)162　　14. 4)284　　15. 6)532　　16. 8)889

17. 134 ÷ 2　　18. 504 ÷ 3　　19. 317 ÷ 9　　20. 587 ÷ 6

 Algebra • **Functions** Copy and complete each table.

Divide by 3	
Input	Output
21. 209	▪
22. 361	▪
23. 577	▪

Divide by 4	
Input	Output
24. 209	▪
25. 361	▪
26. 577	▪

Solve.

27. **Analyze** Look back at your answers in each function table. What patterns do you notice? Explain your thinking.

28. There are 452 insect photos displayed in 4 equal groups. How many photos are in each group?

29. Tim wants to sort 242 butterfly photos into 5 equal groups. How many photos will he have left over?

Go On

Data The bar graph below shows how fast some animals can run.
Use the graph for Problems 30–36.

30. At top speed, how much faster can a cheetah run than a lion?

31. Which animal's top speed is twice as fast as an elephant's?

32. List the animals in order from the slowest to the fastest.

33. **Analyze** Suppose an antelope could run at its fastest speed for 15 minutes. How far would it run?

34. The record speed for a coyote is 43 miles an hour. Which animal runs about as fast as a coyote?

35. **Analyze** Suppose an elephant ran for 10 minutes at its fastest speed. How far could it run?

36. **Challenge** Suppose a grizzly bear can travel 9 miles in 15 minutes. What animal runs about twice as fast as the grizzly bear?

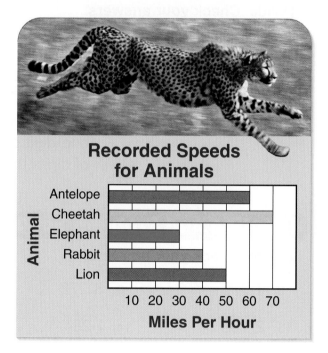

Recorded Speeds for Animals

Animal: Antelope, Cheetah, Elephant, Rabbit, Lion

Miles Per Hour: 10 20 30 40 50 60 70

Mixed Review and Test Prep

Open Response

Write each time to the minute before and after the hour. (Grade 3)

37.

38.

39.

40.

41. Judy, Ron, and Michael have 147 baseball cards to share equally. How many baseball cards will each child receive?

42. Six friends shared 234 pennies equally. Explain how you would estimate the number of pennies each friend received. (Ch. 9, Lesson 2)

Extra Practice See page 249, Set B.

Logical Reasoning
Digit Detective

Solve these division problems by working backwards!
You have the quotient, now find the divisor and the dividend.

Use the digits in each square only once to complete each problem.

1.
$$\begin{array}{r} 1\,3\,\text{R1} \\ \blacksquare \overline{)\,\blacksquare\blacksquare} \end{array}$$

2.
$$\begin{array}{r} 1\,6\,\text{R1} \\ \blacksquare \overline{)\,\blacksquare\blacksquare} \end{array}$$

3.
$$\begin{array}{r} 1\,2\,\text{R2} \\ \blacksquare \overline{)\,\blacksquare\blacksquare} \end{array}$$

4.
$$\begin{array}{r} \blacksquare\,\text{R1} \\ \blacksquare \overline{)\,\blacksquare\blacksquare} \end{array}$$

 3 4 5

 5 4 6

 6 7 8

1 2 4 5

Math Reasoning
Purple Paint Prices

Pierre at the Paint Pot Store told Pat that he could sell her 9 gallons of purple paint for $216. Paco at the Perfect Paints Store said, "I have a better price! I'll sell you 8 gallons for only $208."

Is Paco's price better than Pierre's? Explain how you decided.

Brain Teaser

Shelly is thinking of a number between 100 and 140. It can be divided evenly by 6 and 12, but not by 7. What number is it?

Education Place

Check out **eduplace.com/map** for more brain teasers.

Divide Money

Objective Divide money amounts.

Learn About It

A mother and her three children are spending the day at the petting zoo. She paid $9.80 for their admission. Each ticket cost the same amount. How much was each ticket?

Divide. $9.80 ÷ 4 =   or   4)$9.80

STEP 1 Estimate.

$9.80 is between $8.00 and $12.00.

$$\begin{array}{r} \$2.00 \\ 4)\overline{\$8.00} \end{array} \qquad \begin{array}{r} \$3.00 \\ 4)\overline{\$12.00} \end{array}$$

The quotient will be between $2.00 and $3.00.

STEP 2 Divide as if you were dividing whole numbers.

```
      2 45
  4)$9.80
  − 8
    18
  − 16
    20
  − 20
     0
```

STEP 3 Write the dollar sign and the decimal point in the quotient.

```
    $2.45
 4)$9.80
  − 8
    18
  − 16
    20
  − 20
     0
```

Align the decimal point in the quotient with the decimal point in the dividend.

Solution: Cost of admission for each person was $2.45. Since $2.45 is between $2.00 and $3.00, the answer is reasonable.

Another Example

Zero in the Dividend

Divide.

```
    1 68
 3)$5.04
  − 3
    20
  − 18
    24
  − 24
     0
```

Write the dollar sign and the decimal point.

```
    $1.68
 3)$5.04
  − 3
    20
  − 18
    24
  − 24
     0
```

Guided Practice

Estimate. Then divide.

1. $8\overline{)\$9.20}$

2. $3\overline{)\$756}$

3. $2\overline{)\$0.42}$

4. $2\overline{)\$856}$

5. $3\overline{)\$0.81}$

6. $4\overline{)\$7.92}$

7. $\$1.55 \div 5$

8. $\$252 \div 6$

9. $\$5.39 \div 7$

Explain Your Thinking ▶ How can estimating when dividing money help you be sure the decimal point is in the correct place in the quotient? Use an example to explain.

Practice and Problem Solving

Divide. Check your answers.

10. $6\overline{)\$6.72}$

11. $6\overline{)\$0.78}$

12. $3\overline{)\$0.48}$

13. $4\overline{)\$7.24}$

14. $4\overline{)\$88}$

15. $8\overline{)\$5.76}$

16. $3\overline{)\$6.36}$

17. $2\overline{)\$1.34}$

18. $\$45 \div 3$

19. $\$0.36 \div 2$

20. $\$0.88 \div 8$

21. $\$0.72 \div 6$

22. $\$7.56 \div 6$

23. $\$5.58 \div 9$

24. $\$8.19 \div 9$

25. $\$464 \div 8$

Solve.

26. **What's Wrong?** Look at Vera's work. What did she do wrong?

27. Tina spends $4.38 on 2 key chains at the petting zoo. Each key chain costs the same amount. How much does each key chain cost?

28. On the way to the petting zoo, Mrs. Ellis bought 6 gallons of gasoline for $8.70. How much did she spend on each gallon?

29. Paulo has $9.44 in his pocket. He wants to use the money to buy small gifts for 3 friends, and then keep the rest for himself. If Paulo wants to buy a yo-yo for each of his friends, and yo-yos cost $3.29 after tax, does he have enough money?

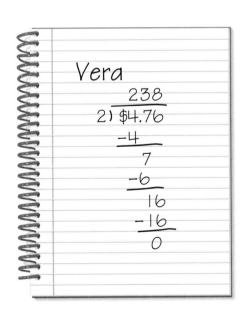

Ask Yourself

- Where should I place the first digit in the quotient?
- Where should I place the decimal point in the quotient?

Go On

𝒳 Algebra • Functions Copy and complete each table.

Rule: $y = x \div 5$	
x	y
30. ▦	$1.21
31. $7.50	▦
32. $0.95	▦
33. ▦	$0.14

Rule: $y = x \div 9$	
x	y
34. ▦	$1.12
35. $9.99	▦
36. ▦	$0.51
37. $4.95	▦

38.

Rule: ____	
x	y
$1.50	$0.75
$0.90	$0.45
$6.80	$3.40
$5.32	$2.66

Compare. Write >, <, or = for each ⬤.

39. $3.99 ÷ 3 ⬤ $1.00

40. $7.92 ÷ 3 ⬤ $2.00

41. $6.63 ÷ 3 ⬤ $3.00

42. $4.98 ÷ 4 ⬤ $2.00

43. $8.46 ÷ 3 ⬤ $3.00

44. $6.20 ÷ 5 ⬤ $1.00

📊 Data Use the ad for Problems 45–49.

45. What is a good estimate of the total cost of 3 T-shirts at the gift shop?

46. Mrs. Rea needs to buy 7 rolls of film. What is the least amount she might pay? What is the greatest amount she might pay?

47. You Decide Tony has $20.00 to spend at the gift shop. What can he buy? Explain how you decided.

48. Kelly wants to buy mugs for her mother and her two aunts. How much money does she need?

49. Multistep Ann wants to send postcards to each of the 8 girls in her club. She also wants to buy one roll of film. How much money does she need?

WILD ANIMAL PARK!
GIFT SHOP
T-shirts...........$19.95
Postcards........75¢
Mugs.........$5.95
Roll of Film..$5.85

Special
2 Rolls
of Film
$11.00

236

Extra Practice See page 249, Set C.

Social Studies Connection
Three Cheers for Division

In the 1800s, Americans could buy things with a Spanish coin worth a dollar. If an item cost less than a dollar, people broke their Spanish coin into eight small pieces, or bits. These are the "bits" in the cheer, "Two bits, four bits, six bits, a dollar…"

1. About how much was 1 bit worth?

2. If you spent 50 cents in the 1800s, how many bits would you need?

3. Suppose an item cost $2.36. You could pay with $2.00 and how many bits?

4. **You Decide** Do you think that it was practical to break off parts of the Spanish coin? What problems might this cause?

WEEKLY WR READER eduplace.com/map

Check your understanding of Lessons 1–3.

Divide. Check your answers. (Lessons 1–2)

1. 2)398

2. 3)736

3. 806 ÷ 5

4. 937 ÷ 4

5. 2)196

6. 3)260

7. 593 ÷ 5

8. 384 ÷ 4

Solve. (Lesson 3)

9. Juan and Roberto spend $5.70 on lunch together. Each lunch costs the same amount. What is the price of each lunch?

10. Anna and her 2 sisters each buy a key chain. They spend $4.35 altogether. If each key chain costs the same amount, what is the price of one key chain?

Lesson 4

Zeros in the Quotient

Objective Decide when to place zeros in the quotient.

Learn About It

Whale Watch Company buys binoculars for visitors to use on their tours. The binoculars are shipped in boxes of 8. If the tour manager orders 824 binoculars, how many boxes should she receive?

Divide. $824 \div 8 = \blacksquare$ or $8\overline{)824}$

STEP 1 Decide where to place the first digit.

$$\text{Think: } 8\overline{)\overset{? \text{ hundreds}}{8 \text{ hundreds}}}$$

$$\begin{array}{r} 1 \\ 8\overline{)824} \\ -\ 8 \\ \hline 0 \end{array}$$

Multiply. 1×8
← Subtract. $8 - 8$
Compare. $0 < 8$

STEP 2 Bring down the tens. Divide the tens.

$$\text{Think: } 8\overline{)\overset{? \text{ tens}}{2 \text{ tens}}}$$

$$\begin{array}{r} 10 \\ 8\overline{)824} \\ -\ 8\downarrow \\ \hline 02 \end{array}$$

Since $2 < 8$, you cannot divide the tens. Write a zero in the tens place.

STEP 3 Bring down the ones. Divide the ones.

$$\text{Think: } 8\overline{)\overset{? \text{ ones}}{24 \text{ ones}}}$$

$$\begin{array}{r} 103 \\ 8\overline{)824} \\ -\ 8\downarrow \\ \hline 024 \\ -\ 24 \\ \hline 0 \end{array}$$

Multiply. 3×8
← Subtract. $24 - 24$
Compare. $0 < 8$

Solution: The manager should receive 103 boxes.

Check.
Multiply.
$8 \times 103 = 824$
The product equals the dividend.

Guided Practice

Divide. Check your answers.

1. $3\overline{)924}$
2. $4\overline{)832}$
3. $5\overline{)547}$
4. $6\overline{)639}$

5. $9\overline{)972}$
6. $8\overline{)884}$
7. $7\overline{)746}$
8. $7\overline{)635}$

Ask Yourself
- Can I divide the hundreds?
- Can I divide the tens?
- Can I divide the ones?

Explain Your Thinking ▶ Look back at Exercise 1. Why must you remember to write the zero in the quotient?

Practice and Problem Solving

Divide. Check your answers.

9. $4\overline{)804}$ **10.** $2\overline{)412}$ **11.** $7\overline{)\$7.56}$ **12.** $6\overline{)361}$

13. $7\overline{)\$8.40}$ **14.** $2\overline{)613}$ **15.** $9\overline{)992}$ **16.** $5\overline{)754}$

17. $162 \div 8$ **18.** $529 \div 5$ **19.** $420 \div 3$ **20.** $\$8.72 \div 8$

21. $\$6.12 \div 3$ **22.** $963 \div 8$ **23.** $947 \div 9$ **24.** $\$9.10 \div 7$

 Algebra • **Expressions** Find the value of each expression when $n = 3$.

25. $66 \div n$ **26.** $96 \div n$ **27.** $849 \div n$ **28.** $342 \div n$

29. $848 \div (n - 1)$ **30.** $(8 \times n) \div 2$ **31.** $742 \div (n + 4)$ **32.** $342 \div (n \times 3)$

Solve.

33. The Whale Watch Company sailed 3 times last Saturday, with the same number of tourists each time. If 324 tourists sailed on Saturday, how many people were on each tour?

 34. Write About It Think about the problem $968 \div 8 = 121$. Without dividing, decide whether there would be a remainder if you divided by 4. Explain your reasoning.

Mixed Review and Test Prep

Open Response

Divide. (Ch. 8, Lesson 4)

35. $8\overline{)60}$ **36.** $4\overline{)70}$ **37.** $5\overline{)60}$

38. $9\overline{)30}$ **39.** $6\overline{)70}$ **40.** $7\overline{)40}$

41. $3\overline{)50}$ **42.** $3\overline{)70}$ **43.** $7\overline{)90}$

44. $7\overline{)30}$ **45.** $5\overline{)70}$ **46.** $8\overline{)50}$

Multiple Choice

47. Jamie divides 321 books equally into 3 boxes. How many books are in each box? (Ch. 9, Lesson 4)

A 17   **C** 648

B 107   **D** 3,752

Extra Practice See page 249, Set D.

Problem-Solving Strategy
Guess and Check

Objective Work backward to solve a problem.

Problem Aurora visited an aquarium. She saw 5 more jellyfish than leafy sea dragons. There were 10 more tropical fish than starfish. Aurora saw twice as many starfish as jellyfish. She saw 120 tropical fish. How many leafy sea dragons did Aurora see?

The leafy sea dragon is found only in Australia. It is a relative of the sea horse and is an endangered species.

UNDERSTAND

This is what Aurora saw.

- 5 more jellyfish than leafy sea dragons
- 10 more tropical fish than starfish
- twice as many starfish as jellyfish
- 120 tropical fish

PLAN

You can use what you know.

You know the number of tropical fish. Work backward and use inverse operations.

Remember
- Addition and subtraction are inverse operations.
- Multiplication and division are inverse operations.

SOLVE

Use inverse operations.

Start with the 120 tropical fish.

tropical fish		starfish		jellyfish		leafy sea dragons
120	− 10	110	÷ 2	55	− 5	50
This is 10 more than the number of starfish.	Work backward. Subtract 10.	This is twice the number of jellyfish.	Work backward. Divide by 2.	This is 5 more than the number of leafy sea dragons.	Work backward. Subtract 5.	

Solution: Aurora saw 50 leafy sea dragons.

LOOK BACK

Look back at the problem. How can you check the answer?

Guided Practice

Use the Ask Yourself questions to help you solve each problem.

1. Twice as many people went on the first aquarium tour as the second tour. Three times as many went on the third tour as the second tour. If 90 people went on the third tour, how many went on the first tour?

   (Hint) What information should you start with?

2. At a zoo, there are 2 more penguins than walruses. There are half as many seals as penguins. There are 6 seals. How many walruses are at the zoo?

Ask Yourself

 **What facts do I know?**

 **What number do I know?**

 **Did I use inverse operations?**

LOOK BACK **Did I check by starting with my answer and working forward?**

Independent Practice

Solve.

3. The Dunns bought aquarium supplies. One angelfish cost 2 times as much as the fish food. The filter cost 3 times as much as the angelfish. The filter cost $12. How much did the fish food cost?

4. At an aquarium there are twice as many sharks as turtles. There are 3 fewer seals than sharks. If there are 15 seals, how many turtles are there?

5. Kelley is thinking of a number. She adds 1, divides by 5, subtracts 2, and multiplies by 5. The result is 40. What is Kelley's number?

6. **Create and Solve** Make up a number puzzle like the one in Problem 5. Give your number puzzle to a classmate to solve.

Go On

Mixed Problem Solving

Solve. Show your work. Tell what strategy you used.

7. Justin is in a parade. There are 4 rows of students in front of him and 12 rows behind him. There are 5 students to his right and 4 to his left. If every row has the same number of students, how many students are there?

8. **Money** Dale buys a book and a bookmark. The bookmark costs half as much as the book. The total cost is $9.75. How much does each item cost?

9. Michael is 5 years older than Liz. Liz is 8 years younger than Carlos. Carlos is 2 years older than Meredith. If Meredith is 12 years old, how old is Michael?

You Choose

Strategy
- Draw a Picture
- Guess and Check
- Work Backward
- Write an Equation

Computation Method
- Mental Math
- Estimation
- Paper and Pencil
- Calculator

Data Use the table for Problems 10–13.

10. Amy, Lisa, and Dwayne skated on different paths. Amy's path was longer than Dwayne's but shorter than Lisa's. Lisa did not skate on Windy Way. Which path did each use?

11. **Explain** Ty skated all of Speedy Street and Twisty Trail. Ed skated all of Bumpy Boulevard and Windy Way. Who skated farther? Explain how you got your answer.

12. **Mental Math** There are 3 feet in a yard. Which path at Skate Park is 960 feet long?

13. **Measurement** A mile is 1,760 yards. Edith skates Windy Way 5 times. Is that more than a mile? Explain.

Skate-Park Paths

Path	Length
Bumpy Boulevard	342 yards
Speedy Street	320 yards
Twisty Trail	208 yards
Windy Way	432 yards

242

Problem Solving on Tests

Multiple Choice

Choose the letter of the correct answer.

1. The Clarks will drive 1,200 miles from Tampa to Chicago. They want to drive the same distance on each of four days. How many miles should they plan to drive each day?

    A 30   C 400

    B 300   D 1,200

    (Chapter 8, Lesson 5)

2. Mateo has 68 bagels. He puts 6 bagels in each bag. When he has filled as many bags as he can, how many bagels will be left over?

    F 12   H 3

    G 11   J 2

    (Chapter 8, Lesson 2)

Open Response

Solve each problem.

3. Mrs. Marcel is planning a party for 208 people. She can use tables that seat 4, 6, or 8 people. What is the fewest number of tables she can use? How do you know?

    (Chapter 9, Lesson 2)

4. Eva has placed 24 photos on her bulletin board. The number in each row is 5 more than the number of rows. How many rows of photos are there? **Explain** What steps did you take to solve the problem?

    (Chapter 6, Lesson 5)

Extended Response

5. Matt, Sean, Eric and Roy sold their used toys at a yard sale. Here are the bills and coins they collected.

The boys compared the money they had in their pockets that evening after supper. How money much did each boy have?

a. Matt bought an ice cream cone for $0.95 with his share of the money.

b. Sean earned $6.50 mowing the neighbor's lawn and shared half of his total with his sister Julie.

c. Eric received his share of the money as coins. He spent three of his quarters at a garage sale.

d. Roy put his share in his pocket where he already had 2 quarters, a dime, and 4 pennies left from his allowance.

    (Chapter 9, Lesson 3)

Education Place

See **eduplace.com/map** for more Test-Taking Tips.

Divide Greater Numbers

Objective Divide greater numbers.

Learn About It

Monarch butterflies can migrate up to 3,000 miles! Suppose a butterfly flew 1,116 miles in 9 days. If it flew the same distance each day, how many miles did it fly in one day?

Estimate. Think $9\overline{)1{,}116}$ → $9\overline{)900}$ ← 100

Divide. $1{,}116 \div 9 = \blacksquare$ or $9\overline{)1{,}116}$

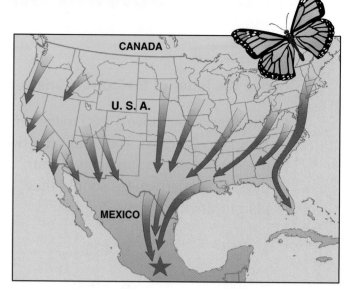

Different Ways to Divide 1,116 by 9

Way ① Use paper and pencil.

STEP 1 Divide the thousands.

Think: $9\overline{)1 \text{ thousand}}$? thousands

$9\overline{)1{,}116}$
↑
not enough thousands

STEP 2 Regroup the thousands as hundreds. Divide the hundreds.

Think: $9\overline{)11 \text{ hundreds}}$? hundreds

$\begin{array}{r} 1 \\ 9\overline{)1{,}116} \\ -9 \\ \hline 2 \end{array}$

Multiply. 1×9
← Subtract. $11 - 9$
Compare. $2 < 9$

STEP 3 Complete the division.

$\begin{array}{r} 124 \\ 9\overline{)1{,}116} \\ -9 \\ \hline 21 \\ -18 \\ \hline 36 \\ -36 \\ \hline 0 \end{array}$

Way ② Use a calculator.

1 1 1 6 ÷ 9 =

$1116 \div 9 = 124$

Solution: The monarch butterfly flew 124 miles in 1 day.
Since 124 is close to 100, the answer is reasonable.

Guided Practice

Estimate. Then divide.

1. $5\overline{)4{,}325}$

2. $4\overline{)7{,}318}$

3. $8\overline{)56{,}912}$

4. $10{,}967 \div 9$

5. $\$502.38 \div 9$

6. $\$15{,}310 \div 2$

Ask Yourself

• Where do I write the first digit in each quotient?

• What steps should I follow each time I divide?

Explain Your Thinking ▷ Think about $9{,}872 \div 7$. Without dividing, how many digits are in the quotient?

Practice and Problem Solving

Use paper and pencil or a calculator to divide.

7. $4\overline{)1{,}356}$

8. $8\overline{)9{,}851}$

9. $3\overline{)\$2{,}136}$

10. $5\overline{)6{,}453}$

11. $9\overline{)\$90.72}$

12. $9\overline{)9{,}160}$

13. $6\overline{)8{,}022}$

14. $7\overline{)11{,}129}$

15. $\$1{,}135 \div 5$

16. $2{,}991 \div 3$

17. $8{,}414 \div 7$

18. $\$270.81 \div 9$

Mental Math Compare. Write >, <, or = for each ⬤.

19. $2{,}000 \div 4$ ⬤ $2{,}000 \div 8$

20. $8{,}000 \div 4$ ⬤ $4{,}000 \times 2$

21. $5{,}000 \div 5$ ⬤ 500×2

22. $9{,}000 \div 3$ ⬤ $2{,}000 \times 1$

23. $3{,}000 \div 3$ ⬤ $3{,}000 \times 3$

24. $800 \div 4$ ⬤ $1{,}000 \div 5$

✸ **Algebra** • **Equations Solve for *n*. Reminder: Use the correct order of operations.**

25. $7{,}000 \div 7 = n$

26. $n \div 6 = 100$

27. $(7{,}896 \div 3) \times 1 = n$

28. $(2{,}500 \div 5) + 3 = n$

29. $2{,}100 \div n = 700$

30. $(7{,}500 \div 6) - 125 = n$

31. $(3{,}544 \div 3) \times 0 = n$

32. $(792 \div 3) \times 2 = n$

Go On ➡

Mental Math • Estimation • Paper and Pencil • Calculator

Solve. Tell which method you choose.

33. A butterfly traveled 728 miles in 7 days. It flew the same number of miles each day. How many miles did it fly each day?

34. Melinda has 7 coins in her pocket. The total value of the coins is $0.48. What are the 7 coins?

35. A caribou can travel up to 2,500 miles in a year. If a caribou traveled 5 miles every day, would it take more or less than 1 year to travel 2,500 miles? Explain your thinking.

36. The Parkers traveled 1,497 miles from Boston to Miami. They visited friends in North Carolina for 2 days. If they drove 520 miles a day, about how many days did it take them to arrive in Miami?

 Data Zion National Park in Southwestern Utah keeps the public informed about history and events in the park. The chart below shows the different ways that park officials gave out this information during one year.

Use the table for Problems 37–39.

37. Information Phone Calls from Zion National Park are made all year long. If about the same number of calls is made each month, about how many calls are made each month?

38. Three volunteers can put together 242 Information Mail-outs in 1 hour. About how many hours would it take the volunteers to put together all of the Mail-outs for the year?

39. **Create and Solve** Write and solve a problem that uses information from the table.

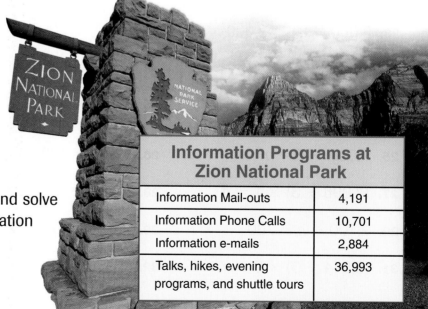

Information Programs at Zion National Park	
Information Mail-outs	4,191
Information Phone Calls	10,701
Information e-mails	2,884
Talks, hikes, evening programs, and shuttle tours	36,993

Extra Practice See page 249, Set E.

Open Response

Divide. Check your answers

(Chapter 9, Lesson 3)

40. $4.83 ÷ 7   **41.** $8.46 ÷ 9

42. $5.60 ÷ 5   **43.** $0.64 ÷ 4

Solve.

44. The Panos family is planning a 7,917 mile trip for next summer. Their trip will be 7 days long. If they travel the same number of miles each day during the trip, how many miles should they travel each day?

(Chapter 9, Lesson 6)

Math Reasoning
Nifty Nines

Problem Solving

Look at the number pattern of nines.

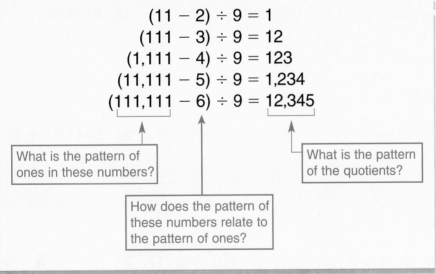

$$(11 - 2) ÷ 9 = 1$$
$$(111 - 3) ÷ 9 = 12$$
$$(1,111 - 4) ÷ 9 = 123$$
$$(11,111 - 5) ÷ 9 = 1,234$$
$$(111,111 - 6) ÷ 9 = 12,345$$

What is the pattern of ones in these numbers?

How does the pattern of these numbers relate to the pattern of ones?

What is the pattern of the quotients?

1. What is the next number sentence in the pattern?

2. What number would you subtract from 1,111,111,111? What would be the quotient?

VOCABULARY

Choose the best word to complete each statement.

1. The answer in a division problem is the _____.

2. If one whole number cannot be divided equally by another, there will be a _____.

3. The number that is divided in a division problem is the _____.

> **Vocabulary**
> divisor
> dividend
> quotient
> remainder

CONCEPTS AND SKILLS

Divide. Check your answers. (Lessons 1–4, pp. 228–239)

4. 2)264

5. 3)975

6. 4)548

7. 4)219

8. 8)173

9. 7)457

10. 4)$4.20

11. 9)$6.48

12. 6)$2.10

13. 3)906

14. 6)638

15. 8)$8.64

Estimate. Then divide. (Lesson 6, pp. 244–246)

16. 9,105 ÷ 3

17. 6,544 ÷ 8

18. 31,268 ÷ 6

19. 50,734 ÷ 7

20. 14,533 ÷ 3

21. $768.64 ÷ 8

22. 53,527 ÷ 5

23. $441.81 ÷ 9

PROBLEM SOLVING

Solve. (Lesson 5, pp. 240–242)

24. Three people got on the bus at Asbury Street. At the next stop, 10 people got on and 5 people got off. Then there were 28 people on the bus. How many people were on the bus before it stopped at Asbury Street?

25. Ali is twice as old as Kevin. Kevin is 10 years older than Pedro. Pedro is 2 years old. How old is Ali?

 **Write About It**

Show You Understand
Explain the steps you would use to solve this problem.

5)600

Use pictures, symbols, or words to explain the steps you used.

Extra Practice

Divide. Check your answers.

1. 3)381 2. 2)246 3. 4)566 4. 7)859 5. 5)605

6. 675 ÷ 5 7. 476 ÷ 3 8. 686 ÷ 4 9. 775 ÷ 6 10. 937 ÷ 8

Set B (Lesson 2, pp. 230–232)

Divide. Check your answers.

1. 5)120 2. 4)396 3. 6)451 4. 8)753 5. 9)327

6. 239 ÷ 3 7. 435 ÷ 7 8. 126 ÷ 4 9. 352 ÷ 8 10. 575 ÷ 6

Set C (Lesson 3, pp. 234–236)

Divide. Check your answers.

1. 2)$0.48 2. 3)$3.96 3. 4)$3.44 4. 5)$6.10 5. 6)$0.78

6. $5.12 ÷ 4 7. $2.66 ÷ 7 8. $1.10 ÷ 5 9. $8.68 ÷ 7 10. $6.48 ÷ 3

Set D (Lesson 4, pp. 238–239)

Divide. Check your answers.

1. 6)639 2. 4)880 3. 3)325 4. 5)524 5. 7)722

6. 188 ÷ 9 7. 510 ÷ 5 8. 612 ÷ 3 9. 427 ÷ 4 10. 962 ÷ 8

Set E (Lesson 6, pp. 244–246)

Estimate. Then divide.

1. 4)1,799 2. 2)2,560 3. 3)3,037 4. 9)4,554 5. 6)4,274

6. 6,413 ÷ 7 7. 15,481 ÷ 3 8. 20,415 ÷ 4 9. 31,985 ÷ 5 10. 65,738 ÷ 8

Number Theory and Mean

Using Data

The table shows how many children used some of the slides at a fair. About how many children would you guess used the red slide on Thursday? What information from the table did you use to make your guess?

Children Using Slides

	Tuesday	Wednesday	Thursday
Red	151	298	?
Blue	160	321	638
Pink	190	399	791
Green	144	288	590

Use What You Know

**Use this page to review and remember
what you need to know for this chapter.**

VOCABULARY

Choose the best word to complete each sentence.

1. In the number sentence $4 \times 7 = 28$, 7 is a ____.

2. In the number sentence $32 \div 4 = 8$, 32 is the ____.

3. The number you divide by is the ____.

4. The answer in a division problem is the ____.

> **Vocabulary**
> factor
> divisor
> product
> quotient
> dividend

CONCEPTS AND SKILLS

Skip count to find the missing numbers.

5. 15, 20, 25, ■, ■, ■

6. 40, 50, ■, ■, 80

7. 4, 8, 12, ■, ■, ■

8. 6, 9, ■, 15, ■, ■

9. ■, 12, 18, ■, ■

10. ■, ■, 32, ■, 48, 56

**Write a division sentence and a multiplication sentence
for each picture.**

11.

12.

13.

Solve.

14. $6 + 134 + 23$

15. $5 + 6 + 21 + 33$

16. $100 + 98 + 178$

17. $1,976 \div 8$

18. $896 \div 7$

19. $50,670 \div 9$

Write About It

20. What do the numbers 5, 10, 15, 20,
25, 30, 35, and 40 have in common?

Facts Practice, See Page 670.

Audio Tutor 1/34 Listen and Understand

Factors and Multiples

Objective Find factors and multiples of whole numbers.

Vocabulary
factor
multiple

Materials
Multiplication Table
(Learning Tool 13)

Work Together

You can use a multiplication table to find **factors**.

Work with a partner.

STEP 1 Find 18 on the multiplication table.

- Look at the number at the top of the column. 6 is a factor of 18.

- Look at the number at the side of the row. 3 is a factor of 18.

$$6 \times 3 = 18$$

factor   factor

column ↓

×	1	2	3	4	5	6	7	8	9	10	11	12
1	1	2	3	4	5	6	7	8	9	10	11	12
2	2	4	6	8	10	12	14	16	18	20	22	24
3	3	6	9	12	15	18	21	24	27	30	33	36
4	4	8	12	16	20	24	28	32	36	40	44	48
5	5	10	15	20	25	30	35	40	45	50	55	60
6	6	12	18	24	30	36	42	48	54	60	66	72
7	7	14	21	28	35	42	49	56	63	70	77	84
8	8	16	24	32	40	48	56	64	72	80	88	96
9	9	18	27	36	45	54	63	72	81	90	99	10
10	10	20	30	40	50	60	70	80	90	100	110	12
11	11	22	33	44	55	66	77	88	99	110	121	13
12	12	24	36	48	60	72	84	96	108	120	132	14

row →

STEP 2 Find 18 in other places on the table. List other factors of 18.

STEP 3 Repeat Steps 1 and 2 to find factors of 24.

- What factors did you find?

- Do you think these are all of the factors of 24? Explain.

You can also use a multiplication table to find multiples.

▶ A **multiple** of a number is a product of that number and any whole number.

Some multiples of 2 are 2, 4, 6, 8, and 10.

Extra Help at **eduplace.com/map**

Follow these steps to find common multiples.

STEP 4

Look at the column that starts with 2. All the numbers in this column are multiples of 2.

• List the multiples of 2 on the table.

Look at the column that starts with 3. All the numbers in this column are multiples of 3.

• List the multiples of 3 on the table.

These numbers that are on both lists are common multiples of 2 and 3.

• List the common multiples of 2 and 3.

×	1	2	3	4	5	6	7	8	9	10	11	12
1	1	2	3	4	5	6	7	8	9	10	11	12
2	2	4	6	8	10	12	14	16	18	20	22	24
3	3	6	9	12	15	18	21	24	27	30	33	36
4	4	8	12	16	20	24	28	32	36	40	44	48
5	5	10	15	20	25	30	35	40	45	50	55	60
6	6	12	18	24	30	36	42	48	54	60	66	72
7	7	14	21	28	35	42	49	56	63	70	77	84
8	8	16	24	32	40	48	56	64	72	80	88	96
9	9	18	27	36	45	54	63	72	81	90	99	108
10	10	20	30	40	50	60	70	80	90	100	110	120
11	11	22	33	44	55	66	77	88	99	110	121	132
12	12	24	36	48	60	72	84	96	108	120	132	144

STEP 5

Repeat Step 4. This time list the multiples of 3 and 6 on the table.

• What common multiples of 3 and 6 did you find?

On Your Own

List the factors on the table for each number.

1. 12   **2.** 45   **3.** 100   **4.** 11   **5.** 72

Use the table to list 10 multiples for each number in each pair. Then circle the common multiples.

6. 2, 5   **7.** 6, 10   **8.** 3, 7   **9.** 9, 10   **10.** 4, 12

Talk About It • Write About It

You learned how to find factors and multiples of numbers.

11. Explain Are all the factors of a number shown on the multiplication table? Are all the multiples shown? Give examples to explain your answers.

12. Reasoning Do you think a number that has 8 as a factor will also have 4 as a factor? Explain your thinking.

Audio Tutor 1/35 Listen and Understand

Prime and Composite Numbers

Objective Tell if a number is prime or composite.

Learn About It

You can use the factors of a number to tell if it is a prime number or a composite number.

> ▶ A **prime number** is a whole number that has exactly two factors, 1 and itself.

Some prime numbers are 19, 29, 31.

Number	Factors
19	1, 19
29	1, 29
31	1, 31

> ▶ A **composite number** is a whole number that has more than two factors.

Some composite numbers are 15, 18, 25.

Number	Factors
15	1, 3, 5, 15
18	1, 2, 3, 6, 9, 18
25	1, 5, 25

Try this activity to tell if a number is prime or composite.

STEP 1 You can make arrays to find the factors of a number. Use 6 counters to make an array like the one shown.

- How many counters are in each row? in each column?
- What are two factors of 6?

STEP 2 Continue to make arrays to find all of the factors of 6.
- What arrays did you make?
- What are the factors of 6?

Record the factors from least to greatest in a chart like the one shown.

Number	Factors
1	
2	
3	
4	
5	
6	1, 2, 3, 6
7	

STEP 3 Repeat Steps 1 and 2 for the numbers 1 through 12.
- Which number has only 1 factor?
- Which numbers have exactly 2 factors?
- Which numbers have more than 2 factors?

 STEP 4 Look at your chart.
- List the prime numbers. List the composite numbers. Explain how you made your lists.
- What number is not on either of your lists? Why not?

Since the number 1 has only 1 factor it is neither prime nor composite.

Guided Practice

Tell if each array represents a prime number or a composite number.

1. ● ● ● ● ●
   ● ● ● ● ●

2. ● ● ● ● ●

3. ● ●
   ● ●
   ● ●

4. ● ● ● ●
   ● ● ● ●
   ● ● ● ●
   ● ● ● ●

5. ● ● ● ● ● ●

6. ● ● ●

Ask Yourself
- Can I make another array with the same number of counters?
- Does the number have more than 2 factors?

List the factors of each number. Use counters if you wish. Then tell if the number is prime or composite.

7. 22   8. 16   9. 42   10. 13   11. 18

12. 23   13. 17   14. 25   15. 31   16. 20

Explain Your Thinking ▶ How does making arrays help you tell if a number is prime or composite?

Go On

List the factors of each number. Use counters if you wish. Then tell if the number is prime or composite.

17. 21	**18.** 19	**19.** 15	**20.** 27	**21.** 100
22. 47	**23.** 24	**24.** 51	**25.** 26	**26.** 28

Tell if each number is prime or composite.

27. 39	**28.** 41	**29.** 37	**30.** 33	**31.** 49
32. 54	**33.** 53	**34.** 95	**35.** 46	**36.** 60
37. 52	**38.** 69	**39.** 71	**40.** 16	**41.** 30

Solve.

42. Analyze Are any even numbers prime? Are all odd numbers prime? Use examples to explain.

43. Are there any whole numbers that have 0 or 5 in the ones place that are prime? Explain your thinking.

44. Explain Do you need to list every factor of a number to tell if it is prime or composite? Why or why not?

45. What's Wrong? Look at Toby's work. She decided that 5 is a composite number because she can make 2 arrays with 5 counters. Explain what is wrong with Toby's reasoning.

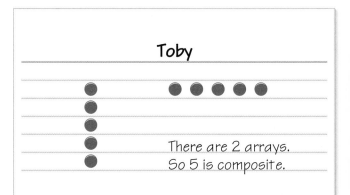

Toby

There are 2 arrays. So 5 is composite.

Open Response

Divide. (Ch. 9, Lessons 3, 6)

46. $0.36 ÷ 3   **47.** $0.92 ÷ 4

48. $7.50 ÷ 6   **49.** 1,230 ÷ 6

Multiple Choice

50. Which is a prime number?

(Ch. 10, Lesson 2)

A 1   **C** 21

B 10   **D** 43

Extra Practice see page 269, Set A.

Math Challenge
The Sieve of Eratosthenes

Materials
Learning Tool 14

Eratosthenes was an ancient Greek mathematician who discovered a way to find prime numbers from 1 to 100.

Follow the steps below to find out how.

1	②	3	4	5	6	7	8	9	10
11	12	13	14	15	16	17	18	19	20
21	22	23	24	25	26	27	28	29	30
31	32	33	34	35	36	37	38	39	40
41	42	43	44	45	46	47	48	49	50

1 Use Learning Tool 14. Draw a box around 1. Circle 2. Cross out all multiples of 2 greater than 2.

2 Circle the least number on the table that is not boxed, circled, or crossed out. Cross out all multiples of that number greater than that number.

3 Repeat Step 2 until all the numbers have been crossed out or circled.

4 List the numbers you circled. What do you notice about these numbers?

The number
1
is not prime
or composite.

Check your understanding of Lessons 1–2.

List five multiples of each number. (Lesson 1)

1. 3
2. 8
3. 6

4. 7
5. 9

List the factors of each number. Tell if the number is prime or composite. (Lesson 2)

6. 43
7. 51
8. 24

9. 77
10. 28

Problem-Solving Strategy
Solve a Simpler Problem

Objective Use a simpler problem to help you solve a problem.

Problem At a fair, 8 teams are in a potato-sack relay race. Each team must race against each of the other teams once. How many races are needed?

UNDERSTAND

This is what you know.

- There are 8 teams.

- Each team must race against each of the other teams once.

PLAN

You can solve a simpler problem and look for a pattern.

SOLVE

Solve the problem for fewer teams.

2 Teams	3 Teams	4 Teams	5 Teams
A ⟷ B			
1 race	3 races	6 races	10 races

Look for a pattern you can use.

Number of Teams: 2   3   4   5   6   7   8

Number of Races: 1   3   6   10   15   21   28
                   +2   +3   +4   +5   +6   +7

- The differences increase by 1 each time.
- Continue the pattern.

Solution: 28 races are needed for 8 teams.

LOOK BACK

How does solving the problem for fewer teams help you?

Guided Practice

Use the Ask Yourself questions to help you solve each problem.

1. There are 6 judges at a race. Each judge shakes hands with every other judge once. How many handshakes is that?

2. A worker is using boards to divide a rectangular animal pen into a row of 12 smaller goat pens. How many boards does the worker need?

   (Hint) How many boards are needed to make 2 pens? 3 pens?

Ask Yourself

UNDERSTAND **What facts do I know?**

PLAN **Can I solve a simpler problem?**

SOLVE • **What simpler problem should I start with?**
  • **What is the pattern?**

LOOK BACK **Does my answer make sense?**

Independent Practice

Use a simpler problem to solve each problem.

3. Cheryl works at a taco stand at a fair. A sign says: "Buy 2 Tacos, Get 3rd FREE!" How many tacos will Cheryl make if customers pay for 20 tacos?

4. Taco shells are stored in boxes. The boxes are labeled on the top and front. How many labels can be seen if the boxes are stacked in 5 rows of 4 boxes?

5. **Measurement** Six 4-foot square boards are placed end to end to make a rectangular stage at the fair. What is the distance around the rectangle they form?

6. Joshua is using straws to make a row of hexagons as shown. How many straws will Joshua need to make a row of 12 hexagons?

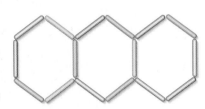

Go On

Mixed Problem Solving

Solve. Show your work. Tell what strategy you used.

7. Children at a picnic eat at a long table made up of 14 small tables placed end to end. Each small table seats 1 person on each side. How many people can sit at the long table?

8. There are 10 hot dogs in a package. Jameel buys 12 packages. Buns come in packages of 8. How many packages of buns should he buy so that he has a bun for every hot dog?

9. The product of two factors is 96. The difference between the factors is 4. What are the factors?

You Choose

Strategy
- Guess and Check
- Solve a Simpler Problem
- Work Backward
- Write an Equation

Computation Method
- Mental Math
- Estimation
- Paper and Pencil
- Calculator

 Data **The graph shows the number and types of pumpkins that are for sale. Use the graph for Problems 10–13.**

10. How many mini pumpkins are for sale?

11. **Money** Mini pumpkins sell for $1 each. Sugar pumpkins sell for $5 each. If the farmer sells all of the mini and sugar pumpkins, how much money will he make?

12. **Analyze** The Cinderella pumpkins are displayed in 5 rows of 6. Can the Giant pumpkins also be displayed in equal rows of 6? How do you know?

13. Next year, the farmer wants to sell 200 pumpkins. How many more pumpkins will she have for sale next year than this year?

Pumpkins for Sale	
Mini	🎃🎃🎃🎃🎃
Cinderella	🎃🎃🎃
Sugar	🎃🎃🎃🎃🎃🎃
Giant	🎃🎃
🎃 = 10 pumpkins	

Problem Solving on Tests

Multiple Choice

Choose the letter of the correct answer. If the correct answer is not here, choose NH.

1. Mr. Lee is buying 11 baseball caps. Each cap costs $11. How much will 11 caps cost?

   A $111

   B $120

   C $121

   D NH

   (Chapter 4, Lesson 6)

2. Which shirt has a prime number?

   F 9

   G 1

   H 7

   J 4

   (Chapter 9, Lesson 6)

Open Response

3. A movie theater has 205 seats. A movie is shown 3 times one day and 4 times a second day. How many people can see the movie in the two days? Explain.

   (Chapter 6, Lesson 6)

4. A box contains 1,215 red, white, and blue beads with the same number of each color. How many red beads are in the box?

   (Chapter 7, Lesson 2)

Extended Response

5. Madisonville soccer team held a bake sale to raise money for a trip to Washington D.C. The team hoped to raise $100 at this sale. Did they reach their goal? How much money did they get toward the trip?

Bake Sale	
Cupcakes	$0.75
Pies	$5.00
Cookies	4 for $1.00
Cakes	$7.00

Information you need:

- They started the sale with 56 cupcakes, 4 pies, 5 cakes, and 36 cookies.

- Gary arrived late, bringing 2 more pies and 48 cookies to sell.

- Mrs. Gray said she didn't need any baked goods, but she donated $10.

- At the end of the day, they had 1 cake and 12 cookies left over.

- The Mayor said the town would match the money they raise from the sale.

Explain How did you solve this problem?

(Chapter 1, Lesson 3)

 Education Place

See **eduplace.com/map** for more Test-Taking Tips.

Model Mean

Objective Use counters to model finding a mean.

Vocabulary

mean
average

Materials
counters

Work Together

Finding a **mean** is one way to find a number that is typical of the numbers in a group. The mean of a group of numbers is sometimes called the **average**.

At a fair, Ana played Topple the Bottles. The first time she played, she hit 5 bottles, the second time 9 bottles, and the third time 7 bottles. What was the mean number of bottles Ana hit?

Work with a partner to use counters to find a mean.

STEP 1

Make a column of counters to show how many bottles Ana hit each time.

- How many columns of counters did you make?

- How many counters are in each column?

STEP 2

To find the mean, move counters from one column to another until there is the same number in each.

- How many counters are in each column?

This number is the mean.

- What is the mean number of bottles Ana hit?

Use counters to find the mean of the numbers in each group.

1. 6, 8   **2.** 4, 8   **3.** 2, 2, 5   **4.** 10, 1, 1

5. 4, 9, 3, 8   **6.** 4, 1, 1, 1, 3   **7.** 8, 3, 4, 5   **8.** 5, 7, 3, 9

9. 6, 3, 4, 1, 1   **10.** 4, 6, 8, 2   **11.** 5, 5, 7, 3, 5   **12.** 9, 8, 7, 4

$\mathcal{X}$ **Algebra • Variables Use counters to find the missing number in each group.**

Mean = 2
13. ⬛ 3, ⬛

Mean = 5
14. ⬛, 7

Mean = 6
15. 5, 3, ⬛

Mean = 6
16. ⬛, 4, 2

Mean = 4
17. 1, 9, ⬛

Mean = 7
18. 12, ⬛, 6

Solve.

19. Matt's scores for a ring-the-bell game were 6, 5, and 10. What was his mean score?

20. Ana's scores for the ring-the-bell game were 8, 8, and 8. What was her mean score? What do you notice about her mean?

21. **Create and Solve** Write a problem for which the answer has a mean of 9. Have a classmate use counters to solve your problem.

Talk About It • Write About It

You learned that a mean is a number that is typical of the numbers in a group.

22. **Predict** Look at the numbers 2, 5, 14, 1, and 3. Will the mean of these numbers be closer to 1 or to 14? Explain. Then use counters to check your prediction.

23. **Analyze** What operations could you use to find the mean of the numbers in a group? Explain your thinking.

Find the Mean

Objective Find the mean of
a group of numbers.

Learn About It

At a county fair 15 ribbons were awarded
in animal contests, 21 in eating contests,
and 12 in baking contests. What was the
mean number of ribbons awarded?

To calculate the **mean** of the numbers
in a group, divide their sum by the number
of addends.

Remember
The mean of a group of
numbers is sometimes
called the average.

Find the mean of 15, 21, and 12.

STEP 1 Find the sum of the numbers.
Count the addends.

$$
\begin{array}{r}
15 \\
21 \\
+\ 12 \\
\hline
48
\end{array}
$$

← 3 addends

STEP 2 Divide the sum by the
number of addends.

$$
\begin{array}{r}
16 \\
3\overline{)48} \\
-\ 3 \\
\hline
18 \\
-\ 18 \\
\hline
0
\end{array}
$$

Solution: The mean number of ribbons awarded is 16.

Guided Practice

Find the mean of the numbers in each group.

1. 6, 8, 9, 33

2. 34, 45, 26

3. 43, 10, 25, 38

4. 41, 39, 29, 19

5. 124, 157, 214

6. 175, 152, 105

Ask Yourself
- What is the sum of
the numbers?
- How many numbers
are in the group?

Explain Your Thinking ▶ Can the mean of the numbers in a group
be greater than the greatest number in the group?
Explain why or why not.

Find the mean of the numbers in each group.

7. 1, 4, 4

8. $3, $4, $8

9. 10, 12, 17

10. $22, $31, $55

11. $3, $5, $6, $6

12. 15, 24, 44, 29

13. 2, 9, 28, 41

14. 50, 25, 10, 15

15. 15, 499, 7, 100, 4

16. $62, $64, $104, $150

17. 11, 12, 16, 17, 19

18. $20, $36, $36, $48, $10

 Predict **Predict the mean for each set of numbers. Then use a calculator to find the mean.**

19. 5, 10, 10, 10, 15

20. 56, 57, 58, 59, 60

21. 35, 40, 45, 50, 55

22. 80, 100, 120, 140

23. 15, 15, 30, 30, 45, 45

24. 100, 200, 300, 400

 Algebra • **Variables** **Find the missing number in each group.**

25. Mean = 36
27, 34, ▪

26. Mean = 9
12, 9, 7, ▪

27. Mean = $225
$240, $189, ▪

28. Mean = 80
95, 89, 50, ▪

29. Mean = 23
25, 20, 16, ▪

30. Mean = 55
16, 26, 99, 18, ▪

31. Can the mean of the numbers in a group be equal to one of the numbers in the group? Use an example to explain.

32. **Create and Solve** List three numbers that have a mean of 121. Explain how you chose the three numbers.

Go On

Choose a Computation Method

Mental Math • Estimation • Paper and Pencil • Calculator

Solve. Tell which method you chose.

33. Sam reads 84 pages of a book about the Illinois State Fair in 4 days. What is the mean number of pages he reads each day?

34. Adele's family's car can travel 28 miles on one gallon of gas. About how many miles can the car travel on 13 gallons of gas?

35. Adele's family took a trip to the state fair. During the trip, Adele's mother drove 275 miles a day for 4 days. How many miles did she drive?

36. A pier in Chicago is open 7 days a week. One week it had 96,586 visitors. What was the mean number of visitors to the pier each day?

 Data Use the table for Problems 37–40.

37. Mental Math What is the average number of tickets needed for a ride?

38. What is the average number of riders?

39. How many more tickets were sold for the most popular ride than for the least popular ride? Explain how you got your answer.

 40. Write About It Suppose a Ferris wheel had 455 riders. How would this affect the average number of riders at the carnival? Explain your answer.

 41. Calculator There were 1,572 people at the fair on Saturday, 1,245 on Sunday, and 420 on Monday. What was the average attendance for the 3 days?

Carnival Rides		
Ride	Number of Riders	Number of Tickets Needed
Twister Coaster	314	5
Flying Saucer	355	3
Spinning Top	129	4

Mixed Review and Test Prep

Open Response

Divide. Check your answers. (Ch. 9, Lesson 3)

42. 5)$11.25

43. 8)$27.60

44. 3)$13.23

45. 5)$10.70

Multiple Choice

46. What is the mean of the numbers 12, 14, 21, 32, and 11?

(Ch. 10, Lesson 5)

A 14   **B** 18   **C** 32   **D** 90

266

 Extra Practice See page 269, Set B.

Math Challenge
Factor Trees

A composite number can be written as the product of its **prime factors**. To find the prime factors of a composite number, you can make a **factor tree**.

Problem Solving

Vocabulary
prime factors
factor tree

STEP 1 Write a pair of factors for 24.

24
4 × 6

STEP 2 Write a pair of factors for each factor until all the factors are prime numbers.

24
4 × 6
2 × 2 × 2 × 3

$2 \times 2 \times 2 \times 3 = 24$, so the prime factors of 24 are 2, 2, 2, 3.

▶ You can often make different factor trees for one number.

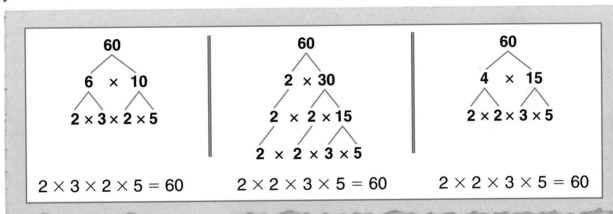

60	60	60
6 × 10	2 × 30	4 × 15
2 × 3 × 2 × 5	2 × 2 × 15	2 × 2 × 3 × 5
	2 × 2 × 3 × 5	
$2 \times 3 \times 2 \times 5 = 60$	$2 \times 2 \times 3 \times 5 = 60$	$2 \times 2 \times 3 \times 5 = 60$

No matter which factors you start with, the prime factors are 2, 2, 3, 5.

Make a factor tree to find the prime factors of each number.

1. 12   2. 27   3. 50   4. 48   5. 65   6. 100

7. **Represent** Look back at Exercises 1–6. Write a number sentence that shows the prime factors of each number.

8. **Explain** Han says that greater numbers have more prime factors than lesser numbers. Is Han correct? Use examples to explain your thinking.

Chapter Review/Test

VOCABULARY

Choose the best term to complete each sentence.

1. A composite number has more than two ____.

2. One way to find the ____ of the numbers in a group is to divide their sum by the number of addends.

3. A ____ of a number is the product of that number and any whole number.

Vocabulary

factors
mean
product
multiple

CONCEPTS AND SKILLS

List 3 multiples of each number. (Lesson 1, pp. 252–253)

4. 3   **5.** 4   **6.** 6   **7.** 8

List the factors of each number. Tell if the number is prime or composite. (Lesson 2, pp. 254–257)

8. 9   **9.** 18   **10.** 24   **11.** 19

12. 2   **13.** 15   **14.** 30   **15.** 11

Find the mean of the numbers in each group. (Lessons 4, 5, pp. 262–266)

16. 3, 5, 7, 9, 11   **17.** $16, $25, $39, $52   **18.** 112, 105, 80, 86, 92

PROBLEM SOLVING

Solve. (Lesson 3, pp. 258–261)

19. One person can sit on each side of a square table. If 10 square tables are placed end-to-end, how many people can be seated?

20. There are 6 people at a meeting. Each person shakes the hand of every other person one time. How many handshakes are there?

Write About It

Show You Understand

Margaret received the following scores on her math test.

70, 80, 95, 75, 80

Explain why Margaret's mean has to be above 70 and below 95.

Extra Practice

Set A (Lesson 2, pp. 254–257)

Tell if each array represents a prime or composite number.

1. ● ● ● ● ●

2. ● ● ●
   ● ● ●

3. ● ● ● ●

4. ● ● ●
   ● ● ●
   ● ● ●

5. ● ● ● ● ● ●

6. ● ● ●

List all the factors of each number. Then tell if the number is prime or composite.

7. 5   8. 9   9. 13   10. 21   11. 27   12. 31

13. 39   14. 42   15. 55   16. 67   17. 74   18. 81

Set B (Lesson 5, pp. 264–267)

Find the mean of the numbers in each group.

1. 19, 27, 53   2. $36, $51, $99   3. 5, 29, 35, 71

4. 16, 36, 44, 76   5. 9, 50, 72, 85, 94   6. 10, 28, 42, 60, 95

Find the missing number in each group.

Mean = 30
7. 14, 28, ■

Mean = 10
8. 15, 6, 3, ■

Mean = $155
9. $140, $199, ■

Use the table for Problems 10–12.

10. What is the mean number of players?

11. What is the average number of tickets needed?

12. Suppose a Can Game had 100 players. How would this affect the mean number of players? Explain.

Carnival Games		
	Number of Players	Number of Tickets Needed
Ring Toss	156	3
Ball Throw	108	7
Water Spray Race	237	5

Extra Practice at **eduplace.com/map**

Divide by Two-Digit Divisors

INVESTIGATION

Using Data

Arbor Day is a national holiday that celebrates trees. The bar graph shows the number of trees that were planted by groups of volunteers on Arbor Day. Ten groups of people planted the same number of trees. How could you find the number of trees that each group planted? Use your method to solve.

Trees Planted on Arbor Day

Use What You Know

**Use this page to review and remember
what you need to know for this chapter.**

VOCABULARY

Choose the best word to complete each sentence.

Vocabulary
divisor
multiple
quotient
dividend

1. In the expression 350 ÷ 5, the number 350 is the _____.

2. In the division sentence 630 ÷ 9 = 70, the number 70 is the _____.

3. The number 30 is a _____ of 6.

CONCEPTS AND SKILLS

Divide.

4. 4)76   5. 7)89   6. 8)97   7. 7)68   8. 3)936

9. 7)787   10. 5)578   11. 4)845   12. 4)396   13. 7)224

14. 8)350   15. 5)128   16. 6)$7.44   17. 4)$1.28   18. 8)$9.84

19. $8.75 ÷ 5   20. $7.74 ÷ 9   21. $6.57 ÷ 3   22. $9.45 ÷ 7   23. $9.08 ÷ 2

 Write About It

24. What basic fact can you use to divide 4,000 by 8? How many zeros will be in the quotient?

25. **What's Wrong?** A van can carry 7 passengers. Danielle says that 4 vans are needed to carry 29 passengers. What is Danielle doing wrong?

Danielle

4 R1
7)29

Facts Practice, See Page 671.

Divide by Multiples of 10

Objective Use division facts to divide by multiples of 10.

Learn About It

A group of students swam a total of 80 laps at a charity swim-a-thon. If each student swam 20 laps, how many students were in the group?

Divide. $80 \div 20 = $ ■

> ▶ **You can use basic facts to help you divide.**
>
> $8 \div 2 = 4$ ← basic fact
>
> $80 \div 20 = 4$ ← Think: 8 tens ÷ 2 tens = 4

Solution: There were 4 students in the group.

Other Examples

A. Basic Fact $21 \div 7 = 3$

$210 \div 70 = 3$

$2,100 \div 70 = 30$

$21,000 \div 70 = 300$

B. Basic Fact $20 \div 4 = 5$

$200 \div 40 = 5$

$2,000 \div 40 = 50$

$20,000 \div 40 = 500$

Guided Practice

Use basic facts to help you divide.

1. $42 \div 6 = $ ■
    $420 \div 60 = $ ■
    $4,200 \div 60 = $ ■
    $42,000 \div 60 = $ ■

2. $40 \div 8 = $ ■
    $400 \div 80 = $ ■
    $4,000 \div 80 = $ ■
    $40,000 \div 80 = $ ■

Ask Yourself

• How many digits will the quotient have?

Explain Your Thinking ▶ In Exercises 1 and 2, how do the number of zeros in the quotients compare to the number of zeros in the dividends?

Use basic facts to help you divide.

3. $25 \div 5 = \blacksquare$
$250 \div 50 = \blacksquare$

4. $14 \div 2 = \blacksquare$
$140 \div 20 = \blacksquare$

5. $6 \div 2 = \blacksquare$
$600 \div 20 = \blacksquare$

6. $81 \div 9 = \blacksquare$
$8{,}100 \div 90 = \blacksquare$

7. $54 \div 6 = \blacksquare$
$5{,}400 \div 60 = \blacksquare$

8. $12 \div 4 = \blacksquare$
$12{,}000 \div 40 = \blacksquare$

9. $80\overline{)640}$

10. $10\overline{)900}$

11. $70\overline{)490}$

12. $30\overline{)1{,}500}$

13. $60\overline{)4{,}200}$

14. $30\overline{)9{,}000}$

15. $50\overline{)40{,}000}$

16. $90\overline{)63{,}000}$

 Algebra • Equations Find each value of n.

17. $2{,}800 \div n = 70$

18. $5{,}400 \div n = 90$

19. $n \div 80 = 50$

20. $n \div 60 = 600$

21. $16{,}000 \div n = 800$

22. $n \div 70 = 700$

Solve.

23. Twenty towns sent 180 swimmers to a charity swim. If each town sent the same number of swimmers, how many swimmers did each town send?

24. Marty swims 3,000 meters in 6 days. Each lap he swims is 50 meters. If he swims the same number of laps each day, how many laps does Marty swim each day?

25. There are 1,800 spectators seated at a regional swim meet. Each row of seats has 60 spectators. How many rows are there?

26. Reasoning In a race, Team D finished ahead of Team A but after Team B. Team C finished ahead of Team B. Which team won?

Mixed Review and Test Prep

Open Response

Compare. Write >, <, or = for each ⬤.
(Ch. 2, Lesson 1)

27. 4,386 ⬤ 4,386

28. 725,000 ⬤ 527,000

29. 136,200,948 ⬤ 136,295,104

Multiple Choice

30. What is the value of n?
(Ch. 11, Lesson 1)

$$720 \div n = 90$$

A 8

C 80

B 9

D 300

Estimate Quotients

Objective Estimate quotients.

Learn About It

Zoe's town held a beach cleanup. On the day of the cleanup, 19 families collected 184 bags of trash. About how many bags of trash did each family collect?

You can estimate to find $184 \div 19$. One way to estimate $184 \div 19$ is to use basic facts and multiples of 10.

Estimate. $19\overline{)184}$

STEP 1 Use basic facts and multiples of 10 to find a new dividend and a new divisor.

$19\overline{)184}$
$\downarrow \quad \downarrow$
$20\overline{)180}$

 The basic fact $18 \div 2 = 9$ can help you.

STEP 2 Divide.

$$\begin{array}{r} 9 \\ 20\overline{)180} \end{array}$$

So $19\overline{)184}$ is about 9.

Solution: Each family collected about 9 bags of trash.

Another Example

Two-Digit Dividend

Estimate $63 \div 29$.

$63 \div 29$
$\downarrow \quad \downarrow$
$60 \div 30 = 2$

The basic fact $6 \div 3 = 2$ can help you.

$63 \div 29$ is about 2.

Ask Yourself
• What basic fact can I use?
• What is the quotient of the new dividend and divisor?

Guided Practice

Use a new dividend and a new divisor to estimate each quotient.

1. $82 \div 18$
$80 \div \blacksquare = \blacksquare$

2. $488 \div 67$
$490 \div \blacksquare = \blacksquare$

3. $158 \div 42$
$\blacksquare \div 40 = \blacksquare$

4. $62\overline{)368}$

5. $43\overline{)250}$

6. $69\overline{)355}$

7. $84\overline{)491}$

Explain Your Thinking ▶ How can an estimate help you decide where to place the first digit in the quotient?

Practice and Problem Solving

Estimate each quotient.

8. $48\overline{)99}$

9. $19\overline{)83}$

10. $63\overline{)379}$

11. $71\overline{)223}$

12. $89\overline{)448}$

13. $68\overline{)559}$

14. $78\overline{)637}$

15. $18\overline{)138}$

16. $98 \div 52$

17. $42 \div 18$

18. $562 \div 81$

19. $308 \div 52$

20. Volunteers collected 719 pounds of trash in 81 bags. About how many pounds of trash did each bag hold?

21. Analyze There are 96 bottles in 12 boxes in Juan's garage. Each box holds the same number of bottles. Juan says that number is 6. Is he right? Explain your thinking.

22. Some creative people make art from trash. Suppose an artist uses 312 pounds of scrap metal to make 36 sculptures. About how much does each sculpture weigh?

This sculpture is made with discarded metal from tool chests, cabinets, and cars.

Mixed Review and Test Prep ✓

Open Response

Use basic facts and patterns to find each product. (Ch. 6, Lesson 1)

23. 7×50

24. 7×500

25. 9×600

26. $4 \times 8,000$

27. What is the best estimate for $481 \div 79$? Explain your thinking.
(Ch. 11, Lesson 2)

Extra Practice See page 291, Set B.

Audio Tutor 1/36 Listen and Understand

Model Division by Two-Digit Divisors

Objective Model division by two-digit divisors.

Work Together

You can use base-ten blocks to model division by a two-digit divisor.

Work with a partner. Use base-ten blocks to find 34 ÷ 11.

STEP 1

Show 34 with the base-ten blocks.

11)‾34‾

- How many tens do you have?
- How many ones?

STEP 2

Estimate to find about how many groups there will be.

- About how many groups will there be?

$$34 \div 11$$
$$\downarrow \qquad \downarrow$$
$$30 \div 10 = 3$$

STEP 3

Use your estimate. Try to divide 3 tens 4 ones into 3 groups of 11.

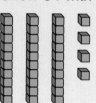

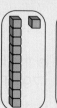

```
        3 R1
11)‾34‾  Multiply. 3 × 11
  − 33   Subtract. 34 − 33 = 1
     1   Compare. 1 < 11
```

- What is the quotient?

Use base-ten blocks to find 158 ÷ 31.

STEP 1
Show 158 with base-ten blocks.

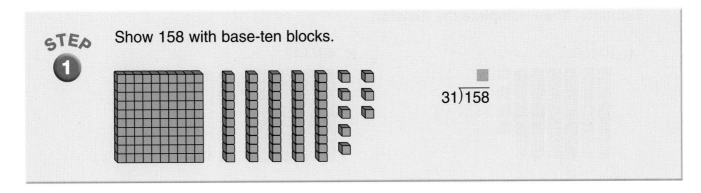

$$31\overline{)158}$$

STEP 2
Estimate to find about how many groups there will be.

158 ÷ 31
↓   ↓
150 ÷ 30 = 5

• About how many groups will there be?

STEP 3
There is 1 hundred. You cannot divide it into five groups. So regroup 1 hundred as 10 tens.

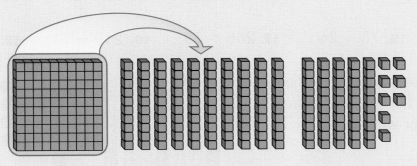

• How many tens do you have now?

STEP 4
Try to divide the tens and ones into 5 groups of 31.

 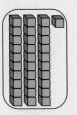 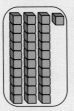 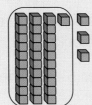

```
        5 R3
31)158   Multiply. 5 × 31
-155     Subtract. 158 − 155 = 3
   3     Compare. 3 < 31
```

• What is the quotient?

Go On

On Your Own

Estimate. Then complete the division.

1. 31)64

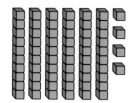

2. 48)149

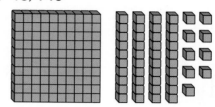

3. 22)45

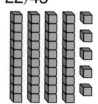

4. 27)168

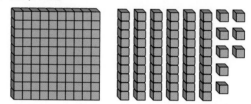

Use models to divide.

5. 17)39   6. 21)84   7. 11)68   8. 31)94   9. 41)88

10. 21)149   11. 29)185   12. 38)204   13. 52)162   14. 43)177

15. 88 ÷ 28   16. 73 ÷ 24   17. 245 ÷ 39   18. 219 ÷ 71   19. 149 ÷ 19

20. Mike says that the model at the right shows 48 ÷ 11 = 4. Is he correct? Explain why or why not.

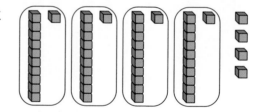

Talk About It • Write About It

You learned how to use base-ten blocks to model division by two-digit divisors.

21. Why is it helpful to estimate before trying to divide with base-ten blocks?

22. Look back at Exercises 5–19. When did you need to regroup?

Social Studies Connection
Old Faithful

Old Faithful is a geyser in Yellowstone National Park. A geyser is a natural hot spring that erupts, sending water and steam into the air. Old Faithful erupts about once every 76 minutes.

1. About how many times does Old Faithful erupt during an eight-hour period?

   (Hint) Find how many minutes there are in 8 hours. Then estimate.

2. About how many times will Old Faithful erupt in a day? in a week? in a year?

One eruption of Old Faithful sends out 3,700 to 8,400 gallons of boiling water.

WEEKLY WR READER eduplace.com/map

Check your understanding of Lessons 1–3.

Use basic facts to help you divide. (Lesson 1)

1. $15 \div 3 = \blacksquare$
   $150 \div 30 = \blacksquare$

2. $42 \div 7 = \blacksquare$
   $420 \div 70 = \blacksquare$

3. $64 \div 8 = \blacksquare$
   $6{,}400 \div 80 = \blacksquare$

4. $72 \div 9 = \blacksquare$
   $72{,}000 \div 90 = \blacksquare$

Use a new dividend and a new divisor to estimate the quotient. (Lesson 2)

5. $79 \div 38$
   ↓   ↓
   $80 \div \blacksquare = \blacksquare$

6. $542 \div 57$
   ↓   ↓
   $\blacksquare \div 60 = \blacksquare$

7. $479 \div 82$
   ↓   ↓
   $\blacksquare \div \blacksquare = \blacksquare$

Use models to divide. (Lesson 3)

8. $12\overline{)62}$

9. $18\overline{)76}$

10. $29\overline{)146}$

One-Digit Quotients

Objective Divide when the quotient has one digit.

Vocabulary

dividend

Learn About It

Isabel's class is making tissue-paper art for the Elder Care Center. There are 235 sheets of tissue paper. If 28 students share the tissue paper equally, how many sheets can each student use? How many sheets will be left?

Divide. $235 \div 28$ or $28\overline{)235}$

STEP 1 Estimate to decide where to place the first digit.

$$28\overline{)235} \rightarrow \overset{8}{30\overline{)240}}$$

Write the first digit of the quotient in the ones place.

STEP 2 Try the estimate. Divide.

$$\begin{array}{r} 8 \text{ R11} \\ 28\overline{)235} \\ -\ 224 \\ \hline 11 \end{array}$$

Multiply. 8×28
Subtract. $235 - 224$
Compare. $11 < 28$

Check your answer.
Multiply. Then add.

$(28 \times 8) + 11 = 235$

The sum equals the **dividend**.

Solution: Each student can use 8 sheets of tissue paper. There will be 11 sheets left.

Another Example
Two-Digit Dividend

Find $43 \div 19$.

Divide.

$$\begin{array}{r} 2 \text{ R5} \\ 19\overline{)43} \\ -\ 38 \\ \hline 5 \end{array}$$

Check your answer.

$(19 \times 2) + 5 = 43$

Guided Practice

Estimate to decide where to place the first digit. Then divide.

1. $17\overline{)62}$ **2.** $37\overline{)124}$ **3.** $92 \div 27$ **4.** $147 \div 28$

Ask Yourself
• How can I estimate the quotient?
• How do I check my answer?

Explain Your Thinking ▶ What does it mean if the remainder is greater than or equal to the divisor?

Divide. Check your answer.

5. $42\overline{)88}$ 6. $32\overline{)99}$ 7. $21\overline{)91}$ 8. $46\overline{)55}$

9. $19\overline{)146}$ 10. $27\overline{)177}$ 11. $61\overline{)250}$ 12. $89\overline{)725}$

13. $73 \div 22$ 14. $81 \div 19$ 15. $34 \div 11$ 16. $74 \div 34$

17. $89 \div 36$ 18. $197 \div 36$ 19. $422 \div 83$ 20. $413 \div 62$

𝒳 Algebra • Symbols Compare. Use >, <, or = for each ⬤.

21. $305 \div 48$ ⬤ $300 \div 48$ 22. $795 \div 37$ ⬤ $785 \div 37$

23. $400 \div 80$ ⬤ $200 \div 40$ 24. $800 \div 20$ ⬤ $80 \div 2$

25. $362 \div 92$ ⬤ $362 \div 90$ 26. $735 \div 81$ ⬤ $735 \div 79$

Solve.

27. **Reasoning** There are 85 paint brushes in a dozen jars. One of the jars contains 1 more brush than the others. How many brushes are in each jar?

28. **Multistep** There are 8 pictures with 6 flowers each and 11 pictures with 7 flowers each. Find the total number of flowers in all the pictures.

29. Elder Care residents made a quilt. There were 84 flowered fabric squares to put in 18 rows. If the residents put an equal number of flowered squares in each row, how many were in each row? How many squares were left?

Mixed Review and Test Prep

Open Response

Decide whether each number is prime or composite. (Ch. 10, Lesson 2)

30. 7   31. 39   32. 16

33. 28   34. 79   35. 59

36. 81   37. 43   38. 87

39. How do you know that 7 is not the correct quotient in the example below? (Ch. 11, Lesson 4)

$$\begin{array}{r} 7 \\ 28\overline{)176} \\ -196 \end{array}$$

Audio Tutor 1/38 Listen and Understand

Two-Digit Quotients

Objective Divide when the quotient has two digits.

Learn About It

Students at Riverside School collected 865 cans to recycle. They are packing the cans in 21 bags. Each bag holds the same number of cans. How many cans are in each bag? Are any cans left?

Divide. $865 \div 21$ or $21\overline{)865}$

 STEP 1   Estimate to decide where to place the first digit in the quotient.

$$21\overline{)865} \rightarrow 20\overline{)800}^{\,40}$$

STEP 2   Try the estimate. Divide.

$$\begin{array}{r} 4 \\ 21\overline{)865} \\ -84 \\ \hline 2 \end{array}$$
Multiply. $4 \times 21 = 84$
Subtract. $86 - 84 = 2$
Compare. $2 < 21$

> **Think**
> $20\overline{)80}^{\,4}$ tens
> 80 tens

STEP 3   Bring down the ones. Divide.

$$\begin{array}{r} 41 \text{ R4} \\ 21\overline{)865} \\ -84\downarrow \\ \hline 25 \\ -21 \\ \hline 4 \end{array}$$
Multiply. $1 \times 21 = 21$
Subtract. $25 - 21 = 4$
Compare. $4 < 21$

STEP 4   Check your answer. Multiply. Then add.

$$\begin{array}{r} 21 \\ \times\ 41 \\ \hline 21 \\ +\ 840 \\ \hline 861 \\ +\ \ \ 4 \\ \hline 865 \end{array}$$
← The sum equals the dividend, so the quotient is correct.

Solution: There are 41 cans in each bag. There are 4 cans left.

▶ You can use the same steps to divide a four-digit dividend.

Divide.   1,278 ÷ 63   or   63)‾1,278

STEP 1 Estimate to decide where to place the first digit in the quotient.

$$\begin{array}{r} 20 \\ 63\overline{)1,278} \rightarrow 60\overline{)1,200} \end{array}$$

STEP 2 Try the estimate. Divide.

Think: $\begin{array}{r} 2 \text{ tens} \\ 60\overline{)120} \text{ tens} \end{array}$

$$\begin{array}{r} 2 \\ 63\overline{)1,278} \\ -\ 126 \\ \hline 1 \end{array}$$
Multiply. 2 × 63 = 126
Subtract. 127 − 126 = 1
Compare. 1 < 63

STEP 3 Bring down the ones.

$$\begin{array}{r} 2 \\ 63\overline{)1,278} \\ -\ 126\downarrow \\ \hline 18 \end{array}$$
← 18 < 63
There are not enough ones to divide.

STEP 4 Write a zero in the ones place. Write the remainder.

$$\begin{array}{r} 20 \text{ R18} \\ 63\overline{)1,278} \\ -\ 126 \\ \hline 18 \\ -\ 0 \end{array}$$

Solution: 1,278 ÷ 63 → 20 R18

Check your answer.
Multiply. Then add.

$$\begin{array}{r} 63 \\ \times\ 20 \\ \hline 1,260 \\ +\ 18 \\ \hline 1,278 \end{array}$$

The sum equals the dividend, so the quotient is correct.

Guided Practice

Divide.

1. 28)‾647

2. 42)‾886

3. 19)‾603

4. 44)‾2,222

5. 28)‾2,537

6. 81)‾6,643

Ask Yourself
• Where do I place the first digit in the quotient?
• Can I divide the tens?

Explain Your Thinking ▶ Why is it helpful to know the number of digits in a quotient before you divide?

Go On

Practice and Problem Solving

Divide. Check your answer.

7. $18\overline{)582}$

8. $33\overline{)769}$

9. $24\overline{)258}$

10. $45\overline{)547}$

11. $51\overline{)4,598}$

12. $69\overline{)2,218}$

13. $77\overline{)6,319}$

14. $86\overline{)8,123}$

15. $657 \div 21$

16. $966 \div 31$

17. $577 \div 28$

18. $672 \div 48$

19. $3,526 \div 68$

20. $1,527 \div 28$

21. $4,769 \div 52$

22. $4,596 \div 89$

Data Use the bar graph for Problems 23–25.

23. There are 6 classes in Grade 5. Each class recycled the same number of cans. How many cans did each class recycle?

24. The cans recycled by Grades 2, 3, and 4 were collected by 12 classes. Each class collected the same number of cans. How many cans did each class collect?

25. **Estimate** To the nearest hundred, about how many more cans were recycled by Grade 5 than by Grade 4?

Mixed Review and Test Prep

Open Response

Find the mean of the numbers.
(Ch. 10, Lesson 5)

26. 2, 5, 8

27. 26, 51, 18, 25

28. $14, $67, $90

29. 3, 9, 20, 41, 82

30. 12, 19, 20, 17

31. 89, 102, 98, 91

Multiple Choice

32. What is the quotient? (Ch. 11, Lesson 5)

$346 \div 23$

A 1 R11

C 15

B 10 R23

D 15 R1

Extra Practice See page 291, Set D.

Math Reasoning
Divide a Different Way

You can use many different strategies to find the answer to a division problem. One strategy is to use repeated subtraction.

Find 224 ÷ 56.

- Start with 224. Subtract 56 repeatedly.

- Count how many times you subtracted 56.

$$
\begin{array}{r}
224 \\
-\ 56 \\ \hline
168 \\
-\ 56 \\ \hline
112 \\
-\ 56 \\ \hline
56 \\
-\ 56 \\ \hline
0
\end{array}
$$
❶ ❷ ❸ ❹

You subtracted 56 four times, so there are 4 groups of 56 in 224. There is no remainder.

$$56 + 56 + 56 + 56 = 224$$
$$4 \times 56 = 224$$
and $224 \div 56 = 4$

Find 296 ÷ 98.

- Start with 296. Subtract 98 repeatedly.

- Count how many times you subtracted 98.

$$
\begin{array}{r}
296 \\
-\ 98 \\ \hline
198 \\
-\ 98 \\ \hline
100 \\
-\ 98 \\ \hline
2
\end{array}
$$
❶ ❷ ❸

You subtracted 98 three times, so there are 3 groups of 98 in 296. The remainder is 2.

$$98 + 98 + 98 + 2 = 296$$
$$(3 \times 98) + 2 = 296$$
and $296 \div 98 \rightarrow 3\ R2$

Use repeated subtraction to find each quotient.

1. $328 \div 82$
2. $350 \div 70$
3. $372 \div 93$

4. $125 \div 25$
5. $450 \div 50$
6. $193 \div 23$

7. $434 \div 62$
8. $729 \div 81$
9. $308 \div 51$

10. $525 \div 63$
11. $227 \div 72$
12. $170 \div 24$

13. **Analyze** What advantages are there in using repeated subtraction to find the quotient? What disadvantages are there?

Lesson 6

Audio Tutor 1/39 Listen and Understand

Adjust the Quotient

Objective Adjust an estimate of the quotient to divide.

Learn About It

If your first estimate of a quotient is too large or too small, you need to adjust your estimate.

▶ **Sometimes the estimate is too large.**

Find $368 \div 23$.

Estimate first. $23\overline{)368}$ → $\overset{20}{20\overline{)400}}$

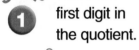

STEP 1 Place the first digit in the quotient.	**STEP 2** Adjust the estimate. Try 1.	**STEP 3** Bring down the next digit. Try 7.	**STEP 4** Try 6.
$\begin{array}{r} 2 \\ 23\overline{)368} \\ -46 \end{array}$ $\begin{array}{l}46 > 36\\ \text{2 is too}\\ \text{large.}\end{array}$	$\begin{array}{r} 1 \\ 23\overline{)368} \\ -23 \\ \hline 13 \end{array}$ $\begin{array}{l}13 < 23\\ \text{1 is correct.}\end{array}$	$\begin{array}{r} 17 \\ 23\overline{)368} \\ -23\downarrow \\ \hline 138 \\ -161 \end{array}$ $\begin{array}{l}161 > 138\\ \text{7 is too}\\ \text{large.}\end{array}$	$\begin{array}{r} 16 \\ 23\overline{)368} \\ -23\downarrow \\ \hline 138 \\ -138 \\ \hline 0 \end{array}$ $\begin{array}{l}0 < 23\\ \text{6 is correct.}\end{array}$

Remember
To adjust something is to change it in order to make it fit.

Solution: $368 \div 23 = 16$

▶ **Sometimes the estimate is too small.**

Find $849 \div 16$.

Estimate first. $16\overline{)849}$ → $\overset{40}{20\overline{)800}}$

STEP 1 Place the first digit in the quotient.	**STEP 2** Adjust the estimate. Try 5.	**STEP 3** Bring down the next digit. Try 2.	**STEP 4** Try 3.
$\begin{array}{r} 4 \\ 16\overline{)849} \\ -64 \\ \hline 20 \end{array}$ $\begin{array}{l}20 > 16\\ \text{4 is too}\\ \text{small.}\end{array}$	$\begin{array}{r} 5 \\ 16\overline{)849} \\ -80 \\ \hline 4 \end{array}$ $\begin{array}{l}4 < 16\\ \text{5 is correct.}\end{array}$	$\begin{array}{r} 52 \\ 16\overline{)849} \\ -80\downarrow \\ \hline 49 \\ -32 \\ \hline 17 \end{array}$ $\begin{array}{l}17 > 16\\ \text{2 is too}\\ \text{small.}\end{array}$	$\begin{array}{r} 53\ \text{R1} \\ 16\overline{)849} \\ -80\downarrow \\ \hline 49 \\ -48 \\ \hline 1 \end{array}$ $\begin{array}{l}1 < 16\\ \text{3 is correct.}\end{array}$

Solution: $\overset{53\ \text{R1}}{16\overline{)849}}$

Extra Help at **eduplace.com/map**

Guided Practice

Write *too large, too small*, or *correct* for each estimate of the quotient. Then find the correct answer.

1. $\dfrac{60}{12\overline{)654}}$

2. $\dfrac{40}{16\overline{)839}}$

3. $\dfrac{20}{26\overline{)583}}$

Ask Yourself
- How many digits will the quotient have?
- Do I need to adjust my estimate?

Explain Your Thinking ▶ What should you do if your estimate is too large?

Practice and Problem Solving

Estimate. Then divide.

4. $18\overline{)619}$ 5. $54\overline{)983}$ 6. $19\overline{)422}$ 7. $31\overline{)342}$ 8. $28\overline{)632}$

9. $42\overline{)794}$ 10. $28\overline{)931}$ 11. $26\overline{)626}$ 12. $48\overline{)527}$ 13. $19\overline{)564}$

14. $840 \div 24$ 15. $611 \div 33$ 16. $843 \div 16$ 17. $771 \div 44$

 Data Use the list for Problems 18–20.

18. For a community-service project, Mr. Li's class made a time capsule. A video was made of 12 classroom activities. How long is each activity if each one is the same length?

19. Fourteen students recorded messages on audiotapes. About how long is each message if each is the same length?

20. **Analyze** The essays fill a 42-page journal. All essays are the same number of pages except for one that is 3 pages longer than each of the others. How many pages long is each essay?

Time-Capsule Items
- One 360-minute video
- 13 student essays
- Two 120-minute audiotapes

essays

Mixed Review and Test Prep

Open Response

Find the mean of the numbers.
(Ch. 10, Lesson 5)

21. 6, 9, 12   22. 5, 12, 9, 26

23. $12, $15, $45   24. 75, 23, 67, 38, 12

Multiple Choice

25. What is $418 \div 21$? (Ch. 11, Lesson 6)

A 18 R40   c 19 R19

B 19   D 24 R14

Problem-Solving Decision
Multistep Problems

Objective Solve multistep problems.

Problem Lucia and her dad will prepare corn on the cob for the volunteer firefighters' dinner. There are 3 bags of corn. Each bag holds 32 ears of corn. If 16 ears of corn fit in a pot, what is the least number of pots needed to cook all the corn at the same time?

It takes more than one step to solve this problem.

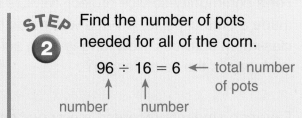

You know these facts.

- There are 3 bags of corn.

- Each bag holds 32 ears of corn.

- Each pot holds 16 ears of corn.

STEP 1 Find the total number of ears of corn.

$$3 \times 32 = 96 \leftarrow \text{total number of ears}$$

↑ number of bags
↑ number in each bag

There are 96 ears in all.

STEP 2 Find the number of pots needed for all of the corn.

$$96 \div 16 = 6 \leftarrow \text{total number of pots}$$

↑ number of ears
↑ number of ears in each pot

Six pots are needed.

Solution: Six pots are needed to cook all the corn.

Try These

1. A firehouse pantry has 144 cans of vegetables and 220 cans of soup. Each shelf holds up to 52 cans. How many shelves are needed for all the cans?

2. An adult's dinner costs $8. A family of 2 adults and 2 children pay $26 for their dinners. How much does a child's dinner cost?

3. Layla's dad bought 10 dozen tomatoes for the dinner. The tomatoes were equally divided among 20 bags. How many tomatoes were in each bag?

4. After the dinner, Ben collected 92 cans and 48 bottles. If he received 5¢ for each can or bottle, about how much money did Ben receive?

Math Challenge
Hit the Target

**Place the digits to find each Target Number.
Use a calculator to help you.**

1. Digits: 2, 2, 4, 7
   Target Number: 3

   ▪▪ ÷ ▪▪ = ▪

2. Digits: 0, 1, 5, 9
   Target Number: 6

   ▪▪ ÷ ▪▪ = ▪

3. Digits: 0, 1, 3, 4, 7
   Target Number: 20

   ▪▪▪ ÷ ▪▪ = ▪▪

4. Digits: 0, 1, 2, 3, 6
   Target Number: 30

   ▪▪▪ ÷ ▪▪ = ▪▪

5. Digits: 2, 2, 4, 6, 7
   Target Number: 16

   ▪▪▪ ÷ ▪▪ = ▪▪

6. Digits: 0, 1, 4, 5, 8
   Target Number: 18

   ▪▪▪ ÷ ▪▪ = ▪▪

7. Digits: 2, 8, 9, 9
   Target Number: 124

   ▪▪▪ ÷ ▪ = ▪▪▪

8. Digits: 4, 4, 6, 7
   Target Number: 124

   ▪▪▪ ÷ ▪ = ▪▪▪

9. **Challenge** Find another way to place the digits in Exercise 4 to find the Target Number.

10. Write your own Hit the Target problem to challenge a classmate. What steps did you take to write your problem?

Chapter Review/Test

VOCABULARY

Choose the best word to complete each sentence.

1. In the division sentence 480 ÷ 12 = 40, the number 40 is the _____.

2. In the division sentence 27 ÷ 3 = 9, the number 27 is the _____.

3. The number by which another number is divided is the _____.

> **Vocabulary**
> divisor
> multiple
> quotient
> dividend

CONCEPTS AND SKILLS

Estimate each quotient. (Lesson 2, pp. 274–275)

4. 99 ÷ 54

5. 152 ÷ 33

6. 349 ÷ 68

Divide. (Lessons 1, 3–6, pp. 272–273, 276–287)

7. $40\overline{)360}$

8. $50\overline{)4,500}$

9. $80\overline{)72,000}$

10. $13\overline{)72}$

11. $24\overline{)92}$

12. $35\overline{)140}$

13. $27\overline{)540}$

14. $42\overline{)635}$

15. $15\overline{)645}$

16. $33\overline{)585}$

17. $29\overline{)8,694}$

18. $46\overline{)9,465}$

PROBLEM SOLVING

Solve. (Lesson 7, p. 288)

19. Mr. Tucker pays a total of $24 for movie tickets. He buys two adult tickets for $6 each. He also buys four tickets for his children. What is the price of a child's ticket?

20. Bree is unpacking boxes of books. She has 6 boxes that each hold 36 books. If 18 books fit on each shelf, what is the least number of shelves needed for the books?

Show You Understand

- Explain how you would estimate to find 3,599 ÷ 62.

- Predict whether the exact answer will be greater than or less than your estimate. Explain your prediction.

- Find the exact answer. Was your prediction correct?

Extra Practice

Set A (Lesson 1, pp. 272–273)

Use basic facts to help you divide.

1. $120 \div 30$
2. $240 \div 60$
3. $6,300 \div 70$
4. $8,100 \div 90$

5. $30\overline{)180}$
6. $40\overline{)3,600}$
7. $80\overline{)5,600}$
8. $50\overline{)25,000}$

9. $3,500 \div n = 50$
10. $n \div 8 = 600$
11. $4,800 \div 60 = n$

Set B (Lesson 2, pp. 274–275)

Estimate each quotient.

1. $58 \div 31$
2. $79 \div 19$
3. $102 \div 49$
4. $542 \div 89$

5. $318 \div 82$
6. $325 \div 44$
7. $447 \div 53$
8. $719 \div 78$

Set C (Lesson 4, pp. 280–281)

Divide. Check your answer.

1. $16\overline{)80}$
2. $28\overline{)34}$
3. $55\overline{)198}$
4. $72\overline{)398}$

5. $84 \div 42$
6. $96 \div 25$
7. $129 \div 14$
8. $230 \div 46$

9. $126 \div 18$
10. $248 \div 62$
11. $620 \div 77$
12. $766 \div 85$

Set D (Lesson 5, pp. 282–284)

Divide. Check your answer.

1. $18\overline{)865}$
2. $28\overline{)569}$
3. $42\overline{)894}$
4. $31\overline{)716}$

5. $31\overline{)2,499}$
6. $47\overline{)3,620}$
7. $19\overline{)1,452}$
8. $29\overline{)1,894}$

Set E (Lesson 6, pp. 286–287)

Estimate. Then divide.

1. $842 \div 23$
2. $943 \div 25$
3. $581 \div 32$
4. $849 \div 16$

5. $467 \div 38$
6. $685 \div 23$
7. $784 \div 44$
8. $587 \div 22$

Aloha
from the
Ring of Fire

Hawaii Volcanoes National Park is one of the most beautiful places in the world. The park contains Earth's largest volcano, Mauna Loa, which is 13,677 feet high. Mount Kilauea, the world's most active volcano, is also within the park.

More than half the park is wilderness, which makes it an exciting place for hiking and camping. Because of its great natural beauty, important landforms, and rainforest habitat, the park was named a World Heritage Site in 1987. This means it is a valuable and protected area.

ISLAND OF HAWAII

Problem Solving

Use the table for Problems 1–3.

Hawaii Volcanoes National Park Trails

Trail	Roundtrip Distance
Naulu	10 miles
Napau	14 miles
Kilauea Crater Rim	11 miles
Pu'u Huluhulu	3 miles

1. Tamanaha hiked on the Naulu and Napau trails. It took him 6 hours to hike both trails. What was the average number of miles he hiked each hour?

2. Henry is writing a story titled "Naulu, Pu'u Huluhulu, and Kilauea Crater Rim." In the story, Henry says that the mean length of the 3 trails is about 8 miles. Is he correct? Explain.

3. Gina hiked the Pu'u Huluhulu trail each day. If she walked 27 miles on this trail, how many days did she hike?

4. Jessica earns $15 per person to guide visitors on the Naulu trail. If she earned $225, how many visitors did she guide?

5. Ms. Wilson is preparing a booklet for the park. She puts 4 pages of information in each booklet. If she has 876 pages, how many booklets can she make?

Education Place

Visit Weekly Reader Connections at **eduplace.com/map** for more on this topic.

Enrichment: Divisibility Rules

A number is **divisible** when it can be divided by another number and there is no remainder.

Divisibility Rules	Examples
Even numbers are divisible by 2. Even numbers end with 0, 2, 4, 6, or 8 in the ones place.	These numbers are divisible by 2. 630 632 634 636 638
Numbers divisible by 5 end with 0 or 5 in the ones place.	These numbers are divisible by 5. 630 635 640 645 650
Numbers divisible by 10 end with 0 in the ones place.	These numbers are divisible by 10. 600 610 620 630 640
If a number is divisible by 3, the sum of the digits is divisible by 3.	The number 630 is divisible by 3. $630 \rightarrow 6 + 3 + 0 = 9$ $9 \div 3 = 3$
If a number is divisible by 9, the sum of the digits is divisible by 9.	The number 630 is divisible by 9. $630 \rightarrow 6 + 3 + 0 = 9$ $9 \div 9 = 1$

Try These!

Tell whether each number is divisible by 2, 3, 5, 9, or 10.

1. 30
2. 45
3. 84
4. 95

5. 130
6. 180
7. 502
8. 2,000

9. **Challenge** If a number is divisible by both 2 and 3, is it divisible by 6? Try some examples. Explain your answer.

10. Can an **odd number** be divisible by 2? by 4? Try some examples.

Divide and Conquer

You can use the base-ten blocks found on Education Place at **eduplace.com/kids/map** to practice division.

Follow these steps to find 153 ÷ 6.

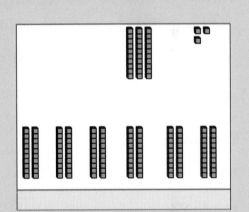

- At **Change Mat,** choose **Empty.**

- To show 153:
  Put your pointer over the **Stamp** tool.
  Click the hundreds block.
  Then click the tens block 5 times.
  Next, click the ones block 3 times.

- To regroup 1 hundred as 10 tens, click the right arrow in the hundreds column.

- Click the **Hand** tool. Put 12 of the tens into 6 equal groups.

- To regroup the remaining 3 tens as 30 ones, click the right arrow in the tens column 3 times.

- Click the **Hand** tool. Divide the 33 ones into the 6 groups.

Solution: There are 2 tens blocks and 5 ones blocks in each group with 3 ones blocks left over. So 153 ÷ 6 = 25 R3.

Use the base-ten blocks to find each quotient.

1. 43 ÷ 3
2. 65 ÷ 2
3. 74 ÷ 3
4. 377 ÷ 6

5. 112 ÷ 5
6. 222 ÷ 4
7. 225 ÷ 3
8. 141 ÷ 4

9. **Create and Solve** Write a word problem that uses division. Use the base-ten blocks to solve.

Unit 4 Test

Choose the best word to complete each sentence.

1. The number that is left after one whole number is divided by another is the _____.

2. The number by which a number is being divided is the _____.

3. The number that is divided in a division problem is the _____.

Vocabulary

divisor
quotient
dividend
remainder

CONCEPTS AND SKILLS Open Response

Use basic facts to help you divide. (Chapters 8, 11)

4. $80 \div 4$

5. $1,200 \div 3$

6. $2,100 \div 7$

7. $5,600 \div 8$

8. $240 \div 60$

9. $1,800 \div 90$

10. $36,000 \div 40$

11. $56,000 \div 80$

Estimate. (Chapters 8, 11)

12. $6\overline{)34}$

13. $9\overline{)350}$

14. $7\overline{)567}$

15. $5\overline{)245}$

16. $48\overline{)97}$

17. $19\overline{)169}$

18. $31\overline{)222}$

19. $68\overline{)349}$

Divide. Check your answers. (Chapters 8, 9, 11)

20. $4\overline{)85}$

21. $3\overline{)67}$

22. $65 \div 5$

23. $76 \div 4$

24. $4\overline{)448}$

25. $7\overline{)938}$

26. $\$5.04 \div 9$

27. $\$6.15 \div 5$

28. $8\overline{)1,128}$

29. $15\overline{)53}$

30. $12\overline{)99}$

31. $5\overline{)32,566}$

32. $23\overline{)576}$

33. $52\overline{)607}$

34. $97\overline{)8,148}$

35. $58\overline{)3,596}$

List two multiples for each number. (Chapter 10)

36. 7

37. 3

38. 9

39. 6

List the factors for each number. Tell if the number is prime or composite. (Chapter 10)

40. 4

41. 5

42. 17

43. 12

Find the mean of the numbers in each group. (Chapter 10)

44. 93, 72, 78   **45.** $57, $24, $99, $108   **46.** 8, 378, 123, 49, 187

PROBLEM SOLVING   Open Response

47. Jenny has 55 CDs in a display case. One shelf has 7 CDs. All the other shelves have 8 CDs each. How many shelves are in the display case?

48. Guitar strings cost 2 times as much as a set of picks. A tuner costs 8 times as much as the picks. The tuner costs $24. How much do the strings cost?

49. A sign says: "Buy 4 post cards, get a 5th post card FREE!" If Hector wants 25 post cards, how many does he have to buy at the regular price?

50. Jo delivers 24 papers to each class on 2 floors. The first floor has 15 classes. She delivers 624 papers. How many classes are on the second floor?

Performance Assessment

Extended Response

Gerald's Action Figures	
Type	**Total Number**
Japanese figures	36
Knights	23
Dinosaurs	33
Movie characters	31
TV characters	32

Task Gerald wants to trade some of his action figures for some action figures that his friend Kevin has. Use the table above and the information on the right.

How should Gerald trade his figures so that he will have an equal number of each type of action figure? How many of each type of figure will Gerard have then? Explain how you solved the problem.

Information You Need

- For every dinosaur, Kevin will give Gerald one movie character or two TV characters.

- For every TV character, Kevin will give Gerald one movie character.

- Kevin will trade 2 knights for 1 Japanese figure or 5 knights for 2 Japanese figures.

- Gerald plans to give one or two action figures to his younger brother.

Cumulative Test Prep

Solve Problems 1–10.

Test-Taking Tip

Sometimes you need to do more than one step to solve a problem.

Look at the example below.

Mr. Benz is slicing bagels into 4 equal pieces. There are 24 students in his class. If each student gets 2 pieces, how many bagels will Mr. Benz slice?

A 6   C 24

B 12   D 48

THINK

Multiply to find the total number of pieces needed.

24 students × 2 pieces = 48 pieces

Now find how many bagels are needed to make 48 pieces.

48 pieces ÷ 4 pieces = 12 bagels

Therefore, you should choose **B**.

Multiple Choice

1. Which shows the prices in order from least to greatest?

A $3.98 $3.76 $3.70 $5.00

B $3.76 $3.70 $3.98 $5.00

C $5.00 $3.98 $3.76 $3.70

D $3.70 $3.76 $3.98 $5.00

(Chapter 2, Lesson 3)

2. What is the value of *n*?

$$(2 + 9) - (6 + 3) = n$$

F 0   G 1   H 2   J 3

(Chapter 5, Lesson 1)

3. One pack of baseball cards contains 10 cards. There are 36 packs in a box and 20 boxes in a case. How many baseball cards are in a case?

A 7,200   C 720

B 3,600   D 360

(Chapter 11, Lesson 7)

4. When the heights of the mountains are rounded to the nearest hundred, about what is the difference in their heights?

Mt. Everest	Mt. Kilimanjaro
29,035 feet	19,340 feet

F 9,000 feet   H 9,700 feet

G 9,500 feet   J 10,000 feet

(Chapter 3, Lesson 3)

For Test-Taking Tips, See Page 658.

Open Response

5. A farmer plants 26 rows of tomato plants, with 105 plants in each row. How many plants does the farmer plant? Write a number sentence to show how to find the answer.

(Chapter 7, Lesson 6)

6. Sharifa went bowling and scored 98, 107, and 98. What was her mean score for the three games?

(Chapter 10, Lesson 5)

7. One page in a photo album holds 8 photos. If Sue has 87 photos, how many pages in the photo album can she fill completely?

(Chapter 8, Lesson 3)

8. The table shows a pattern for the number of divisions and the number of teams in a soccer league. Based on the pattern, how many divisions will there be when there are 32 teams?

Soccer League	
Number of Divisions	**Number of Teams**
2	8
3	12
4	16
5	20

(Chapter 4, Lesson 3)

Extended Response

9. On Day 1, James read 9 pages of a book. On Day 2, he read twice as many pages as on Day 1. At the start of Day 3, he had 35 pages left to read.

  A How many pages are in the book?

  B Explain what steps you used to find the answer.

  C On what day did James finish reading the book if he read 7 pages each remaining day?

(Chapter 9, Lesson 5)

10. The number of fish in a tank is greater than 15 and is equal to the sum of two different odd numbers that are each less than 10.

  A How many fish are in the tank?

  B Explain how you solved the problem.

  C Write a number sentence to show how many fish are in the tank.

(Chapter 6, Lesson 5)

 Education Place

Look for Cumulative Test Prep at **eduplace.com/map** for more practice.

Vocabulary Wrap-Up for **Unit 4**

Look back at the big ideas and vocabulary in this unit.

Big Ideas

Sometimes you need to regroup when you divide.

A multiple of a number is a product of that number and any whole number.

You can use basic facts to help you place the first digit in a quotient.

Key Vocabulary

regroup
multiple
product
quotient

Math Conversations

Use your new vocabulary to discuss these big ideas.

1. Explain how to find the mean of four numbers.

2. Explain how to regroup to divide 98 by 8.

3. Explain how multiplication and division are related.

4. Explain the difference between a prime number and a composite number.

5. **Write About It** Look through catalogs and newspaper ads. Then explain how you can use division when you shop.

What are some multiples of 3?

How about 6, 9, 12, or 18?

UNIT 5

Measurement and Graphing

301

Reading Mathematics

Reviewing Vocabulary

Here are some math vocabulary words that you should know.

capacity	the amount that a container can hold
centimeter (cm)	a metric unit used to measure length
mass	the amount of matter in an object
ounce (oz)	a customary unit used to measure weight

Reading Words and Symbols

You can describe the capacity of an object by using customary units or metric units.

Customary Units

Read: The pitcher holds about one quart.

Write, using symbols: The pitcher holds about 1 qt.

Metric Units

Read: The pitcher holds about one liter.

Write, using symbols: The pitcher holds about 1 L.

Use words and symbols to answer the questions.

1. What is the length of the eraser?

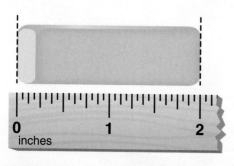

2. What is the mass of the apple?

302

Reading Test Questions

Choose the correct answer for each.

3. What is the approximate weight of the apples?

    a. 1 pound   **c.** 3 pounds

    b. 2 pounds   **d.** 4 pounds

Approximate means "close to" or "about."

4. What unit of measure would you use to determine the height of a tree that is 100 years old?

    a. cups   **c.** feet

    b. degrees   **d.** seconds

Determine means "find out" or "decide."

5. Which word completes this sentence?

Use a ____ to measure temperature.

    a. balance   **c.** ruler

    b. bar graph   **d.** thermometer

Completes means "finishes" or "fills in."

Learning Vocabulary

Watch for these words in this unit. Write their definitions in your journal.

century   interval

decade   outlier

milliliter (mL)

degrees Celsius (°C)

degrees Fahrenheit (°F)

Literature Connection

Read "Lengths of Time" on Page 650. Then work with a partner to answer the questions about the story.

Education Place

At **eduplace.com/map** see eGlossary and eGames—Math Lingo.

Customary and Metric Measurement

INVESTIGATION

Using Data

Sunflowers can grow as high as 3 meters! The table shows how tall one sunflower grew in four weeks. How tall do you think the sunflower would be after 6 weeks? How can you use the information in the chart to make your estimate?

Growth of a Sunflower

Number of Weeks	Height in Centimeters
1	30
2	60
3	90
4	120

Use What You Know

**Use this page to review and remember
what you need to know for this chapter.**

VOCABULARY

Choose the best word to complete each sentence.

1. A pencil weighs about one _____.

2. A grocer sells potatoes by the _____.

3. The amount of water in a swimming pool
   would best be measured in _____.

CONCEPTS AND SKILLS

Measure to the nearest inch.

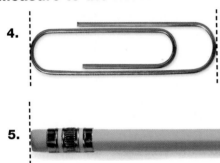

4.

5.

Choose the better unit of measure.

6. the width of a book
   a. meters   **b.** centimeters

7. the length of a car
   a. meters   **b.** kilometers

8. the length of an eraser
   a. inches   **b.** feet

9. the distance between towns
   a. yards   **b.** miles

Write About It

10. Name 4 measuring tools that you have
    used. Describe how to use them and tell
    what you could measure with them.

Facts Practice, See page 670.

Hands On Lesson 1

Explore Customary Units of Length

Objective Estimate and measure lengths, using an inch ruler.

Work Together

Work with a partner to estimate length and then measure, using an inch ruler.

Estimate:	
Nearest inch:	
Nearest half inch:	
Nearest quarter inch:	

STEP 1
Estimate the length of the pea pod above. Record your estimate in a table like the one at the right.

STEP 2
Use an inch ruler to measure the pea pod to the nearest inch. Use a half-inch mark to decide which inch mark is closer to the end of the pea pod. Record the length.

If the end is exactly at the half—inch mark, round to the next inch.

STEP 3
Now measure the pea pod to the nearest half inch. Use a quarter-inch mark to decide which half-inch mark is closer to the end. Record the length.

STEP 4
Measure the pea pod to the nearest quarter inch. Use an eighth-inch mark to decide which quarter-inch mark is closer to the end.

The more marks your ruler has, the more accurately you will be able to measure.

Compare your estimate and the three measurements of the pea pod. Which is closest to the actual length of the pea pod?

STEP 5 Find five objects to measure. Estimate the length of each object to the nearest inch. Then measure each object to the nearest inch, half inch, and quarter inch. Record your work.

On Your Own

Measure to the nearest inch, half inch, and quarter inch.

1.

2.

Estimate the length of each object to the nearest inch. Then measure to the nearest inch, half inch, and quarter inch.

3.

4.

Talk About It • Write About It

You have learned to measure to the nearest inch, half inch, and quarter inch.

5. One green bean is less than 5 inches long, and another is more than 5 inches long. When they are measured to the nearest inch, both are about 5 inches long. Explain how this is possible.

6. What is the length of this green bean to the nearest quarter inch?

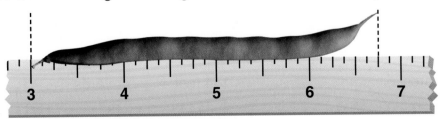

Inch, Foot, Yard, Mile

Objective Change units of length.

Learn About It

The fourth grade planted flowers in the school courtyard. The length of the flower bed is 9 feet. What is the length in inches? in yards?

Inch, foot, yard, and mile are customary units of measure.

Change Feet to Inches

When you change from larger units to smaller units, the number of units increases. So multiply.

Multiply by the number of inches in 1 foot.

$$9 \quad \times \quad 12 \quad = \quad 108$$

| number of feet | inches in foot | inches in 9 feet |

Customary Units of Length
1 foot (ft) = 12 inches (in.)
1 yard (yd) = 3 feet
1 yard (yd) = 36 inches
1 mile (mi) = 1,760 yards
1 mile (mi) = 5,280 feet

Change Feet to Yards

When you change from smaller units to larger units, the number of units decreases. So divide.

Divide by the number of feet in 1 yard.

$$9 \quad \div \quad 3 \quad = \quad 3$$

| number of feet | feet in 1 yard | yards in 9 feet |

Solution: The length of the flower bed is 108 inches, or 3 yards.

Other Examples

A. Miles to Yards

2 miles = _____ yards

$2 \times 1,760 = 3,520$

2 miles = 3,520 yards.

Think
Miles are larger than yards, so multiply.

B. Feet to Yards

144 feet = _____ yards

$144 \div 3 = 48$

144 feet = 48 yards.

Think
Feet are smaller than yards, so divide.

Guided Practice

Find each missing number.

1. 72 ft = _____ yd

2. _____ in. = 6 ft

3. 2 mi = _____ ft

4. _____ yd = 144 in.

> **Ask Yourself**
> • Am I converting to a larger or smaller unit?
> • Should I multiply or divide?

Explain Your Thinking ▶ What unit of measure would you use to measure the length of your classroom?

Practice and Problem Solving

Find each missing number.

5. 72 yd = _____ ft

6. 5 ft = _____ in.

7. 10 yd = _____ ft

8. 4 mi = _____ ft

9. _____ yd = 3 mi

10. 21 ft = _____ yd

Compare. Write >, <, or = for each ●.

11. 3 ft ● 36 in.

12. 2 yd ● 60 in.

13. 5,280 yd ● 2 mi

14. 4 yd ● 108 in.

15. 5 ft ● 60 in.

16. 7 yd ● 28 ft

Copy and complete the tables. Write the rule for each table.

17.

ft	2	3	5	8	9	12
in.	24	36	■	■	■	■

18.

ft	3	6	9	12	15	30
yd	1	■	3	■	■	■

Solve.

19. Alicia has a board that is 2 yards long. She cuts a 4-foot length for a fence. How long is the remaining piece?

20. Seth estimates the length of his garden to be 20 feet. Sarah estimates it to be 7 yards. If the actual length is 19 feet, which is the better estimate?

Mixed Review and Test Prep

Open Response

Solve. (Ch. 4, Lesson 5)

21. 35 ÷ 7

22. 8 × 9

23. 56 ÷ 8

24. 90 ÷ 10

25. 6 × 7

26. 9 × 5

27. 54 ÷ 9

28. 8 × 7

29. 64 ÷ 8

Multiple Choice

30. Which is the best unit for measuring the distance from New York to Chicago?

(Ch. 12, Lesson 2)

A inch

C yard

B foot

D mile

Extra Practice See page 331, Set A.

Lesson 3

Customary Units of Capacity

Objective Change units of capacity.

Learn About It

Angela's watering can holds 8 quarts of water. How many cups is that? how many gallons?

Gallons, quarts, pints, and cups all measure capacity, the amount a container can hold.

Change Quarts to Cups

When you change from larger units to smaller units, the number of units increases. So multiply.

Multiply by the number of cups in 1 quart.

$$8 \quad \times \quad 4 \quad = \quad 32$$

| number of quarts | cups in 1 quart | cups in 8 quarts |

Customary Units of Capacity	
1 pint (pt)	= 2 cups (c)
1 quart (qt)	= 2 pints
1 quart (qt)	= 4 cups
1 gallon (gal)	= 4 quarts
1 gallon (gal)	= 8 pints
1 gallon (gal)	= 16 cups

Change Quarts to Gallons

When you change from smaller units to larger units, the number of units decreases. So divide.

Divide by the number of quarts in 1 gallon.

$$8 \quad \div \quad 4 \quad = \quad 2$$

| number of quarts | quarts in 1 gallon | gallons in 8 quarts |

Solution: The watering can holds 32 cups, or 2 gallons, of water.

Other Examples

A. Cups to Pints

10 cups = _____ pints

$10 \div 2 = 5$

10 cups = 5 pints

> **Think**
> Cups are smaller than pints, so divide.

B. Gallons to Pints

3 gallons = _____ pints

$3 \times 8 = 24$

3 gallons = 24 pints

> **Think**
> Gallons are larger than pints, so multiply.

310

Guided Practice

Find each missing number.

1. 8 c = ____ pt

2. ____ qt = 5 gal

3. 16 pt = ____ qt

4. 2 qt = ____ c

> **Ask Yourself**
> - Am I converting to a larger or smaller unit?
> - Should I multiply or divide?

Explain Your Thinking ▶ Describe how you found the missing number in Exercise 2.

Practice and Problem Solving

Find each missing number.

5. 14 c = ____ pt

6. 8 gal = ____ qt

7. 9 pt = ____ c

8. ____ qt = 10 pt

9. 4 pt = ____ qt

10. 16 c = ____ qt

Choose the unit you would use to measure the capacity of each item. Write *cup, pint, quart,* or *gallon.*

11.

12.

13.

14.

Compare. Write >, <, or = for each ⬤.

15. 4 pt ⬤ 6 c

16. 8 gal ⬤ 30 qt

17. 13 pt ⬤ 8 qt

18. 16 c ⬤ 8 qt

19. 16 pt ⬤ 4 gal

20. 2 qt ⬤ 4 c

21. **Explain** Which is the better buy, 4 quarts of plant food for $5.00 or one half gallon for $3.00? Explain how you got your answer.

22. Jane has 5 cups of water. Al has 3 pints and Bert has 1 quart of water. List amounts in order from least to greatest.

Mixed Review and Test Prep

Open Response

Round each number to the nearest hundred. Then estimate. (Ch. 3, Lesson 3)

23. 5,321 − 2,192

24. 2,896 + 1,419

25. 7,099 − 3,299

26. 4,650 + 4,506

27. How many times must Taylor fill his 1-pint measuring cup to make a recipe calling for $\frac{1}{2}$ gallon of water? Explain how you got your answer. (Ch. 12, Lesson 3)

Extra Practice See page 331, Set B.

Chapter 12 Lesson 3 311

Customary Units of Weight

Objective Estimate and measure, using customary units of weight.

Vocabulary
tons

Materials
balance scale
1-pound weight
1-ounce weight

Learn About It

Ounces, pounds, and **tons** are units of weight. They are used to show how heavy an object is.

A strawberry weighs about one ounce.

A bunch of grapes weighs about one pound.

A tractor weighs about one ton.

Try this activity to measure and compare weight.

STEP 1 Find three objects in the classroom that you estimate weigh about one pound.

STEP 2 Weigh each object and record the weight. List the three objects from heaviest to lightest. Which object weighs closest to one pound?

STEP 3 Use the object closest to one pound to predict what other things in the classroom weigh. Make a list of four things that weigh more than, less than, and about one pound.

STEP 4 Repeat Step 1 and Step 2, looking for four objects in the classroom that weigh about 1 ounce. Which object weighs closest to one ounce?

▶ Look at the truck. How many tons of watermelons are on it?

Change Pounds to Tons

When you change from smaller units to larger units, the number of units decreases. So divide.

Divide by the number of pounds in 1 ton.

$$4{,}000 \div 2{,}000 = 2$$

↑ number of pounds   ↑ pounds in 1 ton   ↑ tons in 4,000 pounds

Customary Units of Weight

1 pound (lb) = 16 ounces (oz)

1 ton (T) = 2,000 pounds

Solution: The truck carries 2 tons of watermelons.

▶ If one watermelon weighs 10 pounds, how many ounces does it weigh?

Change Pounds to Ounces

When you change from larger units to smaller units, the number of units increases. So multiply.

Multiply by the number of ounces in 1 pound.

$$10 \times 16 = 160$$

↑ number of pounds   ↑ ounces in 1 pound   ↑ ounces in 10 pounds

Solution: The watermelon weighs 160 ounces.

Guided Practice

Find each missing number.

1. 8,000 lb = _____ T

2. 5 lb = _____ oz

3. 112 oz = _____ lb

4. _____ lb = 3 T

Ask Yourself

- Am I converting to a larger or smaller unit?
- Should I multiply or divide?

Explain Your Thinking ▶ Do small objects always weigh less than large ones? Give examples to support your answer.

Find each missing number.

5. _____ lb = 16 T

6. 48 oz = _____ lb

7. _____ oz = 2 lb

8. 144 oz = _____ lb

9. 8,000 lb = _____ T

10. 10 lb = _____ oz

What is the best unit to weigh these items?
Write *ounce, pound,* or *ton*.

11. a bunch of bananas

12. a paper clip

13. a car

14. an elephant

15. a handful of blueberries

16. a table

Compare. Write >, <, or = for each ●.

17. 38 oz ● 2 lb

18. 3,000 lb ● 3T

19. 5 lb ● 80 oz

20. 2 lb ● 40 oz

21. 90 oz ● 6 lb

22. 2 T ● 3,000 lb

23. Shonte bought a 9-pound watermelon that cost $0.50 per pound. How much did she pay?

24. Darlene bought 3 pounds of peaches, 6 ounces of cherries and 14 ounces of plums. What was the total weight of her purchases?

25. Mario bought 3 pounds of fruit. He bought strawberries, cherries, grapes, and blueberries. How much did each type of fruit weigh if they weighed the same?

Mixed Review and Test Prep

Open Response

Round each number to the nearest hundred. Then estimate. (Ch. 3, Lesson 3)

26. 7,091 + 2,802

27. 3,399 − 1,239

28. 4,511 + 5,499

29. 1,887 − 1,102

30. 3,271 + 4,010

31. 6,487 − 2,296

Multiple Choice

32. How many ounces are in 5 pounds? (Ch. 12, Lesson 4)

A 16 ounces

C 80 ounces

B 20 ounces

D 2,000 ounces

Extra Practice See page 331, Set C.

Visual Thinking
Balancing Act

Which containers should you move so that each group has the same amount of juice?

Group A

Group B

Science Connection
A Lot of Elephant!

An African elephant can weigh 12 tons. How many pounds is that?

An elephant can drink as much as 40 gallons of water a day. How many quarts is that?

An elephant's tusk can be as long as 8 feet. How many inches is that?

Brain Teaser

A snail is climbing a 15-foot fence. Every day it climbs 3 feet, but slides back 1 foot every night. How long does it take the snail to climb to the top of the fence?

 Education Place

Check out **eduplace.com/map** for more brain teasers.

Problem Solving

Audio Tutor 2/12 Listen and Understand

Problem-Solving Decision

Too Much or Too Little Information

Objective Find the information you need to solve a problem.

Problem Sam sold 38 seed packets. He collected $19.00. April sold four times as many seed packets as Sam. How many seed packets did April sell?

Ask Yourself

What is the question?	What do I need to know?	What do I know?
• How many seed packets did April sell?	• How many packets did Sam sell?	• Sam sold 38 packets. • April sold 4 times as many packets as Sam.

Solve the problem.

$$38 \leftarrow \text{number of packets Sam sold}$$
$$\times\ 4 \leftarrow \text{4 times as many as Sam}$$
$$152 \leftarrow \text{number of packets April sold}$$

Solution: April sold 152 seed packets.

Try These

Solve. If not enough information is given, tell what information is needed to solve the problem.

1. Rebecca's club sold 343 flower and vegetable seed packets altogether. They collected $171.50. Were more flower or vegetable seeds sold?

2. Nate bought 8 one-pound packages of crocus bulbs for $1.50 a pound and a box of fertilizer for $4.00. How much did he spend on bulbs?

3. Ann planted 16 tulips and 12 lilies. She planted twice as many daffodils as tulips. How many daffodils did she plant?

4. Lee planted marigold seeds in pots. Each pot held 20 ounces of soil. What was the weight of all the soil used?

Extra Help at **eduplace.com/map**

Art Connection
Mobile Math

Hanging sculptures like the one in the photo are called mobiles. The artist needs to carefully balance the construction.

Calder might have used an equation like this to balance his mobile.

Use some of the shapes below to construct an imaginary mobile. Draw a picture equation to show how it will balance.

△ 3 oz   ☽ 5 oz   ● 4 oz   ★ 4 oz   ▢ 1 lb   🐟 8 oz   ▮ 2 oz

"Lobster Trap and Fish Tail" by
Alexander Calder (1939)

WEEKLY WR READER eduplace.com/map

Check your understanding of Lessons 1–5.

Measure to the nearest inch, half inch, and quarter inch. (Lesson 1)

1. |——————————————————| 2. |——————| 3. |——|

Compare. Write >, <, or = for each ●. (Lessons 2–4)

4. 2 yd ● 66 in.   5. 72 in. ● 6 ft   6. 9 gal ● 30 qt

7. 8,500 lb ● 8 T   8. 60 oz ● 4 lb   9. 7 lb ● 112 oz

Solve. (Lesson 5)

10. Mrs. Juba used 20 oranges to make 8 cups of juice. How many quarts of juice did she make?

Explore Metric Units of Length

Vocabulary
millimeter (mm)

Objective Estimate and measure lengths using a centimeter ruler.

Work Together

Work with a partner to estimate lengths.
Then use a centimeter ruler to measure lengths.

STEP 1 Estimate the length of the cattail above. Record your estimate in a table like the one shown.

Object	Estimate	Nearest Centimeter	Nearest Millimeter
cattail			

STEP 2 Use a centimeter ruler to measure the length of the cattail to the nearest centimeter. Use a half-centimeter mark to decide which centimeter mark is closer to the end of the cattail. Record the length in your table.

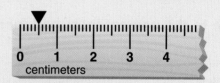

If the end is exactly halfway between centimeters, round to the next centimeter.

STEP 3 Now measure the cattail to the nearest **millimeter**. Decide which millimeter mark is closer to the end of the cattail. Record the length in millimeters in your table.

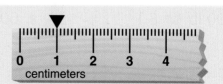

There are 10 millimeters in 1 centimeter.

STEP 4 Find 5 objects to measure. Estimate the length of each object to the nearest centimeter. Then measure each object to the nearest centimeter. Record your work in your table.

On Your Own

Measure the length to the nearest centimeter and millimeter.

1.

2.

Estimate the length. Then measure each object to the nearest centimeter and millimeter.

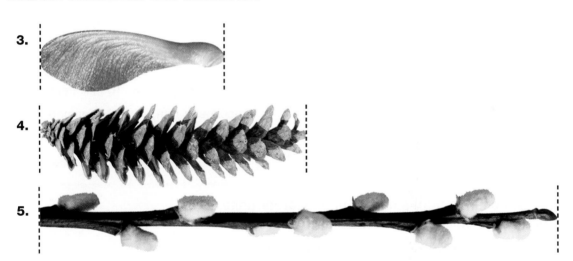

3.

4.

5.

Talk About It • Write About It

You have learned to measure lengths in centimeters and millimeters.

6. Suppose you know how tall a plant is in centimeters. Explain how you can tell how tall it is in millimeters.

7. Suppose you are measuring a piece of wood for a birdhouse. Would it be better to measure in centimeters or in millimeters? Explain your thinking.

<table>
<tr><td>

</td></tr>
</table>

Metric Units of Length

Objective Change metric units of length.

Vocabulary

millimeter (mm)
centimeter (cm)
decimeter (dm)
meter (m)
kilometer (km)

Learn About It

Millimeters, **centimeters**, **decimeters**, **meters**, and **kilometers** are metric units used to measure length.

A corn kernel is about 1 centimeter long.

An ear of corn is about 2 decimeters long.

A young corn plant is about 1 meter tall.

A road can be about 1 kilometer long.

Change Meters to Decimeters

When you change from larger units to smaller units, the number of units increases. So multiply.

Multiply by the number of decimeters in 1 meter.

$$4{,}000 \quad \times \quad 10 \quad = \quad 40{,}000$$

number of meters   decimeters in 1 meter   decimeters in 4,000 meters

4,000 meters = 40,000 decimeters

Metric Units of Length

1 centimeter (cm)	=	10 millimeters (mm)
1 decimeter (dm)	=	10 centimeters
1 meter (m)	=	10 decimeters
1 kilometer (km)	=	1,000 meters

Change Meters to Kilometers

When you change from smaller units to larger units, the number of units decreases. So divide.

Divide by the number of meters in 1 kilometer.

$$4{,}000 \quad \div \quad 1{,}000 \quad = \quad 4$$

number of meters   meters in 1 kilometer   kilometers in 4,000 meters

4,000 meters = 4 kilometers

Other Examples

A. Meters to Centimeters

5 meters = _____ centimeters

$5 \times 100 = 500$

5 meters = 500 centimeters

B. Millimeters to Centimeters

80 millimeters = _____ centimeters

$80 \div 10 = 8$

80 millimeters = 8 centimeters

Find each missing number.

1. 40 cm = _____ mm
2. 200 cm = _____ m
3. 3 km = _____ m
4. 50 cm = _____ dm

> **Ask Yourself**
> • Am I converting to a larger or smaller unit?
> • Should I multiply or divide?

Explain Your Thinking ▶ What is the best unit to use when measuring the distance between two cities?

Practice and Problem Solving

Find each missing number.

5. 50 km = _____ m
6. 600 mm = _____ cm
7. _____ mm = 9 cm
8. 3 m = _____ cm
9. 5,000 m = _____ km
10. _____ dm = 40 cm

Choose the better estimate of length.

11. length of a garden row
    a. 10 m   b. 10 mm

12. width of your fingertip
    a. 1 dm   b. 1 cm

13. the length of a street
    a. 3 km   b. 3 dm

14. the height of a window
    a. 1 m   b. 10 mm

Copy and complete the tables. Write the rule for each table.

15.

km	1	3	5	7	8
m	1,000	■	■	■	■

16.

mm	10	20	30	60	80
cm	1	■	■	■	■

17. **Estimate** Sue estimates that there are 9 dm between plants. Lee estimates 1 m. The actual distance is 97 cm. Who made the closer estimate?

18. Maxine has a piece of string that is 2 m long. If she cuts off a piece that is 105 cm long, will she have at least 35 cm left?

Mixed Review and Test Prep

Open Response

Solve. (Ch. 4, Lesson 5)

19. 72 ÷ 9
20. 36 ÷ 6
21. 56 ÷ 7
22. 49 ÷ 7
23. 27 ÷ 9
24. 72 ÷ 8

Multiple Choice

25. Which length is closest to 1 kilometer? (Ch. 12, Lesson 7)

    A 10 dm   c 1,000 cm

    B 900 m   D 999 m

Hands On Lesson 8

Metric Units of Capacity

Objective Change metric units of capacity.

Vocabulary
liter (L)
milliliter (mL)

Learn About It

Materials
containers of various sizes
liter measure marked in mL
water

Liter and **milliliter** are units used to measure capacity in the metric system.

This bottle
holds 1 liter.

This eyedropper
holds 1 milliliter.

Metric Units of Capacity
1 liter (L) = 1,000 milliters (mL)

Try this activity to measure metric capacity.

STEP 1 Find three containers that you estimate will each hold about a liter of water.

STEP 2 Fill the liter measure with water. Pour it into each of the containers you selected.

Container Estimated	More or Less Than 1 Liter
Container 1	
Container 2	
Container 3	

STEP 3 Decide if the capacity of each container is greater than, less than, or equal to a liter.

• Which container has a capacity closest to one liter? Explain how you know.

322

Other Examples

A. Liters to Milliliters

4 liters = _____ milliliters

4 × 1,000 = 4,000

4 liters = 4,000 milliliters

B. Milliliters to Liters

2,000 milliliters = _____ liters

2,000 ÷ 1,000 = 2

2,000 milliliters = 2 liters

Guided Practice

Find each missing number.

1. 9 L = _____ mL

2. _____ L = 5,000 mL

3. 3,000 mL = _____ L

4. _____ mL = 4 L

Ask Yourself

• Am I converting to a larger or smaller unit?

• Should I multiply or divide?

Explain Your Thinking ▶ Why is it useful to measure capacity by using milliliters and liters instead of by using a small container and a large container?

Practice and Problem Solving

Find each missing number.

5. _____ mL = 3 L

6. _____ L = 2,000 mL

7. 6,000 mL = _____ L

8. 10,000 mL = _____ L

9. 4,000 mL = _____ L

10. 25 L = _____ mL

Choose the better estimate of capacity for each item.

11.

a. 20 mL   b. 20 L

12.

a. 400 mL   b. 400 L

13.

a. 250 mL   b. 25 L

14.

a. 8 mL   b. 8 L

15.

a. 215 mL   b. 215 L

16.

a. 280 mL   b. 28 L

Go On

**Choose the better unit to measure each capacity.
Write *milliliters* or *liters*.**

17. a glass of milk   **18.** a kitchen sink   **19.** the juice from one lemon

20. a bathtub   **21.** a spoon   **22.** a swimming pool

Compare. Write >, <, or = for each ⬤.

23. 6 mL ⬤ 6,000 L   **24.** 8 L ⬤ 8,000 mL   **25.** 30 L ⬤ 300 mL

26. 4,500 mL ⬤ 45 L   **27.** 4 L ⬤ 350 mL   **28.** 2,000 mL ⬤ 2 L

29. 7 L ⬤ 7,000 mL   **30.** 550 mL ⬤ 5 L   **31.** 60 L ⬤ 60,000 mL

Solve.

32. Carla has 4 bottles of water. Each bottle has a capacity of 500 mL. How many liters of water can the bottles hold altogether?

33. It takes 12 average-size oranges to make 1 liter of orange juice. How many mL of juice can be expected from 18 oranges?

34. **Estimate** A recipe calls for 250 mL of apple juice. If the recipe is tripled, will a 1 L container of apple juice be enough?

35. A large cooler can hold 20 L and a small cooler can hold 5 L. How many more milliliters can a large cooler hold than a small cooler?

📊 **Data** **Use the recipe for Problems 36–40.**

36. How many liters will Sonya's punch recipe make?

37. How many 250 mL servings are in this recipe?

38. If each serving is 250 mL, how many liters of punch will be needed for 40 servings?

39. How many more milliliters of lemon-lime soda are in this recipe than orange juice?

40. **Money** How much will each 250 mL serving cost if the ingredients in the recipe cost a total of $5.60?

Sonya's Citrus Punch

750 mL orange juice
250 mL grapefruit juice
600 mL lemonade
400 mL limeade
2 L lemon lime soda

324

Extra Practice See page 331, Set E.

Open Response

Write the time in two ways. (Grade 3)

41.

42.

43. Anna wants to write 7,000 milliliters, using the fewest digits. How else could she write this capacity? (Chapter 12, Lesson 8)

Explain how you got your answer.

Math Reasoning
Using Benchmarks

Activity

Materials: centimeter or inch ruler
yardstick or meter stick

Here are some useful ways to estimate length.

1 centimeter

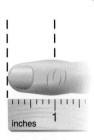

1 inch

1 foot

1 yard or 1 meter

Work with a partner.

STEP 1 Check the measurements shown above to find your personal benchmarks for length.

- Is your finger about 1 centimeter wide?
- Is the first joint in your thumb about 1 inch long?
- Does your arm from elbow to hand measure about 1 foot?
- Does your arm span measure about 1 yard? 1 meter?

STEP 2 Use your personal benchmarks to estimate the length of 5 objects in the classroom. Order and record your estimates. Then measure the objects using metric or customary units. Order and record your measurements.

How close were your estimates?

Metric Units of Mass

Objective Change metric units of mass.

Learn About It

These four pumpkin seeds have a mass of 1 gram. The pumpkin has a mass of 45 kilograms.

Gram and **kilogram** are metric units of mass.

Materials
balance
metric masses

Try this activity to measure and compare mass.

STEP 1 Find three objects in the classroom that you estimate will have a mass of 500 grams, 1 gram, and 100 grams.

STEP 2 Determine each object's mass and record it. List the three objects from heaviest to lightest.

STEP 3 Use the objects you found to predict the mass of other things in the classroom. Make a list of things that have a mass of about 1 gram, about 100 grams, and about 500 grams.

Metric Units of Mass
1 kilogram (kg) = 1,000 grams (g)

Other Examples

A. Kilograms to Grams

3 kilograms = _____ grams

$3 \times 1,000 = 3,000$

3 kilograms = 3,000 grams

B. Grams to Kilograms

2,000 grams = _____ kilograms

$2,000 \div 1,000 = 2$

2,000 grams = 2 kilograms

Find each missing number.

1. 8 kg = _____ g

2. _____ kg = 9,000 g

3. _____ kg = 5,000 g

4. 7 kg = _____ g

Explain Your Thinking ▶ Why is mental math useful in converting kilograms to grams?

Practice and Problem Solving

Find each missing number.

5. 5 kg = _____ g

6. _____ kg = 3,000 g

7. _____ g = 8 kg

8. 10 kg = _____ g

9. _____ g = 4 kg

10. 6 kg = _____ g

Choose the better unit to measure each. Write *gram* or *kilogram*.

11. a paper clip

12. a stapler

13. a desk

14. a dictionary

15. a pencil

16. a cherry

Choose the better estimate of the weight of each.

17.

a. 40 g   b. 4 kg

18.

a. 450 g   b. 45 kg

19.

a. 60g   b. 6 kg

20.

a. 8 g   b. 8 kg

21.

a. 100 g   b. 10 kg

22.

a. 300 g   b. 300 kg

Compare. Write >, <, or = for each ⬤.

23. 95 kg ⬤ 950 g

24. 3 kg ⬤ 3,000 g

25. 1,000 g ⬤ 2 kg

26. 5 g ⬤ 5,000 kg

27. 25 kg ⬤ 2,500 g

28. 700 g ⬤ 7 kg

29. 3 kg ⬤ 6,000 g

30. 125 kg ⬤ 4,000 g

31. 1,990 g ⬤ 19 kg

Solve.

32. Estimate Workers put apples in baskets that hold about 12 kg each. The workers filled 17 baskets. About how many kg of apples did they put in baskets?

33. Write About It A 500-gram bag of peanuts costs $2, and 2-kg bag costs $6.50. What is the least expensive way to buy 5 kg of peanuts?

34. Paul sold 3-kg bags of apples for $3.90 each. He sold pears for $1.20 per kg. He found that he had sold 15 kg of apples and 7 kg of pears. How much money did he collect?

35. Delroy weighed the pumpkins shown below. What is the average mass of the pumpkins?

36. Delroy decided to sell the pumpkins for 1 cent per gram. How much money will he collect if he sells all the pumpkins?

Extra Practice See page 331, Set F.

Open Response

Estimate. Then Divide. (Ch. 11, Lesson 6)

37. 16)339

38. 22)628

39. 893 ÷ 47

40. 990 ÷ 38

41. The local market sells cornmeal in 2,000-gram bags. Kristen needs 5 kilograms of cornmeal to make cornbread for the town fair. How many bags of cornmeal should she buy? Will she have any cornmeal left over?

(Chapter 12, Lesson 9)

Visual Thinking
Crafty Conversions

Problem Solving

Use your calculator to estimate conversions between metric and customary units.

1. 5 yd is about _____ m

2. 12 oz is about _____ g

3. 36 lb is about _____ kg

4. 5 mi is about _____ km

5. 10 cm is about _____ in.

6. 6 qt is about _____ L

7. 3 m is about _____ ft

8. 4 ft is about _____ cm

Estimated Equivalents
Length
1 in. is about 2.5 cm
1 yd is about 0.9 m
1 mi is about 1.6 km
Weight/Mass
1 oz is about 28 g
1 lb is about 0.5 kg
Capacity
1 qt is about 0.9 L

Chapter Review/Test

VOCABULARY

Choose the best word to complete each sentence.

1. A unit used to describe mass is a ____.

2. A unit used to describe length is a ____.

3. A unit used to describe liquid measure is a ____.

CONCEPTS AND SKILLS

Measure this ribbon. (Lessons 1 and 6, pp. 306–307, pp. 318–319)

4. to the nearest inch

5. to the nearest quarter inch

6. to the nearest centimeter

7. to the nearest millimeter

Find each missing number. (Lessons 2–4, pp. 308–314)

8. 4 yd = ____ in.

9. 60 ft = ____ yd

10. 2 mi = ____ ft

11. 5 gal = ____ qt

12. 12 c = ____ pt

13. 2 gal = ____ c

14. 4 lb = ____ oz

15. 2 T = ____ lb

16. 32 oz = ____ lb

Choose the metric unit you would use to describe each. (Lessons 7–9, pp. 320–328)

17. the length of a flea

18. the capacity of a sink

19. the mass of a pencil

PROBLEM SOLVING

Solve. (Lesson 5, p. 316)

20. Maria is 3 feet 9 inches tall. Naeem is 47 inches tall. Paula is 5 feet tall. What is the difference in inches between Paula's height and Naeem's height?

Write About It

Show You Understand

Tony has a 22 gallon aquarium. Ian said that it holds 90 quarts of water. Is Ian correct?

Explain why or why not.

Extra Practice

Set A (Lesson 2, pp. 308–309)

Find each missing number.

1. 3 yd = _____ in.

2. 24 in. = _____ ft

3. _____ in. = 6 ft

4. _____ ft = 1 mi

5. 4 yd = _____ ft

6. 3 mi = _____ yd

Set B (Lesson 3, pp. 310–311)

Find each missing number.

1. 16 c = _____ pt

2. 4 gal = _____ c

3. 8 pt = _____ gal

4. _____ gal = 12 qt

5. 11 pt = _____ c

6. _____ pt = 6 qt

Set C (Lesson 4, pp. 312–314)

Compare. Write >, <, or = for each ⬤.

1. 3,000 lb ⬤ 3 T

2. 6 lb ⬤ 80 oz

3. 36 oz ⬤ 2 lb

Set D (Lesson 7, pp. 320–321)

Find each missing number.

1. 3 dm = _____ cm

2. 5 cm = _____ mm

3. 200 cm = _____ m

4. _____ km = 5,000 m

5. 30 cm = _____ dm

6. 700 mm = _____ cm

Set E (Lesson 8, pp. 322–324)

Find each missing number.

1. 2 L = _____ mL

2. _____ L = 6,000 mL

3. _____ mL = 10 L

4. 4000 mL = _____ L

5. _____ mL = 8 L

6. 5 L = _____ mL

Set F (Lesson 9, pp. 326–328)

Compare. Write >, <, or = for each ⬤.

1. 2 kg ⬤ 2,500 g

2. 17 kg ⬤ 17,000 g

3. 850 g ⬤ 85 kg

Extra Practice at **eduplace.com/map**

Time and Temperature

INVESTIGATION

Using Data

Flamingos are beautiful pink birds that live in tropical climates. Look at the list of facts about flamingos. About how many weeks does it take a flamingo egg to hatch? What information do you need to write each of the Flamingos facts in terms of weeks?

Flamingos

- It takes between 26 and 31 days for a flamingo egg to hatch.

- It takes between 1 and 3 years for the gray flamingo chick to turn pink.

- A flamingo can live up to 50 years.

 **Use What You Know**

Use this page to review and remember
what you need to know for this chapter.

VOCABULARY

Choose the best term to complete each sentence.

1. The tool for measuring temperature is a ____.

2. Temperature can be measured in ____.

3. A ____ shows the days, weeks, and months in a year.

CONCEPTS AND SKILLS

Write each time in two different ways.

4.

5.

6.

Use the calendar for Questions 7–9.

7. The first Monday of September is Labor Day. What is the date?

8. What is the date of the third Wednesday?

9. How many Fridays are there in the month shown?

September

Sun.	Mon.	Tue.	Wed.	Thu.	Fri.	Sat.
				1	2	3
4	5	6	7	8	9	10
11	12	13	14	15	16	17
18	19	20	21	22	23	24
25	26	27	28	29	30	

Write About It

10. Why is 7:30 sometimes called half past seven? Use words or pictures to explain your thinking.

Facts Practice, See page 671.

Calendar

Objective Use a calendar to find elapsed time.

Vocabulary

decade

century

Learn About It

A cardinal laid eggs on Monday, April 25. They hatched 13 days later. On what day and date did the eggs hatch?

You can use a calendar to find elapsed time by counting the number of days.

Find April 25. Start counting forward from the next day. Count 13 days.

APRIL

S	M	T	W	T	F	S
					1	2
3	4	5	6	7	8	9
10	11	12	13	14	15	16
17	18	19	20	21	22	23
24	25	26	27	28	29	30

MAY

S	M	T	W	T	F	S
1	2	3	4	5	6	7
8	9	10	11	12	13	14
15	16	17	18	19	20	21
22	23	24	25	26	27	28
29	30	31				

Solution: The eggs hatched on Sunday, May 8.

Units of Time

1 week = 7 days
1 year = 12 months
1 year = 52 weeks
1 year = 365 days
1 leap year = 366 days

Other Examples

A. A **decade** is equal to 10 years. How many years equal 5 decades?

Think
1 decade = 10 years
So 5 decades = 5 × 10, or 50 years

5 decades = 50 years

B. A **century** is equal to 100 years. How many years equal 5 centuries?

Think
1 century = 100 years
So 5 centuries = 5 × 100 or 500 years

5 centuries = 500 years

Guided Practice

Use the calendars above for Questions 1–4.

1. Write the day and date 10 days after May 3.

2. Write the day and date 5 days after April 29.

3. Write the day and date 2 weeks before May 4.

4. Write the day and date 3 weeks after May 10.

Ask Yourself
- On what day do I begin counting?
- Should I count forward or backward?
- How many days do I count?

Explain Your Thinking ▶ What multiplication fact could you use to find how many years are in 8 decades? 4 centuries?

Practice and Problem Solving

Use the calendars on Page 334. Write the day and date.

5. 2 days before May 4

6. 6 days after May 22

7. 9 days before April 27

8. 1 week after May 10

9. 1 week after April 24

10. 2 weeks before May 9

Find each missing number.

11. 2 weeks = _____ days

12. 3 decades = _____ years

13. 2 years = _____ weeks

14. 5 centuries = _____ years

15. 1 year 2 weeks = _____ weeks

16. 2 years 3 months = _____ months

17. 4 decades 3 years = _____ years

18. 6 centuries = _____ decades

19. How many days is it from February 23 to March 15 in a leap year when February has 29 days?

20. Look at this pattern of leap years.

2004   2008   2012   2016

When is the next leap year?

Use the calendars on Page 334 and the schedule on the right for Problems 21–23.

21. How many meetings are planned for Bird Watching?

22. Jed plans to attend the series on *Habits of Chipmunks* and *Trees and Bushes.* How many meetings will that be?

23. Mark wants to attend the series *Animals of the Night* and one other series. What other series can he attend?

Bird Watching April 4 – May 6
Meets Monday through Friday

Habits of Chipmunks April 2 – April 30
Meets Tuesdays and Saturdays

Trees and Bushes April 4 – May 25
Meets Mondays and Wednesdays

Animals of the Night April 6 – May 27
Meets Wednesdays and Fridays

Mixed Review and Test Prep

Open Response

Write each number in word form.

(Ch. 1, Lesson 2)

24. 406   **25.** 758   **26.** 10,002

27. 4,250   **28.** 9,345   **29.** 16,400

30. 20,250   **31.** 900,050   **32.** 607,844

Multiple Choice

33. On April 7, Edmundo is looking forward to the school trip, which is in 5 days. What is the date of the school trip?

(Ch. 13, Lesson 1)

A April 2   **C** April 12

B April 7   **D** April 13

Extra Practice See page 353, Set A.

Lesson 2

Elapsed Time

Objective Find elapsed times.

Learn About It

Mariah finds that a tour of the Raptor Center is full when she arrives at 11:00 A.M. How long will she have to wait for the next tour?

Elapsed time is the time that passes between one time and another.

A.M. is used for the hours between 12 midnight and 12 noon.

P.M. is used for the hours between 12 noon and 12 midnight.

Next Tour Begins at 1:45 P.M.

▶ **You can use a clock to find how long it will be until the next tour.**

Start at 11:00.

1 h   2 h

Count the hours.
11:00 to 1:00 is 2 hours.

Then count the minutes.
1:00 to 1:45 is 45 minutes.

Solution: Mariah will have to wait 2 hours and 45 minutes.

▶ **If the tour starts at 1:45 P.M. and lasts 50 minutes, at what time does the tour end?**

If you know when the tour starts and how long it lasts, you can find when the tour ends.

Start at 1:45.

Count ahead 50 minutes to 2:35.

Solution: The tour ends at 2:35 P.M.

Extra Help at **eduplace.com/map**

You also can add or subtract to find elapsed time.

Units of Time
60 second(s) = 1 minute (min)
60 minutes = 1 hour (h)
24 hours = 1 day (d)
7 days = 1 week (wk)

▶ **If a tour begins at 1:45 P.M. and lasts 50 minutes, at what time does the tour end?**

$$\begin{array}{r} 1\text{ h } 45\text{ min} \\ +\quad\; 50\text{ min} \\ \hline 1\text{ h } 95\text{ min or } 2\text{ h } 35\text{ min} \end{array}$$

Think
60 min = 1 h

Solution: The tour ends at 2:35 P.M.

▶ **Mariah plans to arrive at the Raptor Center at 11 A.M. It is a 1 hour 15 minute ride by car. At what time should she leave home?**

$$\begin{array}{r} \overset{10}{\cancel{11}}\text{ h }\overset{60}{\cancel{0}}\text{ min} \\ -\;1\text{ h } 15\text{ min} \\ \hline 9\text{ h } 45\text{ min} \end{array}$$

Think
Rename 11 h 0 min as 10 h 60 min.

Solution: Mariah should leave home at 9:45 A.M.

Another Example

Reading Time to the Second

Read or Write 6:23:15
six twenty-three and fifteen seconds, or
twenty-three minutes fifteen seconds after six.

second hand

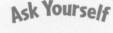

Guided Practice

Tell what time it will be.

1. in 3 hours

2. in 20 minutes

3. in 5 minutes

Ask Yourself
- At what time do I start counting?
- Do I need to count hours?
- Do I need to count minutes?

Explain Your Thinking ▶ How much time will elapse between 3:20 A.M. and 9:45 P.M.? How did you find the elapsed time?

Practice and Problem Solving

Tell what time it will be.

4. in 4 hours

5. in 15 minutes

6. in 13 minutes

7. in 10 hours

10:47

Look at each pair of times. Write how much time has passed.

8. Start: 1:05 P.M.
   End: 6:15 P.M.

9. Start: 6:50 A.M.
   End: 9:57 A.M.

10. Start: 8:35 A.M.
   End: 1:40 P.M.

11. Start: 11:45 A.M.
   End: 3:20 P.M.

12. Start: 9:10 P.M.
   End: 12:34 A.M.

13. Start: 7:40 A.M.
   End: 11:47 P.M.

Write the time shown on the clock before the hour and then after the hour.

14.

15.

16.

17.

Find each missing number.

18. 2 hours = _____ minutes

19. 3 minutes = _____ seconds

20. 90 minutes = 1 hour _____ minutes

21. 1 hour 25 minutes = _____ minutes

22. 4 minutes = _____ seconds

23. 95 minutes = 1 hour _____ minutes

24. Greg spent 2 hours 45 minutes visiting the Raptor Center. He arrived at 11:40 in the morning. What time did he leave?

25. Rita went to the Raptor Center at half-past four in the afternoon. How long was she there if she left at 8:25 P.M.?

26. **What's Wrong?** Bird-watching videos are shown every 20 minutes. The last video was at 2:25 P.M. Ann says that the next videos will be at 2:45 P.M. and 2:65 P.M. What did Ann do wrong?

27. **Analyze** Mr. Motts started working at the Raptor Center at 2:40 P.M. He led a tour for 2 hours 10 minutes. Then he worked in the office for 90 minutes. Was he finished before 7 P.M.?

Extra Practice See page 353, Set B.

Open Response

Round each number to the nearest ten cents. Then estimate. (Ch. 3, Lesson 3)

28. $0.57 + $0.81   **29.** $0.49 − $0.22

30. $4.65 + $8.32   **31.** $9.44 − $0.11

Multiple Choice

32. A yard sale starts at 8:30 A.M. and ends at 1:00 P.M. How long is the yard sale? (Ch. 13, Lesson 2)

A 3 h 30 min   **c** 4 h 30 min

B 4 h   **D** 7 h 30 min

Math Reasoning
Estimating Time

Problem Solving

You don't always need to know the exact time. Sometimes you can use an estimate.

Use the clocks for Problems 1–2.

▶ **You can estimate time to the nearest quarter hour.**

1. Suppose it takes 15 minutes to walk to the library. To the nearest quarter hour, at what time would you arrive?

▶ **You can estimate time to the nearest 5 minutes.**

2. Suppose a friend stops to ask what time it is. If you round to the nearest 5 minutes, what time will you tell your friend?

▶ **You can estimate elapsed time.**

3. The sign at the right lists the movies that are showing at the Raptor Center. How long will each movie last

a. to the nearest quarter hour?

b. to the nearest 5 minutes?

MOVIE TIMES AT THE RAPTOR CENTER

The Eagle Soars	11:00 A.M.–11:22 A.M.
Owls of the Night	1:15 P.M.–2:43 P.M.
Hawks on High	2:10 P.M.–3:24 P.M.

Problem-Solving Strategy
Guess and Check

Objective Use the Guess and Check strategy to solve a problem.

**Sometimes a good way to solve a problem
is to guess and check.**

Problem A nature photographer took some
pictures of puffins and otters. She
photographed 21 animals with 66 legs
altogether. How many puffins and otters did
she photograph?

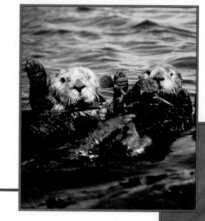

UNDERSTAND

This is what you know.

- The 21 animals have 66 legs altogether.

- Puffins have 2 legs and otters have 4 legs.

PLAN

Use the Guess and Check strategy.

Guess two numbers. Then check to see if they are correct.
If not, use your result to improve your next guess.

SOLVE

Use your result to make your next guess.

1st Guess	2nd Guess	3rd Guess
14 otters → 56 legs 7 puffins → 14 legs 21 animals 70 legs	11 otters → 44 legs 10 puffins → 20 legs 21 animals 64 legs	12 otters → 48 legs 9 puffins → 18 legs 21 animals 66 legs
Check: Too many legs. Guess again.	Check: Too few legs. Guess again.	Check: This is the answer.

Solution: She photographed 9 puffins and 12 otters.

LOOK BACK

Reread the problem.
Does the solution fit the facts of the problem?

Guided Practice

Use the Ask Yourself questions to help you solve each problem.

1. Altogether, there are 10 birds and bees in Ali's garden. If the birds and bees have 48 legs in all, how many birds and bees are there?

   (Hint) A bee has 6 legs.

2. Tim and Jared collect trading cards of rare birds. Tim has 8 more cards than Jared. Together they have 104 cards. How many cards does each boy have?

Ask Yourself

UNDERSTAND **What facts do I know?**

PLAN **What numbers would be a reasonable first guess?**

SOLVE **How can I use my result to improve my next guess?**

LOOK BACK **Did I go back to the problem to check my answer?**

Independent Practice

Use Guess and Check to solve each problem.

3. A photographer said that the only animals he saw on an island were lizards and parrots. He saw 8 animals with 22 legs altogether on that island. How many lizards and parrots did he see?

4. **Money** On a nature tour the guide collects $260 in fares. He collects only $10 bills and $20 bills. He collects 22 bills in all. How many of each kind of bill does the guide collect?

5. Carol has 8 booklets about birds. Some of the booklets have 26 pages and the others have 41 pages. How many of each size booklet does she have if the pages total 253?

6. The product of two numbers is 24. The difference between the numbers is 10. What are the numbers?

Go On

Mixed Problem Solving

Solve. Show your work. Tell what strategy you used.

7. In a bike race, there are judges posted at the beginning and end of each mile. If the race is 10 miles long, how many judges are needed?

8. Ten bicycles and tricycles are lined up at the park. Jerry counts a total of 24 wheels. How many bicycles are there?

9. Tyrone invited 8 friends to his party. He asked each friend to bring two other friends. How many people will come to Tyrone's party?

10. Five friends stood in line. Jamie was fourth in line. Jose stood right behind Ned. Lee was not third or last. Alice was also in line. In what order did the friends stand?

You Choose

Strategy
- Act It Out
- Draw a Picture
- Guess and Check
- Use Logical Reasoning
- Write an Equation

Computation Method
- Mental Math
- Estimation
- Paper and Pencil
- Calculator

Data Use the graph to solve Problems 11–13.

Students at Whitney School planted trees on Arbor Day. The graph at the right shows the number of trees planted by Grades 3–6.

11. How many trees were planted altogether?

12. Suppose it takes 15 minutes to plant each tree. How long will it take the fourth grade to plant all their trees?

13. Altogether, how many more trees did the fifth and sixth graders plant than the fourth graders?

14. **You Decide** Meg has $200 to buy trees. She can choose 2 kinds of trees. Pine trees cost $10, elm trees cost $8, and oak trees cost $12 each. How many of each type of tree can Meg buy?

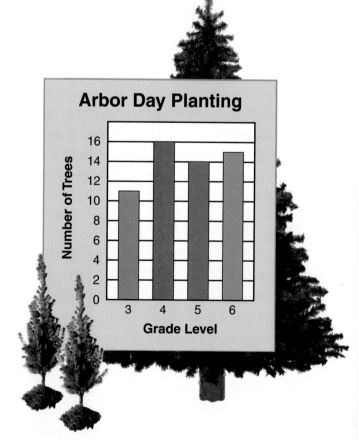

Arbor Day Planting

342

Problem Solving on Tests

Multiple Choice

Choose the letter of the correct answer. If a correct answer is not here, choose NH.

1. The length of a pencil is 16 centimeters. How many millimeters are equal to 16 centimeters?

    A 16,000   **C** 160

    B 1,600   **D** NH

    (Chapter 12, Lesson 7)

2. About how much water can this sink hold?

    F 160 gallons   **H** 10 quarts

    G 10 gallons   **J** 600 quarts

    (Chapter 12, Lesson 3)

Open Response

Solve each problem.

3. Sixty-seven students are taking part in a game. Teams can have no fewer than 3 and no more than 8 members. What is the smallest number of teams possible? Draw a diagram or write an equation to explain your answer.

    (Chapter 8, Lesson 3)

4. A soccer team begins practice at quarter after 3 and ends practice at quarter to 5. How many minutes does the team practice? Explain how you found your answer.

    (Chapter 13, Lesson 2)

Extended Response

5. You and your friend are going to the County Fair. You each have $15.00 to spend on rides. Use the table below to solve this problem.

County Fair Rides	
High Jumper	4 tickets
Crazy Cups	3 tickets
Scrambler	6 tickets
Hidden River	5 tickets
Carousel	2 tickets

    a. You can buy tickets individually for $1.00 each or in blocks of 10 tickets for $7.00. How many tickets can you afford to buy? Will you have any money left over?

    b. What rides could you go on with tickets bought with $15.00?

    c. Suppose you have 21 tickets. Plan your rides so that you don't have any tickets left. You can take the same ride more than one time. Tell how you will use the 21 tickets.

    d. If you could go on a hot-air balloon ride for $12.00, how would you spend your $15.00? Explain why you made your decision.

    (Chapter 6)

Education Place

See **eduplace.com/map** for more Test-Taking Tips.

Lesson 4

Audio Tutor 2/5 Listen and Understand

Temperature and Negative Numbers

Objective Use a thermometer to read temperatures above and below zero.

Vocabulary
- positive numbers
- negative numbers
- degrees Fahrenheit (°F)
- degrees Celsius (°C)

Learn About It

A thermometer can be used to measure temperature in degrees Fahrenheit or degrees Celsius.

°F
°C
220°
210°
200°
190°
180°
170°
160°
150°
140°
130°
120°
110°
100°
90°
80°
70°
60°
50°
40°
30°
20°
10°
0°
⁻10°
⁻20°
100°
90°
80°
70°
60°
50°
40°
30°
20°
10°
0°
⁻10°
⁻20°
⁻30°
water boils (212°F)
water boils (100°C)
normal body temperature (98.6°F)
normal body temperature (37°C)
hot summer day (86°F)
hot summer day (30°C)
room temperature (68°F)
room temperature (20°C)
water freezes (32°F)
water freezes (0°C)
cold winter day (14°F)
cold winter day (⁻10°C)

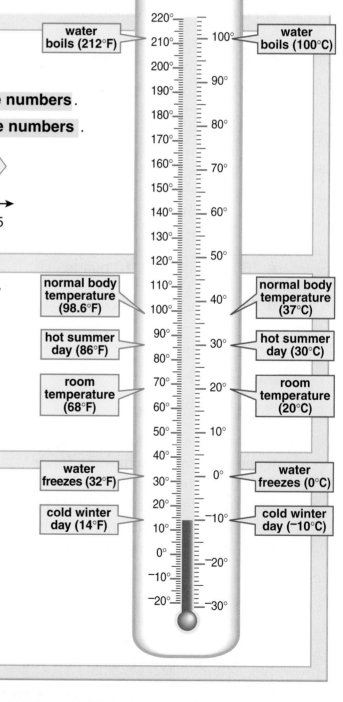

▶ **You can think of a thermometer as a vertical number line.**

- Temperatures above zero are **positive numbers**.
- Temperatures below zero are **negative numbers**.

Negative numbers are less than 0. | **Positive numbers are greater than 0.**

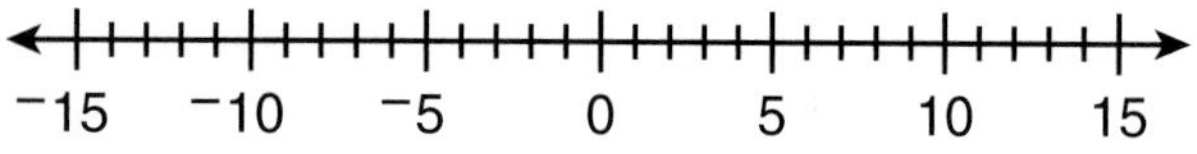

⁻15
⁻10
⁻5
0
5
10
15

▶ **Degrees Fahrenheit (°F)** are customary units of temperature.

The temperature shown on this thermometer is 14°F.

Write: 14°F

Say: fourteen degrees Fahrenheit

▶ **Degrees Celsius (°C)** are metric units of temperature.

The temperature shown on this thermometer is ⁻10°C.

Write: ⁻10°C

Say: negative ten degrees Celsius or ten degrees below zero Celsius

▶ **Use a thermometer to find the difference between two temperatures.**

Count up or down on the thermometer to find the difference.

A. 70°F and 42°F

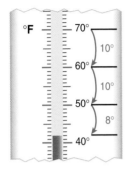

10 + 10 + 8 = 28
The difference is 28°.

B. ⁻15°C and 8°C

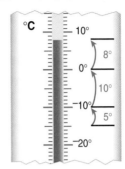

5 + 10 + 8 = 23
The difference is 23°.

Guided Practice

Write each temperature.

1. °F 50° 40°

2. °C 0° ⁻10°

3. °F 90° 80°

Ask Yourself

• What numbers is the temperature between?

• Is the temperature positive or negative?

• Is the temperature in degrees Fahrenheit or degrees Celsius?

Find the difference between the temperatures.

4. 2°C and 4°C

5. ⁻3°F and 2°F

6. 27°F and 45°F

7. ⁻8°F and 15°F

8. ⁻12°C and ⁻26°C

9. 13°C and ⁻2°C

Choose the better estimate of the temperature.

10. a cold day
   a. ⁻10°C   b. 30°C

11. a hot day
   a. 90°F   b. 37°F

12. room temperature
   a. 20°F   b. 70°F

Explain Your Thinking ▶ Which is lower, 5°C or ⁻15°C? How do you know?

Go On

Write each temperature.

13. °F | 20° | 10° 14. °C | 30° | 20° 15. °F | −10° | −20° 16. °C | −20° | −30°

Write the temperature shown on each thermometer.
Then write the difference between the two temperatures.

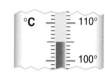 17. °C | 30° | 20°   °C | 110° | 100°

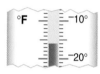 18. °F | 50° | 40°   °F | −10° | −20°

Find the difference between the temperatures.

19. 88°F and 110°F

20. −5°C and 10°C

21. −3°F and −10°F

22. 27°C and 13°C

23. 71°F and 39°F

24. −26°C and −8°C

Choose the better estimate of the temperature.

25. room temperature
  a. 22°C b. 39°C

26. swim at the beach
  a. 32°F b. 85°F

27. cup of hot soup
  a. 73°C b. 14°C

28. build a snowman
  a. 10°C b. −10°C

29. rake leaves
  a. 20°F b. 60°F

30. play baseball
  a. 75°F b. 17°F

 **Data** Use the table for Problems 31–32.

31. Was the difference in temperature greater between 6:00 A.M. and noon or between noon and 6:00 P.M.?

32. **Reasoning** Do you think the temperature at 7:00 A.M. was greater than or less than 70°F? Explain.

33. **Analyze** After the sun rose one morning, the temperature rose 5°. In the afternoon, the temperature fell 3°. If the temperature was 24°C then, what was the temperature when the sun rose?

Temperatures on July 27	
Time	Temperature
6:00 A.M.	64°F
9:00 A.M.	70°F
Noon	87°F
3:00 P.M.	78°F
6:00 P.M.	71°F

Extra Practice See page 353, Set C

Real World Connection
Why Do We Leap?

Earth takes a little more than 365 days to orbit the sun, but our calendars usually have only 365 days. After several hundred years, the extra time would build up, and our seasons would be turned around.

Long ago, people came up with a solution—leap year. Every fourth year, an extra day is added to February.

In leap years, February has 29 days.

- You can use division to find out which years are leap years. Pick any five years from 1904 to 2005. If you can divide the year evenly by 4, it is a leap year.

- How many leap years did you pick?

Quick Check

Check your understanding of Lessons 1–4.

Find each missing number. (Lesson 1)

1. 2 years = _____ weeks
2. 3 weeks = _____ days

Look at each pair of times. Write how much time has passed. (Lesson 2)

3. Start: 2:20 P.M.
   End: 3:05 P.M.

4. Start: 10:35 A.M.
   End: 12:15 P.M.

5. Start: 9:03 A.M.
   End: 10:10 P.M.

Find the difference between the temperatures. (Lesson 4)

6. 15°C and 23°C

7. ⁻4°F and 12°F

8. 7°C and ⁻7°C

Solve. (Lessons 3 and 4)

9. There are 3 more dogs than cats in a pet store. There are 21 cats and dogs altogether. How many cats are there?

10. At 9 A.M. the temperature was ⁻3°F. At 3 P.M. the temperature was 15° warmer. What was the temperature at 3 P.M.?

Extra Practice at **eduplace.com/map**

Problem-Solving Application
Use Temperature
Objective Solve problems about temperature.

You can use what you know about finding temperature to solve problems.

Problem Antarctica is the coldest continent on Earth. The temperature at noon one day is ⁻6°F. The temperature rises 4 degrees over the next two hours. Then by 8:00 P.M. the temperature falls 7 degrees. What is the temperature at 8:00 P.M.?

UNDERSTAND

This is what you know.

- The temperature is ⁻6°F at noon.

- The temperature rises 4 degrees and then falls 7 degrees by 8:00 P.M.

PLAN

You can use a thermometer to count up and down.

SOLVE

Count up or count down.

- Start at ⁻6°F.   • Count up 4 degrees.   • Count down 7 degrees.

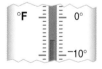 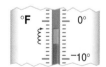 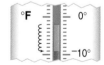

Solution: The temperature is ⁻9°F at 8:00 P.M.

LOOK BACK

Check your answer to see if it's reasonable. Since the temperature fell more than it rose, the answer should be less than ⁻6°F. ⁻9°F is less than ⁻6°F, so the answer is reasonable.

Guided Practice

Use the Ask Yourself questions to help you solve each problem.

1. If it is 68°F inside and 24°F outside, how many degrees lower is the temperature outside than inside?

2. Mina recorded the temperature at noon. It then fell 6 degrees. Later it rose 4 degrees. If the last temperature was 17°C, what was it at noon?

(**Hint**) Should you count up or count down?

Ask Yourself

UNDERSTAND → What do I know?

PLAN → Can I use a thermometer?

SOLVE → Did I count up or count down the correct number of degrees?

LOOK BACK → Does my answer make sense?

Independent Practice

3. The temperature was 70°F in the morning. It rose 17 degrees during the day and then dropped 9 degrees by 6 P.M. What was the temperature at 6 P.M.?

4. At 10 A.M. the temperature was ⁻14°F at a bird research station in Antarctica. If the temperature rose 2 degrees every hour, what was the temperature at 3 P.M.?

5. Suppose the temperature falls 1 degree Celsius for every 100 meters you climb. If your thermometer shows 2°C now, what will it show after you climb 400 meters?

6. A thermometer shows 16°F. The wind makes the air feel 20 degrees colder. How cold does it feel?

7. On Monday the low temperature was ⁻37°C and the high temperature was ⁻12°C. On Tuesday the low temperature was ⁻23°C and the high was 4°C. Which day had the greatest difference in temperature?

Go On

Mixed Problem Solving

Solve. Show your work. Tell what strategy you used.

You Choose

Strategy
- Find a Pattern
- Guess and Check
- Work Backward
- Write an Equation

Computation Method
- Mental Math
- Estimation
- Paper and Pencil
- Calculator

8. Mr. Ordono's class collected a total of 172 cans for a food drive. Jacob collected 16 cans and Lakia collected 9 cans. How many cans did the rest of the class collect?

9. **Money** Ben and Norman earned $63 together last weekend. Norman earned $9 more than Ben. How much did Ben earn?

10. Ashley swam 2 laps on Monday, 4 laps on Tuesday, 7 laps on Wednesday, and 11 laps on Thursday. If she continues at the same rate, how many laps is she likely to swim on Friday?

Solve. Tell which method you used.

11. Arctic terns migrate about 10,000 miles. This is about the same distance as two round trips from New York to Los Angeles. About how many miles apart are New York and Los Angeles?

12. Look at the caption at the right. About how long was it between the time Albert Crary arrived at the North Pole and at the South Pole?

13. **Explain** Marsha plans to cut a piece of string 97 inches long to show the wingspan of the American White Pelican. She has 7 feet of string. Is that enough? How do you know?

Albert Paddock Crary was the first person to reach both the North Pole and the South Pole. He arrived at the North Pole in 1952, and the South Pole in 1961.

Math Reasoning
In Hot Water!

Materials:
1 glass of hot water from the tap
1 glass of cold water from the tap
2 Fahrenheit thermometers

Have you ever left a cold drink outside on a hot day? When you try to drink it later, it's as hot as the air around it.

Try this activity to see how a liquid's temperature changes over time.

1. Make a table like the one at the right.

2. Measure the room temperature and record it.

3. Measure the temperature of each glass of water and record it.

   • What is the difference between each water temperature and the room temperature at the beginning of the experiment?

   • Predict which glass will reach room temperature first.

4. Repeat the water measurements every half hour and record them.

   • At what time did both glasses of water reach the same temperature?

Water Temperature (°F)		
Time	**Cold Water**	**Hot Water**
9:00 A.M.		
9:30 A.M.		
10:00 A.M.		
10:30 A.M.		
11:00 A.M.		
11:30 A.M.		

Room Temperature _____ °F

Chapter Review/Test

VOCABULARY

Choose the best term to complete each sentence.

1. The time that passes between one time and another is ____.

2. A number that is less than 0 is a ____.

3. There are 10 years in a ____.

4. There are 100 years in a ____.

Vocabulary

decade
century
positive number
negative number
elapsed time

CONCEPTS AND SKILLS

Find each missing number. (Lesson 1, pp. 334–335)

5. 4 weeks = ____ days

6. 1 year = ____ days

7. 5 years = ____ months

8. 21 days = ____ weeks

9. leap year = ____ days

10. ____ weeks = 1 year

11. 3 decades 2 years = ____ years

12. 2 centuries 3 decades = ____ years

Look at each pair of times. Write how much time has passed. (Lesson 2, pp. 336–338)

13. Start: 9:00 A.M.
    End: 6:45 P.M.

14. Start: 4:10 P.M.
    End: 5:53 P.M.

15. Start: 8:17 A.M.
    End: 11:00 A.M.

Find the difference between the temperatures. (Lesson 4, pp. 344–347)

16. 25°F and 7°F

17. 12°C and ⁻5°C

18. ⁻8°F and ⁻6°F

PROBLEM SOLVING

Solve. (Lessons 3, 5, pp. 340–342, 348–350)

19. There are 13 children and dogs in the park. Altogether there are 34 legs. How many children and how many dogs are there?

20. Kelly read the temperature at noon. It rose 10 degrees by 3 P.M. then fell 5 degrees by 6 P.M. If the temperature was 3°F at 6 P.M., what was it at noon?

 **Write About It**

Show You Understand

Frank says that when it's 30°C, it is time to wear a warm coat. Is he correct? Explain why or why not.

Extra Practice

Set A (Lesson 1, pp. 334–335)

			January			
Sun.	Mon.	Tue.	Wed.	Thu.	Fri.	Sat.
						1
2	3	4	5	6	7	8
9	10	11	12	13	14	15
16	17	18	19	20	21	22
23	24	25	26	27	28	29
30	31					

Use the calendar.

1. Write the day and date 3 days before January 26.

2. Write the day and date 5 days after January 8.

3. Write the day and date 2 weeks after January 1.

4. Write the day and date 1 week before January 11.

Find each missing number.

5. 3 weeks = _____ days

6. 1 year = _____ days

7. 2 decades = _____ years

8. 52 weeks = _____ year

9. 1 year 6 months = _____ months

10. 3 centuries = _____ years

Set B (Lesson 2, pp. 336–339)

Tell what time it will be.

1. in 3 hours

2. in 20 minutes

3. in 17 minutes

Set C (Lesson 4, pp. 344–347)

Write the temperature shown on each thermometer.
Then write the difference between the two temperatures.

1.

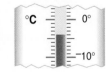

2.

Find the difference between the temperatures.

3. 5°C and 12°C

4. −3°F and 10°F

5. −9°C and −4°C

CHAPTER 14

Collect and Analyze Data

INVESTIGATION

Using Data

Students in a fourth-grade class answered this survey question: "Where would you like to visit?" The tally chart shows the answers. Write 5 facts about the students using the information in the tally chart.

Where Would You Like to Visit?

Country	Tally
Spain	卌 |||
Kenya	卌	
Italy	卌 卌
Japan	||

Use What You Know

**Use this page to review and remember
what you need to know for this chapter.**

VOCABULARY

Choose the best term to complete each sentence.

1. A graph that uses pictures to show data is a ____.

2. One way to collect information is to take a ____.

3. The symbols ⑷⑷ are called ____.

CONCEPTS AND SKILLS

**The tally chart at the right shows the number
of hours Alicia trained for a marathon. Use
the tally chart for Problems 4–6.**

4. In which week did Alicia train the most?

5. How many more hours did she train in
Week 4 than in Week 1?

6. What is the total number of hours Alicia
trained in 4 weeks?

Alicia's Marathon Training

Week	Hours of Training
1	⑷⑷
2	⑷⑷ ⑷⑷ |||
3	⑷⑷ ||
4	⑷⑷ ⑷⑷ ⑷⑷	

Order the numbers from least to greatest.

7. 89   72   86   64

8. 163   314   145   278

9. 948   762   1,045   926

Write About It

10. What would be a good interval on a bar graph
for the following data? Explain your reasoning.

15   16   20   22   25   28

Facts Practice, See page 672.

Collect and Organize Data

Objective Conduct a survey and organize information.

Vocabulary
data
survey

Materials
Tally Charts
(Learning Tool 17)

Work Together

A survey is one way to collect information, or **data**. When you conduct a **survey**, you ask a question and record the answers.

The question for a class survey was, "What do you like to eat?"

- Thirty students answered the question.

- The answer choices were *chicken nuggets, corn, French fries, salad,* and *tuna sandwich.*

- The answer *chicken nuggets* was given most often. Thirteen students liked chicken nuggets best.

Work with a partner. Conduct a survey and organize your data.

What Do You Like to Eat?

Answer	Tally	Number
Chicken nuggets	卌 卌 III	13
Corn	卌 II	7
French fries	卌 I	6
Salad		0
Tuna sandwich	IIII	4

STEP 1 Write a question that has 3 or 4 possible answers. List the possible answers in a tally chart like the one shown.

Question:_____		
Answer	Tally	Number

STEP 2 Survey 20 people. Allow each person to give only one answer. Make a tally mark for each answer. Then add the tally marks for each answer.

STEP 3 Analyze your data.
- How would you describe the results of your survey?

Use the tally chart for Problems 1–6.

1. What is the survey question?

2. Which answer was given most often? least often?

3. How many students answered the survey question?

4. How many students named the two most popular activities?

5. What is the order of activities from most to least popular?

6. **What's Wrong?** Dora says that more than half the class likes swimming or visiting grandparents best. Explain why that is not true.

What Is Your Favorite Summer Activity?		
Activity	**Tally**	**Number**
Bicycling	ЖНТ ЖНТ ||	12
Going to camp	|||	3
Playing video games	ЖНТ |	6
Swimming	ЖНТ ЖНТ ЖНТ |	16
Visiting grandparents	||||	4

Use the list at the right to make a tally chart. Then solve Problems 7–10.

7. What are the possible answers on your tally chart?

8. How many students never bring their lunch to school?

9. How many students sometimes bring their lunch to school?

10. How many students sometimes or always bring their lunch to school?

How Often Do You Bring Your Lunch to School?

Sandy	always
Gina	sometimes
Wilson	never
Paco	sometimes
Joy	sometimes
Rosalie	always
Bob	sometimes
Joanna	sometimes
Will	always

Go On

Conduct your own survey. Use the survey question "What do you like to eat?" or "What is your favorite summer activity?" Use the survey for Problems 11–13.

11. How many students did you survey?

12. Compare your survey results to the survey results on pages 356 or 357. Are the results similar or different? Explain.

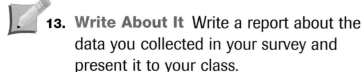
13. **Write About It** Write a report about the data you collected in your survey and present it to your class.

Use the tally chart for Problems 14–19. Write *true* or *false* for each statement.

14. The greatest number of people in the survey recycle newspapers.

15. More people recycle glass than cans.

16. There were a total of 28 answers to the survey question.

17. From least to greatest, the order of recycled items is cardboard, plastic, glass, cans, newspapers.

18. More people recycle newspapers than plastic and cans combined.

19. **Create and Solve** Use the tally chart to write a word problem. Then solve the problem.

What Items Do You Recycle?

Answer	Tally	Number
Cans	ЖⅠ ⅠⅠⅠ	8
Cardboard	Ⅰ	1
Glass	ЖⅠ Ⅰ	6
Newspapers	ЖⅠ ЖⅠ ⅠⅠ	12
Plastic	ⅠⅠ	2

Talk About It • Write About It

You learned to conduct a survey and collect data.

20. Suppose a principal wants to know what color people prefer for the walls of a cafeteria. Does it make sense for the principal to survey only fourth-graders? Why or why not?

21. Can a survey tell you anything about the opinions of people who did not take part in the survey? Explain your answer.

Igba-ita

In parts of Africa, people use small shells called cowries to play *Igba-ita*. You and a partner can play a similar game with pennies instead of cowries.

2 Players

What You'll Need • 20 pennies for each player
• *Igba-Ita* Scoring sheets (Learning Tool 18)

How to Play

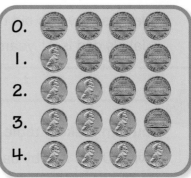

1 Look at the picture to see all the different ways four pennies tossed at the same time can land.

2 Make a scoring sheet. Write the numbers 0–4 in a column down the left side of your paper.

3 Take turns tossing four pennies. After each round, count the number of heads you and your partner tossed. The player with the greater number of heads tossed takes all eight pennies. Toss again if both players toss the same number of heads. Mark the scoring sheet with the number of heads each player tossed.

4 Keep playing until one player has all the pennies.

Problem-Solving Strategy
Make a Table

Objective Organize data in a table to solve a problem.

Problem Jake is 18 years old. Jake's dad is 41 years old. How old will they both be when Jake's dad is twice as old as Jake?

UNDERSTAND

This is what you know.

- Jake is 18 years old now.
- Jake's dad is 41 years old now.

PLAN

You can make a table to help you solve the problem.

Divide Dad's age by Jake's age. When the quotient is 2, Dad's age will be twice Jake's age.

SOLVE

Make a table.

- Divide Dad's age by Jake's age. Write the quotient in the table.
- Keep adding one year to each person's age.
- Divide until you find an exact quotient of 2.

  Think: $2 \times 23 = 46$

Solution: When Jake is 23, his dad will be 46.

Jake's Age	Dad's Age	Dad's Age ÷ Jake's Age
18	41	$41 \div 18 = 2$ R5
19	42	$42 \div 19 = 2$ R4
20	43	$43 \div 20 = 2$ R3
21	44	$44 \div 21 = 2$ R2
22	45	$45 \div 22 = 2$ R1
23	46	$46 \div 23 = 2$

LOOK BACK

Look back at the problem.

Does the solution answer the question?
Does the answer make sense?

Guided Practice

Use the Ask Yourself questions to help you solve each problem.

1. Scott is 9 years old, and his sister is 2 years old. How old will each be when Scott is twice his sister's age?

2. Ellen's aunt is 34 years old. Ellen is 15 years old. At what age will Ellen be exactly half her aunt's age? How old will Ellen's aunt be then?

   (Hint) Ellen's aunt will be twice Ellen's age.

Ask Yourself

UNDERSTAND **What do I know?**

PLAN **Can I make a table?**

SOLVE
- **Did I start with the correct numbers?**
- **Did I choose the correct operation?**

LOOK BACK **Does my solution answer the question?**

Independent Practice

Make a table to solve each problem.

3. Six people are in Steve's family. Each person is 8 inches taller than the next person. The tallest person is 70 inches tall. How tall is the shortest person?

4. Steve has $12. His sister Emily has $7. Steve earns $3 a week, and Emily earns $2 a week doing chores. How much money will each have when Steve has exactly $10 more than Emily?

5. Steve has read 5 books. Each week he reads 3 more books. Emily has read 6 books. Each week she reads 2 more. How many books will each have read when they have read a total of 41 books?

6. A fast-growing weed doubles its height every week. It is now 3 centimeters tall. How tall will it be at the end of 5 weeks?

Go On

Mixed Problem Solving

Solve. Show your work. Tell what strategy you used.

7. Dalia, Jen, and Brad are wearing jackets that are either red, blue, or gray. Each is wearing a different color. Brad's jacket is not red. Jen's jacket is not red or blue. What color is each person's jacket?

8. Susan is 9 years old. Her uncle is 24 years old. At what age will Susan be half her uncle's age? How old will her uncle be then?

9. **Measurement** What is Martha's height in feet and inches if she is 10 inches less than five feet?

10. Copy the table below. Fill in the missing numbers so that the sum of the numbers in each row and column is equal.

6		3
		2
4		17

You Choose

Strategy
- Find a Pattern
- Make a Table
- Use Logical Reasoning
- Work Backward
- Write an Equation

Computation Method
- Mental Math
- Estimation
- Paper and Pencil
- Calculator

Data **Use the graph about class birthdays for Problems 11–14.**

11. Which season has the greatest number of birthdays?

12. How many birthdays are in autumn and winter?

13. How many fewer birthdays are in summer than in the rest of the year?

14. How many people were surveyed?

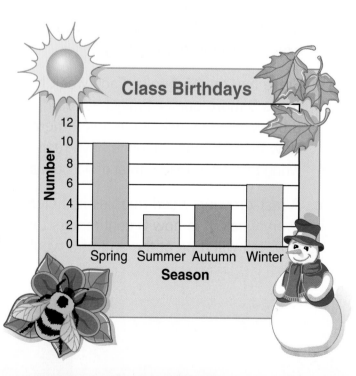

Class Birthdays

Problem Solving on Tests

Choose the letter of the correct answer.

Multiple Choice

1. The temperature at 3:00 P.M. was 2 degrees higher than the temperature at 2:00 P.M. If it was 6°C at 2:00 P.M., what was the temperature at 3:00 P.M.?

   A ⁻2°C   B 2°C   C 4°C   D 8°C

   (Chapter 13, Lesson 4)

2. Marlena can pack 28 books into one box. How many boxes does she need in order to pack 224 books?

   F 7   G 8   H 78   J 196

   (Chapter 11, Lesson 4)

Open Response

Solve each problem.

3. Al uses 8 pins to hang 3 drawings.

   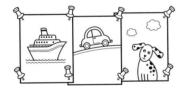

   If Al hangs a total of 6 drawings the same way, how many pins will he use?

   (Chapter 10, Lesson 3)

4. Students estimated a doorway's height.

Name	Estimate
Andrew	2 yd
Sarah	75 in.
Christy	6 ft 1 in.
Mike	2 yd 1 ft

   The actual height is 6 ft 8 in. Whose estimate is closest to the actual height?

   (Chapter 12, Lesson 2)

Extended Response

5. Use the ad to solve the problems.

   Georgia Peaches 3-pound bag $2.19
   Delicious Apples 4-pound bag $1.48
   Florida Oranges 5-pound bag $2.60
   McIntosh Apples 5-pound bag $3.55
   New York Pears 3-pound bag $1.95
   Yellow Bananas 2 pounds $0.98

   a. Shoppers often estimate prices. Estimate the cost of 1 pound of each kind of fruit.

   b. Find the exact price of 1 pound of each fruit.

   c. Find the differences between your estimates and the actual prices. If your estimates were not close to the actual prices, check your division.

   (Chapters 8, 9)

Education Place

See **eduplace.com/map** for more Test-Taking Tips.

Mean, Median, Mode, and Range

Objective Find the mean, median, mode, and range of a set of data.

Work Together

Look at the data in the list. Then work with a partner to describe the data in different ways.

How Tall Are You?	
Name	Height (cm)
Dana	129
Ted	130
Darryl	135
Mason	130
Sadie	131
Lauren	140
Max	136

 STEP 1

Find the **mean** of the data.
First, find the sum of the numbers: 931.

Divide the sum by the number of addends: $931 \div 7$.

- What is the mean height of the students?

 STEP 2

Find the **median** of the data.

When a set of numbers is ordered from least to greatest, the middle number is called the median.

- What is the median height of the students?

> When there are two middle numbers in a data set, the median is the mean of those two numbers. Look at the data.
>
> 12, 12, 13, 15, 15, 15
>
> $13 + 15 = 28$
>
> $28 \div 2 = 14$
>
> The median is 14.

 STEP 3

Find the **mode** of the data.

The number that occurs most often in a data set is called the mode.

- What is the height that occurs most often?

 STEP 4

Find the **range** of the data.

The difference between the greatest number and the least number is the range.

- What is the range of the students' heights?

STEP 5 Use the results of your work to describe the heights of the fourth-graders surveyed.

• Do you think your description would also describe your class? Explain.

On Your Own

Use the data in the table to answer Problems 1–5.

Sandra and her friends play basketball for the Star Hoopsters. Every year, their coach records the heights of the players. The table shows the data for this year.

★ Star Hoopsters ★

Name	Height (cm)
Lee	133
Elise	128
Maya	141
Sandra	137
Vince	141

1. Use a calculator to find the mean height of the players.

2. Sandra says that most of her teammates are taller than she is. Is she correct? Explain how you know.

3. What is the mode of the data?

4. You do not have to be tall to play for the Star Hoopsters. Use the range to tell why that statement is true.

5. **Analyze** Mr. Jordan, the basketball coach, played with the team on Tuesday. Suppose his height was added to the table. He is 184 cm tall. How will this information change the mean, median, mode, and range?

Talk About It • Write About It

You learned to find the mean, median, mode, and range of a set of data.

6. Explain why it is helpful to put the data in order from least to greatest before you find the median, mode, and range.

7. Does the mode or the median give a better description of the Star Hoopsters? Explain your thinking.

Lesson 4

Line Plots

Objective Make a line plot to represent data.

Learn About It

Cindy and Pete surveyed their classmates about family pets. They made a line plot to show the data they collected.

A **line plot** is a way to represent data using X's. You can use a line plot to find the median, mode, and range of a data set.

How many pets do you have?	
Number	**Tally**
0	IIII
1	IIII I
2	II
3	II
4	
5	I

▶ To find the **range**, look at the number line on the line plot. Subtract the least value from the greatest value.

$5 - 0 = 5$ The range is 5.

▶ When a set of numbers is ordered from least to greatest, the middle number is called the **median**.

0 0 0 0 1 1 1 **1** 1 1 2 2 3 3 5

The median, or middle, of the data set is 1.

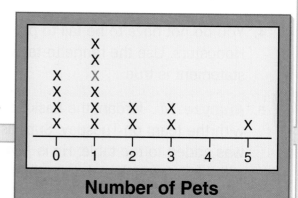

Number of Pets

▶ To find the **mode**, look for the number that has the most X's. Some data sets do not have a mode. Others have one or more modes.

The mode is 1.

Guided Practice

Seven students weighed their dogs. The line plot shows the data. Use it for Problems 1–3.

1. What is the range of the data?

2. What are the median and the mode of the data?

3. Suppose there was another dog weighing 15 kg. What would the median and mode be then?

Ask Yourself

- What do the X's represent?
- What does the number line represent?

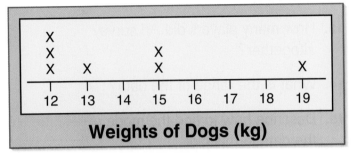

Weights of Dogs (kg)

Explain Your Thinking ▶ What is the mean of the data in the line plot above? How did you find it?

Practice and Problem Solving

Use the line plot at the right for Problems 4–6.

4. How many hours of TV did most fourth-graders watch on Tuesday?

5. What is the range of the data?

6. What are the mean, median, and mode of the data?

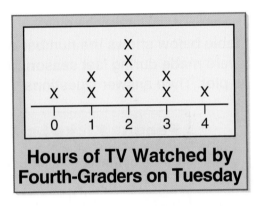

Hours of TV Watched by Fourth-Graders on Tuesday

This line plot shows the hours students spend reading each week. Use the line plot to answer each question.

7. How many students read for 2 hours each week?

8. How many students answered the survey? Explain your answer.

9. Did more students read for 3 hours or for 5 hours?

10. Describe how to find the median number of hours spent reading for the data in this plot.

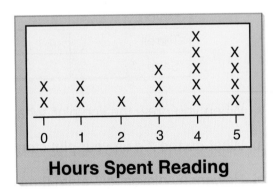

Hours Spent Reading

Ari asked the players on his soccer team how many goals they scored last season. This line plot shows the results. Use the line plot to answer Questions 11–15.

11. How many players scored exactly 4 goals?

12. How many players scored at least 2 goals?

13. How many players did Ari survey altogether?

14. What is the range of the data?

15. Describe how to find the mode of the data in this plot.

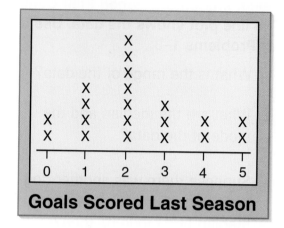

Goals Scored Last Season

16. Decide on a survey question for which the answers are numbers. There should be three or four possible answers. Conduct the survey and record your answers on a line plot.

The table below shows the number of penalty kicks that 5 players made during last season. Use the data to make a line plot. Then answer Questions 17–21.

Penalty Kicks Last Season	
Name of Player	Number of Penalty Kicks
Josh	4
Kristen	5
Louis	8
Terrell	5
Sean	3

17. When you drew the line plot, what numbers did you use?

18. What do the X's on your plot stand for?

19. How many players got more than 1 hit?

20. What is the median of the data?

21. What is the mode of the data?

Math Reasoning
Mode of a Set

Mode can describe data sets that are not numerical. These dog tags are grouped by size. The mode for size is medium.

1. What is the mode for dog-tag shape: octagon, rectangle, or circle?

2. What is the mode for dog-tag color: red, blue, silver, gold, or green?

Check your understanding of Lessons 1–4.

Use the tally chart. (Lesson 1)

What Is Your Favorite Color?	
Color	**Tally**
Blue	IIII III
Green	IIII

1. How many people chose blue?

2. How many people were surveyed?

Use the line plot. (Lessons 3–4)

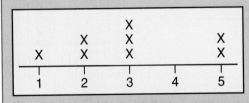

Size of Litters for Eight Animals

3. What is the range of the data set?

4. What is the mean?

Solve. (Lesson 2)

5. Lee saves $3 in Week 1. Each week, he doubles the amount he saves. What is the amount he saves in Week 5?

Audio Tutor 2/7 Listen and Understand

Stem-and-Leaf Plots

Objective Read and make stem-and-leaf plots.

Learn About It

Another way to organize data is with a
stem-and-leaf plot. A stem-and-leaf plot
shows information arranged by place value.

The table at the right shows how many minutes
nine students spent doing chores. You can make
a stem-and-leaf plot of the data.

Minutes Spent Doing Chores	
Name	**Minutes**
Akio	77
Bonnie	30
Daniel	38
Ella	45
Julie	40
Miguel	35
Payat	55
Sarah	50
Tanya	35

• First, order the data from least to greatest.

30	35	35	38	40	45	50	55	77

• Then make a stem-and-leaf plot with
  digits in order from least to greatest.

Minutes Spent Doing Chores	
Stem	**Leaves**
3	0 5 5 8
4	0 5
5	0 5
6	
7	7

Each stem is the tens digit of each number.

Each leaf is the ones digit of each number.

3 | 0 = 30 minutes

The stem 7 and the leaf 7 tell you that one student spent
77 minutes doing chores. The number 77 is called an
outlier because it is far from the other numbers.

You can use a stem-and-leaf plot to find the mean,
median, mode, and range of the data set.

• What are these measures?

Guided Practice

The stem-and-leaf plot shows the amount of money Mia earned baby-sitting. Use the plot for Problems 1–3.

1. What is the median of the data?

2. What is the mode of the data?

3. Is there an outlier? What does that tell you about the data?

Explain Your Thinking ▶ How are the stems and the leaves different in a stem-and-leaf plot?

Ask Yourself
- What place do the stems represent?
- What place do the leaves represent?

Mia's Earnings	
Stem	**Leaves**
1	0 2 3 7 8 8
2	0 0 2 5
3	4

1 | 0 = $10

Practice and Problem Solving

The list on the right shows how many minutes Lionel practiced the piano on 11 different days. Use the list for Problems 4–8.

4. Use the data to make a stem-and-leaf plot. Then use your stem-and-leaf plot for Problems 7–11.

5. How many leaves are in your stem-and-leaf plot? What do they represent?

6. What was the least number of minutes Lionel practiced?

7. What is the median number of minutes Lionel spent practicing?

8. **Analyze** Is the range a good way to describe Lionel's practice time? Why?

Lionel's Piano Practice (minutes)	
60	55
50	30
65	46
48	63
60	57
60	

Mixed Review and Test Prep

Open Response

Find each missing number. (Ch. 12, Lesson 3)

9. 3 pints = _____ cups

10. 1 gallon = _____ quarts

11. 8 cups = _____ quarts

12. Make a stem-and-leaf plot for the data. (Ch. 14, Lesson 5)

My Miniature Golf Scores
35, 40, 39, 45, 41, 32, 38, 44, 57

Chapter Review/Test

VOCABULARY

1. The difference between the greatest number and the least number in a set of data is the ____.

2. A way of displaying data as tens and ones is a ____.

3. When a set of numbers is arranged in order, the middle number is the ____.

Vocabulary

mean
range
median
stem-and-leaf plot

CONCEPTS AND SKILLS

Use the line plot for Problems 4–6.

(Lessons 3, 4, pp. 364–368)

4. What is the median of the data?

5. What is the range of the data?

6. What is the mode of the data?

```
                    X
              X     X
              X     X           X
        X     X     X     X     X
        ┬─────┬─────┬─────┬─────┬─────┬
        0     1     2     3     4     5
```

**Number of Runs
in 11 Games**

Use the stem-and-leaf plot for Problems 7 and 8. (Lesson 5, pp. 370–371)

7. How many scores are there?

8. Is there an outlier? If so, which score is it?

Test Scores	
Stem	**Leaves**
5	0
6	
7	2 4 8
8	3 6 7 7

5 | 0 = 50

PROBLEM SOLVING

Make tables to solve Problems 9 and 10.

(Lesson 2, pp. 360–362)

9. Jamal is 19 years old. Billy is 3 years old. How old will each one be when Jamal is three times as old as Billy?

10. A blue bus leaves every 3 minutes. A red bus leaves every 5 minutes. Both leave at 6:00 P.M. When is the next time a blue bus and a red bus will leave at the same time?

Write About It

Show You Understand

Do you think that a survey of 100 people will give more reliable information than a survey of 10 people? Explain your thinking.

Extra Practice

Set A (Lesson 4, pp. 366–368)

Use the line plot for Problems 1–6.

1. How many campers are there?

2. Are any of the campers younger than 8 years old?

3. What is the age of the oldest camper?

4. What is the range of the data?

5. What is the mode?

6. What is the median?

```
                    X
          X         X
          X         X         X
          X         X         X         X
          X         X         X         X         X
      ————————————————————————————————————————————
          8         9        10        11        12
```

Ages of Campers

Set B (Lesson 5, pp. 370–371)

Use the stem-and-leaf plot at the right for Problems 1–5.

1. How many days are recorded?

2. Which temperature is an outlier?

3. What is the range?

4. What is the median?

5. What is the mode?

Daily High Temperatures in September (°F)	
Stem	Leaves
4	9
5	
6	6 8 9 9
7	0 0 0 1 2 2 3 5 7 9

4 | 9 = 49

Use the stem-and-leaf plot at the right for Problems 6–10.

6. Which measure—the mean, median, mode, or range—helps you understand the difference between the team's best and worst games?

7. What was the highest score?

8. What is the mean of the scores between 80 and 89?

9. What is the median score?

10. Is there an outlier? Explain your reasoning.

Basketball Scores	
Stem	Leaves
6	8 9
7	1 5 6 6
8	4 7 8 8 8
9	0

6 | 8 = 68

Graph Data

INVESTIGATION

Using Data

To estimate the distance between you and a thunderstorm, count the number of seconds between a lightning flash and the sound of thunder. If you see a lightning flash, how could you use the graph to find out how far away the thunderstorm is?

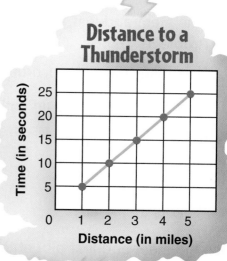

Distance to a Thunderstorm

Time (in seconds) vs. Distance (in miles)

Use What You Know

Use this page to review and remember what you need to know for this chapter.

VOCABULARY

Choose the best term to complete each sentence.

1. When you ask people questions, one way to keep track of the answers is to use a ____.

2. The difference between the greatest number and the least number in a set of data is the ____.

3. A number that names a part of a whole is a ____.

CONCEPTS AND SKILLS

Write a fraction for the shaded part.

4.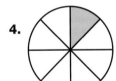

5.

6.

Use the bar graph for Problems 7–9.

7. How many more animal books than sports books does Robin have?

8. Robin has about the same number of sports books as what other type of book?

9. How many animal and mystery books does Robin have altogether?

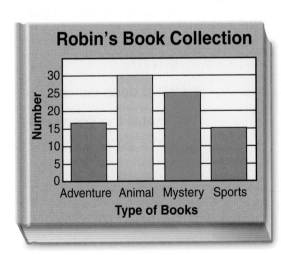

Robin's Book Collection

 Write About It

10. Think about what you know about pictographs and bar graphs. Explain how a bar graph is different from a pictograph.

Facts Practice, See page 665.

Double Bar Graphs

Objective Make a double bar graph to compare two sets of data.

Work Together

A **double bar graph** can be used to compare two sets of data.

The table on the right shows the number of rainy days during May, June, and July in Cleveland, Ohio, and Raleigh, North Carolina.

Work with a partner to make a double bar graph to compare the data.

Number of Rainy Days			
	May	**June**	**July**
Cleveland, OH	13	11	10
Raleigh, NC	10	9	11

STEP 1

Choose a title and labels for the graph. Then choose colors for the **key.** The key shows what each bar stands for.

Next, choose an interval. The difference between two numbers on the scale is the **interval.**

- What is the title of the graph?

- What are the labels on the graph?

- What does the key show?

- What is the interval? Why is that a good interval to use?

Choose two different colors.

Always start at zero.

STEP 2

Use the data from the table to make the graph.

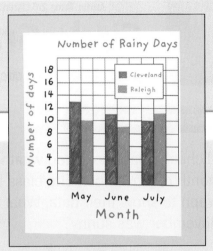

STEP 3

Use the completed graph to compare the data.

• In May, were there more rainy days in Cleveland or in Raleigh?

On Your Own

Use the table below to make a double bar graph. Then use the graph for Problems 1–3.

1. What interval did you choose for your graph? Explain your choice.

Number of Rainy Days			
	August	**September**	**October**
Hilo, Hawaii	26	23	24
Syracuse, New York	11	11	12

2. In which month were there twice as many rainy days in Hilo as in Syracuse?

3. In which city was the number of rainy days the same in August and in September?

4. Choose four rainy-day activities. Ask the girls and boys in your class which activity they like best. Record the data in a table. Use the table to make a double bar graph.

Talk About It • Write About It

You learned that you can make a double bar graph to compare two sets of data.

5. For the same graph, how would the length of the bars change if the interval were changed from 2 to 4?

6. Is a double bar graph a good way to show how much a puppy grew from birth to age 6? Why or why not?

Audio Tutor 2/8 Listen and Understand
Circle Graphs
Objective Use a circle graph to solve problems.

Learn About It

Michael's class collected weather data for the month of November. The class made a circle graph to show their data. What fraction of November was sunny?

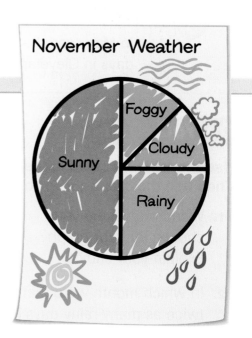

▶ A **circle graph** shows the parts that make up a whole. The circle on the right represents the whole month of November.

Each section of the circle represents the part of the month that was sunny, rainy, cloudy, or foggy. You can use a fraction to represent each part.

Find the section of the graph labeled *Sunny*. You can see that half the circle represents the part of November that was sunny.

Solution: In November, half the month was sunny.

Guided Practice

Use the circle graph above for Problems 1–3.

1. About what fraction of November was rainy?

2. Were there more rainy days than foggy days during November? Explain how you know.

3. Which types of weather are represented about equally in the graph?

Ask Yourself
- What does the circle represent?
- What do the circle's sections represent?

Explain Your Thinking ▶ If *r* represents the number of rainy days, what expression represents the number of sunny days?

Practice and Problem Solving

The circle graph represents the types of clouds Dianne saw in the sky each day in February. Use the circle graph for Problems 4–6.

February Clouds

4. What fraction of the days had cirrus clouds?

5. Did Dianne see stratus clouds or cirrus clouds on more days during February?

6. What was the fraction of the month that the sky was clear of clouds?

7. For a hike on a sunny day, Al packs 4 eight-packs and 3 six-packs of water. If 10 people go on the hike, how many bottles of water are there for each person?

8. **Explain** Kate buys 5 books about the sky and stars. She pays a mean cost of $10 per book. Trina buys 3 books with a mean cost of $20. Does Kate or Trina spend more?

9. **Create and Solve** Conduct a survey of 8 students. Record the answers in a circle graph. Write two questions that can be answered by using the graph. Have a classmate answer the questions.

Mixed Review and Test Prep

Open Response

Write the temperature that is 4° below the temperature shown. (Ch. 13, Lesson 4)

10.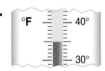

11.

12.

13.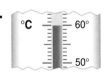

Multiple Choice

14. Which color is the favorite of $\frac{1}{4}$ of the class? (Ch. 15, Lesson 2)

Favorite Colors

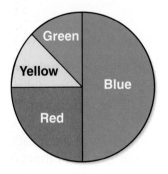

A red

B yellow

C blue

D green

Extra Practice See page 389, Set A.

Problem-Solving Application
Interpret a Line Graph

Objective Get information from a graph even if it does not give exact information.

Sometimes you can get information from a graph even though it does not have numbers or labels.

Jeff hiked on a trail in Great Smoky Mountains National Park with his dad. The **line graph** shows changes in temperature during the hike.

▶ **Use the line graph to understand how data change over time.**

The graph shows the temperature at different times during the hike.

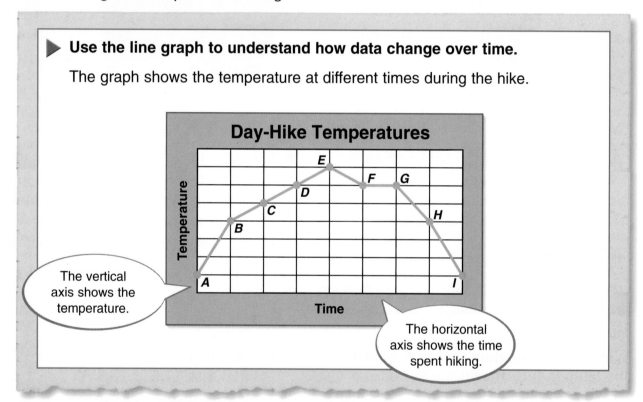

Day-Hike Temperatures

The vertical axis shows the temperature.

The horizontal axis shows the time spent hiking.

▶ **Use the line graph to compare data.**

- The line is flat between points *F* and *G*, which means the temperature did not go up or down. Time is passing, but the temperature is not changing.

- On the *Time* axis, there are more intervals between points *D* and *H* than between points *A* and *C*, so more time elapsed between points *D* and *H*.

Look Back Explain why the graph lines can't go straight up or down.

Guided Practice

Use the graph on Page 380 and the Ask Yourself questions to help you solve each problem.

Ask Yourself
- How can I tell when the temperature is going up?
- How can I tell when time is passing?

1. Explain what happened between Point *A* and Point *B*. Tell how you know.

   Hint How are temperature and time related?

2. Between which two points did the temperature drop the most? What explanation could there be?

Independent Practice

Use the graph at the right for Problems 3–5.

3. Was it colder at the start of the day or at the end of the day?

4. Between which two consecutive points did the greatest change occur? Can you tell how much the temperature changed during that time? Explain.

5. Did more time pass between Point *A* and Point *B* or between Point *C* and Point *E*?

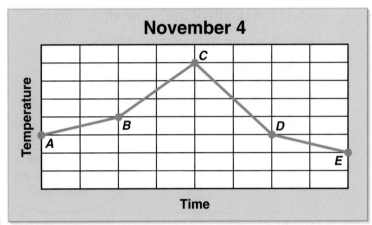

Use the graph at the right for Problems 6 and 7.

6. The graph shows the change in height during a climb and the time spent climbing. Which points show when the climbers probably stopped for lunch?

7. Explain what happened between Point *A* and Point *B*. Tell how you know.

8. **Represent** Make a line graph without numbers. Show that the distance around a tree increases as the tree grows taller.

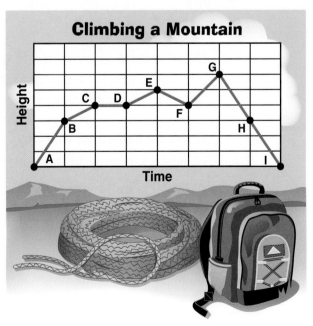

Chapter 15 Lesson 3 381

Audio Tutor 2/9 Listen and Understand

Read and Make Line Graphs

Objective Read and make a line graph.

Materials
Grid Paper
(Learning Tool 21)

Learn About It

You can use a **line graph** to show how data change over time. This line graph shows how much snow fell in 4 hours. How deep was the snow after 2 hours?

To find the depth of the snow after 2 hours,

• Find 2 on the axis labeled *Hours*.

• Move up to the line of the graph.

• Move left to the axis labeled *Depth*. Read the depth in inches.

The vertical axis represents depth in inches.

Depth of Snow

The horizontal axis represents time in hours.

Solution: After 2 hours, the snow was 4 inches deep.

Try this activity to make a line graph.

STEP 1 Use the table to make a line graph. Write a title and labels. Then choose a scale to show the icicle lengths.

STEP 2 Show 24 inches for Monday.
• Locate Monday on the horizontal axis.
• Move up to 24 inches on the vertical axis.
• Place a point where both lines meet.

STEP 3 Continue placing points, then connect them.

Icicle Lengths

Day	Length
Monday	24 inches
Tuesday	20 inches
Wednesday	12 inches
Thursday	16 inches
Friday	20 inches

Guided Practice

Use the *Depth of Snow* graph on Page 382 for Problems 1–3.

1. What was the depth of snow after 3 hours?

2. About what is the depth of snow after $2\frac{1}{2}$ hours?

3. The graph line goes up from left to right. Could the direction of the line ever change? Explain.

Explain Your Thinking ▶ What is the pattern on the Depth of Snow graph? If the pattern continues, what will the depth of the snow be after 5 hours?

Practice and Problem Solving

4. Use the table at the right to make a line graph. Then use your line graph for Problems 5–7.

5. What happened to the temperatures from Thursday through Sunday?

6. **Predict** Would you expect the high temperature on the day after Sunday to be 20°F, 60°F, or 90°F? Explain your answer.

7. What is the range of the temperatures on your graph?

Daily High Temperatures	
Day	**Temperature**
Monday	40°F
Tuesday	45°F
Wednesday	30°F
Thursday	40°F
Friday	35°F
Saturday	30°F
Sunday	25°F

Quick Check ✓

Check your understanding for Lessons 1–4.

Use the graphs for Problems 1 and 2. (Lessons 1, 3, 4)

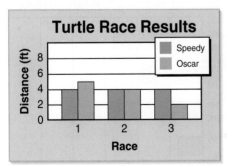

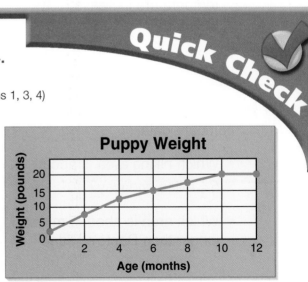

1. How far did Oscar travel in the race he won?

2. How much weight did the puppy gain between 6 months and 1 year?

Hands On Lesson 5

Analyze Graphs

Objective Use graphs to display different types of data.

Materials
Grid Paper
(Learning Tools 19, 20, and 21)

Learn About It

Brian is doing a report on Death Valley, one of the hottest places in the world. These graphs show data about Death Valley in different ways.

On July 10, 1913, a high temperature of 134°F was recorded at Greenland Ranch in California's Death Valley.

> A **line graph** is a good way to show change over time.

- About how hot is it at 9:00 A.M.? How do you know?

- Between which two times does the temperature increase about 20°?

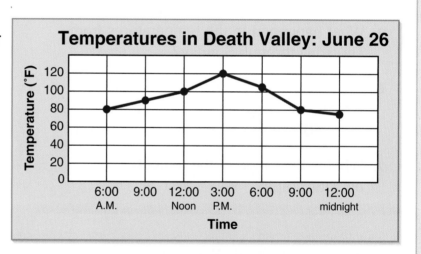

> A **bar graph** lets you compare data.

- Which hiking area is about $5\frac{1}{2}$ miles one way?

- Which area is about 3 miles longer than Dante's Ridge?

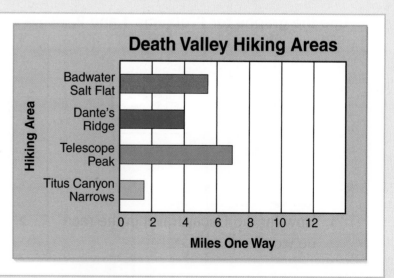

384

▶ A **circle graph** shows the parts of a whole. It is a good choice for showing a budget.

Vacation Budget

- Which item will use about half the vacation budget?

- Which budget item will cost about the same amount as a car rental?

▶ A **pictograph** uses a key instead of a scale. The pictograph shows the results of a survey that asked students to vote on the best month to visit Death Valley.

Best Month to Visit Death Valley	
March	☼ ☼
April	☼ ☼ ☼ ☼ ☼
May	☼ ☼ ☼
June	☼ ☼
July	☼

Each ☼ = 2 votes.

- Which month got the most votes?

- What does the symbol ☼ stand for?

Make a graph to analyze the results of a survey.

STEP 1 — Choose a survey question like the one shown on the right. Then conduct a survey and record the data.
- How many students did you survey?

STEP 2 — Make a graph to display the data you collected.
- Why did you choose the type of graph you did?

STEP 3 — Write two questions about the data that can be answered using your graph.

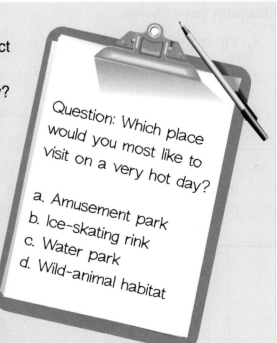

Question: Which place would you most like to visit on a very hot day?

a. Amusement park
b. Ice-skating rink
c. Water park
d. Wild-animal habitat

Go On

Use the graphs on Pages 384 and 385 for Problems 1–4.

1. Between which two times on June 26 does the temperature increase the most?

2. What will cost about twice as much as a car rental?

3. If Brian's family wants to hike a total of about 3 miles out and back, to which hiking area should they go?

4. How many votes were recorded on the pictograph?

Explain Your Thinking ▶ Would a pictograph have been another good way to represent the data about Death Valley hiking areas? Why or why not?

Practice and Problem Solving

Choose a graph to display the data for Exercises 5–10. Write *bar graph*, *circle graph*, *line graph*, or *pictograph*. Explain your choice.

5. the results of an election

6. the growth of a plant

7. compare the heights of cacti

8. rainfall for a week

9. the parts of a day spent hiking, eating, and sleeping

10. the number of books read during the summer by 5 students

11. **Create and Solve** What could the graph below be showing? Create a title, scale, and labels for the graph.

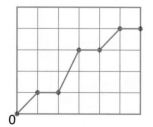

386

Extra Practice See page 389, Set C.

Open Response

Find the mean, median, mode, and range for each set of data. (Ch. 14, Lesson 3)

12. 14, 3, 8, 1, 14

15. 5, 3, 11, 5

13. 13, 1, 13, 6, 2

16. 30, 40, 20, 30

14. 9, 6, 12, 9, 9

17. 15, 23, 17, 25

18. A line graph that shows the distance a bicyclist rode on a 1-hour trip levels off between two points in the middle of the graph. (Ch. 15, Lesson 5)

How could you explain this?

Math Reasoning
Histograms

Problem Solving

A histogram shows how often data occur within equal intervals. This histogram shows the heights of 15 roadside animal statues.

1. Which interval shows the heights of the greatest number of statues?

> **Remember**
> An interval is the amount of space between 2 things.

Heights of Roadside Animal Sculptures

Number of Statues: 6, 4, 2, 0

Height (ft): 10–19, 20–29, 30–39, 40–49, 50–59

2. How many statues are less than 30 feet?

3. How many statues are between 30 and 39 feet high?

Chapter Review/Test

VOCABULARY

Choose the best term to complete each sentence.

1. A _____ uses bars to compare two sets of data.

2. The difference between two numbers on a scale is the _____.

3. A _____ shows the parts that make up a whole.

Vocabulary
key
interval
line graph
circle graph
double bar graph

CONCEPTS AND SKILLS

Use the graphs to answer Problems 4–9. (Lessons 1, 2, 5, pp. 376–379, 384–386)

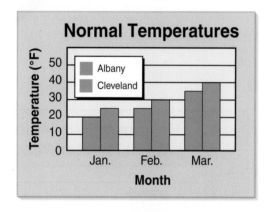

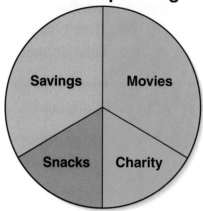

4. In January, which city has the colder temperature?

5. In March, is it warmer in Albany or in Cleveland?

6. Why is a double bar graph a good choice for these data?

7. What fraction of Jamie's money does she save?

8. Does Jamie spend more on movies or on snacks?

9. Why is a circle graph a good choice for these data?

PROBLEM SOLVING

Solve. (Lessons 3, 4, pp. 380–383)

10. Draw a line graph to show the total distance hikers walked in a day.

Write About It

Show You Understand

What kind of graph would best display changes in the high temperature outside a school during one week? Why?

Extra Practice

Set A (Lesson 2, pp. 378–379)

Use the circle graph for Problems 1–3.

1. What fraction of people chose peanut butter?

2. Did more people choose hamburger or tuna salad as their favorite sandwich?

3. Which choice shows about twice as many votes as grilled cheese?

Favorite Sandwich

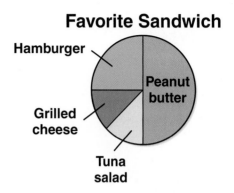

Set B (Lesson 4, pp. 382–383)

Use the line graph for Problems 1–3.

1. On which day was the water level the greatest?

2. On which days was the water level less than 1 inch?

3. Between which two days did the water level decrease the most?

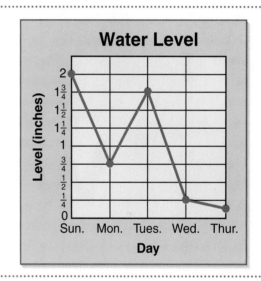

Set C (Lesson 5, pp. 384–386)

Write the letter of the graph that shows the information given in each problem.

A.
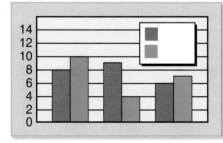

B.
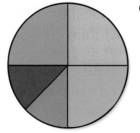

C.
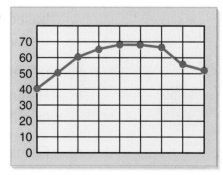

1. the amount spent on party supplies

2. changes in temperature during a day

3. a comparison of scores by two teams in three games

What Time Is It?

Before the late 1800s, it was difficult to know the correct time. That's because each town kept its own "official" time. Train schedules were difficult to use because the time for each stop was based on the local time for that place. People all over the world told time differently.

In 1878, Sir Sanford Fleming solved the time problem. He created a system of worldwide time zones that is still used today.

Fleming divided Earth into 24 time zones. That's one zone for each hour of the day. Each zone has a different time. If it is 1:00 P.M. in one zone, it is 2:00 P.M. in the zone to it's right. Catching a train has never been easier!

Problem Solving

The map shows time zones in the United States. The time in each zone is one hour later than the time in the zone to its left.

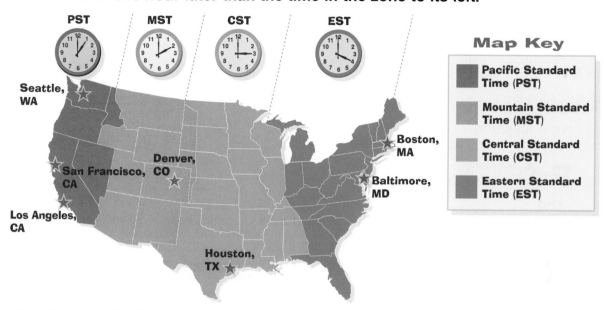

PST **MST** **CST** **EST**

Seattle, WA

San Francisco, CA

Los Angeles, CA

Denver, CO

Houston, TX

Boston, MA

Baltimore, MD

Map Key

- Pacific Standard Time (PST)
- Mountain Standard Time (MST)
- Central Standard Time (CST)
- Eastern Standard Time (EST)

Use the map for Problems 1–4.

1 If it is midnight in Boston, what time is it in Los Angeles? What is the time difference between those two cities?

2 Suppose it is 11:45 P.M. on August 23 in San Francisco. What are the time and date in Baltimore?

3 A flight from Seattle to Houston leaves Seattle at 9:30 A.M. The flight takes 4 hours 5 minutes. What time is it in Houston when the plane arrives?

4 A man in Denver looks at his watch at 4:37 P.M. At the same moment, his aunt in Ohio looks at her watch. What is the time on his aunt's watch?

Education Place

Visit Weekly Reader Connections **eduplace.com/map** for more on this topic.

Enrichment: Time Lines

Toys From The Past

A **time line** can be used to show when events happened.

This time line shows when some popular games and toys were invented.

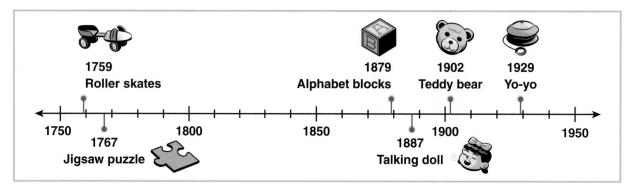

1759
Roller skates

1879
Alphabet blocks

1902
Teddy bear

1929
Yo-yo

1750   1800   1850   1900   1950

1767
Jigsaw puzzle

1887
Talking doll

The space between the marks for 1750 and 1850 represents 100 years, or a century. It is divided into 10 smaller spaces. The amount of time each small space represents is called an interval. On this time line the interval is 10 years, or a decade.

Try These!

Use the time line for Problems 1–5.

1. What games or toys were invented in the 1700s? in the 1800s?

2. How many decades are between the invention of the jigsaw puzzle and the invention of the talking doll?

3. Was there more or less than a century between the invention of alphabet blocks and the yo-yo? Explain.

4. There were 2 decades 3 years between the invention of alphabet blocks and the teddy bear. How many years was that?

5. What interval would you use to create a time line of inventions of the past decade? the past year? How did you choose your interval?

Watch 'em Grow!

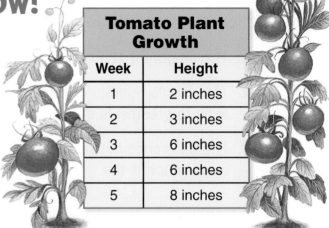

Tomato Plant Growth	
Week	Height
1	2 inches
2	3 inches
3	6 inches
4	6 inches
5	8 inches

Mrs. Spinelli's class is growing vegetables in the school garden. The table on the right shows the growth of one of their tomato plants over 5 weeks.

You can use Graphers to make a line graph of the data.

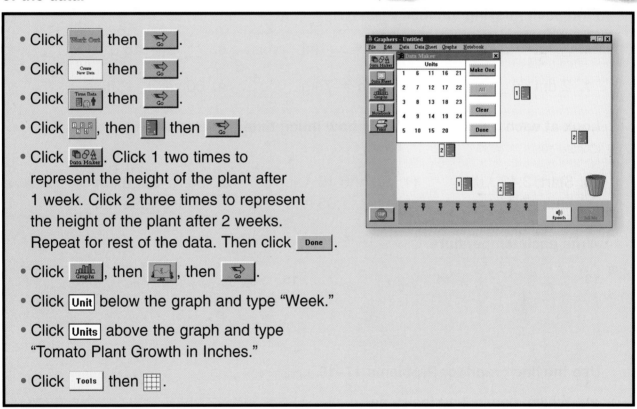

- Click [Work Out] then [Go].
- Click [Create New Data] then [Go].
- Click [Time Data] then [Go].
- Click [▦], then [▯] then [Go].
- Click [Data Maker]. Click 1 two times to represent the height of the plant after 1 week. Click 2 three times to represent the height of the plant after 2 weeks. Repeat for rest of the data. Then click [Done].
- Click [Graphs], then [▱], then [Go].
- Click [Unit] below the graph and type "Week."
- Click [Units] above the graph and type "Tomato Plant Growth in Inches."
- Click [Tools] then [▦].

Use the line graph you created for Problems 1–4.

1. How tall was the tomato plant at the end of Week 4?

2. How many inches did the tomato plant grow between Week 1 and Week 3?

3. Between which two weeks did the growth of the tomato plant show the greatest increase?

4. What are the mean, median, mode, and range of the heights? How did you find the mean?

Unit 5 Test

VOCABULARY （Open Response）

Choose the correct word to complete each sentence.

1. The amount that a container can hold is its ____.

2. The middle number in a set of numbers ordered from least to greatest is the ____.

3. The difference between two numbers on the scale of a bar graph is the ____.

> **Vocabulary**
> mode
> median
> interval
> capacity

CONCEPTS AND SKILLS （Open Response）

Find each missing number. (Chapter 12)

4. ___ pt = 32 c

5. 6 L = ___ mL

6. ___ lb = 48 oz

7. 2 dm = ___ cm

8. ___ g = 7 kg

9. 60 yd = ___ ft

Look at each pair of times. Write how much time has elapsed.

(Chapter 13)

10. Start: 3:42 A.M.
    End: 7:07 A.M.

11. Start: 8:15 A.M.
    End: 1:05 P.M.

12. Start: 10:20 P.M.
    End: 2:35 A.M.

Write each temperature. (Chapter 13)

13. °F 70° 60°

14. °C 20° 10°

15. °F 0° -10°

16. °C 100° 90°

Use the line graph for Problems 17–19. (Chapter 15)

17. Which months had the same amount of rainfall?

18. How much rain fell in the wettest month? Which month was it?

19. About how much rain fell between the beginning of May and the end of July?

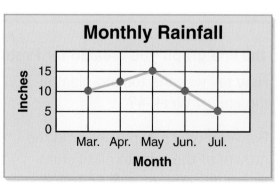

Monthly Rainfall

Inches: 15, 10, 5, 0

Month: Mar. Apr. May Jun. Jul.

Use the data in the table for Problems 20 and 21. (Chapter 14)

20. Use the data to make a stem-and-leaf plot.

21. Find the mean, median, and mode of the data.

Minutes Jacob Played in His Soccer Games				
1	25	13	13	20
13	14	25	20	

PROBLEM SOLVING (Open Response)

22. A comic book doubled in price every 10 years. It cost $20 in 1950. How much did it cost 5 decades later?

23. Jim bought 4 muffins for $2.50 each and 2 snack bars for $1.25 each. How much did he spend on muffins?

24. In a park, there are 25 people and dogs with a total of 70 legs. How many people are there?

25. It is 17°F at 8 P.M. If it gets 4° colder each hour for 3 hours, what will the temperature be then?

Performance Assessment

(Extended Response)

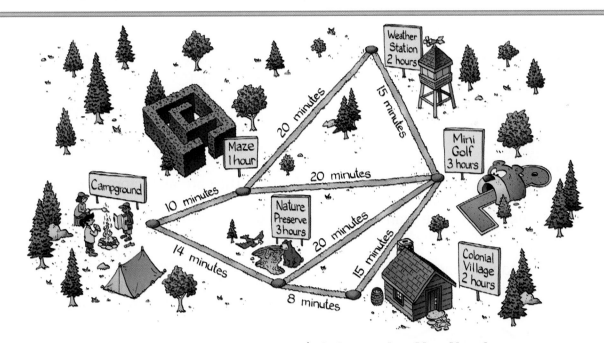

Task A club is planning what activities to do on a two-day camping trip.

Use the map and the information at the right to decide which activities the club should do in the two days. Make a schedule, including the times the club arrives and departs from each activity.

Information You Need

- The club wants to do at least four activities during the two-day trip.

- Club members want to leave the campground at 9 A.M. and be back by 4 P.M. each day.

- The time it takes to travel from activity to activity and the length of each activity are shown the map.

Cumulative Test Prep

Solve Problems 1–10.

Test-Taking Tip

A question may ask you to choose the statement that is true. All parts of the statement must be true for the answer to be true.

Look at the example below.

Which statement is true for these data?

14	18	11	14	14	15	12

A The mean is 13, and the mode is 14.

B The range is 10, and the median is 14.

C The mean is 3 more than the median.

D The mean, the median, and the mode are 14.

THINK

A is **not true** because the mean is not 13.

B is **not true** because the range is not 10.

C is **not true** because the mean and the median are both 14.

D is **true** because the mean, the median, and the mode are all 14.

So choose **D.**

1. Which is the product of 9 × 5,300?

   A 4,770   **c** 47,700

   B 45,900   **D** 50,000

(Chapter 6, Lesson 7)

2. Katrina is 4 feet 7 inches tall. How many inches tall is she?

   F 45 inches   **H** 52 inches

   G 47 inches   **J** 55 inches

(Chapter 12, Lesson 2)

3. Which statement is true of the numbers 3, 5, and 12?

   A They are all factors of 35.

   B They are all prime numbers.

   c They are all factors of 60.

   D They are all composite numbers.

(Chapter 10, Lesson 2)

4. An orbit is the time it takes for a planet to go around the Sun. Mercury's orbit lasts 88 Earth days. How many times does Mercury orbit the Sun in 440 Earth days?

   F 3   **H** 5

   G 4   **J** 6

(Chapter 11, Lesson 4)

For Test-Taking Tips, See page 658.

5. Khai has $12. Each week for 5 weeks, he saves $4. How much money does Khai have at the end of 5 weeks?

(Chapter 4, Lesson 4)

6. Copy and complete the function table.

Rule: _____	
x	**y**
1	6
■	18
10	60
12	■

(Chapter 5, Lesson 6)

7. It took Teresa 16 minutes to walk from her house to school. She arrived at school at 9:05 A.M. At what time did Teresa leave her house?

(Chapter 13, Lesson 2)

8. Use the table.

Game	1	2	3	4	5	6
Runs	2	1	12	3	4	3

What are the mode and the range of the number of runs?

(Chapter 14, Lesson 3)

9. A carton holds 12 eggs. If Jon has 11 cartons of eggs, how many eggs does he have?

(Chapter 4, Lesson 6)

10. Matt has $5.00 and must buy lunch for himself and his sister Gina.

Lunch Menu	
Item	**Price**
Milk	$0.40
Orange Juice	$0.60
Pizza Slice	$1.15
Apple	$0.25
Combo (pizza slice, apple, and milk)	$1.65

A Matt wants 1 combo meal for himself, and 1 slice of pizza and 1 orange juice for his sister. How much will this cost?

B If Matt gives the cashier $5.00, how much change will he get?

C Whose lunch costs more, Matt's or Gina's? Tell how much more.

D How much money is Matt saving by buying the combo meal instead of buying each item in the combo meal separately?

(Chapter 2, Lesson 4)

Education Place

Look for Cumulative Test Prep at **eduplace.com/map** for more practice.

Vocabulary Wrap-Up for Unit 5

Look back at the big ideas and vocabulary in this unit.

Big Ideas

You can use multiplication and division to convert from one unit of measure to another.

You can measure elapsed time on a calendar or a clock.

You can display data in a graph.

You can find the mean, median, and mode of a data set.

Key Vocabulary

data
elapsed time
mean
median
mode

Math Conversations

Use your new vocabulary to discuss these big ideas.

1. Explain how you can find the number of inches in 6 feet.

2. Explain the difference between the mean, median, and mode of a data set.

3. Explain how bar graphs and line graphs are alike and different.

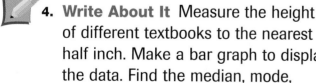

4. **Write About It** Measure the height of different textbooks to the nearest half inch. Make a bar graph to display the data. Find the median, mode, and range of the data.

> I recorded the temperature each day this week.

> You could use a line graph to display your data.

UNIT 6

Geometry and Measurement

Reading Mathematics

Reviewing Vocabulary

Here are some math vocabulary words that you should know.

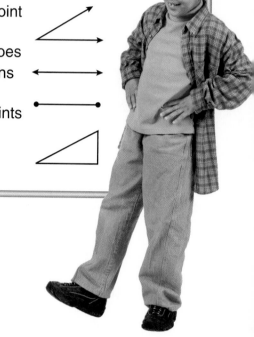

angle	two rays with a common endpoint
line	a straight path of points that goes on without end in both directions
line segment	a part of a line with two endpoints
triangle	a polygon with 3 sides

Reading Words and Symbols

There are many different geometric figures.

Look at the names of these polygons.

3 sides, 3 angles	4 sides, 4 angles	4 equal sides, 4 equal angles

Write: triangle	**Write:** quadrilateral	**Write:** square

Use the figure at the right for Problems 1–2.

1. What figure is shown at the right?

2. Are there other names you could give the figure? Explain your thinking.

Reading Test Questions

Choose the correct answer for each.

3. Which figure is a circle?

a.

c.

b.

d.

Figure means "shape."

4. Which pair of figures appears to be the same size and shape?

a.

c.

b.

d.

Pair means "group of two."

5. How many stars are inside the rectangular figure at the right?

a. 9

c. 18

b. 12

d. 24

Rectangular means "shaped like a rectangle."

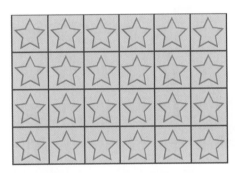

Learning Vocabulary

 Watch for these words in this unit. Write their definitions in your journal.

radius

net

acute angle

reflection

 Education Place

At **eduplace.com/map** see eGlossary and eGames—Math Lingo.

Literature Connection

Read "Dividing the Cheese" on Page 651. Then work with a partner to answer the questions about the story.

Plane Figures

INVESTIGATION

Using Data

The figures you study in math class can be found all around you. The chart shows the number of sides different figures have. How many of each figure can you find in the photo of the playground?

Name of Figure	Number of Sides
Triangle	3
Quadrilateral	4
Pentagon	5
Hexagon	6

Use What You Know

**Use this page to review and remember
what you need to know for this chapter.**

VOCABULARY

Choose the best word to complete each sentence.

1. A straight path of points that goes on without end in both directions is a ____.

2. A polygon with exactly three sides is a ____.

3. A ____ is a polygon with opposite sides parallel and four right angles.

> **Vocabulary**
> line
> circle
> triangle
> rectangle

CONCEPTS AND SKILLS

Tell whether each figure is a line, a line segment, or an angle.

4.    5.   6.

Draw a polygon for each description. Name the polygon you drew.

7. a figure with four equal sides

8. a figure with five sides

9. a figure with two pairs of parallel sides

Write About It

10. Use as many different words as you can to describe this figure. Tell why those words are good descriptions.

Facts Practice, See Page 667.

Points, Lines, and Line Segments

Objective Identify geometric figures.

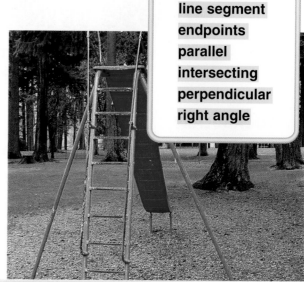

Vocabulary

line segment
endpoints
parallel
intersecting
perpendicular
right angle

Learn About It

Many everyday things can model geometric figures. The period at the end of this sentence is a model of a point. A solid painted stripe in the middle of a straight road is a model of a line. The rungs on a metal ladder are models of parallel line segments.

Geometric Figures

A point is a location in space.

B

Say: point *B*
Write: *B*

You can draw a line through any two points. A line goes on without end in both directions.

C   D

Say: line *CD* or line *DC*
Write: $\overleftrightarrow{CD}$ or $\overleftrightarrow{DC}$

A **line segment** is part of a line. It has two **endpoints**.

R
Q

Say: line segment *QR* or line segment *RQ*
Write: $\overline{QR}$ or $\overline{RQ}$

Lines that are always the same distance apart are **parallel**.

Y   L
Z   K

Say: Line *ZY* is parallel to line *KL*.
Write: $\overleftrightarrow{ZY} \parallel \overleftrightarrow{KL}$

↑
The symbol ∥ means "is parallel to."

Lines that cross each other are **intersecting**.

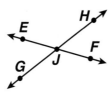

E   H
G   J   F

Say: Line *EF* and line *GH* intersect at point *J*.

Two lines that form right angles are **perpendicular**.

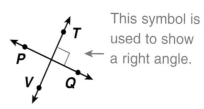

T
P
V   Q

This symbol is used to show a right angle.

Say: Line *PQ* is perpendicular to line *TV*
Write: $\overleftrightarrow{PQ} \perp \overleftrightarrow{TV}$

↑
The symbol ⊥ means "is perpendicular to."

▶ In the picture at the right, the horizontal line is perpendicular to the vertical line. At their intersection, they form right angles.

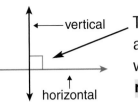

The angle makes a square corner, which is called a **right angle**.

Guided Practice

Use words and symbols to name each figure.

1.

2. • S

3.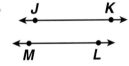

Ask Yourself

• Which point will I write first to name the figure?

• What symbol stands for the figure?

Write *parallel, intersecting,* or *perpendicular* to describe the relationship between each pair of lines.

4.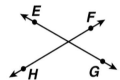

5.

6.

7.

Explain Your Thinking ▶ Can two lines be both intersecting and perpendicular? Can two lines be both intersecting and parallel? Explain your thinking.

Practice and Problem Solving

Use words and symbols to name each figure.

8.

9.

10.

11. • Q

12.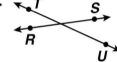

Write *parallel, intersecting,* or *perpendicular* to describe the relationship between each pair of lines.

13.
W• •R
   •
K• •J

14.
A• •B
•Z M•

15.
C• P•
  •N
 •G

16.
  Y•
L• •D
  •F

Draw an example of each.

17. line segment *JK*

18. line *MN*

19. horizontal line segment *WY*

20. $\overleftrightarrow{EF} \parallel \overrightarrow{GH}$

21. $\overleftrightarrow{AB} \perp \overleftrightarrow{CD}$

22. horizontal $\overline{PQ}$ and vertical $\overline{PR}$

23. $\overleftrightarrow{CD}$ intersecting $\overleftrightarrow{ST}$

24. $\overline{VW} \parallel \overline{XY}$

25. $\overline{AB} \perp \overline{QR}$

Write *true* or *false* for each sentence. You can draw a picture to help find the answer.

26. If two lines are parallel, they never meet.

27. If a line is horizontal, it is parallel to a vertical line.

28. If two lines intersect, they are always perpendicular.

29. If two lines are perpendicular, they are also parallel.

Use the drawing at the right for Problems 30–33.

30. Name a line.

31. Name a pair of perpendicular lines.

32. Name a pair of parallel lines.

33. **Explain** Is $\overleftrightarrow{AB}$ is perpendicular to $\overleftrightarrow{FJ}$? Explain your answer.

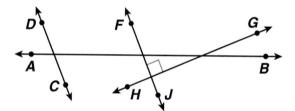

34. **Write About It** Look around your classroom. Describe something that shows a pair of parallel lines. Then describe something that shows a pair of perpendicular lines.

Mixed Review and Test Prep

Open Response

What letter is likely to come next in each pattern? (Grade 3)

35. t u u v v v w w w w x x x x ____

36. a b a b c a b c d a b c d ____

37. m n m n o m n o p m n o p ____

38. a c a c e a c e g a c e g ____

39. Which lines in the diagram below appear to be perpendicular? Explain your answer.

(Ch. 16, Lesson 1)

Extra Practice See page 427, Set A.

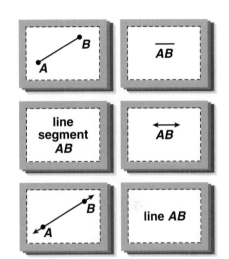

Triple Concentration

2 Players

What You'll Need • **18 Game Cards** (Learning Tool 22)

How to Play

1 Make 3 copies of each card shown on the right.

2 Shuffle the cards. Place them face down in a 3 by 6 array.

3 • The first player turns up three cards.

• If all the cards match (picture, name, and symbol), the player collects those cards.

• If the cards do not match, the player turns the cards face down. The next player takes a turn.

4 Players take turns until all matches have been made. The player with the most cards wins.

Rays and Angles

Objective Name and describe rays and angles.

Vocabulary

ray
angle
sides
vertex
obtuse angle
acute angle
straight angle

Learn About It

You have learned about lines and line segments.

Rays and angles are also geometric figures.

▶ A **ray** is a part of a line. It has one endpoint and goes on without end in one direction.

Say: ray *BA*
Write: $\overrightarrow{BA}$

▶ An **angle** is formed by two rays with a common endpoint. The rays are the **sides** of the angle. The common endpoint is the **vertex** of the angle.

Say	Write
angle *C*	∠*C*
angle *BCD*	∠*BCD*
angle *DCB*	∠*DCB*

← Each of the angle names in the chart can be used to name the angle on the right.

← When naming an angle, the vertex is the middle letter.

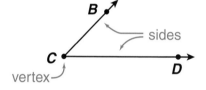

Angles are classified by the size of the opening between the sides.

This angle forms a square corner.

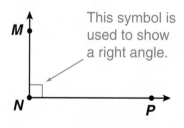

This symbol is used to show a right angle.

∠*MNP* is a right angle.

This angle is greater than a right angle.

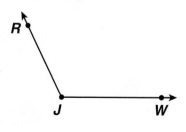

∠*RJW* is an **obtuse angle**.

This angle is less than a right angle.

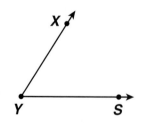

∠*XYS* is an **acute angle**.

This angle forms a straight line.
∠*FGH* is a **straight angle**.

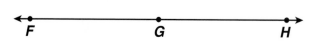

Guided Practice

Name each angle in three ways. Then classify the angle as *acute*, *obtuse*, *right*, or *straight*.

Ask Yourself

• What point will be the middle letter in the name of the angle?

• How does the size of the angle compare to the size of a right angle?

1.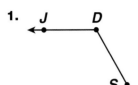

2.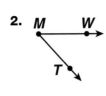

3.

Explain Your Thinking ▶ Can ∠*PQR* also be named ∠*PRQ*? Why or why not?

Practice and Problem Solving

Name each angle in three ways. Then classify the angle as *acute*, *obtuse*, *right*, or *straight*.

4.

5.

6.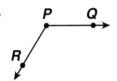

7.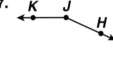

Solve.

8. What is the time on the clock with hands that show

   a. a right angle?   **b.** an obtuse angle?

   c. an acute angle?   **d.** a straight angle?

 9. **Write About It** Draw two angles. Label them ∠*MHP* and ∠*TWZ*. Write a sentence to describe each angle. Use the words *vertex* and *sides*. Then classify your angles.

Mixed Review and Test Prep

Open Response

Add or subtract. (Ch. 3, Lesson 8)

10.   12,438
     + 14,201

11.   23,894
     + 32,784

12.   98,234
     − 23,478

13.   78,036
     − 75,613

14. Copy the angle below. Label the angle. Then describe it in as many ways as you can.

(Ch. 16, Lesson 2)

Extra Practice See page 427, Set B.

Measure Angles

Objective Use a protractor to measure angles.

Vocabulary

degrees
protractor

Materials
protractor

Work Together

An angle can be measured in units called **degrees** (written as °).
You will measure angles between 0° and 180°.

A right angle measures exactly 90°.	An angle that measures less than 90° is an acute angle.	An angle that measures more than 90° is an obtuse angle.	An angle that measures exactly 180° is a straight angle.
90°	50°	120°	180°

Work with a partner to use a **protractor** to measure angles.

Find the number of degrees in ∠*TRU* and ∠*QRT*.

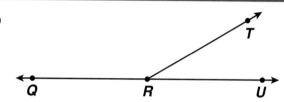

STEP 1
Place the center mark of the protractor on vertex *R*.

> For an acute angle, read the scale that shows less than 90°.

STEP 2
Measure ∠TRU
Align the 0° mark of one of the protractor scales with one ray of the angle to be measured.

STEP 3
Measure ∠QRT
Find where the other ray passes through the same scale. Read the measure of the angle on that scale.

The measure of ∠*TRU* is 30°.

• What is the measure of ∠*QRT*?

> For an obtuse angle, read the scale that shows more than 90°.

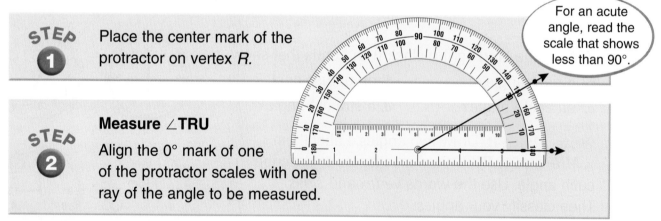

▶ You can also use a protractor to draw angles.
Draw ∠ABC that measures 70°.

STEP 1 Draw $\overrightarrow{BC}$ and label it. Place the center mark of a protractor on point B and align the 0° mark with the ray.

STEP 2 Mark a point at 70° Label the point A.

STEP 3 Draw a ray from the vertex through the point you labeled.
• What is the measure of ∠ABC?

On Your Own

Use a protractor to draw an angle having each measure. Then classify the angle as *right, acute, obtuse,* or *straight.*

1. 90°   **2.** 40°   **3.** 180°   **4.** 130°   **5.** 110°

Talk About It • Write About It

You learned to measure and draw angles.

6. Look at your angles for Exercises 1–5. How can you tell quickly which one is 40°?

7. **Analyze** A protractor has two scales. How do you decide which scale to use to measure an angle?

Audio Tutor 2/10 Listen and Understand

Quadrilaterals and Other Polygons

Objective Classify and identify polygons.

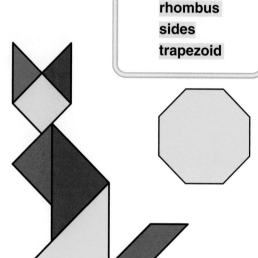

Vocabulary
polygon
rhombus
sides
trapezoid

Learn About It

Look at the shapes in the picture at the right. How would you describe those shapes?

A **polygon** is a flat, closed plane figure made up of three or more line segments called **sides**. The sides meet only at their endpoints.

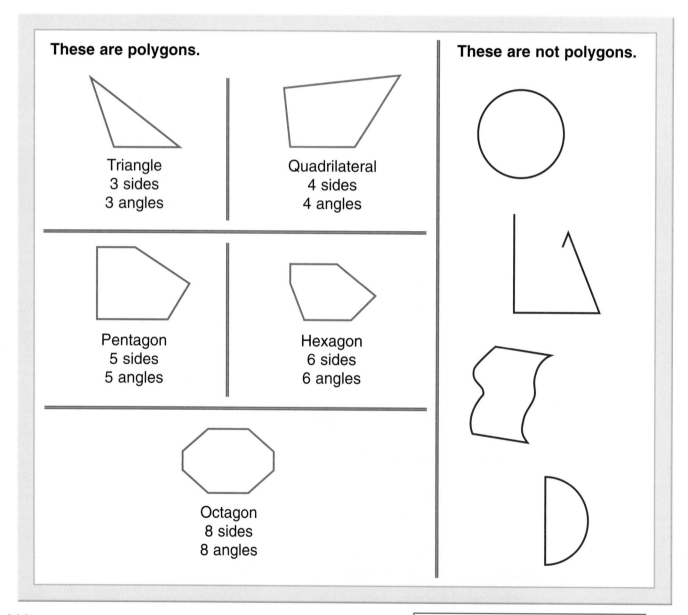

These are polygons.

Triangle
3 sides
3 angles

Quadrilateral
4 sides
4 angles

Pentagon
5 sides
5 angles

Hexagon
6 sides
6 angles

Octagon
8 sides
8 angles

These are not polygons.

Extra Help at **eduplace.com/map**

▶ Some polygons are regular. Some are irregular.

Regular polygons

All sides have equal lengths.
All angles have the same measure.

Regular Hexagon

Irregular polygons

Some sides have different lengths.
Some angles have different measures.

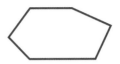

Irregular Hexagon

▶ Some quadrilaterals have special names.

A rectangle has opposite sides parallel and four right angles.

A square has four sides of the same length and four right angles.

A **trapezoid** has only one pair of parallel sides.

A parallelogram has opposite sides parallel and of the same length.

A **rhombus** has opposite sides parallel and four sides of the same length.

▶ Polygons with more than 3 sides have diagonals.

A **diagonal** of a polygon is a line segment that connects two vertices. A diagonal is never a side of a polygon.

Ask Yourself

• How many sides does the polygon have?

• If there are 4 sides, are there any parallel sides or right angles?

Name each polygon. If the polygon is a quadrilateral, write all names that apply.

1.

2.

3.

Explain Your Thinking ▶ Why is a circle not a polygon?

Practice and Problem Solving

Name each polygon. If the polygon is a quadrilateral, write all names that apply.

4.

5.

6.

7.

Tell if each figure is a polygon or not. For a polygon, tell if it appears to be regular or irregular.

8.

9.

10.

11.

Solve.

 12. **Write About It** Describe three different figures you see in the swing set on the right. Include the number of sides and angles.

13. **Analyze** I have an even number of sides. I have more sides than a pentagon, but fewer sides than an octagon. What kind of polygon am I?

Extra Practice See page 427, Set C.

Math Reasoning
Midpoint

The midpoint of a line segment lies halfway between the endpoints.

Look at the diagram. The midpoint of $\overline{XY}$ is Z because it is the same distance from both X and Y.

Identify which points in the diagram below are midpoints. Explain your thinking.

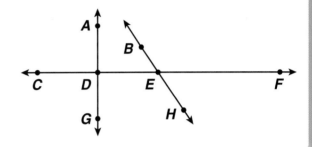

1. Is point D the midpoint of $\overleftrightarrow{AG}$?

2. Is point E the midpoint of $\overleftrightarrow{BH}$?

3. Is point E the midpoint of $\overleftrightarrow{CF}$?

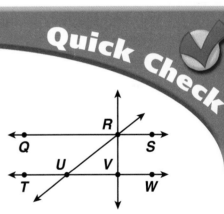

Check your understanding of Lessons 1–4.

Use the drawing on the right for Problems 1–2. (Lesson 1)

1. Name a pair of parallel lines.

2. Name a pair of intersecting lines that are not perpendicular.

Classify each angle as *acute, obtuse, right,* or *straight.* (Lessons 2, 3)

3.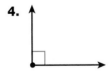

4.

5.

6.

Name each polygon. (Lesson 4)

7.

8.

9.

10.

Classify Triangles

Objective Identify and classify triangles.

Learn About It

Triangles are used to build many things, even jungle gyms! Triangles help make structures rigid and strong.

▶ **You can classify triangles by the lengths of their sides.**

Equilateral Triangle
All sides are
the same length.

Isosceles Triangle
At least two sides
are the same length.

Scalene Triangle
No sides are
the same length.

▶ **You can classify triangles by the measures of their angles.**

Right Triangle
One angle is
a right angle.

Obtuse Triangle
One angle is
an obtuse angle.

Acute Triangle
All angles
are acute angles.

Guided Practice

Ask Yourself
• Are any sides the same length?
• What kinds of angles does the triangle have?

Classify each triangle as *equilateral, isosceles,* or *scalene* and as *right, obtuse,* or *acute.*

1.   2.   3.

Explain Your Thinking ▶ Can a triangle be both isosceles and obtuse? Explain why or why not.

416

Classify each triangle as *equilateral, isosceles,* or *scalene* and as *right, obtuse,* or *acute.*

4.   **5.**    **6.**   **7.**

8.    **9.**    **10.**   **11.**

Draw one example of each triangle described below.

12. an equilateral triangle that is also an acute triangle

13. an isosceles triangle that is also a right triangle

14. a scalene triangle that is also an obtuse triangle

Solve.

15. Analyze A triangle measures 3 cm on one side. The other two sides are twice as long as the first side. Is the triangle equilateral, isosceles, or scalene? Explain your reasoning.

16. Look at the picture of the jungle gym at the right. Draw the triangles you see. Classify each triangle as *acute, obtuse,* or *right.*

Open Response

Find the product. (Ch. 6, Lesson 7)

17. 11,495
× 3

18. 24,459
× 3

19. 45,395
× 8

20. 78,231
× 6

21. Which is **not** an acute triangle?
(Ch. 16, Lesson 5)

A   **C**

B    **D**

Audio Tutor 2/11 Listen and Understand

Problem-Solving Strategy
Find a Pattern

Objective Find patterns to solve problems.

Problem John is using tiles to design a mural for a playground. If he continues the pattern, which group of tiles should he use for the unfinished section?

UNDERSTAND

This is what you know.

• The tiles form a pattern.

• The colors are red, blue, green, and yellow.

PLAN

You can find the pattern and continue it.

SOLVE

Find a pattern.

• Look for a color pattern in the columns from top to bottom. You see a column of red, green, red beside a column of blue, yellow, blue, yellow. This pattern repeats.

• Then look at the diagonal rows. What pattern do you see?

Choose the group of tiles that completes the pattern of the columns and the pattern of the diagonals.

a.   **b.**   **c.**   **d.**

Solution: Choice **c** completes the pattern.

LOOK BACK

Why would the other choices not complete the pattern?

Explore Customary Units of Length

Objective Estimate and measure lengths, using an inch ruler.

Work Together

Work with a partner to estimate length and then measure, using an inch ruler.

STEP 1	Estimate the length of the pea pod above. Record your estimate in a table like the one at the right.	Estimate:
		Nearest inch:
		Nearest half inch:
		Nearest quarter inch:

STEP 2 Use an inch ruler to measure the pea pod to the nearest inch. Use a half-inch mark to decide which inch mark is closer to the end of the pea pod. Record the length.

If the end is exactly at the half–inch mark, round to the next inch.

STEP 3 Now measure the pea pod to the nearest half inch. Use a quarter-inch mark to decide which half-inch mark is closer to the end. Record the length.

STEP 4 Measure the pea pod to the nearest quarter inch. Use an eighth-inch mark to decide which quarter-inch mark is closer to the end.

The more marks your ruler has, the more accurately you will be able to measure.

Compare your estimate and the three measurements of the pea pod. Which is closest to the actual length of the pea pod?

Use What You Know

**Use this page to review and remember
what you need to know for this chapter.**

VOCABULARY

Choose the best word to complete each sentence.

1. A pencil weighs about one _____.

2. A grocer sells potatoes by the _____.

3. The amount of water in a swimming pool
   would best be measured in _____.

> **Vocabulary**
>
> quart
> ounce
> pound
> gallons

CONCEPTS AND SKILLS

Measure to the nearest inch.

4.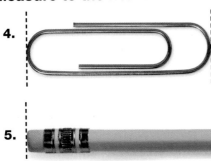

5.

Choose the better unit of measure.

6. the width of a book
   a. meters **b.** centimeters

7. the length of a car
   a. meters **b.** kilometers

8. the length of an eraser
   a. inches **b.** feet

9. the distance between towns
   a. yards **b.** miles

Write About It

10. Name 4 measuring tools that you have
    used. Describe how to use them and tell
    what you could measure with them.

Facts Practice, See page 670.

Use the Ask Yourself questions to help you solve each problem.

1. Describe the pattern. What figures will complete the pattern?

(Hint) Look at the beginning of the sequence. Is the pattern repeated?

2. Which piece completes the pattern?

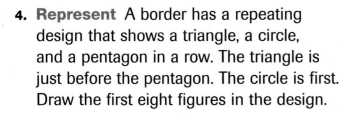

a.   b.   c.   d.

Ask Yourself

UNDERSTAND **What facts do I know?**

PLAN **Can I find the pattern?**

SOLVE **Can I describe how the pattern repeats or changes?**

LOOK BACK **Did I check that my answer completes the pattern?**

Independent Practice

Find the pattern to solve each problem.

3. Nia makes the design on the right. Describe the pattern. What figures will complete the pattern?

4. **Represent** A border has a repeating design that shows a triangle, a circle, and a pentagon in a row. The triangle is just before the pentagon. The circle is first. Draw the first eight figures in the design.

5. The pattern on the right can also be shown as 1, 3, 6, 10. What would be the next two figures and numbers in the pattern?

6. **Analyze** Vincent made a design in which 3 out of every 7 quadrilaterals were green. Vincent colored 56 quadrilaterals. How many quadrilaterals did Vincent color green?

Go On

Mixed Problem Solving

Solve. Show your work. Tell what strategy you used.

7. **Money** Ms. Flores counted 13 bills and found they totaled $110. She had only $5 and $10 bills. How many of each kind of bill did she have?

8. Antoine created a design on the computer. He printed the design, but two figures did not print. What are the missing figures?

9. A fruit stand sells different sizes of fruit baskets. Each piece of fruit costs $3, and the basket costs $11. What is the price of a fruit basket with 6 pieces of fruit?

You Choose

Strategy
- Find a Pattern
- Guess and Check
- Make an Organized List
- Write an Equation

Computation Method
- Mental Math
- Estimation
- Paper and Pencil
- Calculator

 Data **Evan and Ariana used shapes to make puppets. Use the double bar graph for Problems 10–14.**

10. How many shapes did Evan use?

11. Who used more shapes, Evan or Ariana?

12. How many more triangles would Evan have to use in order to use the same number as Ariana?

13. Ariana used equal numbers of which two shapes?

14. **Explain** Since all squares are rectangles, can you use the graph to find how many squares Evan used? Explain your thinking.

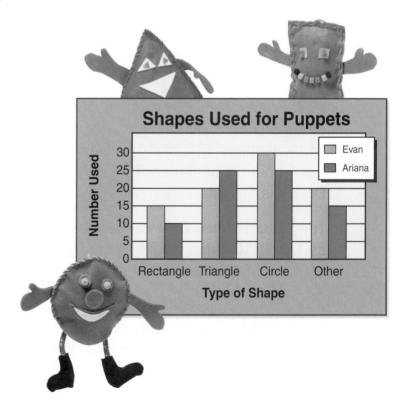

420

Problem Solving on Tests

Choose the letter of the correct answer.

Multiple Choice

1. A library has 42 shelves of books with about 25 books on each shelf. About how many books are there?

   A about 100   **C** about 1,000

   B about 200   **D** about 2,000

   (Chapter 7, Lesson 5)

2. The fourth-grade classes at Hilltop School have 23, 26, 29, and 22 students. What is the average number of students in a fourth-grade?

   F 20   **G** 24   **H** 25   **J** 29

   (Chapter 10, Lesson 5)

Open Response

Solve each problem.

3. This stem-and-leaf plot shows the ages of people at a picnic. How many people are at the picnic? Explain.

Ages of People at a Picnic	
Stem	**Leaves**
3	0 1 4 5
4	2 4 6 7 9
5	0 2
6	0 1

   (Chapter 14, Lesson 5)

4. Dale's family took a trip. They spent the following amounts on T-shirts.

   $10, $14, $10, $16, $50

   Explain Which best describes the cost of a T-shirt: the mean, the median, the mode, or the range? Why?

   (Chapter 14, Lesson 3)

Extended Response

5. The line graph shows the total distance the Dunn family drove during four hours Saturday going to their summer cabin.

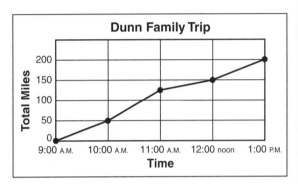

   a. Between what hours did the Dunn family travel the greatest distance? About how far did they travel? How do you know?

   b. The Dunn family stopped at a scenic overlook to take pictures once during their trip. About what time might they have stopped? Explain your reason for selecting that time.

   c. Mr. Dunn thought it cost about $0.05 a mile for gasoline for the trip. About how much did it cost for gasoline to drive to the cabin and back home? Show how you know.

   (Chapter 14, Lesson 5)

Education Place

See **eduplace.com/map** for more Test-Taking Tips.

Circles

Objective Identify parts of a circle.

Vocabulary
circle
center
radius (radii)
diameter
chord

Learn About It

A **circle** is made up of all points in a plane that are the same distance from a given point in that plane, called the center. Point *D* is the **center** of the circle below.

Circles

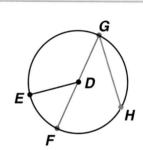

A **radius** is any line segment that joins a point on the circle to the center of the circle.

$\overline{DE}$ or $\overline{ED}$ is a radius of this circle.
$\overline{DG}$ and $\overline{DF}$ are also radii of this circle.

A **diameter** is any line segment that passes through the center of a circle and has its endpoints on the circle.

$\overline{GF}$ or $\overline{FG}$ is a diameter of this circle.

A **chord** is any line segment that has its endpoints on the circle. It does not need to pass through the center.

$\overline{GH}$ or $\overline{HG}$ is a chord of this circle. The diameter, $\overline{GF}$, is also a chord.

▶ The number of degrees (°) in a full circle is 360. You can turn an object around the point that is the center of a circle.

Each turn is measured from the start position. The start position is at the mark for 0°.

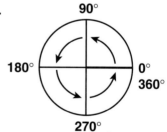

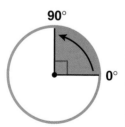

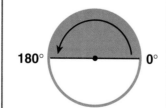

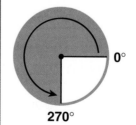

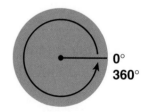

A quarter turn is 90°.

A half turn is 180°.

A three-quarter turn is 270°.

A full turn is 360°.

Guided Practice

Name the parts of the circle. Write *center, radius, diameter,* or *chord.*

1. G

2. $\overline{FH}$

3. $\overline{DE}$

4. $\overline{FG}$

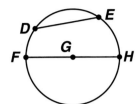

Ask Yourself

- Does the line segment connect a point on the circle to the center?

- Does the line segment pass through the center of the circle?

Explain Your Thinking ▶ How does the length of a diameter of a circle compare to the length of its radius?

Practice and Problem Solving

Name the part of each circle that is shown in red. Write *center, radius, diameter,* or *chord.*

5.

6.

7.

8.

Solve.

9. Look at the circles below. Describe the pattern. Then draw the missing figures in the pattern.

    _____ _____

10. One radius of a circle is 4 meters long. How long would a different radius of the same circle be? Why?

11. If the minute hand of this clock moves from 12 to 6, will it have made a quarter turn, a half turn, or a three-quarter turn? What time will it be when the minute hand has made a full turn?

Go On

Marvin and Lisa are riding the wheel on the right. Use the picture for Problems 12–14.

12. The arrow shows the direction the wheel is turning. Which best describes the turn needed to move Marvin to Lisa's location—half turn, quarter turn, or full turn?

13. From the starting position, which best describes the turn needed to move Lisa to Marvin's position—quarter turn, half turn, or three-quarter turn?

14. How many degrees has the wheel turned each time Lisa arrives back in the same place she started?

For Exercises 15–17, trace around a circular object. Draw the part or parts of the circle described.

15. two radii that do not form a diameter

16. a chord that is not a diameter

17. a horizontal diameter and a vertical diameter

📊 Data Use the circle graph for Problems 18–22.

18. In which activity did the greatest number of students participate?

19. Which activity did about $\frac{1}{4}$ of the students do?

20. **Mental Math** If 50 fourth-graders had recess, about how many of them did either jungle gym or jumping rope?

21. **Analyze** Which two activities had about the same number of students participating?

22. **Create and Solve** Make a circle graph and write two questions about it. Give your questions to a classmate to solve.

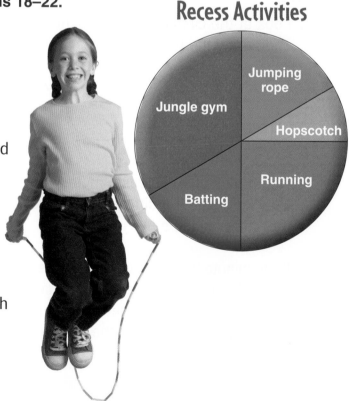

Recess Activities

Jumping rope

Jungle gym

Hopscotch

Running

Batting

Extra Practice See page 427, Set E.

Open Response

Choose a graph to display the data. Write _bar graph_, _circle graph_, _line graph_, or _pictograph_. Explain your choice.

(Ch. 15, Lesson 5)

23. wind speeds during a storm

24. the number of goals scored by 4 hockey players during one month

25. the results of a survey that asked students to choose their favorite

Solve.

26. A circle has a diameter labeled $\overline{FG}$. Could F be the center of the circle? Explain your thinking.

(Ch. 16, Lesson 7)

Art Connection
Be an Artist

Geometry often inspires artists. Painters such as Pablo Picasso, Piet Mondrian, Fernand Léger, and Juan Gris used geometric figures in their paintings.

1. Look at the painting. What geometric figures do you see?

2. **Challenge** Use at least three geometric figures and colored pencils to create a work of art.

Composition, 1924, by Fernand Léger

Chapter Review/Test

VOCABULARY

Choose the best word to complete each sentence.

1. A line segment that joins a point on a circle to the center of the circle is a ____.

2. Two lines that intersect to form right angles are ____.

3. A quadrilateral that has only one pair of parallel sides is a ____.

Vocabulary

radius
triangle
trapezoid
perpendicular

CONCEPTS AND SKILLS

Use words and symbols to name each figure. (Lessons 1–2, pp. 404–409)

4.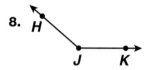

5.

6.

7. •G

Classify each angle as *acute, straight, obtuse,* or *right*. (Lessons 2–3, pp. 408–411)

8.

9.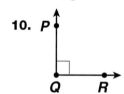

10.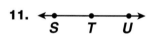

11.

Name each polygon. Write all the names that apply. (Lessons 4–5, pp. 412–417)

12.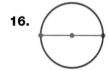

13.

14.

15.

Name the part of each circle that is shown in red. (Lesson 7, pp. 422–424)

16.

17.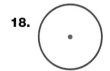

18.

19.

PROBLEM SOLVING

Solve. (Lesson 6, pp. 418–420)

20. Look at the design. If the pattern continues, what kind of polygon should the fifteenth figure be?

Write About It

Show You Understand

How are an equilateral triangle and an isosceles triangle alike? How are they different?

Extra Practice

Set A (Lesson 1, pp. 404–406)

Use words and symbols to name each figure.

1.
K   F

2. • *M*

3.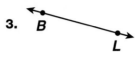
B   L

4.
X
Y

Write *parallel*, *intersecting*, or *perpendicular*.

5.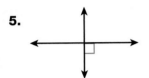

6.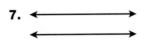

7.

8.

Set B (Lesson 2, pp. 408–409)

Classify each angle as *acute*, *obtuse*, *right*, or *straight*.

1.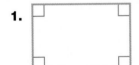

2.

3.

4.

Set C (Lesson 4, pp. 412–414)

Name each polygon. Write all names that apply.

1.

2.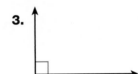

3.

4.

Set D (Lesson 5, pp. 416–417)

Classify each triangle as *equilateral*, *isosceles*, or *scalene*.

1.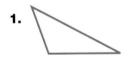

2.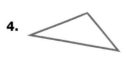

3.

4.

5.

Set E (Lesson 7, pp. 422–424)

Name the part of each circle that is shown in red.

1.

2.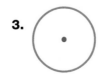

3.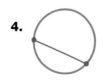

4.

5.

Congruence, Symmetry, and Transformations

Using Data

A ladybug is a small oval-shaped bug with spots on its wings. You can identify the species of ladybug by its pattern of spots. Look at the 6 different species of ladybugs at the right. Describe the pattern of spots shown on each ladybug.

Use What You Know

**Use this page to review and remember
what you need to know for this chapter.**

VOCABULARY

Choose the best term to complete each sentence.

1. A location in space is called a _____.

2. A _____ goes on without end in both directions.

3. A _____ always has four congruent sides.

4. A quadrilateral that has exactly one pair of parallel
   sides is a _____.

> **Vocabulary**
> ray
> line
> point
> rhombus
> trapezoid

CONCEPTS AND SKILLS

**Choose the figure that appears to be the same size
and shape as the first figure. Write *a*, *b*, or *c*.**

5.   a.   b.   c.

6.   a.   b.   c.

**Does the dashed line divide the figure into two parts
that match exactly? Write *yes* or *no*.**

7.   8.   9.

▶ **Write About It**

10. How are a square, rhombus, trapezoid,
    and parallelogram the same? How are
    they different?

Facts Practice, See Page 666.

Audio Tutor 2/13 Listen and Understand

Congruent Figures

Objective Learn about figures that have the same size and shape.

Materials
grid paper
scissors

Learn About It

Sari is designing a puzzle on her computer. Look at the puzzle and the puzzle piece. You can tell that the piece belongs in the puzzle because it is the same size and shape as the empty space.

Plane figures that have the same size and shape are **congruent** figures.

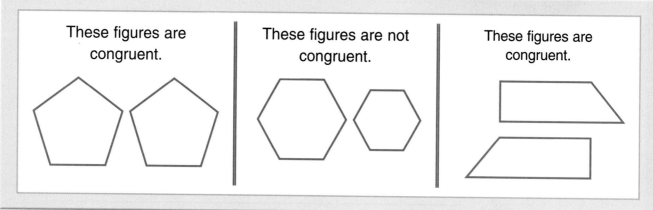

| These figures are congruent. | These figures are not congruent. | These figures are congruent. |

Try this activity to explore congruence.

STEP 1 Copy Figures A, B, C, and D on grid paper. Cut out Figures B, C, and D. Look at the figures. Which figures appear to be congruent?

STEP 2 Place each cut-out figure on top of Figure A, turning it to check for congruence. Which figure is congruent to A? How do you know?

STEP 3 Draw another figure on grid paper. Cut it out. Trace it. Are these two new figures congruent? Explain.

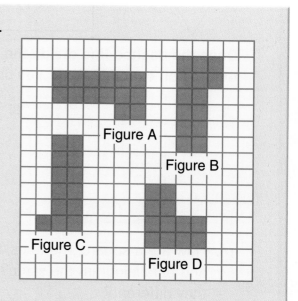

Figure A

Figure B

Figure C

Figure D

Extra Help at eduplace.com/map

Guided Practice

Do the figures in each pair appear to be congruent?
Write *yes* or *no*.

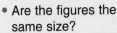

Ask Yourself
- Are the figures the same size?
- Are the figures the same shape?

1.

2.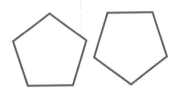

3.

4.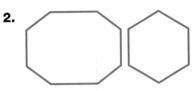

5. Draw a figure congruent to the figures in Exercise 4. Explain how you know it is congruent.

Explain Your Thinking ▶ Are all circles with radii of 4 inches congruent? Why or why not?

Practice and Problem Solving

Do the figures in each pair appear to be congruent?
Write *yes* or *no*. Explain your answer.

6.

7.

8.

9.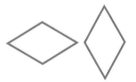

10.

11.

Draw a figure like each shape below. Then draw a figure congruent to the one you drew.

12.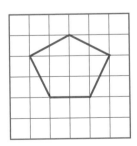

13.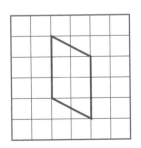

Use the figures at the right for Problems 14–16.

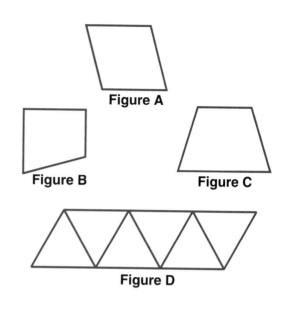

Figure A

Figure B   Figure C

 14. Measurement Parallelograms have 2 pairs of opposite sides that are congruent. Use a centimeter ruler. Which of the figures at the right are parallelograms?

15. Which figure has right angles? Is it a rectangle? a square? Explain your answer.

16. Analyze Six congruent triangles form Figure D. What geometric figure is it? Draw a picture of another way to combine the triangles to make a different geometric figure.

Figure D

17. Reasoning Copy the Venn Diagram at the right. *Trapezoid* and *Square* are the terms that are missing from the diagram. Which term should go in the green section? Which should go in the pink section? Explain how you decided.

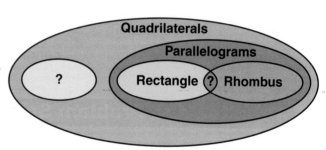

Quadrilaterals

Parallelograms

? | Rectangle ? Rhombus

(**Hint**) What quadrilateral has a special name, but is not a parallelogram?

(**Hint**) What figure is both a rectangle and a rhombus?

Mixed Review and Test Prep

Open Response

Identify each figure. Write all the names that apply. (Ch. 16, Lessons 1, 4–5)

18.

19.

20.

21.

22.

23.

Multiple Choice

24. Which figure appears to be congruent to this figure?
(Ch. 17, Lesson 1)

A   C

B    D

Extra Practice See page 449, Set A.

Math Reasoning
Similar Figures

You have learned that congruent figures are the same size and shape. **Similar** figures are the same shape, but not necessarily the same size.

Vocabulary
similar

Look at the figures below.

Same shape
Not the same size

Similar
Not Congruent

Not the same shape
Not the same size

Not Similar
Not Congruent

Same shape
Same size

Similar
Congruent

Tell if the figures in each pair are *congruent, similar,* or *neither.*

1.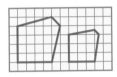

2.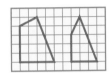

3.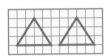

Write *true* or *false* for each sentence. Then draw an example to support your answer.

4. All squares are similar.

5. If shapes are similar, they must be congruent.

6. All hexagons are similar.

7. If shapes are congruent, they must be similar.

8. All circles are similar.

9. If shapes are *not* congruent, they cannot be similar.

Audio Tutor 2/14 Listen and Understand

Rotations, Reflections, and Translations

Objective Learn about rotations, reflections, and translations.

Vocabulary
rotation
reflection
translation
transformations

Materials
trapezoid pattern block
or Learning Tool 25
grid paper

Learn About It

Vincent is a graphic artist. He is designing a logo for his company's product. He moves the figure shown in different ways to create the logo.

There are different ways to move a figure.

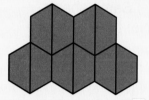

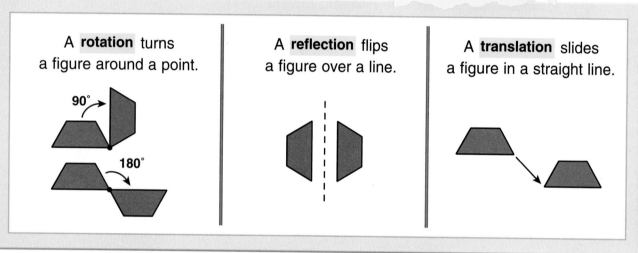

A **rotation** turns a figure around a point.

90°
180°

A **reflection** flips a figure over a line.

A **translation** slides a figure in a straight line.

Rotations, reflections, and translations are called **transformations**.

Try this activity to show rotations, reflections, and translations.

STEP 1 Trace the pattern block on grid paper. Rotate it around the point shown. Trace the resulting figure.

STEP 2 Trace the block again. Flip it across the dotted line shown. Trace the resulting figure.

STEP 3 Trace the block again. Slide it in a line as shown. Trace the resulting figure.

• Are the figures you drew congruent? Explain how you know.

Guided Practice

Tell how each figure was moved. Write *rotation, reflection,* or *translation.*

1.

2.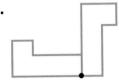

Ask Yourself
- Was the figure turned around a point?
- Was the figure flipped over a line?
- Was the figure slid along a straight line?

Explain Your Thinking ▶ Look at the figures in Exercise 2. Are they congruent? How can you use transformations to find out?

Practice and Problem Solving

Tell how each figure was moved. Write *rotation, reflection,* or *translation.*

3.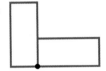

4.

5.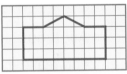

Copy Figure A on grid paper and cut it out. Use the cut-out figure for Problems 6–7.

6. **Represent** Vincent rotated Figure A 90° to the right. What does the figure look like now? Draw a picture to show your answer.

7. **Predict** If you flip Figure A, what will it look like? Draw the resulting figure. Is this the only answer? Explain.

8. Vincent is designing another logo. He started with Figure B. How did he move the figure to make Figure C? Explain your answer.

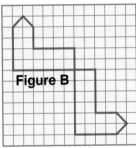

Figure A

Figure B

Figure C

Mixed Review and Test Prep

Open Response

Solve each equation. (Ch. 5, Lesson 4)

9. $12 = n + 4$

10. $16 - n = 9$

11. $40n = 120$

12. $n \div 5 = 27$

13. Suppose the letter P was rotated 180° to the left. What would it look like? Draw a picture to show your answer. (Ch. 17, Lesson 2)

Extra Practice See page 449, Set B.

Problem-Solving Strategy
Act It Out

Objective Learn how to solve a problem by using a model to act it out.

Problem Can these five figures be arranged to form a figure that is congruent to the large square at the right?

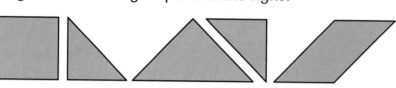

 **UNDERSTAND**

This is what you know.

Congruent figures have the same size and shape.

PLAN

You can make and use models to solve the problem.

SOLVE

Act it out.

• To make models, trace the five figures and the large square on grid paper. Cut out the five figures.

• Now, try to arrange the five figures so that they fit inside the large square without overlapping.

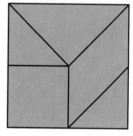

Solution: Yes, the five figures can be arranged to form a figure that is congruent to the large square.

LOOK BACK

Look back at the problem.

How can you be sure your answer is correct?

Guided Practice

Use the figures on Page 436 to solve each problem. Make a drawing to show your answer.

1. Arrange all the figures except the largest triangle to form a figure congruent to the parallelogram below.

2. Arrange the largest triangle, the parallelogram, and one of the small triangles to form a figure congruent to the quadrilateral at the right.

(Hint) Where must right angles be?

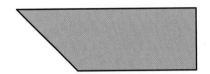

Ask Yourself

UNDERSTAND → What facts do I know?

PLAN → Can I make a model?

SOLVE →
- Did I make and use the correct models?
- Does the figure I made match the figure in the problem exactly?

LOOK BACK → Did I check to see if my answer is correct?

Independent Practice

Use the figures on Page 436 for Problems 3 and 4. Make a drawing to show your answer.

3. Use four of the figures to form a figure congruent to the pentagon shown below.

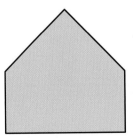

4. Use all five of the figures to form a figure congruent to the triangle shown below.

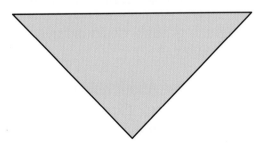

5. Can 12 toothpicks be used to form 4 congruent squares?

6. Can 9 toothpicks be used to form 4 congruent triangles?

Mixed Problem Solving

Solve. Show your work. Tell what strategy you used.

7. A salad costs $1.50 more than a sandwich. Together the salad and sandwich cost $10.50. How much does each cost?

8. Guitar lessons start at 3:30 P.M. Each lesson is 45 minutes long. There are 6 lessons scheduled. At what time does the last lesson start?

9. Lorenzo draws 20 circles in a row. Each circle has a diameter of 25 mm. Each circle touches the next circle at only one point. What is the length of the row of circles?

10. Danny has two buckets. One holds 7 quarts and the other holds 4 quarts. How can Danny use the two buckets to measure 6 quarts?

You Choose

Strategy
- Act it Out
- Draw a picture
- Guess and Check
- Make a Table
- Write an Equation

Computation Method
- Mental Math
- Estimation
- Paper and Pencil
- Calculator

Data Groups of students are using blocks to make designs in art class. The graph shows the number of blocks in four groups' designs. Use the bar graph for Problems 11–14.

11. Which group used the greatest number of blocks? How many did they use?

12. **Explain** Did Group 3 or Group 4 use more blocks? Explain how you know.

13. Which groups' designs have more than 50 blocks?

14. **Estimate** About how many blocks did Group 4 use? Explain how you made your estimate.

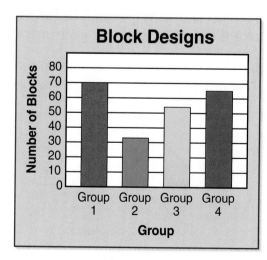

Block Designs

Problem Solving on Tests

Choose the letter of the correct answer.

1. Dan multiplied (5 × 2) × 3. Paul multiplied 5 × (2 × 3). What property says that they both got the same answer?

   A Zero Property

   B Commutative Property

   C Property of One

   D Associative Property

2. A glove costs $25.50. A bat costs $10.45. Jim buys 3 gloves and 4 bats for his club. What is the total cost?

   F $35.95   **H** $133.35

   G $118.30   **J** $147.45

Open Response

Solve each problem.

3.

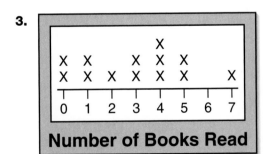

   Number of Books Read

   Explain Which is greater, the median or the mean of the data? Explain.

4. At 10:00 A.M. the temperature was 3°C. By noon, it was 2 degrees higher. By 2:00 P.M., it was 3 degrees lower than it was at noon. What was the temperature at 2:00 P.M.?
   Represent Use a number line to solve the problem.

Constructed Response

5. Toby and Anna work for a florist. Potted flowers are on sale for $4.89 each. A sign reads, "Buy 2 plants and get one free." The pictograph below shows the assortment of plants.

Potted Summer Flowers	
Pansies	✿✿✿✿✿✿
Zinnias	✿✿✿✿✿✿✿✿✿✿✿
Daisies	✿✿✿✿✿✿✿
Petunias	✿✿✿✿
Snapdragons	✿✿✿✿✿✿

✿ = 5 plants

a. Toby and Anna displayed the plants in rows. Decide how many rows of plants they might set up.

b. Mr. Perez wanted 5 potted daisies and 4 potted pansies. How many plants did he pay for? How much will he spend? Show your work.

c. At the end of the sale, Toby and Anna collected almost $420. Make a diagram to show about how many plants were given away free.

Education Place

Check out **eduplace.com/map** for more Test-Taking Tips.

Hands On Lesson 4

Symmetry

Objective Learn how to identify figures that can be folded into matching parts.

Vocabulary

line symmetry

line of symmetry

rotational symmetry

Materials
grid paper

Learn About It

Amir's art class made photo albums. Amir is decorating the front of his album with geometric shapes. He folds the paper in half before he cuts to be sure the two parts of his shape match exactly.

A figure has **line symmetry** if it can be folded in half so the two parts match exactly. The fold line is a **line of symmetry**.

▶ Figures can have one or more than one line of symmetry.

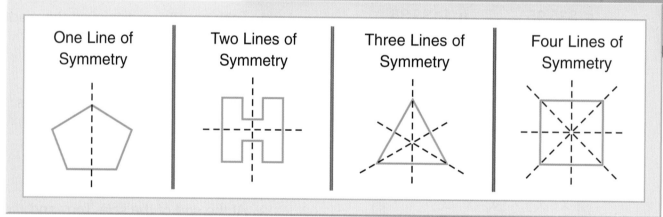

One Line of Symmetry	Two Lines of Symmetry	Three Lines of Symmetry	Four Lines of Symmetry

▶ Some figures have **rotational symmetry**.

A figure has rotational symmetry if you can rotate it less than a full turn (360°) around a point and it looks the same as it did before the turn.

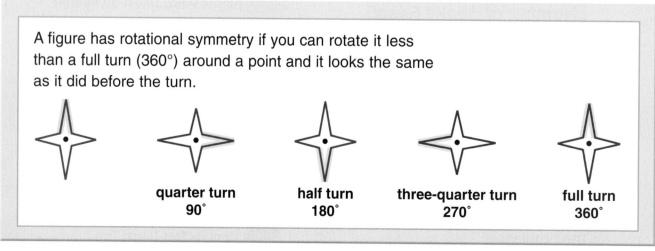

quarter turn 90°	half turn 180°	three-quarter turn 270°	full turn 360°

440

Try this activity to explore symmetry.

STEP 1 Trace Figure A and cut it out. Try to fold it so the two parts match. If you can, draw a line of symmetry on the fold line. Repeat for Figure B.

- Which figure has a line of symmetry?

- Does it have more than one? How can you tell?

STEP 2 On grid paper draw a dashed line of symmetry and the design shown at the right.

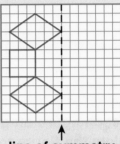

STEP 3 Draw a mirror image of the design on the right side of the line.

- How did you transform the figures on the left to get the figures on the right? Explain.

- How do you know the dashed line is a line of symmetry?

line of symmetry

Guided Practice

Is the dashed line a line of symmetry? Write *yes* or *no*.

1.

2.

Ask Yourself

- Do the two parts match exactly?

- How does the figure look when I turn it less than 360°?

Trace each figure. Does the figure have rotational symmetry? Write *yes* or *no*.

3.

4.

5.

Explain Your Thinking ▶ How can you use a tracing of a figure to find out if it has rotational symmetry?

Practice and Problem Solving

Is the dashed line a line of symmetry? Write *yes* or *no*.

6.

7.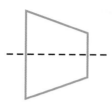

8.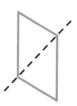

9.

How many lines of symmetry does the figure have?

10.

11.

12.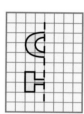

13.

Draw each figure on grid paper. Draw the line of symmetry. Complete the figure to show line symmetry.

14.

15.

16.

17.

18.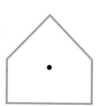

19.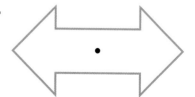

Trace each figure. Does the figure have rotational symmetry? Write *yes* or *no*.

20.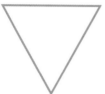

21.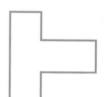

22.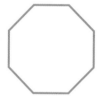

23.

24.

25.

Solve.

26. Represent Suppose each of the letters below is rotated a half turn around the point. Draw a picture to show what each letter would look like.

a.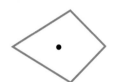
b.
c.
d.

27. Which of the letters in Exercise 26 have rotational symmetry? How do you know?

28. Which of the letters in Exercise 26 have line symmetry? Use a drawing to help you explain.

29. Explain Amir made the figure below in art class. Trace the figure. Turn it. Does the figure have rotational symmetry around the point? Explain how you got your answer.

30. Trace the circle below. Cut it out. Fold it on line segment *NP*. What happens to points *M* and *O*? How many lines of symmetry does a circle have? Explain your thinking.

Quick Check

Check your understanding for Lessons 1–4.

Do the figures in each pair appear to be congruent? Write *yes* or *no*. (Lesson 1)

1.

2.

Tell how each figure was moved. Write *rotation*, *reflection*, or *translation*. (Lesson 2)

3.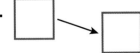

4.

5.

Problem-Solving Application
Visual Thinking

Objective Solve problems using visual thinking.

Sometimes you can use visual thinking to solve problems.

Look at the arrow on the box at the right. What will
the box look like when it is turned upside down?

UNDERSTAND

This is what you know.

- The arrow is in the lower right-hand corner of the box.

- The arrow is pointing up.

- The box is going to be turned upside down.

PLAN

You can use visual thinking to solve the problem.

SOLVE

Use visual thinking to move the box in your mind.

- The arrow will be in the upper left-hand corner of the box.
- The arrow will point down.

Then decide which of the choices below shows
the box after it is turned.

a.    b.    c.

Solution: When the box is turned upside down,
it will look like choice *b*.

LOOK BACK

Look back at the problem.

How else could you have solved this problem?

Guided Practice

Use the Ask Yourself questions to help you solve each problem.

1. What will be the next figure in this pattern? Choose *a, b,* or *c.*

a.   b.   c.

Ask Yourself

UNDERSTAND → **What facts do I know?**

PLAN → **Can I use visual thinking to solve the problem?**

SOLVE → **Did I move the objects correctly in my mind?**

LOOK BACK → **Did I check to be sure my answer is correct?**

2. Willis drew the figure at the right. How many right triangles are in the figure? Explain your solution.

   (Hint) Look for 4 different sizes of triangles.

Independent Practice

Solve.

3. Tammy punched holes in the folded piece of paper at the right. What will the paper look like when it is unfolded? Choose a, b, or c.

   a.    b.    c.

4. Sarah bought some tiles like the one below to fill in the pattern in the floor shown at the right. How many tiles did she buy? Explain your answer.

Go On →

Mixed Problem Solving

Solve. Show your work. Tell what strategy you used.

5. Sammy bought art supplies for $4.95. His mom gave him $5.00. Then he bought paper for $12.50. He had $6.50 left. How much money did Sammy have at the start?

6. At a craft store, 2 pieces of felt cost 75¢. Three pieces of felt cost 95¢, and four pieces of felt cost $1.15. If the prices follow a pattern, how much are seven pieces of felt likely to cost?

7. Five teams are competing in a tournament. Each team must compete against each of the other teams once. How many rounds of competition are needed?

Solve. Show your work. Tell which method you used.

8. Matt is sponge-painting designs on shirts. He buys one shirt for $7.25 and 2 packages of sponges for $2.95 each. He pays with a $20 bill. About how much change does he receive?

9. One shirt has 10 rows with 12 shapes in each row. A second shirt has 13 rows with 10 shapes in each row. Which shirt has the most shapes?

10. **Money** Supplies for another craft project cost $29.99. Matt has $15.50. How much more money does he need?

11. A craft store sold 135,375 sponge stamps in January, 104,476 in February, and 85,904 in March. How many sponge stamps were sold in those 3 months?

You Choose

Strategy
- Find a Pattern
- Guess and Check
- Make an Organized List
- Work Backward

Computation Method
- Mental Math
- Estimation
- Paper and Pencil
- Calculator

Open Response

Name each polygon. (Ch. 16, Lesson 4)

12.

13.

14.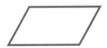

15.

16. Twelve toothpicks are arranged as shown. Can you remove 2 of the toothpicks so that only 2 squares remain? Draw a picture to show your answer.

(Ch. 17, Lesson 5)

Visual Thinking
Kuba Cloth Patterns

Activity

Many of the patterns Kuba weavers use today are the same patterns that have been used for hundreds of years!

You can make your own Kuba pattern.

• Trace pattern blocks or other small objects.

• Cut out the figures you traced.

• Turn, flip, or slide your figures to create a pattern.

The Kuba people of central Africa use geometry to weave patterns into cloth.

Chapter Review/Test

VOCABULARY

Choose the best term to complete each sentence.

1. If a figure can be folded along a line so that the two parts match exactly, it has ____.

2. Figures that have the same size and shape are ____ figures.

3. A change in position resulting from a slide is called a ____.

CONCEPTS AND SKILLS

Do the figures in each pair appear to be congruent? Write *yes* or *no*. (Lesson 1, pp. 430–433)

4.

5.

Tell how each figure was moved. Write *rotation*, *reflection*, or *translation*. (Lesson 2, pp. 434–435)

6.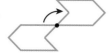

7.

Which figures have both line symmetry and rotational symmetry? (Lesson 4, pp. 440–443)

8. a.   b.   c.   d.

PROBLEM SOLVING

Solve. Draw a picture to show your answer. (Lesson 3, 5, pp. 436–439, 444–447)

9. How can you cut the letter X in half so that the two parts match exactly?

10. What will the letter Y look like if it is turned 90° to the left?

 Write About It

Show You Understand

Consuela thinks that circles are always congruent. Is she correct? Explain why or why not.

Extra Practice

Set A (Lesson 1, pp. 430–433)

**Do the figures in each pair appear to be congruent?
Write *yes* or *no*.**

1.

2.

3.

4.

5.

6.

Set B (Lesson 2, pp. 434–435)

**Tell how each figure was moved. Write *rotation*, *reflection*,
or *translation*.**

1.

2.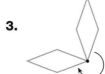

3.

4.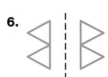

5.

6.

Set C (Lesson 4, pp. 440–443)

Is the dashed line a line of symmetry? Write *yes* or *no*.

1.

2.

3.

4.

5.

6.

Does the figure have rotational symmetry? Write *yes* or *no*.

7.

8.

9.

10.

11.

12.

Perimeter, Area, and Volume

Using Data

An architect draws a blueprint before a house is built. A carpenter then follows the blueprint when building the house. Imagine that you are an interior designer. You need to fit certain items of furniture into the bedrooms. How could you use the blueprint to determine whether you have enough room for the furniture? What other information would you need?

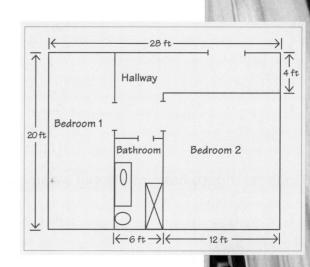

Use What You Know

**Use this page to review and remember
what you need to know for this chapter.**

VOCABULARY

Choose the best word to complete each statement.

1. A polygon with five sides is a ____.

2. A polygon with eight sides is an ____.

3. A polygon with four equal sides is a ____.

4. A polygon with six sides is a ____.

> **Vocabulary**
> square
> hexagon
> octagon
> pentagon
> triangle

CONCEPTS AND SKILLS

Solve.

5. 83×3

6. 45×7

7. 68×44

8. $75 + 24 + 5$

9. $26 + 7 + 14 + 3$

10. $32 + 19 + 23$

Write *regular* or *irregular* for each figure.

11.

12.

13.

Find each missing number.

14. 12 in. = _____ ft

15. _____ yd = 3 ft

16. 36 in. = _____ yd

17. 7 km = _____ m

18. 3 m = _____ cm

19. 500 cm = _____ m

Write About It

20. How are regular polygons and
irregular polygons the same?
How are they different?
Explain your reasoning.

Facts Practice, See Page 668.

Hands On Lesson 1

Explore Perimeter and Area

Objective Use models to explore perimeter and area.

Vocabulary
perimeter
area

Materials
grid paper
(Learning Tool 27)

Work Together

Does the **perimeter**, or distance around a figure, determine the number of square units needed to cover the figure?

Work with a partner to find out.

STEP 1
Look at the figures at the right. Find the perimeter of each figure by counting the number of units around the outside of the figure.

- Record your answers in a table like the one below.

Figure	Perimeter	Area
Square A	12 units	▢ square units
Rectangle B	▢ units	▢ square units

Square A

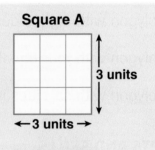

3 units
←3 units→

Rectangle B

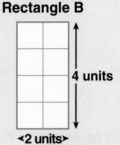

4 units
‹2 units›

STEP 2
Now find the number of square units needed to cover each of the figures.

The number of square units needed to cover a figure is the **area** of the figure.

- Count to find the area of each figure.

- Record your answers in your table.

STEP 3
Look at your table.

- Can a square have the same perimeter as a rectangle?

- Can rectangles and squares with the same perimeter have different areas?

Find the perimeter and area of each figure.
Record your answers in a table like this:

	Figure	Perimeter	Area
1.	Rectangle C	▢ units	▢ square units
2.	Square D	▢ units	▢ square units
3.	Rectangle E	▢ units	▢ square units

Rectangle C

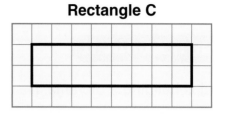

Square D

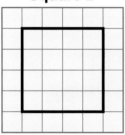

Rectangle E

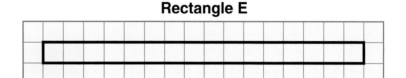

Use your table to answer these questions.

4. Can a square have the same area as a rectangle?

5. Can rectangles and squares with the same area have different perimeters?

Use grid paper for Problems 6–8.

6. Draw a rectangle with an area of 20 square units and a perimeter greater than 20 units.

7. Draw a rectangle with an area of 18 square units and a perimeter of 18 units.

8. **Analyze** If you double the length and width of a figure will its area double also? Double the length and width of figures C, D, and E above. What can you conclude?

Talk About It • Write About It

You learned how perimeter and area can be measured.

9. How are perimeter and area different?

10. Suppose two figures have different shapes. If one figure has a greater perimeter than the other, does it also have a greater area? Explain your thinking.

 **Audio Tutor 2/15** Listen and Understand

Algebra

Perimeter

Objective Find perimeters of polygons.

Learn About It

Paul is building a diorama. He plans to glue a strip of leather around the edge. The diorama is 12 inches long and 8 inches wide. How many inches of leather edging will he need?

To find the length of the edges, find the **perimeter** or distance around the diorama.

Different Ways to Find Perimeter

Way 1 You can add the lengths of the sides.

Perimeter = $l + w + l + w$

P = 12 in. + 8 in. + 12 in. + 8 in.

P = 40 in.

Way 2 You can use the formula to find the perimeter of a rectangle.

Perimeter = $(2 \times l) + (2 \times w)$

$P = (2 \times 12 \text{ in.}) + (2 \times 8 \text{ in.})$

P = 24 in. + 16 in.

P = 40 in.

Remember
Do what is in parentheses first.

Solution: Paul needs 40 inches of leather edging.

Estimate and then find the perimeter of objects.

STEP 1 Choose three objects in your classroom.

STEP 2 Estimate what the perimeter of each might be. Record your estimate.

STEP 3 Use your ruler to find the exact perimeter. Record the actual perimeter.

Find the perimeter of each polygon.

1.
   4 in.

2.
   3 ft

3.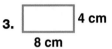
   4 cm
   8 cm

4. 3 cm   7 cm
   5 cm

Ask Yourself
• Is the figure a regular or irregular polygon?
• Can I use a formula?

Explain Your Thinking ▶ Write a formula for finding the perimeter of a square.

Practice and Problem Solving

Find the perimeter of each polygon.

5. 20 cm
   60 cm

6. 2 yd

7. 5 in.
   2 in.

Write a formula to find each perimeter. Then solve.

8. a regular pentagon with sides 8 cm long

9. a regular hexagon with sides 8 cm long

10. a regular octagon with sides 8 cm long

Solve.

11. A rectangular room is 15 feet long and 7 yards wide. Find the perimeter in feet. Then find the perimeter in yards.

12. **Explain** Reggie is making sandals. He traced his foot on grid paper. How can he find its perimeter with a piece of string and a ruler?

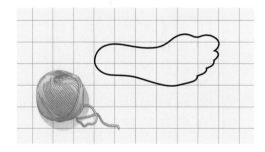

Mixed Review and Test Prep

Open Response

Write >, <, or = for each ⬤. (Ch. 3, Lesson 1)

13. 9 + 4 − 3 ⬤ 7 + 8

14. 13 − 5 ⬤ 2 + 6

15. 5 + 9 − 1 ⬤ 4 + 8

16. 4 + 7 − 2 ⬤ 5 + 8 − 3

Multiple Choice

17. The perimeter of a square is 36 cm. What is the length of one side of the square?

(Ch. 18, Lesson 2)

A 4 cm   C 9 cm

B 32 cm   D 40 cm

Audio Tutor 2/16 Listen and Understand

Algebra

Area

Objective Find the area of a rectangle.

Learn About It

Jake's grandfather is building a patio. He wants to know how many square feet of slate he needs to order.

To find how much slate is needed, you need to find the **area** or square units within the patio. You can find area in two ways.

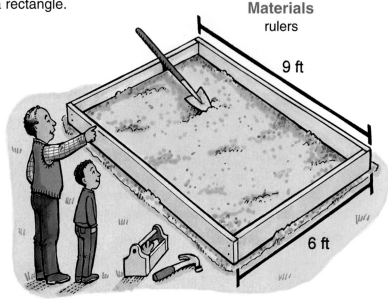

9 ft

6 ft

Different Ways to Find Area

Way ❶ You can draw a model and count the squares.

1	2	3	4	5	6	7	8	9
10	11	12	13	14	15	16	17	18
19	20	21	22	23	24	25	26	27
28	29	30	31	32	33	34	35	36
37	38	39	40	41	42	43	44	45
46	47	48	49	50	51	52	53	54

Each square is 1 square foot or 1 ft².

Way ❷ You can use the formula to find the area of a rectangle.

Area = length × width

Area = $l \times w$

$A = 9$ ft × 6 ft

$A = 54$ ft² or 54 square feet

Solution: The patio will be 54 square feet in area. So, he will need 54 square feet of slate.

Another Example

Area of a Square

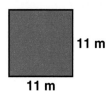

11 m

11 m

$A = s \times s$

$A = 11$ m × 11 m

$A = 121$ m²

Remember
Each side of a square is the same length.

456

Try this activity to estimate and find the area of objects.

STEP 1   Find three flat rectangular objects in your classroom.

STEP 2   Estimate what the area of each might be. Record your estimate.

STEP 3   Use your ruler and a formula to find the area of each object. Record the actual area. How did your estimate compare to the actual area?

Guided Practice

Ask Yourself
• What formula can I use?
• What unit do I need?

Use a formula to find the area of each figure.

1. 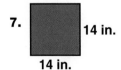 2 mi
3 mi

2. 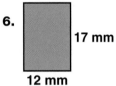 16 ft
16 ft

3. 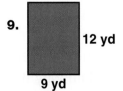 12 in.
25 in.

4. 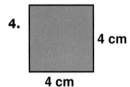 4 cm
4 cm

5. 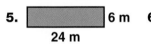 6 m
24 m

6.  17 mm
12 mm

Explain Your Thinking ▶ How could you find the perimeter of a square that has an area of 25 square inches?

Practice and Problem Solving

Find the area of each figure.

7. 14 in.
14 in.

8. 2 mi
5 mi

9. 12 yd
9 yd

10. 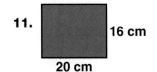 7 m
12 m

11. 16 cm
20 cm

12. 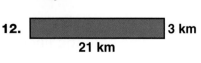 3 km
21 km

Go On ▶

Find the perimeter and area for each rectangle.

13. 14 m long, 6 m wide

14. 3 yd long, 7 yd wide

15. 15 cm long, 4 cm wide

16. 5 ft long, 13 ft wide

17. 2 in. long, 16 in. wide

18. 8 mm long, 26 mm wide

Which of the figures below have the same perimeter but different areas?

19.

a.

5 in.
3 in.

b.

6 in.
2 in.

c.

4 in.
4 in.

d.
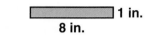
1 in.
8 in.

Solve.

20. The area of Kahli's closet is 15 square feet. One side is 3 feet long. How long is the other side? What did you do to get your answer?

21. Analyze Does the area of a rectangle double when the length and width are doubled? How do you know?

Data Use the floor plan at the right for Problems 22–26.

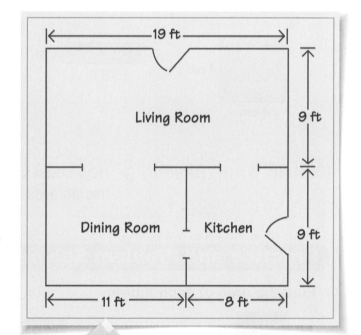

22. Is the floor space of the living room greater or less than 200 square feet? How much greater or less?

23. Money Anna wants to tile the kitchen floor. Each tile is 1 foot square and costs $1.75. How much will it cost for the tiles?

24. The rug in the living room is 10 feet by 8 feet. How much floor space is not covered by the rug?

25. What's Wrong? Ben finds the total perimeter of the three rooms by doubling the perimeter of the living room. Explain why that is not correct.

26. You Decide Suppose you added two rooms onto the floor plan shown. What size might each be? What would the total area of the five rooms become?

Extra Practice See page 475, Set B.

Measurement Sense
Area of a Right Triangle

You can use the area of a rectangle to find the area of this right triangle.

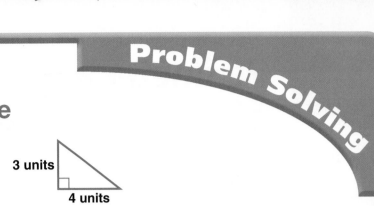

- Think of the right triangle as half of a rectangle.
- Find the area of the rectangle.
  4 units × 3 units = 12 square units
- Now divide the area of the rectangle by 2.
  12 square units ÷ 2 = 6 square units

3 units

4 units

The area of the triangle is 6 square units.

Find the area of each right triangle.

1. 4 cm / 7 cm

2. 10 mm / 10 mm

3. 6 m / 3 m

Check your understanding of Lessons 1–3.

Find the perimeter of each figure. (Lessons 1–2)

1. 6 cm / 2 cm

2. 5 in. / 5 in.

3. 8 cm / 8 cm / 5 cm

4. 4 in. / 3 in. / 6 in. / 7 in.

Find the area of each figure. (Lessons 1 and 3)

5. 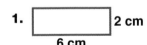 4 yd / 5 yd

6. 7 in. / 2 in.

7. 2 cm / 2 cm

8.  9 ft / 9 ft

**Write a formula to find the perimeter.
Then solve.** (Lesson 2)

9. a regular octagon; each side is 7 cm

**Write a formula to find the area.
Then solve.** (Lesson 3)

10. a rectangle 9 in. long and 7 in. wide

Algebra

Perimeter and Area of Complex Figures

Objective Find the perimeter and area of figures that are not rectangles.

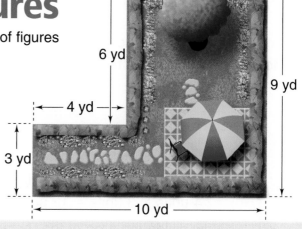

6 yd

6 yd

9 yd

4 yd

3 yd

10 yd

Learn About It

Andy wants to put a fence around his garden. The space he will use is shown at the right. How much fence should he buy? What is the area of his garden?

Find the perimeter.

Add the lengths of the sides.

Perimeter = 10 yd + 3 yd + 4 yd + 6 yd + 6 yd + 9 yd

$P = 38$ yd

Solution: He should buy 38 yards of fence.

Find the area.

STEP 1 Separate the figure into a rectangle and a square.

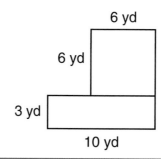

6 yd

6 yd

3 yd

10 yd

STEP 2 Use a formula to find the area of each figure.

Area of the Rectangle

Area = $l \times w$

$A = 10$ yd $\times$ 3 yd

$A = 30$ yd²

Area of the Square

Area = $s \times s$

$A = 6$ yd $\times$ 6 yd

$A = 36$ yd²

STEP 3 Add both areas to find the area of the whole figure.

30 yd² + 36 yd² = 66 yd²

Solution: The area of the garden is 66 square yards.

Ask Yourself
- How can I divide the figure into squares and rectangles?
- How should I label the answer?

Guided Practice

Find the perimeter and area of each figure.

1.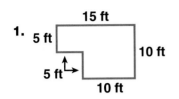
   15 ft
   5 ft
   10 ft
   5 ft
   10 ft

2.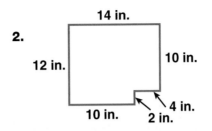
   14 in.
   12 in.
   10 in.
   10 in.
   4 in.
   2 in.

Explain Your Thinking ▶ How could you find the area of your classroom? What tools would you need? What formula would you use?

Practice and Problem Solving

Find the perimeter and area of each figure.

3.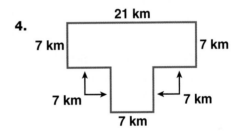
   28 m
   7 m
   21 m
   21 m
   14 m
   7 m

4.
   21 km
   7 km
   7 km
   7 km
   7 km
   7 km

5.
   24 yd
   12 yd
   18 yd
   18 yd
   6 yd
   6 yd

6.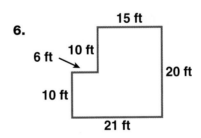
   15 ft
   6 ft
   10 ft
   20 ft
   10 ft
   21 ft

7.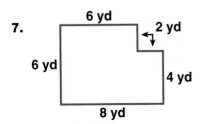
   6 yd
   2 yd
   6 yd
   4 yd
   8 yd

8.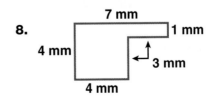
   7 mm
   1 mm
   4 mm
   3 mm
   4 mm

Go On

Find the length of each missing side.

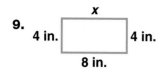
9.
x
4 in. [rectangle] 4 in.
8 in.

Perimeter = 24 inches

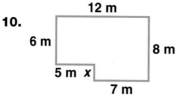
10.
12 m
6 m
5 m x
8 m
7 m

Perimeter = 40 meters

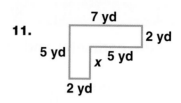
11.
7 yd
5 yd
2 yd
x 5 yd
2 yd

Perimeter = 24 yards

 Data Use the drawing below and the table at the right for Problems 12–15.

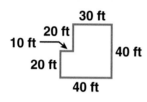
30 ft
20 ft
10 ft
20 ft
40 ft
40 ft

12. **Money** Dee needs to put a fence around this yard. Fencing costs $3 per foot. How many feet of fencing are needed? How much will it cost?

13. **Analyze** Dee wants to put grass seed on the yard. How many pounds of grass seed will she need?

14. Joel purchased 3 pounds of grass seed. What might the length and width of his yard be?

 15. **Write Your Own** Use the data in the table to write a problem. Give your problem to a classmate to solve.

GRASS SEED

How Much Grass Seed to Buy	
Area (ft²)	Pounds of Seed
1,000	1
1,500	2
2,000	3
2,500	4

Mixed Review and Test Prep

Open Response

Is the dashed line a line of symmetry?
Write *yes* or *no*. (Ch. 17, Lesson 4)

16.    17.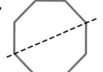

18. Aldo plans to put new tiles on the kitchen floor. How many square yards of tile does he need if the kitchen measures 9 feet by 12 feet? (Ch. 18, Lesson 4)

Explain your thinking.

Visual Thinking
Estimating Area

Look at the shape on the right.

You can use grid paper to help you estimate the area of unusual shapes like this one by counting the square units within the shape.

- If the shape covers $\frac{1}{2}$ or more than $\frac{1}{2}$ of a square, count it as 1 square unit.

- If the shape covers less than $\frac{1}{2}$ of a square, don't count it.

This area is about 15 square units.

Estimate the area of these shapes.

1.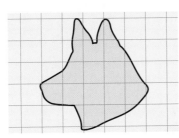

2.

3.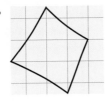

Art Connection
Stencil Patterns

Vivian is stenciling a border on her bedroom wall. Which of the pieces below will complete the unfinished section? Explain how you know.

a.   **b.**   **c.**

Brain Teaser

Mr. Tanz is building a 48-foot fence along one side of his yard. He plans to put a post on each end. He wants to place the remaining posts every 8 feet.

How many posts does he need?

Education Place

Check out **eduplace.com/map** for more brain teasers.

Solid Figures and Nets

Objective Identify and make solid shapes.

Learn About It

Sand castles are fun to make. You create solid figures when you build sand castles. Solid figures are objects that take up space.

This solid figure is called a cube.

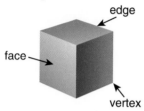

edge

face

vertex

- A cube has 6 **faces**.
- Two faces meet to form an **edge**.
- The point where 3 edges meet is a **vertex**. A cube has 8 vertices.

Here are more solid figures.

Vocabulary

faces

edge

vertex (vertices)

net

Materials
Learning Tools 28–33
scissors
tape

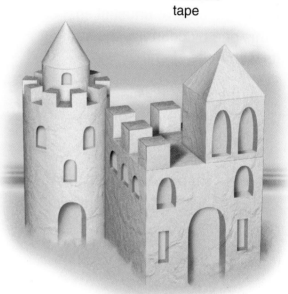

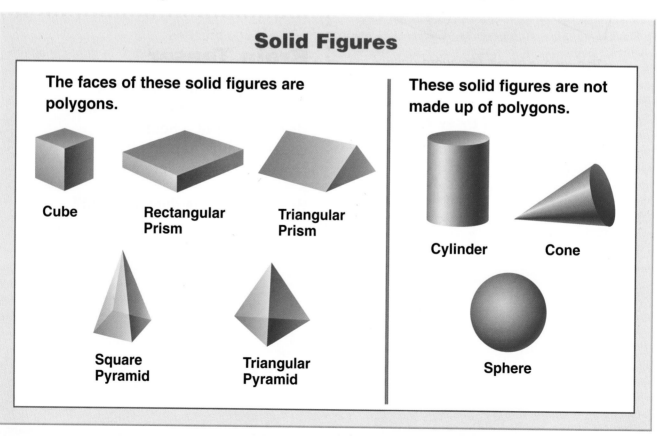

Solid Figures

The faces of these solid figures are polygons.

Cube

Rectangular Prism

Triangular Prism

Square Pyramid

Triangular Pyramid

These solid figures are not made up of polygons.

Cylinder

Cone

Sphere

464

These patterns are **nets**. If you cut out a net and fold it on the dotted lines, you can make a solid figure.

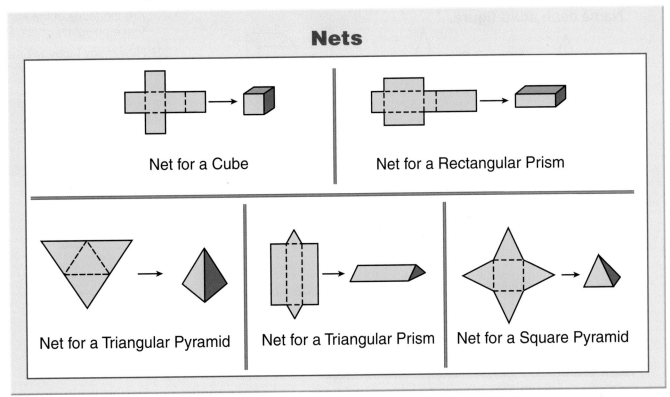

Nets

Net for a Cube

Net for a Rectangular Prism

Net for a Triangular Pyramid

Net for a Triangular Prism

Net for a Square Pyramid

Try this activity to make solid figures.

STEP 1   Cut out three nets from Learning Tools 28–33.

STEP 2   Fold on the dotted lines and tape closed.

STEP 3   Make a table to record the name of each figure you constructed. Then write the number of faces, edges, and vertices of each figure.

Go On

Guided Practice

Name each solid figure.

1.

2.

3.

Ask Yourself

- Are the faces of the solid figure polygons or circles?
- How many faces will the solid figure have when the net is folded?

4. Which net can be folded to make a cube?

a.   b.   c. 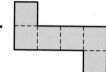   d.

Explain Your Thinking ▶ Which solid figure has faces that are all triangles?

Practice and Problem Solving

Name the solid figure each object looks like.

5.   6.   7.    8.

Name the solid figure that can be made with each net.

9. 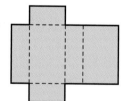   10. 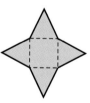   11.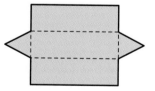

Copy and complete the table.

	Solid Figure	Number of Faces	Number of Edges	Number of Vertices
12.	Cylinder			
13.	Triangular Prism			
14.	Rectangular Prism			
15.	Triangular Pyramid			

Name the solid figure with the following faces.

16.

Top View	Bottom View	Side View

17.

Top View	Bottom View	Side View

Solve.

18. Name 3 solid figures that have curved surfaces.

19. Name a solid figure that has only 4 faces. Draw a picture of it.

20. Analyze Sarah built a pyramid out of sand. The bottom of the pyramid was a square. What shape were the other faces of the pyramid? How many other faces were there?

21. Kari was thinking of a solid figure with 5 faces. Jo guessed it was a square pyramid. Kari said it was another figure that she was thinking of. What figure might it be?

Mixed Review and Test Prep

Open Response

Does the figure have rotational symmetry? Write *yes* or *no*. (Ch. 17, Lesson 4)

22.

23.

24.

25.

Multiple Choice

26. If you tape 4 identical cubes in a row, what figure can be formed? (Ch. 18, Lesson 5)

A cylinder

B rectangular prism

C square pyramid

D large cube

Extra Practice Page 475, Set D.

Audio Tutor 2/17 Listen and Understand

Algebra

Volume

Objective Find the volume of a rectangular prism.

Materials
centimeter cubes
small box

Learn About It

Suppose you need to know how much a box can hold. You need to find the volume of the box.

Volume is the amount of space inside a solid figure. Volume is measured in **cubic units**.

One standard unit used for describing volume is a cube with each edge 1 centimeter long. This unit is called a **cubic centimeter**.

1 cm   1 cm

1 cm

Try this activity to find the volume of a box.

STEP 1 Estimate how many cubes it will take to fill a small box. Record your estimate.

STEP 2 Fill the box with cubes. Count the cubes to find the volume of the box.

STEP 3 Record the number of cubes that fit in the box.
How did your estimate compare to the actual volume?

You can also use a formula to find the volume of a box.

A rectangular prism has three dimensions: length (*l*), width (*w*), and height (*h*). You can find its volume (*V*) by multiplying these dimensions.

The result is the same as counting the number of cubes that would fit in the box.

The volume of the box at the right is 24 cubic centimeters.

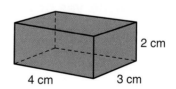

2 cm

4 cm   3 cm

Volume = length × width × height

$V = l \times w \times h$
$V = 4 \text{ cm} \times 3 \text{ cm} \times 2 \text{ cm}$
$V = 24$ cubic centimeters or 24 cm^3

Extra Help at **eduplace.com/map**

Find the volume of each figure.

1. 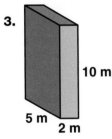 12 in. 12 in. 12 in.

2. 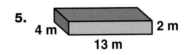 4 in. 2 in. 12 in.

Explain Your Thinking ▶ Why is volume always written as cubic units?

Practice and Problem Solving

Find the volume of each figure.

3. 10 m 5 m 2 m

4. 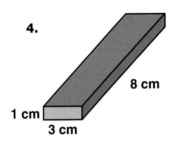 8 cm 1 cm 3 cm

5. 4 m 2 m 13 m

6. 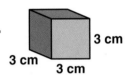 3 cm 3 cm 3 cm

Solve.

7. A box is 27 cm long, 5 cm wide, and 5 cm high. What is the volume of the box?

8. **Explain** Does the volume of a box double if the dimensions are doubled? How do you know?

9. Matt's box measures 3 inches on each edge. Penny's box measures 6 inches on each edge. How much greater is the volume of Penny's box than Matt's box?

10. Peli is putting soil in a terrarium. The space he needs to fill is 9 inches by 13 inches by 2 inches. How many cubic inches of soil will he need to put in the terrarium?

Mixed Review and Test Prep

Open Response
Identify the parts of this circle.
(Ch. 16, Lesson 7)

11. the center

12. a radius

13. the diameter

14. a chord

D, E, A, B, C

15. The volume of a gift box is 36 cubic inches. The height is 3 inches, and the width is 2 inches. What is the length of the box?
(Ch. 18, Lesson 6)

Explain how you found the length.

Problem-Solving Application
Use Formulas

Objective Decide which formula to use to solve a problem.

You can use formulas for perimeter, area, and volume to solve word problems.

Thomas is decorating a treasure box for his sister Sarah. The box is 12 inches long, 8 inches wide, and 6 inches high.

He wants to buy the right amount of decorative materials for it.

▶ **Sometimes you need to find perimeter.**

A row of decals will go around the box along the bottom of the box. How long will the row of decals be?

$P = (2 \times l) + (2 \times w)$
$P = (2 \times 12 \text{ in.}) + (2 \times 8 \text{ in.})$
$P = 24 \text{ in.} + 16 \text{ in.}$
$P = 40 \text{ in.}$

Solution: The row will be 40 inches long.

▶ **Sometimes you need to find area.**

Thomas plans to line the bottom of the box with felt. How much felt should he buy?

$A = l \times w$
$A = 12 \text{ in.} \times 8 \text{ in.}$
$A = 96 \text{ in.}^2$

Solution: He should buy 96 square inches of felt.

▶ **Sometimes you need to find volume.**

How much space will Sarah have for her treasures?

$V = l \times w \times h$
$V = 12 \text{ in.} \times 8 \text{ in.} \times 6 \text{ in.}$
$V = 576 \text{ in.}^3$

Solution: Sarah will have 576 cubic inches of space.

Look Back What is the difference between inches, square inches, and cubic inches?

Guided Practice

Use the Ask Yourself questions to help you solve each problem.

1. Thomas's workbench measures 19 inches by 36 inches. What is the perimeter of his workbench?

2. Sarah will place the treasure box on her desk. The desk measures 24 inches by 30 inches. How much room will be left on the desk?

 Hint Remember to subtract the area of the treasure box.

Ask Yourself

UNDERSTAND → Does the question ask me to find perimeter, area, or volume?

PLAN → What formula should I use?

SOLVE → Did I answer with the correct unit?

LOOK BACK → Did I need inches, square inches or cubic inches?

Independent Practice

Use a formula to solve.

3. Suppose a toolbox is 1 foot high, 20 inches long, and 9 inches wide. How much space is inside the toolbox?

4. A workshop is 10 feet on each side. What area will be left for working if 6 square feet are used for a workbench?

5. **Mental Math** A garage wall that measures 10 feet by 30 feet needs to be painted. How many square feet is that?

6. **Analyze** You have 72 cm of wood to make a picture frame. How can you cut the wood to make a frame with the greatest area for a picture? What shape will it be?

Go On

Mixed Problem Solving

Solve. Show your work. Tell what strategy you used.

7. There are 8 teams competing in a soccer tournament. Each team plays every other team once. How many games are played?

8. Mary planted flowers every 6 inches along a garden path. She planted them at the beginning, end, and along both sides of the 14-foot path. How many flowers did she plant?

9. Steven is thinking of a number. If he multiplies the number by 6 and then adds 123, the result is 621. What number is he thinking of?

You Choose

Strategy
- Draw a Picture
- Make an Organized List
- Work Backward
- Write an Equation

Computation Method
- Mental Math
- Estimation
- Paper and Pencil
- Calculator

Solve. Tell which method you chose.

10. **Money** Mr. Brown's class put 8 small plants and 5 large plants in a terrarium. The small plants cost $2.19 each. The large plants cost $3.86 each. About how much was spent on plants?

11. Sheila is starting a train trip. Her watch indicates that it is now 12 noon. The trip will end 2 days later at 3 P.M. How many hours will she be traveling?

12. Mike is framing a square picture that measures 20 inches on each side. What is the length of wood he will need for the frame?

13. A factory produces birdbaths. Workers can make 50 birdbaths in 30 minutes. How many birdbaths can be made in an 8-hour day? in a 40-hour week?

Visual Thinking
Graphing in a Different Way

The coach drew this graph to show spring sports teams. She uses the graph to schedule games.

- Each dot or vertex stands for a different team: Kickball, Track, Lacrosse, and Soccer.

- Each line segment or edge that connects vertices stands for students who are members of both teams.

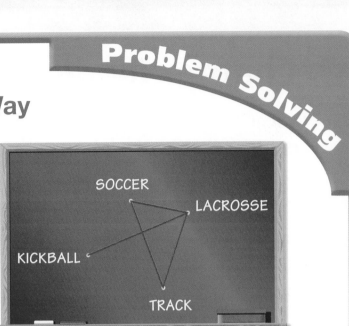

Use the graph to solve.

1. Are there students who play soccer and lacrosse? Are there students who play soccer and kickball? How do you know?

2. Can the coach schedule a kickball game on the same day as a track meet? Why or why not?

3. How could you use a graph to show how many students in your class are involved in more than one after-school activity? What steps would you need to take to get the data? How might a graph be a useful tool?

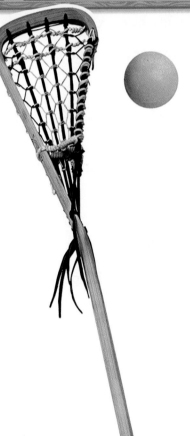

Chapter Review/Test

VOCABULARY

Choose the best word to complete each sentence.

1. The number of cubic units in a solid figure is the _____.

2. The point where 3 edges of a solid figure meet is a _____.

3. The number of square units in a region is the _____.

CONCEPTS AND SKILLS

Find the perimeter and area of each figure. (Lessons 1–4, pp. 452–462)

4.
3 ft
5 ft

5.
14 mm
14 mm

Name the solid figure that can be made with the net. (Lesson 5, pp. 464–467)

6.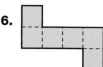

Find the volume of each figure. (Lesson 6, pp. 468–469)

7.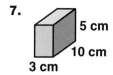
5 cm
10 cm
3 cm

8.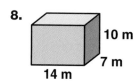
10 m
7 m
14 m

PROBLEM SOLVING

Use a formula to solve. (Lesson 7, pp. 470–472)

9. Mrs. Cortez wants to buy wall-to-wall carpeting. The room is 10 feet wide and 12 feet long. How much carpeting does she need?

10. The volume of a box is 24 cubic inches. The height is 2 inches and the width is 3 inches. What is the length?

Write About It

Show You Understand

Kim has a rectangle with an area of 12 square inches. Mona says the length can only be 6 inches, and the width can only be 2 inches. Is she correct?

Explain your reasoning.

Extra Practice

Set A (Lesson 2, pp. 454–455)

Write a formula to find each perimeter. Then solve.

1. a square with sides
7 centimeters long

2. a regular pentagon with
sides 3 meters long

3. a rectangle with sides
2 feet and 5 feet long

Set B (Lesson 3 pp. 456–458)

Find the area of each figure.

1. a rectangle with sides
4 inches and 6 inches long

2. a square with sides
13 millimeters long

3. a rectangle with sides
5 feet and 9 feet long

Set C (Lesson 4, pp. 460–462)

Find the perimeter and area of each figure.

1.

2 ft
3 ft
5 ft
6 ft
2 ft
8 ft

2.

60 cm
30 cm
50 cm
40 cm
20 cm
20 cm

3.

2 in.
5 in.
8 in.
4 in.
3 in.
6 in.

Set D (Lesson 5, pp. 464–467)

Name the solid figure that can be made with each net.

1.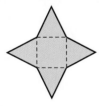

2.

3.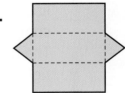

Set E (Lesson 6, pp. 468–469)

Find the volume of each figure.

1.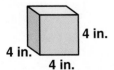

4 in.
4 in.
4 in.

2.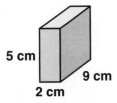

5 cm
9 cm
2 cm

3.

6 ft
8 ft
3 ft

I See a PATTERN

When the same shapes are repeated over and over, they make patterns. Think about the honeycomb in a beehive. It is made up of repeating hexagons that form a pattern. Repeating patterns that completely cover a region are called tessellations. Tessellations have no gaps and no overlaps.

M.C. Escher was a Dutch artist who drew tessellations. He often used animals, such as birds, fish, and lizards to create complex patterns! The picture at the right is one of his works.

"Unicorn" by Maurits Cornelius Escher (1950)

476

Problem Solving

Figure A

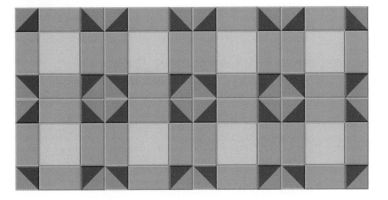

Use the design above for Problems 1–2.

1 Gina is tiling her hallway. She repeated Figure A to make the tessellation above. What geometric shapes are in this tessellation? List all that you can find.

2 What transformations do you see in the design? Use tracings to explain.

3 Look at the tessellation at the right. Does Figure E show a rotation, a reflection, or a translation of Figure D?

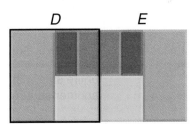

D   *E*

4 Can you make a tessellation using an equilateral triangle? Use drawings to show your answers.

5 Draw your own tessellation on grid paper. What shapes did you use?

Education Place

Visit Weekly Reader Connections at **eduplace.com/map** for more on this topic.

Pentominoes

Pentominoes are flat shapes made up of five congruent squares. They can be put together to make many larger shapes.

A figure is a pentomino if it follows these rules:

- It has five congruent squares.
- Each square shares at least one entire side with another square.

These are pentominoes.

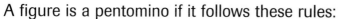

These are not pentominoes.

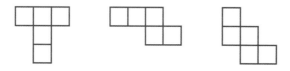

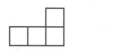

This figure has only four squares.

The yellow square does not share an entire side with another square.

All the squares are not congruent.

Try These!

Are these figures pentominoes? If not, explain why not.

7 **Challenge** There are only 12 possible pentominoes. Draw the five not shown on this page.

Maximize the Size

Use your calculator to explore area and perimeter.

1. Find the area and perimeter of each of the figures below.

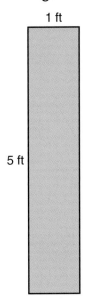

1 ft

5 ft

Figure A

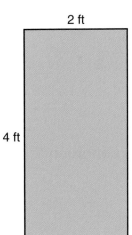

2 ft

4 ft

Figure B

3 ft

3 ft

Figure C

2. What do you notice about the perimeters of the figures above?

3. Which figure has the greatest area?

4. Use graph paper to draw 5 different rectangles that each have a perimeter of 20 centimeters. Which rectangle has the greatest area?

5. Use your calculator to find 5 different rectangles that have a perimeter of 40 centimeters. Which has the greatest area?

6. **Analyze** Look at your answers for Exercises 2–5. What rectangle always seems to have the greatest area for any perimeter?

7. **Challenge** Find the length and width of the rectangle with the greatest area that has a perimeter of 144 meters.

Unit 6 Test

VOCABULARY (**Open Response**)

Choose the best term to complete each sentence.

1. A figure that has only one endpoint and goes on without end in one direction is called a ____.

2. A figure whose sides are congruent and angles are congruent is called a ____.

3. Two lines that form right angles are ____ to each other.

> **Vocabulary**
> ray
> line
> parallel
> parallelogram
> perpendicular
> regular polygon

CONCEPTS AND SKILLS (**Open Response**)

Name each plane figure. (Chapter 16)

4.   5.   6.   7.

Do the figures in each pair appear to be congruent? Write *yes* or *no*. (Chapter 17)

8.    9.    10.

Tell how each figure was moved. Write *rotation*, *reflection*, or *translation*. (Chapter 17)

11. 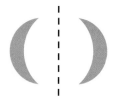   12. 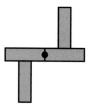   13.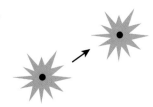

How many lines of symmetry does the figure have? Does the figure have rotational symmetry? Write *yes* or *no*. (Chapter 17)

14.   15.   16.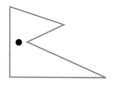

Find the perimeter and area of each figure. (Chapter 18)

17.
8 cm
4 cm

18.
6 in.
3 in.

19.
7 ft
7 ft

Name each solid figure. Then find the volume of each. (Chapter 18)

20.
2 in.
2 in.
2 in.
2 in.

21.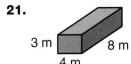
3 m
8 m
4 m

PROBLEM SOLVING   Open Response

22. A repeating design has a circle after a hexagon. A square is first. What are the first 8 figures in the design?

24. A rectangular trunk is 5 ft long, 2 ft wide, and 2 ft high. What is the volume of the trunk? Explain.

23. Can an equilateral triangle, a parallelogram, and a trapezoid be used to make a hexagon? Use a drawing to explain.

25. Can 17 toothpicks be used to form 6 congruent squares? If so, draw the figures.

Performance Assessment

Constructed Response

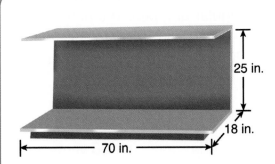

25 in.
18 in.
70 in.

12 in.
RICE PUFFS
5 in.
8 in.

10 in.
OAT BRAN
4 in.
6 in.

8 in.
CORN FLAKES
3 in.
4 in.

Task Mr. Alou needs to fill a supermarket shelf with the cereal boxes shown above. He needs to display some of each kind of cereal.

Use the information above and at the right to find a way Mr. Alou can display the cereal. How many of each kind of cereal are in your display? Explain your thinking. Use the words *across*, *deep*, and *high* to describe your display.

Information You Need

- All boxes must be upright and face forward.
- Only the same kinds of cereal are placed in front of one another.
- Only the same kinds of cereal are stacked on top of one another.

Cumulative Test Prep

Solve Problems 1–10.

Test-Taking Tip

To solve problems that have more than one step, break the problem into smaller steps.

Look at the example below.

Kasib's bedroom is 10 ft wide and 15 ft long. The rug in his bedroom is 9 ft wide and 12 ft long. How many square feet of the floor of Kasib's bedroom are **not** covered by the rug?

A 25 ft² **C** 96 ft²

B 42 ft² **D** 138 ft²

THINK

Area of room: 10 ft × 15 ft = 150 ft²
Area of rug: 9 ft × 12 ft = 108 ft²
Area of room minus area of rug:
150 ft² − 108 ft² = 42 ft²
Choose **B**.

1. If 278,099 > ■, which number could be the value of ■?

   A 279,067 **C** 278,099

   B 278,136 **D** 278,081

   (Chapter 2, Lesson 1)

2. Tani has 2 red pencils. She is given 10 blue, 10 yellow, and 10 green pencils. Which expression represents the number of pencils Tani has now?

   F (2 + 10) × 3 **H** (10 − 2) × 3

   G 2 + (10 × 3) **J** 10 + (2 × 3)

   (Chapter 5, Lesson 2)

3. John is putting a fence around a rectangular dog pen. The pen is 25 feet long and 32 feet wide. John has 20 yards of fencing. How many more yards does he need?

   A 8 yards **C** 32 yards

   B 18 yards **D** 38 yards

   (Chapter 18, Lesson 2)

4. Jeff has a block of wood. He cuts it in half. How many more faces are there now than before Jeff made the cut?

   F 18 **H** 8

   G 12 **J** 6

   (Chapter 18, Lesson 5)

For Test-Taking Tips, See Page 658.

5. Together Rodrigo and Marci earned $86. How much money did they each earn if Marci earned $4 more than Rodrigo?

(Chapter 9, Lesson 3)

6. It is 9° C. What would the temperature be if it were 11 degrees colder?

(Chapter 13, Lesson 4)

7. Look at the figure.

Which angle in the figure is an acute angle?

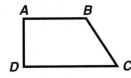

(Chapter 16, Lesson 2)

8. What is the prime factorization for 72?

(Chapter 10, Lesson 2)

9. The table shows how many miles the Vaughn family drove each day during their vacation.

Miles Driven Each Day	
Day	**Miles**
Monday	23
Tuesday	21
Wednesday	13
Thursday	31

What is the average number of miles the Vaughn family drove each day?

(Chapter 10, Lesson 5)

10. The School Store is placing an order for balloons and mugs. A case of balloons costs $4. A case of mugs costs $22. The school needs to order more than 1 case of each.

Let b stand for the number of cases of balloons.

Let m stand for the number of cases of mugs.

A Write an equation to find the total cost of the balloons and mugs ordered.

B Suppose the School Store ordered 3 cartons of balloons and 2 cartons of mugs. Use the equation you wrote to find the total cost of all the items.

C The School Store also needs to order erasers. A case of erasers costs $5. Change the equation you wrote to include the cost of the erasers.

(Chapter 5, Lesson 5)

Education Place

Look for Cumulative Test Prep at **eduplace.com/map** for more practice.

Vocabulary Wrap-Up for Unit 6

Look back at the big ideas and vocabulary in this unit.

Big Ideas

You can rotate, reflect, or translate plane figures.

You can use formulas to find perimeter, area, or volume.

Key Vocabulary

- **rotate**
- **reflect**
- **translate**
- **formula**

Math Conversations

Use your new vocabulary to discuss these big ideas.

1. What are the 3 ways you can move figures? Use drawings to give examples of each way.

2. Use a rectangle and a rectangular prism to describe area, perimeter, and volume. Give a formula for each.

3. Explain the difference between line symmetry and rotational symmetry.

4. Explain how to determine if a pair of figures is congruent.

5. **Write About It** Search for examples of plane and solid figures near your home or school. Identify and describe what you find.

How can we find the perimeter of our classroom?

We can measure its length and width and then use the formula.

UNIT 7

Fractions and Decimals

Reading Mathematics

Reviewing Vocabulary

Here are some math vocabulary words that you should know.

fraction	a number that names a part of a whole or part of a group
denominator	the number below the bar in a fraction that tells how many equal parts there are
numerator	the number above the bar in a fraction that tells how many equal parts have been counted
decimal	a number with one or more digits to the right of a decimal point
decimal point	a symbol (.) used to separate the ones and tenths places in a decimal

Reading Words and Symbols

Fractions and decimals both name parts of a whole.
Look at the rectangle on the right.

Read: Seven tenths of the rectangle is red.

Write as a fraction: $\frac{7}{10}$ of the rectangle is red.

Write as a decimal: 0.7 of the rectangle is red.

Use words and symbols to answer the questions.

1. In the fraction $\frac{7}{10}$, which number is the numerator? What does that number mean?

2. What decimal names the part of the rectangle that is blue? How would you write it as a fraction?

Reading Test Questions

Choose the correct answer for each.

3. Which statement is false?

   a. $\frac{1}{8}$ of the circles are blue.

   b. $\frac{2}{8}$ of the circles are green.

   c. $\frac{1}{2}$ of the circles are red.

   d. $\frac{8}{8}$ of the circles are yellow.

False means "not true" or "wrong."

---

4. Which fraction represents the green part of the rectangle?

   a. $\frac{1}{4}$ c. $\frac{2}{3}$

   b. $\frac{1}{2}$ d. $\frac{3}{4}$

Represents means "stands for," or "shows," or "names."

5. Which decimal represents the shaded part of the rectangle?

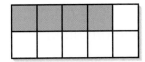

   a. 0.3   c. 0.5

   b. 0.4   d. 0.6

Shaded means "colored in."

Learning Vocabulary

**Watch for these words in this unit.
Write their definitions in your journal.**

> equivalent fractions
>
> improper fraction
>
> tenth
>
> hundredth

Education Place

At **eduplace.com/map**
see eGlossary and
eGames—Math Lingo.

Literature Connection

Read "Hold the Meat!" on
Pages 652–653. Then work
with a partner to answer the
questions about the story.

Understand Fractions

INVESTIGATION

Using Data

The Venn diagram shows the pizza toppings that 10 students chose at lunch. What fraction of the students chose both mushrooms and pepperoni? How might the school lunch staff use this information when preparing pizzas?

Pizza Toppings

Mushrooms   **Pepperoni**

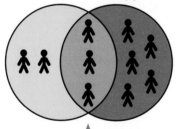

↑
Both mushrooms
and pepperoni

Use What You Know

Use this page to review and remember what you need to know for this chapter.

VOCABULARY

Choose the best term to complete each sentence.

1. The number below the bar in a fraction is the ____.

2. A ____ names a part of a whole.

3. A number that contains a whole number and a fraction is known as a ____.

4. The number above the bar in a fraction is the ____.

Vocabulary
fraction
numerator
denominator
mixed number
whole number

CONCEPTS AND SKILLS

Write a fraction for the shaded part.

5.

6.

7.

Write each as a fraction or mixed number.

8. two thirds	9. one eighth	10. two and one third
11. three fourths	12. one fifth	13. six and three tenths
14. six eighths	15. seven tenths	16. three and two fifths
17. five twelfths	18. eight eighths	19. one and nine tenths

 Write About It

20. Can the fraction $\frac{2}{6}$ be used to represent the shaded part of this circle? Explain why or why not.

Facts Practice, See Page 667.

Represent Fractions

Objective Read, write, and identify fractions.

Vocabulary

fraction

numerator

denominator

Learn About It

John helped his dad make a rectangular pizza for dinner. They used green and yellow peppers as toppings. You can use **fractions** to describe the pizza and the peppers.

▶ **A fraction can describe part of a whole.**

slices with green peppers → $\dfrac{1}{4}$ ← **numerator**
total number of slices → ← **denominator**

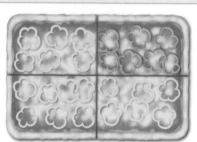

This fraction is read as "one fourth."

What fraction of the pizza is topped with green peppers?
What fraction of the pizza is topped with yellow peppers?

▶ **A fraction can describe part of a group.**

number of yellow peppers → $\dfrac{4}{7}$ ← **numerator**
total number of peppers → ← **denominator**

This fraction is read as "four sevenths."

What fraction of the peppers are yellow?
What fraction of the peppers are green?

Guided Practice

Write a fraction for the shaded part. Then write a fraction for the part that is not shaded.

1.

2.

3. △ △ △
△ △ △

Ask Yourself

- How many equal parts are there?
- How many parts are shaded? not shaded?

Explain Your Thinking ▶ Look back at Exercise 2. What whole number could represent the shaded part of the circle?

Write a fraction for the shaded part. Then write a fraction for the part that is not shaded.

4.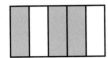

5.

6.

7.

Draw a picture to show each fraction.

8. $\frac{3}{4}$ 9. $\frac{1}{3}$ 10. $\frac{1}{2}$ 11. $\frac{3}{8}$ 12. $\frac{5}{8}$ 13. $\frac{2}{2}$ 14. $\frac{7}{10}$ 15. $\frac{4}{12}$

Match the picture to the description. Write A or B.

16. $\frac{2}{5}$ is orange.

17. $\frac{3}{5}$ is NOT green.

18. $\frac{1}{5}$ is yellow.

19. $\frac{5}{5}$ is orange OR green.

A

B

Solve.

20. Suppose the pizza on page 490 was divided into eighths. Would each slice be larger or smaller than when the pizza was divided into fourths? Explain.

21. A pizza had 6 equal slices. Natalie ate 3 slices. Her brothers shared the remaining slices. What fraction of the pizza did her brothers eat?

22. There are 5 yellow apples, 6 red apples, and 3 green apples in a bowl. What fraction of the apples are red?

23. Suppose the number of red apples in Problem 22 is doubled. Then what fraction of the apples are red?

24. **Represent** Jon and Meg buy a pie and cut it into 8 pieces. They eat 5 pieces. Draw a picture to show the fraction of the pie that is left.

25. At a flower shop, spring flowers cost $2 each, and vases cost $9 each. What is the total cost for a vase with 8 spring flowers?

Mixed Review and Test Prep

Open Response

Solve. (Ch. 12, Lessons 2, 7)

26. 1 yd = ▓ ft

27. 4 ft = ▓ in.

28. ▓ yd = 6 ft

29. ▓ in. = 2 yd

30. 400 cm = ▓ m

31. ▓ m = 2 km

32. 96 in. = ▓ ft

33. ▓ cm = 500 m

Multiple Choice

34. Maria sleeps for 9 hours each night. What fraction of each day (24 hours) is she NOT sleeping?

(Ch. 19, Lesson 1)

A $\frac{9}{24}$ C $\frac{15}{24}$

B $\frac{9}{15}$ D $\frac{3}{8}$

Extra Practice See page 513, Set A.

🔘 **Audio Tutor 2/18** Listen and Understand

Explore Equivalent Fractions

Objective Use models to identify equivalent fractions.

Vocabulary
equivalent fractions

Materials
Fraction Pieces
(Learning Tool 34)

Work Together

Fractions that name the same amount are **equivalent fractions**.

Work with a partner to find fractions that are equivalent to $\frac{1}{2}$.

STEP 1

Line up $\frac{1}{4}$ fraction pieces to fit below a $\frac{1}{2}$ fraction piece.

- How many $\frac{1}{4}$ fraction pieces did you use?

- What fraction names the same amount as $\frac{1}{2}$?

STEP 2

Line up $\frac{1}{8}$ fraction pieces to fit below the $\frac{1}{4}$ fraction pieces.

- How many $\frac{1}{8}$ fraction pieces did you use?

- What fraction names the same amount as $\frac{1}{2}$ and $\frac{2}{4}$?

$\frac{1}{2}$, $\frac{2}{4}$, and $\frac{4}{8}$ are equivalent fractions.

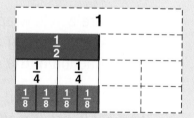

492

STEP 3

Use fraction pieces to find as many other fractions as you can that are equivalent to $\frac{1}{2}$. Make a table like the one shown at the right to record your work.

Fractions Equivalent to $\frac{1}{2}$

Fraction Piece	How many?	Equivalent fractions
$\frac{1}{4}$	2	$\frac{2}{4} = \frac{1}{2}$
$\frac{1}{6}$		$= \frac{1}{2}$
$\frac{1}{8}$		$= \frac{1}{2}$

STEP 4

Now look at the number lines at the right.

- Which fractions are equivalent to $\frac{1}{3}$?

- Which fractions are equivalent to $\frac{2}{3}$?

Use fraction pieces to check your answers.

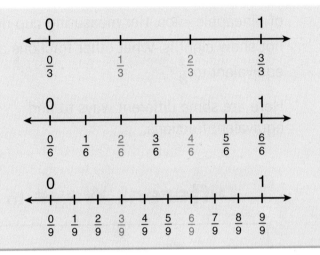

On Your Own

**Decide whether the fractions are equivalent. Write *yes* or *no*.
Use fraction pieces to help you.**

1. $\frac{3}{4}$ and $\frac{6}{8}$ 2. $\frac{7}{10}$ and $\frac{5}{6}$ 3. $\frac{8}{12}$ and $\frac{4}{6}$ 4. $\frac{5}{6}$ and $\frac{10}{12}$

Find a fraction equivalent to each. Draw number lines to help you.

5. $\frac{2}{10}$ 6. $\frac{4}{4}$ 7. $\frac{1}{6}$ 8. $\frac{4}{12}$ 9. $\frac{3}{4}$ 10. $\frac{2}{3}$

Talk About It • Write About It

You learned that equivalent fractions name the same amount.

11. Describe the pattern you see in the equivalent fractions at the right. Then continue the pattern and find two more equivalent fractions.

$$\frac{4}{6} = \frac{6}{9} = \frac{8}{12} = \frac{10}{15}$$

12. If you know that $\frac{4}{5} = \frac{8}{10}$ and $\frac{8}{10} = \frac{16}{20}$, what can you say about $\frac{4}{5}$ and $\frac{16}{20}$? Explain.

Equivalent Fractions and Simplest Form

Vocabulary

simplest form

Objective Find equivalent fractions and write fractions in simplest form.

Learn About It

Reni is making fruit shakes. She needs $\frac{4}{8}$ cup of pineapple juice. Her measuring cup does not show eighths. What other fractions are equivalent to $\frac{4}{8}$?

Here are some different ways to find equivalent fractions.

Different Ways to Find Fractions Equivalent to $\frac{4}{8}$

Way ❶ You can use number lines.

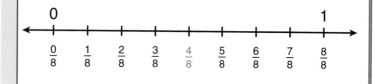

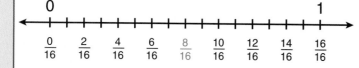

$\frac{4}{8}$, $\frac{8}{16}$, and $\frac{1}{2}$ are equivalent fractions.

Way ❷ You can multiply.

Multiply the numerator and denominator by the same number.

$$\frac{4}{8} \xrightarrow{\times 2} = \xrightarrow{\times 2} \frac{8}{16}$$

$\frac{4}{8}$ and $\frac{8}{16}$ are equivalent fractions.

Way ❸ You can divide.

Divide the numerator and denominator by the same number.

$$\frac{4}{8} \xrightarrow{\div 4} = \xrightarrow{\div 4} \frac{1}{2}$$

$\frac{4}{8}$ and $\frac{1}{2}$ are equivalent fractions.

Solution: $\frac{8}{16}$ and $\frac{1}{2}$ are both equivalent to $\frac{4}{8}$.

▶ A fraction is in **simplest form** when 1 is the only number that divides both the numerator and the denominator with no remainder.

<table>
<tr><td>

These fractions are in simplest form.

$\frac{1}{2}$ $\frac{2}{3}$ $\frac{3}{8}$ $\frac{2}{7}$ $\frac{5}{9}$

</td><td>

These fractions are not in simplest form.

$\frac{2}{4}$ $\frac{4}{8}$ $\frac{3}{15}$ $\frac{6}{9}$ $\frac{8}{12}$

</td></tr>
</table>

Juan and Brooke both used equivalent fractions to write $\frac{12}{18}$ in simplest form.

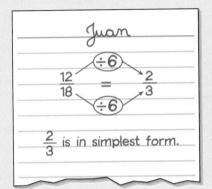

Juan

$$\frac{12}{18} \overset{\div 6}{\underset{\div 6}{=}} \frac{2}{3}$$

$\frac{2}{3}$ is in simplest form.

Brooke

$$\frac{12}{18} = \frac{12 \div 2}{18 \div 2} = \frac{6}{9}$$
$$\frac{6}{9} = \frac{6 \div 3}{9 \div 3} = \frac{2}{3}$$

$\frac{2}{3}$ is in simplest form.

Could Brooke have divided by 3 first?

$\frac{2}{3}$ is in simplest form because 1 is the only number that can divide both 2 and 3 with no remainder.

• How are Juan's work and Brooke's work alike?

• How are they different?

Guided Practice

Write each fraction in simplest form. Then write another equivalent fraction.

1. $\frac{2}{6}$ 2. $\frac{4}{10}$ 3. $\frac{6}{12}$ 4. $\frac{10}{16}$

Complete the equivalent fraction. What number did you multiply or divide the numerator or denominator by?

5. $\frac{1}{2} = \frac{3}{\blacksquare}$ 6. $\frac{15}{20} = \frac{\blacksquare}{4}$ 7. $\frac{4}{10} = \frac{\blacksquare}{5}$ 8. $\frac{2}{3} = \frac{4}{\blacksquare}$

Ask Yourself

• Did I multiply or divide the numerator and the denominator by the same number?

Explain Your Thinking ▶ Can you always multiply or divide to find equivalent fractions?

Go On

Are the fractions in each pair equivalent? Explain how you know.

9. $\frac{2}{8}$ $\frac{4}{16}$

10. $\frac{2}{4}$ $\frac{5}{10}$

11. $\frac{6}{9}$ $\frac{8}{12}$

12. $\frac{5}{5}$ $\frac{8}{8}$

13. $\frac{6}{15}$ $\frac{2}{5}$

14. $\frac{14}{16}$ $\frac{7}{9}$

Write each fraction in simplest form.
Then write another equivalent fraction.

15. $\frac{3}{9}$

16. $\frac{6}{8}$

17. $\frac{9}{12}$

18. $\frac{6}{15}$

19. $\frac{15}{18}$

20. $\frac{4}{14}$

21. $\frac{2}{3}$

22. $\frac{20}{20}$

23. $\frac{9}{21}$

24. $\frac{18}{36}$

X Algebra • Variables Find the value of x.

25. $\frac{x}{4} = \frac{2}{8}$

26. $\frac{9}{12} = \frac{x}{4}$

27. $\frac{x}{5} = \frac{15}{15}$

28. $\frac{10}{x} = \frac{2}{3}$

29. $\frac{18}{27} = \frac{2}{x}$

30. $\frac{x}{42} = \frac{1}{7}$

Use the recipe for Problems 31–33.

31. Are the amounts of cranberry juice and pineapple juice equivalent? Explain.

32. Reni made 12 servings of her fruit shake for her friends. How many bananas did she use?

33. Lila will make one serving of Reni's recipe. How much cranberry juice does she need? Use fraction strips to solve the problem.

34. **Write About It** Justine says that $\frac{2}{3}$ and $\frac{16}{25}$ are equivalent fractions. Is she correct? Explain your thinking.

35. **Reasoning** Can you add the same number to the numerator and denominator to find equivalent fractions? Why or why not?

Reni's Fruit Shake

1 large banana $\frac{3}{4}$ cup cranberry juice

1 cup strawberries $\frac{1}{2}$ cup pineapple juice

1 mango, cubed   1 cup ice cubes

Put all ingredients in blender.

Blend until thick and smooth.

Makes 3 servings.

Extra Practice See page 513, Set B.

Open Response

Solve. (Ch. 6, Lesson 4; Ch. 8, Lesson 2)

36. $4\overline{)78}$ **37.** $8\overline{)26}$ **38.** 18×7

39. $6\overline{)45}$ **40.** 86×3 **41.** 25×9

42. 31×4 **43.** $8\overline{)38}$ **44.** $4\overline{)89}$

45. Dora's team won 10 of 15 games. Pedro's team played 6 games and won the same fraction of their games as Dora's. How many games did Pedro's team win? Explain your thinking. (Ch. 19, Lesson 3)

Fraction Match-up

Game

Activity

2 Players

What You'll Need • 16 index cards (Learning Tool 37)

How to Play

1 Use Learning Tool 37 or make 16 cards like the ones shown.

2 Shuffle the cards. Place them facedown in any order in a 4 × 4 array.

3 A player turns over any two cards. If the cards show two equivalent fractions, the player keeps both cards. If not, the player turns the cards over and places them in the same positions.

4 Players take turns repeating Step 3 until all 8 matches have been made. The player with the greater number of cards is the winner.

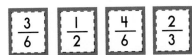
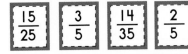
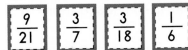

$$\frac{3}{6} \quad \frac{1}{2} \quad \frac{4}{6} \quad \frac{2}{3}$$

$$\frac{15}{25} \quad \frac{3}{5} \quad \frac{14}{35} \quad \frac{2}{5}$$

$$\frac{9}{21} \quad \frac{3}{7} \quad \frac{3}{18} \quad \frac{1}{6}$$

$$\frac{12}{40} \quad \frac{3}{10} \quad \frac{15}{24} \quad \frac{5}{8}$$

Compare and Order Fractions

Objective Compare and order fractions.

Learn About It

Clay used $\frac{2}{6}$ of his garden for pumpkins, $\frac{1}{2}$ for lettuce, and $\frac{1}{6}$ for tomatoes. Was more of his garden used for pumpkins or for tomatoes?

To compare fractions that have the same denominators, just compare the numerators.

Compare $\frac{2}{6}$ and $\frac{1}{6}$.

pumpkins → $\boxed{\frac{1}{6}}\boxed{\frac{1}{6}}$ $\frac{2}{6}$

tomatoes → $\boxed{\frac{1}{6}}$ $\frac{1}{6}$

$2 > 1$, so $\frac{2}{6} > \frac{1}{6}$

Solution: Clay used more of his garden for pumpkins than tomatoes.

▶ You can also compare fractions with different denominators.

Compare $\frac{2}{6}$ and $\frac{1}{2}$.

Different Ways to Compare $\frac{2}{6}$ and $\frac{1}{2}$

Way ① Use a model.

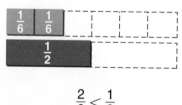

$\frac{2}{6} < \frac{1}{2}$

Way ② Find equivalent fractions. Then compare the numerators.

• Find a fraction equivalent to $\frac{1}{2}$ that has a denominator of 6.

$$\frac{1}{2} \xrightarrow{\times 3} = \frac{3}{6} \xleftarrow{\times 3} \text{ so } \frac{1}{2} = \frac{3}{6}$$

• Then compare the numerators.

$\frac{2}{6} < \frac{3}{6}$, so $\frac{2}{6} < \frac{1}{2}$.

Solution: $\frac{2}{6}$ is less than $\frac{1}{2}$.

Extra Help at **eduplace.com/map**

▶ You can use what you know about comparing fractions to order fractions.

Order $\frac{2}{6}$, $\frac{1}{2}$, and $\frac{1}{6}$ from least to greatest.

Different Ways to Order $\frac{2}{6}$, $\frac{1}{2}$, and $\frac{1}{6}$

Way 1 Find equivalent fractions. Then compare the numerators.

- Find a fraction equivalent to $\frac{1}{2}$ that has a denominator of 6.

$$\frac{1}{2} \xrightarrow{\times 3} = \frac{3}{6}, \text{ so } \frac{1}{2} = \frac{3}{6}.$$

- Then compare the numerators and order the fractions.

$$1 < 2 < 3, \text{ so } \frac{1}{6} < \frac{2}{6} < \frac{1}{2}$$

Way 2 Use a number line.

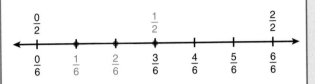

$\frac{1}{6}$ is farthest to the left.

$\frac{1}{2}$ is farthest to the right.

$\frac{2}{6}$ is in the middle.

So $\frac{1}{6} < \frac{2}{6} < \frac{1}{2}$

Solution: The order of the fractions from least to greatest is: $\frac{1}{6}$ $\frac{2}{6}$ $\frac{1}{2}$

Guided Practice

Ask Yourself
- Do the fractions have like denominators?
- If not, how can I find equivalent fractions?

Compare. Write >, <, or = for each ⬤.

1. $\frac{3}{4}$ ⬤ $\frac{5}{8}$

2. $\frac{2}{3}$ ⬤ $\frac{5}{6}$

3. $\frac{4}{6}$ ⬤ $\frac{2}{3}$

Order the fractions from greatest to least. Draw number lines to help if you wish.

4. $\frac{2}{7}$ $\frac{6}{7}$ $\frac{4}{7}$

5. $\frac{3}{4}$ $\frac{7}{8}$ $\frac{5}{8}$

6. $\frac{1}{5}$ $\frac{1}{10}$ $\frac{4}{5}$

7. $\frac{6}{12}$ $\frac{1}{3}$ $\frac{3}{3}$

Explain Your Thinking ▶ Suppose you have to order $\frac{2}{3}$, $\frac{1}{4}$, and $\frac{1}{2}$. What is the smallest denominator you can use to write equivalent fractions for $\frac{2}{3}$, $\frac{1}{4}$, and $\frac{1}{2}$?

Practice and Problem Solving

Compare. Write >, <, or = for each ●.

8. $\frac{2}{6}$ ● $\frac{4}{6}$

$\frac{1}{6}$	$\frac{1}{6}$			
$\frac{1}{6}$	$\frac{1}{6}$	$\frac{1}{6}$	$\frac{1}{6}$	

9. $\frac{1}{2}$ ● $\frac{2}{4}$

$\frac{1}{2}$		
$\frac{1}{4}$	$\frac{1}{4}$	

10. $\frac{1}{4}$ ● $\frac{3}{8}$

$\frac{1}{4}$					
$\frac{1}{8}$	$\frac{1}{8}$	$\frac{1}{8}$			

11. $\frac{6}{7}$ ● $\frac{5}{7}$

12. $\frac{4}{9}$ ● $\frac{1}{3}$

13. $\frac{3}{5}$ ● $\frac{2}{10}$

14. $\frac{2}{3}$ ● $\frac{1}{4}$

Mental Math Write >, <, or = for each ●.

15. 1 ● $\frac{5}{6}$

16. $\frac{2}{4}$ ● $\frac{2}{8}$

17. $\frac{3}{5}$ ● $\frac{3}{8}$

18. 2 ● $\frac{4}{8}$

19. $\frac{2}{5}$ ● $\frac{4}{5}$

20. $\frac{6}{7}$ ● 1

21. $\frac{2}{2}$ ● 2

22. $\frac{3}{3}$ ● $\frac{6}{6}$

Order the fractions from least to greatest.

23. $\frac{1}{5}$ $\frac{4}{5}$ $\frac{2}{5}$

24. $\frac{5}{7}$ $\frac{2}{7}$ $\frac{6}{7}$

25. $\frac{4}{8}$ $\frac{7}{8}$ $\frac{1}{8}$

26. $\frac{7}{12}$ $\frac{10}{12}$ $\frac{3}{4}$

27. $\frac{5}{8}$ $\frac{3}{4}$ $\frac{1}{4}$

28. $\frac{2}{3}$ $\frac{2}{6}$ $\frac{3}{6}$

29. $\frac{1}{2}$ $\frac{4}{6}$ $\frac{5}{12}$

30. $\frac{3}{4}$ $\frac{1}{2}$ $\frac{1}{3}$

Solve.

31. **Write About It** Why is it easier to compare fractions with the same rather than different denominators?

32. **Analyze** Explain why you can compare $\frac{2}{12}$ and $\frac{2}{16}$ without finding equivalent fractions.

Data The table at the right shows results from the longest-green-bean contest at a fair. Use the table for Problems 33–35.

33. Who entered a longer green bean, Sara or Brian?

34. List the lengths of the green beans in order from shortest to longest.

35. Which people entered green beans that were less than $\frac{2}{3}$ yd long?

Longest Green Beans at County Fair	
Name	**Length**
Sara	$\frac{5}{6}$ yd
Tom	$\frac{1}{2}$ yd
Brian	$\frac{7}{12}$ yd

Extra Practice See page 513, Set C.

Social Studies Connection
Flags of Africa

Five students were studying African countries. They each drew and colored the flag of the country they were studying. From the clues, decide who colored each flag.

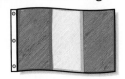

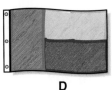
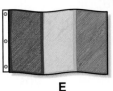

A   B   C   D   E

- José said, "Inga's flag and my flag are both $\frac{1}{3}$ red, with the red stripe on the right."

- Heather said, "My flag has the same colors as José's flag and Ken's flag."

- Ken said, "The thirds on my flag are not the same as the thirds on all the other flags."

- Maribeth said, "My flag is $\frac{2}{3}$ green."

Challenge Do research to find the name of each country being studied.

WEEKLY WR READER eduplace.com/map

Check your understanding of Lessons 1–4.

Write a fraction for the part that is shaded. Then write a fraction for the part that is not shaded. (Lesson 1)

1.

2.

3.

4.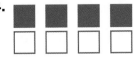

Write each fraction in simplest form. Then write another equivalent fraction. (Lessons 2–3)

5. $\frac{4}{6}$ 6. $\frac{9}{12}$ 7. $\frac{10}{20}$ 8. $\frac{8}{18}$

Order the fractions from greatest to least. (Lesson 4)

9. $\frac{3}{4}$ $\frac{7}{8}$ $\frac{5}{8}$ 10. $\frac{2}{5}$ $\frac{3}{10}$ $\frac{7}{10}$

Find Part of a Number

Objective Find a fractional part of a number.

Learn About It

Maria and her mother use 20 apples to make apple pies. One fourth of the apples are green and three fourths are red. How many apples are red?

How can you find $\frac{3}{4}$ of 20?

Different Ways to Find $\frac{3}{4}$ of 20

Way ➊ You can use a model.

STEP 1 The denominator, 4, tells you to separate the 20 counters into 4 equal groups.

STEP 2 The numerator, 3, tells you to count the number in 3 groups.

$\frac{3}{4}$ of 20 is 15.

4 equal groups

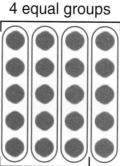

3 groups = 15

Way ➋ You can use division and multiplication.

STEP 1 Divide 20 by 4 to find the number in each group.

number of apples   number of equal groups

$20 \div 4 = 5$

number in each group

STEP 2 Multiply the number in each group by 3.

$5 \times 3 = 15$

$\frac{3}{4}$ of 20 is 15.

Solution: 15 apples are red.

Guided Practice

Find the fractional part of each number.

Ask Yourself
• How many equal parts are there?
• How many equal parts do I need to count?

1. ●●●●
    ●●●●

$\frac{1}{4}$ of 8

2. ▲▲▲▲▲
    ▲▲▲▲▲

$\frac{3}{5}$ of 10

3. $\frac{2}{3}$ of 9   **4.** $\frac{1}{6}$ of 24   **5.** $\frac{2}{5}$ of 20   **6.** $\frac{3}{4}$ of 16   **7.** $\frac{4}{5}$ of 15

Explain Your Thinking ▶ How does knowing $\frac{1}{5}$ of 10 help you find $\frac{2}{5}$ of 10?

Practice and Problem Solving

Find the fractional part of each number.

8. $\frac{1}{2}$ of 14   **9.** $\frac{2}{3}$ of 30   **10.** $\frac{1}{4}$ of 12   **11.** $\frac{3}{7}$ of 14   **12.** $\frac{2}{10}$ of 10

13. $\frac{3}{5}$ of 20   **14.** $\frac{7}{9}$ of 18   **15.** $\frac{3}{8}$ of 16   **16.** $\frac{5}{6}$ of 12   **17.** $\frac{3}{10}$ of 100

Solve.

18. Mina has 21 apples. Two thirds of the apples are green. How many of the apples are green?

19. Keisha's family eats $\frac{3}{4}$ of an 8-piece apple pie. How many pieces are not eaten?

20. **Analyze** Mike's dad has 100 quarters. He tells Mike that he can have either $\frac{3}{4}$ or $\frac{6}{10}$ of them. Which should Mike choose? Explain.

21. **Represent** Show why $\frac{2}{3}$ of 9 and $\frac{1}{3}$ of 18 name the same number. Use counters or draw a picture to explain your reasoning.

Mixed Review and Test Prep

Open Response

Solve. (Ch. 6, Lessons 4, 6; Ch. 9, Lessons 2, 3)

22. 67×8 **23.** 105×6

24. $504 \div 7$ **25.** $\$5.60 \div 5$

26. $317 \div 9$ **27.** $\$7.24 \div 4$

Multiple Choice

28. Donya is $\frac{1}{4}$ as old as her sister, Amy. If Amy is 24, how old is Donya? (Ch. 19, Lesson 5)

   A 4   **B** 6   **C** 8   **D** 14

Extra Practice See page 513, Set D.

Audio Tutor 2/20 Listen and Understand

Problem-Solving Strategy
Draw a Picture

Objective Draw a picture to solve a problem.

Problem Annie Aardvark's dinner was all ants. One half of the ants she ate were black, $\frac{1}{4}$ were red, and 6 were brown. How many ants did Annie eat?

UNDERSTAND

This is what you know.

- $\frac{1}{2}$ were black ants.
- $\frac{1}{4}$ were red ants.
- 6 were brown ants.

PLAN

You can draw a picture to help you solve the problem.

SOLVE

Draw a picture.

- Draw a rectangle. Show the information given in the problem.
- Use what you know about fractions to solve the problem.

You know $\frac{1}{2} = \frac{2}{4}$ and $1 = \frac{4}{4}$.

So 6 brown ants are $\frac{1}{4}$ of all the ants.

Then 4×6, or 24, is the total number of ants.

Why do you multiply by 4?

Solution: Annie ate 24 ants.

All Ants		
$\frac{1}{2}$	$\frac{1}{4}$	6

black ants red ants brown ants

All Ants			
$\frac{1}{4}$	$\frac{1}{4}$	$\frac{1}{4}$	$\frac{1}{4}$

black ants red ants 6 brown ants

LOOK BACK

Look back at the problem.

Does the solution make sense?

Guided Practice

Use the Ask Yourself questions to help you solve each problem.

1. Spencer Spider bought insects. Two sixths were centipedes, $\frac{1}{2}$ were millipedes, and 12 were flies. How many insects did he buy?

2. Betty Bat has a bug collection. Two eighths are flies, $\frac{3}{8}$ are locusts, and 9 are moths. How many flies are in her collection?

   (Hint) The answer is **not** 24.

Ask Yourself

UNDERSTAND — **What facts do I know?**

PLAN — **Can I draw a picture?**

SOLVE —
- **Did I separate the rectangle into equal parts?**
- **Did I label the parts?**
- **Did I find the number each part represents?**

LOOK BACK — **Did I solve the problem?**

Independent Practice

Draw a picture to solve each problem.

3. Rodney spent half of his money on paint and $\frac{1}{6}$ on art paper. He had $8 left. What was his starting amount?

4. All the students in Ann's art class must complete one final project. Three eighths painted, $\frac{1}{4}$ drew charcoal sketches, and 12 made pottery. How many students are there in Ann's class?

5. Tina collects colorful beads. Five twelfths are green, $\frac{1}{3}$ are red, and 9 are yellow. How many beads are red?

6. Carl made fruit punch. Half of it was orange juice, $\frac{2}{6}$ was cranberry juice, and 12 ounces was ginger ale. How many ounces of punch did he make?

Go On

Mixed Problem Solving

Solve. Show your work. Tell what strategy you used.

7. **Money** Suppose you had only nickels and dimes in your pocket. Then you lost 10 coins that totaled 85 cents. How many of each coin did you lose?

8. Rico spent half of his money on admission to the museum and $\frac{1}{4}$ on lunch. He has $5 left. What was his starting amount?

9. Colleen wants a computer game that costs $64. She has $30. If she saves $5 a week, how many weeks will it take until she has enough money to buy the game?

Data Use the graph to solve Problems 10–13.

Each week Steve earns money by helping in art classes for younger students. The graph shows what he does with his money each week.

10. How much money does Steve earn each week?

11. How much more money does Steve spend on food than on art supplies?

12. Steve spends $\frac{1}{2}$ of his food money at school. How much does he spend on food at school?

13. After 9 weeks, how much money will Steve have earned? How much money will he have saved?

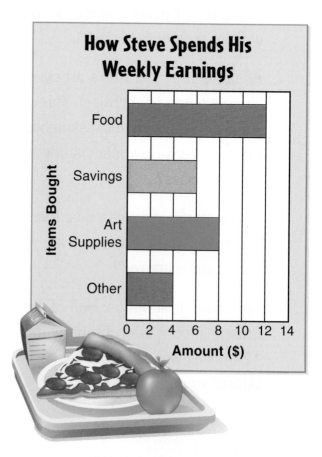

How Steve Spends His Weekly Earnings

Problem Solving on Tests

Multiple Choice
Choose the letter of the correct answer.

1. Tina bought some bottled water for a bike trip. She drank 3 bottles. Then she bought 5 more. After drinking another 2 bottles, she had 4 bottles left. How many bottles of water did Tina start with?

   A 14   c 10

   B 12   D 4

   (Chapter 9, Lesson 5)

2. What is the next likely picture in this pattern?

   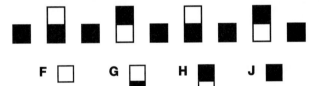

   (Chapter 16, Lesson 6)

Open Response
Solve each problem.

3. In a picture of turtles and parrots, there are 7 animals with 22 legs altogether. How many parrots are in the picture?

   Represent Support your solution with a picture or table.

   (Chapter 13, Lesson 3)

4. Tommy has 36 photos. He wants to put the photos in an album. He puts 4 photos on each page. How many pages will he use?

   Represent Write an equation that can be used to find the number of pages he will need.

   (Chapter 4, Lesson 2)

Extended Response

5. Josh is making a new habitat for his pet turtle. He has a glass aquarium that measures 6 in. long by 12 in. wide by 8 in. high.

   a. One of the long sides of the aquarium was removed and replaced with a piece of screen. What is the area of the screen?

   b. Josh has a plastic dish that measures 4 in. long by 6 in. wide by 1 in. deep. He plans to put $\frac{1}{2}$ inch of water in it so the turtle can swim. What will the volume of the water in the dish be? Show how you know.

   c. After Josh places the dish in the aquarium, he plans to put a mixture of sand and soil around it to the top of the dish. The base of the aquarium will be completely covered. What is the volume of sand and soil that he will use? Explain.

   d. Decide what else Josh might add to the aquarium. Tell why he should add these things.

   (Chapter 18, Lesson 7)

Education Place

See **eduplace.com/map**
for more Test-Taking Tips.

Chapter 19 Lesson 6   **507**

Audio Tutor 2/21 Listen and Understand

Mixed Numbers and Improper Fractions

Objective Write mixed numbers and improper fractions.

Vocabulary

mixed number

improper fraction

Learn About It

There are two whole waffles and one fourth of a waffle. There are nine fourths waffles.

You can write the amount of waffles as a mixed number or as an improper fraction.

▶ A **mixed number** is made up of a whole number and a fraction.

whole number → $2\frac{1}{4}$ ← fraction

To write a mixed number, count the wholes and parts.

$$\frac{4}{4} + \frac{4}{4} + \frac{1}{4} = 2\frac{1}{4}$$

▶ An **improper fraction** has a numerator that is greater than or equal to its denominator.

$\frac{9}{4}$ ← improper fraction

To write an improper fraction, count the parts.

$$\frac{9}{4}$$

508

Here's how to change from one form to another.

To change an improper fraction to a mixed number, you can divide.	To change a mixed number to an improper fraction, you can multiply and add, as shown below.
The fraction bar stands for "divided by." So $\frac{9}{4}$ means "9 divided by 4."	

$$\begin{array}{r} 2 \\ 4\overline{)9} \\ -\ 8 \\ \hline 1 \end{array}$$ ← number of wholes

← number of fourths

So $\frac{9}{4}$ is equal to $2\frac{1}{4}$.

$$2\frac{1}{4} = \frac{9}{4}$$ ← (4 × 2) + 1
← denominator stays the same

So $2\frac{1}{4} = \frac{9}{4}$.

Other Examples

Improper Fractions Equal to Whole Numbers

A.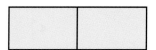

$\frac{2}{2} = 1$, because $2 \div 2 = 1$

B.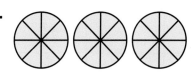

$\frac{24}{8} = 3$, because $24 \div 8 = 3$

Guided Practice

Write an improper fraction for the shaded parts. Then write each as a mixed number or as a whole number.

1.

2.

3.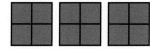

4.

Ask Yourself
- Into how many equal parts is each figure divided?
- How many wholes are represented?

Explain Your Thinking ▶ How can you tell whether a fraction can be rewritten as a mixed number or as a whole number?

Go On

Practice and Problem Solving

Write an improper fraction and a mixed number or whole number to describe the shaded parts.

5.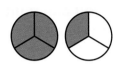

6.

7.

Write a mixed number and an improper fraction for each letter.

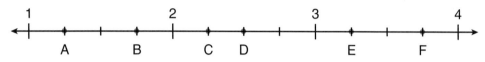

8. A
9. C
10. F
11. D
12. B
13. E

Copy and complete each table.

	Division	Improper Fraction	Mixed Number
14.	16 ÷ 3	$\frac{16}{3}$	
15.	19 ÷ 2		$9\frac{1}{2}$
16.		$\frac{11}{9}$	
17.			$1\frac{7}{8}$

	Division	Improper Fraction	Mixed Number
18.		$\frac{28}{7}$	
19.			$4\frac{4}{5}$
20.	10 ÷ 2		
21.		$\frac{15}{6}$	

Solve.

22. Mr. Alvarez brought 5 oranges to a picnic. All the oranges were cut into halves. Each person ate one half of an orange, and there were no oranges left over. How many people ate oranges?

23. Michael is 5 years older than Elizabeth. Elizabeth is 8 years younger than José. Meredith is 2 years younger than José. If Meredith is 12 years old, how old is Michael?

24. **Reasoning** Ms. Carter made pies for the picnic. She brought enough so that each person could have $\frac{1}{8}$ of a pie. What is the least number of pies she could have made if 20 people were at the picnic?

510

Extra Practice See page 513, Set E.

Open Response

Find the fractional part of each number.

25. $\frac{2}{3}$ of 15

★ ★ ★ ★ ★
★ ★ ★ ★ ★
★ ★ ★ ★ ★

26. $\frac{5}{6}$ of 18

(Ch. 19, Lesson 5)

Solve.

32. Mr. Cronin's class made 4 pecan pies for the school bake sale. Each of the pies is cut into 8 equal pieces. Mr. Cronin bought 10 pieces of pie for a party. What fraction of 1 pie did he buy? Write your answer as an improper fraction in simplest form and as a mixed number.

(Ch. 19, Lesson 7)

Math Reasoning
Pie Pieces

Problem Solving

You can use these pies to help you round fractions.

$\frac{1}{8}$ is close to 0.
Round $\frac{1}{8}$ to 0.

$\frac{3}{8}$ is close to $\frac{1}{2}$.
Round $\frac{3}{8}$ to $\frac{1}{2}$.

$\frac{7}{8}$ is close to 1.
Round $\frac{7}{8}$ to 1.

Write whether the fraction rounds to 0, $\frac{1}{2}$, or 1.

1. $\frac{1}{10}$

2. $\frac{5}{6}$

3. $\frac{4}{5}$

4. $\frac{2}{6}$

5. $\frac{3}{5}$

6. $\frac{9}{8}$

7. $\frac{4}{6}$

8. $\frac{4}{10}$

Chapter Review/Test

VOCABULARY

Choose the best term to complete each sentence.

1. The number 7 in $\frac{4}{7}$ is the _____ of the fraction.

2. If the only number that divides both the numerator and the denominator is 1, then the fraction is in _____.

3. If the denominator is less than the numerator, then the number is a(n) _____.

CONCEPTS AND SKILLS

Draw a picture to show each. (Lesson 1, pp. 490–491; Lesson 7, pp. 508–510)

4. $\frac{6}{7}$
5. $\frac{8}{8}$
6. $1\frac{1}{3}$
7. $\frac{14}{5}$

Write each fraction in simplest form. Then write another equivalent fraction. (Lessons 2–3, pp. 492–497)

8. $\frac{6}{8}$
9. $\frac{3}{9}$
10. $\frac{4}{10}$
11. $\frac{12}{20}$

Compare. Write >, <, or = for each ⬤. (Lesson 4, pp. 498–500)

12. $\frac{3}{10}$ ⬤ $\frac{7}{10}$
13. $\frac{5}{25}$ ⬤ $\frac{1}{5}$
14. $\frac{5}{8}$ ⬤ $\frac{6}{16}$
15. $\frac{2}{2}$ ⬤ $\frac{5}{6}$

Find the fractional part of each number. (Lesson 5, pp. 502–503)

16. $\frac{3}{5}$ of 15
17. $\frac{1}{4}$ of 8
18. $\frac{1}{3}$ of 21

PROBLEM SOLVING

Solve. (Lesson 6, pp. 504–507)

19. Mari collects books. One third of her books are fiction, $\frac{1}{6}$ are nature books, and 12 are mysteries. How many books are in Mari's collection?

20. Cody bought some sports cards. One half were baseball cards, 18 were soccer cards, and $\frac{1}{8}$ were football cards. How many sports cards did Cody buy?

Write About It

Show You Understand

Bob wrote $\frac{13}{5}$ as a mixed number.

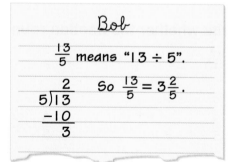

Explain what Bob did wrong. Then solve the problem correctly.

Extra Practice

Set A (Lesson 1, pp. 490–491)

Write the fraction for the shaded part.

1.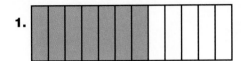

2. ★★★★
   ★☆☆☆

3. ⬤

Set B (Lesson 3, pp. 494–497)

Write each fraction in simplest form. Then write another equivalent fraction.

1. $\frac{2}{16}$ 2. $\frac{6}{12}$ 3. $\frac{4}{20}$ 4. $\frac{3}{9}$ 5. $\frac{10}{15}$ 6. $\frac{2}{14}$

Set C (Lesson 4, pp. 498–500)

Compare. Write >, <, or = for each ⬤.

1. $\frac{2}{5}$ ⬤ $\frac{3}{5}$ 2. $\frac{1}{2}$ ⬤ $\frac{1}{6}$ 3. $\frac{5}{8}$ ⬤ $\frac{3}{4}$ 4. $\frac{2}{3}$ ⬤ $\frac{3}{9}$

Order the fractions from least to greatest.

5. $\frac{4}{10}$ $\frac{7}{10}$ $\frac{9}{10}$ 6. $\frac{3}{4}$ $\frac{2}{8}$ $\frac{2}{4}$ 7. $\frac{2}{5}$ $\frac{4}{15}$ $\frac{2}{3}$ 8. $\frac{1}{2}$ $\frac{3}{7}$ $\frac{5}{14}$

Set D (Lesson 5, pp. 502–503)

Find the fractional part of each number.

1. $\frac{2}{4}$ of 16   2. $\frac{2}{3}$ of 21   3. $\frac{1}{2}$ of 18   4. $\frac{3}{5}$ of 15   5. $\frac{3}{4}$ of 12

Set E (Lesson 7, pp. 508–510)

Write each as an improper fraction.

1. $3\frac{1}{5}$ 2. $4\frac{3}{4}$ 3. $2\frac{3}{7}$ 4. $5\frac{1}{2}$ 5. $1\frac{4}{9}$ 6. $3\frac{2}{3}$

Write a mixed number or a whole number for each improper fraction.

7. $\frac{11}{3}$ 8. $\frac{9}{2}$ 9. $\frac{21}{6}$ 10. $\frac{20}{3}$ 11. $\frac{8}{4}$ 12. $\frac{16}{5}$

INVESTIGATION

Using Data

The chart on the right lists Family Fun Day activities. Plan a day for a family that likes outdoor activities. Plan for at least 5 hours. Tell the total time for activities and for eating.

Family Fun Day

Activity	Time
Hike to River	$\frac{1}{2}$ hour
Rapids Ride	$2\frac{1}{2}$ hours
Lunch or Snack	$\frac{3}{4}$ hour
Canoe Ride	$1\frac{1}{4}$ hours
Hike to Camp	$\frac{3}{4}$ hour

 Use What You Know

Use this page to review and remember
what you need to know for this chapter.

VOCABULARY

Choose the best term to complete each sentence.

1. The fraction $\frac{1}{3}$ is in ____.

2. A number made up of a whole number and a
   fraction is called a ____.

3. Fractions that name the same amount are ____.

Vocabulary

mixed number

simplest form

whole number

equivalent fractions

CONCEPTS AND SKILLS

Write two equivalent fractions for each.

4. $\frac{3}{4}$ 5. $\frac{1}{3}$ 6. $\frac{4}{8}$ 7. $\frac{2}{5}$ 8. $\frac{1}{8}$

9. $\frac{4}{6}$ 10. $\frac{8}{8}$ 11. $\frac{4}{14}$ 12. $\frac{5}{9}$ 13. $\frac{2}{9}$

Write an improper fraction to describe each picture.
Then write the fraction as a mixed number or whole number.

14. 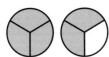   15. 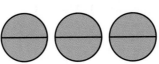   16.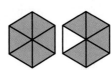

Write a fraction or mixed number for each.
Then write the answer in simplest form.

17. six eighths   18. ten fourths   19. one and three sixths

Write About It ▶

20. Which is greater, $\frac{1}{3}$ of 12 or $\frac{1}{4}$ of 20?
    Use pictures, symbols, or words to
    explain your answer.

Facts Practice, See Page 668.

Add and Subtract Fractions With Like Denominators

Objective Add and subtract fractions that have the same denominators.

Learn About It

Adam and Josh took turns rowing their boat around the pond. Adam rowed $\frac{4}{8}$ of a mile, and Josh rowed $\frac{2}{8}$ of a mile. How far did they row together?

You can add the fractions with **like denominators** to find the distance they rowed.

Add. $\frac{4}{8} + \frac{2}{8} = \blacksquare$

STEP 1 Since the denominators are the same, you can add the numerators and keep the same denominator.

$$\frac{4}{8} + \frac{2}{8} = \frac{6}{8}$$ ← Add numerators.
← Denominator stays the same.

$$\frac{4}{8} + \frac{2}{8} = \frac{6}{8}$$

STEP 2 Write the sum in simplest form.

$$\frac{6}{8} \overset{\div 2}{\underset{\div 2}{=}} \frac{3}{4}$$

$$\frac{6}{8} = \frac{3}{4}$$

Solution: Together they rowed $\frac{3}{4}$ of a mile.

Other Examples

A. Sum equal to 1

$$\begin{array}{r} \frac{2}{6} \\ + \frac{4}{6} \\ \hline \frac{6}{6} = 1 \end{array}$$

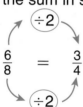

$$\frac{2}{6} \qquad \frac{4}{6}$$

B. Sum greater than 1

$$\begin{array}{r} \frac{2}{5} \\ + \frac{4}{5} \\ \hline \frac{6}{5} = 1\frac{1}{5} \end{array}$$

$$\frac{2}{5} \qquad \frac{4}{5}$$

▶ You can also subtract fractions with **like denominators** .

Subtract. $\frac{4}{8} - \frac{2}{8} = $ ▪

STEP 1 Since the denominators are the same, you can subtract the numerators and keep the same denominator.

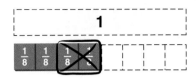

$\frac{4}{8} - \frac{2}{8} = \frac{2}{8}$ ← Subtract numerators.
    ← Denominator stays the same.

$\frac{4}{8} - \frac{2}{8} = \frac{2}{8}$

STEP 2 Write the difference in simplest form.

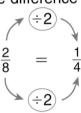

$$\frac{2}{8} = \frac{1}{4}$$

$$\frac{2}{8} = \frac{1}{4}$$

Solution: $\frac{4}{8} - \frac{2}{8} = \frac{1}{4}$

Guided Practice

Add or subtract. Use the fraction pieces to help you.

Ask Yourself
• Should I add or subtract the numerators?
• Do I need to simplify the answer?

1.

$\frac{3}{8} + \frac{3}{8} = $ ▪

2.

$\frac{3}{6} + \frac{4}{6} = $ ▪

3.

$\frac{4}{8} - \frac{1}{8} = $ ▪

4.

$\frac{3}{4} - \frac{2}{4} = $ ▪

5.

$\frac{5}{6} - \frac{3}{6} = $ ▪

Add or subtract. Write your answer in simplest form.

6. $\quad \frac{2}{9} \\ + \frac{4}{9}$

7. $\quad \frac{4}{6} \\ - \frac{2}{6}$

8. $\quad \frac{8}{10} \\ + \frac{9}{10}$

9. $\quad \frac{10}{11} \\ - \frac{5}{11}$

10. $\quad \frac{10}{12} \\ - \frac{4}{12}$

Explain Your Thinking ▶ For like fractions, why can you add or subtract the numerators and keep the same denominator?

Go On

Add or subtract. Write your answer in simplest form.

11.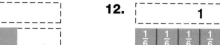

$$\frac{1}{3} + \frac{1}{3} = \blacksquare$$

12.

$$\frac{5}{6} + \frac{2}{6} = \blacksquare$$

13.

$$\frac{7}{8} - \frac{5}{8} = \blacksquare$$

14. $\frac{1}{4}$
$+ \frac{1}{4}$

15. $\frac{3}{8}$
$+ \frac{4}{8}$

16. $\frac{1}{3}$
$+ \frac{2}{3}$

17. $\frac{2}{5}$
$+ \frac{4}{5}$

18. $\frac{2}{10}$
$+ \frac{4}{10}$

19. $\frac{5}{6}$
$- \frac{1}{6}$

20. $\frac{2}{3}$
$- \frac{1}{3}$

21. $\frac{7}{8}$
$- \frac{3}{8}$

22. $\frac{6}{10}$
$- \frac{2}{10}$

23. $\frac{4}{9}$
$- \frac{1}{9}$

24. $\frac{3}{7} + \frac{2}{7}$

25. $\frac{8}{9} - \frac{5}{9}$

26. $\frac{7}{10} + \frac{3}{10}$

27. $\frac{6}{12} - \frac{3}{12}$

28. $\frac{9}{10} - \frac{3}{10}$

29. $\frac{7}{12} + \frac{4}{12}$

30. $\frac{8}{7} - \frac{3}{7}$

31. $\frac{9}{11} + \frac{2}{11}$

Use the triangular sail on the right for Problems 32–36. Show your work. Write each answer in simplest form.

32. What fraction of the sail is either blue or yellow?

33. What fraction of the sail is neither blue nor green?

34. What is the difference between the fraction of the sail that is red and the fraction that is blue?

35. Which colors make up $\frac{7}{8}$ of the sail?

36. **Write About It** There are two answers to the question, "Which two colors make up half of the sail?" Explain why that is true.

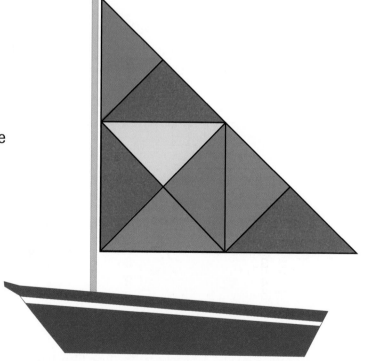

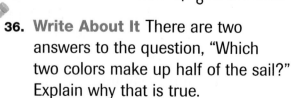

Algebra • Variables Find the value of *n*.

37. $\dfrac{5}{10} + \dfrac{n}{10} = \dfrac{8}{10}$ 38. $\dfrac{n}{5} - \dfrac{4}{5} = \dfrac{1}{5}$ 39. $\dfrac{8}{3} - \dfrac{n}{3} = \dfrac{3}{3}$

40. $\dfrac{5}{9} - \dfrac{n}{9} = \dfrac{0}{9}$ 41. $\dfrac{n}{11} + \dfrac{6}{11} = \dfrac{11}{11}$ 42. $\dfrac{4}{9} + \dfrac{n}{9} = \dfrac{7}{9}$

43. $\dfrac{n}{8} + \dfrac{3}{8} = 1$ 44. $1 - \dfrac{n}{6} = \dfrac{5}{6}$ 45. $\dfrac{n}{5} + \dfrac{3}{5} = \dfrac{11}{5}$

46. $1 - \dfrac{n}{10} = \dfrac{7}{10}$ 47. $\dfrac{9}{12} + \dfrac{n}{12} = 1$ 48. $\dfrac{6}{7} + \dfrac{n}{7} = \dfrac{6}{7}$

 Data Use the table for Problems 49–51.

49. How many miles did Cara swim altogether during the 5 days?

50. Twelve people each donated $1.25 for every fifth of a mile Cara swam. How much money did Cara raise on Monday?

51. **Write About It** How much farther did Cara swim on Thursday than on Wednesday? Explain how you know.

52. Tina has saved $45 to buy binoculars. The 13 bills she has are $1 bills and $5 bills. How many of each kind of bill has she saved?

Cara's Swimming Record

Day	Distance
Monday	$\frac{4}{5}$ mile
Tuesday	$\frac{1}{5}$ mile
Wednesday	$\frac{3}{5}$ mile
Thursday	1 mile
Friday	$\frac{2}{5}$ mile

Mixed Review and Test Prep

Open Response

Match each road sign with the name of its shape. (Ch. 16, Lesson 4)

53. octagon   54. triangle   55. pentagon

A   B   C

56. Kimberly and her 2 friends ate an entire pizza that was cut into 6 equal slices. They each ate an equal amount. What fraction of the pizza did her friends eat?

Explain how you got your answer.
(Ch. 20, Lesson 1)

Extra Practice See page 539, Set A.

Add and Subtract Mixed Numbers

Objective Add and subtract mixed numbers with like denominators.

Learn About It

Steve and Aliya used this recipe to make trail mix for a hike. How many cups of peanuts and raisins did they use in all?

Trail Mix Recipe
$1\frac{3}{4}$ cups peanuts
$\frac{1}{4}$ cup chocolate chips
$1\frac{1}{4}$ cups raisins

Add. $1\frac{3}{4} + 1\frac{1}{4} = \blacksquare$

 STEP 1 Add the fractions.

$$1\frac{3}{4}$$
$$+ 1\frac{1}{4}$$
$$\overline{\frac{4}{4}}$$

 STEP 2 Add the whole numbers.

$$1\frac{3}{4}$$
$$+ 1\frac{1}{4}$$
$$\overline{2\frac{4}{4}} = 2 + 1 = 3$$

> Write the answer in simplest form.

Solution: They used 3 cups of peanuts and raisins.

▶ How many more cups of peanuts than chocolate chips did they use?

Subtract. $1\frac{3}{4} - \frac{1}{4} = \blacksquare$

 STEP 1 Subtract the fractions.

$$1\frac{3}{4}$$
$$- \frac{1}{4}$$
$$\overline{\frac{2}{4}}$$

 STEP 2 Subtract the whole numbers.

$$1\frac{3}{4}$$
$$- \frac{1}{4}$$
$$\overline{1\frac{2}{4}} = 1\frac{1}{2}$$

> Write the answer in simplest form.

Solution: They used $1\frac{1}{2}$ more cups of peanuts.

Guided Practice

Add or subtract. Write your answer in simplest form.

1. $2\frac{1}{2}$
    $+ 1$

2. $3\frac{7}{8}$
    $- \frac{3}{8}$

3. $5\frac{2}{3}$
    $- 4\frac{1}{3}$

4. $4\frac{3}{4}$
    $+ 2\frac{3}{4}$

Ask Yourself
- Did I add or subtract the fractions first?
- Is my answer in simplest form?

Explain Your Thinking ▶ Look back at Exercise 4. Describe how you found the sum in simplest form.

Extra Help at **eduplace.com/map**

Add or subtract. Write your answer in simplest form.

5. $3\frac{1}{3}$
   $+ 1\frac{2}{3}$

6. $1\frac{5}{9}$
   $- \frac{3}{9}$

7. $4\frac{1}{6}$
   $+ 3\frac{2}{6}$

8. $6\frac{1}{2}$
   $- 5$

9. $4\frac{2}{7}$
   $+ 2\frac{5}{7}$

10. $6\frac{3}{4}$
    $- 3\frac{1}{4}$

11. $5\frac{1}{9}$
    $+ 3\frac{2}{9}$

12. $7\frac{5}{6}$
    $- 2\frac{1}{6}$

13. $3\frac{3}{5}$
    $+ \frac{1}{5}$

14. $2\frac{7}{8}$
    $- 1\frac{7}{8}$

𝒳 Algebra • Functions Follow the rule to complete each table.

Rule: Add $1\frac{2}{5}$.	
Input	Output
15. $4\frac{4}{5}$	■
16. ■	$5\frac{2}{5}$

Rule: Subtract $2\frac{1}{6}$.	
Input	Output
17. $6\frac{4}{6}$	■
18. ■	$5\frac{2}{6}$

Rule: Subtract $\frac{2}{3}$.	
Input	Output
19. ■	5
20. $3\frac{2}{3}$	■

21. How many cups of trail mix does the recipe on page 520 make? If it is doubled, how many cups will be made?

22. Pete's water bottle holds $4\frac{3}{4}$ cups of water. He drinks $3\frac{1}{4}$ cups of water while hiking. How much water is left?

23. **Write About It** Use words and diagrams to explain how to subtract $2\frac{4}{8}$ from $4\frac{6}{8}$. Write the difference in simplest form.

24. Mary made $4\frac{3}{4}$ cups of a snack. She used 2 cups of nuts, $1\frac{1}{4}$ cups of granola, and some raisins. How many cups of raisins did she use?

Mixed Review and Test Prep ✓

Open Response

Solve. (Ch. 7, Lesson 4; Ch. 8, Lesson 2)

25. 25×19

26. 16×23

27. 64×41

28. $35 \div 3$

29. $67 \div 2$

30. $48 \div 4$

31. $85 \div 5$

32. 36×28

33. 15×27

34. $84 \div 4$

Multiple Choice

35. Joey took 2 plane trips. The first lasted $5\frac{2}{3}$ hours. The second lasted $2\frac{2}{3}$ hours. How much longer was his first trip? (Ch. 20, Lesson 2)

   A 2 hours

   B 3 hours

   C $3\frac{1}{3}$ hours

   D $8\frac{1}{3}$ hours

Extra Practice See page 539, Set B.

Problem-Solving Application
Decide How to Write the Quotient

Objective Decide how to write the quotient to solve a problem.

You can write the solution to a division problem in different ways.
You should choose the way that makes the most sense.

▶ **Sometimes the remainder is the answer.**

When 23 students went to the safari park, a parent
went with each group of 4 students. The remaining
students went with the teacher. How many students
went with the teacher?

$$\begin{array}{r} 5\ R3 \\ 4\overline{)23} \\ -20 \\ \hline 3 \end{array}$$

The remainder is the number of students that went with the teacher. So the remainder is the answer.

Solution: 3 students went with the teacher.

▶ **Sometimes you need to write the quotient as a mixed number.**

A parent gave 5 oranges to the 4 students in
his group. If the students shared the oranges
equally, what did each student receive?

$$\begin{array}{r} 1\frac{1}{4} \\ 4\overline{)5} \\ -4 \\ \hline 1 \end{array}$$

It is possible to split an orange into parts. So write the quotient as a mixed number.

Solution: Each student received $1\frac{1}{4}$ oranges.

Look Back Why couldn't you write the quotient in the first
problem as a mixed number?

Use the Ask Yourself questions to help you solve each problem.

1. Fred has $10 to ride the jungle train at the zoo. Each ride costs $3. How many rides can he take? How much money will he have left?

2. For lunch at the park, 8 students shared 12 sandwiches. Each student ate the same amount. If all of the sandwiches were eaten, how many sandwiches did each student eat?

    Hint Can you eat a fractional part of a sandwich?

Independent Practice

Solve. Explain how you decided to write each quotient.

3. An animal keeper at the park had 34 fish for the seals to share. The fish came packed 6 to a box. How many full boxes of fish did the animal keeper have?

4. The class learned that 98 pounds of alfalfa is used to feed the 8 rhinoceros at the park. If each rhinoceros is fed the same amount, how many pounds of alfalfa does each rhinoceros eat?

5. The zoo shop has colorful bookmarks for $2 each and animal books for $4 each. How many sets of bookmarks and books can be bought with $22? How much change would be left over?

6. **Analyze** Tom has $15. Camel rides cost $4. Pony rides cost $2. Tom rode each animal an equal number of times. He had enough change to ride one of the animals again. Which animal did he ride again?

7. **Write Your Own** Write two word problems. In one of the problems, the answer must be the remainder. In the other, the quotient must be written as a mixed number.

Estimate With Fractions

Objective Estimate sums of fractions.

Learn About It

Carlos wants to hike at least a mile. Should he take Falls Trail or Mine Trail?

You can estimate to solve this problem. One way to estimate the sum of two fractions is by comparing each addend to $\frac{1}{2}$.

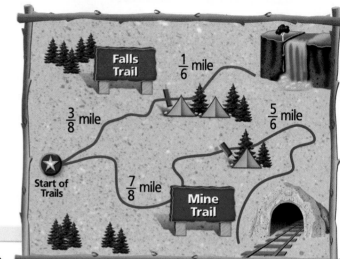

▶ The length of Falls Trail is $\frac{3}{8}$ mile + $\frac{1}{6}$ mile.

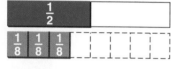

$\frac{3}{8}$ is less than $\frac{1}{2}$.　　$\frac{1}{6}$ is less than $\frac{1}{2}$.

- When both addends are less than $\frac{1}{2}$, their sum is less than 1.

$\frac{3}{8} + \frac{1}{6}$ is less than 1.

So the length of Falls Trail is less than 1 mile.

▶ The length of Mine Trail is $\frac{7}{8}$ mile + $\frac{5}{6}$ mile.

　　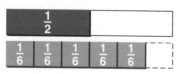

$\frac{7}{8}$ is greater than $\frac{1}{2}$.　　$\frac{5}{6}$ is greater than $\frac{1}{2}$.

- When both addends are greater than $\frac{1}{2}$, their sum is greater than 1.

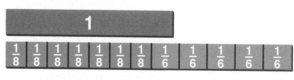

$\frac{7}{8} + \frac{5}{6}$ is greater than 1.

So the length of Mine Trail is greater than 1 mile.

Solution: Carlos should hike Mine Trail.

Estimate each sum. Write *greater than 1* or *less than 1*.

1. $\frac{1}{3} + \frac{1}{4}$ 2. $\frac{3}{4} + \frac{5}{8}$ 3. $\frac{1}{8} + \frac{3}{10}$ 4. $\frac{5}{9} + \frac{2}{3}$

Ask Yourself
• Are both fractions less than $\frac{1}{2}$?
• Are both fractions greater than $\frac{1}{2}$?

Explain Your Thinking ▶ What can you say about the sum of $\frac{3}{4}$ and $\frac{2}{5}$?

Practice and Problem Solving

Estimate each sum. Write *greater than 1* or *less than 1*.

5. $\frac{5}{8} + \frac{7}{10}$ 6. $\frac{3}{8} + \frac{3}{9}$ 7. $\frac{1}{8} + \frac{1}{3}$ 8. $\frac{2}{5} + \frac{2}{5}$ 9. $\frac{4}{5} + \frac{8}{9}$

10. $\frac{4}{9} + \frac{2}{5}$ 11. $\frac{5}{6} + \frac{7}{8}$ 12. $\frac{3}{10} + \frac{3}{8}$ 13. $\frac{1}{2} + \frac{3}{4}$ 14. $\frac{1}{2} + \frac{1}{3}$

Estimate each sum. Write > or < for each ●.

15. $\frac{1}{3} + \frac{3}{8}$ ● $\frac{3}{4} + \frac{5}{8}$ 16. $\frac{3}{8} + \frac{4}{9}$ ● $\frac{2}{3} + \frac{4}{6}$ 17. $\frac{5}{6} + \frac{5}{8}$ ● $\frac{5}{12} + \frac{5}{15}$

18. $\frac{5}{6} + \frac{7}{10}$ ● $\frac{5}{12} + \frac{1}{3}$ 19. $\frac{5}{8} + \frac{3}{4}$ ● $\frac{1}{5} + \frac{2}{10}$ 20. $\frac{2}{5} + \frac{1}{6}$ ● $\frac{4}{5} + \frac{6}{9}$

📊 **Data** Use the table at the right to solve Problems 21–24.

21. On what day did Jen run less than 1 mile?

22. On what day did Jen run more than a mile?

23. How many miles did Jen run on Day 3?

24. On Day 3, how much farther did Jen run in the evening than in the morning?

Jen's Running Log

	Morning	Evening
Day 1	$\frac{1}{4}$ mile	$\frac{3}{8}$ mile
Day 2	$\frac{4}{5}$ mile	$\frac{7}{10}$ mile
Day 3	$\frac{1}{3}$ mile	$\frac{2}{3}$ mile

Mixed Review and Test Prep

Open Response

Find each product or quotient.

(Ch. 7, Lesson 4; Ch. 8, Lesson 2)

25. 21×31 26. 84×42

27. $78 \div 7$ 28. $37 \div 3$

Multiple Choice

29. Which sum is greater than 1?

(Ch. 20, Lesson 4)

A $\frac{1}{3} + \frac{2}{5}$ C $\frac{3}{8} + \frac{1}{9}$

B $\frac{2}{7} + \frac{4}{10}$ D $\frac{4}{5} + \frac{7}{8}$

Problem-Solving Decision
Choose a Method

Objective Choose a method to solve a problem.

Before you solve a problem with fractions, you need to decide what method to use.

Problem Lionel rode $5\frac{7}{8}$ miles on Saturday. He rode $2\frac{2}{8}$ miles on Monday. How much farther did he ride on Saturday?

Ask Yourself

- Should I use mental math?

$$5\frac{7}{8} - 2\frac{2}{8} = 3\frac{5}{8}$$

- Do I need to use paper and pencil?

○
$$5\frac{7}{8}$$
$$- 2\frac{2}{8}$$
_____
○ $3\frac{5}{8}$ miles

- Does it make sense to use a calculator?

Solution: Lionel rode $3\frac{5}{8}$ miles farther on Saturday.
Which method would you have chosen to solve?

Try These

Solve. Explain which method you chose and why.

1. A group of bicyclists rode $\frac{7}{10}$ mile before lunch and $\frac{2}{10}$ mile after lunch. How much farther did they ride before lunch?

2. In three days a cyclist rode $4\frac{1}{5}$ miles, $3\frac{3}{5}$ miles, and $2\frac{1}{5}$ miles. How many miles did she ride in those three days?

3. Helen won $\frac{1}{4}$ of her bicycle races last year. If she competed in 20 races, how many races did she win?

4. Four professional bicyclists rode 3,280 miles in 41 days. What was the mean number of miles that they rode each day?

Art Connection
Pet Projects

In art class, five students made models of their pets.
Match each model with the student who created it.

- Earl's model is $1\frac{5}{8}$ inches taller than Monica's.

- Bob's model is 2 inches taller than Marla's.

- Charlene's model is $\frac{3}{8}$ inch shorter than Monica's.

- Monica's model is $2\frac{3}{8}$ inches tall.

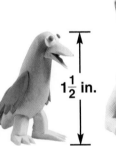
$1\frac{1}{2}$ in.

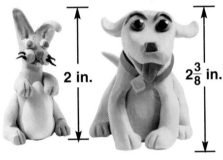
2 in.
$2\frac{3}{8}$ in.

$3\frac{1}{2}$ in.

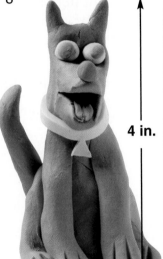
4 in.

WEEKLY (WR) READER eduplace.com/map

Check your understanding of Lessons 1–5.

Find each sum or difference in simplest form. (Lessons 1–2)

1. $\frac{2}{6} + \frac{4}{6}$

2. $\frac{7}{12} - \frac{5}{12}$

3. $3\frac{1}{6} + 5\frac{1}{6}$

4. $4\frac{5}{6} - 1\frac{2}{6}$

Estimate each sum. Write *greater than 1* or *less than 1*. (Lesson 4)

5. $\frac{7}{8} + \frac{3}{4}$

6. $\frac{1}{6} + \frac{1}{4}$

7. $\frac{2}{5} + \frac{3}{10}$

8. $\frac{8}{9} + \frac{3}{5}$

Solve. (Lessons 3, 5)

9. Sarah has $30 to buy books. Each book costs $4. How many books can she buy?

10. An express train leaves at 5:30 P.M. and arrives $1\frac{1}{2}$ hours later. What time does the train arrive?

Extra Practice at **eduplace.com/map**

Add Fractions With Unlike Denominators

Objective Use models to add fractions that have different denominators.

Materials
Fraction Pieces
(Learning Tool 34)

Work Together

You can use fraction pieces to add fractions with different denominators, or **unlike denominators**.

Find $\frac{1}{2} + \frac{1}{4}$.

STEP 1
Use fraction pieces. Place $\frac{1}{2}$ and $\frac{1}{4}$ under 1 whole.

STEP 2
Find like fraction pieces that fit exactly under $\frac{1}{2} + \frac{1}{4}$.

• How many $\frac{1}{4}$ pieces fit exactly under $\frac{1}{2} + \frac{1}{4}$?
• What is $\frac{1}{2} + \frac{1}{4}$?

Now find $\frac{2}{3} + \frac{3}{4}$.

STEP 1
Use fraction pieces to model $\frac{2}{3} + \frac{3}{4}$.

STEP 2
Find like fraction pieces that fit exactly under $\frac{2}{3} + \frac{3}{4}$.

• How many $\frac{1}{12}$ pieces fit exactly under $\frac{2}{3} + \frac{3}{4}$?

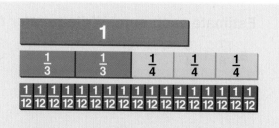

• What is the sum of $\frac{2}{3}$ and $\frac{3}{4}$?

• How do you know that the sum is greater than 1?

• How can you write the sum as a mixed number?

On Your Own

Find each sum. Use fraction pieces to help you.

1.

1

$\frac{1}{3}$	$\frac{1}{3}$	$\frac{1}{6}$

$$\frac{2}{3} + \frac{1}{6}$$

2.

1

$\frac{1}{2}$	$\frac{1}{8}$	$\frac{1}{8}$	$\frac{1}{8}$	$\frac{1}{8}$	$\frac{1}{8}$

$$\frac{1}{2} + \frac{5}{8}$$

3.

1

$\frac{1}{5}$	$\frac{1}{5}$	$\frac{1}{2}$

$$\frac{2}{5} + \frac{1}{2}$$

4. $\frac{3}{4} + \frac{1}{6}$

5. $\frac{1}{3} + \frac{3}{6}$

6. $\frac{3}{8} + \frac{1}{4}$

7. $\frac{5}{12} + \frac{1}{4}$

8. $\frac{5}{6} + \frac{1}{3}$

9. $\frac{2}{3} + \frac{1}{2}$

10. $\frac{1}{3} + \frac{3}{4}$

11. $\frac{3}{5} + \frac{1}{2}$

12. $\frac{5}{6} + \frac{3}{4}$

13. $\frac{3}{4} + \frac{5}{8}$

 Measurement Jan, Erin, and Devin found some arrowheads while hiking. Jan measured her arrowhead. It was $1\frac{1}{4}$ inches long.

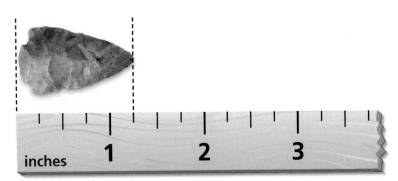

14. Devin found an arrowhead that was $\frac{1}{2}$ inch longer than Jan's. How long was the arrowhead that Devin found?

15. Erin found an arrowhead that was $1\frac{1}{12}$ inches longer than Jan's. How long was the arrowhead that Erin found?

Talk About It • Write About It

You learned how to use models to add fractions with unlike denominators.

16. Explain how adding fractions with unlike denominators is different from adding fractions with like denominators.

17. Explain how you can add $\frac{3}{4}$ and $\frac{1}{3}$. Use words and a picture.

Subtract Fractions With Unlike Denominators

Objective Use models to subtract fractions that have different denominators.

Vocabulary
unlike denominators

Materials
Fraction Pieces
(Learning Tool 34)

Work Together

You can use fraction pieces to subtract fractions that have **unlike denominators**.

Find $\frac{2}{3} - \frac{1}{6}$.

STEP 1

Use fraction pieces.

Place $\frac{1}{6}$ under $\frac{2}{3}$.

The remaining space is the difference.

$\frac{1}{3}$	$\frac{1}{3}$

$\frac{1}{6}$	**?**

STEP 2

Find like fraction pieces that fit exactly in the remaining space.

$\frac{1}{3}$	$\frac{1}{3}$

$\frac{1}{6}$	$\frac{1}{6}$	$\frac{1}{6}$	$\frac{1}{6}$

- How many $\frac{1}{6}$ pieces fill the remaining space?
- What is $\frac{2}{3} - \frac{1}{6}$?

Now find $\frac{3}{4} - \frac{2}{3}$.

STEP 1

Use fraction pieces. Place $\frac{2}{3}$ under $\frac{3}{4}$.
The remaining space is the difference.

$\frac{1}{4}$	$\frac{1}{4}$	$\frac{1}{4}$

| $\frac{1}{3}$ | $\frac{1}{3}$ | **?** |

STEP 2

Use fraction pieces to find equivalent fractions for $\frac{3}{4}$ and $\frac{2}{3}$ that have the same denominators.

| $\frac{1}{4}$ | $\frac{1}{4}$ | $\frac{1}{4}$ |

| $\frac{1}{12}$ $\frac{1}{12}$ $\frac{1}{12}$ $\frac{1}{12}$ $\frac{1}{12}$ $\frac{1}{12}$ $\frac{1}{12}$ $\frac{1}{12}$ $\frac{1}{12}$ |

$$\frac{3}{4} = \frac{9}{12}$$

| $\frac{1}{3}$ | $\frac{1}{3}$ |

| $\frac{1}{12}$ $\frac{1}{12}$ $\frac{1}{12}$ $\frac{1}{12}$ $\frac{1}{12}$ $\frac{1}{12}$ $\frac{1}{12}$ $\frac{1}{12}$ |

$$\frac{2}{3} = \frac{8}{12}$$

STEP 3

Replace the $\frac{1}{4}$ pieces and the $\frac{1}{3}$ pieces with the equivalent fraction pieces.

$\frac{3}{4} = \frac{9}{12} \rightarrow$ [nine $\frac{1}{12}$ pieces]

$\frac{2}{3} = \frac{8}{12} \rightarrow$ [eight $\frac{1}{12}$ pieces] **?**

STEP 4

Find like fraction pieces that fit exactly in the remaining space.

- How many $\frac{1}{12}$ pieces fill the space?

- What is $\frac{3}{4} - \frac{2}{3}$?

[nine $\frac{1}{12}$ pieces]

[eight $\frac{1}{12}$ pieces]

On Your Own

Use the pictures to help you find each difference.

1.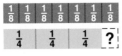

$$\frac{7}{8} - \frac{3}{4}$$

2.

$$\frac{5}{6} - \frac{2}{12}$$

3.

$$\frac{1}{2} - \frac{1}{5}$$

Go On

Use fraction pieces to help you find each difference.

4. $\frac{1}{2} - \frac{1}{3}$

5. $\frac{7}{8} - \frac{3}{4}$

6. $\frac{5}{6} - \frac{1}{3}$

7. $\frac{1}{2} - \frac{1}{4}$

8. $\frac{2}{3} - \frac{1}{2}$

9. $\frac{3}{4} - \frac{1}{2}$

10. $\frac{3}{8} - \frac{1}{4}$

11. $\frac{1}{2} - \frac{1}{6}$

12. $\frac{4}{6} - \frac{1}{4}$

13. $\frac{5}{6} - \frac{7}{12}$

14. $\frac{5}{8} - \frac{1}{4}$

15. $\frac{1}{2} - \frac{3}{8}$

16. $\frac{3}{4} - \frac{1}{3}$

17. $\frac{7}{8} - \frac{1}{4}$

18. $\frac{5}{6} - \frac{3}{4}$

Solve.

19. **Analyze** Jamie and Ray each used fraction pieces to find $\frac{1}{2} - \frac{1}{3}$. Jamie's answer was $\frac{1}{6}$. Ray's answer was $\frac{2}{12}$. They are both correct. Explain why.

20. **Reasoning** Jay lined up three fraction pieces to fit exactly under $\frac{7}{10}$. One of the fraction pieces is a $\frac{1}{2}$ piece. What are the other two fraction pieces?

21. **What's Wrong?** Look at Amy's work below. It shows how Amy subtracted $\frac{1}{3}$ from $\frac{2}{4}$. What did she do wrong? Use words and fraction pieces to explain your answer.

22. Evan lined up fraction pieces that showed $\frac{5}{8}$. Lily lined up fraction pieces that showed $\frac{3}{4}$. They want to make the two rows the same length. What fraction piece should be added?

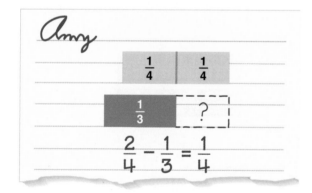

Talk About It • Write About It

You learned how to use fraction pieces to subtract fractions with unlike denominators.

23. Explain how subtracting fractions with unlike denominators is different from subtracting fractions with like denominators.

24. Explain how to find $\frac{1}{2} - \frac{1}{3}$. Use words or a picture.

Music Connection
Musical Fractions

Fractions are used to name some of the notes in music.

Look at the song below. All the notes in each measure are equal to one whole note. But some notes are missing. Use the diagram at the right. Find the missing notes. The first measure has been started for you.

whole note
1

half note
$\frac{1}{2}$

quarter note
$\frac{1}{4}$

eighth note
$\frac{1}{8}$

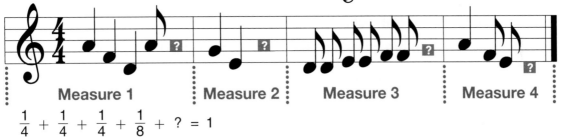

Measure 1   Measure 2   Measure 3   Measure 4

$\frac{1}{4} + \frac{1}{4} + \frac{1}{4} + \frac{1}{8} + ? = 1$

Logical Thinking
Fraction Sense

What's wrong with each statement?

"I ate $\frac{3}{4}$ of a peach. You ate $\frac{1}{8}$ of a watermelon. Since $\frac{3}{4} > \frac{1}{8}$, I ate more fruit than you."

"I'm not very hungry. I only want 1 small slice of pizza. So cut one pizza into 4 slices instead of 8, please."

Write your own silly statements.

Brain Teaser

What fraction of the square is unshaded?

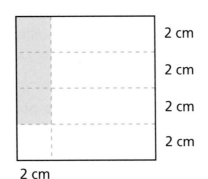

2 cm
2 cm
2 cm
2 cm

2 cm

Ask Yourself
What do I know about the sides of a square?

 Education Place

Check out
eduplace.com/map
for more brain teasers.

Problem-Solving Application
Use a Circle Graph

Objective Use circle graphs to solve problems.

You can use fractions and a circle graph to show a total amount divided into parts.

Problem There are 16 students in one art class. The circle graph shows what fractions of the students chose to use paints, markers, and colored pencils to complete their projects. How many more students chose colored pencils than paints?

paints
$\frac{1}{8}$

colored
pencils
$\frac{1}{2}$

markers
$\frac{3}{8}$

UNDERSTAND

This is what the question asks you to find.

How many more students chose colored pencils than paints?

This is what you know.

- There are 16 students.
- $\frac{1}{8}$ chose paints.

- $\frac{1}{2}$ chose colored pencils.
- $\frac{3}{8}$ chose markers.

PLAN

You can use the information in the graph.
Use the fractions on the circle graph to find how many students chose colored pencils and how many chose paints. Then subtract to find the difference.

SOLVE

Find the fractional parts of the whole.

- Find how many students chose colored pencils and how many chose paints.

$\frac{1}{2}$ of $16 = 8$ ← chose colored pencils $\frac{1}{8}$ of $16 = 2$ ← chose paints

- Then subtract. $8 - 2 = 6$

Solution: Six more students chose colored pencils than chose paints.

LOOK BACK

Look back at the circle graph.

Does your answer seem reasonable?

Use the circle graph on Page 534 to solve each problem.

1. How many more students chose markers than chose paints?

   (Hint) What part of the circle graph shows markers?

2. Suppose the art class has 8 more students, but the circle graph remains the same. Now how many students chose markers?

Ask Yourself

UNDERSTAND What does the question ask me to find?

PLAN Did I use the correct information from the graph?

SOLVE
• Did I find the fractional parts of the whole?

• Did I decide what operation to use?

LOOK BACK Does my answer make sense?

Independent Practice

An art club has 36 members. The circle graph shows the types of projects the students chose to do for an art show.

Use the graph to solve Problems 3–6.

3. How many members chose woodworking projects?

4. How many more students chose pottery than chose drawing?

5. How many more students chose drawing and pottery than chose woodworking and weaving?

6. Suppose there are 72 members, but the graph is the same. Now how many students chose weaving?

7. **Create and Solve** Use real or made-up data to create a circle graph of your own. Then write and solve a problem about the graph you drew.

Art Projects

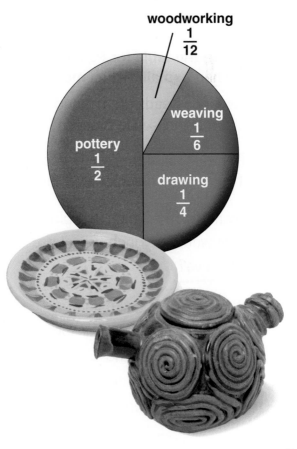

woodworking $\frac{1}{12}$

weaving $\frac{1}{6}$

pottery $\frac{1}{2}$

drawing $\frac{1}{4}$

Go On

Mixed Problem Solving

Solve. Show your work. Tell what strategy you used.

8. Lin painted 6 pictures in art class. He framed $\frac{2}{3}$ of those pictures. How many pictures did he frame?

9. Clemence used red, white, and blue stripes to make a flag. The red stripe is not on the top. The white stripe is not next to the red stripe. In what order from top to bottom are the stripes?

10. Marlena bought apples and oranges. She bought twice as many apples as oranges. Together, she bought 18 pieces of fruit. How many of each type of fruit did she buy?

📊 **Data** Use the table for Problems 11–15. Then explain which method you chose.

11. How many beads are needed to make a 2-inch-wide bracelet?

12. What fraction of the beads needed for a 1-inch-wide bracelet are blue?

13. How many red, white, and blue beads would a $\frac{1}{4}$ inch bracelet likely have?

Beads Needed For 8-Inch Long Bracelets			
Bracelet Width	**Red**	**White**	**Blue**
$\frac{1}{2}$ inch	60	24	36
1 inch	120	48	72
2 inches	240	96	144

14. Robert wants to make a larger bracelet to use as a collar for his dog. Robert wants the collar to be $1\frac{1}{2}$ inches wide and 16 inches long. How many beads will he need?

15. **You Decide** Each color bead comes in a bag of 60 or 200. You want to make 3 bracelets. Decide which size bracelets to make. Then decide how many bags of beads to buy. Explain your thinking.

Social Studies Connection
Egyptian Fractions

A **unit fraction** is a fraction that has 1 as its numerator. All ancient Egyptian fractions were written as unit fractions or as the sum of more than one unit fractions.

Look at the examples below.

- $\frac{1}{4}$ is unit fraction, because its numerator is 1.

- $\frac{3}{4}$ is not a unit fraction, because its numerator is 3, not 1.

- In ancient Egypt $\frac{3}{4}$ was written as the sum of unit fractions: $\frac{1}{2} + \frac{1}{4}$.

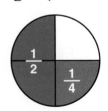

Write each of these fractions as sums of unit fractions.

1. $\frac{5}{8}$ 2. $\frac{8}{15}$ 3. $\frac{7}{12}$ 4. $\frac{7}{8}$

5. $\frac{5}{6}$ 6. $\frac{3}{8}$ 7. $\frac{3}{5}$ 8. $\frac{5}{12}$

Chapter Review/Test

VOCABULARY

Choose the best term to complete each sentence.

1. When you do not need an exact answer, you can ____.

2. The fractions $\frac{4}{6}$ and $\frac{3}{6}$ have ____.

3. The fractions $\frac{2}{7}$ and $\frac{1}{3}$ have ____.

Vocabulary

estimate

like denominators

mixed number

unlike denominators

CONCEPTS AND SKILLS

Add or subtract. Use fraction pieces if you wish. Write your answer in simplest form. (Lessons 1, 2, 6, 7, pp. 516–521, 524–525)

4. $\frac{1}{3} + \frac{1}{3}$

5. $\frac{4}{6} + \frac{2}{6}$

6. $\frac{10}{12} - \frac{5}{12}$

7. $\frac{18}{24} - \frac{12}{24}$

8. $1\frac{1}{4} + 2\frac{1}{4}$

9. $5\frac{3}{5} + 4\frac{2}{5}$

10. $3\frac{2}{6} - 1\frac{1}{6}$

11. $7\frac{1}{9} - 4\frac{1}{9}$

12. $\frac{3}{5} + \frac{1}{10}$

13. $\frac{1}{4} + \frac{3}{8}$

14. $\frac{5}{6} - \frac{1}{2}$

15. $\frac{1}{3} - \frac{2}{12}$

Estimate each sum. Write *greater than 1* or *less than 1*. (Lesson 4, pp. 524–525)

16. $\frac{1}{4} + \frac{3}{8}$

17. $\frac{4}{5} + \frac{3}{4}$

18. $\frac{2}{9} + \frac{4}{12}$

PROBLEM SOLVING

Solve. (Lessons 3, 8, pp. 522–523, 534–536)

19. At an arcade, four friends shared 25 tokens. If each person got the same number of tokens, how many tokens were left?

20. The circle graph shows the different coins Carl has. If Carl has 18 coins, how many of them are pennies?

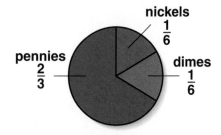

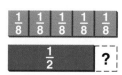

Write About It

Show You Understand

Jim used these fraction strips to solve a subtraction problem.

Jim's answer was $\frac{1}{8}$. What problem did he solve? Explain how you found your answer.

Extra Practice

Set A (Lesson 1, pp. 516–519)

Add or subtract. Write your answer in simplest form.

1. $\dfrac{3}{5}$ $+ \dfrac{2}{5}$

2. $\dfrac{2}{9}$ $+ \dfrac{4}{9}$

3. $\dfrac{3}{4}$ $+ \dfrac{1}{4}$

4. $\dfrac{6}{7}$ $- \dfrac{5}{7}$

5. $\dfrac{2}{3}$ $- \dfrac{2}{3}$

6. $\dfrac{4}{5}$ $- \dfrac{1}{5}$

7. $\dfrac{4}{8} - \dfrac{2}{8}$

8. $\dfrac{4}{5} + \dfrac{4}{5}$

9. $\dfrac{5}{6} - \dfrac{2}{6}$

10. $\dfrac{7}{8} + \dfrac{5}{8}$

11. $\dfrac{3}{4} + \dfrac{3}{4}$

12. $\dfrac{7}{8} - \dfrac{1}{8}$

13. $\dfrac{2}{3} - \dfrac{1}{3}$

14. $\dfrac{5}{7} + \dfrac{4}{7}$

Set B (Lesson 2, pp. 520–521)

Add or subtract. Write your answer in simplest form.

1. $2\dfrac{1}{9}$ $+ 3\dfrac{2}{9}$

2. $5\dfrac{4}{6}$ $+ 3\dfrac{2}{6}$

3. $4\dfrac{5}{12}$ $- 3\dfrac{1}{12}$

4. $7\dfrac{8}{10}$ $- 5\dfrac{3}{10}$

5. $2\dfrac{7}{8}$ $+ 4\dfrac{5}{8}$

6. $9\dfrac{5}{6}$ $- 6\dfrac{4}{6}$

7. $6\dfrac{2}{4} - 4\dfrac{1}{4}$

8. $8\dfrac{3}{5} + 2\dfrac{4}{5}$

9. $5\dfrac{5}{7} - 2\dfrac{3}{7}$

10. $9\dfrac{3}{10} + 6\dfrac{7}{10}$

11. $2\dfrac{9}{10} - 2\dfrac{7}{10}$

12. $4\dfrac{1}{8} + 3\dfrac{5}{8}$

13. $1\dfrac{2}{3} + 2\dfrac{2}{3}$

14. $5\dfrac{5}{8} - 3\dfrac{3}{8}$

Set C (Lesson 4, pp. 524–525)

Estimate each sum. Write *greater than 1* or *less than 1*.

1. $\dfrac{6}{8} + \dfrac{7}{8}$

2. $\dfrac{3}{8} + \dfrac{2}{5}$

3. $\dfrac{3}{10} + \dfrac{1}{3}$

4. $\dfrac{3}{4} + \dfrac{2}{3}$

5. $\dfrac{3}{5} + \dfrac{7}{10}$

6. $\dfrac{1}{5} + \dfrac{3}{12}$

7. $\dfrac{2}{3} + \dfrac{9}{10}$

8. $\dfrac{5}{8} + \dfrac{4}{7}$

9. $\dfrac{6}{10} + \dfrac{8}{15}$

10. $\dfrac{2}{3} + \dfrac{1}{2}$

Estimate each sum. Write > or < for each ●.

11. $\dfrac{1}{5} + \dfrac{3}{8}$ ● $\dfrac{5}{8} + \dfrac{2}{3}$

12. $\dfrac{6}{8} + \dfrac{3}{5}$ ● $\dfrac{7}{18} + \dfrac{4}{10}$

13. $\dfrac{1}{2} + \dfrac{3}{5}$ ● $\dfrac{2}{5} + \dfrac{1}{8}$

14. $\dfrac{3}{4} + \dfrac{4}{5}$ ● $\dfrac{1}{3} + \dfrac{3}{8}$

15. $\dfrac{1}{4} + \dfrac{2}{5}$ ● $\dfrac{4}{5} + \dfrac{7}{10}$

16. $\dfrac{3}{9} + \dfrac{1}{3}$ ● $\dfrac{2}{3} + \dfrac{7}{9}$

CHAPTER 21 Understand Decimals

INVESTIGATION

Using Data

A soccer game is broken up into either 2 or 4 equal sections of time. The table shows how long each section lasts for different age groups. How else could you write the numbers in the *Length of Section* column?

Age Group	Length of Section
Under 12	0.25 hour
12–17	0.50 hour
Over 17	0.75 hour

Use What You Know

Use this page to review and remember what you need to know for this chapter.

VOCABULARY

Choose the best word to complete each sentence.

Vocabulary

tenths

improper

equivalent

hundredths

1. A whole can be divided into 100 equal parts called _____.

2. If two fractions name the same amount, they are called _____ fractions.

3. A whole can be divided into 10 equal parts called _____.

CONCEPTS AND SKILLS

Write a fraction to describe the shaded part.

4. 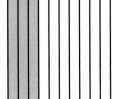   5. 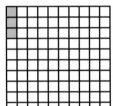   6. 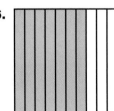   7.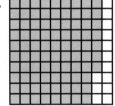

Write each amount, using a dollar sign and a decimal point.

8. 75¢

9. 2 dollars and 53 cents

10. 3 dollars and 4 cents

11. 10 dollars and 1 cent

Find the value for each ▪.

12. $\frac{1}{2} = \frac{\blacksquare}{10}$

13. $\frac{1}{5} = \frac{\blacksquare}{10}$

14. $\frac{3}{5} = \frac{\blacksquare}{10}$

15. $\frac{4}{5} = \frac{\blacksquare}{10}$

16. $\frac{1}{4} = \frac{\blacksquare}{100}$

17. $\frac{1}{2} = \frac{\blacksquare}{100}$

18. $\frac{1}{25} = \frac{\blacksquare}{100}$

19. $\frac{2}{5} = \frac{\blacksquare}{100}$

 Write About It

20. Draw pictures to show $\frac{5}{10}$ and $\frac{50}{100}$. How are these fractions alike? How are they different?

Facts Practice, See Page 669.

Tenths and Hundredths

Objective Use models to show tenths and hundredths.

Work Together

One way to show parts of a whole is to use fractions. Another way is to use decimals.

A **decimal** is a number with one or more digits to the right of the **decimal point**.

Look at the models below.

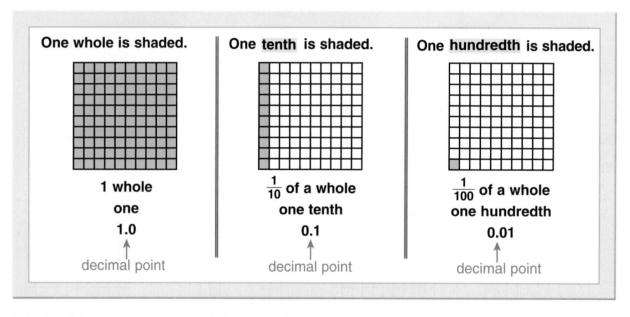

One whole is shaded.

1 whole
one
1.0
↑
decimal point

One tenth is shaded.

$\frac{1}{10}$ of a whole
one tenth
0.1
↑
decimal point

One hundredth is shaded.

$\frac{1}{100}$ of a whole
one hundredth
0.01
↑
decimal point

Work with a partner to model decimals.

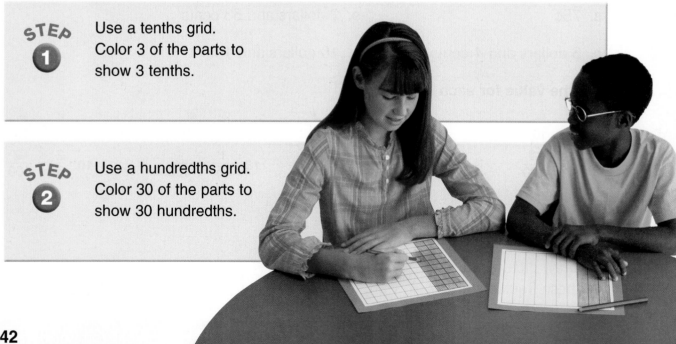

STEP 1
Use a tenths grid.
Color 3 of the parts to show 3 tenths.

STEP 2
Use a hundredths grid.
Color 30 of the parts to show 30 hundredths.

STEP 3 Compare your models.

- Is the same area colored in both models?

- How do you write 3 tenths as a decimal?

- How do you write 30 hundredths as a decimal?

STEP 4 Repeat Steps 1–3. This time show 0.6 and 0.60. Is the same area colored on both models?

On Your Own

Write a fraction and a decimal to describe each model.

1. 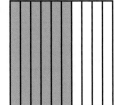   **2.** 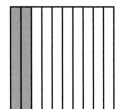   **3.** 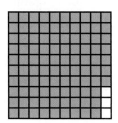   **4.**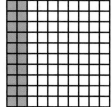

Use grid paper. Draw a model to show each fraction. Then write each fraction as a decimal.

5. $\frac{9}{10}$ **6.** $\frac{1}{10}$ **7.** $\frac{99}{100}$ **8.** $\frac{7}{100}$ **9.** $\frac{70}{100}$

Use grid paper. Draw a model to show each decimal. Then write each decimal as a fraction.

10. 0.3   **11.** 0.5   **12.** 0.01   **13.** 0.76   **14.** 0.54

Talk About It • Write About It

You learned how to represent fractions and decimals.

15. How are 0.9 and 0.90 alike? How are they different?

16. Why is 0.1 greater than 0.01?

Audio Tutor 2/24 Listen and Understand

Thousandths

Objective Write decimals for thousandths.

Vocabulary

thousandths
equivalent decimals

Materials
Decimal Grids or
Learning Tools 38, 39
and 40

Learn About It

A whole can be divided into 1,000 equal parts called
thousandths . Thousandths are even smaller than hundredths.

Look at these models and place-value charts.

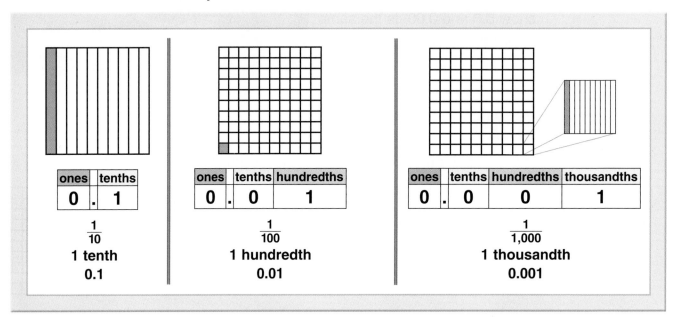

ones	tenths
0 .	1

$\frac{1}{10}$
1 tenth
0.1

ones	tenths	hundredths
0 .	0	1

$\frac{1}{100}$
1 hundredth
0.01

ones	tenths	hundredths	thousandths
0 .	0	0	1

$\frac{1}{1,000}$
1 thousandth
0.001

Try this activity to explore thousandths.

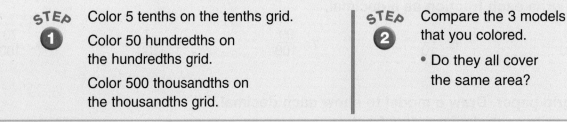

STEP 1 Color 5 tenths on the tenths grid.

Color 50 hundredths on
the hundredths grid.

Color 500 thousandths on
the thousandths grid.

STEP 2 Compare the 3 models
that you colored.

• Do they all cover
the same area?

▶ Decimals that name the same amount are called **equivalent decimals** .

0.5, 0.50, and 0.500 are equivalent decimals.

Other Examples

A. Zero in Tenths Place

Fraction	Decimal	Words
$\frac{21}{1,000}$	0.021	twenty-one thousandths

B. Zero in Tenths and Hundredths Places

Fraction	Decimal	Words
$\frac{9}{1,000}$	0.009	nine thousandths

Guided Practice

Write each as a decimal.

1. $\frac{782}{1,000}$ 2. $\frac{206}{1,000}$ 3. $\frac{45}{1,000}$ 4. $\frac{3}{1,000}$

5. 37 thousandths   6. 222 thousandths

Ask Yourself
- How many equal parts are there?
- How many digits do I put after the decimal point to show thousandths?

Explain Your Thinking ▶ Look at the place-value charts on Page 544. How does the value of the digit change as you move from left to right?

Practice and Problem Solving

Write each as a decimal.

7. $\frac{356}{1,000}$ 8. $\frac{350}{1,000}$ 9. $\frac{49}{1,000}$ 10. $\frac{70}{1,000}$ 11. $\frac{3}{1,000}$

12. 450 thousandths   13. 6 thousandths   14. 15 thousandths

Write each in word form.

15. 0.005   16. 0.023   17. $\frac{455}{1,000}$ 18. 0.302   19. $\frac{300}{1,000}$

20. Mark walks $\frac{4}{10}$ mile to school. Carla walks 0.450 miles to school. Who walks farther? Explain how you know.

21. Cho Yia and her mother drive 0.7 kilometers to the store. Write an equivalent decimal for this distance.

22. **What's Wrong?** Look at Brian's work on the right. What's wrong with his reasoning?

> Brian
> 300 > 30 so
> 0.300 > 0.30

Mixed Review and Test Prep

Open Response

Write all the factors of each number.

(Ch. 10, Lesson 1)

23. 6   24. 24   25. 18

26. 25   27. 14   28. 27

29. 30   30. 20   31. 42

Multiple Choice

32. Marcia's mother tells her that a liter is nine hundred forty-six thousandths of a quart. How do you write this number?

(Ch. 21, Lesson 2)

A 0.946   C 940.006

B 900.046   D 946,000

Extra Practice See page 565, Set A.

Mixed Numbers and Decimals

Objective Read, write, and model amounts greater than 1.

Red Path 2.8 km

Blue Path 2.45 km

Learn About It

Melanie and Elena like to jog every day at their local park. There are two paths. Elena's favorite is the Blue Path. Melanie's favorite is the Red Path. The Red Path is two and eight tenths kilometers long.

Here are different ways to show two and eight tenths.

Models	Mixed Number	Place-Value Chart
	$2\frac{8}{10}$	**ones** | **tenths** **2** . **8**
Standard Form 2.8	**Word Form** two and eight tenths	**Expanded Form** 2 + 0.8

Here are different ways to show two and forty-five hundredths.

Models	Mixed Number	Place-Value Chart
	$2\frac{45}{100}$	**ones** | **tenths** | **hundredths** **2** . **4** **5**
Standard Form 2.45	**Word Form** two and forty-five hundredths	**Expanded Form** 2 + 0.4 + 0.05

▶ Thinking about money can help you understand decimals.

Here are different ways to show $1.49.

Models	Mixed Number	Place Value Chart		
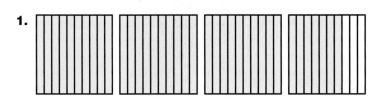	$1\frac{49}{100}$	**dollars (ones)**	**dimes (tenths)**	**pennies (hundredths)**
		1 .	4	9

Standard Form	Word Form	Expanded Form
$1.49	one dollar and 49 cents	$1 + $0.4 + $0.09

Guided Practice

Write a mixed number and a decimal to describe the shaded part in each model.

Ask Yourself

• What part is the whole number?

• What should the numerator be? What should the denominator be?

1.

2.

3.

Write each as a decimal.

4. $5\frac{3}{10}$ **5.** $9\frac{9}{10}$ **6.** $26\frac{7}{10}$ **7.** $15\frac{55}{100}$ **8.** $12\frac{5}{100}$ **9.** $2\frac{17}{1,000}$

10. seven tenths   **11.** twenty-two hundredths   **12** one and 5 thousandths

Explain Your Thinking ▶ Look back at Exercise 7.
Why is the value of each 5 different?

Go On

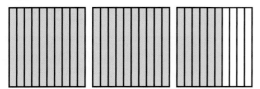

Practice and Problem Solving

Write a mixed number and a decimal to describe the shaded part.

13.

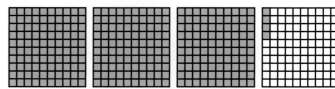

14.

Write each mixed number as a decimal.

15. $1\frac{2}{10}$ **16.** $7\frac{7}{100}$ **17.** $4\frac{54}{100}$ **18.** $4\frac{7}{10}$ **19.** $34\frac{17}{100}$

20. $158\frac{85}{100}$ **21.** $175\frac{8}{100}$ **22.** $19\frac{38}{100}$ **23.** $45\frac{26}{1,000}$ **24.** $56\frac{3}{1,000}$

Write each as a decimal in standard form.

25. sixty-four hundredths   **26.** five and seven tenths

27. forty and four hundredths   **28.** three and sixteen thousandths

29. $7 + 0.5$ **30.** $3 + 0.9 + 0.07$ **31.** $4 + 0.06$ **32.** $2 + 0.2 + 0.03 + 0.004$

Write each decimal in words and in expanded form.

33. 0.4   **34.** 0.65   **35.** 5.03   **36.** 3.07   **37.** $3.98

38. 4.3   **39.** 5.67   **40.** 4.876   **41.** 0.005   **42.** 3.098

 Data Use the table for Problems 43–45.

43. Measurement On which day was there less than 1 inch of snow?

44. Represent Use a ruler to draw a line segment that shows the height of the snow that fell on Tuesday.

45. Analyze Melanie decided not to jog one day because eight and five tenths inches of snow fell on the day before. On which day of the week didn't she jog?

Day	Inches of Snow
Monday	3.0 inches
Tuesday	3.5 inches
Wednesday	0.5 inches
Thursday	4.0 inches
Friday	8.5 inches

Extra Practice See page 565, Set B

Real World Connection
Batting Averages

Did you know that baseball statistics use decimals? Jackie Robinson was the first African-American player in major league baseball. His batting average in 1949 was .342.

A batting average is the number of hits divided by the number of times at bat. It is shown as a decimal in thousandths. Jackie Robinson's .342 means that he made 342 hits out of 1,000 times at bat, on average.

- Roberto Clemente was the first Latin American player to be inducted into baseball's Hall of Fame. He averaged 357 hits out of 1,000 times at bat in 1967. Write his batting average as a decimal.

- Ty Cobb had a batting average of .377. What does that mean?

WEEKLY (WR) READER eduplace.com/map

Check your understanding of Lessons 1–3.

Write a fraction and a decimal to describe each model. (Lesson 1)

1.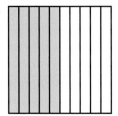

2.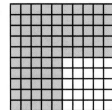

Write each fraction as a decimal. (Lesson 2)

3. $\dfrac{8}{1,000}$ 4. $\dfrac{11}{1,000}$ 5. $\dfrac{139}{1,000}$ 6. $\dfrac{500}{1,000}$

Write each decimal in words. (Lesson 3)

7. 1.2   8. 3.03   9. 9.016   10. 5.179

Extra Practice at **eduplace.com/map**

Lesson 4

Fractions and Decimal Equivalents

Objective Write fractions and decimals that name the same amount.

Learn About It

A decimal that names the same amount as a fraction is the fraction's **decimal equivalent** .

Carrie says that $\frac{1}{2}$ of the grid is orange. Jenny says that $\frac{5}{10}$ is orange. Rosa says that 0.5 is orange, and Marla says that 0.50 of the grid is orange. Which of the girls is correct?

To change a fraction to a decimal, find an equivalent fraction with a denominator of 10, 100, or 1,000.

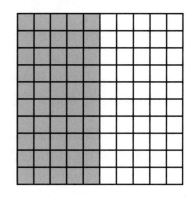

Different Ways to Show Equivalent Amounts

Way 1 You can use models.

$\frac{1}{2}$

$\frac{5}{10}$ or 0.5

$\frac{50}{100}$ or 0.50

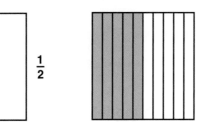

$$\frac{1}{2} \overset{\times 5}{\underset{\times 5}{=}} \frac{5}{10} = 0.5 \qquad \frac{1}{2} \overset{\times 50}{\underset{\times 50}{=}} \frac{50}{100} = 0.50$$

Way 2 You can use number lines.

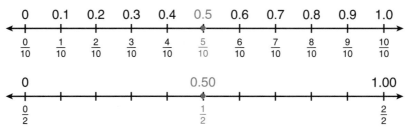

Solution: All four girls are correct.

Extra Help at **eduplace.com/map**

Other Examples

A. Denominator of 100

$$\frac{3}{4} \overset{\times 25}{\underset{\times 25}{=}} \frac{75}{100} = 0.75$$

B. Denominator of 1,000

$$\frac{7}{500} \overset{\times 2}{\underset{\times 2}{=}} \frac{14}{1000} = 0.014$$

Guided Practice

Write a fraction to describe the shaded part of each model. Then write a decimal equivalent.

Ask Yourself
• What part of the square is shaded?
• How do I write that amount as a fraction? as a decimal?

1.

2.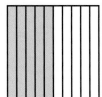

3.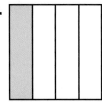

4.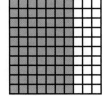

5.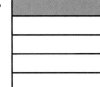

6.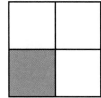

Explain Your Thinking ▶ Describe how you would find the decimal equivalent for $\frac{7}{20}$.

Practice and Problem Solving

Write a fraction to describe the shaded part of each model. Then write a decimal equivalent.

7.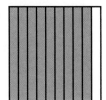

8.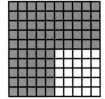

9.

10.

11.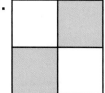

12.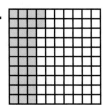

13.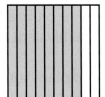

14.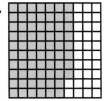

15.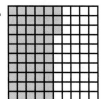

16.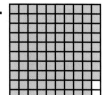

Go On ▶

Practice and Problem Solving

Write each decimal as an equivalent fraction.

17. 0.4 **18.** 0.04 **19.** 0.75 **20.** 0.67 **21.** 0.25

22. 0.34 **23.** 0.98 **24.** 0.30 **25.** 0.500 **26.** 0.005

Write each fraction as an equivalent decimal.

27. $\frac{3}{5}$ **28.** $\frac{4}{50}$ **29.** $\frac{2}{25}$ **30.** $\frac{1}{20}$ **31.** $\frac{1}{25}$

32. $\frac{9}{10}$ **33.** $\frac{27}{100}$ **34.** $\frac{4}{5}$ **35.** $\frac{643}{1,000}$ **36.** $\frac{9}{500}$

Find the missing digit.

37. $\frac{\blacksquare}{10} = 0.30$ **38.** $\frac{42}{100} = 0.\blacksquare2$ **39.** $\frac{3}{5} = 0.\blacksquare0$ **40.** $\frac{1}{5} = 0.\blacksquare$

41. $4\frac{4}{5} = 4.\blacksquare$ **42.** $3\frac{1}{2} = \blacksquare.5$ **43.** $10.\blacksquare5 = 10\frac{1}{20}$ **44.** $7\frac{2}{\blacksquare} = 7.4$

 Data Use the picture for Problems 45–46.

45. Write a decimal that tells the part of the hats that is blue.

46. Write a decimal that tells the part of the hats that is not blue.

47. Analyze Suppose there are 100 hats, and $\frac{4}{10}$ of them are not red. If the rest are red, how many hats are red?

48. What's Wrong? What did Brett do wrong when he tried to write $\frac{1}{25}$ as a decimal?

Brett

$\frac{1}{25} = \frac{1 \times 4}{25 \times 4} = \frac{4}{100} = 0.4$

Mixed Review and Test Prep ✓

Open Response

Write each answer in simplest form.
(Ch. 20, Lesson 1)

49. $\begin{array}{r} \frac{2}{9} \\ + \frac{4}{9} \\ \hline \end{array}$ **50.** $\begin{array}{r} \frac{9}{10} \\ + \frac{7}{10} \\ \hline \end{array}$ **51.** $\begin{array}{r} \frac{5}{12} \\ + \frac{7}{12} \\ \hline \end{array}$

52. Are 5.05, 5.005, and 5.500 equivalent decimals? (Ch. 21, Lesson 4)

Explain your answer using words and models or place-value charts.

Extra Practice See page 565, Set C.

Math Challenge
Percent

Did you ever get 100% on a test? Congratulations! That means that all your answers were correct!

The symbol **%** is read as "**percent**". Percent means per hundred.

100% means 100 out of 100. It means all.
50% means 50 out of 100.
25% means 25 out of 100.

Vocabulary

percent

Look at these examples.

100%	50%	25%
100 out of 100	50 out of 100	25 out of 100
$\frac{100}{100} = 1 = 1.0$	$\frac{50}{100} = \frac{1}{2} = 0.50$	$\frac{25}{100} = \frac{1}{4} = 0.25$

Copy and complete this chart.

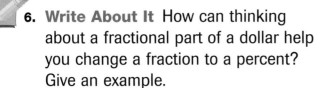

1.	**Fraction**	$\frac{25}{100}$	$\frac{50}{100}$		$\frac{100}{100}$
2.	**Decimal**	0.25		0.75	
3.	**Percent**		50%	75%	

4. A basketball team won $\frac{1}{2}$ of the games it played last season. What percent of the games did it win?

5. Suppose 25% of the students in Amy's class bought lunch today. What fraction of the students bought lunch?

6. Write About It How can thinking about a fractional part of a dollar help you change a fraction to a percent? Give an example.

7. What do you think 10% means? How would you show 10% as a fraction and as a decimal? How would you show 75% as a fraction and as a decimal?

Problem-Solving Strategy
Find a Pattern

Objective Use patterns to solve problems.

Photo Prices	
Number of Packages	**Price**
1	$15.00
2	$29.00
3	$42.00
4	$54.00
5	
6	

Problem An ice-skating club orders photos of the year's skating highlights. The sign on the right shows the prices for photo packages. If the pattern continues, how much do 6 packages of photos cost?

UNDERSTAND

These are the facts that you know.

• 1 package costs $15.00. • 2 packages cost $29.00.

• 3 packages cost $42.00. • 4 packages cost $54.00.

PLAN

You can find a pattern to help you solve the problem.

SOLVE

Find the pattern.

$15.00 $29.00 $42.00 $54.00

+ $14.00   + $13.00   + $12.00

The pattern is: Add $14.00 to the first amount and $1.00 less to each amount after that.

Now use the pattern to solve the problem.

• First, find the cost of 5 packages.
  Add $11.00 to the cost of 4 packages.
  $54.00 + $11.00 = $65.00

• Then find the cost of 6 packages.
  Add $10.00 to the cost of 5 packages.
  $65.00 + $10.00 = $75.00

Solution: It will cost $75.00 for 6 packages.

LOOK BACK

Look back at the problem.

Is your answer reasonable? Tell why.

Use the Ask Yourself questions to help you solve each problem.

1. Look at this pattern of numbers.

| 4 | 7 | 6 | 9 | 8 | 11 | 10 | 13 | 12 |

If the pattern continues, what is the next number likely to be?

(Hint) The pattern is: +■, −■.

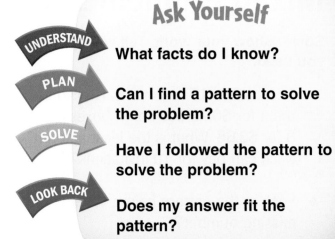

Ask Yourself

UNDERSTAND **What facts do I know?**

PLAN **Can I find a pattern to solve the problem?**

SOLVE **Have I followed the pattern to solve the problem?**

LOOK BACK **Does my answer fit the pattern?**

2. One skating photo enlargement costs $3.50, two cost $5.75, three cost $8.00, and four cost $10.25. If the pattern continues, what is likely to be the cost of seven enlargements?

$3.50

$5.75

$8.00

$10.25

Independent Practice

Find a pattern to solve each problem.

3. Look at this pattern of numbers.

| 4 | 8 | 12 | 16 | 20 | 24 | 28 | 32 |

If the pattern continues, what is the next number likely to be?

5. One wallet-sized photo sells for $1.00, two wallet-sized photos sell for $1.75, and three sell for $2.50. If this pattern continues, how many wallet-sized photos can you buy for $5.00?

7. **Create and Solve** Make up your own number pattern. Have a classmate find the rule and name the next number in the pattern.

4. Look at this pattern of numbers.

| 2 | 6 | 4 | 12 | 10 | 30 | 28 |

If the pattern continues, what is the next number likely to be?

6. One pair of skate laces costs $5.75, two pairs cost $10.00, three pairs cost $14.25, and four pairs cost $18.50. If the pattern continues, how much will eight pairs cost?

Go On

Mixed Problem Solving

Solve. Show your work. Tell what strategy you used.

8. Mick needs 10 invitations. He can buy them for $0.75 each or in boxes of 8 for $3.65. What is the least amount Mick can pay for 10 invitations?

9. Look at the pattern below. What is the missing number?

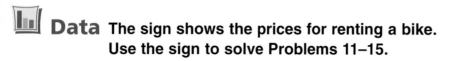

| 3.1 | 6.2 | 9.3 | ____ | 15.5 |

10. John cut a 12 foot board into 3 pieces. The first piece is as long as the second and third pieces together. The third piece is half as long as the second piece. How long is each piece?

You Choose

Strategy
- Draw a Picture
- Find a Pattern
- Solve a Simpler Problem
- Write an Equation

Computation Method
- Mental Math
- Estimation
- Paper and Pencil
- Calculator

Data The sign shows the prices for renting a bike. Use the sign to solve Problems 11–15.

11. What is the cost of renting a bike for 3 hours?

12. What is the cost of renting a bike for 2 weeks and 1 day?

13. Marcy rents a bike for 7 hours. How much less is the daily rate than the hourly rate?

14. Manuel rents a bike at 10:30 A.M. and returns it the same day at 2:30 P.M. How much does he pay?

15. **Analyze** Antonia used this equation to find her cost of renting a bike.

$$C = 6 + (4 \times 2)$$

How long did she rent the bike?

Bob's Bike Shop
Rental Rates

First hour	$ 6
Each additional hour	$ 2
All day	$17
Three days	$35
Weekly	$60

Problem Solving on Tests

Multiple Choice

Choose the letter of the correct answer. If the correct answer is not here, choose NH.

1. Ethan mixes $\frac{3}{4}$ gallon of orange juice with $\frac{1}{4}$ gallon of cranberry juice. How much juice does he now have?

   A $\frac{2}{8}$ gallon   C $\frac{4}{8}$ gallon

   B $\frac{3}{8}$ gallon   D 1 gallon

   (Chapter 20, Lesson 1)

2. A piece of cardboard is 0.015 inch thick. Which shows 0.015 in word form?

   F fifteen thousand

   G fifteen hundredths

   H fifteen thousandths

   J NH

   (Chapter 21, Lesson 2)

Open Response

Solve each problem.

3. What is the area of a room that is 12 ft by 14 ft?

   (Chapter 18, Lesson 4)

4. Gloria collected 3 kinds of toys for a toy drive. Of the toys, $\frac{2}{5}$ were cars, $\frac{1}{5}$ were puppets, and 10 were dolls. How many toys did Gloria collect?

   Represent Support your solution with pictures.

   (Chapter 19, Lesson 6)

Extended Response

5. Mrs. Stewart has $40 to buy food and party supplies for 28 people.

Food and Party Supplies	
Ice Cream ($\frac{1}{2}$ gal)	$3.89
Lemonade (1 gal)	$1.98 (serves 16)
Chips	$2.85
Napkins	$3.49
Plastic Spoons	$0.89 (package of 12)
Paper Plates	$2.99 (package of 15)
Plastic Cups	$0.69 (package of 8)

a. Mrs. Stewart wants to buy 4 half gallons of ice cream, 3 bags of chips, 1 package of napkins, and enough lemonade, plastic spoons, paper plates, and cups for 28 people. Does she have enough money? How do you know?

b. Plan a party for your class using the table above as a guide for your purchases. If each person is served 1 cup of ice cream, how many $\frac{1}{2}$ gallon containers of ice cream will you need to buy? Decide what you will buy and how much it will cost.

   (Chapter 7)

Education Place
Check out **eduplace.com/map** for more test prep practice.

Compare and Order Decimals

Objective Compare and order decimals and recognize equivalent decimals.

Learn About It

At a diving meet, Sue earned these scores. What are her highest and lowest scores? What is the order of the scores from least to greatest?

Different Ways to Compare and Order Decimals

Way ❶ Use a place-value chart.

- Line up the decimal points.

- Start comparing in the ones place. 3 < 4. So, 3.9 is the least.

- Continue comparing in the tenths place. 8 > 6 > 0. So, 4.8 is the greatest.

ones		tenths
4	.	6
3	.	9
4	.	8
4	.	0

4.8 > 4.6 > 4.0 > 3.9

Way ❷ Use a number line.

- Locate all the scores on a number line.

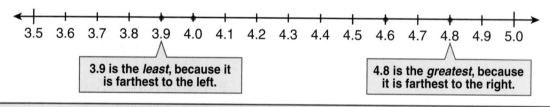

3.9 is the *least*, because it is farthest to the left.

4.8 is the *greatest*, because it is farthest to the right.

Solution: 4.8 is Sue's highest score and 3.9 is her lowest score. The order of her scores is: 3.9 4.0 4.6 4.8.

Another Example

Order 2.59, 2.5, 2.067, and 2.12 from least to greatest.

- Line up the decimal points.

- Start comparing in the ones place.

- Continue until all are ordered.

ones		tenths	hundredths	thousandths	
2	.	5	9	0	
2	.	5	0	0	2.5 = 2.500
2	.	0	6	7	
2	.	1	2	0	2.12 = 2.120

same | 0 < 1, so 2.067 is the least | 0 < 9 so, 2.500 < 2.590

2.067 < 2.120 < 2.5 < 2.59

Compare. Write >, <, or = for each .

1. 3.6 ⬤ 3.8   **2.** 9.25 ⬤ 8.93   **3.** 12.5 ⬤ 12.50

Order the numbers from least to greatest.

4. 2.9   3.5   3.2   2.3   **5.** 4.7   4.78   4.73   4.67

Ask Yourself
- Where would each decimal be on a number line?
- What if the numbers do not have the same number of decimal places?

Explain Your Thinking ▶ How is comparing decimals like comparing whole numbers?

Practice and Problem Solving

𝑿 Algebra • Symbols Compare. Write >, <, or = for each ⬤.

6. 7.8 ⬤ 8.7   **7.** 24.6 ⬤ 24.58   **8.** 6.9 ⬤ 6.90   **9.** 21.003 ⬤ 21.300

Order the numbers from greatest to least.

10. 2.13   2.14   2.24   2.42   **11.** 9.8   6.9   8.299   9.85

12. 6.24   6.2   6.09   6.9   **13.** 3.76   3.07   3.7   3.762

14. Four swim teams have scores of 49.5, 50.0, 47.6, and 47.8. What is the order of the scores from least to greatest?

15. At a diving meet, Alina's mean score was 4.2 and Carmine's mean score was 3.8. Which girl had the greater average score?

16. **Analyze** A decimal number with two digits is between 7.3 and 7.9. It is less than 7.89 and greater than 7.58. The digit in the tenths place is odd. What is the number?

Mixed Review and Test Prep

Open Response

Write all the factors of each number.
(Ch. 10, Lesson 1)

17. 81   **18.** 35   **19.** 18   **20.** 24

21. 20   **22.** 15   **23.** 42   **24.** 36

Multiple Choice

25. Which of the following can be placed in the to make a true sentence? (Ch. 21, Lesson 6)

4.56 ⬤ 4.7

A <   **B** >   **C** =   **D** +

Audio Tutor 2/26 Listen and Understand

Compare and Order Decimals and Mixed Numbers

Objective Compare and order decimals and mixed numbers.

Learn About It

Diane rode her bike $1\frac{1}{2}$ miles to school. Then she rode 1.75 miles to the library. She then rode 1.6 miles to visit her aunt. Her ride home was $1\frac{1}{4}$ miles. What is the order of all the distances from least to greatest?

Different Ways to Compare and Order $1\frac{1}{2}$, 1.75, 1.6, and $1\frac{1}{4}$

Way ① Use a place-value chart.

- Change the fractions to decimals.
- Write the decimals in hundredths.
- Compare.

	ones		tenths	hundredths
$1\frac{1}{2}$ mi	1	.	5	0
1.75 mi	1	.	7	5
1.6 mi	1	.	6	0
$1\frac{1}{4}$ mi	1	.	2	5

Way ② Use a number line.

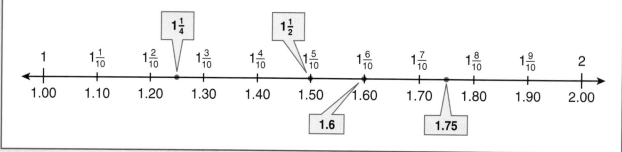

Solution: The order of the distances from least to greatest is:
$1\frac{1}{4}$ miles $1\frac{1}{2}$ miles   1.6 miles   1.75 miles

Guided Practice

Ask Yourself

- Do I use a number line or place value?
- Do I start with the digit in the least place or in the greatest place?

Compare. Write >, <, or = for each ⬤.

1. $1\frac{3}{4}$ ⬤ 1.8

2. $3\frac{1}{2}$ ⬤ 3.21

3. $1\frac{1}{4}$ ⬤ 1.25

Order the numbers from least to greatest.

4. 1.4 $1\frac{9}{10}$ 1.05 $1\frac{15}{100}$

5. $\frac{25}{100}$ 6.1   4.26 $5\frac{8}{10}$

Explain Your Thinking ▶ In Exercise 4, did you use a number line or a place-value chart? Explain your choice.

Practice and Problem Solving

Compare. Write >, <, or = for each ⬤.

6. 2.9 ⬤ $2\frac{3}{4}$

7. 46.7 ⬤ $46\frac{1}{2}$

8. 35.7 ⬤ $53\frac{1}{5}$

9. 34.5 ⬤ 34.26

10. 8.6 ⬤ $8\frac{2}{5}$

11. $3\frac{1}{10}$ ⬤ 3.18

12. 4.5 ⬤ $4\frac{1}{2}$

13. 3.7 ⬤ 3.70

Order the numbers from greatest to least.

14. $1\frac{5}{10}$ 1.9 $1\frac{36}{100}$ 1.63

15. $15\frac{3}{100}$ 18.05   12.9 $19\frac{1}{10}$

16. 23.4 $23\frac{4}{100}$ $24\frac{3}{10}$ 23.34

17. 352.02   293.2 $352\frac{2}{10}$ $293\frac{2}{100}$

✗ Algebra • Symbols Write >, <, or = for each ⬤.

18. 5.2 ⬤ 5.9 ⬤ 7.8

19. 6.5 ⬤ $6\frac{1}{2}$ ⬤ 6.05

20. 5.95 ⬤ 5.29 ⬤ 4.22

21. 3.1 ⬤ $3\frac{1}{2}$ ⬤ $2\frac{1}{2}$

22. 4.6 ⬤ $4\frac{3}{4}$ ⬤ 4.1

23. 2.09 ⬤ 2.25 ⬤ $2\frac{1}{10}$

24. **You Decide** Choose any four numbers from below. Then order them from least to greatest.

$6\frac{1}{2}$

6.09

6.02

6.3

6.75

6.2

$6\frac{1}{4}$

Go On ➡

Solve.

25. **Mental Math** Bob can ride a mile in 8 minutes. If he rides at the same speed, how long will it take to ride $1\frac{1}{2}$ miles?

26. Suppose Sasha starts riding her bike at 10:30 A.M. and ends at 2:00 P.M. How long does she ride her bike?

27. **Measurement** A bicycle rally was held at a town park. The park measures 450 feet long and 700 feet wide. What is the area of the park?

28. **Money** The entrance fee to the bleachers at the bike race is $5.00. There are 10 rows of seats and each row has 14 seats. If all the seats are filled, how much money is collected?

Data The bar graph shows the best standing long jumps for five students. Use the graph for Problems 29–34.

29. Which of the five students jumped the farthest? How far did he jump?

30. Which student's farthest jump was 1.68 meters?

31. Which student's farthest jump was 1.58 meters?

32. Which student jumped closest to 2 meters?

33. Which student jumped closest to $1\frac{1}{2}$ meters?

34. **Analyze** David says that the graph shows that he jumped about twice as far as Jim. Do you agree? Why or why not?

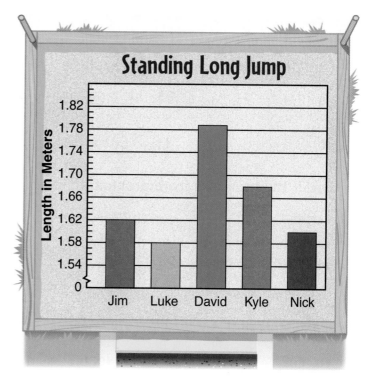

Standing Long Jump

Open Response

Compare. Write >, <, or = for each ⬤.

35. 0.9 ⬤ 0.90

36. 0.071 ⬤ 0.7

37. 0.03 ⬤ 0.30

38. 0.45 ⬤ 0.067

(Chapter 21, Lesson 6)

Solve.

39. Karen measured the temperature in her backyard with a digital thermometer 5 times during one day. The temperatures she recorded were: 52.04°F, 52.12°F, 54.006°F, 54.024°F, 52.121°F, and 52.211°F. How could Karen list the temperatures in order from least to greatest?

(Chapter 21, Lesson 7)

Calculator Connection
Changing Fractions to Decimals

You can use a calculator to find decimal equivalents. The fraction $\frac{1}{2}$ means 1 divided by 2.

To find the decimal equivalent for $\frac{1}{2}$:

• Enter the numerator, 1. Press

• Enter the denominator 2. Press

The calculator display should show 0.5.

Find the decimal equivalent for each fraction.

1. $\frac{4}{5}$ **2.** $\frac{15}{20}$ **3.** $\frac{6}{24}$ **4.** $\frac{9}{36}$ **5.** $\frac{6}{30}$

6. $\frac{14}{28}$ **7.** $\frac{7}{35}$ **8.** $\frac{3}{10}$ **9.** $\frac{43}{100}$ **10.** $\frac{77}{100}$

Chapter Review/Test

VOCABULARY

Choose the best term to complete each sentence.

Vocabulary

tenths
decimal
equivalent
hundredths

1. The decimals 0.5 and 0.50 are ____ decimals.

2. In the decimal 3.075, the 0 is in the ____ place.

3. A number with one or more digits to the right of a decimal point is a ____.

CONCEPTS AND SKILLS

Write each fraction as a decimal. (Lessons 1–2, pp. 542–545)

4. $\frac{3}{10}$ 5. $\frac{9}{10}$ 6. $\frac{37}{100}$ 7. $\frac{99}{100}$

8. $\frac{6}{100}$ 9. $\frac{426}{1,000}$ 10. $\frac{22}{1,000}$ 11. $\frac{306}{1,000}$

Write each mixed number as a decimal. (Lesson 3, pp.546–548)

12. $12\frac{6}{10}$ 13. $3\frac{5}{100}$ 14. $7\frac{566}{1,000}$

15. three and five tenths

16. four and twenty-six hundredths

Write each fraction as an equivalent decimal. (Lesson 4, pp. 550–552)

17. $\frac{1}{2}$ 18. $\frac{3}{4}$ 19. $\frac{77}{100}$ 20. $\frac{14}{1,000}$

Compare. Write >, <, or = for each ⬤. (Lessons 6–7, pp. 558–562)

21. 3 ⬤ 3.2   22. $5\frac{1}{2}$ ⬤ 5.2

23. 4.71 ⬤ 4.071   24. $6\frac{1}{4}$ ⬤ 6.025

PROBLEM SOLVING

Solve. (Lesson 5, pp. 554–556)

25. One yard of velvet fabric sells for $3.00, two yards sell for $5.00, and three yards sell for $7.00. If this pattern continues, how many yards of velvet fabric can Jo buy for $15.00?

Write About It

Show You Understand

The following number is in expanded form.

$$1 + 0.3 + 0.05 + 0.004$$

John wrote the number in standard form as 1.12.

Explain what he did wrong. What should the decimal be?

Extra Practice

Set A (Lesson 2, pp. 544–545)

Write each fraction as a decimal.

1. $\frac{9}{10}$ **2.** $\frac{6}{10}$ **3.** $\frac{4}{100}$ **4.** $\frac{16}{100}$ **5.** $\frac{125}{1,000}$

6. thirteen thousandths   **7.** one hundred seven thousandths

Set B (Lesson 3, pp. 546–548)

Write each mixed number as a decimal.

1. $3\frac{8}{10}$ **2.** $1\frac{30}{100}$ **3.** $16\frac{1}{100}$ **4.** $2\frac{35}{1,000}$ **5.** $9\frac{6}{1,000}$

Write each decimal in words and in expanded form.

6. 3.8   **7.** 9.12   **8.** 6.07   **9.** 15.003   **10.** 2.055

Set C (Lesson 4, pp. 550–552)

Write a fraction to describe the shaded part.
Then write a decimal equivalent.

1.   **2.**   **3.**   **4.**

Set D (Lessons 6, pp. 558–559)

Compare. Write >, <, or = for each ⬤.

1. 0.7 ⬤ 0.3   **2.** 5.65 ⬤ 5.065   **3.** 1.7 ⬤ 1.17   **4.** 1.05 ⬤ 1.5

5. 6.65 ⬤ 6.56   **6.** 8.08 ⬤ 8.80   **7.** 22.9 ⬤ 22.90   **8.** 13.03 ⬤ 13.30

Set E (Lesson 7, pp. (560–562)

Order the numbers from least to greatest.

1. 0.2 $\frac{1}{2}$ $\frac{1}{4}$ 0.6   **2.** $1\frac{1}{2}$ 1.05   1.005   1.55   **3.** $2\frac{3}{4}$ $1\frac{2}{5}$ 1.3   2.09

4. 0.67   1.5   0.007 $2\frac{1}{4}$ **5.** 4.1 $4\frac{1}{5}$ 4.07 $4\frac{1}{2}$ **6.** 6.007   6.070 $6\frac{3}{4}$ 6

Add and Subtract Decimals

INVESTIGATION

Using Data

Knowing the value of the U.S. dollar is very important when you travel. Look at the table. If you were in China, how many yuan would you get for $2.00? What's the best way to find out how much your $2.00 would be worth in each of the other countries?

CURRENCY EXCHANGE RATES*		
$1.00 U.S. =		48.27 Indian Rupees
$1.00 U.S. =		8.23 Chinese Yuan
$1.00 U.S. =		0.63 British Pound
$1.00 U.S. =		31.49 Russian Rubles
$1.00 U.S. =		1.81 Australian Dollars
$1.00 U.S. =		3.51 Peruvian Nuevo Soles

*Rates are constantly changing.

Use What You Know

**Use this page to review and remember
what you need to know for this chapter.**

VOCABULARY

Choose the best term to complete each sentence.

1. When you find an approximate answer, you are making an _____.

2. One of ten equal parts of a whole is a _____.

3. The symbol that separates ones and tenths in a decimal is a _____.

4. You write $3.59 as $4.00 when you _____ to the nearest dollar.

> ### Vocabulary
> **tenth**
> **round**
> **estimate**
> **hundredth**
> **decimal point**

CONCEPTS AND SKILLS

Write a decimal to describe the shaded part.

5.

6.

7.

**Tell whether the underlined digit is in the *ones,
tenths, hundredths,* or *thousandths* place.**

8. 0.4̲21

9. 5.618̲

10. 1.27̲6

11. 2̲.015

Round each number to the place of the underlined digit.

12. 4̲3

13. 25̲7

14. 29̲8

15. 3,1̲39

16. 4̲,622

17. 14̲,372

18. 6̲1,315

19. 309̲,897

20. Why is 0.4 greater than 0.04? Use pictures, symbols, or words to explain your answer.

> Facts Practice, See Page 669.

Audio Tutor 2/27 Listen and Understand

Round Decimals

Objective Use rules or a number line to round decimals.

Learn About It

Ami sells nuts and vegetables at an outdoor market in Ghana. She has 1.35 kilograms of kola nuts to sell. What is the weight of the kola nuts to the nearest whole kilogram?

1.35 kg

Kola Nuts

Kilograms Scale

Here are some different ways to round decimals.

Different Ways to Round 1.35

Way 1 You can use a number line.

rounds to

1.00   1.10   1.20   1.30   ↑   1.40   1.50   1.60   1.70   1.80   1.90   2.00

**1.35 lies between 1 and 2.
1.35 is closer to 1.**

So round 1.35 to 1.

Way 2 You can use rules for rounding.

STEP 1 Find the place you want to **round** to.	STEP 2 Look at the digit to the right.	STEP 3 Round as you do with whole numbers.
1.35 ↑ ones place	1.35 ↑ digit to the right	1.35 ↑ 3 < 5 So 1.35 rounds down to 1.

Solution: The weight of the kola nuts to the nearest whole kilogram is 1 kilogram.

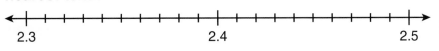

Use the number line to round each decimal to the nearest tenth.

• Which digit do I need to look at in order to round the decimal?

• Should the rounding-place digit change or stay the same?

1. 2.31   **2.** 2.38   **3.** 2.46   **4.** 2.43

Round each decimal to the place of the underlined digit.

5. 3<u>8</u>.6   **6.** 9<u>5</u>.05   **7.** 7.<u>3</u>7   **8.** 6.1<u>9</u>4   **9.** 5.7<u>0</u>4

Explain Your Thinking ▶ Compare rounding decimals to rounding whole numbers.

Practice and Problem Solving

Round each decimal to the nearest whole number.

10. 10.01   **11.** 680.46   **12.** 501.79   **13.** 12.536   **14.** 14.376   **15.** 19.62

16. 238.49   **17.** 302.63   **18.** 5.989   **19.** 199.08   **20.** 498.57   **21.** 5,679.91

Round each decimal to the place of the underlined digit.

22. <u>2</u>.8   **23.** <u>9</u>.4   **24.** 11<u>8</u>.16   **25.** 8<u>9</u>.98   **26.** 7.<u>8</u>6   **27.** 73.<u>5</u>7

28. 6.<u>5</u>1   **29.** 236.<u>4</u>37   **30.** 9.0<u>5</u>4   **31.** 10.4<u>2</u>7   **32.** 9.1<u>3</u>2   **33.** 125.0<u>9</u>6

Solve.

34. Ami has 15.47 kg of yams. What is the weight of the yams to the nearest whole kilogram?

35. Ami lives $1\frac{3}{4}$ km from the market. What is this distance to the nearest tenth of a kilometer?

36. Analyze What is the greatest decimal in tenths that rounds to 83?

37. Explain What is a reasonable rounded estimate for 35.27?

Mixed Review and Test Prep

Open Response

Write a mixed number for each.
(Ch. 19, Lesson 7)

38. $\frac{9}{7}$ **39.** $\frac{7}{3}$ **40.** $\frac{8}{5}$

41. $\frac{5}{4}$ **42.** $\frac{10}{6}$ **43.** $\frac{7}{2}$

Multiple Choice

44. Which is 18.26 rounded to the nearest tenth? (Ch. 22, Lesson 1)

A 18   **C** 18.2

B 19   **D** 18.3

Extra Practice See page 581, Set A.

Estimate Decimal Sums and Differences

Objective Use rounding to estimate sums and differences.

Bamboo Needed	
Top Wing	2.3 meters
Bottom Wing	1.6 meters
Center Support	2.5 meters

Learn About It

Liang is making a kite with his grandfather. He wants to make the kite that uses the least amount of bamboo. Should he pick the butterfly kite or the hawk kite?

You do not need an exact answer. You can solve the problem with an estimate.

Bamboo Needed	
Wings	3.2 meters
Body	2.6 meters

STEP 1 Estimate the amount of bamboo needed for each kite.

Round each **decimal** to the nearest whole number. Then add the rounded numbers.

Butterfly Kite

2.3 rounds to 2
1.6 rounds to 2
+ 2.5 rounds to + 3
7 meters

Hawk Kite

3.2 rounds to 3
+ 2.6 rounds to + 3
6 meters

STEP 2 Compare the two estimates.

7 meters > 6 meters

The butterfly kite needs more bamboo than the hawk kite.

Solution: Liang should pick the hawk kite.

Other Examples

A. Round to the Nearest $10.

$16.25 rounds to $20
+ 12.35 rounds to + 10
$30

B. Round to the Nearest $100.

$306.75 rounds to $300
− 97.25 rounds to − 100
$200

Guided Practice

Ask Yourself
- How do I round each decimal to the nearest whole number?
- Should I add or subtract?

Estimate by rounding to the nearest whole number.

1. 5.1
    − 1.7

2. $44.63
    + 14.35

3. 349.29
    + 34.516

4. 4.7 + 2.5 + 3.1

5. 21.73 − 19.959

6. $157.93 + $104.52

Explain Your Thinking ▶ Would rounding to the nearest $10 or $100 give the most reasonable estimate for Exercise 6?

Practice and Problem Solving

Estimate by rounding to the nearest whole number.

7. 8.6
    + 5.2

8. 8.2
    − 3.9

9. $23.82
    − 20.49

10. 13.534
     + 15.972

11. $349.59
     + 34.25

Estimate by rounding to the nearest $10 and $100.

12. $139.24 + $406.37

13. $274.85 + $135.40

14. $527.49 − $248.21

15. $902.55 − $383.72

16. $727.33 + $91.89

17. $563.50 − $329.90

18. **Money** Tom spent $18.96 on fabric and $15.37 on other supplies to make a kite. About how much did he spend?

19. Kaya has 15 m of silk. She uses 7.15 m for one kite and 5.76 m for another. About how much does she have left?

20. Buses taking people to a kite-flying competition leave every 7 minutes, starting at 9:05 A.M. At what time will the sixth bus leave for the show?

21. **Explain** Give a reasonable estimate for the sum of $4,109,384.75 and $9,834,523.78. What place did you round to?

Mixed Review and Test Prep

Open Response

Write each decimal as a fraction.
(Ch. 21, Lesson 4)

22. 0.1

23. 0.48

24. 0.125

25. 0.70

26. 0.6

27. 0.08

28. Miguel rode his bike 3.3 km, 1.5 km, and 2.8 km. About how much farther does he need to ride to reach 10 km? Explain how you got your answer.
(Ch.22, Lesson 2)

Explore Addition and Subtraction of Decimals

Objective Use models to add and subtract decimals.

Materials
Decimal Models
(Learning Tool 41)
colored pencils in red and blue

Work Together

You can use models to add and subtract decimals.

Work with a partner.
Use models to add.

Find 1.5 + 0.75.

 STEP 1 Shade 1.5 decimal grids red.

STEP 2 Shade an additional 0.75 decimal grids blue.

- How many decimal grids do you need? Why?

 STEP 3 Record your work in a chart like the one on the right.

- How should you line up the numbers?

- Why do you record 0 in the hundredths place for 1.5?

- What is the sum?

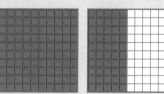

	ones		tenths	hundredths
	1	.	5	0
+	0	.	7	5

Find 2.1 − 1.4.

 STEP 1 Shade 2.1 decimal grids red.

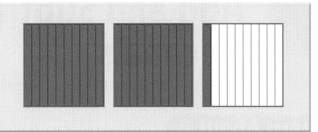

STEP 2 Outline 1.4 on the shaded part of the grids and cross it out.

- Why do you cross out part of your model?

- How many tenths are not crossed out?

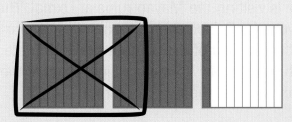

STEP 3 Record your work in a chart like the one on the right.

- What is the difference?

	ones		tenths
	2	.	1
−	1	.	4

On Your Own

Find the sum or difference. Use models if you wish.

1. 1.3 + 1.7
2. 3.2 − 1.4
3. 2.9 + 3.5
4. 4.5 − 2.9

5. 3.71 − 1.47
6. 1.04 + 1.18
7. 2.36 − 1.12
8. 3.27 + 4.96

Talk About It • Write About It

You learned how to use models to add and subtract decimals.

9. What does the decimal point in a number tell you?

10. Look at how the decimals are lined up in the addition chart. What would happen if the decimal points were not lined up?

Add and Subtract Decimals

Objective Add and subtract decimals.

Learn About It

Inez is visiting the Mayan ruins at Uxmal. The Governor's Palace stands on a series of four platforms. One of the platforms is 1.25 meters high. Another is 7.5 meters high. What is the total height of the two platforms?

Add. $1.25 + 7.5 = n$

STEP 1 Line up the decimal points. Add.

$$\begin{array}{r} 1.25 \\ + 7.50 \\ \hline 8\ 75 \end{array}$$ Place a zero in the hundredths place.

STEP 2 Write the decimal point in the answer.

$$\begin{array}{r} 1.25 \\ + 7.50 \\ \hline 8.75 \end{array}$$ decimal point

STEP 3 Estimate to check. Round and add.

1.25 rounds to 1
+ 7.50 rounds to + 8
9

8.75 is close to 9.

Solution: The total height of the two platforms is 8.75 meters.

If the height of all four platforms is 18.05 meters, what is the combined height of the remaining two platforms?

Subtract. $18.05 - 8.75 = n$

STEP 1 Line up the decimal points. Subtract.

$$\begin{array}{r} \overset{\scriptstyle 17}{} \\ \overset{0\ \ 7\ \ 10}{\cancel{18.05}} \\ -\ 8.75 \\ \hline 9\ 30 \end{array}$$

STEP 2 Write the decimal point in the answer.

$$\begin{array}{r} \overset{\scriptstyle 17}{} \\ \overset{0\ \ 7\ \ 10}{\cancel{18.05}} \\ -\ 8.75 \\ \hline 9.30 \end{array}$$ decimal point

STEP 3 Add to check.

$$\begin{array}{r} \overset{1}{}8.75 \\ +\ 9.30 \\ \hline 18.05 \end{array}$$

Solution: The combined height of the remaining two platforms is 9.3 meters.

Extra Help at **eduplace.com/map**

Guided Practice

Ask Yourself

- Should I add or subtract?
- Where do I put the decimal point?

Add or subtract. Check your work.

1. 8.2
    + 2.5

2. $2.32
    + 1.71

3. 12.34
    − 10.125

4. $83.35 − $20.67   5. 24.31 + 2.579   6. 9.31 − 3.4   7. 76.41 − 8.15

Explain Your Thinking ▶ Compare adding and subtracting decimals to adding and subtracting whole numbers.

Practice and Problem Solving

Add or subtract. Check your work.

8.   2.4
    + 7.1

9.   3.25
    + 3.49

10. $91.42
    − 35.21

11. 5.38
    − 0.67

12. 5.384
    − 1.921

Mental Math Place the decimal points in the addends to make the sentences correct.

13. 14 + 32 = 4.6   14. 47 + 189 = 23.6   15. 12 + 258 + 101 = 13.88

16. 451 + 109 = 5.6   17. 237 + 374 = 39.77   18. 12 + 295 + 41 = 45.15

19. When Emilio was on vacation last summer, his family drove 8.25 km to Merida and 78.4 km to Uxmal. How many kilometers did they drive?

20. **Create and Solve** Write a problem that requires adding or subtracting decimals. Give your problem to a classmate to solve.

Quick Check

Check your understanding of Lessons 1–4.

Estimate by rounding to the nearest whole number. (Lessons 1–2)

1. 3.2 + 5.9   2. $12.02 − $8.95

Add or subtract. Check your work. (Lessons 3–4)

3. 10.9 + 12.1   4. $25.10 − $6.37   5. 5.021 + 1.78

Problem-Solving Application
Use Decimals

Objective Use decimals to solve problems.

You can add or subtract decimals to solve problems.

Problem The London subway system is called "The Tube." Victoria and Oxford Circus are two busy Tube stations. In the year 2001, Victoria had 76.5 million passengers and Oxford Circus had 66.1 million passengers.

How many passengers did the two stations have in 2001?

UNDERSTAND

This is what the question asks.

How many passengers did Victoria Station and Oxford Circus Station have in the year 2001?

This is what you know.

• Victoria Station had 76.5 million passengers.

• Oxford Circus Station had 66.1 million passengers.

PLAN

Choose an operation.

Add the number of people who used Victoria Station and the number who used Oxford Circus Station.

SOLVE

Line up the decimal points and add.

$$\begin{array}{r} \overset{1}{76.5} \\ + \ 66.1 \\ \hline 142.6 \end{array}$$ ← Victoria Station
← Oxford Circus Station

Solution: The two stations had 142.6 million passengers in the year 2001.

LOOK BACK

Look back at the problem.

Is your answer reasonable? Explain.

Guided Practice

Use the Ask Yourself questions to help you solve each problem.

1. The average depth below ground of the deep-level Tube lines is 24.4 meters. The maximum depth is 43 meters more. What is the maximum depth?

   (Hint) Are the numbers lined up correctly?

2. The Seikan Tunnel in Japan is 53.9 km long. It is the world's longest rail tunnel. The Tube's longest tunnel is 26.1 km shorter than the Seikan. What is its length?

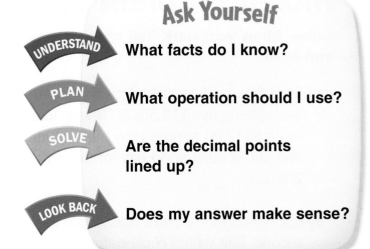

Ask Yourself

UNDERSTAND → **What facts do I know?**

PLAN → **What operation should I use?**

SOLVE → **Are the decimal points lined up?**

LOOK BACK → **Does my answer make sense?**

Independent Practice

3. Inside Gloucester Road Station, one art display measures 2.4 ft across. Another display measures 0.7 ft. What is the difference?

4. The longest trip Bill can make by Tube without changing trains is 54.9 km. If he travels this distance to and from his house, how many kilometers does he travel?

5. **Measurement** A subway has three tunnels that are 1.9 km, 2.7 km, and 1.6 km long. Which two tunnels when placed end-to-end would be between 3 and 4 kilometers long?

6. **Money** Barry needs a Tube pass for 6 days. Suppose a one-day pass costs $8.24 and a week pass costs $29.99. How much money will Barry save if he buys the week pass?

This elephant is part of the Underground Safari Art Exhibition at Gloucester Road Station.

Mixed Problem Solving

Solve. Show your work. Tell what strategy you used.

7. For a trip, each student pays $10.00 and each adult pays $18.50. A 10-seat minibus costs $117.00 to rent. How many students and adults must go to pay for exactly 2 buses?

8. Luz visited four friends. She visited Earl second. She visited Nicki before Joe. She visited Mary right after Earl. In what order did Luz visit her friends?

9. One night in November, the temperature dropped 0.2 degrees every 15 minutes for 2 hours. Then the temperature stayed at 15.6°F. What was the temperature when it began to drop?

You Choose

Strategy
- Guess and Check
- Use Logical Reasoning
- Work Backward
- Write an Equation

Computation Method
- Mental Math
- Estimation
- Paper and Pencil
- Calculator

 Data Use the table for Problems 10–13. Then tell which method you chose and why.

10. What would it cost for 2 adults and 2 children to visit the water park?

11. **Analyze** Lita and her dad have $65. If they pay one adult fee and one child's fee at the amusement park, will they have enough money left to visit the state park? Explain your reasoning.

12. How much more would it cost for 1 adult and 2 children to visit the animal park than to visit the state park?

13. **You Decide** Your family has $100 to spend on any of the attractions. Decide which you would visit and find the total cost for your family.

Park Entrance Fees

Attraction	Adult Fee	Child Fee
Amusement Park	$28.99	$19.99
Animal Park	$12.00	$ 7.00
Water Park	$20.50	$15.50
State Park	$ 5.95	$ 3.95

Calculator Connection
Place Value Pathways

Use your calculator to get from each Start Number to each End Number.

1. **Start Number**
3.21

Add
6 thousandths.

Add
7 tenths.

Subtract
5 hundredths.

End Number

2. **Start Number**
4.096

Subtract
4 hundredths.

Add
8 tenths.

Add
5 thousandths.

End Number

3. **Start Number**
41.387

Subtract
4 tenths.

Add
1 thousandth.

Add
2 hundredths.

End Number

4. **Start Number**
1.309

Add
4 thousandths.

Subtract
2 tenths.

Subtract
5 hundredths.

End Number

5. **Start Number**
23.76

Subtract
2 tenths.

Add
9 hundredths.

Add
2 tenths.

End Number

6. **Start Number**
0.793

Add
3 tenths.

Add
7 thousandths.

Add
9 tenths.

End Number

7. **Challenge** Compare each Start Number with its End Number. Decide which is greater. Then use your calculator to find how much greater.

8. Create your own Place Value Pathway. Start by choosing a decimal number as a Start Number. Then add and subtract tenths, hundredths, and thousandths as in the examples above. What End Number do you end up with? Challenge a classmate to solve your Place Value Pathway and compare your results.

Chapter Review/Test

VOCABULARY

Choose the best term to complete each sentence.

1. A number close to the exact amount is an ____.

2. When you write 4.237 as 4.2 you are rounding to the nearest ____.

3. The symbol between the ones and tenths in a decimal is the ____.

Vocabulary

tenth
estimate
hundredth
decimal point

CONCEPTS AND SKILLS

Round each decimal to the place of the underlined digit. (Lesson 1, pp. 568–569)

4. <u>1</u>.55 5. 4.<u>9</u>2 6. 3.1<u>8</u>9 7. 1<u>6</u>.39

Estimate by rounding to the nearest whole number. (Lesson 2, pp. 570–571)

8.　16.3
　 + 9.8

9.　$25.83
　 − 6.70

10.　199.7
　 − 30.32

11.　212.1
　 + 318.59

Add or subtract. Check your work. (Lessons 3–4, pp. 572–575)

12.　7.3
　 + 6.9

13.　6.5
　 − 3.2

14.　$6.17
　 − 3.53

15.　12.84
　 + 6.925

16. 125.3 + 12.7　　17. 2.9 − 1.64　　18. $15.53 − $6.44

PROBLEM SOLVING

Solve. (Lesson 5, pp. 576–579)

19. Ella's family drove 26.7 miles to visit her grandparents. Then they drove 15.9 miles to visit her cousins. How many miles did they drive?

20. Mr. Jacob's grocery bill is $58.76. He gives the clerk $100. How much change will he get back?

 **Write About It**

Show You Understand

The teacher asked the class to round to estimate.

Rich	6.81 →	6
	5.76 →	5
	+ 7.53 →	+ 7
		18

Explain what Rich did wrong. Then estimate the answer correctly.

Extra Practice

Set A (Lesson 1, pp. 568–569)

Round each decimal to the place of the underlined digit.

1. <u>3</u>.4   **2.** <u>9</u>.7   **3.** 1<u>3</u>.5   **4.** 2<u>1</u>.91   **5.** 7<u>3</u>.15   **6.** 12<u>6</u>.09

7. 4.<u>7</u>6   **8.** 8.<u>3</u>1   **9.** 11.<u>6</u>7   **10.** 35.<u>9</u>2   **11.** 57.<u>9</u>8   **12.** 98.<u>5</u>4

13. 2.1<u>2</u>2   **14.** 5.1<u>0</u>9   **15.** 33.1<u>8</u>9   **16.** 42.2<u>7</u>1   **17.** 61.9<u>9</u>3   **18.** 23.0<u>1</u>7

Set B (Lesson 2, pp. 570–571)

Estimate by rounding to the nearest whole number.

1.	2.7	2.	16.5	3.	35.1	4.	52.9	5.	$23.56
	+ 3.2		− 9.8		− 10.6		+ 9.6		+ 13.10

6.	3.98	7.	4.29	8.	$49.91	9.	100.3	10.	119.18
	− 0.75		− 1.52		+ 25.27		+ 99.98		− 87.04

11. 5.6 + 2.3   **12.** 18.27 − 9.5   **13.** $215.20 − $14.95

Estimate by rounding to the nearest $10 and $100.

14. $267.39 + $361.22   **15.** $807.13 − $698.79   **16.** $316.55 + $628.31

17. $435.17 − $287.29   **18.** $534.78 + $645.35   **19.** $211.21 − $171.89

20. $793.25 + $129.56   **21.** $638.48 + $382.71   **22.** $441.98 + $219.24

Set C (Lesson 4, pp. 574–575)

Add or subtract. Check your work.

1.	9.1	2.	10.7	3.	18.3	4.	21.3	5.	$49.21
	+ 5.6		+ 9.3		− 7.2		− 10.7		+ 13.96

6.	7.25	7.	32.67	8.	16.7	9.	13.5	10.	$176.51
	+ 6.98		− 14.25		+ 9.851		− 11.98		− 49.28

11. 16.5 − 10   **12.** 37.2 − 9.85   **13.** 100 − 2.588

14. $3.15 + $6.98   **15.** $10.19 − $7.00   **16.** $200.00 − $17.25

Under the Sea

The John Pennekamp Coral Reef State Park is located in the Atlantic Ocean off Key Largo, Florida. It contains part of the only living coral reef in the continental United States.

Coral reefs are home to plants, sponges, turtles, lobsters, and hundreds of different kinds of fish. Visitors to Pennekamp can see the reef through glass-bottom boats or by snorkeling or scuba diving.

Florida

Key Largo

Problem Solving

Use the diagram at the right for Problems 1–3.

1 Suppose you see chub swimming $\frac{1}{4}$ of the way down to the bottom. How many feet below the surface is that?

2 You see snapper $\frac{3}{4}$ of the way down, grunts $\frac{6}{8}$ of the way down, and chromis $\frac{1}{5}$ of the way down. Which fish are swimming at the same depth? How do you know?

3 A barracuda is swimming at a depth of 50 feet. What fraction of the way down to the bottom is that?

4 While scuba diving, half the fish you see are grunts, two sixths are snappers, and four are stingrays. How many fish do you see?

5 Look at the pictures of the fish below. List them in order from longest to shortest.

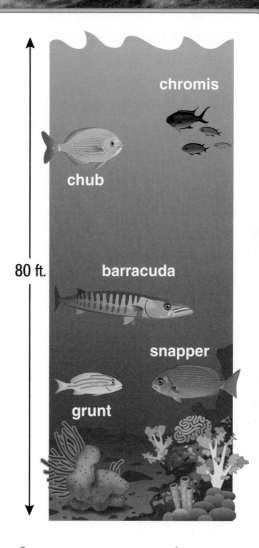

80 ft.

chromis

chub

barracuda

snapper

grunt

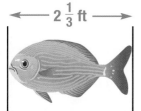

← $2\frac{1}{3}$ ft →

Bermuda Sea Chub

← $2\frac{7}{8}$ ft →

Spotted Moray Eel

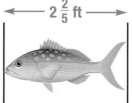

← $2\frac{2}{5}$ ft →

Yellowtail Snapper

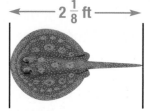

← $2\frac{1}{8}$ ft →

Yellow Stingray

Education Place

Visit Weekly Reader Connections at **eduplace.com/map** for more on this topic.

Enrichment: Use a Scale

A LONG WALK!

The Appalachian Trail is a footpath that runs for 2,167 miles from Katahdin, Maine, to Springer Mountain in Georgia.

The map at the right shows the Appalachian Trail as it passes through North Carolina and parts of Tennessee.

The scale shows 1 inch = 32 miles. That means that every inch of the trail shown on the map represents 32 miles of the actual trail.

Try These!

Use the map, a piece of string, and a ruler.

1. Use the string to find the length of the trail on the map to the nearest half inch. Then use the scale to find the actual length of the trail.

2. Find the actual distances between some of the places along the trail. Copy and complete the table.

3. If a hiking trail started in your hometown, where would it end? Use a U.S. road map and plan a route that has about the same total miles as the Appalachian Trail in North Carolina.

APPALACHIAN TRAIL
(NORTH CAROLINA)

Scale : 1 inch = 32 miles

Places	Distance on Map (to nearest half inch)	Approximate Distance (in miles)
Roan High Knob to Big Bald		
Big Bald to Mt. Guyot		
Mt. Guyot to Wayah Bald		

Fun With Fractions!

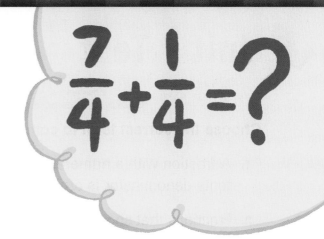

$$\frac{7}{4} + \frac{1}{4} = ?$$

You can use the fraction models found on Education Place at **eduplace.com/map** to add and subtract fractions.

Find $\frac{7}{8} + \frac{1}{4}$.

- At **Change Mat,** choose **Circles.** To divide into eighths, put pointer over the scissors. Choose $\frac{1}{8}$ and click the first circle.

- To show $\frac{7}{8}$, click **Fill.** Then click on 7 of the 8 sections.

- Repeat with the second circle. Divide it into fourths and fill 1 section.

- To make common denominators, put pointer over the scissors, choose $\frac{1}{8}$, and click the second circle.

- Click the **Hand Tool.** Drag 2 sections from the second circle to the first.

$$\frac{7}{8} + \frac{1}{4} = 1\frac{1}{8}$$

Find $\frac{4}{5} - \frac{3}{10}$.

- To divide into fifths, put pointer over the scissors. Choose $\frac{1}{5}$ and click the first circle.

- To show $\frac{4}{5}$, click **Fill.** Then click on 4 of the 5 sections.

- To subtract, first make common denominators. Put pointer over the scissors and choose $\frac{1}{10}$. Click the circle showing $\frac{4}{5}$.

- Click **Fill.** Click on 3 out of the 10 filled sections to empty them.

$$\frac{4}{5} - \frac{3}{10} = \frac{1}{2}$$

Use the fraction models. Write each answer in simplest form.

1. $\frac{1}{3} + \frac{5}{6}$

2. $\frac{7}{8} - \frac{1}{4}$

3. $\frac{10}{12} + \frac{5}{6}$

4. $\frac{5}{6} - \frac{1}{2}$

5. $\frac{1}{2} - \frac{1}{4}$

6. $\frac{2}{3} + \frac{1}{6}$

7. $\frac{3}{4} + \frac{1}{2}$

8. $\frac{7}{10} - \frac{1}{5}$

9. $\frac{2}{3} + \frac{5}{6}$

10. $\frac{1}{2} + \frac{1}{4}$

Unit 7 Test

VOCABULARY Open Response

Choose the correct term to complete each sentence.

1. A fraction with a numerator greater than or equal to its denominator is a(n) ____.

2. Fractions that show equal parts using different numbers are called ____.

3. A number that is made up of a whole number and a fraction is called a(n) ____.

> **Vocabulary**
> decimal
> mixed number
> improper fraction
> equivalent fractions

CONCEPTS AND SKILLS Open Response

Write each fraction in simplest form. Then write another equivalent fraction. (Chapter 19)

4. $\frac{6}{8}$
5. $\frac{10}{15}$
6. $\frac{8}{12}$
7. $\frac{3}{9}$

Write each improper fraction as a mixed number or whole number. (Chapter 19)

8. $\frac{15}{4}$
9. $\frac{10}{3}$
10. $\frac{16}{2}$
11. $\frac{21}{5}$

Add or subtract. Write your answer in simplest form. (Chapter 20)

12. $\frac{4}{6} + \frac{1}{6}$
13. $\frac{5}{12} - \frac{4}{12}$
14. $6\frac{2}{8} + 1\frac{3}{8}$
15. $4\frac{3}{5} - 2\frac{2}{5}$

16. $\frac{3}{8} - \frac{1}{4}$
17. $\frac{5}{6} - \frac{1}{2}$
18. $\frac{3}{5} + \frac{3}{10}$
19. $\frac{7}{12} + \frac{5}{6}$

Write a fraction and a decimal to describe the shaded part. (Chapter 21)

20.
21.
22.
23.

Order the numbers from greatest to least. (Chapter 21)

24. 1.3 $1\frac{8}{10}$ 1.05 $\frac{11}{10}$

25. $1\frac{25}{100}$ 1.1 $1\frac{5}{10}$ $1\frac{3}{5}$

586

Estimate each answer by rounding. Then find the exact answer. (Chapter 22)

26. 2.81
    + 3.75

27. 4.381
    + 7.987

28. 16.53
    − 14.82

29. $ 27.87
    − 12.19

PROBLEM SOLVING (Open Response)

30. After Kim spent $\frac{1}{2}$ of her money on a sandwich, $\frac{1}{6}$ of her money on juice, and $2 for a salad, she had no money left. How much money did Kim spend?

31. A store manager ordered five sizes of bottles: 1.2 oz, 2.4 oz, ? oz, 4.8 oz, and 6.0 oz. She knows the sizes follow a pattern, but forgot one size. What is that size likely to be?

32. Raj has 7 liters of water to share equally with 3 friends. If each person receives the same amount, how much water will each of the four people receive?

33. **Write About It** Pedro has $10.00. Does he have enough money to buy dog food for $4.89, a dog treat for $2.48, and a dog toy for $1.29? Explain how you solved the problem.

Performance Assessment

Extended Response

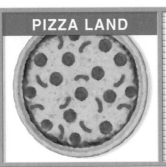

SMALL PIZZA - 4 slices		PIZZA LAND	LARGE PIZZA - 8 slices	
Cheese	$3.99		Cheese	$9.99
Pepperoni	$5.99		Pepperoni	$11.99
Vegetable	$4.99		Vegetable	$10.99
MEDIUM PIZZA - 6 slices			DRINKS - medium/large	
Cheese	$5.99		Soft Drink	$0.75/$0.95
Pepperoni	$7.99		Juice	$1.00/$1.25
Vegetable	$6.99			

Task A class-trip leader has $45 to buy food for himself and 9 students. Use the menu above and the information at the right. How should the leader spend the money so that everyone gets at least 2 slices of pizza and a drink they like? Explain your thinking.

Information You Need

- Two thirds of the students like pepperoni.
- The leader and two of the students like vegetable pizza.
- All the students would be willing to eat cheese pizza.
- Half of the group prefer juice to soft drinks.
- The leader wants a large juice.

Cumulative Test Prep

Solve Problems 1–10.

Test-Taking Tip

Sometimes when you take a test, you can eliminate answer choices that are clearly wrong.

Look at the example below.

Kim has $2\frac{1}{4}$ yards of red ribbon and $1\frac{3}{4}$ yards of blue ribbon. How much ribbon does she have?

A $3\frac{1}{8}$ yards   **C** $4\frac{1}{8}$ yards

B 4 yards   **D** 10 yards

THINK

You know that $1\frac{3}{4}$ is a little less than 2 and $2\frac{1}{4}$ is a little more than 2. So the answer will be about 4 yards. Therefore, you can eliminate choices A and D.

For Test-Taking Tips, See Page 658.

Multiple Choice

1. What is the remainder when you divide 38 by 4?

   A 0   **C** 9

   B 2   **D** 10

   (Chapter 4, Lesson 8)

2. A store sells pencils in packages of 7 and pens in packages of 8. Mrs. Ruíz needs 56 pencils. How many packages of pencils must she buy?

   F 0   **H** 8

   G 7   **J** 56

   (Chapter 12, Lesson 5)

3. In January, the normal temperature in Anchorage, Alaska, is 15°F. The normal temperature in Miami, Florida, is 67°F. What is the difference between these two temperatures?

   A 52 degrees   **C** 72 degrees

   B 60 degrees   **D** 82 degrees

   (Chapter 13, Lesson 4)

4. A rectangular pool is 40 feet long, 15 feet wide, and 8 feet deep. What is the perimeter of the pool?

   F 8 feet   **H** 126 feet

   G 110 feet   **J** 600 feet

   (Chapter 18, Lesson 2)

5. Bob collected 48 cans of food. Sue collected $\frac{2}{3}$ as many cans as Bob. How many cans of food did Sue collect?

(Chapter 19, Lesson 5)

6. Emily wrote this number pattern.

7, 14, 28, 56

If Emily continues the pattern, what will the sixth number be?

(Chapter 21, Lesson 5)

7. Vern gave a clerk $20.00 to pay for a $15.95 shirt. The tax was $0.76. How much change should Vern get?

(Chapter 22, Lesson 4)

8. Travis had a board that was $4\frac{3}{4}$ feet long. He used the board to make a shelf that was $2\frac{1}{4}$ feet long. How much of the board does Travis have left?

(Chapter 20, Lesson 2)

9. How much money will a family of 2 adults, 3 teenagers, and a 10-year-old girl save by buying their tickets to the state fair in advance?

State Fair Admission Prices		
Ages	Bought in Advance	Bought at the Gate
12 years or older	$5	$8
6–11 years	$3	$4
Under 6	Free	Free

(Chapter 11, Lesson 7)

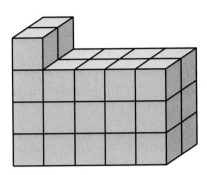

10. Each cube in the drawing above represents 5 tons of trash.

A How many cubes are represented in the drawing?

B How many tons of trash are represented in the drawing?

C Central City produces 230 tons of trash. Make a drawing of cubes to show how to represent that amount. Tell how much each cube represents. Explain how you decided how many cubes to use in your drawing.

D Suppose the amount of trash Central City produces is cut in half. How would your answer to Question C change? Make a new drawing to help you explain your answer.

(Chapter 18, Lesson 6)

Education Place

Look for Cumulative Test Prep at **eduplace.com/map** for more practice.

Vocabulary Wrap-Up for Unit 7

Look back at the big ideas and vocabulary in this unit.

Big Ideas

A fraction or a decimal can represent a number less than 1.

When you write a decimal, you use place-value notation.

You can name the same amount as a fraction or decimal.

Key Vocabulary

fraction
decimal
place-value

Math Conversations

Use your new vocabulary to discuss these big ideas.

1. Explain how the fraction $\frac{4}{8}$ is different from the fraction $\frac{8}{4}$.

2. Explain the relationship between $\frac{3}{2}$, 1.5, and 1.50.

3. Explain how to add $\frac{3}{8}$ and $\frac{1}{2}$.

4. Explain how to subtract 0.31 from 0.9.

5. **Write About It** Search for decimals and fractions in a newspaper or magazine. List the different ways that fractions and decimals are used.

Which is greater, $\frac{3}{5}$ or $\frac{7}{8}$?

We can use a picture or fraction pieces to find out.

Probability/
Algebra
and
Graphing

Reading Mathematics

Reviewing Vocabulary

Here are some math vocabulary words that you should know.

equally likely   having the same chance of occurring

ordered pair   a pair of numbers in which one number is named as the first and the other number is named as the second

outcome   a result in a probability experiment

probability   the chance that an event will occur

Reading Words and Symbols

You can find the probability that something will happen by looking at the possible results. Look at the spinner.

The spinner has 8 parts altogether. 3 parts are blue.

The chance of landing on blue is 3 out of 8.

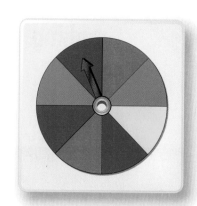

- You can write this in words: three out of eight.

- You can write this as a fraction: $\frac{3}{8}$

Use the spinner to answer these questions.

1. What is the chance that a spin will land on red?

2. What is the chance that a spin will land on yellow?

Reading Test Questions

Choose the correct answer for each.

3. Which statement describes the location of Point *A*?

   a. 2 units right and 3 units up

   b. 3 units right and 2 units up

   c. 1 unit right and 4 units up

   d. 4 units right and 1 unit up

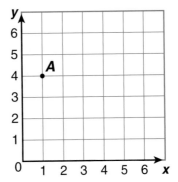

Location means "place" or "position."

---

4. On which spinner is the arrow most likely to land on blue?

   a.   **c.**

   b.   **d.**

Most likely means "having the greatest chance."

5. What is the chance that the outcome "red" will occur on one spin?

   a. 4 out of 5

   b. 3 out of 5

   c. 2 out of 5

   d. 1 out of 5

Occur means "happen."

Learning Vocabulary

 Watch for these words in this unit. Write their definitions in your journal.

   coordinates

   integers

   tree diagram

   x-axis

   y-axis

 Education Place

At **eduplace.com/map**
see eGlossary and
eGames–Math Lingo.

Literature Connection

Read "The Perfect Present" on Pages 654–655. Then work with a partner to answer the questions about the story.

Probability

INVESTIGATION

Using Data

Gabrielle just picked a bag from the treasure chest. Look at the graph. Suppose you were to pick a bag. What type of item are you most likely to pick? How would the graph change if all picks were equally likely?

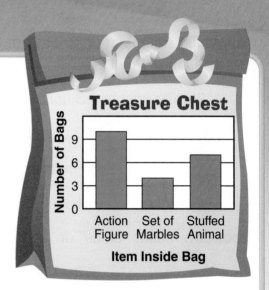

Use What You Know

Use this page to review and remember what you need to know for this chapter.

VOCABULARY

Choose the best word to complete each sentence.

1. If an event will definitely happen, it is ____.

2. A ____ names a part of a whole.

3. In a fraction, the number that tells how many equal parts are in a whole is the ____.

Vocabulary
certain
fraction
impossible
denominator

CONCEPTS AND SKILLS

Write *likely*, *equally likely*, or *unlikely* to describe the probability of picking a red tile without looking.

4.   5.   6.

Write a fraction that represents the red part.

7.   8.   9.

Write About It

10. If you pick one cube from the bag on the right, are you likely to pick a blue cube? Why or why not? Which two colors have the same probablility of being picked?

Facts Practice, See page 670.

Audio Tutor 2/29 Listen and Understand

Probability

Objective Decide the probability that something will happen.

Learn About It

Probability is a mathematical way of describing how likely it is that something will happen. An **outcome** is a result of a probability experiment.

If you pick one cube from the bag at the right without looking, the outcome will be either a red cube or a green cube.

You are more likely to pick a red cube than a green cube, because there are more red cubes than green cubes.

▶ **Look at the spinners below.**

• What are the possible outcomes for each spinner?

• What words can be used to describe the probability that the spinner will land on red?

Possible Outcomes	Red	Red, Green	Green, Red	Green
Probability of Landing on Red	Certain	Likely	Unlikely	Impossible

Another Example

Equally Likely Outcomes

Each of the spinners on the right is divided into congruent regions. On each spinner, the number of regions of each color is equal. So the probability of the arrow landing on each color is equally likely.

Guided Practice

Look at the bag of marbles. Write *certain, likely, equally likely, unlikely,* or *impossible* to describe the probability of picking each color without looking.

Ask Yourself
- How many marbles of each color are there?
- Are there more marbles of one color than another?

1. blue

2. yellow

3. red

4. blue or red

Explain Your Thinking ▶ How would you change the colors in the bag above to make it likely that red would be picked?

Practice and Problem Solving

Write *certain, likely, equally likely, unlikely,* or *impossible* to describe the probability of landing on blue.

5.   6.   7.   8.

 Data Use the chart for Problems 9 and 10.

9. **Predict** Which number of tiles is more likely to be found in the bag?
   - 5 yellow, 5 orange, and 5 brown
   - 10 yellow, 10 orange, and 5 brown

10. **Write About It** Is it likely that exactly 6 brown tiles, 11 orange tiles, and 13 yellow tiles are in the bag? Explain.

Picking Tiles		
Outcome	Tally	Number
Brown	卌 I	6
Orange	卌 卌 I	11
Yellow	卌 卌 III	13

The tally chart shows the results of picking tiles from a bag. The chosen tile was replaced after each pick.

Mixed Review and Test Prep ✓

Open Response

Divide. (Ch. 11, Lessons 4 and 5)

11. $25\overline{)178}$

12. $13\overline{)247}$

13. $19\overline{)182}$

14. $32\overline{)384}$

15. $770 \div 35$

16. $729 \div 81$

17. $145 \div 11$

18. $468 \div 26$

19. On which two colors is the arrow equally likely to land? Explain.
(Ch. 23, Lesson 1)

Probability as a Fraction

Objective Write probabilities in words and as fractions.

Learn About It

You can use words or fractions when you describe probability.

The spinner on the right has eight equally likely outcomes: 1, 2, 3, 4, 5, 6, 7, and 8. A **favorable outcome** is a result that you are looking to find. When you use a fraction to describe a probability, it is written as:

$$\frac{\text{favorable outcomes}}{\text{total possible outcomes}}$$

Favorable Outcome	Explanation
3	The probability of landing on 3 is 1 out of 8. Probability = $\frac{1}{8}$ ← favorable outcome (3) ← total possible outcomes (1, 2, 3, 4, 5, 6, 7, 8) It is **unlikely** that a spin will land on 3.
a number greater than 3	The probability of landing on a number greater than 3 is 5 out of 8. Probability = $\frac{5}{8}$ ← favorable outcomes (4, 5, 6, 7, 8) ← total possible outcomes (1, 2, 3, 4, 5, 6, 7, 8) It is **likely** that a spin will land on a number greater than 3.
9	The probability of landing on 9 is 0 out of 8. Probability = $\frac{0}{8}$ ← favorable outcome (none, 9 is not possible) ← total possible outcomes (1, 2, 3, 4, 5, 6, 7, 8) It is **impossible** that a spin will land on 9.
1 or greater	The probability of landing on 1 or greater is 8 out of 8. Probability = $\frac{8}{8}$ ← favorable outcomes (1, 2, 3, 4, 5, 6, 7, 8) ← total possible outcomes (1, 2, 3, 4, 5, 6, 7, 8) It is **certain** that a spin will land on 1 or greater.

▶ The number line below shows that the probability of an outcome ranges from 0 (impossible) to 1 (certain).

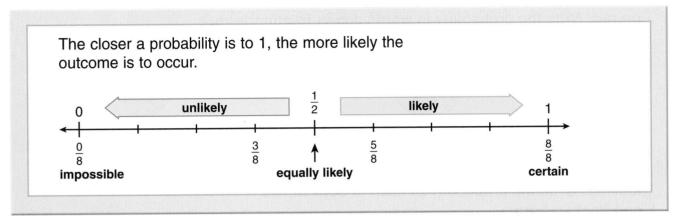

The closer a probability is to 1, the more likely the outcome is to occur.

Guided Practice

Suppose you pick a tile in the word below without looking. Write the probability of each favorable outcome in words and in fraction form.

M A T H E M A T I C S

1. T   **2.** C   **3.** H or A   **4.** a vowel   **5.** a consonant

Ask Yourself

• How many tiles are there altogether?

• How many tiles have the letter or letters I am looking for?

For each spinner, write the probability that a spin will land on blue. Write the probability in both words and fraction form.

6.   **7.**   **8.**   **9.**

Explain Your Thinking ▶ If the probability of spinning blue is $\frac{3}{8}$, does this mean that you will always spin blue 3 out of 8 times? Explain why or why not.

For each spinner, write the probability that a spin will land on red. Write the probability in words and in fraction form.

10.   **11.**   **12.**   **13.**

Suppose you pick one tile from this bag without looking. Write the probability of each in both words and fraction form.

14. picking 1

15. picking a multiple of 3

16. picking 3 or 5

17. picking a number greater than 4

Solve.

18. A bag holds 5 red marbles and 3 blue marbles. How many and what color marbles would you add to the bag so that the probability of picking a blue marble is $\frac{1}{2}$?

19. Represent Draw a spinner for which the probability of spinning yellow is $\frac{1}{6}$ and it is more likely to spin red than blue.

20. Reasoning The six sides of the number cube on the right are numbered 1, 2, 3, 4, 5, and 6. Write a fraction that tells the probability of tossing a number greater than 4

21. After winning the class spelling bee, Natalia picks from a bag of prizes. The bag contains 4 pencil sets, 3 notepads, and 3 magnet sets. If Natalia picks from the bag without looking, what is the probability that she will pick a pencil set? Write the probability in simplest form.

22. Write Your Own Imagine that you were to pick your classmates' names from a hat. Write 2 probability problems and solve them. Write your solutions as a fraction.

Extra Practice See page 613, Set B.

Fair Game

Activity

2 Players

What You'll Need • Playing Board (Learning Tool 43)
• Spinners (Learning Tools 44–47), colored as shown
• 1 red counter and 1 yellow counter

How to Play

1 Players pick a color and place their counters in the center section of the board. The first player picks the spinner for the first game.

2 Players take turns spinning. If the spinner lands on yellow, the player who chose yellow moves the yellow counter 1 space toward the yellow goal. If the spinner lands on red, the player who chose red moves 1 space toward the red goal.

3 The game continues until a player reaches his or her goal. That player wins.

4 Repeat Steps 2 and 3 to play the game three more times. Use a different spinner each time.

Write About It Which of the spinners are fair? Did using a fair spinner mean that each color moved toward its goal an equal number of times? Explain.

Quick Check

Check your understanding of Lessons 1–2.

Write _certain, likely, equally likely, unlikely,_ or _impossible_ to describe the probability of picking each color. (Lesson 1)

1. green   2. blue   3. yellow

Write the probability that a spin will land on red.

(Lesson 2)

4.
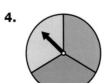

5.

Make Predictions

Objective Predict outcomes in a probability experiment.

Vocabulary
prediction

Materials
paper bag
Probability Cards
(Learning Tool 48)
number cube

Work Together

Sometimes you can use probability to make a
prediction about what may happen.

STEP 1 Work with a partner. Make 12 cards like
the ones shown and put them in a bag.

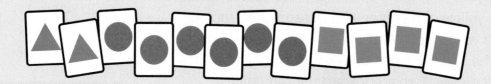

STEP 2 Predict what may happen if you pick
one card from the bag without looking.

- What is the probability of picking each
  kind of card?

- Suppose you pick from the bag
  48 times and put the card back each
  time. Predict how many times you will
  pick each shape. Put your predictions
  in a chart like the one below.

Card Experiment			
Outcome	**Prediction**	**Tally**	**Number**
Circle			
Square			
Triangle			

STEP 3 Pick a card without looking. Make a tally mark
to record the result in your chart. Put the card
back in the bag. Do this 47 more times.

- How did your predictions compare to your
  actual results?

▶ **You can use the results of an experiment to make predictions.**

The bar graph shows the results of a card experiment. Each time a card was picked, it was returned to the bag.

- How many times was a blue card picked? a red card? a green card?

- If 12 cards were in the bag, how many of each color would you predict there were?

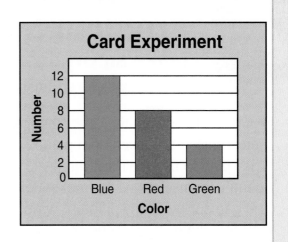

Card Experiment

On Your Own

Follow these steps for a probability experiment.

1. Label the faces of a cube with the letters *R, E, C, E, S*, and *S*.

   a. Predict how many times the cube will land on each letter if you toss the cube 30 times.

   b. Toss the cube. Record the result on a line plot like the one at the right. Do this 29 more times.

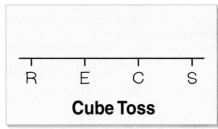

Cube Toss

2. Compare your prediction with your results. Was your prediction accurate? Explain your thinking.

3. If you tossed the cube 600 times, about how many times do you think you would toss an *S?* Explain.

Talk About It • Write About It

You learned how to predict outcomes in a probability experiment.

4. Suppose you toss a cube with the numbers 1, 2, 3, 4, 5, and 6. Why would you predict that you would toss a number less than 4 more often than a number greater than 4?

Audio Tutor 2/30 Listen and Understand

Problem-Solving Strategy
Make an Organized List

Objective: Use an organized list to solve a problem.

Problem Peggy Smith, Janet Chan, and Pete Tobias have invented a game. They plan to use their last names to identify themselves as the makers of the game. How many different ways can the names be arranged?

UNDERSTAND

This is what you know.

- The last names are *Smith, Chan,* and *Tobias.*

PLAN

You can make an organized list to help you solve the problem.

SOLVE

List all the items.

Begin with one name.

- There are two ways to arrange the names when *Smith* is first.

- There are two ways to arrange the names when *Chan* is first.

- There are two ways to arrange the names when *Tobias* is first.

Solution: There are six ways to arrange the names.

> Smith, Chan, Tobias
> Smith, Tobias, Chan
> Chan, Smith, Tobias
> Chan, Tobias, Smith
> Tobias, Smith, Chan
> Tobias, Chan, Smith

LOOK BACK

Look back at the problem. Is your answer reasonable?

Extra Help at **eduplace.com/map**

Use the Ask Yourself questions to help you solve each problem.

1. A gardener is planting tulip, daffodil, lily, and hyacinth bulbs in clusters along a sidewalk. How many different ways can he arrange the four kinds of bulbs?

2. Ann, Sue, Jo, and Nina are in line. How many ways can the girls be arranged if Ann has to be first in line?

(Hint) Which names cannot be first?

Ask Yourself

UNDERSTAND **What facts do I know?**

PLAN **Can I make an organized list?**

SOLVE
- **Did I list all the items?**
- **Did I try every possible arrangement?**

LOOK BACK **Did I solve the problem?**

Independent Practice

Make an organized list to solve each problem.

3. A painter is hanging a portrait, a landscape, and a still life in a row. What are all the different arrangements he can make?

4. Lena wants to use the four letters of her name as part of an e-mail address. How many different ways can she arrange the letters of her name?

5. Nick is using the digits 5, 6, 7, and 8 to make as many four-digit numbers as he can. What are all the numbers Nick can make?

6. A conductor is organizing players in a row.
   - He has people who play violins, cellos, flutes, saxophones, and drums.
   - The violins have to be on the left end.
   - The cellos have to be on the right end.
   How many ways can the conductor arrange the players?

Go On

Mixed Problem Solving

Solve. Show your work. Tell what strategy you used.

7. Mr. Rios is 31 years old. His son Luis is 7 years old. How old will each of them be when Mr. Rios's age is three times Luis's age?

8. Half of Sal's hats are red, $\frac{1}{6}$ are blue, and 4 are black. How many hats does Sal have?

9. Luz has post cards from New Jersey, Delaware, North Carolina, and Connecticut. How many different ways can she arrange them in a row?

10. Mark has saved $131. He has saved the same amount for four months. If he started with $15, how much did he save each month?

Data Use the line plot for Problems 11–14.

The line plot at the right shows the number of gold medals won by 11 countries during the 2002 Winter Olympic Games.

11. What do the three X's above the number 4 tell you?

12. What are the range, median, and mode of the data?

13. What is the mean of the data? What does the mean tell you?

14. Why are there no X's above the numbers 5, 7, 8, and 9?

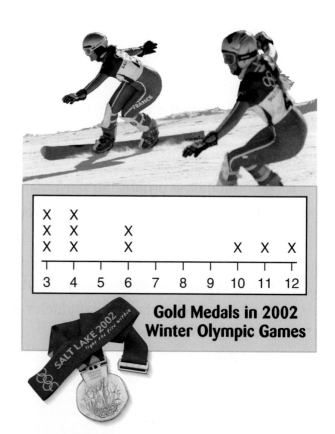

Gold Medals in 2002 Winter Olympic Games

You Choose

Strategy
- Draw a Picture
- Make an Organized List
- Make a Table
- Work Backward
- Write an Equation

Computation Method
- Mental Math
- Estimation
- Paper and Pencil
- Calculator

606

Problem Solving on Tests

(Multiple Choice)

Choose the letter of the correct answer.

1. How many 100-gram weights are needed to balance the scale?

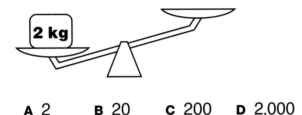

   A 2   **B** 20   **C** 200   **D** 2,000

   (Chapter 12, Lesson 9)

2. Look at this pattern of numbers.

5, 10, 6, 12, 8, 16, 12, 24

   If the pattern continues, what is the next number likely to be?

   F 16   **G** 20   **H** 28   **J** 48

   (Chapter 21, Lesson 5)

(Open Response)

Solve each problem.

3. Look at the spinner below. What is the probability that the arrow will land on the shaded area?

   (Chapter 23, Lesson 2)

4. A spinner is divided into more than 4 equal sections. The colors on the spinner are red, yellow, and blue.

   Represent Draw a spinner so that the probability of spinning blue is $\frac{1}{4}$ and it is more likely to spin red than yellow.

   (Chapter 23, Lesson 2)

(Extended Response)

5. At the National Storytelling Festival in Tennessee, people from all over the world come to hear great stories.

National Storytelling Festival		
	1-day ticket	3-day ticket
Child 6–12	$80.00	$115.00
Adult	$90.00	$135.00
Senior Citizen	$85.00	$120.00

a. Mr. and Mrs. Peterson and their two young sons plan to attend for three days. How much will it cost for their tickets?

b. Mr. and Mrs. Nguyen are both senior citizens. They will be able to attend only 2 days. Should they buy 2 one-day tickets each, or 1 three-day ticket each? Which would be the better buy? How do you know?

c. Mr. and Mrs. Patel will go to the festival for 3 days. They will stay at a motel for 4 nights. The motel will cost them $119 each night. How much will they spend for tickets and their motel room? Show your work.

   (Chapter 7)

Education Place

See **eduplace.com/map** for more Test-Taking Tips.

Audio Tutor 2/31 Listen and Understand

Find Probability

Objective Find the probability of outcomes, using a grid or a tree diagram.

Vocabulary
grid
tree diagram

Learn About It

A coin is tossed twice. What is the probability that it will land heads-up once and tails-up once?

Here are two ways you can represent all the outcomes.

▶ **You can use a grid .**

• Write the possible outcomes for the first toss at the left.

• Write the possible outcomes for the second toss at the top.

• Put the possible outcomes for both tosses in each part of the grid.

	Second Toss	
	heads	**tails**
First Toss **heads**	heads, heads	heads, tails
tails	tails, heads	tails, tails

▶ **You can use a tree diagram .**

• Use branches to show the possible outcomes for the first toss.

• Show the possible outcomes for the second toss.

• List the possible outcomes for both tosses.

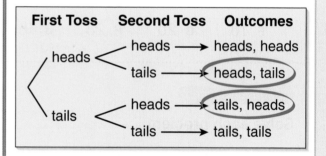

Solution: The probability is 2 out of 4, or $\frac{2}{4}$.

Guided Practice

A bag holds two cards, one with the letter _T_ and one with the letter _Y_. A card is picked and put back each time.

1. Make a tree diagram or a grid to show all possible outcomes when a card is picked twice.

2. What is the probability of spelling the name TY?

Ask Yourself

• What are all the possible outcomes?

• How many ways can the outcome I want occur?

Explain Your Thinking ▶ Why is it helpful to use a tree diagram or a grid?

Practice and Problem Solving

The tree diagram shows the possible outcomes when a coin is tossed and a four-part spinner is spun.

3. Make a grid to show the same outcomes.

4. How many outcomes show heads and red or heads and blue?

5. Write the probability of tails and blue as a fraction and in words.

6. What is the probability of heads and yellow or heads and green?

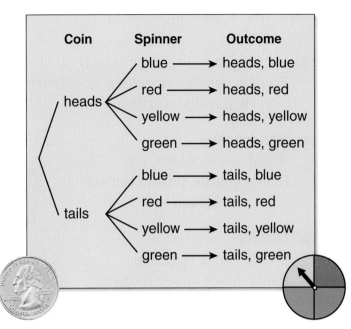

Coin	Spinner	Outcome
heads	blue	heads, blue
	red	heads, red
	yellow	heads, yellow
	green	heads, green
tails	blue	tails, blue
	red	tails, red
	yellow	tails, yellow
	green	tails, green

Use Spinners A and B for Problems 7–9.

7. Make a grid to show all the possible outcomes of spins on both spinners.

8. Find the probability of spins on both spinners landing on red. Write the probability as a fraction and in words.

9. What is the probability of Spinner A landing on blue and Spinner B landing on green or red?

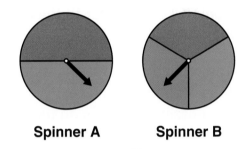

Spinner A   **Spinner B**

10. Ed and Kim will each glaze the inside of a mug red or yellow, the outside green or blue, and the handle black or white. What are all the ways the mug can be glazed? Use a tree diagram or an organized list.

Go On

For Problems 11–13, make a grid or a tree diagram to show the total number of possible outcomes when one of each is chosen.

11. **Ice Cream**
    Flavors: vanilla, chocolate, strawberry
    Way of serving: cup, cone

12. **Sandwiches**
    Bread: white, wheat, rye
    Filling: cheese, peanut butter,
             tuna, ham

13. **Outfits**
    Shirts: white, red, blue
    Pants: black, green, brown

Tina and a friend are playing a game with a six-sided number cube. Problems 14–17 all refer to the same number cube.

14. The probability of tossing a number greater than 13 and less than 24 is $\frac{6}{6}$, or 1. What are the possible numbers on the cube?

15. The probability of tossing a number that is divisible by 5 is $\frac{2}{6}$, or $\frac{1}{3}$. What does this tell you about the numbers on the cube?

16. The probability of tossing an odd number greater than 17 is $\frac{3}{6}$, or $\frac{1}{2}$. What additional information does this give you about the numbers on the cube?

17. The probability of tossing a number that can be divided evenly by 3 is $\frac{3}{6}$, or $\frac{1}{2}$. What information does this give you about the numbers?

18. **Create and Solve** Design a probability experiment that uses a fair spinner, a number cube, or both. Work with a partner to list all the possible outcomes and the probability of each. Then do the experiment.

Reading Connection
Give Me an E!

Materials: newspapers or magazines, colored pens or pencils

It is said that the letter *e* is the vowel that is used most often. Is this true? Do your own test to find out.

1. Choose a paragraph in a newspaper or magazine and cut it out.

2. Use colored pencils to circle each of the vowels (*a, e, i, o,* and *u*). Use a different color for each vowel.

3. Make a tally chart showing how many times each of the vowels is used.

4. Try again, using other paragraphs.

Dominoes
Old Game, New Uses

Domino games have been played all over the world for centuries. No one knows who invented dominoes, but a set of tiles like dominoes was found in the tomb of Tutankhamen, the king of Egypt in 1355 B.C. That's more than 3,300 years ago. Today dominoes are used for many games, but they also are used to build mazes that fall in intricate patterns when one domino is knocked over.

Number of Vowels	
E	IIIII IIIII IIIII IIIII IIIII IIIII IIIII II
A	
O	
U	
I	

5. **Write About It** Is the letter *e* the most frequently used vowel? Why do you think so?

6. Which vowel is used least, according to your tally? Did this result surprise you? Explain.

Chapter Review/Test

VOCABULARY

1. A ____ is the chance of an event occurring.

2. A result in a probability experiment is an ____.

3. Combinations of outcomes can be shown on a ____.

CONCEPTS AND SKILLS

**Write *certain*, *likely*, *equally likely*, *unlikely*, or *impossible*
to describe the probability of landing on blue.** (Lesson 1, pp. 596–597)

4.   5.   6.   7.

**Suppose you pick one tile from this bag without looking.
Write the probability of each.** (Lesson 2, pp. 598–600)

8. picking 11 or 15

9. picking an odd number

10. picking a multiple of 10

Use the tree diagram for Problems 11–13.

(Lesson 5, pp. 608–610)

11. What are the possible outcomes for the second spinner?

12. What are the possible outcomes for both spinners?

13. What is the probability of landing on two different colors for both spins?

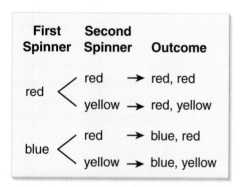

First Spinner	Second Spinner	Outcome
red	red	red, red
	yellow	red, yellow
blue	red	blue, red
	yellow	blue, yellow

PROBLEM SOLVING

Solve. (Lesson 4, pp. 604–606)

14. How many different ways can Joe, Beth, and Chad be arranged in a line?

15. How many different ways can four people be arranged in a line?

Write About It

Show You Understand

The probability of tossing 2 on a number cube is $\frac{1}{6}$. If the cube is tossed 48 times, can you predict how many times a 2 will be tossed? Explain your thinking.

Extra Practice

Set A (Lesson 1, pp. 596–597)

Write *certain, likely, equally likely, unlikely,* or *impossible*
to describe the probability of landing on red.

1.

2.

3.

4.

....

Set B (Lesson 2, pp. 598–600)

Look at the spinner on the right. Write the probability of each
outcome in both words and fraction form.

1. purple

2. red

3. yellow

4. yellow or red

5. purple or red

6. green

....

Set C (Lesson 5, pp. 608–610)

Use the tree diagram on the right for Problems 1–4.

1. Write all the possible outcomes for two picks.

2. What is the probability of picking the star twice?

3. What is the probability of picking a star and a square?

4. What is the probability of picking the square first and
the star second?

First Pick	Second Pick	Outcome
★	★	★, ★
	■	★, ■
■	★	■, ★
	■	■, ■

Use the grid on the right for Problems 5–7.

5. What is the probability of the coin landing
heads up and the spinner landing on 3?

6. What is the probability of the coin landing
tails up and the spinner landing on 1, 2,
or 3?

7. What is the probability of the coin landing
heads up or tails up and the spinner landing
on 1?

		Spinner		
		1	2	3
Coin	heads	heads, 1	heads, 2	heads, 3
	tails	tails, 1	tails, 2	tails, 3

Algebra and Graphing

INVESTIGATION

Using Data

Pretend you are in charge of setting up a park for Independence Day. Make a grid like the one at the right to show the park. Show where you would put carnival rides, games, picnic area, food tent, and fireworks. Mark each location with a dot where two lines cross.

Use What You Know

**Use this page to review and remember
what you need to know for this chapter.**

VOCABULARY

Choose the best term to complete each sentence.

1. A table of pairs that follows a rule is a ____.

2. A number greater than zero is ____.

3. A number less than zero is ____.

Vocabulary

positive
negative
ordered pair
function table

CONCEPTS AND SKILLS

Copy and complete each function table.

Rule: $y = 7 + x$	
Input	**Output**
x	***y***
4. 4	■
5. 19	■
6. 33	■

Rule: $y = x - 3$	
Input	**Output**
x	***y***
7. 10	■
8. 17	■
9. 45	■

Rule: $y = 3x$	
Input	**Output**
x	***y***
10. 2	■
11. 5	■
12. ■	24

Write the number for each letter.

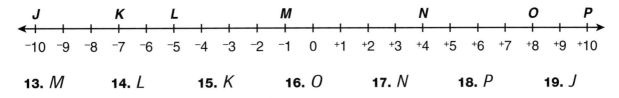

13. *M*   14. *L*   15. *K*   16. *O*   17. *N*   18. *P*   19. *J*

Write About It

20. How are 3 and ⁻3 different? Use a
number line, symbols, or words to
explain your answer.

Facts Practice, See page 671.

Locate Points on a Grid

Objective Use ordered pairs to name points on a grid.

Vocabulary
coordinate
ordered pair

Learn About It

Jana is having a treasure hunt at her birthday party. She made a map of her backyard. Guests will use the map to locate the prizes.

How can you use the map to locate the crown?

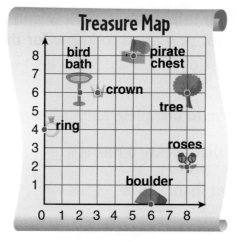

Treasure Map

Different Ways to Locate the Crown

Way 1 Use directions.

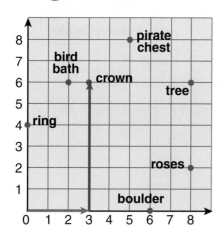

• Start at 0.
• Move right 3 units.
• Then move up 6 units.

Way 2 Use an ordered pair.

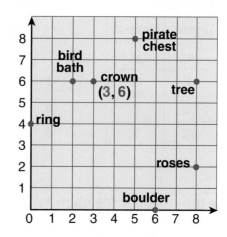

• The **ordered pair** for the crown is (3, 6).
  right ↑ ↑ up
• The numbers in an ordered pair are called **coordinates**.

Solution: You can use directions or an ordered pair. (3, 6) is the ordered pair that names the location of the crown.

Other Examples

A. Zero as the First Coordinate
The location of the ring is (0, 4).
• Start at 0. Move right 0 units. Then move up 4 units.

B. Zero as the Second Coordinate
The location of the boulder is (6, 0).
• Start at 0. Move right 6 units. Then move up 0 units.

Extra Help at **eduplace.com/map**

Guided Practice

Use the treasure map on Page 616 to solve.

Ask Yourself
- Did I start at zero?
- Did I move to the right first?

1. What is described by the following directions?
- Start at 0.
- Move right 5 units.
- Then move up 8 units.

2. Complete the directions for the tree.
- Start at ■.
- Move right ■ units.
- Then move up ■ units.

Explain Your Thinking ▶ Why does knowing both coordinates of an ordered pair help you locate a point?

Practice and Problem Solving

Use the graph on the right for Exercises 3–12.
Write the letter of the point for each ordered pair.

3. (1, 1)   **4.** (3, 6)   **5.** (6, 2)

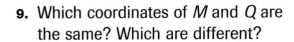

Write the ordered pair for each point.

6. *Q*   **7.** *M*   **8.** *L*

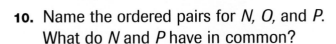

9. Which coordinates of *M* and *Q* are the same? Which are different?

10. Name the ordered pairs for *N, O,* and *P.* What do *N* and *P* have in common?

11. Write directions explaining how to go from (0, 0) to *R* and then from *R* to *L.*

 12. Write About It Does the ordered pair (3, 4) name point *Q*? Explain.

Mixed Review and Test Prep

Open Response

Use order of operations to evaluate each expression. (Ch. 5, Lesson 1)

13. $3 \times (6 + 2)$ **14.** $19 - (7 \times 2)$

15. $24 \div (7 - 3)$ **16.** $48 + (8 \times 4)$

17. Write directions for locating a point whose coordinates are (9, 7). (Ch. 24, Lesson 1)

Extra Practice See page 633, Set A.

Algebra

Graph Ordered Pairs

Objective Use ordered pairs to plot points on a grid.

Vocabulary

plot

Learn About It

Mia and Luis are playing *Sink the Ship* at a party. They each color 4 rectangles on a grid. Then they take turns naming coordinates of a point. If the point is inside a rectangle, they have hit a ship.

To check, players **plot** the points on their grid. The first coordinate tells the horizontal distance from 0. The second coordinate tells the vertical distance from 0.

Mia names (5, 7). Did she hit one of Luis's ships?

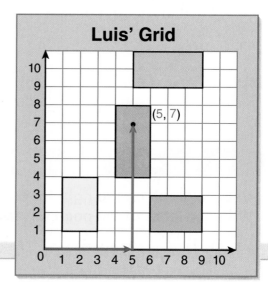

Luis' Grid

▶ **Plot the point named by (5, 7).**

- Start at 0. Move 5 units to the right.
- Next, move 7 units up.
- Then make a dot on the point.
- Label the point (5, 7).

Solution: Yes, Mia hit a ship. The point named by (5, 7) is inside a rectangle.

Guided Practice

Is the point named by each ordered pair in a rectangle?

1. (5, 2)　　2. (9, 4)　　3. (2, 3)

4. (9, 8)　　5. (5, 5)　　6. (7, 10)

Ask Yourself

- Did I move the correct number of units horizontally?
- Did I move the correct number of units vertically?

Explain Your Thinking ▶ Do (3, 5) and (5, 3) name the same point? Why or why not?

Copy the grid. Plot each point and label it with the correct letter.

7. E (1, 4)   8. R (6, 6)

9. W (0, 1)   10. L (6, 1)

11. T (4, 3)   12. M (1, 6)

13. X (4, 1)   14. S (6, 4)

15. Z (6, 3)   16. P (3, 1)

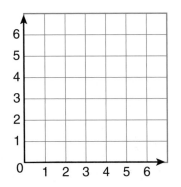

17. Karen collected rainfall data for a science experiment. She wants to make a line graph of her data, which is shown at the right.

   a. Rewrite the data as ordered pairs. Use the day as the first coordinate and the inches of rainfall as the second coordinate.

   b. Copy the grid below. Then plot and connect the points to make a line graph.

Karen

Rainfall Data

Day	Rainfall (in.)
1	2
2	0
3	0
4	3
5	4
6	1

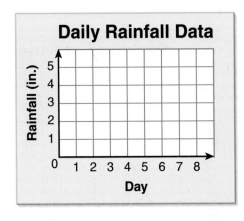

Daily Rainfall Data

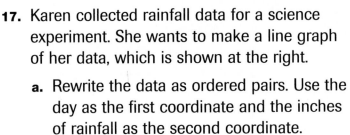

Check your understanding of Lessons 1–2.

Use the table for Problems 1–2. (Lessons 1–2)

1. Write the pairs of data as ordered pairs. Use the number of bags as the first coordinate. Then plot and connect the points named by the ordered pairs.

2. How many toys would be in 5 bags?

Grab Bags	
Number of Bags	Number of Toys
1	3
2	6
3	9

Algebra

Graph Functions

Objective Plot ordered pairs from a function table and draw a line to help you solve problems.

Vocabulary
origin
x-axis
y-axis
axes

Learn About It

Hiroko is buying fans to use as party favors. Each package has 2 fans. She wants to know how many fans are in 5 packages.

Hiroko could find the answer by extending the table on the right or by solving the equation $y = 2x$. She could also find the answer by graphing points.

Packages of Fans $y = 2x$	
Number of Packages (*x*)	Number of Fans (*y*)
1	2
2	4
3	6

Here's how to graph points to find the number of fans in 5 packages.

STEP 1 Plot and connect the points from the table. Use the number of packages as the first coordinate and the number of fans as the second coordinate.

STEP 2 Observe that the points appear to lie on a line. Extend the line.

The vertical number line is the **y-axis.**

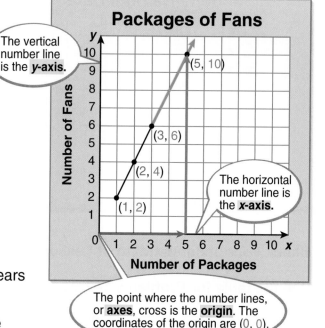

Packages of Fans

The horizontal number line is the **x-axis.**

STEP 3 Find the point on the line for 5 packages.

- Start at 0.

- Move 5 units to the right.

- Then move up until you meet the line at (5, 10).

The point named by (5, 10) appears to lie on the same line.

This suggests that extending the table would lead to more points that lie on the same line.

The point where the number lines, or **axes**, cross is the **origin**. The coordinates of the origin are (0, 0).

Solution: There are 10 fans in 5 packages.

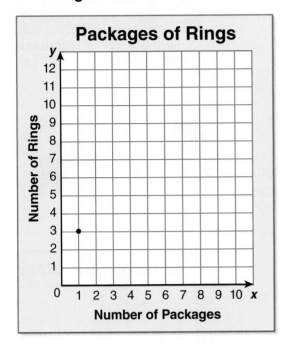

Guided Practice

Use the grid and the table below for Problems 1–3.

Ask Yourself
- Did I record ordered pairs in the correct order?
- Are all points on a line?

Packages of Rings $y = 3x$	
Number of Packages (x)	Number of Rings (y)
1	3
2	6
3	9

1. Write the data in the table as ordered pairs. Use the number of packages as the first coordinate. Use the number of rings as the second coordinate.

2. Copy the grid and the point named by the first ordered pair. Plot and connect the other points. Extend the line. Check that the points lie on a line.

3. Use the graph to find the number of rings in 4 packages.

Explain Your Thinking ▷ Do you think the point named by (6, 16) lies on the line?

Practice and Problem Solving

4. Copy the table at the right and extend it to 6 packages. Then write the pairs of data as ordered pairs. Use the number of packages as the first coordinate.

5. Make a grid. Label the x-axis to 10 and the y-axis to 34. Plot and connect the points named by the ordered pairs. Check that the points lie on a line.

6. Extend the line. Find the number of noisemakers in 8 packages.

Packages of Noisemakers $y = 4x$	
Number of Packages (x)	Number of Noisemakers (y)
1	4
2	8
3	12

Go On

Practice and Problem Solving

Use the table to complete Exercises 7–9.

7. There are 6 party hats in a package. Copy and complete the table.

8. Make a grid. Label the *x*-axis to 7 and the *y*-axis to 38. Plot ordered pairs from the table. Use the number of packages as the first coordinate and the number of hats as the second coordinate.

9. Check that the ordered pairs lie on the same line. Extend the line. How many hats are in 6 packages?

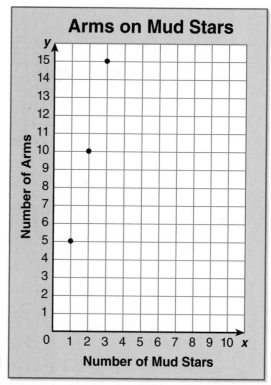

Packages of Party Hats $y = 6x$	
Number of Packages (*x*)	Number of Hats (*y*)
1	6
2	
3	

 Data **Use the graph for Problems 10–13. Assume the points lie on the same line.**

10. One mud star has 5 arms. How many arms do 3 mud stars have?

11. How many more arms do 3 mud stars have than 1 mud star?

12. How many mud stars have a total of 10 arms? How can you tell from the graph?

13. **Analyze** Let *x* stand for the number of mud stars. Let *y* stand for the number of arms. Write a rule for calculating the number of arms on *x* number of mud stars.

14. Research the number of arms on a squid. Make a table showing the number of arms on up to 3 squids. Graph the data in the table. Then extend the line to find the number of arms on 4 squids.

Mixed Review and Test Prep

Open Response

Write the probability of spinning blue as a fraction. (Ch. 23, Lesson 2)

15.

16.

Multiple Choice

17. The points (1, 6), (2, 12), and (3, 18) lie on the same line. Which of the following ordered pairs also lies on this line? (Ch. 24, Lesson 3)

A (24, 4) **C** (6, 30)

B (6, 35) **D** (6, 36)

622

Extra Practice See page 633, Set B.

Visual Thinking
Research at Sea

A group of scientists are working at a research station. Use ordered pairs to describe the location of each of the following.

1. Research station

2. Sea lions

3. Research boat

4. Killer whales

5. Bottle-nosed dolphins

6. **Challenge** The shortest distance between two points on a flat surface is a straight line. Draw a straight line between the research boat and the research station. What 4 ordered pairs lie on this line?

(graph showing points)
- Bottle-nosed Dolphins (at approx. 1, 6)
- Research Station (at approx. 10, 5)
- Killer Whales (at approx. 7, 2)
- Sea Lions (at approx. 11, 1)
- Research Boat (at approx. 1, 1)
x-axis: 1 2 3 4 5 6 7 8 9 10 11 12
y-axis: 0 1 2 3 4 5 6

Algebraic Thinking
What's My Rule?

Choose the equation that shows the rule for the graph. Let *x* stand for the first coordinate. Let *y* stand for the second coordinate.

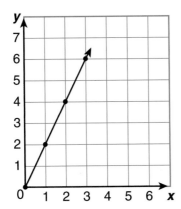

a. $y = x + 2$ **b.** $y = 2x$

Brain Teaser

Use the clues to find each ordered pair.

- The first coordinate is 8 times the only even prime number. The second coordinate is 3 more than the first.

- The first coordinate is 4 more than the second coordinate. The sum of the coordinates is the product of 2 and 7.

Education Place
Check out
eduplace.com/map
for more brain teasers.

Algebra

Integers

Objective Learn about integers.

Learn About It

Carlos and Sara are playing a game at a party. In the first round, Carlos lost 4 points and Sara won 5 points. How will they record their scores?

To show he lost 4 points, Carlos writes ⁻4. To show she gained 5 points, Sara writes ⁺5.

The numbers ⁻4 and ⁺5 are **integers**. ⁻4 is a **negative integer**. ⁺5 is a **positive integer**. Positive 5 can be written either as ⁺5 or as 5.

▶ Integers include 0, the positive whole numbers, and the negative whole numbers.

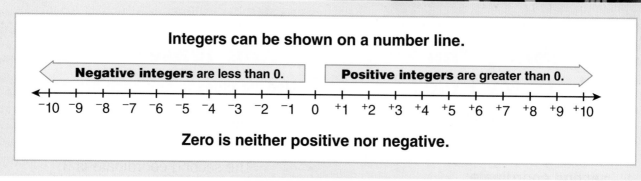

Integers can be shown on a number line.

Negative integers are less than 0.   Positive integers are greater than 0.

⁻10 ⁻9 ⁻8 ⁻7 ⁻6 ⁻5 ⁻4 ⁻3 ⁻2 ⁻1 0 ⁺1 ⁺2 ⁺3 ⁺4 ⁺5 ⁺6 ⁺7 ⁺8 ⁺9 ⁺10

Zero is neither positive nor negative.

▶ All integers have an **opposite**. An integer's opposite is the same distance from 0 as the integer, but in the opposite direction. Zero is its own opposite.

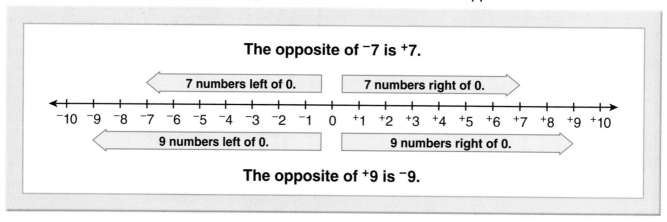

The opposite of ⁻7 is ⁺7.

7 numbers left of 0.   7 numbers right of 0.

⁻10 ⁻9 ⁻8 ⁻7 ⁻6 ⁻5 ⁻4 ⁻3 ⁻2 ⁻1 0 ⁺1 ⁺2 ⁺3 ⁺4 ⁺5 ⁺6 ⁺7 ⁺8 ⁺9 ⁺10

9 numbers left of 0.   9 numbers right of 0.

The opposite of ⁺9 is ⁻9.

▶ You can use a number line to compare integers. When comparing integers, the number farther to the right is greater.

Which is greater, ⁻5 or ⁻2?

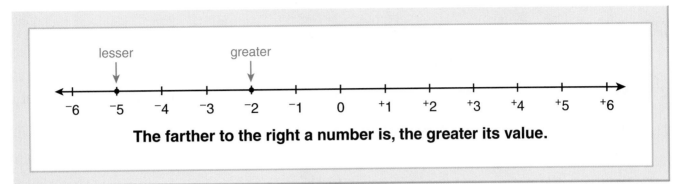

The farther to the right a number is, the greater its value.

Solution: ⁻2 is greater than ⁻5.

Other Examples

A. Positive Integers

- 17 feet above sea level is ⁺17.
- 50 degrees above zero is ⁺50.
- 4 floors above street level is ⁺4.
- $12 earned is ⁺12.

B. Negative Integers

- 5 feet below sea level is ⁻5.
- 14 degrees below zero is ⁻14.
- 3 floors below street level is ⁻3.
- $2 owed is ⁻2.

Guided Practice

Ask Yourself
- Is the number greater than 0?
- Is the number less than 0?

Write the integer for each letter on the number line.

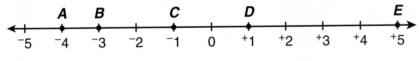

1. *A*　　　2. *B*　　　3. *C*　　　4. *D*　　　5. *E*

Explain Your Thinking ▶ Locate ⁺3 and ⁻3 on a number line. Why are these numbers called opposites?

Practice and Problem Solving

For each letter, write the integer from the number line.

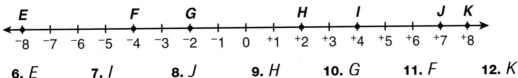

6. *E*　　　7. *I*　　　8. *J*　　　9. *H*　　　10. *G*　　　11. *F*　　　12. *K*

Go On

Algebra • Inequalities Compare. Use >, <, or = for each ⬤.
Use a number line if you wish.

13. ⁻3 ⬤ ⁺3   **14.** 7 ⬤ ⁺7   **15.** ⁻2 ⬤ ⁻5   **16.** ⁻8 ⬤ ⁻4

17. ⁺6 ⬤ 3   **18.** ⁺5 ⬤ ⁻4   **19.** ⁻1 ⬤ 0   **20.** ⁻3 ⬤ ⁺2

Write the integer for each situation.

21. $3 earned   **22.** 9 degrees below zero   **23.** 2 stories above street level

24. $4 spent   **25.** 7 feet below sea level   **26.** 6 points won in a game

27. Analyze One day the temperature ranged from ⁻3 to ⁻15. Which was the low temperature for the day? How far from 0 was the high temperature?

28. Write About It On a number line, Mavis started at 0, moved 4 spaces to the right, and then moved 9 spaces to the left. On what number did she end?

Data Use the table for Problems 29–32.
The elevation at sea level is 0 feet.

29. On which continent is the lowest elevation closest to sea level?

30. On which continent is the lowest elevation farthest from sea level?

31. Order the elevations from least to greatest.

32. Write the integer that is the opposite of the lowest elevation in Europe.

Lowest Continental Elevations	
Continent	**Elevation (in feet)**
Africa	⁻512
Antarctica	⁻8,327
Asia	⁻1,348
Australia	⁻52
Europe	⁻92
North America	⁻282
South America	⁻131

Mixed Review and Test Prep

Open Response

Find the total number of outcomes when one of each is chosen. (Ch. 23, Lesson 5)

33. Pants: tan, black, white
Shirt: red, blue

34. Meal: chicken, fish, beef
Drink: milk, orange juice, water, soda

35. Joe said that ⁻6 is greater than 2, because 6 is greater than 2.
(Ch. 24, Lesson 4)

Explain why he is right or wrong.

Extra Practice See page 633, Set C.

Math Reasoning
Coordinate Plane

The coordinate plane is formed by two perpendicular number lines.

- Points are located and plotted using ordered pairs of integers.

- When plotting a point in a coordinate grid, always start at the **origin** (0, 0).

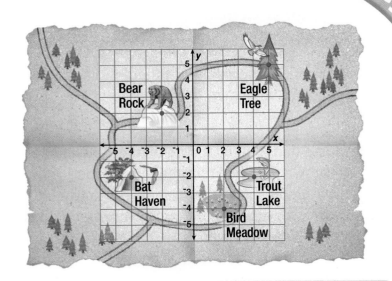

▶ **The sign of the integers in an ordered pair tells you in what direction to move.**

The first number in an ordered pair is called the **x-coordinate**.

If the x-coordinate is:

- **positive**, move **right**.
- **negative**, move **left**.

The second number in an ordered pair is called the **y-coordinate**.

If the y-coordinate is:

- **positive**, move **up**.
- **negative**, move **down**.

▶ **Here's how to locate and plot points on a coordinate plane.**

To locate Bat Haven:

- Start at the origin (0, 0).
- Move **left** 4 units.
- Move **down** 2 units.

To plot the point (3, ⁻1):

- Start at the origin (0, 0).
- Move **right** 3 units.
- Move **down** 1 unit.

Write the ordered pair for each location.

1. Eagle Tree
2. Bear Rock
3. Trout Lake
4. Bird Meadow

Draw an x-axis and a y-axis on graph paper. Label each axis from ⁻10 to 10. Then plot and label the points below.

5. M (⁻8, 4)
6. S (0, ⁻6)
7. A (5, ⁻7)
8. Q (⁻3, ⁻1)

Problem-Solving Application
Use a Graph

Objective Solve a problem by extending a line graph.

When data can be represented by points that lie on a line, you can sometimes solve a problem by extending the line.

Problem Lee had a party at a miniature-golf course. The table shows the price for different numbers of players. The graph shows the relationship between the number of players and the price. How much does it cost for 4 players to play golf?

UNDERSTAND

This is what the question asks.

What is the price for 4 players?

This is what the graph shows.

The blue line shows the price for 1 to 3 players.

Miniature Golf Prices	
Number of Players	**Price**
1	$5
2	$7
3	$9

PLAN

You can find the answer by extending the line.

SOLVE

Use a ruler to extend the line.

• The point (4, 11) is on the graph.

Solution: It should cost $11 for 4 people, if the pattern continues.

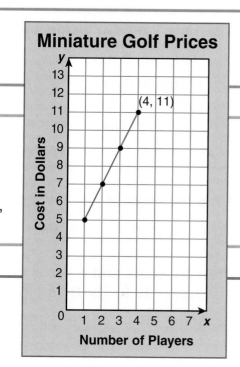

Miniature Golf Prices

LOOK BACK

Look back at the problem.

How does the graph relate to the table?

Guided Practice

Use the graph on Page 628 for Problems 1–2.

1. How much does it cost for 5 people to play miniature golf?

2. Lee has $10 to spend on his party. What is the greatest number of players he can afford?

   (Hint) Where on the line is the *y*-coordinate 10? Is the other point a whole number?

Ask Yourself

UNDERSTAND
• What does the question ask?
• What does the graph represent?

PLAN
Do I need to extend the line?

SOLVE
Do the points lie on the line?

LOOK BACK
Does my answer make sense?

Independent Practice

Alta has a party at a science museum. The museum offers a craft activity for an additional fee. The graph shows the relationship between the number of people and the cost.

Use the graph for Problems 3–7.

3. What would a craft activity for Alta and 3 of her friends cost?

4. **Money** How much more would it cost for 4 people to do a craft than for 2 people to do a craft?

5. Alta's parents spent $15 on the craft activities for the party. They spent $4 per person on goody bags. How much did they spend on goody bags?

6. Tom is also having a party at the museum. He has $16 to spend on crafts. What is the greatest number of people that can do a craft, including himself?

7. **Predict** If you extend the line, will the point (10, 35) be on it?

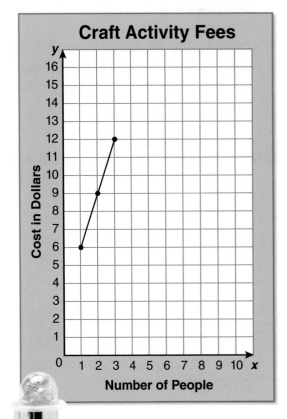

Craft Activity Fees

Cost in Dollars (y-axis, 0–16)
Number of People (x-axis, 0–10)

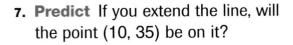

Go On

Mixed Problem Solving

Solve. Show your work. Tell what strategy you used.

8. Al's used bike costs $3 more than Rosa's. Ed's bike costs $2 less than Rosa's. If Ed's bike costs $24, how much does Al's bike cost?

9. Leon is arranging 3 model cars on a shelf. The cars are red, silver, and blue. How many different ways can the cars be arranged in a line?

10. The product of two numbers is 128. One factor is half the other factor. What are the factors?

11. Four teams are competing in a soccer tournament. Each team plays each of the other teams once. How many games will be played?

You Choose

Strategy
- Guess and Check
- Make an Organized List
- Use Logical Reasoning
- Work Backward
- Write an Equation

Computation Method
- Mental Math
- Estimation
- Paper and Pencil
- Calculator

Data Use the table for Problems 12–15. Then explain which method you chose.

12. **Analyze** All of the children in the basketball program are taking vans to see a game. How many vans are needed, if 7 children fit in each van?

13. **Money** The fee for soccer is $8.95 per child. The fee for ceramics is $14.95 per child. Which program made more money, soccer or ceramics?

14. What is the total number of children signed up for programs at the Town Recreation Center?

15. How many more children signed up for drama and computers than for gymnastics?

Town Recreation Center	
Program	Number of Children
Basketball	89
Ceramics	32
Computers	25
Drama	60
Gymnastics	40
Soccer	58

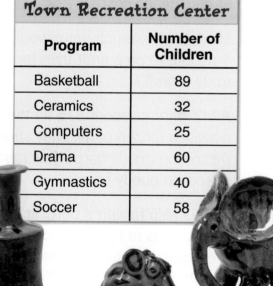

Real World Connection
Chess Challenge

Chess players use a set of ordered pairs with a letter and a number to tell the location of any piece.

Each chess piece moves differently. Knights make L-shaped moves. They move 2 squares in one row and then 1 square in a perpendicular row.

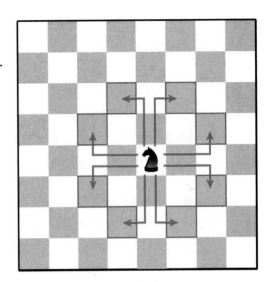

> **Here are some examples of a move that a knight might make.**
>
> At the start of the game, the 4 knights are located at b1, g1, b8, and g8.
>
> The knight at b1 moves forward 2 spaces and then left 1 space to a3.

Use the chessboard on the right. Decide if each describes a move that a knight could make.

1. d5 to f6

2. c3 to b5

3. c5 to f4

4. h3 to g5

5. f6 to f3

6. b1 to e1

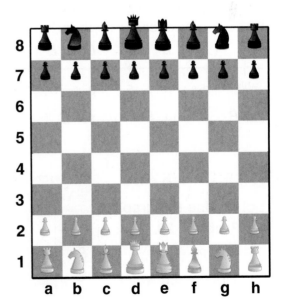

7. Write three moves that a knight might make, using ordered pairs.

Chapter Review/Test

VOCABULARY

1. The set of positive whole numbers, their opposites, and 0 are called ____.

2. An ordered pair of numbers that locate a point on a coordinate grid are called ____.

3. The vertical number line on a coordinate grid is the ____.

CONCEPTS AND SKILLS

Write the letter of the point for each. (Lesson 1, pp. 616–617)

4. (5, 5)   5. (3, 6)   6. (4, 2)   7. (1, 1)

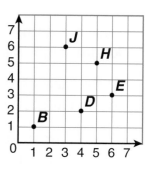

Draw a coordinate grid. Plot each point and label it with the correct letter. (Lesson 2, pp. 618–619)

8. *Q* (2, 5)   9. *R* (3, 7)   10. *S* (4, 4)   11. *T* (0, 6)

Use the table to answer Exersise 12. (Lesson 3, pp. 620–623)

12. If *x* stands for the number of packages, and *y* stands for the number of cards, what is the rule for calculating the number of cards in *x* packages?

Packages of Game Cards			
Number of Packages	3	4	5
Number of Cards	15	20	25

Write the integer for each letter. (Lesson 4, pp. 624–627)

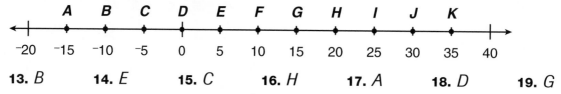

13. *B*   14. *E*   15. *C*   16. *H*   17. *A*   18. *D*   19. *G*

PROBLEM SOLVING

Solve. Use the graph for Problem 20.

(Lesson 5, pp. 628–631)

20. How much water flows out of the pipe in 1 minute? 2 minutes?

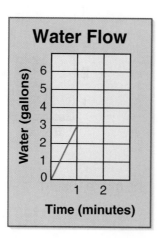

Water Flow

Write About It

Show You Understand

At sunrise, the temperature was 10°F. At noon, it rose 5°. At sunset, it went down 19°. Draw a number line to determine the temperature at sunset.

Extra Practice

Set A (Lessons 1–2, pp. 616–619)

Use the grid at the right for Exercises 1–8.
Write the ordered pair for each point.

1. E **2.** F **3.** D **4.** A

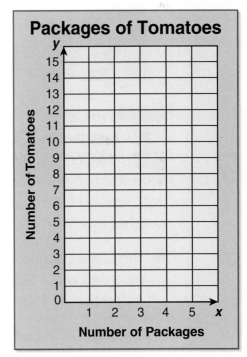

Copy the grid. Plot and label each point.

5. G (5, 0)   **6.** H (3, 4)   **7.** I (8, 3)   **8.** J (5, 5)

Set B (Lesson 3, pp. 620–623)

Use the table to complete Exercises 1–3.

1. Write the data in the table as ordered pairs. Use the number of packages as the first coordinate.

Packages of Tomatoes

Number of Packages	1	2	3	4	5
Number of Tomatoes	3	6	9	12	15

2. Copy the grid. Plot the coordinates from Exercise 1. Then connect the points.

3. Extend your grid. Label the *x*-axis to 10 and the *y*-axis to 30. How many tomatoes would be in 7 packages? in 9 packages?

Packages of Tomatoes

(grid: y-axis "Number of Tomatoes" labeled 0–15, x-axis "Number of Packages" labeled 1–5)

Set C (Lesson 4, pp. 624–627)

Write an integer for each situation.

1. sea level

2. $15 owed

3. 14 floors above street level

4. 89 feet below sea level

5. $25 won

6. 75° above zero

Weather Records

Think about the most extreme weather you've ever seen. Maybe you remember a blinding snowstorm, a powerful hurricane, or the dark funnel of a tornado. Some extreme weather has set records.

◆ The lowest temperature ever recorded was ⁻128.6°F in Vostok, Antarctica, in 1983.

◆ The highest temperature ever recorded was 136°F on the Sahara Desert in Libya, in 1922.

◆ The fastest wind speed ever recorded was 231 miles per hour on Mount Washington, New Hampshire, in 1934.

Problem Solving

Use the coordinate grid for Problems 1–2.

1 The coordinate grid shows the location of three tornado strikes. Write an ordered pair for each of the locations.

2 Suppose another tornado struck at (6, 7). Describe how you would graph the location of this tornado on the grid.

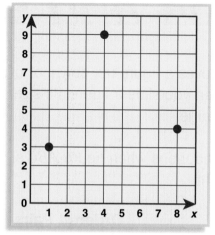

Use the table for Problems 3–5.

3 An unexpected rainstorm sends people rushing to buy umbrellas. The table shows the number of umbrellas one store sells and the amount of money the store takes in. Write an equation for the values of x and y in the table.

4 Write the pairs of data from the table as ordered pairs. Use the number of umbrellas as the first coordinate. Then graph the ordered pairs on a grid. Connect all the points.

5 Extend the line on your graph. How much money will the store take in if 6 people buy umbrellas?

Umbrella Sales

Number of Umbrellas (x)	Money Store Takes In (y)
1	$3
2	$6
3	$9
4	$12

Education Place

Visit Weekly Reader Connections at **eduplace.com/map** for more on this topic.

Enrichment: Transformations

Slips and Slides

A **slide** moves a figure up, down, or over along a line. When you slide a figure, its size and shape do not change.

See what happens when figure *ABC* slides 5 units right.

	Ordered Pairs		
Original Figure	*A* (2, 2)	*B* (4, 4)	*C* (5, 3)
Image	*A′* (7, 2)	*B′* (9, 4)	*C′* (10, 3)

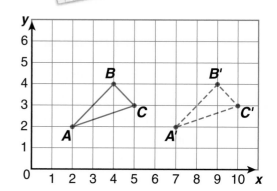

After you slide *ABC* to the right:

- *A* becomes *A′*, *B* becomes *B′*, and *C* becomes C′.
- The first coordinate of each point increases by 5.
- The second coordinate of each point does not change.

The numbers in the coordinate change depending on how you slide.

When you slide right or left,

- The first coordinate increases or decreases.
- The second coordinate stays the same.

When you slide up or down,

- The first coordinate stays the same.
- The second coordinate increases or decreases.

Try These!

Graph triangle *ABC* on grid paper. Slide triangle *ABC* the number of units given. Write the ordered pairs for the Points *A′*, *B′*, and *C′*.

 1 unit left   2 units down   2 units up   4 units right

Get On Line!

Qwan was playing a game on the computer. In Round 1 he won 6 points. In Round 2 he lost 9 points. In Round 3 he won 4 points. How many points did Qwan have at the end of Round 3?

You can use the number line found on Education Place at eduplace.com/kids/map to work with integers.

- Click on 0 on the number line to start.

- To show Qwan's points at the end of Round 1, at **Choose Jump Size,** click on 6. Then click the **Jump Right** arrow.

- To show Qwan's points at the end of Round 2, change **Choose Jump Size.** Since Qwan lost 9 points, choose 9. Click the **Jump Left** arrow.

- To show Qwan's points at the end of Round 3, change **Choose Jump Size.** Since Qwan won 4 points, choose 4. Click the **Jump Right** arrow.

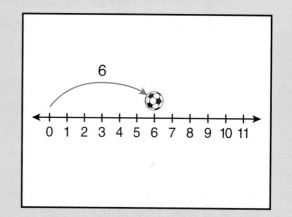

Solution: At the end of Round 3, Qwan had 1 point.

Use the number line to help you solve each problem.

1. Mia owes her brother $3. She earns $9. After paying her brother back, she spends $5 on a book. How much money does Mia have left?

2. A scuba diver dove 9 feet below sea level. She swam up 6 feet. Next she dove down 2 feet. How many feet below sea level was the scuba diver?

3. One day, the temperature at 10 A.M. was 83°F. By 3 P.M. it had risen 9°. At 8 P.M. the temperature was 7° lower than it was at 3 P.M. What was the temperature at 8 P.M?

4. One day, the elevator in a building starts on the ground floor. It goes up 9 floors, down 3 and then up 2. How many floors above or below ground is the elevator?

Unit 8 Test

Choose the best term to complete each sentence.

> | Vocabulary |
> | --- |
> | *x*-axis |
> | *y*-axis |
> | origin |
> | outcome |
> | tree diagram |

1. You can use a ____ to show all the possible combinations of outcomes for an event.

2. The point with the coordinates (0, 0) is called the ____.

3. A result of a probability experiment is an ____.

4. The horizontal number line on a coordinate grid is the ____.

CONCEPTS AND SKILLS (Open Response)

For each spinner, write the probability that a spin will land on green, in both words and fraction form. (Chapter 23)

5.   6.   7.

Suppose you have a cube with sides numbered 1, 2, 3, 4, 5, and 6. If the cube is tossed 30 times, predict how many times you will toss each. (Chapter 23)

8. an even number   9. 3 or 4   10. a number less than 5

Make a grid or tree diagram to show the total number of outcomes when one of each is chosen. (Chapter 23)

11. **Lunches**

Drink: juice, milk

Sandwich: cheese, egg salad, hot dog

12. **Outfits**

Dress: pink, blue, yellow

Shoes: black, blue, white

Write the integer for each situation. (Chapter 24)

13. 5 floors up   14. $10 spent   15. 6 degrees below zero

Use the table and grid paper for Problems 16–18.

16. Write pairs of data in the table as ordered pairs. Use the number of hours as the first coordinate.

17. Plot the ordered pairs on a coordinate graph.

18. How many hours does Carla have to work to earn $12?

Carla's Baby-sitting Earnings	
Hours Worked	Dollars Earned
1	4
2	8
3	12

PROBLEM SOLVING Open Response

19. Use the digits 2, 4, and 8 to make as many three-digit numbers as you can. What are all the numbers?

20. Extend the graph you made for Problem 17. How much will Carla earn if she baby-sits for 4 hours?

Performance Assessment

Constructed Response

Task Trisha has invented a game that will use a spinner. The information at the right describes the kind of spinner that she wants for her game.

Use the information above and at the right to design a spinner for Trisha's game.

What is the probability of spinning each of the six colors on your spinner?

Information You Need

• The spinner should have 6 or 8 equal sections.

• The probability of landing on red must be more likely than the probability of landing on blue.

• The probability of landing on at least one of the colors is impossible.

• The probability of landing on two of the colors must be the same.

Spinner Section Colors		
Must Use	May Use	
red	green	orange
blue	yellow	purple

Cumulative Test Prep

Solve Problems 1–10.

Test-Taking Tip

Sometimes a problem asks you to explain your thinking. It can help to remind yourself about what you know about the subject.

Look at the example below.

Samantha drew a triangle with sides measuring 3 inches, 4 inches, and 3 inches. How should she classify the triangle? Explain your thinking.

THINK

You know that an isosceles triangle has two equal sides. You also know that all the angles in an acute triangle are less than 90°.

Draw a triangle with two sides that are 3 units long and one side that is 4 units long. You can see that all the angles are less than 90°.

So, you can classify the triangle as acute isosceles.

Multiple Choice

1. What is the value of this expression?

$$4 + (14 - 6) \div 4$$

A 3   **c** 6

B 4   **D** 8

(Chapter 5, Lesson 1)

2. Which figures appear to be congruent?

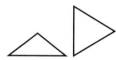

(Chapter 17, Lesson 1)

3. What shape will this net create?

A cube   **c** rectangular prism

B cone   **D** triangular prism

(Chapter 18, Lesson 5)

4. Which set of numbers is listed from greatest to least?

F 0.09 $5\frac{2}{5}$ $3\frac{1}{4}$

G 2.3 $2\frac{1}{8}$ $1\frac{1}{8}$

H 0.75 $4\frac{5}{6}$ $1\frac{1}{2}$

J 0.2 $1\frac{1}{2}$ $1\frac{3}{4}$

(Chapter 21, Lesson 7)

For Test-Taking Tips, See page 658.

5. Which unit of measure, milliliters or liters, would be better to measure the capacity of a dropper full of vitamins for a cat? Explain your thinking.

(Chapter 12, Lesson 8)

6. What fraction can be used to represent the shaded part of the figure below?

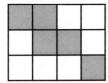

(Chapter 19, Lesson 1)

7. Which of the following factors of 48 are composite numbers? Explain how you know.

1, 2, 3, 4, 6, 8, 12, 16, 24, 48

(Chapter 10, Lesson 2)

8. Neal and Joe paid a total of $10 for lunch. They each had 2 slices of pizza and 1 can of juice. Each can of juice cost $1. Write and solve an equation to find the cost of each slice of pizza.

(Chapter 5, Lesson 5)

9. Write the coordinates for Point *A*.

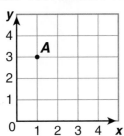

(Chapter 24, Lesson 2)

10. Rashad puts 10 marbles in a bag. He picks 1 marble without looking, records its color, and puts it back in the bag. He does this 30 times. His results are shown in the line plot.

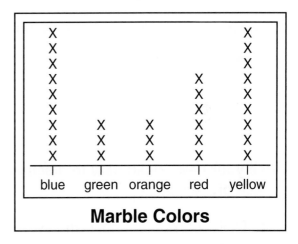

Marble Colors

A How many times was a blue marble picked? a red marble?

B Predict how many marbles of each color are in the bag. Explain your thinking.

C Based on your prediction, what is the probability of choosing each color marble?

D Suppose Rashad does the same experiment 40 times. Predict how many times each color marble will be picked.

(Chapter 23, Lesson 3)

Education Place

Look for Cumulative Test Prep at **eduplace.com/map** for more practice

Vocabulary Wrap-Up for Unit 8

Look back at the big ideas and vocabulary in this unit.

Big Ideas

You can use a fraction to represent the probability of an outcome.

You can use coordinates to locate points on a grid.

Key Vocabulary

probability
outcome
coordinates

Math Conversations

Use your new vocabulary to discuss these big ideas.

1. Explain how you know whether a probability is certain or impossible.

2. Suppose you put all of the letters in the word HAWAII in a bag. Explain how to describe the probability of picking each letter without looking.

3. Explain how to find the opposite of 7 on a number line.

4. Explain how to plot the ordered pairs in the table on the right to form a line.

x	y
1	1
2	3
3	5
4	7

5. **Write About It** Survey the students in your class to see how many students are wearing blue socks. Show your data and write how you would find the probability that a student is wearing blue socks.

I surveyed 20 students. Now how should I show my data?

Think about making a bar graph.

Student Resources

BEYOND
PLUTO

Scientists know quite a bit about most of the planets in the solar system. And then there is Pluto.

Even powerful telescopes don't reveal much about Pluto except that it is a distant, barely visible cold point of light. Pluto remains the only planet not yet visited by an Earth-launched spacecraft.

If Congress approves a $546 million mission, NASA will build a spacecraft called *New Horizons*. Even if the launch goes smoothly and according to plan, *New Horizons* won't reach Pluto until 2016.

TIMING IS EVERYTHING

Pluto takes almost 248 Earth-years to orbit the sun. If the *New Horizons* mission is delayed by only a year, scientists said, their next best hope to gather valuable information about Pluto might not be until after 2200!

After snapping pictures of Pluto during a six-month period, *New Horizons* would travel for ten more years deep into the Kuiper Belt, a ring of icy rocks beyond Neptune's orbit. Many scientists believe the Kuiper Belt is where many comets originate. Comets are dirty snowballs of ice that hurtle through the solar system.

Some astronomers believe Pluto should be counted as a Kuiper Belt object rather than as the ninth planet. *New Horizons* could settle that issue once and for all. Then again, if Congress scraps the mission, Pluto—and astronomers—will be left out in the cold.

Quaoar is the biggest object scientists have found in the Kuiper Belt so far. It is more than half the size of Pluto.

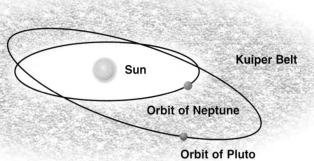

Sun

Kuiper Belt

Orbit of Neptune

Orbit of Pluto

1 About how long should it take *New Horizons* to reach Pluto?

2 Is 248 an exact number as it is used in this article? Explain.

Kid Camp

from American Girl

Last summer, Sarah Hennigsen of California knew she wanted to spend time with little kids. But at age ten, she felt she was too young to baby-sit by herself. So Sarah, her sister Molly, and their friend Aimee opened Sunshine Summer Camp. Each day for a week, 11 neighborhood kids came for an afternoon of crafts, snacks, and games.

"Mom was close by in case anything went wrong," Sarah says. "But everything went great!" By the end of the week, the girls had made more than $100 — plus tips!

Thinking about hosting a day camp? "Don't try games where very young kids have to take turns and only one person wins," warns Sarah. "Group games work better!"

1 Suppose Sarah and her camp partners charged $50 per camper for four weeks of camp. They wanted to earn $500 for that period of time. About how many campers would they need?

2 If the girls earned $20 in tips, about how much would each girl get if they split the tips evenly?

READING MATH

GONE PRAWNING

from Weekly Reader

Many farms in the Midwest have cornfields that cover the landscape for miles. However, for the past few years, lack of rain has caused great concern. As corn crops dry up, so do the farmers' wallets.

In an attempt to save their farms, farmers who have ponds on their farms are trying alternate ways to bring in money. These farmers have begun stocking their ponds with prawns, which are shrimp-like animals. They can raise about 400 prawns in a pond that covers about a $\frac{1}{2}$ acre. The prawns sell for about \$8 a pound. Farmers can earn about ten times more money raising a $\frac{1}{2}$ acre of prawns than they can growing a $\frac{1}{2}$ acre of corn.

Many farmers across the drought-stricken Corn Belt plan to raise prawns to keep their farms afloat. Experts say that the United States imports about \$2 billion worth of shrimp per year, which is a good enough reason for the farmers to be hopeful.

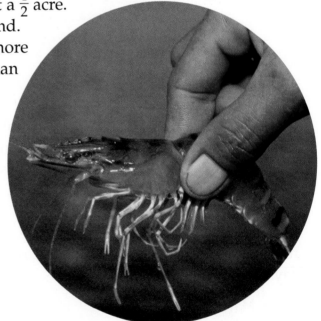

A farmer holding a prawn

1 Suppose there are 15 prawns in a pound and a customer wants to buy 6 pounds. How many prawns would that be? How much would they cost?

2 Write a short letter from a farmer who has switched from corn to prawns. Have him or her explain the reasons for switching.

But I'm Not Tired

"**J**ust five more minutes!" "I'm tired!" "I can't get up." If you have ever had trouble getting up in the morning, you are not alone. A new report says many U.S. kids do not get enough sleep.

Your body needs sleep and lots of it! "Evidence shows that elementary-age children need at least nine hours of sleep per night," says sleep expert Dr. Carl Hunt.

Sleep Matters

Kids who do not sleep enough cannot do their best, experts say. A tired kid may

- be moody,
- forget things,
- act badly,
- have trouble learning,
- have trouble playing a sport.

Not sleeping enough can also affect kids' safety. Experts say children who are tired are more likely to suffer injuries.

Lots of kids lose sleep because they are busy. Many take part in after-school activities. Then they go home, eat dinner, and do homework. Afterward, many kids watch TV, play video games, and surf the Internet. That leaves less time for sleep.

Sometimes you may not be able to go to bed early. But, if you get a choice whether to stay up late, think twice. A good night's sleep can help you feel your best!

Get a Good Night's Sleep!

Here are some tips for getting a good night's sleep.

- Relax with quiet time before bed.

- Go to bed at the same time each night.

- Don't eat a big meal right before going to sleep.

1 If Lauren gets 50 hours of sleep in a week, about how much sleep does she get each night?

2 To get the amount of sleep you need, how many hours must you sleep in a week?

3 Do you get enough sleep?

Lengths of Time

BY PHYLLIS McGINLEY *from Wonderful Time*

Time is peculiar
And hardly exact.
Though minutes are minutes,
You'll find for a fact
(As the older you get
And the bigger you grow)
That time can
Hurrylikethis
Or plod, plod, slow.

Waiting for your dinner when you're hungry?
Down with the sniffles in your bed?
Notice how an hour crawls along and crawls along
Like a snail with his house on his head.

But when you are starting
A game in the park.
It's morning,
It's noon,
And suddenly it's dark.
And hours like seconds
Rush blurringly by.
Whoosh!
Like a plane in the sky.

1. What periods of time are mentioned in the poem?

2. Suppose the poet had placed numbers in the last stanza instead of using the words *morning*, *noon*, and *dark*. Would you have the same impression of time rushing by? Explain.

DIVIDING THE CHEESE

Retold by Jackson Smith

Two foolish cats stole a piece of cheese. Neither cat trusted the other, so they agreed to ask the monkey to divide the cheese for them.

The monkey was glad to help. He fetched a scale. Then he started to divide the cheese. But instead of cutting the cheese in equal pieces, he made one portion larger than the other. He put both pieces on the scale. "Oh dear," said the monkey. "I'll just make it even."

The monkey began to eat the cheese from the heavier side. As he ate, the heavier piece became lighter than the other piece. Then the monkey ate from the other side. The cats became alarmed as they watched their snack disappear. "We've changed our minds," they said to the monkey. "We will divide the rest of the cheese ourselves."

"No, I must finish the job I started," said the monkey. And he continued to eat, first on one side, and then on the other, until the cheese was gone.

1 If the piece of cheese is square, how many ways could this be divided evenly between the two cats? How could it be divided evenly if the cats and the monkey were to share the piece? Draw a picture to show your solution.

2 What lesson does this folktale teach?

Unit 6 Literature: Folktale   **651**

HOLD THE MEAT!

from American Girl

" I became a vegetarian about six years ago. It isn't too hard for me. My mom doesn't eat much meat, so she and I fix veggies or tofu. And my dad and brother cook their own meat. If I'm going to someone's house, I tell him or her ahead of time that I don't eat meat so it won't be awkward. At restaurants, I can usually order a veggie plate.

"A few of my friends think it's strange that I'm a vegetarian, but most of them are supportive. I really don't remember how most meat tastes, except for seafood — I'm still looking for a good substitute for that! I'm happy with my choice, though, and I don't think I'll ever go back to eating meat." — Celeste, age 13, Ohio.

continued on the next page

Great Shake

Whether or not you eat meat, you'll love this chocolatey treat. It's made with soy milk — and it packs as much protein as a hot dog!

You will need:

- An adult to help you

- A blender

- 2 peeled, frozen bananas, cut into chunks (peel and cut the bananas before freezing)

- $\frac{1}{2}$ cup chocolate soy milk

- 2 tablespoons chocolate syrup

- 2 tablespoons peanut butter

Ask an adult to blend ingredients until smooth.

Enjoy your soy!

---

1 Suppose you want to make this shake twice. How many cups of chocolate soy milk would you use? How many bananas?

2 If you decided to put in $1\frac{1}{2}$ tablespoons less peanut butter, how many tablespoons would you use?

3 How much chocolate syrup would be in the shake if you added $1\frac{1}{2}$ more tablespoons of chocolate syrup instead of the peanut butter?

The Perfect Present

BY E. RENEE HEISS

from Highlights

"A cow? You got me a cow for my birthday?" Grandma threw her arms up in the air when she saw what I had brought from the farm.

"But you said you wanted something to keep you company, Grandma. And I know you love milk."

"I don't have enough room for a cow," Grandma said.

I looked around the yard and had to agree with Grandma. So I took the cow away, and a few days later, I returned with a different birthday present.

"A pig? Now you're bringing me a pig?" Grandma threw her arms up in the air again. "I don't know how to care for a pig!"

"But the pig is smaller than the cow," I argued.

"I can't keep your pig, but I appreciate the thought," Grandma said.

A few days after that, I brought another gift from the farm for Grandma. But once again she threw her arms up in the air.

"A duck? I would need a pond in my backyard for a duck," Grandma explained.

"I'm sorry, Grandma," I said. "Next time I'm sure I'll have the perfect present for you."

The next time I rang the doorbell, Grandma didn't throw her arms in the air. She squealed with delight when she saw the present I had brought. It had a big red ribbon wrapped around it.

"This present will keep me company," she said. "It's not too big for my yard. It's not too difficult to care for. And it doesn't even need a pond in the backyard. It's perfect!"

Grandma smiled and put her arms around her perfect present — me!

1 What was the "perfect present"? Why is it perfect?

2 If the narrator brought his Grandma a horse, would she have been more likely, less likely, or equally likely to like the present as the "perfect present"? Explain your reasoning.

Being a good math student includes reading carefully and doing your best on tests. On the next few pages, you'll find reading strategies, study hints, and test-taking tips to help you learn.

Use Reading Strategies to Think About Math

What you learn during reading class can help you understand how to solve word problems.

Understand What the Question Is

Read the problem once to be sure it makes sense to you. Ask yourself the question in your own words. Picture the situation and make a drawing if it helps.

Think About the Words

As you read, pay attention to the mathematical terms. If you don't understand a word, try to decide what it means by looking at the words around it.

Be Sure You Have Enough Information

Identify the information you need. Look at tables or graphs as well as the words. Think about what you already know that may help.

Plan What You Will Do

Think about the problem-solving plan and strategies. Decide what computation method is needed. Then make a plan and follow it.

Evaluate Your Work

Look back at what the question asked, and check that your answer really answers that question. Be sure you have labeled your answer.

Strategies for Taking Tests

You need to think differently about how to answer various kinds of questions.

All Questions

If you can't answer a question, go on to the next question. You can return to it if there is time.

Always check your computation.

Multiple-Choice Questions

Estimate the answer. This can help eliminate any unreasonable choices.

On bubble sheets, be sure you mark the bubble for the right question and for the right letter.

Short-Answer Questions

Follow the directions carefully. You may need to show your work, write an explanation, or make a drawing.

If you can't give a complete answer, show what you do know. You may get credit for part of an answer.

Long-Answer Questions

Take time to think about these questions because you often need to explain your answer.

When you finish, reread the question and answer to be sure you have answered the question correctly.

Student Scoring Rubric

Your teacher may use a scoring rubric to evaluate your work. An example is on the next page. Not all rubrics are the same, so your teacher may use a different one.

Scoring Rubric

Rating	My work on this problem
Exemplary (full credit)	• has no errors, has the correct answer, and shows that I checked my answer. • is explained carefully and completely. • shows all needed diagrams, tables, or graphs.
Proficient (some credit)	• has small errors, has a close answer, and shows that I checked only the math. • is explained but may have missing parts. • shows most needed diagrams, tables, or graphs.
Acceptable (little credit)	• has some errors, has an answer, and shows that I did not check my answer. • is not explained carefully and completely. • shows few needed diagrams, tables, or graphs.
Limited (very little credit)	• has many errors and may not have an answer. • is not explained at all. • shows no needed diagrams, tables, or graphs.

TWO Important Things You Can Do Before a Test

• Get plenty of sleep the night before.
• Eat a good breakfast in the morning.

Your Plan for Problem Solving!

Follow this four-part plan, and you'll become a problem-solving superstar!

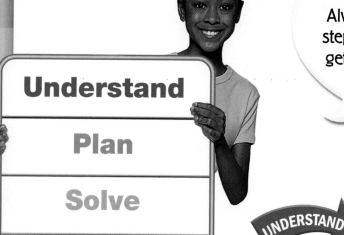

Remember!

Always START at the "Understand" step and move on. But if you can't get an answer, don't give up. Just go back and start again.

Understand

Plan

Solve

Look Back

UNDERSTAND →

Always be sure you know what the question means. Here are some hints to help you:

- Read the problem and imagine the situation. Draw a picture if it helps.

- Replace any hard names you can't read with easier ones.

- Identify what the question is asking and say it in your own words.

- Look for words that help you decide whether to add, subtract, multiply, or divide.

PLAN

Start by making a plan.
Ask yourself:

- What strategy should I use?
- Do I have too much or too little information?
- Should I do more than one step?
- Which operation should I use?
- Should I use estimation, paper and pencil, mental math, or a calculator?

You Choose

Strategy
- Act It Out
- Draw a Picture
- Find a Pattern
- Guess and Check
- Make an Organized List
- Make a Table
- Solve a Simpler Problem
- Use Logical Reasoning
- Work Backward
- Write an Equation

SOLVE

Finally! Now you're ready to solve the problem.

- Carry out your plan.
- Adjust your plan if needed.
- Check your calculations.

LOOK BACK

Congratulations! You've solved the problem. But is it correct? Once you have an answer, ask:

- Is my answer reasonable?
- Is my answer labeled correctly?
- Did I answer the question that was asked?
- Do I need to explain how I found the answer?

Study Skills

Knowing how to study math will help you do well in math class.

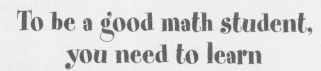

To be a good math student, you need to learn

★ **how to listen when your teacher is teaching.**

★ **how to work alone and with others.**

★ **how to plan your time.**

Listening Skills

Listen carefully when your teacher is showing the class how to do something new. Try to understand what is being taught, as well as how to do each step.

If you don't understand what your teacher is showing the class, ask a question. Try to let your teacher know what you don't understand.

Listening carefully will also help you be ready to answer any questions your teacher may ask. You may be able to help another student by explaining how you understand what your teacher is saying.

Working Alone and with Others

When you work alone, try to connect the math you are learning to math you already know. Knowing how parts of mathematics fit together helps you remember and understand.

When you work with others, help as much as you can. *Cooperating* is another word for working together. When people cooperate, they often learn more because they share ideas.

Planning Your Time

Doing your homework on time is part of being a good math student. Make sure that you take the assignment home with you.

Have a place at home to do your homework—it could be in your room or at the kitchen table or anywhere that works for you and your family.

Get extra help if you are having trouble. Write questions about what you don't understand. This will help your teacher give you the extra help you need.

Addition and Subtraction

- To practice counting on or counting back, do columns A and B.
- To practice adding doubles or doubles plus one and the related subtraction facts, do columns C and D.
- To practice making a ten, do columns E and F.
- For mixed practice, choose rows to do.

	Column A	Column B	Column C	Column D	Column E	Column F
Row 1.	4 + 2	6 − 2	0 + 0	9 − 4	7 + 5	11 − 4
Row 2.	7 + 1	5 − 1	3 + 4	4 − 2	3 + 8	15 − 6
Row 3.	3 + 6	9 − 2	5 + 5	11 − 6	4 + 6	14 − 8
Row 4.	2 + 5	8 − 3	9 + 9	16 − 8	5 + 8	13 − 9
Row 5.	1 + 8	10 − 3	7 + 6	15 − 7	9 + 6	10 − 3
Row 6.	9 + 3	7 − 1	8 + 9	17 − 8	8 + 4	16 − 9
Row 7.	8 + 2	11 − 2	6 + 6	14 − 7	7 + 9	14 − 5

More Practice

Work with a partner. Make flash cards for the facts that give you trouble. Practice your facts by quizzing each other with the flash cards.

More Addition and Subtraction

- **For addition practice, do columns A, C, and E.**
- **For subtraction practice, do columns B, D, and F.**
- **For mixed practice, choose rows to do.**

	Column A	Column B	Column C	Column D	Column E	Column F
Row 1.	5 + 5	13 − 4	7 + 2	15 − 7	7 + 7	12 − 3
Row 2.	4 + 3	14 − 6	5 + 8	10 − 9	7 + 9	16 − 8
Row 3.	7 + 8	15 − 9	6 + 6	14 − 9	8 + 1	13 − 9
Row 4.	8 + 9	11 − 4	9 + 5	17 − 8	6 + 7	12 − 8
Row 5.	7 + 5	16 − 7	4 + 7	12 − 6	3 + 3	18 − 9
Row 6.	9 + 4	12 − 9	2 + 2	10 − 4	8 + 8	11 − 6
Row 7.	6 + 8	14 − 7	9 + 2	13 − 5	9 + 6	15 − 8

More Practice

See how many fact families you can write in 3 minutes.

Addition and Subtraction

- To practice adding, do columns A, B, and C of rows 1–5.
- To practice subtracting, do columns D, E, and F of rows 1–5.
- For mixed practice, choose rows to do.

	Column A	Column B	Column C	Column D	Column E	Column F
Row 1.	5 + 9	6 + 6	8 + 7	14 − 8	13 − 4	15 − 6
Row 2.	4 + 6	7 + 9	9 + 1	16 − 8	9 − 9	12 − 5
Row 3.	6 + 8	3 + 0	4 + 4	7 − 0	14 − 7	11 − 6
Row 4.	4 + 7	3 + 9	6 + 9	11 − 8	17 − 9	10 − 5
Row 5.	9 + 8	6 + 7	2 + 9	15 − 7	13 − 5	16 − 9
Row 6.	6 + 0	8 + 3	0 + 0	9 − 9	7 + 7	12 − 3
Row 7.	5 + 7	13 − 8	9 + 7	11 − 2	4 + 9	9 + 6
Row 8.	18 − 9	8 + 5	14 − 9	2 + 2	6 − 0	15 − 8
Row 9.	7 + 8	8 − 8	12 − 4	8 + 8	17 − 8	14 − 6
Row 10.	13 − 7	16 − 7	11 − 7	15 − 9	9 + 0	13 − 9

More Practice

Make 20 pairs of practice facts on index cards. Write an addition or subtraction fact on a card. Write the answer on another card. Arrange the cards face down in an array. Players turn over 2 cards. If they match, the player collects the cards. If they do not match, they are turned over. Play continues until no cards remain. The player with the most cards wins.

Multiplication Facts

- To practice skip counting by 2 and 3, do column A.
- To practice multiplying by 0 and 1, do column B.
- To practice skip counting by 5 and 10, do column C.
- To practice using doubles, do columns D and E.
- To practice multiplying by 7 and 9, do column F.
- For mixed practice, choose rows to do.

	Column A	Column B	Column C	Column D	Column E	Column F
Row 1.	2 × 3	0 × 0	5 × 3	3 × 3	3 × 4	7 × 7
Row 2.	5 × 3	1 × 1	10 × 8	6 × 6	6 × 7	2 × 9
Row 3.	2 × 4	1 × 0	7 × 5	4 × 4	4 × 5	7 × 3
Row 4.	6 × 3	9 × 1	10 × 1	8 × 8	8 × 9	9 × 5
Row 5.	8 × 2	0 × 8	5 × 9	5 × 5	5 × 6	7 × 4
Row 6.	3 × 7	5 × 1	10 × 4	7 × 7	7 × 6	9 × 6
Row 7.	2 × 6	0 × 4	5 × 8	9 × 9	9 × 8	7 × 8

More Practice

Work with a partner. Make flash cards for the facts
that give you trouble. Practice your facts by quizzing
each other with the flash cards.

More Multiplication

- To practice with 0, 1, and 2, do column A.
- To practice with 3, 4, and 5, do column B.
- To practice with 6 and 7, do column C.
- To practice with 8 and 9, do column D.
- For mixed practice, choose columns E and F or choose rows to do.

You Choose

Strategy
- Use skip counting.
- Use doubles.
- Draw an array.

	Column A	Column B	Column C	Column D	Column E	Column F
Row 1.	2 × 2	4 × 7	7 × 6	8 × 8	3 × 7	6 × 8
Row 2.	5 × 0	9 × 3	6 × 6	0 × 9	0 × 0	5 × 9
Row 3.	1 × 8	5 × 6	6 × 9	8 × 5	3 × 8	1 × 1
Row 4.	4 × 1	8 × 4	3 × 6	9 × 4	7 × 9	8 × 5
Row 5.	2 × 9	3 × 5	7 × 7	9 × 8	3 × 6	0 × 7
Row 6.	7 × 2	4 × 4	4 × 6	8 × 6	9 × 7	6 × 4
Row 7.	0 × 6	5 × 5	8 × 7	9 × 9	7 × 5	4 × 8

More Practice

Make a multiplication table. See how fast you can complete all the multiplication facts.

Division

- To practice dividing by 1, 2, and 3, do column A.
- To practice dividing by 4 and 5, do column B.
- To practice dividing by 6 and 7, do column C.
- To practice dividing by 8 and 9, do column D.
- For mixed practice, choose columns E and F or rows to do.

	Column A	Column B	Column C	Column D	Column E	Column F
Row 1.	2)16	4)4	6)24	9)0	5)10	3)21
Row 2.	3)3	5)30	7)7	8)24	1)1	4)12
Row 3.	2)0	5)45	6)48	9)36	7)49	2)14
Row 4.	1)2	4)36	6)6	8)32	4)20	9)54
Row 5.	3)12	5)5	7)56	8)8	6)54	5)35
Row 6.	1)7	4)8	7)14	9)9	2)18	9)63
Row 7.	2)4	5)40	6)42	9)72	8)64	7)35
Row 8.	3)27	4)32	7)63	8)56	6)36	9)81

More Practice

Work with a partner. Make flash cards for the facts
that give you trouble. Practice your facts by quizzing
each other with the flash cards.

More Division

- To practice with 1, 2, and 3 do column A.
- To practice with 4 and 5, do column B.
- To practice with 6 and 7, do column C.
- To practice with 8 and 9, do column D.
- For mixed practice, choose columns E and F or choose rows to do.

You Choose

Strategy
- Use related multiplication facts.
- Use doubles.
- Draw a picture.

	Column A	Column B	Column C	Column D	Column E	Column F
Row 1.	$1\overline{)9}$	$5\overline{)25}$	$7\overline{)0}$	$8\overline{)16}$	$5\overline{)35}$	$4\overline{)28}$
Row 2.	$3\overline{)6}$	$4\overline{)0}$	$7\overline{)21}$	$9\overline{)45}$	$6\overline{)18}$	$3\overline{)27}$
Row 3.	$1\overline{)3}$	$4\overline{)16}$	$6\overline{)12}$	$8\overline{)48}$	$2\overline{)12}$	$9\overline{)72}$
Row 4.	$2\overline{)8}$	$5\overline{)15}$	$6\overline{)30}$	$9\overline{)18}$	$1\overline{)0}$	$5\overline{)40}$
Row 5.	$3\overline{)15}$	$4\overline{)32}$	$7\overline{)42}$	$9\overline{)81}$	$4\overline{)24}$	$8\overline{)56}$
Row 6.	$2\overline{)2}$	$4\overline{)36}$	$6\overline{)36}$	$8\overline{)40}$	$3\overline{)24}$	$7\overline{)63}$
Row 7.	$3\overline{)18}$	$5\overline{)20}$	$7\overline{)28}$	$9\overline{)27}$	$8\overline{)72}$	$6\overline{)54}$
Row 8.	$2\overline{)18}$	$5\overline{)45}$	$6\overline{)6}$	$8\overline{)64}$	$7\overline{)56}$	$9\overline{)0}$

More Practice

Make triangular flash cards for multiplication and division fact families. Place all cards face down. Without looking at the numbers, pick up a card by a corner so that one number is covered up. Use the numbers you can see to decide what the unknown number is.

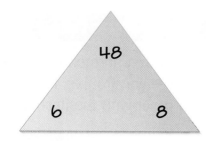

Multiplication and Division

- For mixed multiplication and division practice, choose columns or rows to do.

	Column A	Column B	Column C	Column D	Column E	Column F
Row 1.	5×5	$27 \div 3$	6×7	8×3	$0 \div 2$	$36 \div 9$
Row 2.	$48 \div 6$	5×8	$45 \div 5$	7×5	$21 \div 7$	$4 \div 4$
Row 3.	8×2	7×7	$32 \div 8$	$56 \div 7$	$18 \div 2$	9×8
Row 4.	9×4	$15 \div 5$	9×7	$16 \div 8$	8×6	$45 \div 9$
Row 5.	$64 \div 8$	6×6	5×9	$20 \div 4$	$72 \div 9$	7×8
Row 6.	8×2	$40 \div 8$	$8 \div 8$	9×0	5×3	$63 \div 7$
Row 7.	$54 \div 6$	8×9	$42 \div 6$	$25 \div 5$	4×7	9×3
Row 8.	2×3	$36 \div 4$	$63 \div 9$	2×9	$49 \div 7$	9×9
Row 9.	$56 \div 8$	4×8	3×3	$72 \div 8$	8×5	$48 \div 8$
Row 10.	$81 \div 9$	$35 \div 5$	6×9	8×8	$36 \div 6$	7×9
Row 11.	4×4	$0 \div 6$	3×7	$42 \div 7$	7×0	$24 \div 4$
Row 12.	6×8	5×7	$9 \div 9$	7×4	$54 \div 9$	9×5

Table Of Measures

Length

1 foot (ft)	=	12 inches (in.)	1 centimeter (cm)	=	10 millimeters (mm)
1 yard (yd)	=	36 inches	1 decimeter (dm)	=	10 centimeters
1 yard	=	3 feet	1 meter (m)	=	100 centimeters
1 mile (mi)	=	5,280 feet	1 meter	=	10 decimeters
1 mile	=	1,760 yards	1 kilometer (km)	=	1,000 meters

Capacity

1 pint (pt)	=	2 cups (c)	1 liter (L)	=	1,000 milliliters (mL)
1 quart (qt)	=	2 pints			
1 gallon (gal)	=	4 quarts			

Weight/Mass

1 pound (lb)	=	16 ounces (oz)	1 gram (g)	=	1,000 milligrams (mg)
1 ton (T)	=	2,000 pounds	1 kilogram (kg)	=	1,000 grams

Units of Time

1 minute (min)	=	60 seconds (s)	1 year	=	52 weeks
1 hour (h)	=	60 minutes	1 year	=	365 days
1 day (d)	=	24 hours	1 leap year	=	366 days
1 week (wk)	=	7 days	1 decade	=	10 years
1 year (yr)	=	12 months (mo)	1 century	=	100 years
			1 millennium	=	1,000 years

Money

1 penny	=	1 cent (¢)	1 quarter	=	25 cents
1 nickel	=	5 cents	1 half-dollar	=	50 cents
1 dime	=	10 cents	1 dollar ($)	=	100 cents

Glossary

acute angle An angle that measures less than 90°.

acute triangle A triangle in which each of the three angles is acute.

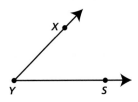

addend A number to be added in an addition problem.

$$Example: 5 + 8 = 13$$

addends

A.M. The time between 12:00 midnight and 12:00 noon.

angle A figure that is formed by two rays with the same endpoint.

area The number of square units in a region.

array An arrangement of objects, pictures, or numbers in columns and rows.

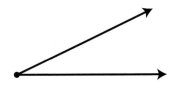

Associative Property of Addition The property which states that the way in which addends are grouped does not change the sum. It is also called the *Grouping Property of Addition*.

Example: $(3 + 4) + 5 = 3 + (4 + 5)$

Associative Property of Multiplication The property which states that the way in which factors are grouped does not change the product. It is also called the *Grouping Property of Multiplication*.

Example: $(6 \times 7) \times 9 = 6 \times (7 \times 9)$

average *See mean.*

bar graph A graph in which information is shown by means of rectangular bars.

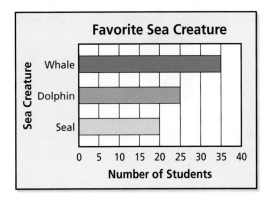

base ten A place-value system in which each digit has a value that is ten times greater than the digit to the right of it.

breaking apart A mental math strategy used to add and subtract.

Example:
$$\begin{array}{r} 28 = 20 + 8 \\ + 35 = 30 + 5 \\ \hline 50 + 13 = 63 \end{array}$$

So, 28 + 35 = 63

capacity The amount a container can hold.

certain An event that will always happen is certain.

chord A line segment that connects two points on a circle.

circle A closed figure in which every point is the same distance from a given point called the **center** of the circle.

circle graph A graph that represents data as part of a circle. (sometimes called a **pie graph**)

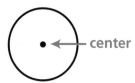

clustering An estimation strategy for finding sums.

Example:
Estimate 125 + 101 + 92
          100 + 100 + 100 = 300

Commutative Property of Addition The property which states that the order of addends does not change the sum. It is also called the *Order Property of Addition*.
Example: 2 + 4 = 4 + 2

Commutative Property of Multiplication The property which states that the order of factors does not change the product. It is also called the *Order Property of Multiplication*.
Example: 3 × 5 = 5 × 3

compare To decide if one number is greater than, less than, or equal to another number.

compensation Adding one amount to an addend and subtracting an equal amount from another addend to add mentally.

composite number A whole number that has more than two factors.

cone A solid that has a circular face and comes to a point called the vertex.

congruent figures Figures that have the same size and the same shape.

coordinates The numbers in an ordered pair.

cube A solid figure that has six square faces of equal size.

cubic unit A unit used to measure volume.

cylinder A solid that has parallel, congruent circular faces.

data A set of information.

decimal A number with one or more digits to the right of a decimal point.

decimal equivalent A decimal that is equal to a whole number, a fraction, or another decimal.

decimal point (.) A symbol used to separate dollars and cents in money amounts or to separate ones and tenths in decimals.

Example: $1.55
↑
decimal point

degree (°) A unit for measuring angles or temperature.

degrees Celsius (°C) The metric temperature scale.

degrees Fahrenheit (°F) The customary temperature scale.

denominator The number below the bar in a fraction.

Example: $\frac{1}{3}$ ← denominator

diameter of a circle A line segment that connects two points on a circle and passes through the center.

difference The answer in a subtraction problem.

Example: $12 - 5 = 7$
↑
difference

digit Any one of the ten number symbols 0, 1, 2, 3, 4, 5, 6, 7, 8, and 9

Distributive Property of Multiplication The property which states that when two addends are multiplied by a factor, the product is the same as when each addend is multiplied by the factor and those products are added.

Example: $(2 + 3) \times 4 = (2 \times 4) + (3 \times 4)$

dividend The number that is divided in a division problem.

Example: $35 \div 7 = 5$
↑
dividend

divisible Describes a number that can be divided into equal parts and has no remainder.

divisor The number by which the dividend is divided in a division problem.

Example: $35 \div 7 = 5$
↑
divisor

double bar graph A graph in which data is compared by means of pairs of rectangular bars drawn next to each other.

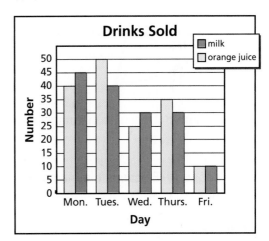

doubles A strategy for finding products.

Example: Since $2 \times 3 = 6$
Then $4 \times 3 = 6 + 6$
So $4 \times 3 = 12$

edge The line segment where two faces of a solid figure meet.

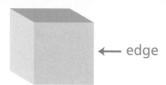

← edge

elapsed time The time that passes between the beginning and the end of an activity.

endpoint The point at either end of a line segment or the beginning point of a ray.

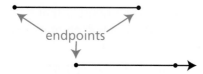

endpoints

equal Having the same value.

equation A mathematical sentence with an equal sign.

Examples: $3 + 1 = 4$ and $2x + 5 = 9$

equilateral triangle A triangle that has three congruent sides.

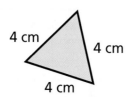

4 cm
4 cm
4 cm

equivalent decimals Decimals that name the same amount.

equivalent fractions Fractions that name the same amount.

Example: $\frac{1}{2}$ and $\frac{3}{6}$

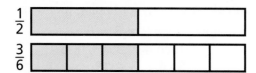

$\frac{1}{2}$

$\frac{3}{6}$

estimate A number close to an exact amount; to find about how many.

evaluate To find the value of an expression.

even number A whole number that is a multiple of 2. The ones digit in an even number is always 0, 2, 4, 6, or 8.

expanded form A number written to show the value of each digit.

Example: The expanded form of 2,345 is $2,000 + 300 + 40 + 5$.

expression A number or group of numbers with operation symbols. An expression may have a variable.

Example: $3 + n$

face A flat surface of a solid figure.

fact family Facts that are related, using the same numbers.

Examples: $1 + 4 = 5$; $4 + 1 = 5$
$5 - 4 = 1$; $5 - 1 = 4$

$3 \times 5 = 15$; $5 \times 3 = 15$
$15 \div 3 = 5$; $15 \div 5 = 3$

factor The numbers used in a multiplication problem.

Example: $7 \times 5 = 35$

↑ ↑
factors

factor tree A visual representation of the prime factors of a number.

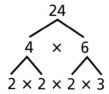

24

4 × 6

$2 \times 2 \times 2 \times 3$

favorable outcome A desired result in a probability experiment.

formula An expression that shows a mathematical rule.

fraction A number that names a part of a whole, a part of a collection, or a part of a region.
Examples: $\frac{1}{2}$, $\frac{3}{4}$, and $\frac{2}{3}$

front-end estimation A method of estimating sums, differences, products, and quotients using front digits.

function table A table of ordered pairs that follows a rule.

Rule: $t = p \times 2$	
Input (p)	Output (t)
4	8
6	12
10	20

grid A chart that shows combinations of outcomes of an event.

		Second Toss	
		heads	**tails**
First Toss	**heads**	heads, heads	heads, tails
	tails	tails, heads	tails, tails

Grouping Property of Addition *See Associative Property of Addition*

Grouping Property of Multiplication *See Associative Property of Multiplication*

hexagon A polygon with six sides.

horizontal axis *See x-axis.*

horizontal line A line that lies straight across.
Example:

hundredth One of the equal parts when a whole is divided into 100 equal parts.

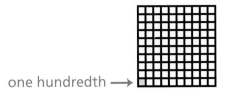

one hundredth →

impossible An event that can not happen is impossible.

improper fraction A fraction that is greater than or equal to 1. The numerator in an improper fraction is greater than or equal to the denominator.

inequality Two expressions that are not equal. The symbols >, <, and ≠ show an inequality.

integers The set of positive whole numbers, their opposites (negative numbers), and 0.

intersecting lines Lines that meet or cross at a common point.

interval The difference between two numbers on a scale.

inverse operations Opposite operations.

Examples: Addition and subtraction are inverse operations. Multiplication and division are inverse operations.

isosceles triangle A triangle that has two congruent sides and two congruent angles.

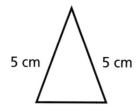

key A part of a map, graph, or chart that explains what symbols mean.

like denominators Denominators in two or more fractions that are the same.

line A straight path that extends in opposite directions with no endpoints.

line graph A graph that uses a line to show changes in data over time.

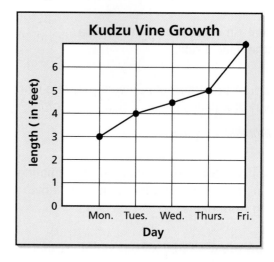

line plot A diagram that organizes data using a number line.

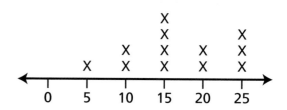

line segment A part of a line that has two endpoints.

line symmetry Describes whether a figure can be folded in half and its two parts match exactly.

line of symmetry The line along which a figure can be folded so that the two halves match exactly.

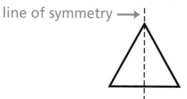

mass A measure of the amount of matter in an object.

mean The number found by dividing the sum of a group of numbers by the number of addends. Also called *average*.

Example:
6 + 2 + 1 = 9   9 ÷ 3 addends = 3
The average of 6, 2, and 1 is 3.

median The middle number when a set of numbers is arranged in order from least to greatest. For an even number of numbers, the median is the mean of the two middle numbers.

Examples: The median of 2, 5, 7, 9, and 10 is 7. The median of 2, 5, 7, and 12 is (5 + 7) ÷ 2, or 6.

mixed number A number containing a whole number part and a fraction part.

Example: $3\frac{1}{2}$

mode The number or numbers that occur most often in a set of data.

Example: The mode of 2, 3, 4, 4, and 6 is 4.

multiple A number that is the product of the given number and another number.

negative numbers Numbers that are less than 0.
Examples: ⁻2, ⁻5, and ⁻26

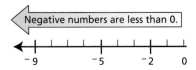

net A flat pattern that can be folded to make a solid.

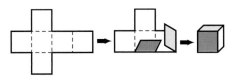

number sentence A mathematical sentence written in numerals and mathematical symbols. A number sentence always includes a greater than, less than, or equal sign.

Examples: 5 × 5 = 19 + 6
            2n ÷ 4 = 16

numerator The number above the bar in a fraction.

Example: $\frac{1}{3}$ ← numerator

obtuse angle An angle that measures more than 90° and less than 180°.

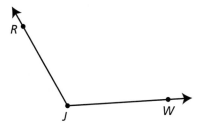

obtuse triangle A triangle that has one obtuse angle.

octagon A polygon with eight sides.

odd number A whole number that is not a multiple of 2. The ones digit in an odd number is 1, 3, 5, 7, or 9.

order To list numbers or items according to their value.

order of operations The order in which operations must be performed in order to arrive at a correct answer.
- First, do operations in parentheses.
- Then, do multiplication and division in order from left to right.
- Finally, do addition and subtraction in order from left to right.

Order Property of Addition *See Commutative Property of Addition.*

Order Property of Multiplication *See Commutative Property of Multiplication.*

ordered pair A pair of numbers used to locate a point on a grid such as (4, 5).

ordinal number A number used to show position.

origin A point assigned to zero on the number line or the point where the *x*- and *y*-axes intersect in a coordinate system.

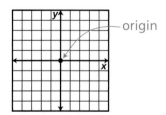

outcome A result in a probability experiment.

outlier A number or numbers that are at one or the other end of a set of data, arranged in order, where there is a gap between the end numbers and the rest of the data.

P.M. The time between 12:00 noon and 12:00 midnight.

parallel lines Lines that lie in the same plane and do not intersect. They are always the same distance apart.

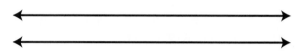

parallelogram A quadrilateral in which both pairs of opposite sides are parallel.

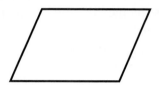

parentheses Used to show which operations should be done first.

pentagon A five-sided polygon.

percent (%) Per hundred. The ratio of a number to 100.

Example: 9% means 9 out of 100 or $\frac{9}{100}$

perimeter The distance around the outside of a figure.

period Each group of 3 digits separated by a comma in a number.

perpendicular lines Two lines or line segments that cross or meet to form right angles.

pictograph A graph in which information is shown by means of pictures or symbols.

Book Sale	
Year 1	📖 📖 📖 📖 📖 📖 📖
Year 2	📖 📖 📖 📖 📖
Year 3	📖 📖 📖 📖 📖 📖
Year 4	📖 📖 📖 📖 📖
Each 📖 stands for 5 books sold.	

place value The value of a digit in a number.

Example: The place value of 2 in 421,000 is 20,000.

plane A flat surface that extends in all directions without end.

plane figure A shape that is on a plane, such as an octagon or a triangle.

plot To place points in the coordinate plane.

point An exact location in space, represented by a dot.

polygon A simple closed plane figure made up of three or more line segments.

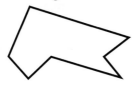

positive numbers Numbers that are greater than zero.

Examples: $^{+}2$, $^{+}5$, and $^{+}9$

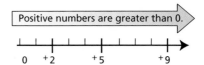

Positive numbers are greater than 0.

0   $^{+}2$ $^{+}5$ $^{+}9$

prediction A guess about the likelihood that an event will occur.

prime factor A factor that happens to also be a prime number.

prime number A whole number that has only itself and 1 as factors, such as 7 or 13.

probability A mathematical way of describing how likely it is that something will happen. A probability can be any number from 0 through 1.

product The answer in a multiplication problem.

Example: $7 \times 5 = 35$

product

proper fraction *See fraction.*

Property of One for Multiplication The property which states that the product of 1 and any number is that number.

Example: $4 \times 1 = 4$

protractor A device used to measure and draw angles.

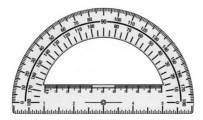

pyramid A solid figure whose base can be any polygon and whose faces are triangles.

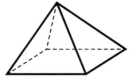

quadrilateral A polygon with four sides.

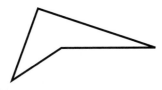

quotient The answer in a division problem.

Example: 35 ÷ 7 = 5
↑
quotient

radius (radii) A segment that connects the center of a circle to any point on the circle.

range The difference between the greatest and least numbers in a set of data.

Example: The range of 2, 3, 6, 8, and 9 is 7

Because 9 − 2 = 7

ray Part of a line that starts at an endpoint and goes on forever in one direction.

rectangle A parallelogram with four right angles.

rectangular prism A solid figure with six faces that are rectangles.

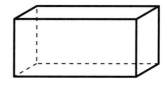

rectangular pyramid A solid figure whose base is a rectangle and whose faces are triangles.

reflection A move that makes a figure face in the opposite direction. It is also called a *flip.*

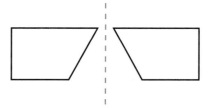

regroup To use place value to exchange equal amounts when renaming a number.

regular polygons Polygons whose sides are all the same length, and whose angles are the same measure.

remainder The number that is left after one whole number is divided by another.

rhombus A parallelogram with all four sides the same length.

right angle An angle made when two line segments meet to form a square corner. It measures 90°.

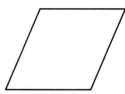

right triangle A triangle that has one right angle.

rotation A move that turns a figure around a point.

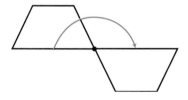

rotational symmetry A figure has rotational symmetry if, after the figure is rotated about a point, the figure is the same as when in its original position.

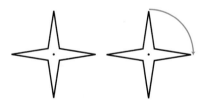

round To find about how many or how much by expressing a number to the nearest ten, hundred, thousand, and so on.

scale An arrangement of numbers in order with equal intervals.

scalene triangle A triangle with all sides of different length.

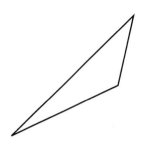

short word form A way to write a number by using digits and words to describe the periods of the number.

Example: The short word form of 2,345 is 2 thousand, 345.

side (of a polygon) One of the line segments that make up a polygon.

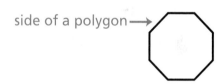

side (of an angle) One of the rays that make up an angle.

similar figures Figures that have the same shape but not necessarily the same size.

simplest form of a fraction A fraction whose numerator and denominator have the number 1 as the only common factor.

sphere A solid figure that is shaped like a round ball.

square A polygon with four right angles and four congruent sides.

square number The product of a number and itself.

square pyramid A pyramid that has a square base.

standard form The usual or common way of writing a number using digits.

Example: The standard form of two hundred twenty-seven is 227.

stem-and-leaf plot A table that organizes information by place value.

sum The answer in an addition problem.
Example: 5 + 8 = 13
            ↑
           sum

survey One method of collecting information.

symmetric figure A figure that has symmetry. *(See line symmetry, rotational symmetry.)*

tenth One of the equal parts when a whole is divided into 10 equal parts.

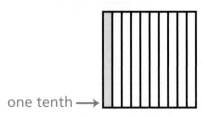

one tenth →

thermometer An instrument that measures temperature.

thousandth One of the equal parts when a whole is divided into 1,000 equal parts.

transformation The collective name that describes rotations, reflections, and translations.

translation An action that slides a figure in a straight line.

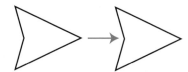

trapezoid A quadrilateral with two parallel sides.

tree diagram A diagram that lists the outcomes of an event.

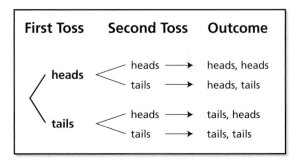

triangle A polygon with three sides and three vertices.

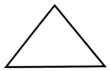

triangular prism A prism that has 2 triangular and 3 rectangular faces.

triangular pyramid A pyramid whose base is a triangle.

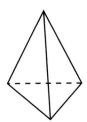

unit fraction A fraction whose numerator is 1.
Examples: $\frac{1}{3}, \frac{1}{5}, \frac{1}{8}$

unlike denominators Denominators that are not equal.

variable A letter or a symbol that represents a number in an algebraic expression.

vertex of an angle (vertices) A point common to the two sides of an angle.

vertex of an angle ⟶

vertex of a polygon (vertices) A point common to two sides of a polygon.

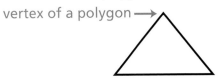
vertex of a polygon ⟶

vertical line A line that lies straight up and down.

volume The number of cubic units that can fit inside a container or a solid figure.

weight The measure of how heavy something is.

whole number Any of the numbers 0, 1, 2, 3, 4, 5, and so on.

word form A way of using words to write a number.
Example: The number 12,345 in word form is twelve thousand three hundred forty-five.

***x*-axis** The horizontal number line in a coordinate system. *Also called horizontal axis.*

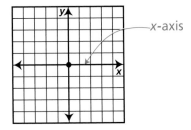
x-axis

x-coordinate The first number of an ordered pair of numbers that names a point in a coordinate system.

y-axis The vertical number line in a coordinate system. Also called *vertical axis.*

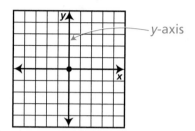

y-coordinate The second number of an ordered pair of numbers that names a point in a coordinate system.

Zero Property of Addition The property which states that the sum of any number and 0 is that number.

Examples: $9 + 0 = 9$ and $0 + 5 = 5$

Zero Property of Multiplication The property which states that the product of any number and 0 is 0.

Examples: $9 \times 0 = 0$ and $0 \times 5 = 0$

Index

Approximate, meaning of, 303

Area
of a complex figure, 460–463
estimating, 457, 463
formulas, 456, 470–472
modeling, 452–453
of a rectangle, 456–458, 484
of a right triangle, 459
of a square, 456–458

Array
division, 88, 89, 94, 95, 202
meaning of, 56
multiplication, 88, 89, 94, 95, 142, 143, 202, 251, 254–255

Assessment, *See also* Test Prep
Chapter Test, 20, 44, 80, 106, 130, 168, 190, 224, 248, 268, 290, 330, 352, 372, 388, 426, 448, 474, 512, 538, 564, 580, 612, 632
Performance Assessment, 51, 137, 197, 297, 395, 481, 587, 639
Quick Check, 9, 33, 69, 97, 121, 155, 183, 213, 237, 257, 279, 317, 347, 369, 383, 415, 443, 459, 501, 527, 549, 601
Unit Test, 50–51, 136–137, 196–197, 296–297, 394–395, 480–481, 586–587, 638–639
Use What You Know, 3, 23, 59, 83, 109, 145, 171, 205, 227, 251, 271, 305, 333, 355, 375, 403, 429, 451, 489, 515, 541, 567, 595, 615

Associative Property
of addition, 60–61
of multiplication, 84–86, 100–101, 178–180

Audio Tutor, 4–5, 6–7, 24–25, 26–27, 64–65, 70–71, 72–73, 74–75, 84–85, 88–89, 92–93, 102–103, 110–111, 112–113, 118–119, 148–149, 150–151, 152–153, 174–175, 176–177, 178–179, 184–185, 206–207, 208–209, 220–221, 228–229, 230–231, 238–239, 252–253, 254–255, 276–277, 280, 282–283, 286–287, 308–309, 320–321, 336–337, 344–345, 366–367, 370–371, 378–379, 382–383, 422–423, 430–431, 434–435, 454–455, 456–457, 468–469,

492–493, 498–499, 508–509, 516–517, 520–521, 544–545, 550–551, 560–561, 568–569, 574–575, 596–597, 604–605, 608, 616–617, 618

Average, *See* Mean
batting, 549

Axes, coordinate, 620–622

Bar graph
double
making, 376–377
using, 420
select an appropriate graph, 384–386
using, 40–42, 43, 44, 49, 53, 139, 180, 216, 232, 270, 284, 342, 362, 375, 387, 438, 506, 562, 603

Base five, 19

Base ten, 6–8, 19

Base two, 19

Basic facts
estimates and, 148–149, 220–221, 274–275
patterns and, 146–147, 172–173, 218–219
practice, 664–671

Benchmarks
capacity, 322
fraction, 524–525
length, 320, 325
mass, 326
number, 9
temperature, 344
weight, 312

Braille numbers, 33

Brain teasers, 29, 87, 163, 233, 315, 463, 533, 623

Breaking apart, mental math strategy, 62–63

Calculator, *See also* Calculator Connection; Technology Time
addition, 76

area and perimeter, 484
average, 265, 266
check multiplication, 165
choose a computation method, 42, 78, 166, 188, 212, 222, 246, 266, 350, 446, 472, 526, 536, 578, 630
division, 244, 245
game, 87
measures of central tendency, 365
multiple operations, 200
multiplication, 180, 186, 187
multiplication patterns, 163
order of operations, 140
subtraction, 77

Calculator Connection
change fractions to decimals, 563
convert between customary and metric units, 329
decimal addition and subtraction, 579
division, 289
multiplication patterns, 163

Calendar, elapsed time, 334–335

Capacity
benchmarks, 322
customary units of, 310–311
meaning of, 302
metric units of, 322–324

Celsius temperature, 344–349
benchmarks for, 344

Center, of a circle, 422

Centimeter, 318–321
cubic, 468

Century, 334–335

Certain outcome, 596–597, 598–600

Challenge
division, one-digit divisors, 213
exercises, 9, 91, 155, 232, 289, 297, 425, 481, 484, 501, 579, 623
percent, 553
Sieve of Erathosthenes, 257
square numbers, 105

Change, making, 34–36, 54

Checking
addition, 76, 186, 574
division, 215, 228, 230, 238, 280, 282, 283
multiplication, 165, 182

survey, 356–358
too much or too little, 316
using
from an ad, 236
from a diagram, 450, 458, 462, 488, 583
from a graph, 22, 40, 41, 49, 96, 170, 180, 188, 216, 232, 260, 270, 284, 304, 342, 362, 370, 374, 420, 424, 438, 506, 535, 562, 594, 622, 635
from a line plot, 12, 606
from a list, 66, 71, 287, 586
from a map, 166, 391, 393, 587, 614
from a menu, 585
from a picture, 28, 32, 124, 222, 428, 552, 556
from a recipe, 58, 135, 324, 496
from a schedule, 335
from a table, 8, 18, 25, 36, 47, 82, 101, 108, 144, 158, 185, 195, 196, 204, 226, 242, 246, 250, 266, 293, 295, 332, 346, 365, 376, 377, 383, 402, 462, 500, 514, 519, 525, 536, 548, 566, 578, 621, 626, 630, 635
from a tally chart, 354, 597

Data Sense
histograms, 387
mode of a non-numerical set, 371

Day, 334–335

Decade, 334–335

Decimal points, 486, 542
aligning to compare decimals, 558
placing in a product, 160

Decimals
adding, 572–573, 574–578
comparing, 558–562
definition of, 486, 542
equivalent, 544–545, 558–559
estimating differences, 570–571
estimating sums, 570–571
extra practice, 581
fraction equivalents, 542–545, 550–553
greater than one, 546–548
mixed numbers and, 546–548
modeling, 542–543

modeling with money, 547
ordering, 558–562
as percents, 553
place value, 542–545
rounding, 568–569
subtracting, 573, 574–578
word form of, 542–545

Decimeter, 320–321

Degrees
angle measure, 410–411
Celsius, 344–349
in a circle, 422
Fahrenheit, 344–349

Denominators, 486, 490
like, 516, 517
unlike, 528

Diagonal, 412–414

Diagrams
using data from, 450, 458, 462, 488, 583
grid, 608–610
tree, 257, 608–610
Venn, 79, 167, 432, 488

Diameter, of a circle, 422

Different Ways
to add greater numbers, 76
to compare fractions, 498
to compare and order decimals, 558
to compare whole numbers, 24
to divide, 92, 95, 244
to find area of a rectangle, 456
to find equivalent fractions, 494
to find a fraction of a number, 502
to find perimeter, 454
to locate a point in the coordinate plane, 616
to multiply, 92, 94, 154, 186
to order decimals and mixed numbers, 560
to order fractions, 499
to round decimals, 568
to round whole numbers, 38
to show decimals greater than one, 546–548
to show equivalent amounts, 550
to solve an equation, 118, 119
to subtract, 77
to write a number, 6

Distributive Property, 176–177, 178–180

Divide, definition of, 202

Dividend, definition of, 56, 202, 214

Divisibility rules, 297

Division
adjusting the quotient, 286–287
checking, 215, 228, 230, 238, 280, 282, 283
choose how to write the quotient, 522–523
dividend, 56, 202, 214
divisibility rules, 294
divisor, 202, 214
estimating quotients, 220–223, 274–275
extra practice, 107, 225, 249, 291
facts practice, 669, 670, 671
fact families, 88–89
facts, 92–96, 98–99
to find equivalent fractions, 494
to find a fraction of a number, 502
greater numbers, 244–247
interpreting remainders, 210–212
as inverse of multiplication, 119–120, 240
mental math, 218–219
modeling, 92, 95, 206–207, 208, 214, 276–278, 300
with money, 234–236
by multiples of 10, 100, and 1,000, 218–219
by multiples of 10, 272–273
with a multiplication table, 90–91, 98–99
by one, 85–86
one-digit divisors, 226–249
one-digit quotients, 280–281
patterns, 218–219, 272–273
placing the first digit of the quotient, 230–232
quotient, 202, 214
regrouping in, 214–217
relationship to multiplication, 88–89, 90–91, 92, 95
remainder, 207, 208
with remainders, 102–103, 208–209
repeated subtraction and, 92, 285
rules, 85–86
three-digit quotients, 228–229
by two-digit divisors, 272–287
two-digit quotients, 282–287
with zero, 85–86
zero in the quotient, 238–239

modeling, 516–517, 518, 524, 528, 529, 590
    unlike denominators, 524–525, 528–529
comparing, 498–500
decimal equivalents, 543–545, 550–553
denominator, 486, 490
Egyptian, 537
equivalent, 492–493, 494–497
to express probability, 598–600
extra practice, 513, 539
game, 497
improper, 508–510
meaning of, 486
mixed numbers and, 508–510
numerator, 486, 490
ordering, 498–500
part of a group, 490–491
part of a number, 502–503
part of a whole, 490–491
as percents, 553
representing, 490–491
rounding, 511
simplest form, 495–497
subtraction with
    like denominators, 517–521
    modeling, 517, 518, 590
    unlike denominators, 530–532
unit, 537

Front-end estimation, 67

Functions
addition, 75, 521
division, 96, 162, 216, 231, 236
graphing, 620–622, 628–629
multiplication, 96, 162
subtraction, 75, 521

Function tables, 126–127
exercises, 75, 96, 109, 130, 131, 162, 216, 231, 236, 521, 600, 620, 621, 622

Gallon, 310–311

Games, *See also* Activities
division by one-digit divisors, 217
equivalent fractions, 497
fair and unfair games, 601
making one dollar, 37
match expressions, 115

multiplication, 181
name geometric figures, 407
record outcomes, 359

Geometry, *See also* Measurement
angles, 408–409, 410–411
circles, 422–424
congruent figures, 430–432
endpoint, 404–406
extra practice, 427, 475
game, 407
intersecting lines, 404–406
line, 404–406
line segment, 404–406
nets, 464–467
parallel lines, 404–406
perpendicular lines, 404–406
plane figures, 402–427
point, 404–406
polygons, 412–414
quadrilaterals, 412–414
rays, 408–409
similar figures, 433
solid figures, 464–467
symmetry, 440–443
tessellation, 476–477
transformations, 434–435, 447
triangles, 416–417

Gram, 326–329

Graphs
bar, using, 40–42, 43, 44, 49, 53, 139, 180, 216, 232, 270, 284, 342, 362, 375, 387, 438, 506, 562, 603
circle, using, 378–379, 424, 534–536, 538
coordinate
    graphing functions, 620–622, 628–629
    plotting points, 616–619, 627
    using, 622, 628–629, 635
double bar
    making, 376–377
    using, 420
histogram, 387
line
    extending, 628–629
    interpreting, 380–382
    making, 382–383
    reading, 382–383
    using software to make, 398
    using, 304, 387, 421
pictograph, using, 96, 188, 260, 370

selecting appropriate, 384–386
step graph, 386
without numbers, 380–381, 389

Grid, for probability outcomes, 608–610

Guess and Check, strategy, 156–158, 340–342

Half inch, 306–307

Half turn, 422

Hands-On Lessons *See* Activities

Hexagon, 412, 413

Histogram, 387

Horizontal line, 405

Hundredths, 542–543

Identity Property
for addition, 60–61
for multiplication, 84–86

Impossible outcome, 596–597, 598–600

Improper fractions, 508–510

Inch, 306–309

Inequality (Inequalities), *See also* Comparing; Ordering, 25, 66, 78, 86, 116–117, 166, 173, 281, 559, 561, 626

Input/output table *See* Function table

Integers
adding, 345–346, 348, 349
comparing, 625, 626
on a coordinate plane, 627
modeling, 624–625
opposite, 624–625
subtracting, 345–346, 348, 349
temperature and, 344–349
zero, 624

Internet *See* Technology; Technology Time

Interpreting remainders, 210–212

Intersecting lines, 404–406

Negative integers, 624–626

Negative numbers
temperature and, 344–349

Nets, 464–467

Non-examples
congruent figures, 430, 433
pentominoes, 478
polygons, 412
similar figures, 433
simplest form fractions, 495

Non-numerical set, mode of, 369

Number line
to compare numbers, 24, 558
to model equivalent fractions, 493
to model integer addition, 642
to model integers, 624, 625
to model integer subtraction, 642
to model multiplication, 92
to model repeated subtraction, 92
to order fractions, 499
to order numbers, 26, 560
to round numbers, 38, 39, 568, 569
to show equivalent fractions, 494
to show equivalent fractions and decimals, 550
to show probability, 599
thermometers as, 344–349
as time lines, 395

Numbers
Braille, 33
composite, 254–257
even and odd, 183
expanded form, 6–7, 16–18
exponents, 105
one million, 14–15
ordinal, 4–5
prime, 254–257
Roman numerals, 48
short word form, 6–7, 16–18
square, 90, 105
standard form, 6–7, 16–18
Thai, 29
uses of, 4–5
word form, 6–7, 16–18, 544–545, 546–548

Number Sense
adjusting the quotient, 286–287

clustering, 67
common multiples, 97
different bases, 9
division patterns, 247
factor trees, 257
front-end estimation, 67
integers on a coordinate plane, 627
interpreting remainders, 210–212
missing products, 189
subtracting to divide, 285

Number theory
divisibility rules, 294
factors, 252–253
multiples, 252–253
prime and composite numbers, 254–257
prime factors, 267
Sieve of Erathosthenes, 257

Numerator, 486, 490

Obtuse angle, 408–409

Obtuse triangle, 416–417

Octagon, 412

Odd numbers, 183

One, Property of, 84–86

Opposites, integer, 624–625

Ordered pair
locating on a coordinate plane, 616–617, 618–619, 620–622, 627, 631
meaning of, 592, 616

Ordering
decimals, 558–562
decimals and mixed numbers, 560–562
fractions, 498–500
money amounts, 31–32
whole numbers, 26–28

Order of operations, 110–111
on a calculator, 140

Ordinal numbers, 4–5

Organized list, making to solve problems, 604–606

Origin, on the coordinate plane, 620

Ounce, 312–314

Outcomes
grid for, 608–610
likelihood of, 592, 593, 596–597, 598–600
meaning of, 592, 596
probability of, 598–600
tree diagram for, 608–610

Outlier, 368–369

Parallel lines, 404–406
symbol for, 404

Parallelogram, 413–414, 432

Parentheses, order of operations and, 110

Patterns
division, 90–91, 98–99, 218–219, 247
finding to solve problems, 258–260, 418–420, 554–556
Kuba cloth, 447
multiplication, 90–91, 98–99, 146–147, 163, 172–173
tessellation, 476–477
tiling, 476–477

Pentagon, 412

Pentominoes, 478

Percent, 553

Performance Assessment *See* Assessment

Perimeter
of a complex figure, 460–462
estimating, 454, 455
meaning of, 452, 454
modeling, 452–453
of a polygon, 454–455, 484

Period, in place value, 6

Perpendicular lines, 404–406
symbol for, 404

Pictograph
select an appropriate graph, 384–386
using, 96, 188, 260, 370

Pictures, using data from, 28, 32, 124, 222, 428, 552, 556

Pint, 310–311

Place value
base five, 9
base two, 9
to compare numbers, 24, 558, 560
decimal, 542–545
division patterns and, 218–219
extra practice, 21
multiplication patterns and, 146–147, 172–173
to order numbers, 26, 558, 560
periods, 6
to round numbers, 38
whole numbers, 6–8, 16–18

Place-value chart
adding decimals on, 572
base five, 19
base ten, 6–8, 19
base two, 19
to compare decimals, 558
for decimals greater than one, 546–547
to order decimals and mixed numbers, 560
subtracting decimals on, 573
through hundred millions, 16–18
through hundred thousands, 6–8
through thousandths, 544

Plane figures, 402–427
circles, 422–424
game, 407
polygons, 412–414
quadrilaterals, 412–414
triangles, 416–417

Plots
line plot, 366–368
stem-and-leaf plot, 370–372

P.M., 336

Point, 404–406
on a coordinate plane, 616–619

Polygons
classifying, 412–414
irregular, 413–414
perimeter of, 454–455
regular, 413–414

Positive integers, 624–626

Positive numbers, 344–349

Pound, 312–314

Practice Games *See* Games

Predict, exercises, 263, 265, 383, 435, 597, 629

Prediction
from a graph, 628–629
with probability, 602–603

Prime factors, 257

Prime numbers, 254–257
Sieve of Erathosthenes and, 257

Prism, 464–467

Probability, 594–613
definition of, 592, 596
experiment, 602–603
extra practice, 613
fair and unfair games, 601
as a fraction, 598–600
grids for outcomes, 608–610
likelihood of an outcome, 592, 593, 596–597, 598–600
predicting with, 602–603
tree diagrams for outcomes, 608–610

Problem solving *See* Choose a computation method; Choose a strategy; Problem-solving applications; Problem-solving decisions; Problem-solving strategies; Test-Taking Tips

Problem-solving applications
use a bar graph, 40–42
use a circle graph, 534–536
use a coordinate graph, 628–629
decide how to write a quotient, 522–523
use decimals, 576–578
use formulas, 470–472
interpret a line graph, 380–381
interpret remainders, 210–212
use temperature, 348–350
visual thinking, 444–446

Problem-solving decisions
choose a method, 526
choose the operation, 104
estimate or exact answer, 68
explain your solution, 128
multistep problems, 288
reasonable answers, 182
too much or too little information, 316

Problem-solving features, 29, 233, 315, 463, 623

Problem-solving strategies
act it out, 436–438
draw a picture, 504–506
find a pattern, 418–420, 554–556

guess and check, 156–158, 340–342
use logical reasoning, 10–12
make an organized list, 604–606
make a table, 360–362
solve a simpler problem, 258–260
work backward, 240–242
write an equation, 122–124

Product, 142
estimating, 148–149, 152–154, 160–161, 164–166, 174–175, 186

Properties
addition, 60–61
associative, 60–61, 84–86, 100–101, 178–180
commutative, 60–61, 84–86
distributive, 176–177, 178–180
multiplication, 84–86, 100–101, 178–180
of one, 84–86
zero, 60–61, 84–86

Proportional Reasoning
equivalence in measurement, 308–309, 310–311, 312–313, 320–321, 322–323, 326–327, 334–335
equivalent fractions, 492–493, 498
functions, 126–127
percent, 553
probability, 598–600
scale, 584

Protractor, 410–411

Pyramid, 464–467

Quadrant, 627

Quadrilaterals
classifying, 413–414

Quart, 310–311

Quarter-inch, 306–307

Quarter-turn, 422

Quick Check *See* Assessment

Quotient
adjusting, 286–287
definition of, 56, 202, 214
estimating, 220–222, 274–275, 276–278, 280–284
ways to write, 522–523

Radius (Radii), of a circle, 422

Range, 364–365, 366–367

Ray, 408–409
naming, 408

Reading Mathematics, 1B, 56, 142, 202, 302, 400, 486, 592

Reading Test Questions, 1C, 57, 143, 203, 303, 401, 487, 593

Reading Words and Symbols, 1B, 56, 142, 202, 302, 400, 486, 592

Real-World Connections
batting averages, 549
Braille numbers, 33
chess, 631
exercises, 55, 141, 201, 301, 399, 485, 591, 643
leap years, 347

Reasoning, *See also* Logical Reasoning, Number Sense; Visual Thinking
always, sometimes, never, 129
area of a right triangle, 459
balancing equations, 121
bases other than ten, 9
benchmark lengths, 325
benchmark numbers, 19
clustering to estimate, 67
common multiples, 97
concept map, 473
division patterns, 247
estimating time, 339
exercises, 5, 12, 13, 36, 42, 49, 86, 149, 216, 253, 261, 273, 281, 346, 414, 432, 496, 510, 532, 600
factor trees, 267
front-end estimation, 67
histogram, 387
integers on a coordinate plane, 627
interpreting remainders, 210–212
Kuba cloth patterns, 447
logic statements, 134
midpoint of a line segment, 415
missing products, 189
mode of a non-numerical set, 369
reasonable answers, 182

rounding fractions, 511
similar figures, 433
subtracting to divide, 285
temperature change, 347
Venn diagram, 79, 167

Rectangle, 413–414
area of, 456–458, 484
perimeter of, 454, 484

Rectangular, meaning of, 401

Rectangular prism, 464–467
net for, 465

Rectangular solid, 468–469

Reflection, 434–435

Regrouping
to add, 70–71, 76–78
definition of, 56
to divide, 214–217
to multiply, 151–154, 160–162
to subtract, 72–78

Regular polygons, 413–414

Remainders
definition of, 102, 202, 207, 208
division with, 102–103
interpreting, 210–212, 522–523

Repeated subtraction
to divide, 92, 285

Represent
exercises, 89, 125, 151, 162, 257, 343, 381, 419, 435, 439, 443, 491, 503, 507, 548, 557, 600
meaning of, 487

Representation *See* Different Ways; Drawing; Graphs; Modeling; Number line; Plots

Rhombus, 413–414

Right angle, 408–409
symbol for, 404

Right triangle, 416–417
area of, 459

Roman numerals, 48

Rotation, 434–435

Rotational symmetry, 440–443

Rounding
decimals, 568–569
to estimate differences, 64–66, 570–571
to estimate products, 148–149, 164–166, 174–175

to estimate sums, 64–66, 570–571
to estimate to check answers, 77, 161
fractions, 511
rules for, 568
whole numbers, 38–39

Rules
division, 85–86
for rounding, 568
subtraction, 60–61

Scale, 584

Scalene triangle, 416–417

Short word form number, 6–7, 16–18

Sides
of an angle, 408
of a polygon, 412

Sieve of Erathosthenes, 257

Similar, meaning of, 433

Similar figures, 433

Simplest form fractions, 494–496

Skip counting, to multiply, 92

Solid figures
classifying, 464, 466
nets for, 464–467
parts of, 464
views of, 467
volume of, 468–469

Solve a Simpler Problem, strategy, 258–260

Space figures *See* Solid figures

Sphere, 464–466

Square, 413–414
area of, 456–458
perimeter of, 452–453, 455

Square number, 90, 142

Square pyramid, 464–467
net for, 465

Standard form number, 6–7, 16–18

Square unit, 456–458, 459, 463

Standards, correlation, 692–696

decade, 334–335, 395
elapsed, 334–335, 336–339
estimating, 339
P.M., 336
subtracting units of, 337–339

Time line, 392

Time zones, 390–391

Ton, 312–314

Trading *See* Regrouping

Transformations, 434–435, 447, 639

Translation, 434–435, 639

Trapezoid, 413–414

Tree diagram
to find factors, 257
to find outcomes, 608–610

Triangles
classifying, 416–417
definition of, 400, 412

Triangular prism, 464–467
net for, 465

Triangular pyramid, 464–467
net for, 465

Turns
half, 422
quarter, 422
three-quarter, 422

Two-dimensional figures, *See* Plane figures

Unfair and fair games, 601

Unit fraction, 537

Unlike denominators, 528

Unlikely outcome, 596–597, 598–600

Variable
definition of, 112, 118, 203
equations and, 118–120
using, 118, 203, 263, 265, 496, 519

Venn diagram, 79, 167, 432, 488

Vertex (Vertices)
of an angle, 408
of a solid figure, 464, 466

Vertical line, 405

Views, of a solid figure, 467

Visual Thinking, *See also* Diagrams; Drawing; Graphs; Patterns
balancing equations, 121
benchmark numbers, 19
concept map, 473
Kuba cloth patterns, 447
midpoint of a line segment, 415
modeling integer operations, 345, 346, 348
pentominoes, 478
rounding fractions, 511
similar figures, 433
to solve problems, 444–446
Venn diagram, 79

Vocabulary
Reading Mathematics, xxx, 56, 142, 202, 302, 400, 486, 592
Wrap-Up, 54, 140, 200, 300, 398, 484, 590, 642

Volume, 468–469, 470–471
estimating, 468
units of, 468

Week, 334–335

Weight, 312–314
benchmarks for, 312

What's Wrong? *See* Error analysis

Whole numbers
comparing, 24–25
ordering, 26–28
place value, 6–8, 16–18
rounding, 38–39

Word form
for angles, 408–409
for decimals, 542–545, 546–548
for geometric figures, 404
for ordered pairs, 616
for whole numbers, 6–7, 16–18

Work Backward, strategy, 240–242

Write About It, 3, 8, 15, 17, 20, 23, 32, 44, 55, 59, 80, 83, 91, 99, 106, 109, 130, 141, 145, 151, 154, 168, 171, 177, 180, 190, 201, 205, 207, 219, 221, 224, 227, 239, 246, 248, 251, 253, 263, 266, 268, 271, 278, 290, 301, 305, 307, 319, 328, 330, 333, 352, 355, 358, 365, 372, 375, 377, 388, 399, 403, 406, 409, 411, 414, 426, 429, 448, 451, 453, 474, 485, 489, 493, 496, 500, 512, 515, 518, 519, 521, 529, 532, 538, 541, 543, 553, 564, 567, 573, 580, 585, 591, 595, 597, 601, 603, 611, 612, 615, 617, 619, 626, 632, 643

Write Your Own, 462, 523

x-axis, 620

Yard, 308–309

y-axis, 620

Year, 334–335
leap, 334–335, 351

You Decide, 25, 222, 236, 237, 342, 343, 458, 536, 561, 578

Zero
in addition, 60–61
in the coordinate plane, 616
division with, 85–86
as an integer, 624
multiplication with, 84–86
in subtraction, 60–61, 74–75

Zero Property
for addition, 60–61
for multiplication, 84–86

Credits

PERMISSIONS ACKNOWLEDGMENTS
Houghton Mifflin Mathematics © 2007, Grade 4 PE/TE

"Beyond Pluto," is adapted from "Postcards from Pluto?" from *Weekler Reader Senior*, March 15, 2002 Issue. Copyright © by Weekly Reader Corporation. Reprinted by permission of Weekly Reader Corporation. Weekly Reader is a federally registered trademark of Weekly Reader Corp.

"But I'm Not Tired!," is adapted from "Do Kids Need More Sleep?" from *Weekly Reader 3*, January 10, 2003 Issue. Copyright © by Weekly Reader Corporation. Reprinted by permission of Weekly Reader Corporation. Weekly Reader is a federally registered trademark of Weekly Reader Corp.

"Gone Prawning" from *Weekly Reader Magazine*, October 2, 2002 issue. Copyright © 2002 by Weekly Reader Corporation. Reprinted by permission of Weekly Reader Corporation. Weekly Reader is a federally registered trademark of Weekly Reader Corp.

"Hold the Meat!," from *American Girl Magazine*, March/April 2002. Copyright © 2002 by Pleasant Company. Reprinted by permission of Pleasant Company.

"Kid Camp" from *American Girl Magazine*, July/August 2001. Copyright © 2001 by Pleasant Company. Reprinted by permission of Pleasant Company.

"Lengths of Time," by Phyllis McGinley, originally appeared in *Wonderful Time*, originally published by J.P. Lippincott Co. Copyright © 1965, 1966 by Phyllis McGinley. Reprinted by permission of Curtis Brown, Ltd.

"The Perfect Present," by E. Renee Heiss from *Highlights for Children Magazine*, September 2002 Issue. Copyright © 2002 by Highlights for Children, Inc., Columbus, Ohio. Reprinted by permission of Highlights for Children.

Cover © HMCo./Bruton Stroube Studios. (turtle) © Dave King/DK Images.

PHOTOGRAPHY

vi © Gail Mooney/Masterfile. **vii** (t) Steve Vidler/SuperStock. (b) Image Ideas. **ix** © Jeff Foott/Discovery Images/PictureQuest. **xiv** (b) Bob Elsdale/agefotostock. **xi** (b) Gary Mason/agefotostock. **xv** © Tom Bean/CORBIS. **xvii** © Coco McCoy/Rainbow/PictureQuest. **xxi** © NRSC Ltd./Photo Researchers Inc. **2** © Gail Mooney/Masterfile. **4** (t) © Jim Pickerell/Stock Connection/PictureQuest. (tm) © James Lemass. (m) © Pictor International, Ltd./PictureQuest. (bm) © James Lemass. (b) © Joseph Nettis/Stock, Boston Inc./PictureQuest. **8** © Chabruken/Getty Images. **10** (b) © Janet Haas/Rainbow/PictureQuest. (mr) © Carol Christensen/Stock South/PictureQuest. (ml) Joyce Wilson/Earth Scenes. (t) © Lucy Ash/Rainbow/PictureQuest. **12** © Michael Newman/PhotoEdit. **18** Grant Heilman Photography. **22** © Tom Bean. **24** (r) Barbara von Hoffman/Earth Scenes. (l) Tim Fitzharris/Index Stock. **26** Jim Wark/Index Stock. **27** © Archive Photos/PictureQuest. **31** (r) Image Ideas. **33** © Garry Gay/Stock Connection/PictureQuest. **34** © David Muench/CORBIS.

36 ComstockKLIPS. **38** © Lester Lefkowitz/CORBIS. **46-7** Bob Thomas/Getty Images. **46** (b) Library of Congress. **48** (cr) Angelo Cavalli/Firstlight.ca. (cr) Heatons/Firstlight.ca. **58** Frank Siteman/Getty Images. **64** Artville. **65** PhotoSpin. **68** © Dorling Kindersley. **72** © Paul Hardy/CORBIS. **74** © Natalie Fobes/CORBIS. **75** © James A. Sugar/CORBIS. **76** John Elk/Stock Boston. **78** © Tom Bean/CORBIS. **82** Shubroto Chattopadhyay/Index Stock. **94** Eulenspiegel Puppet Theatre Company. **100** © Jim Craigmyle/CORBIS. **102** Dave Bartruff/Stock Boston. **103** nowitz.com. **108** Jim Tuten. **110** Patricia Caufield/Animals Animals. **111** © Jeff Foott/Discovery Images/PictureQuest. **112** © Jeff Foott/Discovery Images/PictureQuest. **114** © Frank Krahmer/Pictor International, Ltd./PictureQuest. **116** Keren Su/Getty Images. **118** News Ltd. **119** PhotoDisc/Getty Images. **120** News Ltd. **123** © Kimball/Premium Stock/PictureQuest. **126** (b) Gary Griffen/Animals Animals. (t) © Elena Rooraid/PhotoEdit. **128** (l) Gerry Ellis/Minden. (r) Manaj Shah/Animals Animals. **132-3** © Bettmann/CORBIS. **133** (t) © Bettmann/CORBIS. **144** © Layne Kennedy. **172** Gary Mason/agefotostock. **174** Royalty-Free/CORBIS. **179** DK Images. **180** (l) © James L. Amos/CORBIS. (r) PhotoDisc/Getty Images. **184** Lawrence Migdale/Stock Boston. **192-3** Courtesy of NASA. **193** (b) © Denis Scott/CORBIS. **204** © Mug Shots/CORBIS. **210** (t) © Lake County Museum/CORBIS. (b) Lake County (IL) Discovery Museum, Curt Teich Postcard Archives. Courtesy collection of Jonathan Yonan. **216** (r) PhotoDisc/Getty Images. (l) Royalty Free/CORBIS. **220** Ralph Krubner/Index Stock. **221** sedonawolf.com. **226** Mike Hill/agefotostock. **230** (ml) Essueve/agefotostock. **230** (bl) Martin Rugner/agefotostock. (t) Mark Moffett/Minden. (br) © Mark Tomalty/Masterfile. (mr) © John Serrao/Photo Researchers Inc. **231** © Syracuse Newspapers/Al Campanie/The Image Works. **232** Digital Vision/Getty Images. **234** © Kevin Dodge/Masterfile. **237** Spanish-American Dollars, (eight reales), 18th-19th c. Mexico City mint. Cut pieces countermarked for Trinidad. Silver. Collection of The Newark Museum, Marcus L. Ward Bequest 1921. Inv.:TR.16985W. The Newark Museum/Art Resource, NY. **238** Michael S. Nolan/Seapics.com. **239** Michael S. Nolan/agefotostock. **240** David Hall/agefotostock. **245** Runk/Schoenberger/Grant Heilman Photography, Inc. **250** © Richard Cummins/CORBIS. **257** Bernardo Strozzi, Eratosthenes Teaching in Alexandria (detail). The Montreal Museum of Fine Arts, purchase, Horsley and Annie Townsend Bequest. Photo: The Montreal Museum of Fine Arts, Christine Guest. **258** © Paul Barton/CORBIS. **260** PhotoDisc/Getty Images. **264** © Peter Beck/CORBIS. **266** (t) Royalty-Free/CORBIS. (b) Robin Smith/Getty Images. **270** © Jonathan Nourok/PhotoEdit. **272** David Madison Sports Images, Inc. **274** (t) Johann Schumacher. **275** Linda Raynsford, Link, made from discarded tool chests and shelves. **279** © B. Taylor/Robertstock.com. **281** AP Photo/Longview News-Journal, Kevin Green. **292-3** G. Brad Lewis/Getty Images. **304** © Tom Stewart/CORBIS. **306** PhotoDisc/Getty Images. **307** (mbl) Artville. (b) PhotoDisc/Getty Images. (mbr) PhotoDisc/Getty Images. **308** © Michael J. Doolittle/The Image Works. **310** © Tom Stewart/CORBIS. **312** (tl) (tm) FoodPix/Getty Images. (tr) DK Images. **315** (b) Karl Ammann/naturepl.com. **317** Lobster Trap and Fish Tail. 1939. Hanging mobile, painted steel wire and sheet aluminum, 8'6" × 9'6". Commissioned by the Advisory Committee for the stairwell of the Museum. (590.1939.a-d) The Museum of Modern Art. Digital Image ©The Museum of Modern Art/Licensed by SCALA/Art Resource, NY. **318** Dianne Huntress/Index Stock. **319** (tmr) (tml) (b) PhotoDisc/Getty Images. (m) Fred Whitehead/Earth Scenes. **323** (tl) (bl)

Credits continued

701